STUDY GUIDE *to accompany*

INTERMEDIATE FINANCIAL MANAGEMENT

STUDY GUIDE *to accompany*

INTERMEDIATE FINANCIAL MANAGEMENT

Sixth Edition

EUGENE F. BRIGHAM
UNIVERSITY OF FLORIDA

LOUIS C. GAPENSKI
UNIVERSITY OF FLORIDA

PHILLIP R. DAVES
UNIVERSITY OF TENNESSEE

THE DRYDEN PRESS
HARCOURT BRACE COLLEGE PUBLISHERS

FORT WORTH PHILADELPHIA SAN DIEGO NEW YORK ORLANDO AUSTIN SAN ANTONIO
TORONTO MONTREAL LONDON SYDNEY TOKYO

Portions of this work were published in previous editions.

Address for Domestic Orders
Harcourt College Publishers, 6277 Sea Harbor Drive, Orlando, FL 32887-6777
800-782-4479

Address for Editorial Correspondence
Harcourt College Publishers, 301 Commerce Street, Suite 3700, Fort Worth, TX 76102

Web Site Address
http://www.harcourtcollege.com

Printed in the United States of America

ISBN: 0-03-023461-1

0 1 2 3 4 5 6 7 8 9   202   11 10 9 8 7 6 5 4 3

Harcourt College Publishers

TABLE OF CONTENTS

PREFACE

This *Study Guide* is designed primarily to help you develop a working knowledge of the concepts and principles of financial management. Additionally, it will familiarize you with the types of true/false and multiple-choice test questions that are being used with increasing frequency in finance courses.

The *Study Guide* follows the outline of *Intermediate Financial Management*, Sixth Edition. You should read carefully the next section, "Suggestions for Students Using *Study Guide*," to familiarize yourself with its specific contents and to gain some insights into how it can be used most effectively.

We would like to thank Dana Aberwald Clark, Tim Smith, Susan Purcell Whitman, and Tina Goforth for their considerable assistance in the preparation of this edition and Bob LeClair for his helpful ideas in prior editions which we carried over to this one.

We have tried to make the *Study Guide* as clear and error-free as possible. However, some mistakes may have crept in, and there are almost certainly some sections that could be clarified. Any suggestions for improving the *Study Guide* would be greatly appreciated and should be addressed to Phillip Daves at the address given below. Since instructors almost never read study guides, we address this call for help to students!

Eugene F. Brigham
Louis C. Gapenski

Phillip R. Daves

College of Business Administration
PO Box 117167
University of Florida
Gainesville, FL 32611-7167

Finance Department, SMC 435
University of Tennessee
Knoxville, TN 37996-0540

November 1998

SUGGESTIONS FOR STUDENTS USING STUDY GUIDE

Different people will tend to use the *Study Guide* in somewhat different ways. This is natural because both finance courses and individual students' needs vary widely. However, the tips contained in this section should help all students use the *Study Guide* more effectively, regardless of these differences.

Each chapter contains (1) an overview, (2) an outline, (3) definitional self-test questions, (4) conceptual self-test questions, (5) self-test problems, and (6) answers and solutions to the self-test questions and problems. You should begin your study by reading the overview; it will give you an idea of what is contained in the chapter and how this material fits into the overall scheme of things in financial management.

Next, read over the outline to get a better fix on the specific topics covered in the chapter. It is important to realize that the outline does not list every facet of every topic covered in the textbook. The *Study Guide* is intended to highlight and summarize the textbook, not to supplant it. Also, note that chapter extension material is clearly marked as such within the outline. Thus, if your instructor does not assign a particular chapter extension, you may not want to study that portion of the outline.

The definitional self-test questions are intended to test your knowledge of, and also to reinforce your ability to work with, the terms and concepts introduced in the chapter. If you do not understand the definitions thoroughly, review the outline prior to going on to the conceptual questions and problems.

The conceptual self-test questions focus on the same kinds of ideas that the textbook end-of-chapter questions address, but in the *Study Guide*, the questions are set out in a true/false or multiple-choice format. Thus, for many students these questions can be used to practice for the types of tests that are being used with increasing frequency. However, regardless of the types of tests you must take, working through the conceptual questions will help drive home the key concepts of financial management.

The numeric problems are also written in a multiple-choice format. Generally, the problems are arranged in order of increasing difficulty. Also, note that some of the *Study Guide* problems are convoluted in the sense that information normally available to financial managers is withheld and information normally unknown is given. Such problems are designed to test your knowledge of a subject, and you must work "backwards" to solve them. Furthermore, such problems are included in the *Study Guide* in part because they provide a good test of how well you understand the material and in part because you may well be seeing similar problems on your exams.

Finally, each *Study Guide* chapter provides the answers and solutions to the self-test questions and problems. The rationale behind a question's correct answer is explained where necessary, but the problem solutions are always complete. Note that the problems in the early chapters generally provide both "table-based" and "financial calculator" solutions. In later chapters, only calculator solutions are shown. You should not be concerned if your answer differs from ours by a small amount due to rounding errors.

Of course, each student must decide how to incorporate the *Study Guide* in his or her overall study program. Many students begin an assignment by reading the *Study Guide* overview and outline to get the "big picture," then read the chapter in the textbook. Naturally, the *Study Guide* overview and outline is also used extensively to review for exams. Most students work the textbook questions and problems, using the latter as a self-test and review tool. However, if you are stumped by a text problem, try the *Study Guide* problems first because their detailed solutions can get you over stumbling blocks.

OVERVIEW

This chapter provides an overview of financial management and should give you a better understanding of the following: (1) what the goals of a firm are, (2) what agency relationships are, and (3) the primary agency relationships that exist within the financial management context.

Financial management explains both how managers can increase their firms' value and why it is essential for them to do so. Today more than ever, investors are forcing managers to focus on value maximization, so companies want to hire people who understand how to help in this regard. Therefore, students who are "clued in" on what potential employees are seeking have a major advantage over clueless students. Narrowly focused people who don't understand the firm's broader goals and the actions necessary to achieve those goals are at best marginal employees, and no one wants to hire marginal people.

OUTLINE

Management's basic, overriding goal is to create value for stockholders.

■ Stockholders own the firm—it legally belongs to them.
   □ Stockholders elect directors, who then hire the managing executives.
   □ The directors, as representatives of the stockholders, determine managers' compensation, rewarding them if performance is superior or replacing them if performance is poor.
   • Stockholders will remove the directors if they fail in their fiduciary duty.
   • Years ago, stockholders "voted with their feet," i.e., selling the stock if they thought a particular firm's management wasn't doing a good job.
   • Today, stock ownership is increasingly concentrated in the hands of institutional investors, who use *proxy fights* and *takeovers* to force changes in poorly performing companies.

■ The goal of stock price maximization is indeed the proper foundation for our economic system. The same actions that maximize stock prices also benefit society. Reasons include:

☐ Consumers benefit because stock price maximization requires efficient, low-cost businesses that produce high-quality goods and services at the lowest possible cost.

● If businesses are indeed successful and earn above-normal profits, those very profits will attract competition, which will eventually drive prices down, so the main long-term beneficiary is the consumer.

☐ Employees benefit because companies that successfully increase stock prices also grow and add more employees, thus benefiting society.

☐ To a large extent, the owners of stock are society. Most members of society have an important stake in the stock market.

● Strong stock prices benefit even those who have no direct or indirect ownership interest in the market, because strong markets stimulate both individual spending (through the "wealth effect") and corporate investment (because of lower capital costs and higher consumer spending).

An agency relationship arises whenever one or more individuals (the principals) hires another individual or organization (the agent) to perform some service delegating decision-making authority to that agent. Within the financial management context, the primary agency relationships are those (1) between stockholders and managers, (2) between managers and debtholders, and (3) among managers, stockholders, and debtholders in times of financial distress.

■ A potential *agency problem* arises whenever the manager of a firm owns less than 100 percent of the firm's common stock.

☐ Since the firm's earnings do not go solely to the manager, he or she may not concentrate exclusively on maximizing shareholder wealth.

■ A potential *moral hazard* problem, wherein agents take unobserved actions in their own behalf, arises, because it is virtually impossible for shareholders to monitor all managerial actions.

■ In general, to reduce both agency conflicts and the moral hazard problem, stockholders must incur *agency costs*, which include all costs borne by shareholders to encourage managers to maximize the firm's stock price rather than act in their own self-interests.

☐ There are three major categories of agency costs: (1) expenditures to monitor managerial actions, such as audit costs; (2) expenditures to structure the organization in a way that will limit undesirable managerial behavior, such as appointing outside investors to the board of directors; and (3) opportunity costs which are incurred when shareholder-imposed restrictions, such as requirements for stockholder votes on certain issues, limit the ability of managers to take timely actions that would enhance shareholder wealth.

☐ Agency costs should be incurred as long as each dollar spent returns more than a dollar in shareholder wealth.

■ The optimal solution for dealing with agency conflicts is tying executive compensation to performance but also doing some monitoring of managerial actions. Specific mechanisms are used to motivate managers to act in shareholders' best interests. These include: (1) managerial compensation plans, (2) direct intervention by shareholders, (3) the threat of firing, and (4) the threat of takeover.

☐ The structure of the compensation package should be designed to meet two primary objectives:

● To attract and retain able managers.

● To align managers' actions as closely as possible with the interests of stockholders, who are primarily interested in stock price maximization.

☐ A *performance share* is stock that is awarded to executives on the basis of the company's actual performance and the executive's continued service.

☐ *Executive stock options* are granted to an executive as part of his or her compensation package and allow them to purchase stock at some future time at a given price.

● A relatively new measure of managerial performance, *economic value added (EVA)*, is being used by more and more firms to tie executive compensation to stockholder wealth maximization.

● EVA is found by subtracting from after-tax operating profit the annual cost of all the capital a firm uses. The higher its EVA, the more wealth the firm is creating for its shareholders.

☐ Institutional money managers have the clout, if they choose to use it, to exercise considerable influence over most firms' operations.

☐ A *hostile takeover* is the acquisition of a company over the opposition of its management. Hostile takeovers are most likely to occur when a firm's stock is undervalued relative to its potential because of poor management.

■ Another agency problem involves conflicts between stockholders (through managers) and creditors.

☐ Conflicts arise if (a) management, acting for its stockholders, takes on projects that have greater risk than was anticipated by creditors or (b) the firm increases debt to a level higher than was anticipated. Both of these actions decrease the value of the debt outstanding.

☐ To best serve their shareholders in the long run, managers must play fairly with creditors. Managers, as agents of both shareholders and creditors, must act in a manner that is fairly balanced between the interest of the two classes of security holders.

- Similarly, management actions which would expropriate wealth from any of the firm's other *stakeholders* will ultimately be to the detriment of its shareholders.
- In our society, stock price maximization requires fair treatment for all parties whose economic positions are affected by managerial decisions.

■ When a firm is in financial distress, a decision by management to reorganize may put it in conflict with either the stockholders or the creditors, or both, because an objective analysis might lead to the conclusion that the company would be worth more dead than alive.

☐ If a company really is worth more alive than dead, then it should be reorganized.

- This means that the assets, while worth less than the book value of the securities, would be worth more if operated than if they were sold off piecemeal.

☐ All bankruptcy reorganizations involve intense negotiations between various creditors, stockholders, and managers, and these different parties have different vested interests.

- The creditors generally want the firm to be liquidated, for then they will get their funds relatively quickly.
- Management and stockholders typically want to keep the firm alive, so they argue for reorganization.
- To get court approval for a reorganization, at least some of the creditors must support the plan. Thus, management is tempted to offer creditors more than perhaps they should get, to the detriment of the stockholders.
- Stockholders may be able to replace the managers if they give away too much.

SELF-TEST QUESTIONS

Definitional

1. Management's basic, overriding goal is to create _____ for _____.

2. The same actions that maximize _____ _____ also benefit society.

3. If businesses are successful and earn above-normal _____, this will attract _____, which will eventually drive prices down, so the main long-term beneficiary is the _____.

4. Today, stock ownership is increasingly concentrated in the hands of institutional investors, who use _____ _____ and _____ to force changes in poorly performing companies.

5. A(n) _____ relationship arises whenever one or more individuals (the principals) hire another individual or organization (the agent) to act on their behalf, delegating decision-making authority to that agent.

6. Potential agency problems exist between a firm's shareholders and its _____ and also between managers and _____.

7. A(n) _____ _____ is stock which is awarded to executives on the basis of the company's performance.

8. _____ _____ _____ allow managers to purchase stock at some future time at a given price.

9. A(n) _____ _____ is the acquisition of a company over the opposition of its management.

10. A potential _____ _____ problem, wherein agents take unobserved actions in their own behalf, arises, because it is virtually impossible for shareholders to monitor all managerial actions.

11. A relatively new measure of managerial performance, _____ _____ _____, is being used by more and more firms to tie executive compensation to stockholder wealth maximization.

12. A potential _____ _____ arises whenever the manager of a firm owns less than 100 percent of the firm's common stock.

Conceptual

13. The primary objective of the firm is to maximize EPS.

   a. True   **b.** False

14. The types of actions that help a firm maximize stock price are generally not directly beneficial to society at large.

   a. True   **b.** False

15. Which of the following factors tend to encourage management to pursue stock price maximization as a goal?

    a. Shareholders link management's compensation to company performance.
    b. Managers' reactions to the threat of firing and hostile takeovers.
    c. Managers do not have goals other than stock price maximization.
    d. Statements a and b are both correct.
    e. Statements a, b, and c are correct.

ANSWERS TO SELF-TEST QUESTIONS

1.	value; stockholders	**7.**	performance share
2.	stock price	**8.**	Executive stock options
3.	profits; competition; consumer	**9.**	hostile takeover
4.	proxy fights; takeovers	**10.**	moral hazard
5.	agency	**11.**	economic value added
6.	managers; creditors (or debtholders)	**12.**	agency problem

13.   b. An increase in earnings per share will not necessarily increase stock price. For example, if the increase in earnings per share is accompanied by an increase in the riskiness of the firm, stock price might fall. *The primary objective is the maximization of stock price.*

14.   b. The actions that maximize stock price generally also benefit society by promoting efficient, low-cost operations; encouraging the development of new technology, products, and jobs; and requiring efficient and courteous service.

15.   d. Specific mechanisms which tend to force managers to act in shareholders' best interests include (1) the proper structuring of managerial compensation, (2) direct intervention by shareholders, (3) the threat of firing, and (4) the threat of takeover.

CHAPTER 2
BASIC FINANCIAL TOOLS: A REVIEW

OVERVIEW

The building blocks of finance include the time value of money, risk and its relationship with rates of return, and stock and bond valuation models. These topics are covered in introductory finance courses, but because of their fundamental importance, we review them in this chapter.

OUTLINE

Finding the future value (FV), or compounding, is the process of going from today's values (or present values) to future amounts (or future values). It can be calculated as

$$FV_n = PV(1 + i)^n = PV(FVIF_{i,n}).$$

■ PV = present value, or beginning amount; i = interest rate per year; and n = number of periods involved in the analysis.
   □ The term $FVIF_{i,n}$ is called the *future value interest factor*.
   □ The future value of a series of cash flows is the sum of the future values of each individual cash flow.
   □ An *ordinary annuity* has equal payments, given the symbol PMT, that occur at the end of each period.
      ● Its future value (FVA$_n$) is found as:

$$FVA_n = PMT \left[\frac{(1+i)^n - 1}{i} \right]$$
$$= PMT(FVIFA_{i,n}).$$

      ● The term $FVIFA_{i,n}$ is called the future value interest factor of an annuity at i percent for n periods.

Finding present values is called discounting, and it is simply the reverse of compounding. In general, the present value of a cash flow due n years in the future is the amount which, if

it were on hand today, would grow to equal the future amount. By solving for PV in the future value equation, the present value, or discounting, equation can be developed and written in several forms:

$$PV = \frac{FV_n}{(1+i)^n} = FV_n \left(\frac{1}{1+i}\right)^n = FV_n(PVIF_{i,n}).$$

■ $PVIF_{i,n}$ is the *present value interest factor* at i percent due in n periods.

■   The present value of an annuity is the sum of the present values of the individual payments.

      ☐   The formula is written as:

$$PVA_n = PMT\left[\frac{1 - \frac{1}{(1+i)^n}}{i}\right]$$
$$= PMT(PVIFA_{i,n}).$$

      • $PVIFA_{i,n}$ is the present value interest factor for an annuity of i percent for n periods.

■   An important application of the annuity formula is finding the set of equal payments necessary to amortize a loan.

      ☐   In an *amortized loan* the payment is set so that the present value of the series of payments, when discounted at the loan rate, is equal to the amount of the loan.

      •   Loan amount = $PMT(PVIFA_{i, n})$, or

$$PMT = \frac{\text{Loan amount}}{PVIFA_{i, n}}.$$

      •   Each payment consists of two elements: (1) interest on the outstanding balance and a repayment of principal which reduces the loan balance.

      •   The *amortization schedule* shows for each month the amount paid as interest and the amount applied to reduce principal.

Semiannual, quarterly, and other compounding periods more frequent than an annual basis are often used in financial transactions. Compounding on a nonannual basis requires an adjustment to both the compounding and discounting procedures discussed previously.

■ The *effective,* or *equivalent, annual rate* (EAR or EFF%) is the rate that would have produced the final compounded value under annual compounding. The effective annual percentage rate is given by the following formula:

$$\text{Effective annual rate (EAR)} = \text{EFF\%} = (1 + i_{Nom}/m)^m - 1.0,$$

where i_{Nom} is the nominal, or quoted, interest rate and m is the number of compounding periods per year.

☐ The larger the value of m, the greater the difference between the nominal and effective rates.

☐ If m = 1, which means annual compounding, then the nominal and effective rates are equal.

If we know the current price of an asset (its PV) and the expected cash flows, we can find the rate of return on the asset, or its yield.

■ $$PV = \sum_{t=1}^{n} \frac{CF_t}{(1+i)^t}$$

☐ The cash flows in this equation can be equal, in which case $CF_t = PMT = $ constant, so there is an annuity.

☐ The cash flows can also be unequal and vary from period to period.

■ The value of i that solves the equation is defined as the asset's expected rate of return, or *yield.*

The price of a bond is the present value of its payments, discounted at the current market interest rate appropriate for the bond, given its risk, maturity, and other characteristics.

■ Finding the value of a bond is a straightforward application of the discounted cash flow process.

☐ A bond's *par value* is its stated face value, which is the amount the issuer must pay to the bondholder at maturity.

☐ The *coupon payment* is the periodic interest payment that the bond provides.

☐ The total annual payment as a percentage of the par value is called the *coupon interest rate.*

■ The price of the bond can be found as the present value of an annuity plus the present value of a lump sum.

$$P = \sum_{t=1}^{N} \frac{\text{Coupon}}{(1+k_d)^t} + \frac{\text{Par}}{(1+k_d)^N}.$$

- □ If the going interest rate is greater than the coupon rate, the price of the bond will be less than par so it will sell at a *discount*.
- □ If the going interest rate is less than the coupon rate, the price will be greater than par so it will sell at a *premium*.
- □ If the going interest rate is equal to the coupon rate, the bond will sell at its par value.

■ The *yield to maturity* is defined as the discount rate that sets the present value of all of the cash flows until maturity equal to the bond's current price.

■ Fluctuations in interest rates give rise to changes in bond prices, and this sensitivity is called *interest rate risk*.
- □ The percentage price change in response to a change in interest rates depends on (1) the maturity of the bond and (2) its coupon rate.
  - • Other things held constant, a longer-term bond will experience larger price changes than a shorter-term bond, and a lower coupon bond will have a larger change than a higher coupon bond.
  - • A bond's interest risk also depends on its coupon—the lower the coupon, other things held constant, the greater the interest risk.

Risk is the possibility that an outcome will be different from what is expected. For an investment, risk is the possibility that the actual return will be less than the expected return.

■ Two types of risk for assets will be considered.
- □ *Stand-alone risk* is the risk an investor would bear if he or she held only a single asset.
- □ *Portfolio risk* is the risk that an asset contributes to a well-diversified portfolio.

■ *Discrete probabilities* assumes a finite number of possible events and probabilities.
- □ The list of possible events, and their probabilities, is called a *probability distribution*.

■ The *expected rate of return* on a stock with possible returns k_i and probabilities P_i is found with this equation:

$$\text{Expected rate of return} = \hat{k} = P_1k_1 + P_2k_2 + ... + P_nk_n$$
$$= \sum_{i=1}^{n} P_i k_i.$$

■ *Variance* measures the extent to which actual returns are likely to deviate from the expected value, and it is defined as the average of the squared deviations.

$$\text{Variance} = \sigma^2 = \sum_{i=1}^{n}(k_i - \hat{k})^2 P_i.$$

☐ The *standard deviation,* σ, is the square root of the variance, and it measures how far the actual future return is likely to deviate from the expected return.
  • σ is often used as a measure of risk.
  • The higher the standard deviation of a stock's return, the more stand-alone risk it has.

■ The *coefficient of variation* facilitates comparisons between returns that have different expected values.

$$\text{Coefficient of variation} = CV = \frac{\sigma}{\hat{k}}.$$

☐ The CV measures the amount of risk per unit of expected return.

■ Most investors do not keep all of their money invested in just one asset; instead, they hold collections of assets called *portfolios.*
  ☐ The *expected return on a portfolio,* $\hat{k}_p$, is the weighted average of the expected return on the individual assets:

$$\hat{k}_p = w_1\hat{k}_1 + w_2\hat{k}_2 + ... + w_n\hat{k}_n$$
$$= \sum_{i=1}^{n} w_i\hat{k}_i.$$

  ☐ The variance and standard deviation of a portfolio depend not only on the variances and weights of the individual assets in the portfolio, but also on the *correlation* between the individual assets.
    • The *correlation coefficient* between two assets can range from −1 to +1.
    • Returns on positively correlated assets tend to move up and down together, while returns on negatively correlated assets tend to move in opposite directions.
  ☐ For a two-asset portfolio, the *portfolio standard deviation,* σ_p, is calculated as:

$$\sigma_p = \sqrt{w_1^2\sigma_1^2 + w_2^2\sigma_2^2 + 2w_1 w_2\sigma_1\sigma_2 r_{1,2}}.$$

    • Combining assets that have low correlations results in a portfolio with low risk.
  ☐ As the number of stocks in the portfolio increases, the total amount of risk decreases, but at a lower and lower rate, and it approaches a lower limit.
    • This lower limit is called the *market risk* inherent in stocks, and no amount of diversification can eliminate it.

- The risk that the portfolio has above the market risk is called *diversifiable risk*, and investors can reduce or even eliminate it by holding more and more stocks.

- Investors who do not like risk are called *risk averse*, and such investors will choose to hold portfolios that consist of many stocks rather than only a few so as to eliminate the diversifiable risk in their portfolios.

- Portfolios where only market risk remains are called *well-diversified portfolios*.

■ The *optimal portfolio* has the highest possible return for a given level of risk.

■ The *Capital Market Line (CML)* shows the expected return that investors can expect at each risk level, assuming that they behave optimally by splitting their investments between the market portfolio and the risk-free asset. The equation is:

$$\hat{k}_p = k_{RF} + \left(\frac{\hat{k}_M - k_{RF}}{\sigma_M} \right) \sigma_p.$$

☐ Note that the expected return on the market is greater than the risk-free rate, hence the CML is upward sloping.

- Investors who are willing to accept more risk are rewarded with higher expected returns as compensation for bearing this additional risk.

■ If investors hold only optimal portfolios (i.e., portfolios that have only market risk and are on the CML), then the only type of risk associated with an individual stock that should be of concern to investors is the risk the stock adds to the portfolio.

☐ The correct measure of an individual stock's contribution to the risk of the market portfolio is its *beta coefficient*. It is calculated as:

$$\text{Beta of stock i} = b_i = \frac{r_{i,M} \sigma_i \sigma_M}{\sigma_M^2} = \frac{r_{i,M} \sigma_i}{\sigma_M}.$$

☐ By definition, the market portfolio has a beta of 1.

- Adding a stock with a beta of 1 to the market portfolio will not change the portfolio's overall risk.

- Adding a stock with a beta less than 1 will reduce the portfolio's risk, hence reduce its expected rate of return.

- Adding a stock with a beta greater than 1 will increase the portfolio's risk and expected return.

☐ The CAPM shows the relationship between the risk that a stock contributes to a portfolio and the return that it must provide.

- The *required rate of return* on a stock is related to its beta as follows:

Required rate of return on Stock i = k_i = k_{RF} + $b_i(k_M - k_{RF})$.

☐ For given values of k_{RF} and k_M, the graph of k_i versus b_i is called the *Security Market Line (SML)*.
- The extra return associated with higher betas is called the *risk premium*, and the risk premium on a given stock is equal to $b_i(k_M - k_{RF})$.
- The term $(k_M - k_{RF})$ is called the *market risk premium*, and it amounts to the extra required return an investor requires for bearing the market's risk.
☐ The CML shows the best available set of portfolios, based on risk and return, available to investors. The SML, on the other hand, shows the relationship between the required rate of return on individual stocks and their market risk as measured by beta.

■ The historical relationship between the stock's return and the market's return is used to calculate beta.
☐ The slope of the regression line that best fits these points measures the overall sensitivity of the stock's return to the market return, and it is the stock's beta estimate.
- The regression line is called the stock's *characteristic line*.

■ A stock's risk can be broken down into market risk and diversifiable risk.

Total risk = Variance = Market risk + Diversifiable risk

$$\sigma_J^2 = b_J^2 \sigma_M^2 + \sigma_{eJ}^2.$$

■ The betas of a portfolio can be calculated as the weighted average of the betas of the individual assets in the portfolio.

The techniques used earlier in this chapter to value bonds can also be used, with a few modifications, to value stocks.

■ The general equation to value common stocks is:

$$\text{Price} = \text{PV} = \frac{D_1}{(1+k)} + \frac{D_2}{(1+k)^2} + ... + \frac{D_n}{(1+k)^n} = \sum_{t=1}^{\infty} \frac{D_t}{(1+k)^t}.$$

☐ Here the D_t terms represent the dividend expected in each Year t, and k is the stock's required rate of return.

■ The *dividend growth model* can be used if our best guess is that the firm's earnings and dividends will grow at a constant rate g on into the foreseeable future.

$$\hat{P}_0 = \frac{D_0(1+g)}{k-g} = \frac{D_1}{k-g}.$$

☐ The equation is called the *constant growth model*, or the *Gordon model*.

■ *Perpetuities* are securities that are expected to pay a constant amount each period forever.
  ☐ Preferred stock is an example of a perpetuity.
  ☐ The valuation equation for perpetuities is:

$$P = \frac{D}{k}.$$

■ Often it is inappropriate to assume that a company's dividends will grow at a constant rate forever. The best way to deal with a changing dividend growth rate is to use the *nonconstant growth model*.
  ☐ The following steps are required for this model:
  - Estimate each dividend during the nonconstant growth period.
  - Determine the present value of each of the nonconstant growth dividends.
  - Use the constant growth model to find the discounted value of all of the dividends expected once the nonconstant growth period has ended, which is the expected stock price at the end of the nonconstant growth period.
  - Find the present value of the expected future price.
  - Sum the PVs of the nonconstant dividends and the PV of the expected future price to find the value of the stock today.

SELF-TEST QUESTIONS

Definitional

1. Finding the _____ value, or _____, is the process of going from today's values to future amounts.

2. A(n) _____ _____ has equal payments, given the symbol PMT, that occur at the end of each period.

3. Finding _____ values is called _____, and it is simply the reverse of compounding.

4. In a(n) _____ loan the payment is set so that the present value of the series of payments, when discounted at the loan rate, is equal to the amount of the loan.

5. A(n) _____ _____ shows for each month the amount paid as interest and the amount applied to reduce principal.

6. The _____, or _____, _____ rate is the rate that would have produced the final compounded value under annual compounding.

7. If we know the current price of an asset and the expected cash flows, we can find the rate of return on the asset, or its _____.

8. A bond's _____ _____ is its stated face value, which is the amount the issuer must pay to the bondholder at maturity.

9. The _____ _____ is the periodic interest payment that the bond provides.

10. If the going interest rate is less than the coupon rate, the price will be greater than par so the bond will sell at a(n) _____.

11. The _____ ____ _____ is defined as the discount rate that sets the present value of all of the cash flows until maturity equal to the bond's current price.

12. Fluctuations in interest rates give rise to changes in bond prices, and this sensitivity is called _____ _____ _____.

13. The percentage price change of a bond in response to a change in interest rates depends on (1) the _____ of the bond and (2) its _____ _____.

14. _____ is the possibility that an outcome will be different from what is expected.

15. _____-_____ risk is the risk an investor would bear if he or she held only a single asset, while _____ risk is the risk that an asset contributes to a well-diversified portfolio.

16. The list of possible events, and their probabilities, is called a(n) _____ _____.

17. _____ measures the extent to which actual returns are likely to deviate from the expected value, and it is defined as the average of the squared deviations.

18. The _____ ____ _____ measures the amount of risk per unit of return.

19. A(n) _____ is a collection of assets.

20. The _____ _____ between two assets can range from −1 to +1.

21. The risk that a portfolio has above the _____ risk is called _____ risk, and investors can reduce or even eliminate it by holding more and more stocks.

22. The _____ _____ _____ shows the expected return that investors can expect at each risk level, assuming that they behave optimally by splitting their investments between the market portfolio and the risk-free asset.

23. The historical relationship between a stock's return and the market's return is used to calculate _____.

24. _____ are securities that are expected to pay a constant amount each period forever.

25. The best way to deal with a changing dividend growth rate is to use the _____ _____ model.

Conceptual

26. If a bank uses quarterly compounding for savings accounts, the nominal rate will be greater than the effective annual rate (EAR).

   a. True   **b.** False

27. If money has time value (that is, i > 0), the future value of some amount of money will always be more than the amount invested. The present value of some amount to be received in the future is always less than the amount to be received.

   a. True   **b.** False

28. Changes in economic conditions cause interest rates and bond prices to vary over time.

   a. True   **b.** False

29. If the appropriate rate of interest on a bond is greater than its coupon rate, the market value of that bond will be above par value.

   a. True   **b.** False

30. If a stock has a beta of zero, it will be riskless when held in isolation.

    a. True   **b.** False

31. A group of 200 stocks each has a beta of 1.0. We can be certain that each of the stocks was positively correlated with the market.

    a. True   **b.** False

32. According to the valuation model developed in this chapter, the value that an investor assigns to a share of stock is independent of the length of time the investor plans to hold the stock.

    a. True   **b.** False

33. As the discount rate increases without limit, the present value of a future cash inflow

    a. Gets larger without limit.
    b. Stays unchanged.
    c. Approaches zero.
    d. Gets smaller without limit; that is, approaches minus infinity.
    e. Goes to e^{in}.

34. Which of the following statements is most correct?

    a. Except in situations where compounding occurs annually, the periodic interest rate exceeds the nominal interest rate.
    b. The effective annual rate always exceeds the nominal rate, no matter how few or many compounding periods occur each year.
    c. If compounding occurs more frequently than once a year, and if payments are made at times other than at the end of compounding periods, it is impossible to determine present or future values, even with a financial calculator. The reason is that under these conditions, the basic assumptions of discounted cash flow analysis are not met.
    d. Assume that compounding occurs quarterly, that the nominal interest rate is 8 percent, and that you need to find the present value of $1,000 due 6 months from today. You could get the correct answer by discounting the $1,000 at 2 percent for 2 periods.
    e. Statements a, b, c, and d are false.

35. Which of the following statements is most correct?

    a. Ignoring interest accrued between payment dates, if the required rate of return on a bond is less than its coupon interest rate, and k_d remains below the coupon rate until maturity, then the market value of that bond will be below its par value until the bond matures, at which time its market value will equal its par value.

    b. Assuming equal coupon rates, a 20-year original maturity bond with one year left to maturity has more interest rate risk than a 10-year original maturity bond with one year left to maturity.

    c. Regardless of the size of the coupon payment, the price of a bond moves in the same direction as interest rates; for example, if interest rates rise, bond prices also rise.

    d. For bonds, price sensitivity to a given change in interest rates generally increases as years remaining to maturity increases.

    e. Because short-term interest rates are much more volatile than long-term rates, you would, in the real world, be subject to more interest rate risk if you purchased a 30-_day_ bond than if you bought a 30-_year_ bond.

36. If a company's bonds are selling at a _discount_, then:

    a. The YTM is the return investors probably expect to earn.

    b. The YTC is probably the expected return.

    c. Either a or b could be correct, depending on the yield curve.

    d. The current yield will exceed the expected rate of return.

    e. The after-tax cost of debt to the company will have to be less than the coupon rate on the bonds.

37. Which is the best measure of risk for an asset held in a well-diversified portfolio?

    a. Variance   **d.** Semi-variance

    b. Standard deviation   **e.** Expected value

    c. Beta

38. If investors expected inflation to increase in the future, and they also became more risk averse, what could be said about the change in the Security Market Line (SML)?

    a. The SML would shift up and the slope would increase.

    b. The SML would shift up and the slope would decrease.

    c. The SML would shift down and the slope would increase.

    d. The SML would shift down and the slope would decrease.

    e. The SML would remain unchanged.

39. Assume that a company's dividends are expected to grow at a rate of 25 percent per year for 5 years and then to slow down and to grow at a constant rate of 5 percent thereafter. The required (and expected) total return, k_s, is expected to remain constant at 12 percent. Which of the following statements is most correct?

    a. The dividend yield will be higher in the early years and then will decline as the annual capital gains yield gets larger and larger, other things held constant.

    b. Right now, it would be easier (require fewer calculations) to find the dividend yield expected in Year 7 than the dividend yield expected in Year 3.

    c. The stock price will grow each year at the same rate as the dividends.

    d. The stock price will grow at a different rate each year during the first 5 years, but its average growth rate over this period will be the same as the average growth rate in dividends; that is, the average stock price growth rate will be (25 + 5)/2.

    e. Statements a, b, c, and d are false.

40. Which of the following statements is most correct?

    a. The constant growth model is especially useful in situations where g is greater than 15 percent and k_s is 10 percent or less.

    b. The constant growth model can be used as one part of the process of finding the value of a stock which is expected to experience a very rapid rate of growth for a few years and then to grow at a constant ("normal") rate.

    c. The constant growth model cannot be used unless g is greater than zero.

    d. The constant growth model cannot be used unless the constant g is greater than k.

    e. Statements a, b, c, and d are correct.

SELF-TEST PROBLEMS

(Note: In working these problems, you may get an answer which differs from ours by a few cents due to differences in rounding. This should not concern you; just pick the closest answer.)

1. At an inflation rate of 9 percent, the purchasing power of $1 would be cut in half in just over 8 years (some calculators round to 9 years). How long, to the nearest year, would it take for the purchasing power of $1 to be cut in half if the inflation rate were only 4 percent?

    a. 12 years   **b.** 15 years   **c.** 18 years   **d.** 20 years   **e.** 23 years

2. Calculate the present value of $1,000 to be received at the end of 8 years. Assume an interest rate of 7 percent.

   a. $582.00   **b.** $1,718.19   **c.** $531.82   **d.** $5,971.30   **e.** $649.37

3. You have applied for a mortgage of $60,000 to finance the purchase of a new home. The bank will require you to make annual payments of $7,047.55 at the end of each of the next 20 years. Determine the interest rate in effect on this mortgage.

   a. 8.0%   **b.** 9.8%   **c.** 10.0%   **d.** 5.1%   **e.** 11.2%

4. What is the effective annual percentage rate (EAR) of 12 percent compounded monthly?

   a. 12.00%   **b.** 12.55%   **c.** 12.68%   **d.** 12.75%   **e.** 13.00%

5. The present value (t = 0) of the following cash flow stream is $11,958.20 when discounted at 12 percent annually. What is the value of the missing t = 2 cash flow?

   ```
   0          1        2        3        4
       12%
   ├────────┼────────┼────────┼────────┤
   PV = 11,958.20  2,000     ?      4,000    4,000
   ```

   a. $4,000.00   **b.** $4,500.00   **c.** $5,000.00   **d.** $5,500.00   **e.** $6,000.00

6. Today is your birthday, and you decide to start saving for your college education. You will begin college on your 18th birthday and will need $4,000 per year at the _end_ of each of the following 4 years. You will make a deposit 1 year from today in an account paying 12 percent annually and continue to make an identical deposit each year up to and including the year you begin college. If a deposit amount of $2,542.05 will allow you to reach your goal, what birthday are you celebrating today?

   a. 13   **b.** 14   **c.** 15   **d.** 16   **e.** 17

7. Delta Corporation has a bond issue outstanding with an annual coupon rate of 7 percent and 4 years remaining until maturity. The par value of the bond is $1,000. Determine the current value of the bond if present market conditions justify a 14 percent required rate of return. The bond pays interest annually.

   a. $1,126.42   **b.** $1,000.00   **c.** $796.06   **d.** $791.00   **e.** $536.42

8. Refer to Self-Test Problem 7. Suppose the bond had a semiannual coupon. Now what would be its current value?

    a. $1,126.42   **b.** $1,000.00   **c.** $796.06   **d.** $791.00   **e.** $536.42

9. Refer to Self-Test Problem 7. Assume an annual coupon but 20 years remaining to maturity. What is the current value under these conditions?

    a. $1,126.42   **b.** $1,000.00   **c.** $796.06   **d.** $791.00   **e.** $536.42

10. Refer to Self-Test Problem 9. What is the bond's current yield?

    a. 12.20%   **b.** 13.05%   **c.** 13.75%   **d.** 14.00%   **e.** 14.50%

11. Acme Products has a bond issue outstanding with 8 years remaining to maturity, a coupon rate of 10 percent with interest paid annually, and a par value of $1,000. If the current market price of the bond issue is $814.45, what is the yield to maturity, k_d?

    a. 12%   **b.** 13%   **c.** 14%   **d.** 15%   **e.** 16%

12. The Graf Company needs to finance some new R&D programs, so it will sell new bonds for this purpose. Graf's currently outstanding bonds have a $1,000 par value, a 10 percent coupon rate, and pay interest semiannually. The outstanding bonds have 25 years remaining to maturity, are callable after 5 years at a price of $1,090, and currently sell at a price of $700. The yield curve is expected to remain flat. On the basis of these data, what is the best estimate of Graf's _nominal interest rate_ on the new bonds it plans to sell? (Hint: You will need a financial calculator to work this problem.)

    a. 21.10%   **b.** 14.48%   **c.** 15.67%   **d.** 16.25%   **e.** 18.29%

13. If $k_{RF} = 5\%$, $k_M = 11\%$, and b = 1.3 for Stock X, what is k_X, the required rate of return for Stock X?

    a. 18.7%   **b.** 16.7%   **c.** 14.8%   **d.** 12.8%   **e.** 11.9%

14. The Apple Investment Fund has a total investment of $450 million in five stocks.

Stock	Investment (Millions)	Beta
1	$130	0.4
2	110	1.5
3	70	3.0
4	90	2.0
5	50	1.0
Total	$450	

What is the fund's overall, or weighted average, beta?

a. 1.14   **b.** 1.22   **c.** 1.35   **d.** 1.46   **e.** 1.53

15. Refer to Self-Test Problem 14. If the risk-free rate is 12 percent and the market risk premium is 6 percent, what is the required rate of return on the Apple Fund?

a. 20.76%   **b.** 19.92%   **c.** 18.81%   **d.** 17.62%   **e.** 15.77%

16. You are managing a portfolio of 10 stocks which are held in equal dollar amounts. The current beta of the portfolio is 1.8, and the beta of Stock A is 2.0. If Stock A is sold and the proceeds are used to purchase a replacement stock, what does the beta of the replacement stock have to be to lower the portfolio beta to 1.7?

a. 1.4   **b.** 1.3   **c.** 1.2   **d.** 1.1   **e.** 1.0

17. You are given the following distribution of returns:

Probability	Return
0.4	$30
0.5	25
0.1	-20

What is the coefficient of variation of the expected dollar returns?

a. 206.2500   **b.** 0.6383   **c.** 14.3614   **d.** 0.7500   **e.** 1.2500

18. If the risk-free rate is 8 percent, the expected return on the market is 13 percent, and the expected return on Security J is 15 percent, then what is the beta of Security J?

a. 1.40   **b.** 0.90   **c.** 1.20   **d.** 1.50   **e.** 0.75

19. The Canning Company has been hard hit by increased competition. Analysts predict that earnings (and dividends) will decline at a rate of 5 percent annually into the foreseeable future. If Canning's last dividend (D_0) was $2.00, and investors' required rate of return is 15 percent, what will be Canning's stock price *in 3 years*?

    a. $8.15   **b.** $9.50   **c.** $10.00   **d.** $10.42   **e.** $10.96

20. The Club Auto Parts Company has just recently been organized. It is expected to experience no growth for the next 2 years as it identifies its market and acquires its inventory. However, Club will grow at an annual rate of 5 percent in the third year and, beginning with the fourth year, should attain a 10 percent growth rate which it will sustain thereafter. The first dividend (D_1) to be paid at the end of the first year is expected to be $0.50 per share. Investors require a 15 percent rate of return on Club's stock. What is the current equilibrium stock price?

    a. $5.00   **b.** $8.75   **c.** $9.56   **d.** $12.43   **e.** $15.00

21. Johnson Corporation's stock is currently selling at $45.83 per share. The last dividend paid (D_0) was $2.50. Johnson is a constant growth firm. If investors require a return of 16 percent on Johnson's stock, what do they think Johnson's growth rate will be?

    a. 6%   **b.** 7%   **c.** 8%   **d.** 9%   **e.** 10%

22. Assume that the average firm in your company's industry is expected to grow at a constant rate of 7 percent and its dividend yield is 8 percent. Your company is about as risky as the average firm in the industry, but it has just successfully completed some R&D work which leads you to expect that its earnings and dividends will grow at a rate of 40 percent [$D_1 = D_0(1 + g) = D_0(1.40)$] this year and 20 percent the following year, after which growth should match the 7 percent industry average rate. The last dividend paid (D_0) was $1. What is the current value per share of your firm's stock?

    a. $22.47   **b.** $24.15   **c.** $21.00   **d.** $19.48   **e.** $22.00

23.   Assume that as investment manager of Maine Electric Company's pension plan (which is exempt from income taxes), you must choose between Exxon bonds and GM preferred stock. The bonds have a $1,000 par value; they mature in 20 years; they pay $35 each 6 months; they are callable at Exxon's option at a price of $1,150 after 5 years (ten 6-month periods); and they sell at a price of $815.98 per bond. The preferred stock is a perpetuity; it pays a dividend of $1.50 each quarter, and it sells for $75 per share. Assume interest rates do not change. What is the most likely *effective annual rate of return (EAR)* on the *higher* yielding security? (Hint: You will need a financial calculator to work this problem.)

   a. 9.20%   **b.** 8.24%   **c.** 9.00%   **d.** 8.00%   **e.** 8.50%

24.   Chadmark Corporation is expanding rapidly, and it currently needs to retain all of its earnings, hence it does not pay any dividends. However, investors expect Chadmark to begin paying dividends, with the first dividend of $0.75 coming 2 years from today. The dividend should grow rapidly, at a rate of 40 percent per year, during Years 3 and 4. After Year 4, the company should grow at a constant rate of 10 percent per year. If the required return on the stock is 16 percent, what is the value of the stock today?

   a. $16.93   **b.** $17.54   **c.** $15.78   **d.** $18.87   **e.** $16.05

ANSWERS TO SELF-TEST QUESTIONS

1. future; compounding
2. ordinary annuity
3. present; discounting
4. amortized
5. amortization schedule
6. effective; equivalent; annual
7. yield
8. par value
9. coupon payment
10. premium
11. yield to maturity
12. interest rate risk
13. maturity; coupon rate

14. Risk
15. Stand-alone; portfolio
16. probability distribution
17. Variance
18. coefficient of variation
19. portfolio
20. correlation coefficient
21. market; diversifiable
22. Capital Market Line
23. beta
24. Perpetuities
25. nonconstant growth

26.   b.   The EAR is always greater than or equal to the nominal rate.

27.   a.   Both these statements are correct.

28.   a.   For example, if inflation increases, the interest rate (or required return) will increase, resulting in a decline in bond price.

29.   b.   It will sell at a discount.

30.   b.   A zero beta stock could be made riskless if it were combined with enough other zero beta stocks, but it would still have company-specific risk and be risky when held in isolation.

31.   a.   By definition, if a stock has a beta of 1.0 it moves exactly with the market. In other words, if the market moves up by 7 percent, the stock will also move up by 7 percent, while if the market falls by 7 percent, the stock will fall by 7 percent.

32.   a.   The model considers all future dividends. This produces a current value which is appropriate for all investors independent of their expected holding period.

33.   c.   As the discount rate increases, the present value of a future sum decreases and eventually approaches zero.

34.   d.   Statement a is false because the periodic interest rate is equal to the nominal rate divided by the number of compounding periods, so it will be equal to or smaller than the nominal rate. Statement b is false because the EAR will equal the nominal rate if there is one compounding period per year (annual compounding). Statement c is false because we can determine present or future values under the stated conditions. Statement d is correct; using a financial calculator, enter $N = 2$, $I = 2$, $PMT = 0$, and $FV = 1000$ to find $PV = -961.1688$.

35.   d.   Statement a is false because the bond would have a premium and thus sell above par value. Statement b is false because both bonds would have the same interest rate risk because they both have one year left to maturity. Statement c is false because the price of a bond moves in the opposite direction as interest rates. Statement e is false because the 30-year bond would have more interest rate risk than the 30-day bond. Statement d is correct. As years to maturity increase for a bond, the number of discount periods used in finding the current bond value also increases. Therefore, bonds with longer maturities will have more price sensitivity to a given change in interest rates.

36.   a.   When bonds sell at a discount, the going interest rate (k_d) is above the coupon rate. If a company called the old discount bonds and replaced them with new bonds, the new coupon would be above the old coupon. This would increase a firm's interest cost; hence, the company would not call the discount bonds. Therefore, the YTM would be the expected rate of return. The shape of the yield curve would have no effect on the situation described in this question, but if the bonds had been selling at a premium, making the YTC the relevant yield, then the yield curve in a sense would have an effect. The YTC would be below the cost if the company were to sell new long-term bonds, if the yield curve were steeply upward sloping. Statement d is false because the expected rate of return would include a current yield component and a capital gains component (because the bond's price will rise from its current discounted price to par as maturity approaches). Therefore, the current yield will _not_ exceed the expected rate of return. The after-tax cost of debt is the expected rate adjusted for taxes, $k_d(1 - T)$. Because the bonds are selling at a discount, the coupon rate could be quite low, even zero, so we know that statement e is false. Therefore, statement a is correct.

37.   c.   The best measure of risk is the beta coefficient, which is a measure of the extent to which the returns on a given stock move with the stock market.

38.   a.   The increase in inflation would cause the SML to shift up, and investors becoming more risk averse would cause the slope to increase.

39.   b.   Statement b is correct. We know that after Year 5, the stock will have a constant growth rate, and the capital gains yield will be equal to that growth rate. We also know that the total return is expected to be constant. Therefore, we could find the expected dividend yield in Year 7 simply by subtracting the growth rate from the total return: Dividend yield = 12% – 5% = 7% in Year 7.

The other statements are all false. This could be confirmed by thinking about how the dividend growth rate starts high, ends up at the constant growth rate, and must lie between these two rates and be declining between Years 1 and 5. The average growth rate in dividends during Years 1 through 5 will be (25 + 5)/2 = 15%, which is above k_s = 12%, so statements c and d must be false.

40.   b.   Statement b is correct. In the case of a nonconstant growth stock which is expected to grow at a constant rate after Year N, we would find the value of D_{N+1} and use it in the constant growth model to find P_N. The other statements are all false. Note that the constant growth model can be used for g = 0, g < 0, and g < k.

SOLUTIONS TO SELF-TEST PROBLEMS

1. c.   0   N = ?
         ├───4%────────┤

        1.00   0.50

    With a financial calculator, input I = 4, PV = -1.00, PMT = 0, and FV = 0.50. Solve for N = 17.67 ≈ 18 years.

2. a.

    PV = ?   1,000

    $PV = FV_8(PVIF_{7\%,8}) = \$1,000(0.5820) = \$582.00$.

    With a financial calculator, input N = 8, I = 7, PMT = 0, FV = 1000, and solve for PV = -$582.01.

    (Note: Annual compounding is assumed if not otherwise specified.)

3. c.   0   1   2   3   20
         ├─i = ?─┼────────┼────────┼───── ··· ─────┤

        60,000 -7,047.55 -7,047.55 -7,047.55   -7,047.55

    The amount of the mortgage ($60,000) is the present value of a 20-year ordinary annuity with payments of $7,047.55. Therefore,

    $PVA_{20} = PMT(PVIFA_{i,20})$
    $\$60,000 = \$7,047.55(PVIFA_{i,20})$
    $PVIFA_{i,20} = 8.5136$
    $i = 10.00\%$ exactly.

    With a financial calculator, input N = 20, PV = 60000, PMT = -7047.55, FV = 0, and solve for I = 10.00%.

4. c. $\text{EAR} = (1 + i_{Nom}/m)^m - 1.0$
$= (1 + 0.12/12)^{12} - 1.0$
$= (1.01)^{12} - 1.0$
$= 1.1268 - 1.0$
$= 0.1268 = 12.68\%.$

With a financial calculator, enter P/YR = 12 and NOM% = 12, and then solve for EFF% = 12.68%.

5. e. $\$11,958.20 = \$2,000(\text{PVIF}_{12\%,1}) + \text{CF}_2(\text{PVIF}_{12\%,2})$
$+ \$4,000(\text{PVIF}_{12\%,3}) + \$4,000(\text{PVIF}_{12\%,4})$
$\$11,958.20 = \$2,000(0.8929) + \text{CF}_2(0.7972) + \$4,000(0.7118) + \$4,000(0.6355)$
$\$11,958.20 = \$7,175.00 + (0.7972)\text{CF}_2$
$(0.7972)\text{CF}_2 = \$4,783.20$
$\text{CF}_2 = \$6,000.00.$

With a financial calculator, input cash flows into the cash flow register, using -11,958.20 as the cash flow for time 0 (CF₀), and using 0 as the value for the unknown cash flow, input I = 12, and then press the NPV key to solve for the present value of the unknown cash flow, $4,783.29. This value should be compounded by $(1.12)^2$, so that $\$4,783.29(1.2544) = \$6,000.16$.

6. b. First, how much must you accumulate on your 18th birthday?

$\text{PVA}_n = \$4,000(\text{PVIFA}_{12\%,4}) = \$4,000(3.0373) = \$12,149.20.$
Present birthday = ?

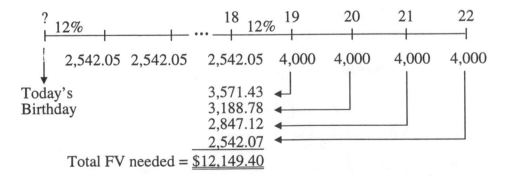

Total FV needed = $\underline{\$12,149.40}$

Using a financial calculator (with the calculator set for an ordinary annuity), enter $N = 4$, $I = 12$, PMT = 4000, FV = 0, and solve for PV = -\$12,149.40. This is the amount (or lump sum) that must be present in your bank account on your 18th birthday in order for you to be able to withdraw \$4,000 at the end of each year for the next 4 years.

Now, how many payments of \$2,542.05 must you make to accumulate \$12,149.20?

$$FVA_n = \$12,149.20 = \$2,542.05(FVIFA_{12\%,n}).$$
$$FVIFA_{12\%,n} = 4.7793$$
$$n = 4, \text{ from Table A-4 in text.}$$

Using a financial calculator, enter $I = 12$, PV = 0, PMT = -2542.05, FV = 12149.40, and solve for $N = 4$. Therefore, if you make payments at 18, 17, 16, and 15, you are now 14.

7.   c. $V_B = INT(PVIFA_{k_d,N}) + M(PVIF_{k_d,N})$
         $= \$70(PVIFA_{14\%,4}) + \$1,000(PVIF_{14\%,4})$
         $= \$70(2.9137) + \$1,000(0.5921) = \$796.06.$

Calculator solution: Input $N = 4$, $I = 14$, PMT = 70, FV = 1000, and solve for PV = -\$796.04.

8.   d. $V_B = (INT/2)(PVIFA_{k_d/2,2N}) + M(PVIF_{k_d/2,2N})$
         $= \$35(PVIFA_{7\%,8}) + \$1,000(PVIF_{7\%,8})$
         $= \$35(5.9713) + \$1,000(0.5820) = \$791.00.$

Calculator solution: Input $N = 8$, $I = 7$, PMT = 35, FV = 1000, and solve for PV = -\$791.00.

9.   e. $V_B = INT(PVIFA_{k_d,N}) + M(PVIF_{k_d,N})$
         $= \$70(PVIFA_{14\%,20}) + \$1,000(PVIF_{14\%,20})$
         $= \$70(6.6231) + \$1,000(0.0728) = \$536.42.$

Calculator solution: Input $N = 20$, $I = 14$, PMT = 70, FV = 1000, and solve for PV = -\$536.38.

10. b. From Self-Test Problem 9 we know that the current price of the bond is $536.38.

Therefore, the current yield $= \dfrac{\text{Annual Interest}}{\text{Current Price}}$

$$= \dfrac{\$70}{\$536.38}$$

$$= 13.05\%.$$

11. c. $\qquad V_B = INT(PVIFA_{k_d,N}) + M(PVIF_{k_d,N})$

$\$814.45 = \$100(PVIFA_{k_d,8}) + \$1,000(PVIF_{k_d,8}).$

Now use trial and error techniques. Try $I = k_d = 12\%$:
$\$814.45 = \$100(4.9676) + \$1,000(0.4039) = \$900.66.$

Since $\$814.45 \ne \$900.66$, the yield to maturity is not 12 percent. The calculated value is too large. Therefore, increase the value of I to 14 percent to lower the calculated value: $\$814.45 = \$100(4.6389) + \$1,000(0.3506) = \$814.49.$ This is close enough to conclude that $k_d =$ yield to maturity $= 14\%$.

Calculator solution: Input N = 8, PV = -814.45, PMT = 100, FV = 1000, and solve for $I = k_d = 14.00\%$.

12. b. Investors would expect to earn either the YTM or the YTC, and the expected return on the old bonds is the cost Graf would have to pay in order to sell new bonds.

YTM: Enter N = 2(25) = 50; PV = -700; PMT = 100/2 = 50; and FV = 1000. Press I to get $I = k_d/2 = 7.24\%$. Multiply 7.24%(2) = 14.48% to get the YTM.

YTC: Enter N = 2(5) = 10, PV = -700, PMT = 50, FV = 1090, and then press I to get I=10.55%. Multiply by 2 to get YTC = 21.10%.

Would investors expect the company to call the bonds? Graf currently pays 10 percent on its debt (the coupon rate). New debt would cost at least 14.48 percent. Because $k_d > 10\%$ coupon rate, it would be stupid for the company to call, so investors would not expect a call. Therefore, they would expect to earn 14.48 percent on the bonds. This is k_d, so 14.48 percent is the rate Graf would probably have to pay on new bonds.

13.   d. $k_X = k_{RF} + (k_M - k_{RF})b_X = 5\% + (11\% - 5\%)1.3 = 12.8\%$.

14.   d. $b_p = \sum_{i=1}^{5} w_i\, b_i$

$$= \frac{\$130}{\$450}(0.4) + \frac{\$110}{\$450}(1.5) + \frac{\$70}{\$450}(3.0) + \frac{\$90}{\$450}(2.0) + \frac{\$50}{\$450}(1.0) = 1.46.$$

15.   a. $k_p = k_{RF} + (k_M - k_{RF})b_p = 12\% + (6\%)1.46 = 20.76\%$.

16.   e.   First find the beta of the remaining 9 stocks:

$1.8 = 0.9(b_R) + 0.1(b_A)$
$1.8 = 0.9(b_R) + 0.1(2.0)$
$1.8 = 0.9(b_R) + 0.2$
$1.6 = 0.9(b_R)$
$b_R = 1.78$.

Now find the beta of the new stock that produces $b_p = 1.7$.

$1.7 = 0.9(1.78) + 0.1(b_N)$
$1.7 = 1.6 + 0.1(b_N)$
$0.1 = 0.1(b_N)$
$b_N = 1.0$.

17.   b.   Use the given probability distribution of returns to calculate the expected value, variance, standard deviation, and coefficient of variation.

P_i	k_i	$P_i k_i$	k_i	$\hat{k}$		$(k_i - \hat{k})$	$(k_i - \hat{k})^2$	$P(k_i - \hat{k})^2$
0.4	× $30	= $12.0	$30	- $22.5	=	$ 7.5	$ 56.25	$ 22.500
0.5	× 25	= 12.5	25	- 22.5	=	2.5	6.25	3.125
0.1	× -20	= -2.0	-20	- 22.5	=	-42.5	1,806.25	180.625
	$\hat{k}$	= $22.5					σ^2 = Variance =	$206.250

The standard deviation (σ) of $\hat{k}$ is $\sqrt{\$206.25} = \$14.3614$.

Use the standard deviation and the expected return to calculate the coefficient of variation: $14.3614/$22.5 = 0.6383.

18. a. Use the SML equation, substitute in the known values, and solve for beta.
$k_{RF} = 8\%$; $k_M = 13\%$; $k_J = 15\%$.

$$k_J = k_{RF} + (k_M - k_{RF})b_J$$
$$15\% = 8\% + (13\% - 8\%)b_J$$
$$7\% = (5\%)b_J$$
$$b_J = 1.4.$$

19. a. $\hat{P}_0 = \dfrac{D_0(1+g)}{k_s - g} = \dfrac{\$2.00(0.95)}{0.15 - (-0.05)} = \dfrac{\$1.90}{0.20} = \$9.50.$

$\hat{P}_3 = \hat{P}_0(1+g)^3 = \$9.50(0.95)^3 = \$9.50(0.8574) = \$8.15.$

The Gordon model can also be used:

$$\hat{P}_3 = \frac{D_4}{k_s - g} = \frac{D_0(1+g)^4}{0.15 - (-0.05)} = \frac{\$2.00(0.95)^4}{0.20} = \frac{\$2.00(0.8145)}{0.20} = \$8.15.$$

20. b. To calculate the current value of a nonconstant growth stock, follow these steps:

1. Determine the expected stream of dividends during the nonconstant growth period. Also, calculate the expected dividend at the end of the first year of constant growth that will be used later to calculate stock price.

$$D_1 = \$0.50.$$
$$D_2 = D_1(1 + g) = \$0.50(1 + 0.0) = \$0.50.$$
$$D_3 = D_2(1 + g) = \$0.50(1.05) = \$0.525.$$
$$D_4 = D_3(1 + g) = \$0.525(1.10) = \$0.5775.$$

2. Discount the expected dividends during the nonconstant growth period at the investor's required rate of return to find their present value.

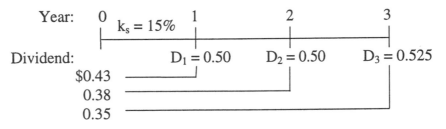

3. Calculate the expected stock price at the end of the final year of nonconstant growth. This occurs at the end of Year 3. Use the Gordon model for this calculation.

$$\hat{P}_3 = \frac{D_4}{k_s - g} = \frac{\$0.5775}{0.15 - 0.10} = \$11.55.$$

Then discount this stock price back 3 periods at the investor's required rate of return to find its present value.

$$PV = \$11.55(PVIF_{15\%,3}) = \$11.55(0.6575) = \$7.59.$$

4. Add the present value of the stock price expected at the end of Year 3 plus the dividends expected in Years 1, 2, and 3 to find the present value of the stock, P_0.

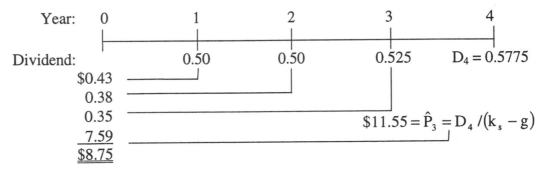

Alternatively, input 0, 0.5, 0.5, 12.075(0.525 + 11.55) into the cash flow register, input I = 15, and then solve for NPV = $8.75.

21. e.

$$P_0 = \frac{D_0(1+g)}{k_s - g}$$

$$\$45.83 = \frac{\$2.50(1+g)}{0.16 - g}$$

$$\$7.33 - \$45.83g = \$2.50 + \$2.50g$$
$$\$48.33g = \$4.83$$
$$g = 0.0999 \approx 10\%.$$

22. d. $D_0 = \$1.00$; $k_s = 8\% + 7\% = 15\%$; $g_1 = 40\%$; $g_2 = 20\%$; $g_n = 7\%$.

$$*\hat{P}_2 = \frac{\$1.7976}{0.15 - 0.07} = \$22.47.$$

23. a. Exxon bonds: Price = \$815.98, Maturity = 20 years, PMT = \$35 per 6 months, and they are callable at \$1,150 after 10 periods (5 years).

Will the bond's YTM or YTC be applicable? The bond is selling at a discount, so k_d > Coupon interest rate. Therefore, the bond is not likely to be called, so calculate the YTM.

Input N = 40, PV = -815.98, PMT = 35, FV = 1000, and solve for I = $k_d/2$ = 4.5%. EAR = $(1.045)^2 - 1 = 9.2\%$.

Preferred: D = \$1.50 per quarter and P_0 = \$75.
k_{ps} = \$1.50/\$75 = 2% = periodic rate. EAR = $(1.02)^4 - 1 = 8.24\%$.

Thus, the Exxon bonds provide the higher effective annual rate of return.

24. a. To calculate Chadmark's current stock price, follow the following steps: (1) Determine the expected stream of dividends during the nonconstant growth period. You will need to calculate the expected dividend at the end of Year 5, which is the first year of constant growth. This dividend will be used in the next step to calculate the stock price. (2) Calculate the expected stock price at the end of the final year of nonconstant growth. This occurs at the end of Year 4. Use the Gordon model for this calculation. (3) Add the value obtained in Step 2 to the dividend expected in Year 4. (4) Put the values obtained in the prior steps on a time line and discount them at the required rate of return to find the present value of Chadmark's stock. These steps are shown below.

$D_0 = \$0$; $D_1 = \$0$; $D_2 = \$0.75$; $D_3 = \$0.75(1.4) = \$1.05$; $D_4 = \$0.75(1.4)^2 = \$1.47$; $D_5 = \$0.75(1.4)^2(1.10) = \$1.617$.

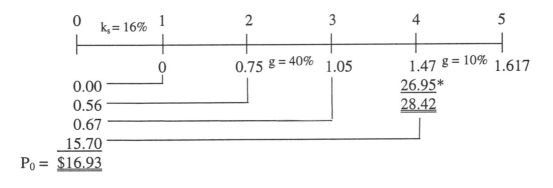

$* \hat{P}_4 = \$1.617/(0.16 - 0.10) = \$26.95$.

$CF_0 = 0$; $CF_1 = 0$; $CF_2 = 0.75$; $CF_3 = 1.05$; $CF_4 = 28.42$.

Alternatively, using a financial calculator you could input the cash flows as shown above into the cash flow register, input I = 16, and press NPV to obtain the stock's value today of $16.93.

OVERVIEW

A manager's primary goal is to maximize the value of his or her firm's stock. Value is based on the stream of earnings and cash flows the firm will generate in the future. But how does an investor go about estimating future earnings and cash flows, and how does a manager decide which actions are most likely to increase future earnings and cash flows? The answers to both questions lie in a study of the financial statements which publicly traded firms must provide to investors. Here "investors" include both institutions and individuals. Thus, this chapter discusses what the basic financial statements are, how they are used, and what kinds of financial information users need.

Much of the material in this chapter reviews concepts covered in basic accounting courses. Accounting is used to "keep score," and if a firm's managers do not know the score, they cannot tell how their actions will affect the stock's price. If a firm's managers—whether they are in marketing, personnel, production, or finance—do not understand financial statements, they will not be able to judge the effects of their actions. Although only accountants need to know how to make financial statements, everyone involved with business needs to know how to interpret them.

OUTLINE

A firm's annual report to shareholders presents two important types of information. The first is a verbal statement of the company's operating results during the past year and discusses new developments that will affect future operations. The second is a set of quantitative financial statements that report what actually happened to the firm's financial position, earnings, and dividends over the past few years.

■ The information contained in an annual report is used by investors to help form expectations about future earnings and dividends.

The balance sheet shows the firm's assets and the claims against those assets. Assets, found on the left-hand side of the balance sheet, are typically shown in the order of their liquidity.

Claims, found on the right-hand side, are generally listed in the order in which they must be paid.

■ Only cash represents actual money.
  ☐ Non-cash assets should produce cash flows eventually, but they do not represent cash in hand.
  ☐ Note, though, that some types of marketable securities have a very short time until maturity, and can be converted very quickly into cash at prices close to their book values. These securities are called *cash equivalents*, and are included with cash.
  ☐ Other types of marketable securities have a longer time until maturity, and their market values are less predictable. These securities are classified as *short-term investments*.

Claims against the assets consist of liabilities and stockholders' equity:

   Assets – Liabilities – Preferred stock = Common stockholders' equity (Net worth).

Preferred stock is a hybrid, or a cross between common stock and debt. In the event of bankruptcy, preferred stock ranks below debt but above common stock.

■ The common equity section of the balance sheet is divided into two accounts: common stock and retained earnings.
  ☐ The common stock account arises from the issuance of stock to raise capital.
  ☐ Retained earnings are built up over time as the firm "saves" a part of its earnings rather than paying all earnings out as dividends.

■ Different methods, such as FIFO and LIFO, can be used to determine the value of inventory. These methods, in turn, affect the reported cost of goods sold, profits, and EPS.

Companies often use the most accelerated method permitted under the law to calculate depreciation for tax purposes but use straight-line depreciation, which results in a lower depreciation expense, for stockholder reporting.

The balance sheet may be thought of as a snapshot of the firm's financial position *at a point in time* (for example, end of year). The balance sheet changes every day as inventory is increased or decreased, as fixed assets are added or retired, as bank loans are increased or decreased, and so on.

The income statement summarizes the firm's revenues and expenses over a period of time (for example, the past year).

Earnings per share (EPS) is called "the bottom line," denoting that of all the items on the income statement, EPS is the most important.

The income statement reports on operations *over a period of time*.

The statement of retained earnings reports changes in the equity accounts between balance sheet dates.

The balance sheet account "retained earnings" represents a claim against assets, not assets per se.

Retained earnings as reported on the balance sheet do not represent cash and are not "available" for the payment of dividends or anything else.

☐ Retained earnings represent funds that have already been reinvested in the firm's operating assets.

The statement of cash flows summarizes the changes in a company's cash position. It is used to help answer questions such as: Is the firm generating enough cash to purchase the additional assets required for growth? Is the firm generating any extra cash that can be used to repay debt or to invest in new products?

Net income, noncash adjustments to net income, changes in working capital, fixed assets, and security transactions are reflected in the statement of cash flows.

Since depreciation is a noncash charge, it must be added back to net income when calculating the firm's cash flow.

The statement of cash flows separates activities into three categories: operating activities, investing activities, and financing activities.

Financial managers generally use this statement, along with the cash budget, when forecasting their companies' cash positions.

Net cash flow is the sum of net income plus noncash adjustments.

Financial statements are used to help predict the firm's future earnings and dividends. From an investor's standpoint, predicting the future is what financial statement analysis is all about. From management's standpoint, financial statement analysis is useful both to help anticipate future conditions and, more important, as a starting point for planning actions that will affect the future course of events. Financial ratios are designed to help one evaluate a firm's financial statements. Ratio analysis raises a red flag as to the questions managers and analysts should ask.

■ Financial ratios are used by three main groups:
  ☐ Managers, who employ ratios to help analyze, control, and thus improve their firm's operating performance.
  ☐ Credit analysts, such as bank loan officers or bond rating analysts, who analyze ratios to help ascertain a company's ability to pay its debts.
  ☐ Stock analysts and stockholders, who are interested in a company's efficiency, risk, and growth prospects to forecast earnings, dividends, and stock prices.

Liquidity ratios are used to measure a firm's ability to meet its current obligations as they come due.

■ The *current ratio* measures the extent to which the claims of short-term creditors are covered by assets that are expected to be converted to cash fairly quickly. It is determined by dividing current assets by current liabilities. It is the most commonly used measure of short-term solvency.

■ The *quick,* or *acid test, ratio* is calculated by deducting inventories from current assets and then dividing the remainder by current liabilities. Inventories are excluded because they are typically the least liquid of a firm's current assets, hence they are the assets on which losses are most likely to occur in the event of liquidation.

Asset management ratios measure how effectively a firm is managing its assets and whether or not the level of those assets is properly related to the level of operations as measured by sales.

■ The *inventory turnover ratio* is defined as sales divided by inventories. It is often necessary to use average inventories rather than year-end inventories, especially if a firm's business is highly seasonal, or if there has been a strong upward or downward sales trend during the year.

■ The *days sales outstanding (DSO),* also called the "average collection period" (ACP), is used to appraise accounts receivable, and it is calculated by dividing accounts receivable by average daily sales to find the number of days' sales tied up in receivables.
  ☐ The DSO represents the average length of time that the firm must wait after making a sale before receiving cash, which is the average collection period.
  ☐ The DSO can also be evaluated by comparison with the terms on which the firm sells its goods.
    • If the trend in DSO is up, but the credit policy has not been changed, this would be strong evidence that steps should be taken to expedite the collection of receivables.

■ The *fixed assets turnover ratio* is the ratio of sales to net fixed assets. It measures how effectively the firm uses its plant and equipment.

■ The *total assets turnover ratio* is calculated by dividing sales by total assets. It measures the utilization, or turnover, of all the firm's assets.

Debt management ratios measure the extent to which a firm is using debt financing, or financial leverage, and the degree of safety afforded to creditors.

■ Financial leverage has three important implications: (1) By raising funds through debt, stockholders can maintain control of a firm while limiting their investment. (2) Creditors look to the equity, or owner-supplied funds, to provide a margin of safety, so if the stockholders have provided only a small proportion of the total financing, the firm's risks are borne mainly by its creditors. (3) If the firm earns more on investments financed with borrowed funds than it pays in interest, the return on the owners' capital is magnified, or "leveraged."
  □ Firms with relatively high debt ratios have higher expected returns when the economy is normal, but they are exposed to risk of loss when the economy goes into a recession.
  □ Firms with low debt ratios are less risky, but also forego the opportunity to leverage up their return on equity.
  □ Decisions about the use of debt require firms to balance higher expected returns against increased risk.

■ The text discusses two procedures analysts use to examine the firm's debt: (1) They check the balance sheet to determine the extent to which borrowed funds have been used to finance assets, and (2) they review the income statement to see the extent to which fixed charges are covered by operating profits.

■ The *debt ratio*, or ratio of total debt to total assets, measures the percentage of funds provided by creditors. Total debt includes both current liabilities and long-term debt. The lower the ratio, the greater the protection afforded creditors in the event of bankruptcy. Stockholders, on the other hand, like the fact that it magnifies expected earnings.

■ The *times-interest-earned (TIE) ratio* is determined by dividing earnings before interest and taxes (EBIT) by the interest charges. The TIE measures the extent to which operating income can decline before the firm is unable to meet its annual interest costs.
  □ Failure to meet this obligation can bring legal action by the firm's creditors, possibly resulting in bankruptcy.
  □ Note that EBIT, rather than net income, is used in the numerator. Because interest is paid with pre-tax dollars, the full amount of EBIT is available to pay interest.

■   The *fixed charge coverage ratio* is similar to the TIE ratio, but it is more inclusive because it recognizes that many firms lease assets and also must make sinking fund payments.

Profitability ratios show the combined effects of liquidity, asset management, and debt on operating results.

■   The *profit margin on sales* is calculated by dividing net income by sales. It gives the profit per dollar of sales.

■   The *basic earning power (BEP) ratio* is calculated by dividing earnings before interest and taxes (EBIT) by total assets. It shows the raw earning power of the firm's assets, before the influence of taxes and leverage, and it is useful for comparing firms with different tax situations and different degrees of financial leverage.

■   The *return on total assets (ROA)* is the ratio of net income to total assets; it measures the return on all the firm's assets after interest and taxes.

■   The *return on common equity (ROE)* measures the rate of return on stockholders' investment. It is equal to net income divided by common equity.

Market value ratios relate the firm's stock price to its earnings and book value per share, and thus give management an indication of what investors think of the company's past performance and future prospects. If the liquidity, asset management, debt management, and profitability ratios are all good, then the market value ratios will be high, and the stock price will probably be as high as can be expected.

■   The *price/earnings (P/E) ratio*, or price per share divided by earnings per share, shows how much investors are willing to pay per dollar of reported profits. P/E ratios are higher for firms with strong growth prospects, other things held constant, but they are lower for riskier firms.

■   The *market/book (M/B) ratio*, defined as market price per share divided by book value per share, gives another indication of how investors regard the company. Higher M/B ratios are generally associated with firms with relatively high rates of return on common equity.

It is important to analyze trends in ratios as well as their absolute levels. Trend analysis can provide clues as to whether the firm's financial situation is likely to improve or to deteriorate.

■ *Common size analysis* and *percent change analysis* are two other techniques that can be used to identify trends in financial statements. The Extensions to Chapter 3 of the text explain these techniques.

A modified Du Pont chart shows how return on equity is affected by assets turnover, profit margin, and leverage.

■ The profit margin times the total assets turnover is called the *Du Pont equation*. This equation gives the rate of return on assets (ROA):

ROA = Profit margin × Total assets turnover.

■ The ROA times the *equity multiplier* (total assets divided by common equity) yields the return on equity (ROE). This equation is referred to as the *extended Du Pont equation:*

ROE = Profit margin × Total assets turnover × Equity multiplier.

☐ Firms which use a large amount of debt financing will necessarily have a high equity multiplier.

■ If a company is financed only with common equity, the return on assets (ROA) and the return on equity (ROE) are the same because total assets will equal common equity. This equality holds only if the company uses no debt.

Ratio analysis involves comparisons because a company's ratios are compared with those of other firms in the same industry, that is, to industry average figures. Comparative ratios are available from a number of sources which include Dun & Bradstreet, Robert Morris Associates, and the U. S. Commerce Department. Benchmarking is the process of comparing the ratios of a particular company with those of a smaller group of "benchmark" companies, rather than with the entire industry.

■ Many companies also benchmark various parts of their overall operation against top companies, whether they are in the same industry or not.

■ Each of the data-supplying organizations uses a somewhat different set of ratios designed for its own purposes. So, when you select a comparative data source, you should be sure that your emphasis is similar to that of the agency whose ratios you plan to use.
☐ Be sure to verify the exact definitions of the ratios to ensure consistency with your own work.

There are some inherent problems and limitations to ratio analysis that necessitate care and judgment.

- Ratios are often not useful for analyzing the operations of large firms which operate in many different industries because comparative ratios are not meaningful.

- The use of industry averages may not provide a very challenging target for high-level performance.

- Inflation affects depreciation charges, inventory costs, and therefore the value of both balance sheet items and net income. For this reason, the analysis of a firm over time, or a comparative analysis of firms of different ages, can be misleading.

- Ratios may be distorted by seasonal factors, or manipulated by management to give the impression of a sound financial condition (*window dressing techniques*).

- Different operating policies and accounting practices, such as the decision to lease rather than to buy equipment, can distort comparisons.

- Many ratios can be interpreted in different ways, and whether a particular ratio is good or bad should be based upon a complete financial analysis rather than the level of a single ratio at a single point in time.

While it is important to understand and interpret financial statements, sound financial analysis involves more than just calculating and interpreting numbers. Good analysts recognize that certain qualitative factors must be considered when evaluating a company. Some of these factors are listed below.

- Are the company's revenues tied to one key customer?

- To what extent are the company's revenues tied to one key product?

- To what extent does the company rely on a single supplier?

- What percentage of the company's business is generated overseas?

- Competition.

- Future prospects.

- Legal and regulatory environment.

The Extensions to Chapter 3 discuss common size analysis and percentage change analysis.

■ In a *common size analysis*, all income statement items are divided by sales, and all balance sheet items are divided by total assets. Common size analysis facilitates comparisons of balance sheets and income statements over time and across companies.

■ In a *percentage change analysis*, growth rates are calculated for all income statement items and balance sheet accounts. This type of analysis pinpoints "problem" areas more quickly than looking at dollar amounts.

■ The conclusions reached in common size and percentage change analyses generally parallel those derived from ratio analysis. It is often useful to have all three analyses to drive home to management, in slightly different ways, the need to take corrective actions. Thus, a thorough financial statement analysis will include ratio, percentage change, and common size analyses, as well as a Du Pont analysis.

SELF-TEST QUESTIONS

Definitional

1. Of all its communications with shareholders, a firm's _____ report is generally the most important.

2. The income statement reports the results of operations during the past year, the most important item being _____ _____ _____.

3. The _____ _____ lists the firm's assets as well as claims against those assets.

4. Typically, assets are listed in order of their _____, while liabilities are listed in the order in which they must be paid.

5. Assets – Liabilities – Preferred stock = _____ worth, or _____ _____ equity.

6. The two accounts that normally make up the common equity section of the balance sheet are _____ _____ and _____ _____.

7. _____ _____ as reported on the balance sheet represent income earned by the firm in past years that has not been paid out as dividends.

8. The _____ ____ _____ _____ is designed to summarize the changes in a company's cash position.

9.   The three major categories of the statement of cash flows are cash flows associated with _____ activities, _____-_____ _____ activities, and _____ activities.

10.   The _____ _____ account arises from the issuance of stock to raise capital.

11.   The _____ ____ _____ _____ reports changes in the equity accounts between balance sheet dates.

12.   _____ _____ _____ is the sum of net income plus noncash adjustments.

13.   The current ratio and acid test ratio are examples of _____ ratios. They measure a firm's ability to meet its _____-_____ obligations.

14.   The days sales outstanding (DSO) ratio is found by dividing average sales per day into accounts _____. The DSO is the length of time that a firm must wait after making a sale before it receives _____.

15.   Debt management ratios are used to evaluate a firm's use of financial _____.

16.   The debt ratio, which is the ratio of _____ _____ to _____ _____, measures the percentage of funds supplied by creditors.

17.   The _____-_____-_____ ratio is calculated by dividing earnings before interest and taxes by the amount of interest charges.

18.   The combined effects of liquidity, asset management, and debt on operating results are measured by _____ ratios.

19.   Dividing net income by sales gives the _____ _____ on sales.

20.   The _____/_____ ratio measures how much investors are willing to pay for each dollar of a firm's reported profits.

21.   Firms with higher rates of return on stockholders' equity tend to sell at relatively high ratios of _____ price to _____ value.

22.   Individual ratios are of little value in analyzing a company's financial condition. More important are the _____ of a ratio over time and the comparison of the company's ratios to _____ average ratios.

23.   A(n) _____ _____ chart shows how return on equity is affected by total assets turnover, profit margin, and leverage.

24.   Return on assets is a function of two variables, the profit _____ and _____ _____ turnover.

25.   Analyzing a particular ratio over time for an individual firm is known as _____ analysis.

26.   The process of comparing a particular company with a smaller set of companies in the same industry is called _____.

27.   Financial ratios are used by three main groups: (1) _____, who employ ratios to help analyze, control, and thus improve their firm's operating performance; (2) _____ _____, who analyze ratios to help ascertain a company's ability to pay its debts; and (3) _____ _____ and _____, who are interested in a company's efficiency, risk, and growth prospects to forecast earnings, dividends, and stock prices.

28.   The _____ _____ _____ ratio measures how effectively the firm uses its plant and equipment.

29.   The _____ _____ _____ ratio measures the utilization of all the firm's assets.

30.   Two procedures analysts use to examine the firm's debt: (1) They check the _____ _____ to determine the extent to which borrowed funds have been used to finance assets, and, (2) they review the _____ _____ to see the extent to which fixed charges are covered by operating profits.

31.   The _____ _____ _____ ratio is similar to the TIE ratio, but it is more inclusive because it recognizes that many firms lease assets and also must make sinking fund payments.

32.   The _____ _____ _____ ratio is useful for comparing firms with different tax situations and different degrees of financial leverage.

33.   If a company is financing only with common equity, the firm's return on assets and return on equity will be _____.

34.   _____ _____ raises a red flag as to the questions managers and analysts should ask.

35.   _____ _____ _____ facilitates comparisons of balance sheets and income statements over time and across companies.

36.   In a(n) _____ _____ analysis, growth rates are calculated for all income statement items and balance sheet accounts.

Conceptual

37.   The equity multiplier can be expressed as $1 - (Debt/Assets)$.

    a. True   **b.** False

38.   A high quick ratio is *always* a good indication of a well-managed liquidity position.

    a. True   **b.** False

39.   International Appliances Inc. has a current ratio of 0.5. Which of the following actions would improve (increase) this ratio?

    a. Use cash to pay off current liabilities.
    b. Collect some of the current accounts receivable.
    c. Use cash to pay off some long-term debt.
    d. Purchase additional inventory on credit (accounts payable).
    e. Sell some of the existing inventory at cost.

40.   Refer to Self-Test Question 39. Assume that International Appliances has a current ratio of 1.2. Now, which of the following actions would improve (increase) this ratio?

    a. Use cash to pay off current liabilities.
    b. Collect some of the current accounts receivable.
    c. Use cash to pay off some long-term debt.
    d. Purchase additional inventory on credit (accounts payable).
    e. Use cash to pay for some fixed assets.

41.   Examining the ratios of a particular firm against the same measures for a small group of firms from the same industry, at a point in time, is an example of

    a. Trend analysis.
    b. Benchmarking.
    c. Du Pont analysis.
    d. Simple ratio analysis.
    e. Industry analysis.

42. Which of the following statements is most correct?

a. Having a high current ratio and a high quick ratio is always a good indication that a firm is managing its liquidity position well.

b. A decline in the inventory turnover ratio suggests that the firm's liquidity position is improving.

c. If a firm's times-interest-earned ratio is relatively high, then this is one indication that the firm should be able to meet its debt obligations.

d. Since ROA measures the firm's effective utilization of assets (without considering how these assets are financed), two firms with the same EBIT must have the same ROA.

e. If, through specific managerial actions, a firm has been able to increase its ROA, then, because of the fixed mathematical relationship between ROA and ROE, it must also have increased its ROE.

43. Which of the following statements is most correct?

a. Suppose two firms with the same amount of assets pay the same interest rate on their debt and earn the same rate of return on their assets and that ROA is positive. However, one firm has a higher debt ratio. Under these conditions, the firm with the higher debt ratio will also have a higher rate of return on common equity.

b. One of the problems of ratio analysis is that the relationships are subject to manipulation. For example, we know that if we use some cash to pay off some of our current liabilities, the current ratio will always increase, especially if the current ratio is weak initially, for example, below 1.0.

c. Generally, firms with high profit margins have high asset turnover ratios and firms with low profit margins have low turnover ratios; this result is exactly as predicted by the extended Du Pont equation.

d. Firms A and B have identical earnings and identical dividend payout ratios. If Firm A's growth rate is higher than Firm B's, then Firm A's P/E ratio must be greater than Firm B's P/E ratio.

e. Each of the above statements is false.

SELF-TEST PROBLEMS

(The following data apply to the next two Self-Test Problems.)

Ryngaert & Sons, Inc. has operating income (EBIT) of $2,250,000. The company's depreciation expense is $450,000, its interest expense is $120,000, and it faces a 40 percent tax rate.

1. What is the company's net income?

 a. $1,008,000   **b.** $1,278,000   **c.** $1,475,000   **d.** $1,728,000   **e.** $1,800,000

2. What is its net cash flow?

 a. $1,008,000   **b.** $1,278,000   **c.** $1,475,000   **d.** $1,728,000   **e.** $1,800,000

3. Info Technics Inc. has an equity multiplier of 2.75. The company's assets are financed with some combination of long-term debt and common equity. What is the company's debt ratio?

 a. 25.00%   **b.** 36.36%   **c.** 52.48%   **d.** 63.64%   **e.** 75.00%

4. Refer to Self-Test Problem 3. What is the company's common equity ratio?

 a. 25.00%   **b.** 36.36%   **c.** 52.48%   **d.** 63.64%   **e.** 75.00%

5. Cutler Enterprises has current assets equal to $4.5 million. The company's current ratio is 1.25, and its quick ratio is 0.75. What is the firm's level of current liabilities (in millions)?

 a. $0.8   **b.** $1.8   **c.** $2.4   **d.** $2.9   **e.** 3.6

6. Refer to Self-Test Problem 5. What is the firm's level of inventories (in millions)?

 a. $0.8   **b.** $1.8   **c.** $2.4   **d.** $2.9   **e.** $3.6

(The following financial statements apply to the next seven Self-Test Problems.)

Roberts Manufacturing Balance Sheet
December 31, 1998
(Dollars in Thousands)

Cash	$ 200	Accounts payable	$ 205
Receivables	245	Notes payable	425
Inventory	625	Other current liabilities	115
Total current assets	$1,070	Total current liabilities	$ 745
Net fixed assets	1,200	Long-term debt	420
		Common equity	1,105
Total assets	$2,270	Total liabilities and equity	$2,270

Roberts Manufacturing Income Statement
for Year Ended December 31, 1998
(Dollars in Thousands)

Sales		$2,400
Cost of goods sold:		
Materials	$1,000	
Labor	600	
Heat, light, and power	89	
Indirect labor	65	
Depreciation	80	1,834
Gross profit		$ 566
Selling expenses		175
General and administrative expenses		216
Earnings before interest and taxes (EBIT)		$ 175
Less interest expense		35
Earnings before taxes (EBT)		$ 140
Less taxes (40%)		56
Net income (NI)		$ 84

7. Calculate the liquidity ratios, that is, the current ratio and the quick ratio.

  a. 1.20; 0.60   **b.** 1.20; 0.80   **c.** 1.44; 0.60   **d.** 1.44; 0.80   **e.** 1.60; 0.60

8. Calculate the asset management ratios, that is, the inventory turnover ratio, fixed assets turnover, total assets turnover, and days sales outstanding.

  a. 3.84; 2.00; 1.06; 36.75 days   **d.** 3.84; 2.00; 1.24; 34.10 days
  b. 3.84; 2.00; 1.06; 35.25 days   **e.** 3.84; 2.20; 1.48; 34.10 days
  c. 3.84; 2.00; 1.06; 34.10 days

9. Calculate the debt management ratios, that is, the debt and times-interest-earned ratios.

  a. 0.39; 3.16   **b.** 0.39; 5.00   **c.** 0.51; 3.16   **d.** 0.51; 5.00   **e.** 0.73; 3.16

10. Calculate the profitability ratios, that is, the profit margin on sales, return on total assets, return on common equity, and basic earning power of assets.

  a. 3.50%; 4.25%; 7.60%; 8.00%
  b. 3.50%; 3.70%; 7.60%; 7.71%
  c. 3.70%; 3.50%; 7.60%; 7.71%
  d. 3.70%, 3.50%; 8.00%; 8.00%
  e. 4.25%; 3.70%; 7.60%; 8.00%

11. Calculate the market value ratios, that is, the price/earnings ratio and the market/book value ratio. Roberts had an average of 10,000 shares outstanding during 1998, and the stock price on December 31, 1998, was $40.00.

    a. 4.21; 0.36   **b.** 3.20; 1.54   **c.** 3.20; 0.36   **d.** 4.76; 1.54   **e.** 4.76; 0.36

12. Use the extended Du Pont equation to determine Roberts' return on equity.

    a. 6.90%   **b.** 7.24%   **c.** 7.47%   **d.** 7.60%   **e.** 8.41%

13. Lewis Inc. has sales of $2 million per year, all of which are credit sales. Its days sales outstanding is 42 days. What is its average accounts receivable balance?

    a. $233,333   **b.** $266,667   **c.** $333,333   **d.** $350,000   **e.** $366,667

14. Southeast Jewelers Inc. sells only on credit. Its days sales outstanding is 60 days, and its average accounts receivable balance is $500,000. What are its sales for the year?

    a. $1,500,000   **b.** $3,000,000   **c.** $2,000,000   **d.** $2,750,000   **e.** $3,225,000

15. A firm has total interest charges of $20,000 per year, sales of $2 million, a tax rate of 40 percent, and a profit margin of 6 percent. What is the firm's times-interest-earned ratio?

    a. 10   **b.** 11   **c.** 12   **d.** 13   **e.** 14

16. Refer to Self-Test Problem 15. What is the firm's TIE, if its profit margin decreases to 3 percent and its interest charges double to $40,000 per year?

    a. 3.0   **b.** 2.5   **c.** 3.5   **d.** 4.2   **e.** 3.7

17. A fire has destroyed many of the financial records at Anderson Associates. You are assigned to piece together information to prepare a financial report. You have found that the firm's return on equity is 12 percent and its debt ratio is 0.40. What is its return on assets?

    a. 4.90%   **b.** 5.35%   **c.** 6.60%   **d.** 7.20%   **e.** 8.40%

18. Refer to Self-Test Problem 17. What is the firm's debt ratio if its ROE is 15 percent and its ROA is 10 percent?

    a. 67%   **b.** 50%   **c.** 25%   **d.** 33%   **e.** 45%

19. Rowe and Company has a debt ratio of 0.50, a total assets turnover of 0.25, and a profit margin of 10 percent. The president is unhappy with the current return on equity, and he thinks it could be doubled. This could be accomplished (1) by increasing the profit margin to 14 percent and (2) by increasing debt utilization. Total assets turnover will not change. What new debt ratio, along with the 14 percent profit margin, is required to double the return on equity?

   a. 0.55   b. 0.60   c. 0.65   d. 0.70   e. 0.75

20. Altman Corporation has $1,000,000 of debt outstanding, and it pays an interest rate of 12 percent annually. Altman's annual sales are $4 million, its federal-plus-state tax rate is 40 percent, and its net profit margin on sales is 10 percent. If the company does not maintain a TIE ratio of at least 5 times, its bank will refuse to renew the loan, and bankruptcy will result. What is Altman's TIE ratio?

   a. 9.33   b. 4.44   c. 2.50   d. 4.00   e. 6.56

21. Refer to Self-Test Problem 20. What is the maximum amount Altman's EBIT could decrease and its bank still renew its loan?

   a. $186,667   b. $45,432   c. $66,767   d. $47,898   e. $143,925

22. Pinkerton Packaging's ROE last year was 2.5 percent, but its management has developed a new operating plan designed to improve things. The new plan calls for a total debt ratio of 50 percent, which will result in interest charges of $240 per year. Management projects an EBIT of $800 on sales of $8,000, and it expects to have a total assets turnover ratio of 1.6. Under these conditions, the federal-plus-state tax rate will be 40 percent. If the changes are made, what return on equity will Pinkerton earn?

   a. 2.50%   b. 13.44%   c. 13.00%   d. 14.02%   e. 14.57%

(The following financial statements apply to the next three Self-Test Problems.)

Baker Corporation Balance Sheet
December 31, 1998

Cash and marketable securities	$ 50	Accounts payable	$ 250
Accounts receivable	200	Accruals	250
Inventory	250	Notes payable	500
Total current assets	$ 500	Total current liabilities	$1,000
Net fixed assets	1,500	Long-term debt	250
		Common stock	400
		Retained earnings	350
Total assets	$2,000	Total liabilities and equity	$2,000

23. What is Baker Corporation's current ratio as of December 31, 1998?

    a. 0.35   **b.** 0.65   **c.** 0.50   **d.** 0.25   **e.** 0.75

24. If Baker uses $50 of cash to pay off $50 of its accounts payable, what is its new current ratio after this action?

    a. 0.47   **b.** 0.44   **c.** 0.54   **d.** 0.33   **e.** 0.62

25. If Baker uses its $50 cash balance to pay off $50 of its long-term debt, what will be its new current ratio?

    a. 0.35   **b.** 0.50   **c.** 0.55   **d.** 0.60   **e.** 0.45

(The following financial statements apply to the next Self-Test Problem.)

Whitney Inc. Balance Sheet
December 31, 1998

		Total current liabilities	$ 100
		Long-term debt	250
		Common stockholders' equity	400
Total assets	$750	Total liabilities and equity	$750

Whitney Inc. Income Statement
for Year Ended December 31, 1998

Sales		$1,000
Cost of goods sold (excluding depreciation)	$550	
Other operating expenses	100	
Depreciation	50	
Total operating costs		700
Earnings before interest and taxes (EBIT)		$ 300
Less interest expense		25
Earnings before taxes (EBT)		$ 275
Less taxes (40%)		110
Net income		$ 165

26. What are Whitney Inc.'s basic earning power and ROA ratios?

    a. 30%; 22%   **b.** 40%; 30%   **c.** 50%; 22%   **d.** 40%; 22%   **e.** 40%; 40%

(The following financial statements apply to the next Self-Test Problem.)

Cotner Enterprises Balance Sheet
December 31, 1998

		Total current liabilities	$ 300
		Long-term debt	500
		Common stockholders' equity	450
Total assets	$1,250	Total liabilities and equity	$1,250

Cotner Enterprises Income Statement
for Year Ended December 31, 1998

Sales		$1,700
Cost of goods sold (excluding depreciation)	$1,190	
Other operating expenses	135	
Depreciation	75	
Total operating costs		1,400
Earnings before interest and taxes (EBIT)		$ 300
Less interest expense		54
Earnings before taxes (EBT)		$ 246
Less taxes (35%)		86
Net income		$ 160

27.   What are Cotner Enterprise's basic earning power and ROA ratios?

    a. 20%; 12.8%   **d.** 17.5%; 12.8%
    b. 24%; 12.8%   **e.** 24%; 10.5%
    c. 24%; 15.8%

28.   Dauten Enterprises is just being formed. It will need $2 million of assets, and it expects to have an EBIT of $400,000. Dauten will own no securities, so all of its income will be operating income. If it chooses to, Dauten can finance up to 50 percent of its assets with debt which will have a 9 percent interest rate. Dauten has no other liabilities. Assuming a 40 percent federal-plus-state tax rate on all taxable income, what is the difference between the expected ROE if Dauten finances with 50 percent debt versus the expected ROE if it finances entirely with common stock?

    a. 7.2%   **b.** 6.6%   **c.** 6.0%   **d.** 5.8%   **e.** 9.0%

ANSWERS TO SELF-TEST QUESTIONS

1.	annual		**19.**	profit margin
2.	earnings per share		**20.**	price/earnings
3.	balance sheet		**21.**	market; book
4.	liquidity		**22.**	trend; industry
5.	Net; common stockholders'		**23.**	Du Pont
6.	common stock; retained earnings		**24.**	margin; total assets
7.	Retained earnings		**25.**	trend
8.	statement of cash flows		**26.**	benchmarking
9.	operating; long-term investing; financing		**27.**	managers; credit analysts; stock analysts; shareholders
10.	common stock		**28.**	fixed assets turnover
11.	statement of retained earnings		**29.**	total assets turnover
12.	Net cash flow		**30.**	balance sheet; income statement
13.	liquidity; short-term (or current)		**31.**	fixed charge coverage
14.	receivable; cash		**32.**	basic earning power
15.	leverage		**33.**	equal
16.	total debt; total assets		**34.**	Ratio analysis
17.	times-interest-earned		**35.**	Common size analysis
18.	profitability		**36.**	percentage change

37.   **b.** $1 - (\text{Debt/Assets}) = \text{Equity/Assets}$. The equity multiplier is equal to Assets/Equity.

38.   b.   Excess cash resulting from poor management could produce a high quick ratio. Similarly, if accounts receivables are not collected promptly, this could also lead to a high quick ratio.

39.   d.   This question is best analyzed using numbers. For example, assume current assets equal $50 and current liabilities equal $100; thus, the current ratio equals 0.5. For answer a, assume $5 in cash is used to pay off $5 in current liabilities. The new current ratio would be $45/$95 = 0.47. For answer d, assume a $10 purchase of inventory on credit (accounts payable). The new current ratio would be $60/$110 = 0.55, which is an increase over the old current ratio of 0.5. (Self-Test Problems 23 through 25 were set up to help visualize this question.)

40.   a.   Again, this question is best analyzed using numbers. For example, assume current assets equal $120 and current liabilities equal $100; thus, the current ratio equals 1.2. For answer a, assume $5 in cash is used to pay off $5 in current liabilities. The new current ratio would be $115/$95 = 1.21, which is an increase over the old current ratio of 1.2. For answer d, assume a $10 purchase of inventory on credit (accounts payable). The new current ratio would be $130/$110 = 1.18, which is a decrease over the old current ratio of 1.2.

41.   b.   The correct answer is benchmarking. A trend analysis compares the firm's ratios over time, while a Du Pont analysis shows how return on equity is affected by assets turnover, profit margin, and leverage.

42.   c.   Excess cash resulting from poor management could produce high current and quick ratios; thus statement a is false. A decline in the inventory turnover ratio suggests that either sales have decreased or inventory has increased, which suggests that the firm's liquidity position is _not_ improving; thus statement b is false. ROA = Net income/Total assets, and EBIT does not equal net income. Two firms with the same EBIT could have different financing and different tax rates resulting in different net incomes. Also, two firms with the same EBIT do not necessarily have the same total assets; thus statement d is false. ROE = ROA × Assets/Equity. If ROA increases because total assets decrease, then the equity multiplier decreases, and depending on which effect is greater, ROE may or may not increase; thus statement e is false. Statement c is correct; the TIE ratio is used to measure whether the firm can meet its debt obligation, and a high TIE ratio would indicate this is so. (Self-Test Problems 26 and 27 were set up to help visualize statement d of this question.)

43. a. Ratio analysis is subject to manipulation; however, if the current ratio is less than 1.0 and we use cash to pay off some current liabilities, the current ratio will decrease, _not_ increase; thus statement b is false. Statement c is just the reverse of what actually occurs. Firms with high profit margins have low turnover ratios and vice versa. Statement d is false; it does not necessarily follow that if a firm's growth rate is higher that its stock price will be higher. Statement a is correct. From the information given in statement a, one can determine that the two firms' net incomes are equal; thus, the firm with the higher debt ratio (lower equity ratio) will indeed have a higher ROE.

SOLUTIONS TO SELF-TEST PROBLEMS

1. b.

EBIT	$2,250,000
Interest	120,000
EBT	$2,130,000
Taxes (40%)	852,000
Net Income	$1,278,000

2. d. Net cash flow = Net income + Depreciation
$$= \$1,278,000 + \$450,000$$
$$= \$1,728,000.$$

3. d. $2.75 = A/E$
$E/A = 1/2.75$
$E/A = 36.36\%.$

$D/A = 1 - E/A$
$\quad\quad = 1 - 36.36\%$
$\quad\quad = 63.64\%.$

4. b. From #3 above, $E/A = 36.36\%.$

5. e. CA = $4.5 million; CA/CL = 1.25.
$4.5/CL = 1.25$
1.25 CL = $4.5
    CL = $3.6 million.

6.   b.   QR $\;= 0.75$; CA $= \$4.5$ million ; CL $= \$3.6$ million.

$$QR \;= \frac{CA - I}{CL}$$

$$0.75 = \frac{\$4.5 - I}{\$3.6}$$

$$\$2.7 = \$4.5 - I$$

$$I = \$1.8 \text{ million.}$$

7.   c. $\text{Current ratio} = \dfrac{\text{Current assets}}{\text{Current liabilities}} = \dfrac{\$1,070}{\$745} = 1.44.$

$\text{Quick ratio} = \dfrac{\text{Current assets} - \text{Inventory}}{\text{Current liabilities}} = \dfrac{\$1,070 - \$625}{\$745} = 0.60.$

8.   a. $\text{Inventory turnover} = \dfrac{\text{Sales}}{\text{Inventory}} = \dfrac{\$2,400}{\$625} = 3.84.$

$\text{Fixed assets turnover} = \dfrac{\text{Sales}}{\text{Net fixed assets}} = \dfrac{\$2,400}{\$1,200} = 2.00.$

$\text{Total assets turnover} = \dfrac{\text{Sales}}{\text{Total assets}} = \dfrac{\$2,400}{\$2,270} = 1.06.$

$\text{DSO} = \dfrac{\text{Accounts receivable}}{\text{Sales}/360} = \dfrac{\$245}{\$2,400/360} = 36.75 \text{ days}.$

9.   d.   Debt ratio = Total debt/Total assets = $\$1,165/\$2,270 = 0.51.$

TIE ratio = EBIT/Interest = $\$175/\$35 = 5.00.$

10. b. $\text{Profit margin} = \dfrac{\text{Net income}}{\text{Sales}} = \dfrac{\$84}{\$2,400} = 0.0350 = 3.50\%.$

$\text{ROA} = \dfrac{\text{Net income}}{\text{Total assets}} = \dfrac{\$84}{\$2,270} = 0.0370 = 3.70\%.$

$\text{ROE} = \dfrac{\text{Net income}}{\text{Common equity}} = \dfrac{\$84}{\$1,105} = 0.0760 = 7.60\%.$

$\text{BEP} = \dfrac{\text{EBIT}}{\text{Total assets}} = \dfrac{\$175}{\$2,270} = 0.0771 = 7.71\%.$

11. e. $\text{EPS} = \dfrac{\text{Net income}}{\text{Number of shares outstanding}} = \dfrac{\$84,000}{10,000} = \$8.40.$

$\text{P/E ratio} = \dfrac{\text{Price}}{\text{EPS}} = \dfrac{\$40.00}{\$8.40} = 4.76.$

$\text{Market/Book value} = \dfrac{\text{Market price}}{\text{Book value}} = \dfrac{\$40(10,000)}{\$1,105,000} = 0.36.$

12. d. $\text{ROE} = \text{Profit margin} \times \text{Total assets turnover} \times \text{Equity multiplier}$

$= \dfrac{\$84}{\$2,400} \times \dfrac{\$2,400}{\$2,270} \times \dfrac{\$2,270}{\$1,105} = 0.035 \times 1.057 \times 2.054$

$= 0.0760 = 7.60\%.$

13. a. $\text{DSO} = \dfrac{\text{Accounts receivable}}{\text{Sales/360}}$

$42 \text{ days} = \dfrac{\text{AR}}{\$2,000,000/360}$

$\text{AR} = \$233,333.$

14. b. $\qquad$ DSO = Accounts receivable/(Sales/360)
$\qquad$ 60 days = \$500,000/(Sales/360)
$\qquad$ 60(Sales/360) = \$500,000
$\qquad$ Sales = \$3,000,000.

15. b. Net income = \$2,000,000(0.06) = \$120,000.

Earnings before taxes = \$120,000/(1 − 0.4) = \$200,000.

EBIT = \$200,000 + \$20,000 = \$220,000.

TIE = EBIT/Interest = \$220,000/\$20,000 = 11.

16. c. Net income = \$2,000,000(0.03) = \$60,000.

Earnings before taxes = \$60,000/(1 − 0.4) = \$100,000.

EBIT = \$100,000 + \$40,000 = \$140,000.

TIE = EBIT/Interest = \$140,000/\$40,000 = 3.5.

17. d. If Total debt/Total assets = 0.40, then Total equity/Total assets = 0.60, and the equity multiplier (Assets/Equity) = 1/0.60 = 1.667.

$$\frac{NI}{E} = \frac{NI}{A} \times \frac{A}{E}$$

ROE = ROA × EM

12% = ROA × 1.667

ROA = 7.20%.

18. d. $\qquad$ ROE = ROA × Equity multiplier
$\qquad$ 15% = 10% × TA/Equity
$\qquad$ 1.5 = TA/Equity
$\qquad$ Equity/TA = 0.67.

Debt/TA = 1 − Equity/TA = 1 − 0.67 = 0.33 = 33%.

19.   c.   If Total debt/Total assets = 0.50, then Total equity/Total assets = 0.50 and the equity multiplier (Assets/Equity) = 1/0.50 = 2.0.

ROE = PM × Total assets turnover × EM.

Before: ROE = 10% × 0.25 × 2.00 = 5.00%.

After: 10.00% = 14% × 0.25 × EM; thus EM = 2.8571.

$$\text{Equity multiplier} = \frac{\text{Assets}}{\text{Equity}}$$
$$2.8571 = \frac{1}{\text{Equity}}$$
$$0.35 = \text{Equity}.$$

Debt = Assets − Equity = 100% − 35% = 65%.

20.   e.   TIE = EBIT/Interest, so find EBIT and Interest.

Interest = $1,000,000(0.12) = $120,000.

Net income = $4,000,000(0.10) = $400,000.

Pre-tax income = $400,000/(1 − T) = $400,000/0.6 = $666,667.

EBIT = $666,667 + $120,000 = $786,667.

TIE = $786,667/$120,000 = 6.56×.

21.   a.   TIE = EBIT/INT
              5 = EBIT/$120,000
        EBIT = $600,000.

From Self-Test Problem 20, EBIT = $786,667, so EBIT could decrease by $786,667 − $600,000 = $186,667.

22. b. ROE = Profit margin × Total assets turnover × Equity multiplier
= NI/Sales × Sales/TA × TA/Equity.

Now we need to determine the inputs for the equation from the data that were given. On the left we set up an income statement, and we put numbers in it on the right:

Sales (given)	$8,000
Cost	NA
EBIT (given)	$ 800
Interest (given)	240
EBT	$ 560
Taxes (40%)	224
Net income	$ 336

Now we can use some ratios to get some more data:

Total assets turnover = S/TA = 1.6 (given).

D/A = 50%, so E/A = 50%, and therefore TA/E = 1/(E/A) = 1/0.5 = 2.00.

Now we can complete the extended Du Pont equation to determine ROE:

ROE = $336/$8,000 × 1.6 × 2.0 = 13.44%.

23. c. Baker Corporation's current ratio equals Current assets/Current liabilities = $500/$1,000 = 0.50.

24. a. Baker Corporation's new current ratio equals ($500 – $50)/($1,000 – $50) = $450/$950 = 0.47.

25. e. Only the current asset balance is affected by this action. Baker's new current ratio = ($500 – $50)/$1,000 = $450/$1,000 = 0.45.

26. d. Whitney's BEP ratio equals EBIT/Total assets = $300/$750 = 40%.

Whitney's ROA equals Net income/Total assets = $165/$750 = 22%.

27. b. Cotner's BEP ratio equals EBIT/Total assets = $300/$1,250 = 24%.

Cotner's ROA equals Net income/Total assets = $160/$1,250 = 12.8%.

28.   b.   Known data: Total assets = $2,000,000; EBIT = $400,000; k_d = 9%, T = 40%.

D/A = 0.5 = 50%, so Equity = 0.5($2,000,000) = $1,000,000.

	D/A = 0%	D/A = 50%
EBIT	$400,000	$400,000
Interest	0	90,000*
Taxable income	$400,000	$310,000
Taxes (40%)	160,000	124,000
Net income (NI)	$240,000	$186,000

For D/A = 0%, ROE = NI/Equity = $240,000/$2,000,000 = 12%. For D/A = 50%, ROE = $186,000/$1,000,000 = 18.6%. Difference = 18.6% − 12.0% = 6.6%.

*If D/A = 50%, then half of the assets are financed by debt, so Debt = 0.5($2,000,000) = $1,000,000. At a 9 percent interest rate, INT = 0.09($1,000,000) = $90,000.

CHAPTER 4
VALUING THE FIRM: THE CASH FLOW MODEL

OVERVIEW

One fundamental goal of financial analysis is to determine the price at which a share of stock should trade. Clearly, an accurate model of stock prices would be a valuable tool for people trying to exploit market inefficiencies. Moreover, an accurate model of stock prices would be most useful to managers who want to maximize their firm's stock prices as they plan the actions that will determine their firms' futures.

One model for determining the value of a share of stock is the dividend growth model. This model is reasonably accurate for firms (1) that pay dividends, (2) that have a relatively slow and constant growth rate in earnings, (3) that have a relatively constant payout ratio, (4) that maintain a relatively constant capital structure, and (5)

that are expected to continue on into the indefinite future rather than to merge with some other company. Many firms meet these specifications, but many more do not, and for these firms the dividend growth model is not appropriate. Some other valuation must be used.

In this chapter, we develop a general cash flow model for valuing either entire corporations or divisions. In order to do so, we must first modify standard accounting data and put it on a cash flow, as opposed to an accounting profit, basis. Next, we discuss the tax environment, because taxes have a major effect on cash flows. Finally, we put it all together in the form of a cash flow model of a firm's value.

OUTLINE

The traditional financial statements are designed more for use by creditors and tax collectors than for managers and equity (stock) analysts. Certain modifications are used for corporate decision making and stock valuation. Financial analysts combine stock prices and accounting data to evaluate and reward managerial performance.

- To judge managerial performance one needs to compare managers' ability to generate operating income (EBIT) with the operating assets under their control.
  - *Operating assets* consist of cash, accounts receivable, inventories, and fixed assets necessary to operate the business.

☐ *Nonoperating assets* include marketable securities, investments in subsidiaries, land held for future use, and the like.

☐ Operating assets can be further divided into *working capital* and *plant and equipment*.

☐ Those current assets used in operations are called *operating working capital*, and operating working capital less accounts payable and accruals is called *net operating working capital (NOWC)*.

- Short-term investments are normally excluded when calculating NOWC because they generally result from investment decisions made by the treasurer, and are not used in the core operations.

☐ *Total operating capital* is the sum of net operating working capital and net fixed assets.

■ Net income does not always reflect the true performance of a company's operations or the effectiveness of its operating managers and employees.

☐ A better measure for comparing managers' performance is *net operating profit after taxes (NOPAT)*, which is the amount of profit a company would generate if it had no debt and held no financial assets.

$$NOPAT = EBIT(1 - T).$$

■ The value of a company's operations depends on all the future expected free cash flows.

☐ *Free cash flow* is the cash flow actually available for distribution to investors after the company has made all the investments in fixed assets and working capital necessary to sustain ongoing operations.

- Free cash flow is defined as after-tax operating profit minus the amount of investment in working capital and fixed assets necessary to sustain the business.

☐ *Operating cash flow* is NOPAT plus any noncash adjustments as shown on the statement of cash flows, such as depreciation.

☐ Free cash flow is calculated as operating cash flow less gross investment in operating capital. It also equals NOPAT less net investment in operating capital.

■ Negative free cash flow is not always bad. If free cash flow is negative because NOPAT is negative, this is a bad sign, because the company probably is experiencing operating problems.

☐ Exceptions to this might be start-up companies; companies that are incurring significant current expenses to launch a new product line; or high growth companies, which will have large investments in capital that cause low current free cash flow, but that will increase future free cash flow.

Two additional ratios can be used to evaluate a firm's operating performance.

■ The *operating capital requirement ratio* measures the relationship between operating capital and sales. It is calculated as:

$$\text{Operating capital requirement ratio} = \frac{\text{Operating capital}}{\text{Sales}}.$$

☐ If a firm can reduce its investment in operating capital without lowering sales, its capital costs would decline, its return on capital would increase, and its stock price would rise.

■ A second useful ratio is the *operating profit margin after taxes*. It is calculated as:

$$\text{Operating profit margin after taxes} = \frac{\text{NOPAT}}{\text{Sales}} = \frac{\text{EBIT}(1-T)}{\text{Sales}}.$$

☐ A low after-tax operating profit margin will drag down free cash flows, as will a high capital requirement ratio.

Neither traditional accounting data nor the modified data discussed earlier deal with stock prices. This is a serious omission, since the primary goal of management is to maximize the firm's stock price. In response to these limitations, financial analysts have developed two new performance measures, Market Value Added (MVA) and Economic Value Added (EVA).

■ Shareholders' wealth is maximized by maximizing the difference between the market value of the firm's equity and the amount of equity capital that was supplied by shareholders. This difference is called the *Market Value Added (MVA)*.

MVA = Market value of equity – Equity capital supplied by shareholders
= (Shares outstanding)(Stock price) – Total common equity.

■ Whereas MVA measures the effects of managerial actions since the very inception of a company, *Economic Value Added (EVA)* focuses on managerial effectiveness in a given year.

EVA = NOPAT – After-tax dollar cost of capital used to support operations
= EBIT (1 – T) – (Operating Capital)(After-tax percentage cost of capital).

☐ EVA is an estimate of a business's true economic profit for the year.
☐ EVA differs sharply from accounting profit. EVA represents the residual income that remains after the cost of all capital, including equity capital, has been deducted, whereas accounting profit is determined without imposing a charge for equity capital.
☐ EVA provides a good measure of the extent to which the firm has added to shareholder value.

☐ EVA can be determined for divisions as well as for the company as a whole, so it provides a useful basis for determining managerial compensation at all levels.

■ There is a relationship between MVA and EVA, but it is not a direct one.
☐ If a company has a history of negative EVAs, then its MVA will probably be negative, and vice versa if it has a history of positive EVAs.
☐ A company with a history of negative EVAs could have a positive MVA, provided investors expect a turnaround in the future.

■ When EVAs or MVAs are used to evaluate managerial performance as part of an incentive compensation program, EVA is the measure that is typically used.
☐ MVA is used primarily to evaluate top corporate officers over periods of five to ten years, or longer.

Individuals pay taxes on wages and salaries, on investment income (dividends, interest, and profits from the sale of securities), and on the profits of proprietorships and partnerships.

■ U. S. income taxes are *progressive*; that is, the higher the income, the larger the percentage paid in taxes. Marginal tax rates begin at 15 percent and can go up to 39.6 percent.
☐ The *marginal tax rate* is the tax applicable to the last unit of income.
☐ The *average tax rate* is calculated as taxes paid divided by taxable income.
☐ *Taxable income* is gross income minus exemptions and allowable deductions as set forth in the Tax Code.
☐ *Bracket creep* is a situation that occurs when progressive tax rates combine with inflation to cause a greater portion of each taxpayer's real income to be paid as taxes.

■ Because dividends are paid from corporate income that has already been taxed (at rates going up as high as 39 percent), there is *double taxation* of corporate income.
☐ Interest on most state and local government securities, which are often called "*municipals*," is not subject to federal income taxes. This creates a strong incentive for individuals in high tax brackets to purchase such securities.

■ Gains and losses on the sale of *capital assets* such as stocks, bonds, and real estate have historically received special tax treatment.
☐ Capital gains tax rates have varied over time, but they have generally been lower than rates on ordinary income. The reason is simple. Congress wants the economy to grow, for growth we need investment in productive assets, and low capital gains tax rates encourage investments.
☐ *Short-term capital gains,* where the asset is sold within one year of the time it was purchased, are added to such ordinary income as wages, dividends, and interest and then are taxed at the same rate as ordinary income.

☐ If an asset has been held longer than a year, any profit is defined to be a *long-term capital gain*, and its rate is capped at 20 percent.

Corporations pay taxes on profits.

■ Corporate tax rates are also progressive up to $18,333,333 of taxable income, but are constant thereafter at a rate of 35 percent. Marginal tax rates range from 15 to 39 percent.

■ Interest and dividend income received by a corporation are taxed.
  ☐ Interest is taxed as ordinary income at regular corporate tax rates.
  ☐ However, 70 percent of the dividends received by one corporation from another is excluded from taxable income. The remaining 30 percent is taxed at the ordinary rate. Thus, the effective tax rate on dividends received by a 35 percent marginal tax bracket corporation is $0.30(35\%) = 10.5\%$.

■ The tax system favors debt financing over equity financing.
  ☐ Interest paid is a tax-deductible business expense.
  ☐ Dividends on common and preferred stock are not deductible. Thus, a 40 percent federal-plus-state tax bracket corporation must earn $\$1/(1.0 - 0.40) = \$1/0.60 = \$1.67$ before taxes to pay $1 of dividends, but only $1 of pretax income is required to pay $1 of interest.

■ Before 1987, long-term corporate capital gains were taxed at lower rates than ordinary income. However, at present, long-term corporate capital gains are taxed as ordinary income.

■ Ordinary corporate operating losses can be *carried back* to each of the preceding 2 years and *forward* for the next 20 years in the future to offset taxable income in those years. The purpose of permitting this loss treatment is to avoid penalizing corporations whose incomes fluctuate substantially from year to year.

■ The Internal Revenue Code imposes a penalty on corporations that improperly accumulate earnings if the purpose of the accumulation is to enable stockholders to avoid personal income tax on dividends.

■ If a corporation owns 80 percent or more of another corporation's stock, it can aggregate profits and losses and file a *consolidated* tax return. Thus, losses in one area can offset profits in another.

■ Small businesses which meet certain restrictions may be set up as *S corporations* which receive benefits of the corporate form—especially limited liability—yet are taxed as proprietorships or partnerships rather than as corporations. This treatment would be preferred by owners of small corporations in which all or most of the income earned each year is distributed as dividends because the income would be taxed only once at the individual level.

The total company, or corporate, valuation model can be used to value (1) companies that don't pay dividends, (2) privately held businesses, and (3) particular divisions that a company may want to sell.

■ A firm's value is determined by its ability to generate cash flow, both now and in the future.

■ A firm's total value can be calculated as the present value of its expected future free cash flows (FCF) from operations, discounted at its cost of capital, k_c, plus the value of its nonoperating assets.

■ Once a company's free cash flows stabilize at time N and begin to grow at a constant rate, then the value of the firm's operations can be calculated as:

$$V_{op\,(at\,time\,N)} = \frac{FCF_N\left(1+g\right)}{k_c - g}.$$

■ The company's *terminal*, or *horizon, value* is its value at the end of the forecast period.

■ Even if a company is paying steady dividends much can be learned from the corporate value model, so many analysts today use it for all types of valuations.
  ☐ The process of projecting the future financial statements can reveal quite a bit about the company's operations and financing needs.
  ☐ This type of analysis can provide insights into actions that might be taken to increase the company's value. This is called *value-based management*.

SELF-TEST QUESTIONS

Definitional

1. The traditional financial statements are designed more for use by _____ and tax collectors than for _____ and equity analysts.

2. _____ _____ consist of cash, accounts receivable, inventories, and fixed assets necessary to operate the business.

3.   _____ _____ include marketable securities, investments in subsidiaries, and land held for future use.

4.   Those current assets used in operations are called _____ _____ _____.

5.   Operating working capital less accounts payable and accruals is called _____ _____ _____ _____.

6.   _____ _____ _____ is the sum of net operating working capital and net fixed assets.

7.   A better measure for comparing managers' performance than net income is _____ _____ _____ _____ _____, which is the amount of profit a company would generate if it had no debt and held no financial assets.

8.   _____ _____ _____ is the cash flow actually available for distribution to investors after the company has made all the investments in fixed assets and working capital necessary to sustain ongoing operations.

9.   _____ _____ _____ is calculated as net operating profit after taxes plus any noncash adjustments as shown on the statement of cash flows, such as depreciation.

10.   Shareholder wealth is maximized by maximizing the difference between the market value of the firm's equity and the amount of equity that was supplied by shareholders. This difference is called _____ _____ _____.

11.   _____ _____ _____ focuses on managerial effectiveness in a given year and is an estimate of a business's true economic profit for the year.

12.   A(n) _____ tax system is one in which tax rates are higher at higher levels of income.

13.   A progressive tax structure, which when combined with inflation increases the government's share of GDP without any change in tax rates, is called _____ _____.

14.   The marginal tax rate on the largest corporations, those with taxable incomes exceeding $18,333,333, is ____ percent, while that on the wealthiest individuals can go up as high as _____ percent.

15.   Interest received on _____ bonds is generally not subject to federal income taxes. This feature makes them particularly attractive to investors in _____ tax brackets.

16. In order to qualify as a long-term capital gain or loss, an asset must be held for more than _____ months.

17. Gains or losses on assets held less than one year are referred to as _____-_____ transactions.

18. Interest income received by a corporation is taxed as _____ income. However, only ____ percent of dividends received from another corporation is subject to taxation.

19. Another important distinction exists between interest and dividends paid by a corporation. Interest payments are _____ _____, while dividend payments are not.

20. Ordinary corporate operating losses can first be carried back ___ years and then forward _____ years.

21. A firm that refuses to pay dividends in order to help stockholders avoid personal income taxes may be subject to a penalty for _____ _____ of earnings.

22. A corporation that owns 80 percent or more of another corporation's stock may choose to file _____ tax returns.

23. The Tax Code permits a corporation (that meets certain restrictions) to be taxed at the owners' personal tax rates and to avoid the impact of _____ taxation of dividends. This type of corporation is called a(n) ___ corporation.

24. The _____ _____, or _____, _____ model can be used to value companies that don't pay dividends, privately held businesses, and particular divisions that a company may want to sell.

25. A firm's value is determined by its ability to generate _____ _____, both now and in the future.

26. A firm's _____ _____ can be calculated as the present value of its expected future free cash flows from operations, discounted at its cost of capital, plus the value of its nonoperating assets.

27. The company's _____, or _____, value is its value at the end of the forecast period.

Conceptual

28. The fact that 70 percent of intercorporate dividends received by a corporation is excluded from taxable income has encouraged debt financing over equity financing.

  a. True   **b.** False

29. An individual with substantial personal wealth and income is considering the possibility of opening a new business. The business will have a relatively high degree of risk, and losses may be incurred for the first several years. Which legal form of business organization would probably be best?

  a. Proprietorship   **d.** S corporation
  b. Corporation   **e.** Limited partnership
  c. Partnership

30. Which of the following statements is most correct?

  a. In order to avoid double taxation and to escape the frequently higher tax rate applied to capital gains, stockholders generally prefer to have corporations pay dividends rather than to retain their earnings and reinvest the money in the business. Thus, earnings should be retained only if the firm needs capital very badly and would have difficulty raising it from external sources.
  b. Under our current tax laws, when investors pay taxes on their dividend income, they are being subjected to a form of double taxation.
  c. The fact that a percentage of the interest received by one corporation, which is paid by another corporation, is excluded from taxable income has encouraged firms to use more debt financing relative to equity financing.
  d. If the tax laws stated that $0.50 out of every $1.00 of interest paid by a corporation was allowed as a tax-deductible expense, this would probably encourage companies to use more debt financing than they presently do, other things held constant.
  e. Statements b and d are both correct.

SELF-TEST PROBLEMS

1. Ryngaert & Sons, Inc. has operating income (EBIT) of $2,250,000. The company's depreciation expense is $450,000, its interest expense is $120,000, and it faces a 40 percent tax rate. What is its operating cash flow?

  a. $1,008,000   **b.** $1,278,000   **c.** $1,475,000   **d.** $1,728,000   **e.** $1,800,000

2. Wayne Corporation had income from operations of $385,000, it received interest payments of $15,000, it paid interest of $20,000, it received dividends from another corporation of $10,000, and it paid $40,000 in dividends to its common stockholders. What is Wayne's federal income tax?

   a. $122,760   b. $130,220   c. $141,700   d. 155,200   e. $163,500

3. A firm purchases $10 million of corporate bonds that paid a 16 percent interest rate, or $1.6 million in interest. If the firm's marginal tax rate is 35 percent, what is the after-tax interest yield?

   a. 7.36%   b. 8.64%   c. 10.40%   d. 13.89%   e. 14.32%

4. Refer to Self-Test Problem 3. The firm also invests in the common stock of another company having a 16 percent before-tax dividend yield. What is the after-tax dividend yield?

   a. 7.36%   b. 8.64%   c. 10.40%   d. 13.89%   e. 14.32%

5. The Carter Company's taxable income and income tax payments are shown below for 1995 through 1998:

Year	Taxable Income	Tax Payment
1995	$10,000	$1,500
1996	5,000	750
1997	12,000	1,800
1998	8,000	1,200

   Assume that Carter's tax rate for all 4 years was a flat 15 percent; that is, each dollar of taxable income was taxed at 15 percent. In 1999, Carter incurred a loss of $17,000. Using corporate loss carry-back, what is Carter's adjusted tax payment for 1998?

   a. $850   b. $750   c. $610   d. $550   e. $450

6. A firm can undertake a new project that will generate a before-tax return of 20 percent or it can invest the same funds in the preferred stock of another company that yields 13 percent before taxes. If the only consideration is which alternative provides the highest relevant (after-tax) return and the applicable tax rate is 35 percent, should the firm invest in the project or the preferred stock?

    a. Preferred stock; its relevant return is 12 percent.
    b. Project; its relevant return is 1.36 percentage points higher.
    c. Preferred stock; its relevant return is 0.22 percentage points higher.
    d. Project; its after-tax return is 20 percent.
    e. Either alternative can be chosen; they have the same relevant return.

7. Cooley Corporation has $20,000 that it plans to invest in marketable securities. It is choosing between MCI bonds which yield 10 percent, state of Colorado municipal bonds which yield 7 percent, and MCI preferred stock with a dividend yield of 8 percent. Cooley's corporate tax rate is 25 percent, and 70 percent of its dividends received are tax exempt. What is the after-tax rate of return on the highest yielding security?

    a. 7.4%   b. 7.0%   c. 7.5%   d. 6.5%   e. 6.0%

    (The following data apply to the next two Self-Test Problems.)

    GPD Corporation has operating income (EBIT) of $300,000, total assets of $1,500,000, and its capital structure consists of 40 percent debt and 60 percent equity. Total assets were equal to total operating capital. The firm's after-tax cost of capital is 10.5 percent and its tax rate is 40 percent. The firm has 50,000 shares of common stock currently outstanding and the current price of a share of stock is $27.00.

8. What is the firm's Market Value Added (MVA)?

    a. $22,500   b. $87,575   c. $187,740   d. $450,000   e. $575,000

9. What is the firm's Economic Value Added (EVA)?

    a. $22,500   b. $87,575   c. $187,740   d. $450,000   e. $575,000

(The following data apply to the next four Self-Test Problems.)

You have just obtained financial information for the past two years for the Smith Brothers Corporation.

Smith Brothers Corporation
Income Statements for Year Ending December 31
(Millions of Dollars)

	1998	1997
Sales	$360	$300
Oper. costs excluding deprec.	306	255
Depreciation	9	7
EBIT	$ 45	$ 38
Interest	7	6
EBT	$ 38	$ 32
Taxes (40%)	15	13
NI available to common stockholders	$ 23	$ 19
Common dividends	16	10

Smith Brothers Corporation
Balance Sheets as of December 31
(Millions of Dollars)

Assets	1998	1997
Cash & equivalents	$ 4	$ 3
ST investments	0	0
Accts. receivable	54	45
Inventories	54	60
Total CA	$112	$108
Net plant & equip.	90	75
Total assets	$202	$183
Liabilities and Equity		
Accts. payable	$ 32	$ 28
Notes payable	20	16
Accruals	22	18
Total CL	$ 74	$ 62
LT bonds	45	45
Total debt	$119	$107
Common stock (50,000,000 shares)	15	15
Retained earnings	68	61
Common equity	$ 83	$ 76
Total liabilities and equity	$202	$183

10.   What is the net operating profit after taxes (NOPAT) in millions of dollars for 1998?

    a. $18   **b.** $27   **c.** $34   **d.** $40   **e.** $45

11.   What is the net operating working capital in millions of dollars for 1998?

    a. $38   **b.** $54   **c.** $58   **d.** $87   **e.** $112

12.   What is the total operating capital in millions of dollars for 1998?

    a. $90   **b.** $128   **c.** $144   **d.** $148   **e.** $177

13.   What is the free cash flow in millions of dollars for 1998?

    a. $11   **b.** $16   **c.** $20   **d.** $25   **e.** $27

14.   HBT Corporation has never paid a dividend. Its current free cash flow is $1,200,000 and is expected to grow at a constant rate of 4 percent. The overall cost of capital is $k_c = 10$ percent. What is HBT's value of operations (in millions)?

    a. $22.00   **b.** $20.80   **c.** $12.48   **d.** $20.00   **e.** $10.00

(The following data apply to the next two Self-Test Problems.)

Cane Enterprises has never paid a dividend. Free cash flow is projected to be $40,000 and $50,000 for the next two years, and after the second year it is expected to grow at a constant rate of 6 percent. The company's weighted average cost of capital is $k_c = 11\%$.

15.   What is the terminal, or horizon, value of operations (in millions)? (Hint: First find the value of all free cash flows beyond Year 2 discounted back to Year 2.)

    a. $0.363   **b.** $0.848   **c.** $1.000   **d.** $1.060   **e.** $1.500

16.   What is the value of Cane's operations?

    a. $848,492   **b.** $936,937   **c.** $1,136,617   **d.** $1,500,000   **e.** $1,724,898

17.   Given the following information, what is Garret Starr Inc.'s free cash flow for 1999?

Income Statement:

	1999	1998
Net sales	$1,569.0	$1,500.0
Costs (except depreciation)	1,200.0	1,140.0
Depreciation	69.0	75.0
Total operating costs	$1,269.0	$1,215.0
EBIT	300.0	285.0
Less interest	69.0	63.0
EBT	$ 231.0	$ 222.0
Taxes (40%)	92.4	88.8
Net income	$ 138.6	$ 133.2

Balance sheet:

Assets	1999	1998
Cash	$ 84.0	$ 81.0
Marketable securities	207.0	198.0
Accounts receivable	252.0	240.0
Inventories	336.0	318.0
Total current assets	$ 879.0	$ 837.0
Net plant and equipment	843.0	795.0
Total assets	$1,722.0	$1,632.0

Liabilities and Equity		
Accounts payable	$ 168.0	$ 156.0
Notes payable	414.0	390.0
Accruals	84.0	84.0
Total current liabilities	$ 666.0	$ 630.0
Long-term bonds	$ 519.0	$ 492.0
Common stock	300.0	300.0
Retained earnings	237.0	210.0
Common equity	$ 537.0	$ 510.0
Total liabilities and equity	$1,722.0	$1,632.0

a. $276   b. $399   c. $420   d. $180   e. $111

(The following data apply to the next three Self-Test Problems.)

Alday Corporation is a fast growing supplier of office products. Analysts project the following free cash flows (FCF) during the next three years, after which FCF is expected to grow at a constant 5 percent rate. Alday's cost of capital is $k_c = 12\%$.

Time	1	2	3
Free cash flow ($ millions)	-$10	$15	$20

18.   What is Alday's terminal, or horizon, value (in millions)? (Hint: Find the value of all free cash flows beyond Year 3 discounted back to Year 3.)

    a. $300   **b.** $167   **c.** $420   **d.** $266   **e.** $500

19.   What is the current value of operations (in millions) for Alday?

    a. $175.60   **b.** $230.80   **c.** $300.00   **d.** $420.00   **e.** $489.98

20.   Suppose Alday has $5 million in marketable securities, $50 million in debt, and 5 million shares of stock. What is the price per share?

    a. $40.50   **b.** $33.00   **c.** $28.95   **d.** $43.79   **e.** $37.16

ANSWERS TO SELF-TEST QUESTIONS

1.   creditors; managers
2.   Operating assets
3.   Nonoperating assets
4.   operating working capital
5.   net operating working capital
6.   Total operating capital
7.   net operating profit after taxes
8.   Free cash flow
9.   Operating cash flow
10.   Market Value Added (MVA)
11.   Economic Value Added (EVA)
12.   progressive
13.   bracket creep
14.   35; 39.6

15.   municipal; high
16.   12
17.   short-term
18.   ordinary; 30
19.   tax deductible
20.   2; 20
21.   improper accumulation
22.   consolidated
23.   double; S
24.   total company; corporate; valuation
25.   cash flow
26.   total value
27.   terminal; horizon

28. b. Debt financing is encouraged by the fact that interest payments are tax deductible while dividend payments are not.

29. d. The S corporation limits the liability of the individual, but permits losses to be deducted against personal income.

30. b. Statement a is incorrect. To avoid double taxation, stockholders would prefer that corporations retain more of its earnings because long-term capital gains are taxed at a rate of 20 percent. Statement c is incorrect. Debt financing has been encouraged by the fact that interest on debt is tax deductible. Statement d is incorrect. Currently, interest on debt is fully tax deductible; allowing 50 percent of interest to be tax deductible would discourage debt financing.

SOLUTIONS TO SELF-TEST PROBLEMS

1. e. Operating cash flow $= \text{NOPAT} + \text{Depreciation}$
$= \text{EBIT}\,(1 - T) + \text{Depreciation}$
$= \$2,250,000(0.6) + \$450,000$
$= \$1,800,000.$

2. b. The first step is to determine taxable income:

Income from operations	$385,000
Interest income (fully taxable)	15,000
Interest expense (fully deductible)	(20,000)
Dividend income (30% taxable)	3,000
Taxable income	$383,000

(Note that dividends are paid from after-tax income and do not affect taxable income.)

Based on the current corporate tax table, the tax calculation is as follows:

$$\text{Tax} = \$113,900 + 0.34(\$383,000 - \$335,000) = \$113,900 + \$16,320 = \$130,220.$$

3. c. The after-tax yield (or dollar return) equals the before-tax yield (or dollar return) multiplied by one minus the effective tax rate, or $\text{AT} = \text{BT}(1 - \text{Effective } T)$. Therefore,

$$\text{AT} = 16\%(1 - 0.35) = 16\%(0.65) = 10.40\%.$$

4. e. Since the dividends are received by a corporation, only 30 percent are taxable, and the Effective T = Tax rate × 30%:

$$AT = BT(1 - \text{Effective T})$$
$$= 16\%[1 - 0.35(0.30)]$$
$$= 16\%(1 - 0.105)$$
$$= 16\%(0.895)$$
$$= 14.32\%.$$

5. e.

Year	Taxable Income	Tax Payment	Adjusted Taxable Income	Adjusted Tax Payment
1995	$10,000	$1,500	$10,000	$1,500
1996	5,000	750	5,000	750
1997	12,000	1,800	0	0
1998	8,000	1,200	3,000	450

The carry-back can only go back 2 years. Thus, there were no adjustments made in 1995 and 1996. After a $12,000 adjustment in 1997, there was a $5,000 loss remaining to apply to 1998. The 1998 adjusted tax payment is $3,000(0.15) = $450. Thus, Carter received a total of $2,550 in tax refunds after the adjustment.

6. b. The project is fully taxable; thus its after-tax return is as follows:

$$AT = 20\%(1 - 0.35) = 20\%(0.65) = 13\%.$$

But only 30 percent of the preferred stock dividends are taxable; thus, its after-tax yield is $AT = 13\%[1 - 0.35(0.30)] = 13\%(1 - 0.105) = 13\%(0.895) = 11.64\%$. Therefore, the new project should be chosen since its after-tax return is 1.36 percentage points higher.

7.   c.   AT yield on Colorado bond = 7%.

AT yield on MCI bond = 10% – Taxes = 10% – 10%(0.25) = 7.5%.

Check: Invest $20,000 at 10% = $2,000 interest.
Pay 25% tax, so AT income = $2,000(1 – T) = $2,000(0.75) = $1,500.
AT rate of return = $1,500/$20,000 = 7.5%.

AT yield on MCI preferred stock = 8% – Taxes = 8% – 0.3(8%)(0.25)
$$= 8\% - 0.6\% = 7.4\%.$$

Therefore, invest in MCI bonds.

8.   d.   Market Value Added = (Shares outstanding)(P_0) – Total common equity
$$= 50{,}000(\$27.00) - (0.6)(\$1{,}500{,}000)$$
$$= \$1{,}350{,}000 - \$900{,}000$$
$$= \$450{,}000.$$

9.   a.   Economic Value Added $= \text{NOPAT} - \dfrac{\text{AT dollar cost of capital}}{\text{used to support operations}}$

$$= \text{EBIT}(1 - T) - (\text{Operating Capital})\left(\begin{array}{c}\text{After - tax}\\\text{percentage cost}\\\text{of capital}\end{array}\right)$$

$$= \$300{,}000(0.6) - (\$1{,}500{,}000)(0.105)$$
$$= \$180{,}000 - \$157{,}500$$
$$= \$22{,}500.$$

10.   b.   NOPAT = EBIT(1 - Tax rate)
$$= \$45(0.6)$$
$$= \$27.$$

11.   c. $\dfrac{\text{Net operating}}{\text{working capital}_{98}} = \dfrac{\text{Non - interest bearing}}{\text{current assets}} - \dfrac{\text{Non - interest charging}}{\text{current liabilities}}$

$$= \dfrac{\text{Operating current}}{\text{assets}} - \dfrac{\text{Operating current}}{\text{liabilities}}$$

$$= (\$4 + \$54 + \$54) - (\$32 + 22)$$
$$= \$112 - \$54 = \$58.$$

12.   d.   Operating capital$_{98}$ = $\dfrac{\text{Net plant}}{\text{and equipment}}$ + $\dfrac{\text{Net operating}}{\text{working capital}}$

$$= \$90 + \$58$$
$$= \$148.$$

13.   b.   FCF = NOPAT – Net investment in operating capital

$$= \$27 - (\$148 - \$137)$$
$$= \$16.$$

14.   b.   Value of operations = V_{op} = PV of expected future free cash flow.

$$V_{op} = \frac{FCF(1+g)}{k_c - g} = \frac{\$1,200,000(1.04)}{0.10 - 0.04} = \$20,800,000.$$

15.   d. $V_{op_2} = \dfrac{\$50,000(1.06)}{0.11 - 0.06} = \$1,060,000.$

16.   b.

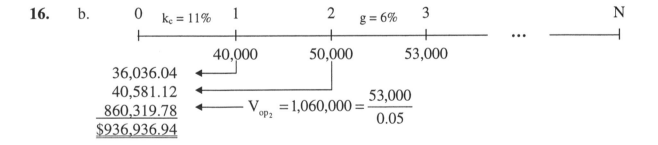

17.   e.   NOPAT $= $ EBIT$(1 - \text{T})$
$= \$300(1 - 0.4) = \$180.$

Net operating $WC_{98} = (\$81 + \$240 + \$318) - (\$156 + \$84)$
$= \$639 - \$240 = \$399.$

Operating capital$_{98} = \$399 + \$795 = \$1,194.$

Net operating $WC_{99} = (\$84 + \$252 + \$336) - (\$168 + \$84)$
$= \$672 - \$252 = \$420.$

Operating capital$_{99} = \$420 + \$843 = \$1,263.$

FCF $=$ NOPAT $-$ Net investment in operating capital
$= \$300(0.6) - (\$1,263 - \$1,194)$
$= \$111.$

18.   a. $V_{op_3} = \dfrac{\$20(1.05)}{0.12 - 0.05} = \$300.$

19.   b.

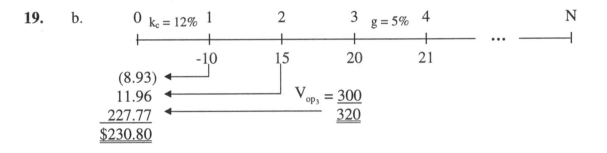

20.   e.   Total value$_{t=0} = \$230.80 + \$5.0 = \$235.80.$

Value of common equity $= \$235.80 - \$50 = \$185.80.$

Price per share $= \dfrac{\$185.80}{5.0} = \$37.16.$

CHAPTER 5
DETERMINING THE COST OF CAPITAL

OVERVIEW

Most important business decisions require capital, and a firm's primary financial objective is to maximize shareholder value. Companies can increase shareholder value by investing in projects that earn more than the cost of capital. For this reason, the cost of capital is sometimes referred to as a hurdle rate: for a project to be accepted, it must earn more than its hurdle rate.

Although its most important use is in capital budgeting, the cost of capital is also used for other purposes. The cost of capital is a key factor in decisions relating to the use of debt versus equity capital. It is also important in the regulation of electric, gas,

and telephone companies. These utilities are natural monopolies in the sense that one firm can supply service at a lower cost than could two or more firms. Since it has a monopoly, your electric or telephone company could, if it were unregulated, exploit you. Therefore, regulators (1) determine the cost of the capital investors have provided the utility and (2) then set rates designed to permit the company to earn its cost of capital, no more and no less.

The same factors that affect required rates of return on securities by investors also determine a firm's cost of capital, so exactly the same models are used by investors and by corporate treasurers.

OUTLINE

Most firms employ several types of capital, called capital components, with common and preferred stock, along with debt, being the three most frequently used types. All capital components have one feature in common: The investors who provided the funds expect to receive a return on their investment.

■ The required rate of return on each capital component is called its *component cost*, and the cost of capital used to analyze capital budgeting decisions should be a *weighted average* of the various components' costs.

☐ This weighted average is the weighted average cost of capital, or WACC.

■ Most firms set target percentages for the different financing sources. This is called the firm's *target capital structure*.

■ Firms try to stay close to their target capital structures; however, they frequently deviate from them in the short run for several reasons.

  □ Market conditions may be more favorable in one market than another at a particular time.

  □ The second, and probably more important, reason for deviations relates to *flotation costs*, which are the costs that a firm must incur to issue securities.

   • It is inefficient and expensive to issue relatively small amounts of debt, preferred stock, and common stock.

   • Therefore, companies tend to finance with common stock one year, with debt the next, and with preferred the following year, thus fluctuating around their target capital structure rather than staying right on it all the time.

■ Managers should view companies as ongoing concerns, and calculate their costs of capital as weighted averages of the various types of funds they use, regardless of the specific source of financing employed in a particular year.

The cost of each capital component can be determined as follows:

■ The after-tax cost of debt, $k_d(1 - T)$, is defined as the interest rate on new, or marginal, debt, k_d, less the tax savings that result because interest is tax deductible.

  □ If a firm has issued debt in the past, and it is publicly traded, the market price can be used to find either the yield to maturity (YTM) or yield to call (YTC), whichever is appropriate. This will provide a good estimate of k_d.

  □ If a firm has no publicly traded debt, yields on publicly traded debt of similar firms should provide a reasonable estimate of k_d.

  □ If a firm has a tax rate of 40 percent and can borrow at a rate of 11 percent, then its after-tax cost of debt is $k_d = 11\%(1 - 0.40) = 11\%(0.60) = 6.6\%$.

  □ Since interest payments are deductible, the government in effect pays part of the total cost.

   • k_d is the marginal cost of new debt to be raised during the planning period.

■ The component cost of preferred stock, k_{ps}, is the preferred dividend, D_{ps}, divided by the net issuing price of the preferred stock, P_n: $k_{ps} = D_{ps}/P_n$.

  □ P_n is the price the firm receives after deducting flotation costs.

  □ No tax adjustments are made when calculating k_{ps} because preferred dividends, unlike interest expense on debt, are not deductible, and hence there are no tax savings.

■ Companies can raise common equity in two ways: (1) by issuing new shares and (2) by retaining earnings.

■   Companies must earn more than k_s on new shares because it incurs flotation costs to issue new stock.
    ☐   In addition, an increase in the supply of stock will put pressure on the stock price, forcing the company to sell new stock at a lower price than existed before the new issue was announced.
    ☐   The combined effects of flotation costs and price pressure inhibit companies from issuing additional common stock.

■   Raising new equity capital by retaining earnings has a cost.
    ☐   If some of a firm's earnings are reinvested, then its stockholders incur an *opportunity cost*—the earnings could have been paid out as dividends (or used to repurchase stock).
    ☐   The firm should earn on its reinvested earnings at least as much as its stockholders themselves could earn on alternative investments of equivalent risk.

■ k_s is the cost of common equity raised by reinvesting earnings.
    ☐   If a company cannot earn at least k_s on reinvested earnings, then it should pass those earnings on to its stockholders and let them invest the money themselves in assets that do provide k_s.

■   There are three methods typically used to estimate k_s:
    ☐   The Capital Asset Pricing Model (CAPM) works as follows:
        •   Estimate the risk-free rate, k_{RF}, generally taken to be the yield on a long-term U. S. Treasury bond.
        •   Estimate the stock's beta coefficient as an index of the stock's risk.
        •   Estimate the current expected rate of return on the market, or on an "average" stock, k_M.
        •   Substitute the preceding values into the CAPM equation, $k_s = k_{RF} + (k_M - k_{RF})b$, to estimate the required rate of return on the stock in question.
        •   Thus, if $k_{RF} = 8\%$, $k_M = 14\%$, and the beta is 1.1, then $k_s = 8\% + (14\% - 8\%)1.1 = 14.6\%$.
    ☐   The *bond-yield-plus-risk-premium approach* is a subjective, ad hoc procedure that estimates k_s by adding a judgmental risk premium of three to five percentage points to the interest rate on the firm's own long-term debt. Thus, k_s = Bond yield + Risk premium.
        •   If the firm uses a risk premium of 4 percentage points, and its bond rate is 11 percent, then $k_s = 11\% + 4\% = 15\%$.
        •   It is logical to think that firms with risky, low-rated, and consequently high-interest-rate debt will also have risky, high-cost equity.

- Because the risk premium is a judgmental estimate, this method is not likely to produce a precise cost of equity; however, it does get us "into the right ballpark."

☐ The required rate of return, k_s, may also be estimated by the *discounted cash flow (DCF) approach*. This approach combines the expected dividend yield, D_1/P_0, with the expected future growth rate, g, of earnings and dividends, or

$$k_s = \hat{k}_s = \frac{D_1}{P_0} + \text{Expected g.}$$

- The DCF approach assumes that stocks are normally in equilibrium and that growth is expected to be at a constant rate. If growth is not constant, then a nonconstant growth model must be used.

- The expected growth rate may be based on projections of past growth rates, if they have been relatively stable, or on expected future growth rates as projected by security analysts.

- Another method for estimating g is called the *retention growth rate method*. First, the firm's average future dividend payout ratio and its complement, the *retention rate*, are forecasted, and then the retention rate is multiplied by the company's expected future rate of return on equity (ROE):

$$g = (\text{Retention rate})(\text{ROE}) = (1.0 - \text{Payout rate})(\text{ROE}).$$

- If the firm's next expected dividend is $2.40, its expected growth rate is 7 percent per year, and its stock is selling for $32 per share, then

$$k_s = \hat{k}_s = \frac{\$2.40}{\$32} + 7.0\% = 14.5\%.$$

☐ When faced with the task of estimating a company's cost of equity, we generally use all three methods and then choose among them on the basis of our confidence in the data used for each in the specific case at hand.

Estimating the inputs for the CAPM and DCF approaches is difficult.

■ To estimate the required rate of return, k_s, under the CAPM we must obtain estimates of (1) the risk-free rate, k_{RF}, (2) the firm's beta, b_i, and (3) the required rate of return on the market, k_M.

☐ There is a question as to which rate (T-bond or T-bill) should be used as the risk-free rate in the CAPM because there is really no such thing as a truly riskless asset in the U. S. economy.

☐ The market risk premium, $RP_M = k_M - k_{RF}$, can be estimated on the basis of (1) ex post, or historical, data or (2) ex ante, or forward-looking, data.

- Historical risk premiums should be approached with caution because the choice of the beginning and ending periods can have a major impact on the calculated risk premiums.

  - Ex ante risk premiums are not stable: They vary over time. Therefore, when using the CAPM to estimate the cost of equity, it is best to use a current estimate of the ex ante RP_M.

  ☐ Historical betas may not be good predictors of future risk, so researchers have sought ways to improve them. This has led to the development of two different types of betas:

  - *Adjusted betas* make an adjustment for an expected future movement towards 1.0.

  - *Fundamental betas* are constantly adjusted to reflect changes in a firm's operations and capital structure.

  ☐ Several different sets of data can be used to calculate historical betas, and the different data sets produce different results.

■ Three inputs are required by the DCF approach: the current stock price, the current dividend, and the expected growth in dividends.

  ☐ The growth rate is by far the most difficult of these inputs to estimate. The most commonly used approaches for estimating it are (1) historical growth rates, (2) the retention growth model, and (3) analysts' forecasts.

The target proportions of debt, preferred stock, and common equity, along with the component costs of capital, are used to calculate the firm's weighted average cost of capital (WACC).

■ The weighted average cost of capital calculation is shown below for a firm which finances 30 percent with debt, 10 percent with preferred stock, and 60 percent with common equity and which has the following after-tax component costs:

Component	Weight	×	After-tax Cost	=	Weighted Cost
Debt	0.3	×	6.6%	=	1.98%
Preferred	0.1	×	10.3	=	1.03
Common	0.6	×	14.7	=	8.82
			WACC	=	11.83%

■ In more general terms, and in equation format,

$$WACC = w_d k_d (1 - T) + w_{ps} k_{ps} + w_{ce} k_s.$$

■ The WACC is the weighted average cost of each new, or *marginal*, dollar of capital—it is not the average cost of all dollars raised in the past.

☐ We are primarily interested in obtaining a cost of capital for use in capital budgeting, and for this purpose the cost of the new money that will be invested is the *relevant* cost.

■ The percentage capital components, called weights, could be based on (1) accounting values as shown on the balance sheet (book values), (2) current market values of the capital components, or (3) management's target capital structure, which is presumably an estimate of the firm's optimal capital structure.

☐ The correct weights are those based on the firm's target capital structure, since this is the best estimate of how the firm will, on average, raise money in the future.

The weighted average cost of capital is affected by a variety of factors. Some are beyond the firm's control, but others are influenced by its financing and investment policies.

■ The two most important factors which are beyond a firm's direct control are (1) the level of interest rates and (2) taxes.

☐ If interest rates in the economy rise, the cost of debt increases because firms will have to pay bondholders a higher interest rate. Higher interest rates also increase the cost of common and preferred equity capital.

☐ Tax rates are used in the calculation of the cost of debt in the WACC, and there are other less apparent ways in which tax policy affects the cost of capital.

● Lowering the capital gains tax rate relative to the rate on ordinary income would make stocks more attractive, which would reduce the cost of equity relative to that of debt. That would lead to a change in a firm's optimal capital structure.

■ A firm can affect its cost of capital through (1) its capital structure policy, (2) its dividend policy, and (3) its investment (capital budgeting) policy.

☐ The firm can change its capital structure, and such a change can affect its cost of capital. If a firm decides to use more debt and less common equity, this change to the weights in the WACC equation will tend to lower the WACC. However, an increase in the use of debt will increase the riskiness of both debt and equity, and increases in component costs will tend to offset the effects of the change in the weights.

☐ The percentage of earnings paid out in dividends may affect a stock's required rate of return, k_s. Also, if a firm's payout ratio is so high that it must issue new stock to fund its capital budget, this will force it to incur flotation costs, and this too will affect its cost of capital.

☐ When we estimate the cost of capital, we use as the starting point the required rates of return on the firm's outstanding stock and bonds. Those cost rates reflect the riskiness of the firm's existing assets. Therefore, we have implicitly been assuming that new capital will be invested in assets of the same type and with the same degree of risk as is embedded in the existing assets. This assumption is generally correct, as most firms do invest in assets similar to those it currently uses. However, it would be incorrect if the firm dramatically changed its investment policy.

The cost of capital is a key element in the capital budgeting process. A project should be accepted if and only if its estimated return exceeds its cost of capital. For this reason, the cost of capital is sometimes referred to as a "hurdle rate"—project returns must jump the "hurdle" to be accepted.

■   Investors require higher returns for riskier investments. Consequently, a company that is raising capital to take on risky projects will have a higher cost of capital than a company that is investing in safer projects.

■   The hurdle rate for each project should reflect the risk of the project itself, not necessarily the risk associated with the firm's average project as reflected in its composite WACC. The relevant hurdle rate is the project's WACC.

■   Applying a specific hurdle rate to each project ensures that every project will be evaluated properly.

■   If a company has different divisional costs of capital, then it would be incorrect to use the company's overall cost of capital to find the NPV of all the company's projects.

Three separate and distinct types of risk can be identified: (1) stand-alone risk, (2) corporate (within-firm) risk, and (3) market (beta) risk.

■   *Stand-alone risk* is the risk an asset would have if it were a firm's only asset. It is measured by the variability of the project's expected returns.

■   *Corporate (within-firm) risk* is the project's risk to the corporation, giving consideration to the fact that the project represents only one of the firm's portfolio of assets. It is measured by a project's impact on uncertainty about the firm's future earnings.

■   *Market (beta) risk* is the riskiness of the project as seen by a well-diversified stockholder who recognizes that the project is only one of the firm's assets and that the firm's stock is but one part of the investor's total portfolio. It is measured by the project's effect on the firm's beta coefficient.

■   Taking on a project with a high degree of either stand-alone or corporate risk will not necessarily affect the firm's beta. However, if the project has highly uncertain returns, and if those returns are highly correlated with returns on the firm's other assets and with most other assets in the economy, then the project will have a high degree of all types of risk.

■ Of the three measures, market risk is theoretically the most relevant measure because of its direct effect on stock prices. Unfortunately, the market risk for a project is also the most difficult to estimate.

☐ In practice, most decision makers consider all three risk measures in a judgmental manner, and then they classify projects into subjective risk categories.

☐ *Risk-adjusted costs of capital* are developed for each category using the composite WACC as a starting point.

■ Risk adjustments are necessarily subjective and somewhat arbitrary. Unfortunately, there is no completely satisfactory way to specify exactly how much higher or lower we should go in setting risk-adjusted costs of capital.

Many firms use the CAPM to estimate the cost of capital for specific projects or divisions.

■ The required rate of return on equity, k_s, is equal to the risk-free rate of return, k_{RF}, plus a risk premium equal to the market risk premium, $k_M - k_{RF}$, times the firm's beta coefficient, b:

$$k_s = k_{RF} + (k_M - k_{RF})b.$$

☐ This is the Security Market Line (SML) equation that expresses the risk/return relationship.

☐ For example, if a firm has a beta of 1.1, $k_M = 12\%$, and $k_{RF} = 8\%$, then its required rate of return would be $k_s = 8\% + (12\% - 8\%)1.1 = 12.4\%$. Stockholders would be willing to let the firm invest their money if the firm could earn 12.4 percent on their equity capital.

■ The acceptance of a particular capital budgeting project may cause a firm's overall beta to rise or fall, causing a change in the required rate of return.

☐ The impact of any one project on a firm's beta will depend upon the size of the project relative to the firm's existing "portfolio" of projects.

☐ The beta of any portfolio is a weighted average of the betas of its individual assets.

☐ An increase in a firm's beta coefficient will cause the stock price to decline unless the increased beta is offset by a higher expected rate of return.

■ If the beta coefficient for each project could be determined, then a *project cost of capital* for each individual project could be found as follows:

$$k_{Project} = k_{RF} + (k_M - k_{RF})b_{Project}.$$

High-beta, or high-risk, projects will have a relatively high cost of equity capital, while low-beta projects will have a correspondingly low cost of equity capital.

■ If the expected rate of return on a given capital project lies above the SML, the expected rate of return on the project is more than enough to compensate for its risk, and the project should be accepted. Conversely, if the project's rate of return lies below the SML, it should be rejected.

■ The discount rate applied in capital budgeting is the firm's weighted average cost of capital. When debt financing is used, the project's cost of equity must be combined with the cost of debt to obtain the *project's overall cost of capital*.

The estimation of project betas is even more difficult than that for stocks. However, two approaches have been used to estimate individual asset's betas: the pure play method and the accounting beta method.

■ In the *pure play method*, the company tries to find several single-product companies in the same line of business as the project being evaluated, and it then averages those companies' betas to determine the cost of capital for its own project.
   □ The pure play approach can be used only for major assets such as whole divisions, and even then it is frequently difficult to implement because it is often impossible to find pure play proxy firms.

■ In the *accounting beta method*, a company's return on assets (ROA) is regressed against the average ROA for a large sample of firms, say the S&P 500. The resulting *accounting beta* is then used as a proxy for the market beta.
   □ In practice, accounting betas are normally calculated for divisions or other large units, not for single assets, and divisional betas are then used for the division's projects.

For many firms, depreciation is the largest source of funds as shown in their statement of cash flows, and these depreciation-generated funds are available to support the capital budget.

■ A good approximation of the firm's internally-generated cash flow is:

$$\text{Internal cash flow} = \text{Net income} - \text{Cash dividends} + \text{Depreciation}$$
$$= \text{Retained earnings} + \text{Depreciation}.$$

   □ This approximation is accurate if the firm does not liquidate assets and if its policies regarding working capital are stable.

■ The capital used to buy the depreciating assets was provided by all the firm's investors. Since depreciation-generated funds, if they are not reinvested in the company, must be distributed to all the firm's investors, the cost of depreciation funds should reflect the opportunity costs of all three groups. Therefore, the *opportunity cost* of depreciation funds is the same as the basic WACC.

■ So long as the firm (1) obtains its new common equity by reinvesting earnings rather than by issuing new common stock, (2) does not change its target capital structure, and (3) invests in assets that have about the same risk as its existing assets, then the WACC as we calculated it can be used for capital budgeting purposes.

Most debt is privately placed and most equity is raised internally as retained earnings. Therefore, no flotation costs are incurred. If companies issue debt or new stock to the public, then the issue of flotation costs can become important.

■ The following formula is used to find the after-tax cost of debt including flotation costs.

$$M(1 - F) = \sum_{t=1}^{N} \frac{INT(1 - T)}{(1 + k_d)^t} + \frac{M}{(1 + k_d)^N}.$$

  □ M is the bond's maturity value, F is the flotation percentage, N is the bond's maturity, T is the firm's tax rate, INT is the dollars of interest per period, and k_d is the after-tax cost of debt adjusted for flotation.
  □ The after-tax cost of debt should reflect the *expected* cost of debt.
  □ Flotation costs raise the true costs of debt, while default possibilities lower the true cost. Since these two factors have opposite effects, ignoring both of them is, to some extent, a situation where "two wrongs make a right."

■ The cost of new common equity, k_e, or external equity, is higher than the cost or retained earnings, k_s, because of flotation costs involved in issuing new common stock.

$$k_e = \frac{D_1}{P_0(1 - F)} + g.$$

  □ F is the percentage flotation cost incurred in selling the new stock, so $P_0(1 - F)$ is the net price per share received by the company.

■ The *marginal cost of capital (MCC)* is the cost of the last dollar of new capital the firm raises, and the marginal cost rises as more and more capital is raised during a given period.
  □ A graph which shows how the WACC changes as more and more new capital is raised during a given year is called the *marginal cost of capital schedule*.

■ Short-term debt is not included in the capital structure.

☐ The cost of capital is used in the capital budgeting process, which involves long-term assets, and those assets are financed with long-term capital. Thus, current liabilities do not enter the calculation.

The *retained earnings break point (BP_{RE})* represents the total financing that can be done before a firm is forced to sell new common stock.

$$BP_{RE} = \frac{Retained\ earnings}{Equity\ fraction}.$$

The *Investment Opportunity Schedule (IOS)* shows the rate of return expected on each potential investment opportunity.

☐ The WACC at the point where the Investment Opportunity Schedule intersects the MCC curve is defined as the "corporate cost of capital"—this point reflects the marginal cost of capital to the corporation.

A number of difficult issues relating to the cost of capital are listed below. These topics are covered in advanced finance courses.

As a general rule, the same principles of cost of capital estimation apply to both *privately held* and publicly owned firms, but the problems of obtaining input data are somewhat different for each.

One cannot overemphasize the practical difficulties encountered when estimating the cost of equity. As a result, we can never be sure just how accurate our estimated cost of capital is.

It is difficult to assign risk-adjusted discount rates to capital budgeting projects of differing degrees of riskiness.

Establishing the target capital structure is a major task in itself.

Managers and students often make four common mistakes when estimating the cost of capital. Here are four common mistakes to avoid:

Do not use the coupon rate on a firm's existing debt as the pre-tax cost of debt.

When applying the CAPM method, never use the historical average return on stocks with the current risk-free rate to estimate $(k_M - k_{RF})$.

■ If you don't know the target capital structure weights, it is better to estimate weights based on the current market values of the capital components than to use book value weights to calculate WACC.

■ Do not include accounts payable and accruals as components in the calculation of WACC. If it's not a source of funding from an investor, then it's not a capital component.

SELF-TEST QUESTIONS

Definitional

1. The firm should calculate its cost of capital as a(n) _____ _____ of the after-tax costs of the various types of funds it uses.

2. There are _____ methods that can be used to determine the cost of common equity.

3. Assigning a cost to reinvested earnings is based on the _____ _____ principle.

4. Companies must earn more than k_s on new shares because they incur _____ _____ to issue new stock.

5. Using the Capital Asset Pricing Model (CAPM), the required rate of return on common stock is found as a function of the _____-_____ _____, the firm's _____ _____, and the required rate of return on an average _____.

6. The cost of common equity may also be found by adding a(n) _____ _____ to the interest rate on the firm's own long-term debt.

7. The required rate of return on common equity may also be estimated as the expected _____ _____ on the common stock plus the expected future _____ _____ of the dividends.

8. The proportions of _____, _____ _____, and _____ _____ in the target capital structure should be used to calculate the _____ _____ cost of capital.

9. The component cost of preferred stock is calculated as the _____ _____ divided by the _____ _____ _____ of preferred stock.

10. One method for estimating g involves multiplying the _____ _____ by the company's expected future rate of return on equity (ROE).

11. The two most important factors that affect the cost of capital and which are beyond the firm's direct control are the level of _____ rates and _____.

12. A firm can affect its cost of capital through its _____ _____ policy, its _____ policy, and its _____ (capital budgeting) policy.

13. The cost of capital is sometimes referred to as the _____ rate because projects must jump over it to be accepted.

14. The hurdle rate for each project should reflect the _____ of the project itself, not necessarily those associated with the firm's _____ project as reflected in the firm's composite WACC.

15. Three separate and distinct types of risk can be identified: _____-_____ risk, _____ risk, and _____ risk.

16. Of the three risk measures, _____ risk is theoretically the most relevant measure because of its direct effect on stock prices.

17. If the expected rate of return on a given capital project lies _____ the SML, the expected rate of return on the project is more than enough to compensate for its risk, and the project should be accepted.

18. _____-_____ risk is the risk an asset would have if it were a firm's only asset.

19. Two approaches have been developed for estimating project betas: the _____ _____ and the _____ _____ methods.

20. Projects are classified into subjective risk categories and then _____-_____ _____ ____ _____ are developed for each category using the composite WACC as a starting point.

21. Most firms employ several types of capital, called _____ _____, with common and preferred stock, along with debt, being the three most frequently used types.

22. k_d is the _____ cost of new debt to be raised during the planning period.

23. The combined effects of _____ _____ and _____ _____ inhibit companies from issuing additional common stock.

24. The correct weights to use in the WACC calculation are those based on the firm's _____ capital structure, since this is the best estimate of how the firm will, on average, raise money in the future.

25. For many firms, _____ is the largest source of funds as shown in their statement of cash flows and is available to support the capital budget.

26. The opportunity cost of depreciation is the _____ _____ _____ ____ _____.

Conceptual

27. Funds acquired by the firm through preferred stock have a cost to the firm equal to the preferred dividend divided by the net issuing price, P_n, the price the firm receives on preferred after deducting flotation costs.

    a. True   b. False

28. Which of the following statements could be true concerning the costs of debt and equity?

    a. The cost of debt for Firm A is greater than the cost of equity for Firm A.
    b. The cost of debt for Firm A is greater than the cost of equity for Firm B.
    c. The cost of reinvested earnings for Firm A is less than its cost of new equity.
    d. The cost of reinvested earnings for Firm A is less than its cost of debt.
    e. Statements b and c could both be true.

29. Which of the following statements is most correct?

    a. If Congress raised the corporate tax rate, this would lower the effective cost of debt but probably would also reduce the amount of earnings available to reinvest, so the effect on the marginal cost of capital is uncertain.

    b. For corporate investors, 70 percent of the dividends received on both common and preferred stocks is exempt from taxes. However, neither preferred nor common dividends may be deducted by the issuing company. Therefore, the dividend exclusion has no effect on a company's cost of capital, so its WACC would probably not change at all if the dividend exclusion rule were rescinded by Congress.

    c. The calculation for a firm's WACC includes an adjustment to the cost of debt for taxes, since interest is deductible, and includes the cost of short-term debt.

    d. Each of the above statements is true.

    e. Each of the above statements is false.

SELF-TEST PROBLEMS

1. Roland Corporation's next expected dividend (D_1) is $2.50. The firm has maintained a constant payout ratio of 50 percent during the past 7 years. Seven years ago its EPS was $1.50. The firm's beta coefficient is 1.2. The required return on an average stock in the market is 13 percent, and the risk-free rate is 7 percent. Roland's A-rated bonds are yielding 10 percent, and its current stock price is $30. Which of the following values is the most reasonable estimate of Roland's cost of common equity, k_s?

    a. 10%   **b.** 12%   **c.** 14%   **d.** 20%   **e.** 26%

2. The director of capital budgeting for See-Saw Inc., manufacturers of playground equipment, is considering a plan to expand production facilities in order to meet an increase in demand. He estimates that this expansion will produce a rate of return of 11 percent. The firm's target capital structure calls for a debt/equity ratio of 0.8. See-Saw currently has a bond issue outstanding which will mature in 25 years and has a 7 percent annual coupon rate. The bonds are currently selling for $804. The firm has maintained a constant growth rate of 6 percent. See-Saw's next expected dividend is $2 and its current stock price is $40. Its tax rate is 40 percent. Should it undertake the expansion? (Assume that there is no preferred stock outstanding and that any new debt will have a 25-year maturity.)

    a. No; the expected return is 2.5 percentage points lower than the cost of capital.
    b. No; the expected return is 1.0 percentage point lower than the cost of capital.
    c. Yes; the expected return is 0.5 percentage point higher than the cost of capital.
    d. Yes; the expected return is 1.0 percentage point higher than the cost of capital.
    e. Yes; the expected return is 2.5 percentage points higher than the cost of capital.

3. The management of Florida Phosphate Industries (FPI) is planning next year's capital budget. The company's earnings and dividends are growing at a constant rate of 5 percent. The last dividend, D_0, was $0.90; and the current equilibrium stock price is $7.73. FPI can raise new debt at a 14 percent before-tax cost. FPI is at its optimal capital structure, which is 40 percent debt and 60 percent equity, and the firm's marginal tax rate is 40 percent. FPI has the following independent, indivisible, and equally risky investment opportunities:

Project	Cost	Rate of Return
A	$15,000	17%
B	15,000	16
C	12,000	15
D	20,000	13

    What is FPI's optimal capital budget?

    a. $62,000   b. $42,000   c. $30,000   d. $15,000   e. $0

4. Gator Products Company (GPC) is at its optimal capital structure of 70 percent common equity and 30 percent debt. GPC's WACC is 14 percent. GPC has a marginal tax rate of 40 percent. Next year's dividend is expected to be $2.00 per share, and GPC has a constant growth in earnings and dividends of 6 percent. The cost of common equity used in the WACC is based on retained earnings, while the before-tax cost of debt is 12 percent. What is GPC's current equilibrium stock price?

    a. $12.73   **b.** $17.23   **c.** $18.33   **d.** $20.37   **e.** $23.70

(The following data apply to the next four Self-Test Problems.)

Sun Products Company (SPC) uses only debt and equity. It can borrow unlimited amounts at an interest rate of 12 percent so long as it finances at its target capital structure, which calls for 45 percent debt and 55 percent common equity. Its last dividend was $2.40, its expected constant growth rate is 5 percent, and its stock sells for $24. SPC's tax rate is 40 percent. Four projects are available: Project A has a cost of $240 million and a rate of return of 13 percent, Project B has a cost of $125 million and a rate of return of 12 percent, Project C has a cost of $200 million and a rate of return of 11 percent, and Project D has a cost of $150 million and a rate of return of 10 percent. All of the company's potential projects are independent and equally risky.

5. What is SPC's cost of common equity?

    a. 15.50%   **b.** 13.40%   **c.** 7.20%   **d.** 12.50%   **e.** 16.00%

6. What is SPC's weighted average cost of capital? In other words, what WACC cost rate should it use to evaluate capital budgeting projects (these four projects plus any others that might arise during the year, provided the WACC remains as it is currently)?

    a. 12.05%   **b.** 13.40%   **c.** 11.77%   **d.** 12.50%   **e.** 10.61%

7. What is SPC's optimal capital budget (in millions)?

    a. $240   **b.** $325   **c.** $365   **d.** $565   **e.** $715

8. Assume now that all four projects are independent; however, Project A has been judged a very risky project, while Projects C and D have been judged low-risk projects. Project B remains an average-risk project. If SPC adjusts its WACC by 2 percentage points up or down to account for risk, what is its optimal capital budget (in millions) now?

    a. $365   **b.** $390   **c.** $440   **d.** $475   **e.** $715

(The following data apply to the next two Self-Test Problems.)

On January 1, the total market value of the Haberdasher Company was $20 million. During the year, the company plans to raise and invest $10 million in new projects. The firm's present market value capital structure, shown below, is considered to be optimal. Assume that there is no short-term debt.

Debt	$10,000,000
Common equity	10,000,000
Total capital	$20,000,000

New bonds will have a 7 percent coupon rate, and they will be sold at par. Common stock is currently selling at $25 a share. Stockholders' required rate of return is estimated to be 13 percent, consisting of a dividend yield of 5 percent and an expected constant growth rate of 8 percent. (The next expected dividend is $1.25, so $1.25/$25 = 5%.) The marginal corporate tax rate is 40 percent.

9. To maintain the present capital structure, how much of the new investment (in millions) must be financed by common equity?

   a. $1.75   **b.** $2.25   **c.** $3.45   **d.** $5.00   **e.** $10.00

10. Assume that there is sufficient cash flow such that Haberdasher can maintain its target capital structure without issuing additional shares of equity. What is the WACC?

   a. 7.0%   **b.** 8.6%   **c.** 9.2%   **d.** 10.1%   **e.** 13.0%

(The following data apply to the next two Self-Test Problems.)

The following tabulation gives earnings per share figures for Gustafson Manufacturing during the preceding 10 years. The firm's common stock, 100,000 shares outstanding, is now selling for $40 a share, and the expected dividend for the coming year (1999) is 40 percent of EPS for the year. Investors expect past trends to continue, so g may be based on the historical earnings growth rate.

Year	EPS
1989	$1.60
1990	1.73
1991	1.86
1992	2.02
1993	2.18
1994	2.35
1995	2.54
1996	2.74
1997	2.96
1998	3.20

The current interest rate on new debt is 7.5 percent. The firm's marginal federal-plus-state tax rate is 40 percent. The firm's market value capital structure, considered to be optimal, is as follows:

Debt	$2,400,000
Common equity	5,600,000
Total capital	$8,000,000

11. What is the firm's after-tax cost of new debt and common equity, assuming new equity comes only from reinvested cash flow? Calculate the cost of equity assuming constant growth; that is, $\hat{k}_s = D_1 / P_0 + g = k_s$.

   a. 4.5%; 11.5% **b.** 4.8%; 11.5% **c.** 4.5%; 12.3% **d.** 4.8%; 12.3% **e.** 4.0%; 11.5%

12. What is the firm's WACC, assuming no new common stock is sold?

   a. 8.05%   **b.** 8.75%   **c.** 9.40%   **d.** 9.80%   **e.** 10.05%

(The following data apply to the next two Self-Test Problems.)

Suppose the Williamson Company has this *book value* balance sheet:

Current assets	$45,000,000	Notes payable	$ 15,000,000
Fixed assets	75,000,000	Long-term debt	45,000,000
		Common stock (1.5 million shares)	1,500,000
		Retained earnings	58,500,000
Total assets	$120,000,000	Total claims	$120,000,000

The interest rate on the notes payable is 10 percent, the same as the rate on new bank loans. The long-term debt consists of 45,000 bonds, each of which has a par value of $1,000, carries an annual coupon interest rate of 6 percent, and matures in 20 years. The going rate of interest on new long-term debt, k_d, is 10 percent, and this is the present yield to maturity on the bonds. The common stock sells at a price of $30 per share.

13. What is the market value of the firm's long-term debt?

    a. $24,231,145 **b.** $29,675,585 **c.** $30,148,667 **d.** $32,498,885 **e.** $33,415,625

14. What is the market value weight of common equity in the firm's capital structure, if short-term debt is included?

    a. 25.00%   **b.** 38.75%   **c.** 42.45%   **d.** 50.18%   **e.** 63.00%

ANSWERS TO SELF-TEST QUESTIONS

1. weighted average
2. three
3. opportunity cost
4. flotation costs
5. risk-free rate (k_{RF}); beta coefficient (b); stock (k_M)
6. risk premium
7. dividend yield; growth rate
8. debt; preferred stock; common equity; weighted average
9. preferred dividends; net issuing price
10. retention rate
11. interest; taxes
12. capital structure; dividend; investment

13. hurdle
14. risk; average
15. stand-alone; corporate (within-firm); market (beta)
16. market
17. above
18. Stand-alone
19. pure play; accounting beta
20. risk-adjusted costs of capital
21. capital components
22. marginal
23. flotation costs; price pressure
24. target
25. depreciation
26. weighted average cost of capital

27. a. This statement is true.

28. e. If Firm A has more business risk than Firm B, Firm A's cost of debt could be greater than Firm B's cost of equity. Also, the cost of reinvested earnings is less than the cost of new equity because of flotation costs.

29. a. Statement a is correct. If Congress were to raise the tax rate, this would lower the cost of debt; however, a bigger chunk of the firm's earnings would go to Uncle Sam. The effect on the WACC would depend on which had the greater effect on the WACC. Statement b is false. Preferred stock generally has a lower before-tax cost than debt due to the dividend exclusion; however, if the dividend exclusion were omitted, preferred stock would have an increased before-tax cost. Statement c is false because short-term debt is not considered in the calculation of WACC.

SOLUTIONS TO SELF-TEST PROBLEMS

1. c. Use all three methods to estimate k_s.

CAPM: $k_s = k_{RF} + (k_M - k_{RF})b = 7\% + (13\% - 7\%)1.2 = 14.2\%$.

Risk Premium: $k_s =$ Bond yield + Risk premium $= 10\% + 4\% = 14\%$.

DCF: $k_s = D_1/P_0 + g = \$2.50/\$30 + g$, where g can be estimated as follows:
$$\$0.75 = \$2.50(PVIF_{k,7})$$
$$PVIF_{k,7} = \$0.75/\$2.50 = 0.3000.$$

Thus k, which is the compound growth rate, g, is about 19%, or, using a calculator, 18.8%. Therefore, $k_s = 0.083 + 0.188 = 27.1\%$.

Roland Corporation has apparently been experiencing supernormal growth during the past 7 years, and it is not reasonable to assume that this growth will continue. The first two methods yield a k_s of about 14 percent, which appears reasonable.

2. e. Cost of equity $= k_s = \$2/\$40 + 0.06 = 0.11 = 11\%$.

Cost of debt $= k_d =$ Yield to maturity on outstanding bonds based on current market price.

$$V_B = INT(PVIFA_{k_d,25}) + M(PVIF_{k_d,25})$$
$$\$804 = \$70(PVIFA_{k_d,25}) + \$1,000(PVIF_{k_d,25}).$$

Solving by trial and error gives $k_d = 9\%$.

Alternatively, with a financial calculator: Input N = 25, PV = -804, PMT = 70, FV = 1000, and solve for I = k_d = 9%.

In determining the capital structure weights, note that Debt/Equity = 0.8 or, for example, 4/5. Therefore, Debt/Assets is

$$\frac{D}{A} = \frac{Debt}{Debt + Equity} = \frac{4}{4+5} = \frac{4}{9},$$

and Equity/Assets = 5/9. Hence, the weighted average cost of capital is calculated as follows:

$$\begin{aligned} WACC &= k_d(1-T)(D/A) + k_s(1-D/A) \\ &= 0.09(1-0.4)(4/9) + 0.11(5/9) \\ &= 0.024 + 0.061 = 0.085 = 8.5\%. \end{aligned}$$

The cost of capital is 8.5 percent, while the expansion project's rate of return is 11 percent. Since the expected return is 2.5 percentage points higher than the cost, the expansion should be undertaken.

3.   b.   The cost of common equity is as follows:

$$k_s = \frac{D_0(1+g)}{P_0} + g = \frac{\$0.90(1.05)}{\$7.73} + 0.05 = 0.1723 = 17.23\%.$$

Now, determine the weighted average cost of capital.

$$\begin{aligned} WACC &= w_d(k_d)(1-T) + w_{ce}(k_s) \\ &= 0.4(14\%)(0.6) + 0.6(17.23\%) = 13.70\%. \end{aligned}$$

To determine FPI's optimal capital budget, we must determine those projects whose rate of return > WACC. (Note that all projects being considered are independent.) Since Projects A, B, and C all have rates of return > WACC, they should be accepted. Therefore, the optimal capital budget is $42,000.

4.   c.   GPC's WACC = 14%. Therefore,

$$\begin{aligned} 14\% &= w_d(k_d)(1-T) + w_{ce}(k_s) \\ 14\% &= 0.3(12\%)(0.6) + 0.7(k_s) \\ k_s &= 16.91\%. \end{aligned}$$

Now, at equilibrium:

$$\hat{k}_s = k_s = \frac{D_1}{P_0} + g$$

$$0.1691 = \frac{\$2.00}{P_0} + 0.06$$

$$0.1091 = \frac{\$2.00}{P_0}$$

$$P_0 = \$18.33.$$

5. a. $k_s = [\$2.40(1.05)]/\$24 + 5\% = 0.1050 + 0.05 = 0.1550 = 15.50\%.$

6. c. $k_d = 12\%; k_d(1 - T) = 12\%(0.6) = 7.2\%.$

    $k_s = [\$2.40(1.05)]/\$24 + 5\% = 15.50\%.$

    WACC $= 0.45(7.2\%) + 0.55(15.50\%) = 11.77\%.$

7. c. Since all projects are equally risky and are independent, those projects whose rate of return > WACC should be chosen. Projects A and B have returns > 11.77%; therefore, the firm's optimal capital budget is $365 million.

8. d.

Project	Cost (Millions)	Return	Risk Level	Risk-Adjusted Cost of Capital
A	$240	13%	High	13.77%
B	125	12	Average	11.77
C	200	11	Low	9.77
D	150	10	Low	9.77

From Self-Test Problem 6 we know that SPC's WACC is 11.77%. We adjust the firm's WACC up by 2% for risky projects and lower it by 2% for low-risk projects. Note that once the WACC is risk-adjusted, Projects B, C, and D are acceptable as their returns are greater than the risk-adjusted WACC. Therefore, the firm's optimal capital budget is $475 million.

9. d. Common equity needed:

0.5($10,000,000) = $5,000,000.

10. b. Cost using k_s:

	Percent	×	After-tax Cost	=	Product
Debt	0.50		4.2%*		2.1%
Common equity	0.50		13.0		6.5
				WACC =	8.6%

*7%(1 – T) = 7%(0.6) = 4.2%.

11. a. After-tax cost of new debt = $k_d(1 - T)$:

$k_d(1 - T) = 0.075(1 - 0.4) = 0.045 = 4.5\%.$

Cost of common equity = k_s:

$k_s = D_1/P_0 + g.$

Using the point-to-point technique, g = 8.01%. Thus,

$k_s = \$3.20(0.4)(1.08)/\$40.00 + 8\% = 3.5\% + 8\% = 11.5\%.$

12. c. WACC calculation:

Component	% Capital Structure	×	After-tax Cost	=	Component Cost
Debt	0.30		4.5%		1.35%
Common equity	0.70		11.5		8.05
	1.00			WACC =	9.40%

13. b. The bonds have a value of

$V_B = \$60(PVIFA_{10\%, 20}) + \$1,000(PVIF_{10\%, 20}) = \$60(8.5136) + \$1,000(0.1486)$
$= \$510.82 + \$148.60 = \$659.42.$

Alternatively, using a financial calculator, input $N = 20$, $I = 10$, $PMT = 60$, and $FV = 1000$ to arrive at a $PV = \$659.46$.

The total market value of the long-term debt is 45,000($659.46) = $29,675,585.

14. d. The book and market value of the current liabilities are both $15,000,000.

There are 1.5 million shares of stock outstanding, and the stock sells for $30 per share. Therefore, the market value of the equity is $30(1,500,000) = $45,000,000. From Self-Test Problem 13 we know that the market value of the bonds is $29,675,585.

The market value capital structure is thus:

Short-term debt	$15,000,000	16.73%
Long-term debt	29,675,585	33.09
Common equity	45,000,000	50.18
Total capital	$89,675,585	100.00%

CHAPTER 6
CAPITAL BUDGETING DECISION CRITERIA

OVERVIEW

This chapter discusses investment decisions involving fixed assets, or capital budgeting. The term capital refers to long-term assets used in production, while a budget is a plan which details projected inflows and outflows during some future period. Thus, the capital budget is an outline of planned investments in fixed assets, and capital budgeting is the whole process of analyzing projects and deciding which ones to include in the capital budget.

Capital budgeting is similar in principle to security valuation in that future cash flows are estimated, risks are appraised and reflected in a cost of capital discount rate, and all cash flows are evaluated on a present value basis. Seven primary methods can be used to determine which projects should be included

in a firm's capital budget: (1) payback, (2) discounted payback, (3) Accounting Rate of Return (ARR), (4) Net Present Value (NPV), (5) Internal Rate of Return (IRR), (6) Modified IRR (MIRR), and (7) Profitability Index (PI).

Both payback methods have deficiencies, and thus should not be used as the sole criterion for making capital budgeting decisions. The NPV, IRR, PI, and MIRR methods all lead to the same accept/reject decisions on independent projects. However, the methods may conflict when ranking mutually exclusive projects which differ in scale or timing. Under these circumstances, the NPV method should be used to make the final decision.

OUTLINE

The capital budget is an outline of planned investments in fixed assets, and capital budgeting is the process of planning expenditures on assets whose cash flows are expected to extend beyond one year.

■ A number of factors combine to make capital budgeting perhaps the most important function financial managers and their staffs must perform.

- ☐ Since the results of capital budgeting decisions continue for many years, investments in fixed assets cause the firm to lose some of its flexibility.
- ☐ A firm's capital budgeting decisions define its strategic direction because moves into new products, services, or markets must be preceded by capital expenditures.

■ The same general concepts that are used in security valuation are also involved in capital budgeting; however, whereas a set of stocks and bonds exists in the securities market from which investors select, capital budgeting projects are created by the firm.

■ Analyzing capital expenditure proposals has a cost, so firms classify projects into different categories to help differentiate the level of analysis required:
- ☐ Replacement: maintenance of business
- ☐ Replacement: cost reduction
- ☐ Expansion of existing products or markets
- ☐ Expansion into new products or markets
- ☐ Safety and/or environmental projects
- ☐ Research and development
- ☐ Other miscellaneous projects

■ Normally, a more detailed analysis is required for cost-reduction replacements, expansion of existing product lines, and new product decisions than for simple replacement and maintenance decisions. Also, projects requiring larger investments will be analyzed more carefully than smaller projects.

■ Once a potential capital budgeting project has been identified, its evaluation involves the same steps that are used in security analysis.
- ☐ The cost of the project must be determined.
- ☐ Cash flows from the project are estimated.
- ☐ The riskiness of projected cash flows must be estimated.
- ☐ Given the project's riskiness, the appropriate cost of capital at which cash flows are to be discounted must be determined.
- ☐ Cash flows are discounted to their present value to obtain an estimate of the asset's value to the firm.
- ☐ The present value of the expected cash flows is compared with the required outlay, or cost. If the PV of the cash flows exceeds the cost, the project should be accepted; otherwise, it should be rejected. (Alternatively, if the expected rate of return on the project exceeds its cost of capital, the project is accepted.)

Seven key methods are used to rank projects and to decide whether or not they should be accepted for inclusion in the capital budget: (1) payback, (2) discounted payback, (3) Accounting Rate of Return (ARR), (4) Net Present Value (NPV), (5) Internal Rate of

Return (IRR), (6) Modified Internal Rate of Return (MIRR), and (7) Profitability Index (PI). The MIRR and PI are discussed in later sections.

■ The *payback period* is defined as the expected number of years required to recover the original investment in the project, and it was the first formal method used to evaluate capital budgeting projects.

  □ Payback is a type of "breakeven" calculation in the sense that if cash flows come in at the expected rate until the payback year, then the project will break even.

  □ The payback method's flaws are that cash flows beyond the payback period are ignored and it does not take into account the cost of capital.

  □ Although the payback method has some serious faults as a ranking criterion, it does provide information on how long funds will be tied up in a project. Thus, the shorter the payback period, other things held constant, the greater the project's *liquidity*.

  □ Also, since cash flows expected in the distant future are generally riskier than near-term cash flows, the payback is often used as one indication of a project's *riskiness*.

■ A variant of the regular payback, the *discounted payback period* discounts the expected cash flows by the project's cost of capital, thus taking into account the effects of capital costs. Thus, the discounted payback period is defined as the number of years required to recover the investment from discounted net cash flows.

■ The *Accounting Rate of Return (ARR)* focuses on a project's net income rather than its cash flows, and it is the second oldest capital budgeting evaluation technique. In its most commonly used form, the ARR is measured as the ratio of the project's average annual expected net income to its average investment.

$$ARR = \frac{\text{Average annual income}}{\text{Average investment}}.$$

  □ The ARR ignores the time value of money.

  □ Because it doesn't provide complete information on the project's contribution to the firm's value, it could lead to an incorrect capital budgeting decision.

■ The *Net Present Value (NPV)* method is a discounted cash flow (DCF) technique that accounts for the time value of all cash flows from a project.

  □ To implement the NPV, proceed as follows: (a) Find the present value of each cash flow discounted at the project's cost of capital, (b) sum these discounted cash flows to obtain the project's NPV, and (c) accept the project if the NPV is positive.

  □ The NPV is defined as follows:

$$NPV = \sum_{t=0}^{n} \frac{CF_t}{(1+k)^t}.$$

Here, CF_t is the expected net cash flow in Period t and k is the project's cost of capital. Cash outflows are treated as negative cash flows.

☐ If the NPV is positive, the project should be accepted; if negative, it should be rejected. If two projects are *mutually exclusive* (that is, only one can be accepted), the one with the higher NPV should be chosen, assuming that the NPV is positive. If both projects have negative NPVs, neither should be chosen.

☐ Finding the NPV with a financial calculator is efficient and easy. Simply enter the different cash flows into the "cash flow register" along with the value of k = I, and then press the NPV key for the solution.

☐ Financial analysts generally use spreadsheets when dealing with capital budgeting projects. Once a spreadsheet has been set up, it is easy to change input values to see what would happen as inputs are changed.

☐ An NPV of zero signifies that the project's cash flows are just sufficient to repay the invested capital and to provide the required rate of return on that capital. If a project has a positive NPV, then it is generating more cash than is needed to service its debt and to provide the required return to shareholders, and this excess cash accrues solely to the firm's stockholders.

☐ There is a direct relationship between NPV and EVA. NPV is equal to the present value of the project's future EVAs. Therefore, accepting positive NPV projects should result in a positive EVA for the company, and in a positive MVA.

☐ A reward system that compensates managers for producing positive EVA will encourage the use of NPV for making capital budgeting decisions.

■ The *Internal Rate of Return (IRR)* is defined as the discount rate which equates the present value of a project's expected cash inflows to the present value of the project's costs.

☐ The equation for calculating the IRR is shown below:

$$\sum_{t=0}^{n} \frac{CF_t}{(1+IRR)^t} = 0.$$

This equation has one unknown, the IRR, and we can solve for the value of the IRR that will make the equation equal to zero. The solution value of IRR is defined as the internal rate of return.

☐ The IRR formula is simply the NPV formula solved for the particular discount rate that causes the NPV to equal zero.

☐ The IRR can be found by trial and error, but most financial calculators and computers with financial analysis software can easily calculate IRRs and NPVs.

☐ To find the IRR with a financial calculator, simply enter the different cash flows into the cash flow register, making sure to input the t = 0 cash flow, and then press the IRR key for the solution.

☐ The IRR rule indicates that a project with an IRR greater than its cost of capital, or *hurdle rate*, should be accepted.

☐ If the IRR exceeds the cost of the funds used to finance the project, a surplus remains after paying for the capital, and that surplus accrues to the firm's stockholders. Therefore, taking on a project whose IRR exceeds its cost of capital increases shareholders' wealth.

☐ Its "breakeven" characteristic makes the IRR useful in evaluating capital projects.

■ In many respects the NPV method is better than the IRR method. However, the IRR is widely entrenched in industry. Therefore, it is important to understand the IRR method including its problems.

■ A *net present value profile* is a graph which plots a project's NPV against different discount rates.

☐ The NPV profile crosses the Y-axis at the *undiscounted* NPV, while it crosses the X-axis at the IRR.

☐ The *crossover rate* is the discount rate at which the NPV profiles of two projects cross and, thus, at which the projects' NPVs are equal.

☐ If an *independent* project is being evaluated, then the NPV and IRR criteria always lead to the same accept/reject decision.

☐ If two *mutually exclusive* projects have NPV profiles which intersect in the upper right-hand quadrant, then there may be a conflict in rankings between NPV and IRR methods. A conflict between the NPV and IRR decision rules exists for mutually exclusive projects if the cost of capital is *less than* the crossover rate. Two basic conditions can lead to conflicts between NPV and IRR:

   • *Project size* (or *scale*) differences exist; that is, the cost of one project is larger than that of the other.

   • *Timing differences* exist such that cash flows from one project come in the early years and most of the cash flows from the other project come in the later years.

☐ The critical issue in resolving conflicts between mutually exclusive projects is to determine how useful it is to generate cash flows earlier rather than later. Thus, the value of early cash flows depends on the *opportunity cost rate* at which we can reinvest these cash flows.

   • The NPV method implicitly assumes that the opportunity cost rate at which project cash flows are reinvested is the project's cost of capital.

   • The IRR method implicitly assumes that project cash flows are reinvested at the project's IRR.

   • The opportunity cost of a project's cash flows is the project's cost of capital. If these cash flows were not available to the firm and if the firm needed capital to invest in new projects, then the funds would be obtained from the firm's capital suppliers; the cost would be the overall cost of capital. Thus, the assumption of reinvestment at the cost of capital is the best *reinvestment rate assumption*, and NPV is the preferred method.

☐ In summary, when projects are independent, the NPV and IRR methods both make exactly the same accept/reject decision. However, when evaluating mutually exclusive projects, especially those that differ in scale and/or timing, the NPV method should be used.

■ Besides ranking conflicts, other problems can arise when using the IRR method.

☐ A *normal* capital project is one that has one or more cash outflows (costs) followed by a series of cash inflows. If a project calls for a large cash outflow either sometime during or at the end of its life, then it is a *nonnormal* project.

☐ Nonnormal projects can present three unique difficulties when evaluated by the IRR criterion: (1) The IRR criterion can lead to a decision which does not maximize the firm's value; (2) the project may have no IRR; and (3) the project may have multiple IRRs.

● In all these cases, the NPV criterion could be easily applied, and the NPV method leads to conceptually correct capital budgeting decisions.

Business executives often prefer to work with percentage rates of return, such as IRR, rather than dollar amounts of NPV when analyzing investments. To overcome some of the IRR's limitations a Modified IRR, or MIRR, has been devised.

■ The MIRR is defined as the discount rate which forces PV costs = PV terminal value, where *terminal value (TV)* is the future value of the inflows compounded at the project's cost of capital. Thus,

$$\sum_{t=0}^{n} \frac{COF_t}{(1+k)^t} = \frac{\sum_{t=0}^{n} CIF_t (1+k)^{n-t}}{(1+MIRR)^n}$$

$$PV \ costs = \frac{TV}{(1+MIRR)^n}.$$

■ Most spreadsheets have a function for finding the MIRR.

■ MIRR assumes that cash flows are reinvested at the cost of capital rather than the project's own IRR, making it a better indicator of a project's true profitability.

■ NPV and MIRR will lead to the same project selection decision for mutually exclusive projects if the two projects are of equal size and have the same life.

- ☐ If the projects are of equal size, but differ in lives, the MIRR will always lead to the same decision as the NPV if the MIRRs are both calculated using as the terminal year the life of the longer project.
- ☐ However, conflicts can still occur when projects differ in scale, and in this case, NPV should be used.

■ MIRR also avoids the problem of multiple IRRs, which can arise when a project has nonnormal cash flows or has negative cash flows after the project has gone into operation. NPV can be easily applied to such situations; however, MIRR can also overcome the multiple IRR problem because there is only one MIRR for any set of cash flows.

■ MIRR is superior to the regular IRR as an indicator of a project's "true" rate of return, or "expected long-term rate of return," but the NPV method is still better for choosing among mutually exclusive projects because it provides a better indicator of how much each project will increase the firm's value.

Another method used to evaluate projects is the Profitability Index (PI), or the benefit/cost ratio.

■ The equation for the *profitability index* is:

$$PI = \frac{PV\ benefits}{PV\ costs} = \frac{\sum_{t=0}^{n} \dfrac{CIF_t}{(1+k)^t}}{\sum_{t=0}^{n} \dfrac{COF_t}{(1+k)^t}}.$$

■ CIF_t represents the expected cash inflows, or benefits, and COF_t represents the expected cash outflows, or costs.

■ The PI shows the relative profitability of any project, or the present value of benefits per present value dollar of costs.

■ A project is acceptable if its PI is greater than 1.0, and the higher the PI, the higher the project's ranking.

■ Mathematically, the NPV, IRR, MIRR, and PI methods will always lead to the same accept/reject decisions for *independent* projects; however, these methods can give conflicting rankings for *mutually exclusive* projects.

In making the accept/reject decision, each of the seven capital budgeting decision methods provides decision makers with a somewhat different piece of relevant information.

■   Payback and discounted payback provide an indication of both the *risk* and the *liquidity* of a project.

■   NPV is important because it gives a direct measure of the dollar benefit (on a present value basis) of the project to shareholders, so it is regarded as the best single measure of *profitability*.

■   IRR also measures profitability, but expressed as a percentage rate of return, which many decision makers prefer. Further, IRR contains information regarding a project's *safety margin*.

■   The modified IRR has all the virtues of the IRR, but it incorporates *a better reinvestment rate assumption*, and it avoids the multiple rate of return problem.

■   The PI measures profitability relative to the cost of a project—it shows the *bang per buck*. Like the IRR, it gives an indication of the project's risk, for a high PI means that cash flows could fall quite a bit and the project would still be profitable.

■   Quantitative methods such as NPV and IRR should be considered as an aid to informed decisions but not as a substitute for sound managerial judgment.

■   In a perfectly competitive economy, there would be no positive NPV projects—all companies would have the same opportunities, and *competition* would quickly eliminate any positive NPV.

■   Positive NPV projects must be due to some imperfection in the marketplace, and the longer the life of the project, the longer that imperfection must last. Therefore, managers should be able to identify the imperfection and explain why it will persist before accepting that a project will really have a positive NPV.

         ☐   If you can't identify the reason a project has a positive projected NPV, then its actual NPV will probably not be positive.

         ☐   Positive NPV projects don't just happen—they result from hard work to develop some competitive advantage.

         ☐   Some competitive advantages last longer than others, with their durability depending on competitors' abilities to replicate them.

A number of studies regarding firms' use of capital budgeting methods have been published. The general conclusion one can reach from these studies is that large firms should and do use the procedures we recommend, and that managers of small firms, especially managers with aspirations for future growth, should at least understand DCF procedures well enough to make rational decisions about using or not using them.

Moreover, as computer technology makes it easier and less expensive for small firms to use DCF methods, and as more and more of their competitors begin using these methods, survival will necessitate increased DCF usage.

An important aspect of the capital budgeting process is the post-audit, which involves comparing actual results with those predicted by the project's sponsors and explaining why any differences occurred. The results of the post-audit help to improve forecasts, increase efficiency of the firm's operations, and identify abandonment/termination opportunities.

■ The *post-audit* is not a simple process—a number of factors can cause complications.
   □ Each element of the cash flow forecast is subject to uncertainty, so a percentage of all projects undertaken by any reasonably aggressive firm will necessarily go awry.
   □ Projects sometime fail to meet expectations for reasons beyond the control of the operating executives and for reasons that no one could realistically be expected to anticipate.
   □ Although some projects stand alone and permit ready identification of costs and revenues, the actual cost savings that result from projects that are part of a larger system may be very hard to measure.
   □ It is often hard to hand out blame or praise because the executives who were responsible for launching a given investment may have moved on by the time the results are known.

■ The results of post-audits often conclude that (1) the actual NPVs of most cost reduction projects exceed their expected NPVs by a slight amount, (2) expansion projects generally fall short of their expected NPVs by a slight amount, and (3) new product and new market projects fall short by relatively large amounts.

■ The best-run and most successful organizations put great emphasis on post-audits.

The techniques developed in this chapter can help managers make a number of different types of decisions.

■ Two examples of decisions which use capital budgeting techniques are evaluating corporate mergers and deciding whether to downsize personnel or to sell off particular assets or divisions.

■ Most decisions should be based on whether they contribute to shareholder value, and that, in turn, can be determined by estimating the net present value of a set of cash flows.

SELF-TEST QUESTIONS

Definitional

1. A firm's _____ _____ outlines its planned expenditures on fixed assets.

2. The number of years necessary to return the original investment in a project is known as the _____ _____ .

3. The primary advantage of payback analysis is its _____ .

4. One important weakness of payback analysis is the fact that _____ _____ beyond the payback period are _____ .

5. The Net Present Value (NPV) method of evaluating investment proposals is a(n) _____ cash flow technique.

6. A capital investment proposal should be accepted if its NPV is _____ .

7. If two projects are _____ _____ , the one with the _____ positive NPV should be selected.

8. In the IRR approach, a discount rate is sought which makes the NPV equal to _____ .

9. A net present value profile plots a project's _____ against different _____ _____ .

10. If an independent project's _____ is greater than the project's cost of capital, it should be accepted.

11. If two mutually exclusive projects are being evaluated and one project has a higher NPV while the other project has a higher IRR, the project with the higher _____ should be preferred.

12. The NPV method implicitly assumes reinvestment at the project's _____ ___ _____ , while the IRR method implicitly assumes reinvestment at the _____ _____ ___ _____ .

13. The MIRR method assumes reinvestment at the _____ ____ _____ , making it a better indicator of a project's profitability than IRR.

14.   The process of comparing a project's actual results with its projected results is known as a(n) _____-_____.

15.   The objective of the post-audit is to improve _____, _____, and identify _____ and _____ opportunities.

16.   The internal rate of return (IRR) is the _____ rate that equates the present value of the _____ _____ with the present value of the _____ _____.

17.   The MIRR is defined as the discount rate which forces the present value of costs to equal the present value of the _____ _____.

18.   The shorter the payback period, other things held constant, the greater the project's _____.

19.   The NPV profile crosses the Y-axis at the _____ NPV, while it crosses the X-axis at the _____.

20.   The _____ _____ ____ _____ focuses on a project's net income rather than its cash flows.

21.   If a(n) _____ project is being evaluated, then the NPV and IRR criteria always lead to the same accept/reject decisions.

22.   Two basic conditions can lead to conflicts between NPV and IRR: _____ and _____ differences.

23.   A normal capital project is one that has one or more cash _____ followed by a series of cash _____.

24.   _____ _____ can result when the IRR criterion is used with a project that has nonnormal cash flows.

25.   In addition to measuring a project's liquidity, the payback is often used as one indication of a project's _____.

26.   There is a direct relationship between NPV and _____. NPV is equal to the present value of the project's future _____.

27.   The _____ _____ is the discount rate at which the NPV profiles of two projects cross and, thus, at which the projects' NPVs are equal.

28. The _____ _____ shows the relative profitability of any project, or the present value of benefits per present value dollar of costs.

29. _____ contains information regarding a project's safety margin.

30. _____ gives a direct measure of the dollar benefit of the project to shareholders.

31. The ____ shows the "bang per buck."

32. A conflict between the NPV and IRR decision rules exists for mutually exclusive projects if the cost of capital is _____ than the crossover rate.

Conceptual

33. The NPV of a project with cash flows that accrue relatively slowly is *more sensitive* to changes in the discount rate than is the NPV of a project with cash flows that come in more rapidly.

    a. True   **b.** False

34. The NPV method is preferred over the IRR method because the NPV method's reinvestment rate assumption is better.

    a. True   **b.** False

35. When you find the yield to maturity on a bond, you are finding the bond's net present value (NPV).

    a. True   **b.** False

36. Other things held constant, a decrease in the cost of capital (discount rate) will cause an *increase* in a project's IRR.

    a. True   **b.** False

37. The IRR method can be used in place of the NPV method for all independent projects.

    a. True   **b.** False

38. The NPV and MIRR methods lead to the same decision for mutually exclusive projects regardless of the projects' relative sizes.

    a. True   **b.** False

39. Projects with nonnormal cash flows sometimes have multiple MIRRs.

    a. True   **b.** False

40. Projects A and B each have an initial cost of $5,000, followed by a series of positive cash inflows. Project A has total undiscounted cash inflows of $12,000, while B has total undiscounted inflows of $10,000. Further, at a discount rate of 10 percent, the two projects have identical NPVs. Which project's NPV will be *more sensitive* to changes in the discount rate? (Hint: Projects with steeper NPV profiles are more sensitive to discount rate changes.)

    a. Project A.
    b. Project B.
    c. Both projects are equally sensitive to changes in the discount rate since their NPVs are equal at all costs of capital.
    d. Neither project is sensitive to changes in the discount rate, since both have NPV profiles which are horizontal.
    e. The solution cannot be determined unless the timing of the cash flows is known.

41. Which of the following statements is most correct?

    a. The IRR of a project whose cash flows accrue relatively rapidly is more sensitive to changes in the discount rate than is the IRR of a project whose cash flows come in more slowly.
    b. There are many conditions under which a project can have more than one IRR. One such condition is where an otherwise normal project has a negative cash flow at the end of its life.
    c. The phenomenon called "multiple internal rates of return" arises when two or more mutually exclusive projects with different lives are being compared.
    d. The modified IRR (MIRR) method has wide appeal to professors, but most business executives prefer the NPV method to either the regular or modified IRR.
    e. Each of the above statements is false.

42. Which of the following statements is most correct?

    a. If a project has an IRR greater than zero, then taking on the project will increase the value of the company's common stock because the project will make a positive contribution to net income.

    b. If a project has an NPV greater than zero, then taking on the project will increase the value of the firm's stock.

    c. Assume that you plot the NPV profiles of two mutually exclusive projects with normal cash flows and that the cost of capital is greater than the rate at which the profiles cross one another. In this case, the NPV and IRR methods will lead to contradictory rankings of the two projects.

    d. For independent (as opposed to mutually exclusive) normal projects, the NPV and IRR methods will generally lead to conflicting accept/reject decisions.

    e. Statements b, c, and d are all true.

43. Which of the following statements is most correct?

    a. Underlying the MIRR is the assumption that cash flows can be reinvested at the firm's cost of capital.

    b. Underlying the IRR is the assumption that cash flows can be reinvested at the firm's cost of capital.

    c. Underlying the NPV is the assumption that cash flows can be reinvested at the firm's cost of capital.

    d. The discounted payback method always leads to the same accept/reject decisions as the NPV method.

    e. Both statements a and c are correct.

SELF-TEST PROBLEMS

1. Your firm is considering a fast-food concession at the World's Fair. The cash flow pattern is somewhat unusual since you must build the stands, operate them for 2 years, and then tear the stands down and restore the sites to their original conditions. You estimate the net cash flows to be as follows:

Time	Expected Net Cash Flows
0	($800,000)
1	700,000
2	700,000
3	(400,000)

What is the approximate IRR of this venture?

a. 5% **b.** 15% **c.** 25% **d.** 35% **e.** 45%

(The following data apply to the next four Self-Test Problems.)

Toya Motors needs a new machine for production of its new models. The financial vice president has appointed you to do the capital budgeting analysis. You have identified two different machines that are capable of performing the job. You have completed the cash flow analysis, and the expected net cash flows are as follows:

Year	Expected Net Cash Flows	
	Machine B	Machine O
0	($5,000)	($5,000)
1	2,085	0
2	2,085	0
3	2,085	0
4	2,085	9,677

2. What is the payback period for Machine B?

a. 1.0 year **b.** 2.0 years **c.** 2.4 years **d.** 2.6 years **e.** 3.0 years

3. The cost of capital is uncertain at this time, so you construct NPV profiles to assist in the final decision. The profiles for Machines B and O cross at what cost of capital?

a. 6% **d.** 24%

b. 10% **e.** They do not cross in the upper righthand quadrant.

c. 18%

4. If the cost of capital for both projects is 14 percent at the time the decision is made, which project would you choose?

    a. Project B; it has the higher positive NPV.
    b. Project O; it has the higher positive NPV.
    c. Neither; both have negative NPVs.
    d. Either; both have the same NPV.
    e. Project B; it has the higher IRR.

5. If the cost of capital is 14 percent, what is the profitability index (PI) for Machine A?

    a. 0.750   b. 0.995   c. 1.150   d. 1.215   e. 1.333

(The following data apply to the next eight Self-Test Problems.)

The director of capital budgeting for Giant Inc. has identified two mutually exclusive projects, L and S, with the following expected net cash flows:

	Expected Net Cash Flows	
Year	Project L	Project S
0	($100)	($100)
1	10	70
2	60	50
3	80	20

Both projects have a cost of capital of 10 percent.

6. What is the payback period for Project S?

    a. 1.6 years   b. 1.8 years   c. 2.1 years   d. 2.5 years   e. 2.8 years

7. What is Project L's NPV?

    a. $50.00   b. $34.25   c. $22.64   d. $18.79   e. $10.06

8. What is Project L's IRR?

    a. 18.1%   b. 19.7%   c. 21.4%   d. 23.6%   e. 24.2%

9. What is Project L's PI?

    a. 0.955   b. 1.050   c. 1.188   d. 1.215   e. 1.346

10. What is Project S's PI?

    a. 0.875   **b.** 0.964   **c.** 1.000   **d.** 1.100   **e.** 1.200

11. What is Project L's MIRR?

    a. 15.3%   **b.** 16.5%   **c.** 16.9%   **d.** 17.1%   **e.** 17.4%

12. What is Project S's MIRR?

    a. 15.3%   **b.** 16.5%   **c.** 16.9%   **d.** 17.1%   **e.** 17.4%

13. Plot the NPV profiles for the two projects. Where is the crossover point?

    a. 6.9%   **b.** 7.8%   **c.** 8.7%   **d.** 9.6%   **e.** 9.9%

14. Your company is considering two mutually exclusive projects, X and Y, whose costs and cash flows are shown below:

Year	Project X	Project Y
0	($2,000)	($2,000)
1	200	2,000
2	600	200
3	800	100
4	1,400	100

The projects are equally risky, and their cost of capital is 10 percent. You must make a recommendation, and you must base it on the modified IRR (MIRR). What is the MIRR of the better project?

    a. 11.50%   **b.** 12.00%   **c.** 11.70%   **d.** 12.50%   **e.** 13.10%

15. A company is analyzing two mutually exclusive projects, S and L, whose cash flows are shown below:

Year	Project S	Project L
0	($2,000)	($2,000)
1	1,800	0
2	500	500
3	20	800
4	20	1,600

The company's cost of capital is 9 percent, and it can get an unlimited amount of capital at that cost. What is the regular IRR (not MIRR) of the better project? (Hint: Note that the better project may or may not be the one with the higher IRR.)

a. 11.45%   b. 11.74%   c. 13.02%   d. 13.49%   e. 12.67%

16. The stock of Barkley Inc. and "the market" provided the following returns over the last 5 years:

Year	Barkley	Market
1994	-5%	-3%
1995	21	10
1996	9	4
1997	23	11
1998	31	15

Barkley finances only with retained earnings, and it uses the CAPM with a historical beta to determine its cost of equity. The risk-free rate is 7 percent, and the market risk premium is 5 percent. Barkley is considering a project which has a cost at $t = 0$ of $2,000 and which is expected to provide cash inflows of $1,000 per year for 3 years. What is the project's MIRR?

a. 23.46%   b. 18.25%   c. 22.92%   d. 20.95%   e. 21.82%

17. CDH Worldwide's stock returns versus the market were as follows, and the same relative volatility is expected in the future:

Year	CDH	Market
1995	12%	15%
1996	-6	-3
1997	25	19
1998	18	12

The T-bond rate is 6 percent; the market risk premium is 7 percent; CDH finances only with equity from retained earnings; and it uses the CAPM to estimate its cost of capital. Now CDH is considering two alternative trucks. Truck S has a cost of $12,000 and is expected to produce cash flows of $4,500 per year for 4 years. Truck L has a cost of $20,000 and is expected to produce cash flows of $7,500 per year for 4 years. By how much would CDH's value rise if it buys the better truck, and what is the MIRR of the better truck?

a. $803.35; 17.05%
b. $1,338.91; 17.05%
c. $1,896.47; 16.06%
d. $1,338.91; 16.06%
e. $803.35; 14.41%

18. Assume that your company has a cost of capital of 14 percent and that it is analyzing the following project:

```
         0        1       2       3       4
            14%
Project M: |----+-------+-------+-------+----|
        -250     140     140     170    -100
```

What are the project's IRR and MIRR?

a. 24.26%; 16.28%
b. 23.12%; 17.19%
c. 23.12%; 16.28%
d. 24.26%; 17.19%
e. None of the above.

ANSWERS TO SELF-TEST QUESTIONS

1. capital budget
2. payback period
3. simplicity
4. cash flows; ignored
5. discounted
6. positive
7. mutually exclusive; higher
8. zero
9. NPV; discount rates
10. IRR

11.	NPV	21.	independent
12.	cost of capital; internal rate of return	22.	scale; timing
13.	cost of capital	23.	outflows; inflows
14.	post-audit	24.	Multiple IRRs
15.	forecasts; operations; abandonment; termination	25.	riskiness
		26.	EVA; EVAs
16.	discount; cash inflows; cash outflows (or initial cost)	27.	crossover rate
		28.	profitability index (PI)
17.	terminal value	29.	IRR
18.	liquidity	30.	NPV
19.	undiscounted; IRR	31.	PI
20.	Accounting Rate of Return (ARR)	32.	less

33. a. The more the cash flows are spread over time, the greater is the effect of a change in discount rate. This is because the compounding process has a greater effect as the number of years increases.

34. a. Project cash flows are substitutes for outside capital. Thus, the opportunity cost of these cash flows is the firm's cost of capital, adjusted for risk. The NPV method uses this cost as the reinvestment rate, while the IRR method assumes reinvestment at the IRR.

35. b. The yield to maturity on a bond is the bond's IRR.

36. b. The computation of IRR is independent of the project's cost of capital.

37. a. Both the NPV and IRR methods lead to the same accept/reject decisions for independent projects. Thus, the IRR method can be used as a proxy for the NPV method when choosing independent projects.

38. b. NPV and MIRR may not lead to the same decision when the projects differ in scale.

39. b. Multiple IRRs occur in projects with nonnormal cash flows, but there is only one MIRR for each project.

40. a. If we were to begin graphing the NPV profiles for each of these projects, we would know two of the points for each project. The Y-intercepts for Projects A and B would be $7,000 and $5,000, respectively, and the crossover rate would be 10 percent. Thus, from this information we can conclude that Project A's NPV profile would have the steeper slope and would be more sensitive to changes in the discount rate.

41.   b.   Statement a is false because the IRR is independent of the discount rate. Statement b is true; the situation identified is that of a project with nonnormal cash flows, which has multiple IRRs. Statement c is false; multiple IRRs occur with projects with nonnormal cash flows, not with mutually exclusive projects with different lives. Statement d is false; business executives tend to prefer the IRR because it gives a measure of the project's safety margin.

42.   b.   Statement b is true; the others are all false. Note that IRR must be greater than the cost of capital; that conflicts arise if the cost of capital is to the left of the crossover rate; and that for some projects with nonnormal cash flows there are two IRRs, so NPV and IRR could lead to conflicting accept/reject decisions, depending on which IRR we examine.

43.   e.   Statement e is correct, because both statements a and c are true. The IRR assumes reinvestment at the IRR, and since the discounted payback ignores cash flows beyond the payback period, it could lead to rejections of projects with high late cash flows and hence NPV > 0.

SOLUTIONS TO SELF-TEST PROBLEMS

1.   c.   Unless you have a calculator that performs IRR calculations, the IRR must be obtained by trial and error or graphically. (Calculator solution: Input CF_0 = -800000, CF_{1-2} = 700000, CF_3 = -400000. Output: IRR = 25.48%.) Note that this project actually has multiple IRRs, with a second IRR at about -53 percent.

2.   c.   After Year 1, there is $5,000 - $2,085 = $2,915 remaining to pay back. After Year 2, only $2,915 - $2,085 = $830 is remaining. In Year 3, another $2,085 is collected. Assuming that the Year 3 cash flow occurs evenly over time, then payback occurs $830/$2,085 = 0.4 of the way through Year 3. Thus, the payback period is 2.4 years.

3. b. To solve graphically, construct the NPV profiles:

The Y-intercept is the NPV when k = 0%. For B, 4($2,085) − $5,000 = $3,340. For O, $9,677 − $5,000 = $4,677. The X-intercept is the discount rate when NPV = $0, or the IRR. For B, $5,000 = $2,085 × PVIFA$_{IRR,4}$; IRR ≈ 24%. For O, $5,000 = $9,677 × PVIF$_{IRR,4}$; IRR ≈ 18%. The graph is an approximation since we are only using two points to plot lines that are curvilinear. However, it shows that there is a crossover point and that it occurs somewhere in the vicinity of k = 10%. (Note that other data points for the NPV profiles could be obtained by calculating the NPVs for the two projects at different discount rates.)

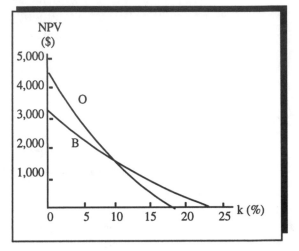

Alternatively,

Year	B	O	Project Δ (B − O)
0	($5,000)	($5,000)	$ 0
1	2,085	0	2,085
2	2,085	0	2,085
3	2,085	0	2,085
4	2,085	9,677	(7,592)

The IRR of Project Δ, 10.00 percent, is the crossover point.

4. a. Refer to the NPV profiles. When k = 14%, we are to the right of the crossover point and Project B has the higher NPV. You can verify this fact by calculating the NPVs. When k = 14%, NPV$_B$ = $1,075 and NPV$_O$ = $730. Note that Project B also has the higher IRR. However, the NPV method should be used when evaluating mutually exclusive projects. Note that had the project cost of capital been 8 percent, then Project O would be chosen on the basis of the higher NPV.

5. d. $PI_A = \dfrac{PV \text{ benefits}}{PV \text{ costs}} = \dfrac{\$6,075.09}{\$5,000} = 1.215.$

6.   a.   After the first year, there is only $30 remaining to be repaid, and $50 is received in Year 2. Assuming an even cash flow throughout the year, the payback period is 1 + $30/$50 = 1.6 years.

7.   d. $NPV_L = -\$100 + \$10/1.10 + \$60/(1.10)^2 + \$80/(1.10)^3 = -\$100 + \$9.09 + \$49.59 + \$60.11 = \$18.79$. Financial calculator solution: Input the cash flows into the cash flow register, $I = k = 10$, and solve for $NPV = \$18.78$.

8.   a.   Input the cash flows into the cash flow register and solve for IRR = 18.1%.

9.   c. $PI_L = \dfrac{PV \text{ benefits}}{PV \text{ costs}} = \dfrac{\$118.78}{\$100} = 1.188.$

10.   e. $PI_S = \dfrac{PV \text{ benefits}}{PV \text{ costs}} = \dfrac{\$119.98}{\$100} = 1.200.$

11.   b. $\displaystyle\sum_{t=0}^{n}\dfrac{COF_t}{(1+k)^t} = \dfrac{\displaystyle\sum_{t=0}^{n}CIF_t(1+k)^{n-t}}{(1+MIRR)^n}.$

$$PV \text{ cost} = \dfrac{TV}{(1+MIRR)^n}$$

$$\$100 = \dfrac{\$10(1.10)^2 + \$60(1.10)^1 + \$80(1.10)^0}{(1+MIRR)^3}$$

$$= \dfrac{\$12.10 + \$66.00 + \$80.00}{(1+MIRR)^3}$$

$$= \dfrac{\$158.10}{(1+MIRR)^3}$$

MIRR = 16.50%.

Alternatively, input N = 3, PV = -100, PMT = 0, FV = 158.10, and solve for I = MIRR = 16.50%.

12. c. $$\$100 = \frac{\$70(1.10)^2 + \$50(1.10)^1 + \$20(1.10)^0}{(1+MIRR)^3}$$

$$= \frac{\$84.70 + \$55.00 + \$20.00}{(1+MIRR)^3}$$

$$= \frac{\$159.70}{(1+MIRR)^3}$$

$MIRR_S = 16.89\% \approx 16.9\%.$

Alternatively, input N = 3, PV = -100, PMT = 0, FV = 159.70, and solve for I = MIRR = 16.89%.

13. c. The NPV profiles plot as follows:

k	NPV_L	NPV_S
0%	$50	$40
5	33	29
10	19	20
15	7	12
20	(4)	5
25	(13)	(2)

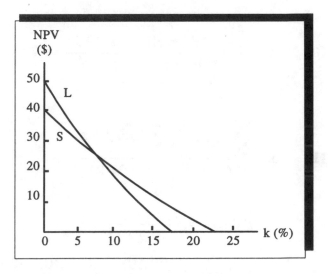

By looking at the graph, the approximate crossover point is 8 to 9 percent. Now, to find the precise crossover point, determine the cash flows for Project Δ, which is the difference between the two projects' cash flows:

Year	L	S	Project Δ (L - S)
0	($100)	($100)	$ 0
1	10	70	(60)
2	60	50	10
3	80	20	60

The crossover point is the IRR of Project Δ, or 8.7 percent.

14.   e.   Project X:

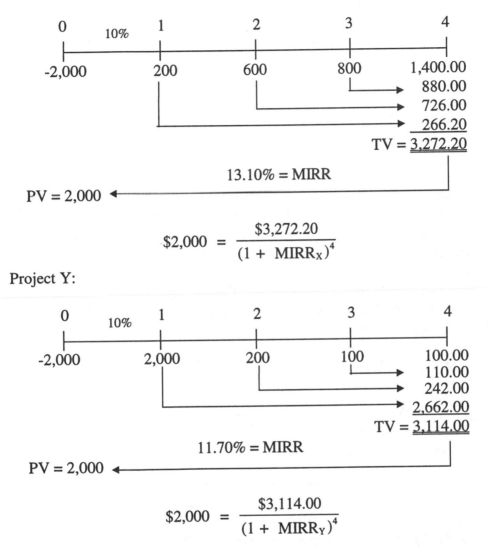

$$\$2,000 \ = \ \frac{\$3,272.20}{(1 + \ MIRR_X)^4}$$

Project Y:

$$\$2,000 \ = \ \frac{\$3,114.00}{(1 + \ MIRR_Y)^4}$$

Project X has the higher MIRR; $MIRR_X$ = 13.10%.

Alternate step: You could calculate NPVs, see that X has the higher NPV, and just calculate $MIRR_X$. NPV_X = \$234.96 and NPV_Y = \$126.90.

15. b. Put the cash flows into the cash flow register, and then calculate NPV at 9% and IRR: Project S: $NPV_s = \$101.83$; $IRR_s = 13.49\%$.

Project L: $NPV_L = \$172.07$; $IRR_L = 11.74\%$.

Because $NPV_L > NPV_S$, it is the better project. $IRR_L = 11.74\%$.

Alternatively, the PVIF table could be used to calculate the NPVs of both projects; however, calculating the IRR by trial and error would be tedious.

16. d. First, calculate the beta coefficient. Barkley's stock has been exactly twice as volatile as the market; thus, beta = 2.0. This can be calculated as $[21 - (-5)]/[10 - (-3)] = 26/13 = 2.0$. (Alternatively, you could use a calculator with statistical functions to determine the beta.)

Next, enter the known values in the CAPM equation to find the required rate of return, or the cost of equity capital. Since the company finances only with equity, this is the cost of capital:

$$CAPM = k_{RF} + (k_M - k_{RF})b = 7\% + (5\%)b = 7\% + 5\%(2.0) = 17\% = k_s.$$

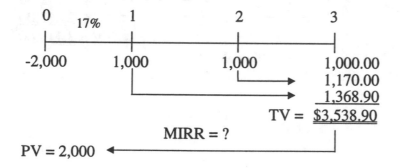

Find TV: $N = 3$; $I = 17$; $PV = 0$; $PMT = -1000$; $FV = \$3,538.90$.

Find MIRR: $N = 3$; $PV = -2000$; $PMT = 0$; $FV = 3538.90$; $I = MIRR = 20.95\%$.

17.   b.   First, we must find the cost of capital. Run a regression between the market and CDH stock returns to get beta = 1.31. Then apply the SML:

$$k_{CDH} = 6\% + (7\%)1.31 = 15.17\%.$$

(1) Now set up the time lines, insert the proper data into the cash flow register of the calculator, and find the NPVs and IRRs for the trucks.

Truck S: NPV = $803.35; IRR = 18.45%.

Truck L: NPV = $1,338.91; IRR = 18.45%.

$NPV_L > NPV_S$, thus $Truck_L$ is the better truck.

(2) To find Truck L's MIRR, compound its cash inflows at 15.17 percent to find the TV, then find the MIRR = I that causes PV of TV = $20,000:

Find TV: Enter N = 4; I = 15.17; PV = 0; PMT = -7500; and solve for FV = $37,543.07.

Find MIRR: Enter N = 4; PV = -20000; PMT = 0; FV = 37543.07; and solve for I = MIRR = 17.05%.

It is interesting to note that both trucks have the same IRR and MIRR; however, the NPV rule should be used so Truck L is the better truck. This problem shows that the NPV method is superior when choosing among competing projects that differ in size.

18.   d.   IRR = 24.26%; MIRR = 17.19%.

To calculate the IRR, enter the given values into the cash flow register and press the IRR key to get IRR = 24.26%.

Enter N = 4; PV = -309.21; PMT = 0; FV = 583.16; and solve for MIRR = I = 17.19%.

CHAPTER 7
CASH FLOW ESTIMATION

OVERVIEW

One of the most critical steps in capital budgeting analysis is *cash flow estimation*—the investment outlays and the annual net cash inflows after a project goes into operation. The key to correct cash flow estimation is to consider only *incremental cash flows*. However, the process is complicated by such factors as sunk costs, opportunity costs, externalities, and salvage values.

Cash flow estimation for replacement projects is similar to that for expansion projects, except that there are more flows to consider when analyzing replacement projects. Adjustments to the analysis must be made for projects with unequal lives as well as for the effects of inflation.

Capital budgeting analysis is in many respects straightforward. A project is deemed acceptable if it has a positive NPV, where the NPV is calculated by discounting the estimated cash flows at the project's risk-adjusted cost of capital. However, things often get more complicated in the real world. Complications include option values, abandonment value, and the effects of inflation.

OUTLINE

The most important, but also the most difficult, step in capital budgeting is estimating projects' cash flows—the investment outlays and the annual net cash inflows after a project goes into operation. Two key concepts in the process are important to recognize: (1) capital decisions must be based on cash flows, not accounting income, and (2) only incremental cash flows are relevant to the accept/reject decision.

- The financial staff's role in the forecasting process includes (1) obtaining information from various departments, (2) ensuring that everyone involved with the forecast uses a consistent set of economic assumptions, and (3) making sure that no biases are inherent in the forecasts.

- *Relevant cash flows* are defined as the specific set of cash flows that should be considered in the decision at hand.

□ The relevant cash flow for a project is the *additional* free cash flow that the company expects if it implements the project.

-   *Free cash flow* is the cash flow available for distribution to investors.

■ The value of a project depends on its free cash flow. There are four major ways that project cash flows differ from accounting income:

□ *Costs of fixed assets.* Asset purchases represent a negative project cash flow; however, accountants do not show the purchase of fixed assets as a deduction from accounting income. Instead, they deduct a depreciation expense each year throughout the asset's life.

□ *Noncash charges.* In calculating net income, accountants usually subtract some noncash charges from revenues. One example is depreciation. Depreciation is added back when estimating a project's cash flow.

□ *Changes in net operating working capital.* The difference between the required increase in current assets and the spontaneous increase in current liabilities is the change in net operating working capital. If this change is positive, then additional financing, over and above the cost of fixed assets, will be needed. The investment in working capital will be returned by the end of the project's life.

□ *Interest expenses are not included in project cash flows.* In calculating accounting income, interest expenses are subtracted because accountants attempt to measure the profit available for stockholders. Project cash flow is the cash flow available for all investors, bondholders as well as stockholders, so interest expenses are not subtracted. The discounting process reduces the cash flows to account for capital costs, both debt and equity costs. If interest charges were first deducted and then the resulting cash flows were discounted, this would result in a double counting of the cost of debt.

■ In evaluating a capital project, we focus on those cash flows that occur if and only if we accept the project. These *incremental cash flows* represent the change in the firm's total cash flow that occurs as a direct result of accepting the project. There are three special problems that occur when determining incremental cash flows:

□ A *sunk cost* is an outlay that has already occurred or has been committed, and hence is not affected by the decision under consideration. Sunk costs are not incremental, and hence should not be included in the analysis.

□ *Opportunity costs*, which are cash flows that could be generated from an asset the firm already owns provided it is not used for the project in question, must be included in the analysis.

□ *Externalities* involve the effects of a project on other parts of the firm, and their effects need to be considered in the incremental cash flows. For example, *cannibalization* occurs when the introduction of a new product causes sales of existing products to decline. This is an externality that must be considered in the analysis.

■ We must account properly for the timing of cash flows.
   □ In most cases, we simply assume that all cash flows occur at the end of every year. However, for some projects, it may be useful to assume that cash flows occur at mid-year, or even quarterly or monthly.

Taxes can have a major impact on cash flows, and the improper treatment of taxes can have serious consequences. Therefore, it is critical that taxes be dealt with properly when a project's cash flows are being analyzed.

■ For tax purposes, the entire cost of an asset is expensed over its depreciable life. An asset's depreciation expense is calculated using the *Modified Accelerated Cost Recovery System (MACRS)*.
   □ A major effect of the MACRS system has been to shorten the depreciable lives of assets, thus giving businesses larger tax deductions and thereby increasing their cash flows available for investment.
   □ Assets are categorized into one of several MACRS class lives. Then the depreciation expense in each year is found by multiplying the asset's *depreciable basis* by the appropriate allowance percentage. Here are the allowance percentages for personal property:

	MACRS Class			
Year	3-Year	5-Year	7-Year	10-Year
1	33%	20%	14%	10%
2	45	32	25	18
3	15	19	17	14
4	7	12	13	12
5		11	9	9
6		6	9	7
7			9	7
8			4	7
9				7
10				6
11				3
	100%	100%	100%	100%

   □ Under MACRS, the assumption is generally made that property is placed in service in the middle of the first year. Then, the remaining half-year's depreciation is taken at the end. The effect of the *half-year convention* is to extend the recovery period out one more year. Thus, a 3-year class life asset is depreciated over 4 years, and so on.

☐ The depreciable basis is the purchase price of the asset plus any shipping and installation costs. Note that, under MACRS, the depreciable basis is *not* reduced by the asset's expected *salvage value* (which is the estimated market value of the asset at the end of its useful life).

■ When a depreciable asset is sold, the actual sales price (the realized salvage value) minus the then-existing book value is multiplied by the tax rate to determine the applicable taxes. The net salvage value, salvage value minus the applicable taxes, is then added to after-tax operating income.

A project creates value for the firm's shareholders if and only if the net present value of its incremental cash flows is positive.

■ In general, incremental cash flows from a project can be classified in one of three ways:
   ☐ *Initial investment outlay.* This includes the up-front cost of fixed assets associated with the project plus any increases in net working capital.
   ☐ *Operating cash flows over the project's life.* These are the incremental cash inflows over the project's economic life.
   ☐ *Terminal year cash flows.* These include the salvage value of the fixed assets, adjusted for taxes if assets are not sold at their book value, plus the return of the net working capital.

■ For each year of the project's economic life, the *net cash flow* is determined as the sum of the cash flows from each of the three categories.

Two types of capital budgeting decisions are (1) expansion project analysis and (2) replacement project analysis. The relevant cash flows for expansion projects are different from those for replacement projects.

■ An expansion project is one that calls for the firm to invest in new facilities to increase sales. Steps in the capital budgeting analysis for an expansion project include:
   ☐ Summarize the investment outlays required for the project. Changes in net working capital should be included as an outflow here; however, they should be considered as an inflow at the end of the project.
   ☐ Forecast the operating cash flows that will occur once production begins, including the effects of depreciation.
   ☐ Estimate the cash flows generated by salvage values.
   ☐ Summarize the data by combining all the net cash flows on a time line and evaluate the project by payback period, IRR, MIRR, and NPV (at the appropriate cost of capital).
   ☐ The cost of capital may need to be increased if the project is deemed riskier than the firm's average project.

■ Capital budgeting decisions are actually based on both quantitative factors such as the calculated NPV, IRR, and MIRR plus qualitative, subjective factors such as the firm's strategic long-run plans.

■ The cash flows and cost of capital estimates used to develop the NPV are based on a number of assumptions, and if those assumptions turn out to be incorrect, then the *actual* NPV can turn out to be quite different from the *forecasted* NPV.

■ Replacement project analysis is different from that for expansion projects because the cash flows from the old asset must be considered in addition to those from the new assets.
   □ The following additional cash flows to the initial investment outlay must be considered at time 0:
      ● The cash received from the sale of the old equipment is an inflow.
      ● However, the sale of the old machine will usually have tax effects. If the old equipment is sold below book value, there will be a tax savings; if the equipment is sold at a profit, taxes must be paid. The tax effect is equal to the loss or gain on the sale times the firm's marginal tax rate.
   □ The calculation for operating cash flows must be modified.
      ● First, look at the effects of the new equipment on revenues and costs. An incremental increase in revenues would produce a cash inflow, while an incremental increase in costs would produce a cash outflow, just as before. After combining the revenue and cost effects into a single incremental cash inflow, multiply by $(1 - T)$ to obtain the after-tax cash inflow.
      ● The depreciation expense on the old equipment must be subtracted from the depreciation expense on the new equipment to get the net change in depreciation. This amount is then multiplied by the tax rate to find the tax savings or loss from the change in depreciation.
   □ The calculation of terminal year cash flows must also be modified.
      ● Any salvage value on the old machine, including tax effects, must be included as a cash outflow at the end of the project's life. Accepting the new project causes the firm to forgo the old machine's salvage value. Thus, it must be included as an *opportunity cost*. Of course, any salvage value on the new machine must also be included in the analysis.

■ The analysis here assumes that the replacement project has the same expected life as the remaining years of usage on the old machine. If this is not true, an adjustment must be made to account for differing project lives.

Several studies indicate that capital budgeting cash flow forecasts are often biased; that is, many managers tend to be overly optimistic, so revenues tend to be overstated and costs

understated. **The end result is an upward bias in net operating cash flows and thus an upward bias in estimated NPVs.**

■ If bias exists, then the acceptance of a project with a zero estimated NPV will likely result in a realized loss and, hence, a decrease in shareholders' wealth.

■ A first step in identifying cash flow estimation bias, especially for projects that are estimated to be highly profitable, is to ask this question: What is the underlying cause of this project's high profitability?
   □ If the firm has some inherent advantage such as patent protection or unique production or marketing expertise, then projects that utilize this advantage may truly be extraordinarily profitable.
   □ However, in the long run, above-normal profits will probably be eroded by competition, and hence, project returns will be driven down to a normal level, which is equal to the firm's cost of capital.

■ If management believes that cash flow estimation bias exists, and historical performance can be used as an indicator, then those managers' estimates should be adjusted, either by raising the cost of capital or by lowering the cash flow estimates.

Cash flow estimation bias can cause a project's profitability to be overstated, but failure to recognize a project's additional opportunities, or options, can cause the project's profitability to be understated.

■ Real assets are not passive investments—managerial actions can influence their results.

■ Any project that expands the set of opportunities facing a firm has positive option value, and any project that reduces the set of future opportunities has negative option value. A project's impact on the firm's opportunities, or the project's option value, may not be captured by conventional NPV analysis. Therefore, option value should be considered separately.

■ Another type of option that can add value is the ability to *abandon*, or discontinue, a project, either to cut losses or because the operation is more valuable to some other party and can be sold for more than the present value of the remaining cash flows.

■ Conventional NPV analysis can at times overstate the value of a project. This occurs because accepting a certain type of project today "kills off" future opportunities.
   □ In these instances, decision makers should insist on an NPV that is both positive and also large enough to offset the option value given up.
   □ Some companies set hurdle rates that are above the calculated cost of capital when evaluating projects that contain *timing options*.

■ The true values of projects which include embedded options may exceed those shown in a straightforward NPV calculation, while the NPVs of projects which limit future opportunities may be overstated. *Decision trees* provide one method for formally dealing with options. Also, *option pricing models* can be used in certain situations.

■ As a result of embedded options, some projects have more or less value than is indicated by their NPVs, and this value should, at a minimum, be subjectively considered when making capital budgeting decisions.

If two mutually exclusive projects have significantly different lives, the analysis must include an adjustment. Two procedures have been developed to deal with this problem: (1) the replacement chain method and (2) the equivalent annual annuity method.

■ The *replacement chain (common life) method* extends one, or both, projects until an equal life is achieved.
 ☐ Suppose two mutually exclusive projects are being considered: Project A with a 2-year life, and Project B with a 3-year life. The projects' lives would be extended to a 6-year common life.
 ☐ Project A would have an extended NPV equal to NPV_A plus NPV_A discounted for 2 years at the project's cost of capital, plus NPV_A discounted for 4 years at the project's cost of capital. Project B would have an extended NPV equal to NPV_B plus NPV_B discounted for 3 years at the project's cost of capital.
 ☐ The project with the highest extended NPV would be chosen.
 ☐ This method assumes that the project can be repeated and that there is no change in cash flows.

■ Another way to deal with unequal lives is the *equivalent annual annuity (EAA) method.*
 ☐ First, find each project's NPV over its original life. Then find the constant annuity cash flow that has the same present value.
  ● With a financial calculator, enter N, I, and PV to solve for PMT.
 ☐ The project with the higher EAA (PMT) would be chosen, because the project with the higher EAA will always have the higher NPV when extended out to any common life.

■ As a general rule, the unequal life issue does not arise for independent projects. Also, common life techniques can only be applied when the shorter-life project is actually expected to be replicated.

■ A serious weakness of the analysis techniques discussed is that changing revenues and/or costs have not been considered. These complications are handled by building the new revenue/cost estimates directly into the cash flow estimates and then using the replacement chain approach.

Thus far, all the capital budgeting examples have been based on a well-defined economic life. However, in most situations, the economic life, or that life which maximizes the project's NPV, is not the same as the project's physical, or engineering, life. The concept of abandonment value recognizes that abandonment of a project before the end of its physical life can have a significant impact on the project's profitability and risk.

- Two very different types of abandonment can occur:
  - □ Sale by the original user of a still-valuable asset to some other party who can extract more value from the asset.
  - □ Abandonment of an asset because the project is losing money.

- Abandonment value should be considered both when projects are originally evaluated and also during routine post-audits of ongoing projects.

- In general, the opportunity to abandon projects allows companies to limit downside losses but reap upside gains. Thus, the abandonment option reduces the riskiness of projects and thus increases their value.

When inflation occurs, the analysis must either explicitly adjust for inflation or treat all variables in real terms.

- Investors recognize that inflation erodes purchasing power; they demand an inflation premium in addition to the real required rate of return, and hence they consider expected inflation rates when setting required rates of return. Thus, a firm's market-determined overall cost of capital is a nominal rate.
  - □ Inflation can be explicitly considered in capital budgeting analysis by expressing all cash flows in nominal terms (NCF_t) and then by using the nominal cost of capital (k_n):

$$NPV = \sum_{t=0}^{n} \frac{NCF_t}{\left(1 + k_n\right)^t}.$$

  - □ The same result can be obtained by expressing all cash flows in real terms (RCF_t) and then by using the real cost of capital (k_r):

$$NPV = \sum_{t=0}^{n} \frac{RCF_t}{\left(1 + k_r\right)^t}.$$

- This approach is relatively simple, but to produce an unbiased NPV it requires (1) that all project cash flows be affected identically by inflation, and (2) that this rate of increase equals the inflation rate built into investors required returns.

■ Occasionally, real, or constant dollar, cash flows are not adjusted for inflation and are used with the nominal cost of capital. If this occurs, the calculated NPV will be biased downward.

■ In practice, it is best to express the cash flows in nominal dollars; that is, to include inflation effects in the cash flow estimates and then to discount by the nominal cost of capital. This procedure is preferred because it allows various cash flow components to be adjusted at differing inflation rates.

■ We cannot estimate future inflation rates with precision, so errors are bound to be made. Thus, inflation adds to the uncertainty, or riskiness, of capital budgeting as well as to its complexity.

SELF-TEST QUESTIONS

Definitional

1. An increase in net working capital would show up as a cash _____ at time 0 and then again as a cash _____ at the _____ of the project's life.

2. A(n) _____ _____ is a cash outlay which has already occurred or has been committed.

3. In replacement analysis, two cash flows that occur at t = 0 that are not present in expansion projects are the price received from the sale of the _____ equipment and the _____ effects of the sale.

4. In replacement analysis, the depreciation tax savings or loss is based on the _____ in depreciation expense between the old and new asset.

5. A(n) _____ cash flow represents the change in the firm's total cash flow that occurs as a direct result of project acceptance.

6. If two projects are _____, the fact that they have unequal lives will not affect the analysis.

7. If two mutually exclusive projects have unequal lives, either the _____ _____ or the _____ _____ _____ method may be used for the analysis.

8. If the cash flows are real, but the cost of capital is nominal, there will be a(n) _____ bias to the calculated NPV.

9. Riskier projects should be evaluated with a higher _____ ____ _____ than average-risk projects.

10. _____ _____, which are cash flows that could be generated from assets the firm already owns, provided they are not used for the project in question, must be included in the analysis.

11. _____ involve the effects of a project on other parts of the firm, and their effects need to be considered in the incremental cash flows.

12. _____ is an externality that occurs when the introduction of a new product causes sales of existing products to decline.

13. If _____ exists, then the acceptance of a project with a zero estimated NPV will likely result in a realized loss, and hence, a decrease in shareholders' wealth.

14. Cash flow estimation bias can cause a project's profitability to be overstated, but failure to recognize a project's additional opportunities, or _____, can cause the project's profitability to be understated.

15. Another type of option that can add value to a project is the ability to _____, or discontinue the project, either to cut losses or because the operation is more valuable to some other party and can be sold for more than the present value of the remaining cash flows.

16. In dealing with inflation in capital budgeting, cash flows and the cost of capital must both be in _____ terms or both be in _____ terms.

17. The _____ cash flow for a project is the additional free cash flow that the company expects if it implements the project.

18. For tax purposes, an asset's depreciation expense is calculated using the _____ _____ _____ _____ _____.

19. The _____ _____ is the purchase price of the asset plus any shipping and installation costs.

20. In general, incremental cash flows from a project can be classified in one of three ways: _____ _____ _____, _____ cash flows, and _____ year cash flows.

Conceptual

21. In general, the value of land currently owned by a firm is irrelevant to a capital budgeting decision because the cost of that property is a sunk cost.

   a. True   **b.** False

22. McDonald's is planning to open a new store across from the student union. Annual revenues are expected to be $5 million. However, opening the new location will cause annual revenues to drop by $3 million at McDonald's existing stadium location. The relevant sales revenues for the capital budgeting analysis are $2 million per year.

   a. True   **b.** False

23. In replacement project analysis, the salvage value of the old asset need not be considered since the current market value of the asset is included in the analysis.

   a. True   **b.** False

24. Abandoning a project before the end of its useful physical life may result in a higher NPV for the project.

   a. True   **b.** False

25. Two corporations are formed. They are identical in all respects except for their methods of depreciation. Firm A uses MACRS depreciation, while Firm B uses the straight line method. Both plan to depreciate their assets for tax purposes over a 5-year life (6 calendar years), which is equal to the useful life, and both pay a 35 percent tax rate. (Note: The half-year convention will apply, so the firm using the straight line method will take 10 percent depreciation in Year 1 and 10 percent in Year 6.) Which of the following statements is *false*?

    a. Firm A will generate higher cash flows from operations in the first year than B.

    b. Firm A will pay more Federal corporate income taxes in the first year than B.

    c. If there is no change in tax rates over the 6-year period, and if we disregard the time value of money, the total amount of funds generated from operations by these projects for each corporation will be the same over the 6 years.

    d. Firm B will pay the same amount of federal corporate income taxes, over the 6-year period, as A.

    e. Firm A could, if it chose to, use straight line depreciation for stockholder reporting even if it used MACRS for tax purposes.

26. A company owns a building, free and clear, which had a cost of $100,000. The building is currently unoccupied, but it can be sold at a net price of $50,000, after taxes. Now the company is thinking of using the building for a new project. Which of the following statements is most correct?

    a. The building is unoccupied, and its cost was incurred in the past, and hence, is a sunk cost. Therefore, no cost for the building should be charged to the new project.

    b. A cost should be charged to the new project, and that cost should be $100,000.

    c. A cost should be charged to the new project, and that cost should be $50,000.

    d. The cost charged to the building would vary depending on the expected profitability of the new project and hence on the new project's ability to help carry the corporation's overhead.

    e. A cost for the building should be charged to the new project only if the NPV on the new project without considering the building is less than zero.

27. Which of the following statements is most correct?

   a. Since capital budgeting involves fixed assets, current assets (also called "working capital") should never be reflected in a capital budgeting analysis.
   b. If Congress changed the tax law such that depreciation allowances were reduced in the early years of an asset's life and then were increased in later years, this would increase net income in the early years and lower it in the later years. Such a change would stimulate investment in the economy because, other things held constant, it would raise projects' NPVs and IRRs.
   c. Either the replacement chain approach or the equivalent annual annuity approach can be used to evaluate mutually exclusive, repeatable projects which have unequal lives.
   d. If expected inflation is ignored when cash flows are estimated, this will generally cause the calculated NPV, IRR, and MIRR to be overstated, and that could cause projects which should be rejected to be accepted.
   e. Both statements c and d are correct.

SELF-TEST PROBLEMS

1. The capital budgeting director of National Products Inc. is evaluating a new project that would decrease operating costs by $30,000 per year without affecting revenues. The project's cost is $50,000. The project will be depreciated using the MACRS method over its 3-year class life. It will have a *zero salvage value* after 3 years. The marginal tax rate of National Products is 35 percent, and the project's cost of capital is 12 percent. What is the project's NPV?

   a. $7,068   b. $8,324   c. $10,214   d. $11,010   e. $12,387

2. Your firm has a marginal tax rate of 40 percent and a cost of capital of 14 percent. You are performing a capital budgeting analysis on a new project that will cost $500,000. The project is expected to have a useful life of 10 years, although its MACRS class life is only 5 years. The project is expected to increase the firm's net income by $61,257 per year and to have a salvage value of $35,000 at the end of 10 years. What is the project's NPV?

   a. $95,356   b. $108,359   c. $135,256   d. $162,185   e. $177,902

3. The Board of Directors of National Brewing Inc. is considering the acquisition of a new still. The still is priced at $600,000 but would require $60,000 in transportation costs and $40,000 for installation. The still has a useful life of 10 years but will be depreciated over its 5-year MACRS life. It is expected to have a salvage value of $10,000 at the end of 10 years. The still would increase revenues by $120,000 per year and increase yearly operating costs by $20,000 per year. Additionally, the still would require a $30,000 increase in net working capital. The firm's marginal tax rate is 40 percent, and the project's cost of capital is 10 percent. What is the NPV of the still?

   a. $18,430   b. -$12,352   c. -$65,204   d. -$130,961   e. -$203,450

(The following data apply to the next three Self-Test Problems.)

As the capital budgeting director of Union Mills Inc. you are analyzing the replacement of an automated loom system. The old system was purchased 5 years ago for $200,000; it falls into the MACRS 5-year class; and it has 5 years of remaining life and a $50,000 salvage value five years from now. The current market value of the old system is $100,000. The new system has a price of $300,000, plus an additional $50,000 in installation costs. The new system falls into the MACRS 5-year class, has a 5-year economic life, and a $100,000 salvage value. The new system will require a $40,000 increase in the spare parts inventory. The primary advantage of the new system is that it will decrease operating costs by $40,000 per year. Union Mills has a 12 percent cost of capital and a marginal tax rate of 35 percent.

4. What is the net cash investment at Year 0?

   a. $350,000   b. $320,800   c. $295,000   d. $40,000   e. $23,200

5. What is the annual net operating cash inflow in Year 1?

   a. $46,300   b. $43,950   c. $39,825   d. $33,350   e. $50,200

6. What is the net cash flow in the final year (Year 5)?

   a. $31,360   b. $43,060   c. $119,325   d. $121,930   e. $117,200

(The following data apply to the next two Self-Test Problems.)

Buckeye Foundries builds railroad cars and then leases them to railroads and shippers. The company has some old boxcars which it plans to convert into specialized carriers. Its analysts foresee demand in two areas—cars to carry coal and cars to carry livestock. Each type of car will cost $50,000 per car to convert. Because of the greater weight they will carry, the coal cars will last only 10 years but will provide an after-tax cash flow of $9,500 per year. The livestock cars will last for 15 years, and their annual after-tax cash flow is estimated at $8,140. Buckeye's cost of capital is 10 percent. At the end of each car's original life, it can be rebuilt into "like new" condition at a cost expected to equal the original conversion cost. Also, since Buckeye has only a limited number of cars to convert, regard the two types of cars as being mutually exclusive.

7. Using the replacement chain method of evaluation, find the adjusted NPV for each alternative.

    a. $8,373; $11,913   c. $8,373; $16,212   e. $12,846; $14,765
    b. $8,373; $14,765   d. $12,846; $11,913

8. Which alternative should be taken according to the equivalent annual annuity method?

    a. Livestock cars, since their EAA equals $1,363 versus the coal cars' EAA of $1,200.
    b. Coal cars, since their EAA equals $1,363 versus the livestock cars' EAA of $1,200.
    c. Livestock cars, since their EAA equals $1,566 versus the coal cars' EAA of $1,363.
    d. Coal cars, since their EAA equals $1,566 versus the livestock cars' EAA of $1,363.
    e. Coal cars, since their EAA equals $2,000 versus the livestock cars' EAA of $1,566.

9. Central City Electric is considering two alternative ways to meet demand: It can build a coal-fired plant (Project C) at a cost of $1,000 million. This plant would have a 20-year life and would provide net cash flows of $120 million per year over its life. Alternatively, the company can build a gas-fired plant (Project G) that would cost $400 million and would produce net cash flows of $68 million per year for 10 years, after which the plant would have to be replaced. The power will be needed for exactly 20 years; the cost of capital for either plant is 10 percent; and inflation and productivity gains are expected to offset one another so as to leave expected costs and cash flows constant over time. What is the NPV of the better project, that is, how much (in millions) will the better project add to Central City's total value?

    a. $17.83   b. $21.63   c. $20.03   d. $24.70   e. $19.57

10. A firm is considering a project with a cost of $5,000 and operating cash flows of $2,000 for 3 years. The expected abandonment cash flows for Years 0, 1, 2, and 3 are $5,000, $3,500, $2,000, and $0, respectively. If the firm's cost of capital is 10 percent, what should the firm do?

   a. Do not accept the project.
   b. Abandon after Year 1; NPV is $0.
   c. Abandon after Year 2; NPV is $56.
   d. Abandon after Year 2; NPV is $124.
   e. Continue the project until the end of its 3-year physical life.

11. As financial vice president, you are evaluating a potential new project. The VP-manufacturing and VP-sales have provided the following real revenue, operating cost, and depreciation data, all stated in constant Year 0 dollars:

Year	Revenue	Cost	Depreciation
0	$ 0	$90,000	$ 0
1	40,000	10,000	30,000
2	40,000	10,000	30,000
3	40,000	10,000	30,000

   The cost of capital to the firm is 14 percent, including the current inflation premium. You estimate that the reported real costs will escalate by 10 percent per year over the project's life, starting at $t = 0$, while revenues will increase by only 5 percent per year. The firm's marginal tax rate is 40 percent. The $90,000 cost in Year 0 is the net after-tax cost of the project, while the $40,000 annual revenues and $10,000 annual costs are before taxes. The project has no salvage value and does not require a change in net working capital. What is the project's NPV?

   a. $10,593   b. $3,297   c. -$5,586   d. -$17,689   e. -$20,351

12. Wild West Air is considering two alternative planes. Plane A has an expected life of 5 years, will cost $200, and will produce net cash flows of $60 per year. Plane B has a life of 10 years, will cost $245, and will produce net cash flows of $48 per year. Wild West plans to serve the route for 10 years. Inflation in operating costs, airplane costs, and fares is expected to be zero, and the company's cost of capital is 14 percent. Assume all costs are in millions. By how much (in millions) would the value of the company increase if it accepted the better project (plane)?

   a. $12.76   b. $9.78   c. $5.37   d. $6.65   e. $9.09

ANSWERS TO SELF-TEST QUESTIONS

1. outflow; inflow; end
2. sunk cost
3. old; tax
4. difference
5. incremental
6. independent
7. replacement chain (common life); equivalent annual annuity
8. downward
9. cost of capital
10. Opportunity costs
11. Externalities
12. Cannibalization
13. bias
14. options
15. abandon
16. nominal; real
17. relevant
18. Modified Accelerated Cost Recovery System (MACRS)
19. depreciable basis
20. initial investment outlay; operating; terminal

21. b. The net market value of land currently owned is an opportunity cost of the project. If the project is not undertaken, the land could be sold to realize its current market value less any taxes and expenses. Thus, project acceptance means forgoing this cash inflow.

22. a. Incremental revenues, which are relevant in a capital budgeting decision, must consider the effects on other parts of the firm.

23. b. In an incremental analysis, the cash flows assuming replacement are compared with the cash flows assuming the old asset is retained. If the old asset is retained, it will produce a salvage value cash flow which must be included, with tax effects, in the replacement analysis.

24. a. The NPV of a project may be maximized by abandoning at some point, thus making the economic life of the project shorter than the physical life.

25. b. Statement a is true; MACRS is an accelerated depreciation method, so Firm A will have a higher depreciation expense than Firm B. We are also given that both firms are identical except for depreciation methods used. Net cash flow is equal to net income plus depreciation. In Year 1, Firm A's depreciation expense is twice as great as Firm B's; however, Firm A's lower net income is more than compensated for by the addition of depreciation (which is twice as high as Firm B's). Thus, in Year 1, Firm A's net cash flow is greater than Firm B's. Statement b is false; because Firm A's depreciation expense is larger, its earnings before taxes will be lower, and thus it will pay less income taxes than Firm B. Statements c, d, and e are all true.

26. c. Statement c is correct. The opportunity cost of the building should be assessed against the new project, and that cost is what the company could get for the building, $50,000. All of the other statements are incorrect.

27. c. Statement c is correct. Statement a is incorrect because the required investment in working capital is often reflected in capital budgeting decision analyses. Statement b is incorrect because higher early depreciation reduces taxes, increases cash flows, and thus leads to higher NPVs and IRRs. Statement d is incorrect because generally considering inflation will increase projected cash flows and thus increase the NPV.

SOLUTIONS TO SELF-TEST PROBLEMS

1. d. Cash flow = Net income + Depreciation. The first step is to set up the income statement for Years 1 through 3. (Note that a reduction in operating costs increases revenues.)

	1	2	3
Revenues	$30,000	$30,000	$30,000
Depreciation[a]	16,500	22,500	7,500
EBT	$13,500	$ 7,500	$22,500
Taxes (35%)	4,725	2,625	7,875
Net income	$ 8,775	$ 4,875	$14,625
Depreciation	16,500	22,500	7,500
	$25,275	$27,375	$22,125
SV tax savings[b]			1,225
Net cash flow	$25,275	$27,375	$23,350

[a]Depreciation schedule: Cost basis = $50,000.

Year	Allowance Percentages	Depreciation	Ending Book Value
1	0.33	$16,500	$33,500
2	0.45	22,500	11,000
3	0.15	7,500	3,500
4	0.07	3,500	0
		$50,000	

[b]At the end of Year 3, the project's book value is $3,500; however, its salvage value is zero. Thus, National can reduce its taxable income by $3,500, producing a 0.35($3,500) = $1,225 tax savings.

The project's cash flows are then placed on a time line as follows and discounted at the project's cost of capital:

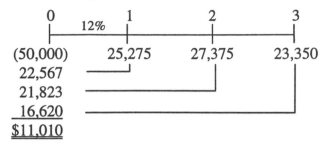

Alternatively, input the cash flows into the cash flow register, input I = 12, and then solve for NPV = $11,010.

2.   e.   In this case, the *net income* of the project is $61,257. Net cash flow = Net income + Depreciation = $61,257 + Depreciation. The depreciation allowed in each year is calculated as follows:

$Dep_1 = \$500,000(0.20) = \$100,000.$
$Dep_2 = \$500,000(0.32) = \$160,000.$
$Dep_3 = \$500,000(0.19) = \$95,000.$
$Dep_4 = \$500,000(0.12) = \$60,000.$
$Dep_5 = \$500,000(0.11) = \$55,000.$
$Dep_6 = \$500,000(0.06) = \$30,000.$
$Dep_{7-10} = \$0.$

In the final year (Year 10), the firm receives $35,000 from the sale of the machine. However, the book value of the machine is $0. Thus, the firm would have to pay 0.4($35,000) = $14,000 in taxes; and the net salvage value is $35,000 - $14,000 = $21,000. The time line is as follows:

0	1	2	3	4	5	6	7	8	9	10
14%										
(500,000)	61,257	61,257	61,257	61,257	61,257	61,257	61,257	61,257	61,257	61,257
	100,000	160,000	95,000	60,000	55,000	30,000				21,000
(500,000)	161,257	221,257	156,257	121,257	116,257	91,257	61,257	61,257	61,257	82,257

The project's NPV can be found by discounting each of the cash flows at the firm's 14 percent cost of capital. The project's NPV, found by using a financial calculator, is $177,902.

3.   d.   Cash flow = Net income + Depreciation. The first step to this problem is to set up the income statement for Years 1 through 10. (Note that the return of NWC is not shown in the income statement here, but is shown on the time line that follows.)

	1	2	3	4	5	6	7-9	10
Revenues	120,000	120,000	120,000	120,000	120,000	120,000	120,000	120,000
Operating costs	20,000	20,000	20,000	20,000	20,000	20,000	20,000	20,000
Depreciation[a]	140,000	224,000	133,000	84,000	77,000	42,000		
EBT	(40,000)	(124,000)	(33,000)	16,000	23,000	58,000	100,000	100,000
Taxes (40%)	(16,000)	(49,600)	(13,200)	6,400	9,200	23,200	40,000	40,000
Net income	(24,000)	(74,400)	(19,800)	9,600	13,800	34,800	60,000	60,000
Depreciation	140,000	224,000	133,000	84,000	77,000	42,000		
	116,000	149,600	113,200	93,600	90,800	76,800	60,000	60,000
SV (AT)[b]								6,000
Cash flow	116,000	149,600	113,200	93,600	90,800	76,800	60,000	66,000

[a]Depreciation schedule:
  Cost basis = Price + Transportation + Installation = $600,000 + $60,000 + $40,000 = $700,000.

Year	Allowance Percentages	Depreciation	Ending Book Value
1	0.20	$140,000	$560,000
2	0.32	224,000	336,000
3	0.19	133,000	203,000
4	0.12	84,000	119,000
5	0.11	77,000	42,000
6	0.06	42,000	0
		$700,000	

[b]At the end of Year 10 the still has a salvage value of $10,000; however, it has been fully depreciated so the firm must pay taxes of 0.4($10,000) = $4,000. Therefore, the still's after-tax salvage value is $10,000 - $4,000 = $6,000.

The still's cash flows are then placed on a time line as follows and discounted at the project's cost of capital:

	0	1	2	3	4	5	6	7	8	9	10
10%	(700,000)	116,000	149,600	113,200	93,600	90,800	76,800	60,000	60,000	60,000	66,000
	(30,000)*										+30,000*
	(730,000)	116,000	149,600	113,200	93,600	90,800	76,800	60,000	60,000	60,000	96,000

*An increase in net working capital is required in Year 0, so this must be added back to the cash flow at the end of the project's life.

At a 10% cost of capital, the still's NPV is -$130,961.

4. b. Price of new machine ($300,000)

Installation (50,000)

Sale of old machine +100,000

Tax on sale* (30,800)

Increase in net working capital (40,000)

($320,800)

*The old machine has been depreciated down to $12,000, since it falls into the MACRS 5-year class and it has been in operation for 5 years. Now, the old machine has a market value of $100,000. The $88,000 (market value minus book value) is treated as ordinary income and is taxed at 35 percent. Thus, Union Mills must pay a tax of 0.35($88,000) = $30,800 on the sale of the old asset.

5. a. The after-tax revenue/cost component is 0.65($40,000) = $26,000. As for the tax savings due to depreciation, the depreciable basis for the new machine is $350,000. Further, the MACRS depreciation allowance for Year 1 of a 5-year class asset is 20 percent. Thus, the depreciation expense on the new machine is 0.20($350,000) = $70,000. The old machine has not been fully depreciated, so its depreciation expense in Year 1 is $12,000, and the change in depreciation due to the replacement decision is an increase of $58,000. The tax savings is 0.35($58,000) = $20,300. Therefore, the Year 1 net cash flow from operations is $26,000 + $20,300 = $46,300.

6. c. In the final year, Year 5, the net cash flow is composed of 0.65($40,000) = $26,000 in after-tax cost decrease and 0.35(0.11)($350,000) = $13,475 in depreciation tax savings, for a total of $39,475, plus the applicable nonoperating cash flows. Thus, we have the following:

From operations	$ 39,475
Salvage value of new machine	100,000
Tax on new machine salvage value	(27,650)
Salvage value of old machine	(50,000)
Tax on old machine salvage value	17,500
Change in working capital	40,000
Net cash flow	$119,325

Note that the salvage value of the old machine is a cash outflow. This is an opportunity cost, since buying the new machine deprives Union Mills of the salvage value of the old machine. Additionally, salvage tax effects must be considered. Also, note that the change in working capital considered at t = 0, an outflow, is exactly offset by an inflow at the end of the project. This is because it is assumed that the project will terminate and the increase in working capital is no longer required.

7. e. First, find each car's original NPV as follows:

$NPV_C = \$9,500(PVIFA_{10\%,10}) - \$50,000 = \$8,373.$
$NPV_L = \$8,140(PVIFA_{10\%,15}) - \$50,000 = \$11,913.$

Now look at the projects at a common life of 30 years:

Adjusted $NPV_C = \$8,373 + \$8,373(PVIF_{10\%,10}) + \$8,373(PVIF_{10\%,20}) = \$12,846.$
Adjusted $NPV_L = \$11,913 + \$11,913(PVIF_{10\%,15}) = \$14,765.$

Alternatively, once you've found the original NPV of each car, then the replication of the cars can be shown on the time line.

Coal:

```
    0          10         20         30
       10%
    |----------|----------|----------|

  8,373      8,373      8,373
  3,228  ◄─────┘
  1,245  ◄────────────────┘
 12,846
```

Livestock:

```
    0              15             30
       10%
    |--------------|--------------|

 11,913         11,913
  2,852  ◄────────┘
 14,765
```

8. c. The original NPVs were calculated above. Now:

$EAA_C = \$8,373/PVIFA_{10\%,10} = \$8,373/6.1446 = \$1,363.$ Alternatively, input N = 10, I = 10, PV = -8373, FV = 0, and solve for PMT = $1,363.

$EAA_L = \$11,913/PVIFA_{10\%,15} = \$11,913/7.6061 = \$1,566.$ Alternatively, input N = 15, I = 10, PV = -11913, FV = 0, and solve for PMT = $1,566.

Because $EAA_L > EAA_C$ the livestock cars should be chosen.

9.   d.   Project C (in millions):

With a financial calculator, input the cash flows into the cash flow register, input I = 10, and then solve for NPV = \$21.63 million.

Project G (in millions):

With a financial calculator input the cash flows for the first replication of the project into the cash flow register, input I = 10, and then solve for NPV = \$17.83 million. However, this NPV must be adjusted for a 20-year common life. The NPV for the next replication can be calculated by inputting N = 10, I = 10, PMT = 0, FV = 17.83, and then solving for PV = \$6.87. Thus, the extended NPV for Project G = \$17.83 + \$6.87 = \$24.70 million:

$$\text{Extended NPV}_G = \$17.83 + (\text{PVIF}_{10\%,10})\$17.83$$
$$= \$17.83 + \$6.87 = \$24.70 \text{ million.}$$

10.   d.

Year	Initial Investment & Operating Cash Flows	Abandonment Value in Year t
0	(\$5,000)	\$5,000
1	2,000	3,500
2	2,000	2,000
3	2,000	0

NPV of project with no abandonment:
-\$5,000 + \$2,000/(1.10)^1 + \$2,000/(1.10)^2 + \$2,000/(1.10)^3 = -\$26.30.

NPV of project if abandoned after Year 1:
-\$5,000 + \$2,000/(1.10)^1 + \$3,500/(1.10)^1 = \$0.

NPV of project if abandoned after Year 2:
-\$5,000 + \$2,000/(1.10)^1 + \$2,000/(1.10)^2 + \$2,000/(1.10)^2 = \$124.

11.   d.   The first step is to recast the given data in nominal terms since the cost of capital is nominal:

Year	Revenues	Costs	Depreciation
0	$ 0	$90,000	$ 0
1	42,000	11,000	30,000
2	44,100	12,100	30,000
3	46,305	13,310	30,000

Now apply standard capital budgeting procedures. The initial investment is $90,000. The operating cash flows are 0.6($42,000 − $11,000) = $18,600 for Year 1, 0.6($44,100 − $12,100) = $19,200 for Year 2, and 0.6($46,305 − $13,310) = $19,797 for Year 3. The tax savings from depreciation is 0.4($30,000) = $12,000 in Years 1 through 3. Now putting this on a time line gives the following:

```
0    14%      1          2          3
├─────────────┼──────────┼──────────┤
-90,000      18,600     19,200     19,797
             12,000     12,000     12,000
             30,600     31,200     31,797
 26,842  ◄──────┘
 24,007  ◄─────────────────┘
 21,462  ◄────────────────────────────┘
($17,689)
```

12.   e.   Plane A: Expected life = 5 years; Costs = $200; NCF = $60; COC = 14%.

       Plane B: Expected life = 10 years; Costs = $245; NCF = $48; COC = 14%.

Enter these values into the cash flow register: CF_0 = -200; CF_1 = 60, 4 times; CF_2 = -140; CF_3 = 60, 5 times.   Then enter I = 14, and press the NPV to get NPV_A = $9.0932 ≈ $9.09.

                   0   14%   1   2   3   4   5   6   7   8   9   10

B: -245   48   48   48   48   48   48   48   48   48   48

Enter these values into the cash flow register, along with the interest rate, and press the NPV key to get NPV_B = $5.3736 ≈ $5.37.

Project A is the better project and will increase the company's value by $9.09.

CHAPTER 8
RISK ANALYSIS AND REAL OPTIONS

OVERVIEW

In the real world cash flows are not known with certainty, and many times it is not even known for sure that a project's forecasted "inflows" will be positive. Firms use different techniques to determine a project's risk and then to decide whether its profit potential is worth the risk. Those techniques are illustrated, and as a part of this analysis, the impact of real options on project's risks and returns is examined.

Real options allow managers to intervene and make changes in a project after it has been implemented, in response to changing market conditions. Real options increase a project's expected cash flows and

decrease the project's risk. Therefore, real options add value to a project.

The optimal capital budget is the set of projects that maximizes firm value. Establishing the optimal capital budget is complicated in practice by an increasing marginal cost of capital and capital rationing. The marginal cost of capital increases due to flotation costs and because investors often perceive extremely large capital investments to be riskier. Capital rationing occurs when a firm forgoes value-adding projects. Several explanations for it are: (1) reluctance to issue new equity, (2) constraints on nonmonetary resources, and (3) controlling estimation bias.

OUTLINE

Three separate and distinct types of risk can be identified in capital budgeting: (1) stand-alone risk, (2) corporate (within-firm) risk, and (3) market (beta) risk.

■ *Stand-alone risk* is the risk an asset would have if it were a firm's only asset. It is measured by the variability of the asset's expected returns.

■ *Corporate (within-firm) risk* is the project's risk to the corporation, giving consideration to the fact that the project represents only one of the firm's portfolio of assets. It is measured by a project's impact on uncertainty about the firm's future earnings.
  □ Corporate risk is important for three reasons.

- Undiversified stockholders are more concerned about corporate risk than about market risk.
- Empirical studies generally find that both market and corporate risk affect stock prices.
- The firm's stability is important to its managers, workers, customers, suppliers, and creditors, as well as to the community in which it operates.

■ *Market (beta) risk* is the riskiness of the project as seen by a well-diversified stockholder who recognizes that the project is only one of the firm's assets and that the firm's stock is but one small part of the investor's total portfolio. It is measured by the project's effect on the firm's beta.

Stand-alone risk is by far the easiest to measure and may be done so in a number of ways. Because all three types of risk are usually highly correlated, stand-alone risk is generally a good proxy for hard-to-measure corporate and market risk. Three techniques for assessing a project's stand-alone risk are: (1) sensitivity analysis, (2) scenario analysis, and (3) Monte Carlo simulation.

■ *Sensitivity analysis* is a technique which indicates how much a project's NPV will change in response to a given change in an input variable, other things held constant.
- □ The analysis begins with expected values for unit sales, sales price, fixed costs, and variable costs to give an expected, or *base case*, NPV. A series of "what if" questions may then be asked to find the change in NPV, given a change in one of the input variables.
- □ Each variable is changed by several specific percentage points above and below the expected value, holding other things constant. The resulting set of NPVs is plotted against the variable that was changed.
- □ The *steeper* the slope, the *more sensitive* NPV is to changes in each of the input variables.
- □ When comparing two projects, the one with the steeper sensitivity lines would be regarded as riskier, because for that project a relatively small error in estimating the input variable would produce a large error in the project's expected NPV.
- □ Sensitivity analysis can provide useful insights into the riskiness of a project.
- □ Spreadsheet computer models are ideally suited for performing sensitivity analysis.
- □ Although sensitivity analysis is probably the most widely used risk analysis technique, it does have limitations.

■ *Scenario analysis* provides a more complete analysis than sensitivity analysis, because in addition to the sensitivity of NPV to changes in key variables, it considers the range of likely values of these variables. A project's stand-alone risk depends on both of these factors.

☐ Worst-case and best-case scenarios are estimated and the input values from these scenarios are used to find the worst-case NPV and the best-case NPV.

☐ Probabilities can be assigned to the best, worst, and base-case NPVs to obtain the expected NPV.

☐ The project's coefficient of variation can be compared to the coefficient of variation of the firm's "average" project to determine the relative stand-alone riskiness of the project.

☐ Scenario analysis is limited in that it only considers a few discrete outcomes, even though there are an infinite number of possibilities.

■ *Monte Carlo simulation*, which ties together sensitivities and input variable probability distributions, requires a computer along with an efficient financial planning software package.

☐ The computer repeatedly selects a random value for each uncertain variable based on its specified probability distribution, along with values for fixed factors. The end result is a continuous NPV probability distribution with its own expected value and standard deviation.

☐ A simulation is more comprehensive than scenario analysis because it considers an infinite number of possible outcomes.

☐ In spite of its obvious appeal, Monte Carlo simulation has not been as widely used in industry as one might expect. The major problem is specifying each uncertain variable's probability distribution and the correlations among the distributions.

■ A problem with both scenario and simulation analysis is that even when the analysis has been completed, no clear-cut decision rule emerges.

☐ The analysis provides no criterion to indicate whether a project's profitability as measured by its expected NPV is sufficient to compensate for its risk as measured by σ_{NPV} or CV_{NPV}.

☐ In addition, scenario and simulation analysis both focus on a project's stand-alone risk—they ignore the effects of diversification, both among projects within the firm and by investors in their personal investment portfolios.

■ Managers, not computers, make the final decision on whether to accept or reject projects. Unlike computers, managers bring qualitative judgment into the decision process, and the stand-alone risk profile of a project can provide some extremely valuable insights.

The wisdom of corporate diversification to reduce risk has been questioned. Why should a firm diversify when stockholders can easily diversify themselves?

■ A project's corporate risk is the project's contribution to the firm's overall corporate risk, or, put another way, *project corporate risk* reflects the impact of the project on uncertainty about the firm's total cash flows.

■ *Corporate risk* is a function of (1) the project's standard deviation and (2) its correlation with returns on the firm's other assets.

■ Although stockholders could directly obtain some of the risk-reducing benefits through personal diversification, other benefits can be gained only by diversification at the corporate level.

The CAPM offers useful insights into risk analysis in capital budgeting.

■ In theory, each project has its own beta, which defines the rate of return that shareholders require on their investment in that particular project.
  □ The estimation of project betas is even more difficult than the estimation of stock betas, and more fraught with uncertainty.
  □ Two approaches are used to estimate individual assets' betas—the *pure play method* and the *accounting beta method*.
  □ The pure play method is more frequently used.

■ The pure play method assumes initially that all projects within a single division have the same type of risk, and therefore, the same beta.
  □ The *divisional beta* is the beta a company would have if the company consisted of only this single division.
  □ The beta of a company is the weighted average of its divisional betas.
  □ The company's overall cost of equity is a weighted average of its divisional costs of equity, and its overall WACC is a weighted average of its divisional WACCs.

■ An *asset beta* is equal to the beta of an unleveraged, single-asset minifirm.
  □ The beta of a firm with an all-equity capital structure (which means that the firm has zero financial leverage) is defined as an *unlevered beta*.
  □ If the firm then begins to use debt, the riskiness inherent in its equity, and also its *levered beta*, will begin to rise.

■ *Robert Hamada's equation* for the relationship between levered and unlevered betas is:

$$b_L = b_U[1 + (1 - T)(D / S)].$$

  □ b_L is the beta given that the firm uses debt.
  □ b_U is the beta it would have if it used no debt.
  □ T is its tax rate.

- ☐ D is its dollars of debt.
- ☐ S is the market value of its stock.

■ b_U for an unlevered, single-project firm would also be the beta of the firm's single asset.
  - ☐ Thus, b_U can be thought of as an unlevered asset's beta.

■ The *equity beta* of a single-asset firm is a function of both the asset's business risk as measured by b_U and how the asset is financed, and it can be approximated by the Hamada equation.

■ The Hamada equation enables us to convert asset betas to leveraged stock betas, and vice versa.
  - ☐ This equation is also used to estimate project betas.

■ In the pure play method, the company tries to find one or more nonintegrated, single-product companies in the same line of business as the project being evaluated to determine a proxy for the project's beta.
  - ☐ The Hamada equation is used to adjust the *proxy beta* for differences between the firms due to financial leverage and tax rates.

■ The pure play approach is often difficult to implement because it is difficult to find pure play proxy firms.

From a theoretical standpoint, well-diversified investors should be concerned only with market risk, managers should be concerned only with stock price maximization, and these two factors should lead to the conclusion that market (beta) risk ought to be given virtually all the weight in capital budgeting decisions. However, if investors are not well diversified, if the CAPM does not operate exactly as theory says it should, or if measurement problems keep managers from having confidence in the CAPM approach in capital budgeting, it may be appropriate to give stand-alone and corporate risk more weight than financial theorists suggest.

■ CAPM ignores bankruptcy costs, and the probability of bankruptcy depends on a firm's corporate risk, not on its beta risk. Therefore, one can easily conclude that even well-diversified investors should want a firm's management to give at least some consideration to a project's stand-alone risk and corporate risk instead of concentrating entirely on market risk.

Two methods are used to incorporate project risk into capital budgeting: the certainty equivalent approach and the risk-adjusted discount rate approach.

■ With the *certainty equivalent approach* all cash flows that are not known with certainty are scaled down, and the riskier the flows, the lower their certainty equivalent values.

■ With the *risk-adjusted discount rate approach* differential project risk is dealt with by changing the discount rate.

  ☐ Average-risk projects are discounted at the firm's average cost of capital, higher-risk projects are discounted at a higher cost of capital, and lower-risk projects are discounted at a rate below the firm's average cost of capital.

■ Risk adjustments are necessarily judgmental and somewhat arbitrary.

■ In many cases, it is impossible to accurately assess a project's market risk, or even its corporate risk. Therefore, managers are often left with only an estimate of the project's stand-alone risk.

  ☐ Stand-alone, corporate, and market risk are usually highly correlated.

  ☐ Managers can get a feel for the relative risk of most projects on the basis of sensitivity, scenario, simulation, and/or decision tree analyses, even though these procedures measure only stand-alone risk.

  ☐ Capital structure must also be taken into account if a firm finances different assets in different ways.

■ The first step in developing a project's cost of capital calls for adjusting the corporate cost of capital to reflect divisional risk and debt capacity.

  ☐ Divisional costs of capital are usually based on divisional betas using Hamada's equation to account for any differences in divisional debt capacity.

  ☐ Each project is then assigned to a risk category on the basis of its own risk relative to its division's average risk.

  ☐ Also, adjustments should be made when projects have debt capacities which differ widely from the divisional average.

  ☐ The end result of the process is a project cost of capital and an NPV which incorporates, to the extent possible, the project's debt capacity and relative riskiness.

  ☐ Managers may also have to consider other risk factors. Such additional factors must be considered subjectively in making the final accept/reject decision.

■ Capital budgeting decisions require a mix of objective and subjective analyses.

■ Despite the imprecision and subjectivity, risk should be assessed and incorporated into the capital budgeting process.

Projects often have negative cash flows during their lives, and when this occurs, special problems may arise.

■ Whereas it is appropriate to increase the discount rate applied to risky cash inflows to adjust for their risk, we must use a *lower discount rate* to reflect *higher risks* for *cash outflows*.

■ This situation also comes up in other types of DCF analyses.
　□ In certain leasing problems the salvage value at the end of a lease is more uncertain than the payment stream during the life of the lease. At times, the salvage value must be treated as an outflow.

Traditional capital budgeting theory says nothing about actions that can be taken after the project has been accepted and placed in operation that might cause the cash flows to change.

■ Chance plays a continuing role throughout the life of the project and managers can respond to changing market conditions and to competitors' actions.

■ Opportunities to respond to changing circumstances are called *managerial options* because they give managers the option to influence the outcome of a project.
　□ They are also called *strategic options* because they are often associated with large, strategic projects rather than routine maintenance projects.
　□ They are also called *real options* and are differentiated from financial options because they involve real, rather than financial, assets.

Three key issues are associated with real options: (1) identifying the optimal response to changing conditions, (2) determining the value of a real option, and (3) structuring projects so as to create real options.

■ Managers are generally more interested in reducing risk than in measuring it.

■ Sometimes projects can be structured so that expenditures can be made in stages over a period of years. This reduces risk by giving managers the opportunity to reevaluate decisions using new information and then either investing additional funds or abandoning the project.

■ *Decision trees* are used to analyze multistage, or sequential, decisions.
　□ A decision tree defines the decision nodes and the branches that leave the nodes.
　□ There are two types of nodes: decision nodes and outcome nodes.
　　● *Decision nodes* are the points at which management can respond to new information.
　　● The *outcome nodes* show the possible results if a particular decision is taken.

☐ The decision tree also shows the probabilities of moving into each branch that leaves a node.

■ Complex decision trees are used to analyze projects. Even more important, they are used to help structure projects and to help identify any real options that might be embedded in the projects.

The valuation of real options is a complex subject. However, it is important for managers to know something about real options.

■ Value of option = New NPV - Old NPV, where the old NPV is calculated with the traditional DCF analysis before the real option has been added.
   ☐ The *option to abandon* is an example of a real option.
   ☐ Real options can lower the stand-alone risk of a project resulting in a lower project cost of capital. Consequently, the value of the real option could be greater than the equation above implies.

■ In general, DCF techniques will not give perfectly accurate estimates of the value of a real option, because real options change a project's risk and resulting cost of capital.

■ Some additional points about decision tree analysis and real options are listed below.
   ☐ Managers can reduce project risk if they can structure the decision process to include several decision points rather than just one.
   ☐ Once production begins, if the firm can shut down or spin off the operation, this could dramatically reduce its risk.
   ☐ The cost of abandonment is generally reduced if the firm has alternative uses for the project's assets.
   ☐ Capital budgeting is a dynamic process. Virtually all input values change over time, so firms must periodically review both their capital expenditure plans and their operating assets.

■ The key concept to remember is that decisions can often be structured with multiple decision points. If so, and if the company has the willpower to admit it when a project is not working out as initially planned and then abandons it, risks can be reduced and profitability increased.

Real options can add value to a project. Managers should be able to identify all real options embedded in projects, they should know which types of options can be valued using quantitative techniques, and they should have some intuition about the qualitative aspects of options.

■ There are many types of real options.
  ☐ The *flexibility option* allows managers to switch inputs in a manufacturing process.
  ☐ The *capacity option* allows firms to manage their productive capacity in response to changing market conditions.
  ☐ The *abandonment option* allows the firm to discontinue a project.
  ☐ Many projects can be structured so that they contain *options to reduce or temporarily suspend operations* rather than completely close them down.
  ☐ Other projects can be structured so they contain an *option to expand*.
  ☐ Projects can also contain an *option to expand into a new geographical market*.
  ☐ *New product options* can be very valuable. A company might accept a negative NPV project if it has embedded in it the option to add complementary projects, or successive "generations" of the original product.
  ☐ Another important type of option is the *timing option*, or *option to delay*.
    • This is valuable during periods of volatile interest rates, since the ability to wait can allow firms to raise capital for projects when interest rates are lower.
    • The option to delay is valuable only if it more than offsets any harm that might come from delaying.
    • Usually, the option to delay is most valuable to firms with proprietary technology, patents, licenses, or other barriers to entry.

■ The addition of a real option to a project alters the risk of the project's cash flows, which makes it impossible to estimate perfectly the project's cost of capital.
  ☐ This makes it difficult to use DCF methods to estimate the value of a real option with precision.

■ An alternative valuation approach, *replicating portfolio*, creates a portfolio of financial securities in such a way that the cash flows of the financial portfolio are identical to the cash flows of the project.
  ☐ Since the securities in the replicating portfolio all have observable prices, it is straightforward to calculate the total value of the portfolio.
  ☐ Therefore, since the project and the replicating portfolio have identical cash flows, the project must have the same value as the portfolio.
  ☐ One advantage of this approach is that it does not require the financial analyst to estimate the project's cost of capital.

■ There are three steps to applying the replicating portfolio approach:
  ☐ Identify each source of risk that affects the real option and that risk's impact on the project's cash flows.
  ☐ Find financial assets that trade in efficient public markets whose cash flows and values depend on the same risks as those that affect the project.

☐ Determine the mix of financial assets so that the portfolio of financial assets replicates the cash flows of the project, and then "crunch the numbers." In general, this is more difficult than traditional DCF analysis.

■ The true NPV of a project can be thought of as the value of the project without any embedded real options plus the value of the options:

True NPV = NPV without options + NPV of options.

■ Sometimes it is not possible to quantify the value of a project with real options. However, managers should still think about real options within the framework of the above equation.
  ☐ Real options often add considerable value to projects, so ignoring them could lead to downward-biased NPVs and systematic underinvestment.
  ☐ In general, the longer before a real option must be exercised, the more valuable it is.
  ☐ The more volatile the underlying source of risk, the more valuable the option.
  ☐ If interest rates rise, the values of real options will increase.

The optimal capital budget is the set of projects that maximizes the value of the firm. Finance theory states that all projects with positive NPVs should be accepted. These positive NPV projects comprise the optimal capital budget. However, two complications arise in practice: (1) an increasing marginal cost of capital and (2) capital rationing.

■ The cost of capital can depend on the size of the capital budget.
  ☐ Because of flotation costs associated with issuing new equity or public debt, the cost of capital increases as soon as a company invests all of its internally generated cash.
  ☐ Investors often perceive extremely large capital investments to be riskier, which also serves to drive up the cost of capital as the size of the capital budget increases.

■ *Capital rationing* occurs when a firm limits capital expenditures to less than the amount required to fund the optimal capital budget.

■ Some potential explanations for capital rationing and possible solutions are:
  ☐ Reluctance to issue new equity
    • A company might be better off to explicitly incorporate the costs of raising external capital into its cost of capital. If there are still positive NPV projects even with the higher cost of capital, then the company should go ahead and raise external equity and accept the projects.
  ☐ Constraints on non-monetary resources
    • By employing *linear programming*, a company can identify the set of projects that maximizes NPV subject to the constraint that the total amount of support required for these projects doesn't exceed the available resources.

☐ Controlling estimation bias
- Implement a post-audit program and link the accuracy of forecasts to the compensation of the managers who initiated the projects.

A firm's capital budgeting decision process combines quantitative measures and qualitative judgment.

The financial vice-president obtains an estimate of the firm's investment opportunities from the director of capital budgeting and an estimate of the WACC from the treasurer.

The corporate WACC is scaled up or down for each division to reflect the division's capital structure and risk characteristics.

Each project within each division is classified into one of three groups—high risk, average risk, and low risk.

Each project's NPV is then determined, using its risk-adjusted project cost of capital.
☐ The optimal capital budget consists of all independent projects with positive risk-adjusted NPVs plus those mutually exclusive projects with the highest positive risk-adjusted NPVs.

These steps implicitly assume that the projects taken on have, on average, about the same debt capacity and risk characteristics, and, consequently, the same weighted average cost of capital as the firm's existing assets.

This procedure forces the firm to think carefully about each division's relative risk, about the risk of each project within the divisions, and about the relationship between the total amount of capital raised and the cost of that capital.

In addition, this procedure forces the firm to adjust its capital budget to reflect capital market conditions—if the costs of debt and equity rise, this fact will be reflected in the cost of capital used to evaluate projects, and projects that would be marginally acceptable when capital costs were low would be ruled unacceptable when capital costs were high.

The Extensions to Chapter 8 discuss the topics of incorporating risk into capital budgeting decisions and the optimal capital budget.

Two alternative methods have been developed for incorporating project risk into the capital budgeting decision process.

- ☐ The *certainty equivalent (CE) method* adjusts the expected cash flows to reflect project risk—risky cash flows are scaled down, and the riskier the flows, the lower their certainty equivalent values.
- ☐ The *risk-adjusted discount rate (RADR) method* deals with differential project risk by changing the discount rate. Average-risk projects are discounted at the firm's corporate cost of capital, above-average risk projects are discounted at a higher cost of capital, and below-average risk projects are discounted at a rate below the corporate cost of capital.

■ The RADR method dominates in practice because people find it far easier to estimate suitable discount rates based on current market data than to derive certainty equivalent cash flows.

■ One cannot determine the cost of capital until the size of the capital budget is determined, and the size of the capital budget cannot be determined until the cost of capital is determined.

■ A firm's *investment opportunity schedule (IOS)* is a plot of each project's IRR, in descending order, versus the dollars of new capital required to finance it.

■ A firm's *marginal cost of capital schedule (MCC)* is a plot of the firm's weighted average cost of capital versus the dollars of new capital raised.

■ The IOS and MCC schedules are combined to find the cost of capital for use in determining an average-risk project's NPV.
- ☐ All independent projects that have rates of return in excess of the cost of the capital that will be used to finance them should be accepted.

■ The corporate cost of capital used in the capital budgeting process is determined at the intersection of the IOS and MCC schedules.
- ☐ This cost is called the firm's *marginal cost of capital (MCC)*, and if it is used in capital budgeting, then the firm will make correct accept/reject decisions, and its level of investment will be optimal.

SELF-TEST QUESTIONS

Definitional

1. The _____ the risk associated with an investment, the greater the _____ ____ _____ needed to compensate investors.

2.   Three separate and distinct types of risk can be identified in capital budgeting: market risk, _____-_____ risk, and _____ risk.

3.   A commonly used method of risk analysis is based on constructing optimistic, pessimistic, and expected value estimates for the key variables. This method is called _____ _____.

4.   In project analysis, changing one key variable at a time and determining the effect on its NPV is known as _____ _____.

5.   One purpose of sensitivity analysis is to determine which of the _____ have the greatest influence on the project's NPV.

6.   Unless the cash flows are negative, riskier projects should be evaluated with a higher _____ ____ _____ than average-risk projects.

7.   The _____ _____ _____ is a plot of the firm's proposed projects, ranked in descending order of IRR, versus the dollars of new capital required.

8.   The marginal cost of capital schedule is a plot of the firm's _____ _____ _____ ____ _____ versus the dollars of new capital raised.

9.   The firm's _____ _____ ____ _____ is defined by the intersection of the MCC and IOS schedules.

10.   All projects of _____ risk should be evaluated at the firm's marginal cost of capital.

11.   _____ _____ occurs when a firm limits its capital expenditures to less than the amount required to fund the optimal capital budget.

12.   _____-_____ risk is the risk an asset would have if it were a firm's only asset.

13.   _____ risk is the riskiness of the project as seen by a well-diversified stockholder who recognizes that the project is only one of the firm's assets and that the firm's stock is but one small part of the investor's total portfolio.

14.   _____ _____ _____ ties together sensitivities and input variable probability distributions, and requires a computer along with an efficient financial planning software package.

15. The _____ _____ approach is one method used to incorporate project risk into capital budgeting, where all cash flows that are not known with certainty are scaled down.

16. _____ risk is measured by a project's impact on uncertainty about the firm's future earnings.

17. Corporate risk is a function of the project's _____ _____ and its _____ with returns on the firm's other assets.

18. Two approaches are used to estimate individual assets' betas: the _____ _____ and the _____ _____ methods.

19. The beta of a firm with an all-equity capital structure is defined as a(n) _____ beta.

20. The _____ equation enables one to convert asset betas to leveraged stock betas, and vice versa.

21. Two methods are used to incorporate project risk into capital budgeting: the _____ _____ and _____-_____ _____ _____ approaches.

22. Whereas it is appropriate to increase the discount rate applied to risky cash inflows to adjust for their risk, we must use a(n) _____ discount rate to reflect higher risks for cash outflows.

23. Opportunities to respond to changing circumstances are called _____ _____ because they give managers the option to influence the outcome of a project.

24. Three key issues are associated with real options: (1) _____ the optimal response to changing conditions, (2) determining the _____ of a real option, and (3) _____ projects so as to create real options.

25. _____ _____ are used to analyze multistage, or sequential, decisions.

26. _____ nodes are the points indicated on the decision tree where management can respond to new information, while _____ nodes show the possible results if a particular decision is taken.

27. In general, DCF techniques will not give perfectly accurate estimates of the value of a(n) _____ _____, because it changes a project's risk and resulting cost of capital.

28. An alternative approach to the DCF method for valuing a project with embedded options is a(n) _____ _____ approach, which creates a portfolio of financial securities in such a way that the cash flows of the financial portfolio are identical to the cash flows of the project.

29. Real options often add considerable value to projects, so ignoring them could lead to _____-biased NPVs and systematic _____.

30. The _____ _____ _____ is the set of projects that maximizes the value of the firm.

Conceptual

31. Even if the beta of a project being considered has a value of zero, acceptance of the project will affect the market risk of the firm.

    a. True   **b.** False

32. When independent projects of different risk are to be considered in capital budgeting, any project will be acceptable to the firm if the project's IRR is greater than the firm's weighted average cost of capital.

    a. True   **b.** False

33. If a cash *outflow* is judged to be riskier than average, then the firm's marginal cost of capital must be adjusted *downward* to reflect this differential.

    a. True   **b.** False

34. A problem with both scenario and simulation analysis is that even when the analysis has been completed, no clear-cut decision rule emerges.

    a. True   **b.** False

35. The cost of abandonment is generally increased if the firm has alternative uses for the project's assets.

    a. True   **b.** False

36. Which of the following statements about real options is *false*?

    a. The more volatile the underlying source of risk, the more valuable the option.
    b. In general, the longer before a real option must be exercised, the more valuable it is.
    c. If interest rates fall, the values of real options will increase.
    d. Real options often add considerable value to projects, so ignoring them could lead to downward-biased NPVs and systematic underinvestment.
    e. While sometimes it is not possible to quantify the value of a project with real options, managers should still think about real options within the framework of this equation: True NPV = NPV without options + NPV of options.

37. Which of the following is *not* a potential explanation for capital rationing?

    a. Controlling estimation bias.
    b. Reluctance to issue new equity.
    c. Constraints on non-monetary resources.
    d. Increasing marginal cost of capital due to flotation expenses.
    e. None of the above; all are potential explanations for capital rationing.

38. In capital budgeting decisions, corporate risk will be of *least* interest to:

    a. Employees.
    b. Stockholders with few shares.
    c. Institutional investors.
    d. Creditors.
    e. The local community.

39. Which of the following steps are commonly used in practice to establish a firm's optimal capital budget?

    a. Analysts estimate a project's stand-alone risk.
    b. The corporate cost of capital is scaled up or down to reflect each division's capital structure and risk characteristics.
    c. Each division's cost of capital is scaled up or down to reflect differential project risk.
    d. Each project's NPV is then determined using its appropriate risk-adjusted cost of capital.
    e. All the above steps are used.

40. The Pennsylvania Company is evaluating two mutually exclusive pollution control processes. Since the company's revenue stream will not be affected by the choice of control process, the projects are being evaluated by finding the PV of each set of costs. The firm's cost of capital is 10 percent, and it adds or subtracts 2 percentage points to adjust for project risk differences. Process A is judged to be a high-risk project—it might end up costing much more to operate than is expected. Process A's risk-adjusted cost of capital is

   a. 8 percent; this might seem illogical at first, but it correctly adjusts for risk where outflows, rather than inflows, are being discounted.
   b. 10 percent; the firm's cost of capital should not be adjusted when evaluating outflow-only projects.
   c. 12 percent; since A is more risky, its cash flows should be discounted at a higher rate, because this correctly penalizes the project for its high risk.
   d. somewhere between 8 and 12 percent, with the answer depending on the riskiness of the relevant inflows.
   e. indeterminate, or, more accurately, irrelevant, because for such projects we would simply select the process that meets the requirements with the lowest required investment.

SELF-TEST PROBLEMS

1. Initially, United Products has a beta of 1.30. The risk-free rate is 12 percent, and the required rate of return on the market is 18 percent. The firm now sells 10 percent of its assets, having a beta of 1.30, and uses the proceeds to purchase a new product line with a beta of 1.00. What is the new overall required rate of return for United Products?

   a. 15.11%   **b.** 16.24%   **c.** 17.48%   **d.** 18.00%   **e.** 19.62%

2. Consolidated Inc. uses a weighted average cost of capital of 12 percent to evaluate average-risk projects and adds/subtracts two percentage points to evaluate projects of greater/lesser risk. Currently, two mutually exclusive projects are under consideration. Both have a net cost of $200,000 and last 4 years. Project A, which is riskier than average, will produce annual after-tax net cash flows of $71,000. Project B, which has less-than-average risk, will produce an after-tax net cash flow of $146,000 in Years 3 and 4 only. What should Consolidated do?

    a. Accept Project B with an NPV of $9,412.
    b. Accept both projects since both NPVs are greater than zero.
    c. Accept Project A with an NPV of $6,874.
    d. Accept neither project since both NPVs are less than zero.
    e. Accept Project A with an NPV of $15,652.

3. Union Industries, an all equity-financed firm, is considering the purchase of a plant that produces plastic products. The plant is expected to generate a rate of return of 17 percent, and the plant's estimated beta is 2.00. The risk-free rate is 12 percent, and the market risk premium is 6 percent. Union should make the investment.

    a. True   b. False

4. Diversified Products (DP) is considering the formation of a new division which will double the assets of the firm. DP is an all-equity firm which has a current required rate of return of 20 percent. The risk-free rate is 10 percent, and the market risk premium is 5 percent. If DP wants to reduce its required rate of return to 18 percent, what is the maximum beta the new division could have?

    a. 1.00   b. 1.10   c. 1.20   d. 1.25   e. 1.30

5. Midwest Motors is choosing between two automobile washing/waxing machines on the basis of cost. The expected net costs of the two machines are as follows:

Year	Machine A	Machine B
0	($20,000)	($10,000)
1	(5,000)	(8,000)
2	(5,000)	(8,000)
3	(5,000)	(8,000)
4	(5,000)	(8,000)

The firm's cost of capital is 10 percent. Machine B is judged to be a riskier-than-average project, while Machine A is considered less risky than average. The firm's policy is to add or subtract 2 percentage points to adjust for risk. The firm should choose Machine B.

a. True   b. False

6. Consolidated Industries' overall cost of capital (WACC) is 10 percent. Division HR is riskier than average, Division AR has average risk, and Division LR is less risky than average. Consolidated adjusts for risk by adding or subtracting 2 percentage points. What is the risk-adjusted project cost of capital for a low-risk project in the HR division?

a. 6%   b. 8%   c. 10%   d. 12%   e. 14%

7. Florida Phosphate Company (FPC) can control ground water pollution using either "Project Average" or "Project Risky." Both will do the job, but the actual costs involved with Project Risky could be much higher than the expected cost levels. The cash outflows associated with "Project Average" are about as uncertain as the cash flows associated with the firm's average project. FPC's cost of capital for average-risk projects is *normally* set at 12 percent, and the company adds 3 percent for high-risk projects but subtracts 3 percent for low-risk projects. The two projects in question meet the criteria for high and average risk, but the financial manager is concerned about applying the normal rule to such cost-only projects. You must decide which project to recommend, and you should recommend the one with the lower PV of costs. What is the PV of costs of the better project?

Year	Project Risky	Project Average
0	($1,000)	($400)
1	(210)	(400)
2	(210)	(400)
3	(210)	(400)
4	(210)	(400)

a. -$1,680.34   b. -$1,599.55   c. -$1,614.94   d. -$1,541.99   e. -$1,637.84

(The following data apply to the next three Self-Test Problems.)

The Carlisle Corporation is considering a proposed project for its capital budget. The company estimates that the project's NPV is $5 million. This estimate assumes that the economy and market conditions will be average over the next few years. The company's CFO, however, forecasts that there is only a 40 percent chance that the economy will be average. Recognizing this uncertainty, she has also performed the following scenario analysis:

Economic Scenario	Probability of Outcome	(NPV)
Recession	0.05	($28 million)
Below Average	0.25	(10 million)
Average	0.40	5 million
Above Average	0.25	8 million
Boom	0.05	15 million

8. What is the project's expected NPV (in millions)?

   a. $0.25   **b.** $0.85   **c.** $1.20   **d.** $1.50   **e.** $2.00

9. What is the project's standard deviation?

   a. $10.04   **b.** $12.78   **c.** $15.65   **d.** $21.37   **e.** $29.43

10. What is the project's coefficient of variation?

   a. 5.02   **b.** 2.75   **c.** 6.39   **d.** 1.25   **e.** 11.81

(The following data apply to the next three Self-Test Problems.)

The San Francisco Yacht Company (SFYC), a prominent sailboat builder in San Francisco, may design a new 30-foot sailboat based on the "winged" keels first introduced on the 12-meter yachts that raced for the America's Cup.

First, SFYC would have to invest $20,000 at t = 0 for the design and model tank testing of the new boat. SFYC's managers believe that there is a 55 percent probability that this phase will be successful and the project will continue. If Stage 1 is not successful, the project will be abandoned with zero salvage value.

The next stage, if undertaken, would consist of making the molds and producing two prototype boats. This would cost $1,000,000 at t = 1. If the boats test well, SFYC would go into production. If they do not, the molds and prototypes could be sold for $200,000. The managers estimate that the probability is 75 percent that the boats will pass testing, and that Stage 3 will be undertaken.

Stage 3 consists of converting an unused production line to produce the new design. This would cost $2,000,000 at t = 2. If the economy is strong at this point, sales would be $6,000,000, while if the economy is weak, sales would be $3,000,000. Sales occur at t = 3, and each state of the economy has a probability of 0.5. SFYC's corporate cost of capital is 13 percent.

11.   What is the project's expected NPV?

     a. $94,298   **b.** $117,779   **c.** $155,189   **d.** $184,291   **e.** $203,471

12.   What is the project's standard deviation of NPV?

     a. $445,060   **b.** $575,011   **c.** $617,050   **d.** $731,295   **e.** $819,647

13.   What is the project's coefficient of variation (CV) of NPV?

     a. 1.50   **b.** 5.28   **c.** 2.75   **d.** 4.45   **e.** 3.89

ANSWERS TO SELF-TEST QUESTIONS

1.	greater; rate of return	17.	standard deviation; correlation
2.	stand-alone; corporate (within-firm)	18.	pure play; accounting beta
3.	scenario analysis	19.	unlevered
4.	sensitivity analysis	20.	Hamada
5.	variables	21.	certainty equivalent; risk-adjusted discount rate
6.	cost of capital (or discount rate)		
7.	investment opportunity schedule	22.	lower
8.	weighted average cost of capital	23.	managerial options
9.	marginal cost of capital	24.	identifying; value; structuring
10.	average	25.	Decision trees
11.	Capital rationing	26.	Decision; outcome
12.	Stand-alone	27.	real option
13.	Market	28.	replicating portfolio
14.	Monte Carlo simulation	29.	downward; underinvestment
15.	certainty equivalent	30.	optimal capital budget
16.	Corporate		

31.   a.   The addition of an asset with a beta of zero would normally lower the beta of the firm, thus lowering the firm's market risk. (The starting beta of most firms is greater than zero.)

32. b. The only time this statement holds is when all independent projects being evaluated have the same risk as the firm's current average project. Otherwise, the cost of capital must be adjusted for project risk.

33. a. The present value of a cash *outflow* (cash cost) must be *increased* to penalize it for above-average risk, and the present value will be increased only if the discount rate is *decreased*.

34. a. This statement is true. Neither provides any criterion to indicate whether a project's profitability as measured by its expected NPV is sufficient to compensate for its risk as measured by σ_{NPV} or CV_{NPV}.

35. b. The cost of abandonment is reduced if the firm has alternative uses for the project's assets.

36. c. If interest rates rise, the values of real options will increase.

37. e. All the statements listed are potential explanations for capital rationing.

38. c. Institutional investors are well diversified and, therefore, more concerned with market risk.

39. e. In fact, responses (a) through (d) are the steps normally followed, in the correct sequence.

40. a. When cash outflows are judged to be riskier than average, a project's marginal cost of capital must be adjusted downward to reflect this fact.

SOLUTIONS TO SELF-TEST PROBLEMS

1. e. New b = 0.9(1.30) + 0.1(1.00) = 1.27.

New k_s = 12% + (18% − 12%)1.27 = 19.62%.

2. a. Look at the time lines:

Project A:

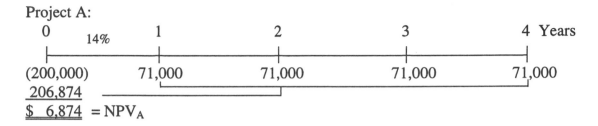

$$206,874$$
$$\underline{\$ \ 6,874} = NPV_A$$

Alternatively, input the cash flows in the cash flow register, enter I = 14, and then solve for NPV$_A$ = \$6,873.57.

Project B:

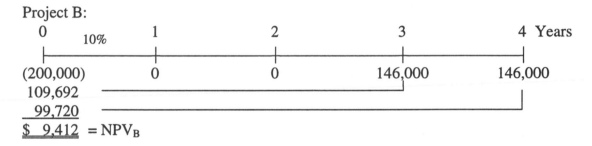

$$109,692$$
$$\underline{\ \ \ 99,720}$$
$$\underline{\$ \ 9,412} = NPV_B$$

Alternatively, input the cash flows in the cash flow register, enter I = 10, and then solve for NPV$_B$ = \$9,411.93.

Note that both discount rates are adjusted for risk. Since the projects are mutually exclusive, the project with the higher NPV is chosen.

3. b. The project's required rate of return on equity and overall cost of capital is 24 percent: $k_{s(Project)}$ = 12% + (6%)2 = 24%. Since the expected return is only 17 percent, the plant should not be purchased.

4. c. First, find the current beta of the firm: k_s = 10% + (5%)b = 20%, so b = 2.00.

Now find the beta required to lower the required rate of return to 18 percent:

k_s = 10% + (5%)b = 18%, so b = 1.60.

Finally, if the firm doubles its size with the formation of the new division, 50 percent of the expanded firm's assets will be old assets, while 50 percent will be assets from the new division. Thus, 0.5(2.00) + 0.5($b_{Div.}$) = 1.60; $b_{Div.}$ = 1.20.

5. b. These are cash outflows, so the risk adjustment process is reversed. Thus, the project cost of capital for Machine A is 12 percent, while the project cost of capital for B is 8 percent. $PV_{Project\ A} = -\$35,187$, and $PV_{Project\ B} = -\$36,497$.

    We see that with the correct risk adjustment, the PV of costs for Machine A is less than the PV of costs for Machine B, and hence Machine A should be selected.

6. c. $k_{HR} = 10\% + 2\% = 12\%$; $k_{Project} = 12\% - 2\% = 10\%$.

7. c. Recognize that (1) risky *outflows* must be discounted at lower rates and (2) since Project Risky is risky, it must be discounted at a rate of $12\% - 3\% = 9\%$. Project Average must be discounted at 12 percent. At these rates:

    $NPV_R = -\$1,680.34$ and $NPV_A = -\$1,614.94$.

    Thus, Project Average is the better project because it has the lower PV of costs.

8. b. $E(NPV) = 0.05(-\$28) + 0.25(-\$10) + 0.40(\$5) + 0.25(\$8) + 0.05(\$15)$
    $= -\$1.40 + -\$2.50 + \$2.00 + \$2.00 + \$0.75$
    $= \$0.85$ million.

9. a. $\sigma = [0.05(-\$28 - \$0.85)^2 + 0.25(-\$10 - \$0.85)^2 + 0.40(\$5 - \$0.85)^2 +$
    $0.25(\$8 - \$0.85)^2 + 0.05(\$15 - \$0.85)^2]^{1/2}$
    $\sigma = [\$41.62 + \$29.43 + \$6.89 + \$12.78 + \$10.01]^{1/2}$
    $\sigma = [\$100.73]^{1/2}$
    $\sigma = \$10.04$.

10. e. $CV = \dfrac{\$10.04}{\$0.85}$
    $CV = 11.81$.

11. c. The resulting decision tree is:

						NPV
t = 0	t = 1	t = 2	t = 3	P	NPV @13%	Product
			$6,000,000	0.20625	$1,687,052	$347,954
		($2,000,000) P = 0.5				
		P = 0.75 $3,000,000		0.20625	(392,099)	(80,870)
	($1,000,000)	P = 0.5				
	P = 0.55 $200,000			0.1375	(748,326)	(102,895)
($20,000)	P = 0.25					
	0			0.45	(20,000)	(9,000)
	P = 0.45			1.00	Exp. NPV =	$155,189
					(@ 13%)	

The NPV of the top path is:

$$\frac{\$6,000,000}{(1.13)^3} - \frac{\$2,000,000}{(1.13)^2} - \frac{\$1,000,000}{(1.13)^1} - \$20,000 = \$1,687,052.$$

Using a financial calculator, input the following: CF_0 = -20000, CF_1 = -1000000, CF_2 = -2000000, CF_3 = 6000000, and I = 13 to solve for NPV = $1,687,051.85 ≈ $1,687,052.

The other NPVs were determined in the same manner. If the project is of average risk, it should be accepted because the expected NPV of the total project is positive.

12. e. σ^2_{NPV} = 0.20625($1,687,052 - $155,189)^2 + 0.20625(-$392,099 - $155,189)^2
   + 0.1375(-$748,326 - $155,189)^2 + 0.45(-$20,000 - $155,189)^2
   = 671,821,678,595.
σ_{NPV} = $819,647.

13. b. $CV_{NPV} = \dfrac{\$819,647}{\$155,189} = 5.2816.$

CHAPTER 9
LONG-TERM FINANCIAL PLANNING

OVERVIEW

Managers are vitally concerned with *future financial statements* and with the effects of alternative assumptions and policies on these *projected*, or *pro forma*, statements. A firm's strategic plan forms the foundation for the pro forma statements, while the construction of pro forma statements begins with a *sales forecast*. On the basis of the sales forecast, the amount of assets necessary to support this sales level is determined. Although some liabilities will increase *spontaneously* with increased sales, if the sales growth rate is rapid, then external capital will be required to support the growth in sales.

Pro forma financial statements have three very important uses in the value creation process. Their first use is for estimating future free cash flows. These are necessary to implement the corporate valuation model, which enables management to measure the firm's current value, and, more importantly, to investigate the impact of proposed changes in strategy and operations. Second, pro forma statements can be used to plan for the financing that will be required to execute the operating plans. Last, pro forma statements provide a basis for setting targets used in the firm's compensation plan.

OUTLINE

Most companies have a mission statement, which is in many ways a condensed version of the firm's strategic plan.

- Strategic plans usually begin with a statement of the overall *corporate purpose*.

- The *corporate scope* defines a firm's lines of business and geographic area of operations.

- The corporate purpose and scope state the general philosophy of the business, but they do not provide managers with operational objectives.

- The *corporate objectives* set forth specific goals for management to attain.

    ☐ These include both qualitative and quantitative objectives.
    ☐ Companies have multiple objectives.
    ☐ Companies revise their objectives as business conditions change.

■ A firm needs to develop a strategy for achieving its goals. *Corporate strategies* are broad approaches rather than detailed plans.
    ☐ Strategies should be both attainable and compatible with the firm's purpose, scope, and objectives.

Operating plans can be developed for any time horizon, but most companies use a five-year horizon.

☐ A five-year plan is most detailed for the first year, with each succeeding year's plan becoming less specific.

☐ The plan is intended to provide detailed implementation guidance, based on the corporate strategy, in order to meet the corporate objectives.
    ☐ Large, multidivisional companies break down their operating plans by divisions.
    ☐ Each division has its own goals, mission, and plan for meeting its objectives, and these plans are then consolidated to form the corporate plan.

The financial planning process can be broken down into six steps.

■ Set up a system of projected financial statements to analyze the effects of the operating plan on projected profits and various financial ratios.

■ Determine the funds needed to support the five-year plan.

☐ Forecast funds availability over the next five years.

☐ Establish and maintain a system of controls governing the allocation and use of funds within the firm.

■ Develop procedures for adjusting the basic plan if the economic forecasts upon which the plan was based do not materialize.

■ Establish a performance-based management compensation system.
    ☐ The EVA system is generally regarded as an especially effective procedure for rewarding managers for maximizing share prices.

Well-run companies generally base their operating plans on a set of forecasted financial statements. A sales forecast for the next five years or so is developed, the assets required to meet the sales target are determined, and a decision is made concerning how to finance the required assets. These forecasts represent the "base case" and are a standard by which to judge alternate forecasts.

■ The *sales forecast* generally begins with a review of sales for the past 5 to 10 years.

■ If the sales forecast is off, the consequences can be serious. Thus, an accurate sales forecast is critical to the well being of the firm.
   ☐ If the market expands more than the firm has geared up for, the company will not be able to meet demand.
   ☐ If a firm's projections are overly optimistic, the firm could end up with too much plant, equipment, and inventory.

Any forecast of financial requirements involves (1) determining how much money the firm will need during a given period, (2) determining how much money the firm will generate internally during the same period, and (3) subtracting the funds generated from the funds required to determine the external financial requirements.

■ Two methods are used to estimate external requirements: the *percent of sales method,* which develops pro forma financial statements, and the *formula method.*

The most commonly used technique for forecasting future balance sheets and income statements is the percent of sales method.

■ This method begins with a sales forecast, expressed as an annual growth rate in dollar sales revenues.
   ☐ Population growth and inflation determine the *long-term sustainable growth rate* for most companies. Reasonable values for the sustainable growth rate are from 5 to 7 percent for most companies.
   ☐ Companies often have a *competitive advantage period*, during which they can grow at rates higher than the long-term sustainable growth rate.

■ With the percent of sales forecasting method, many items on the income statement and balance sheet are assumed to increase proportionally with sales.
   ☐ Items that are not tied directly to sales depend on the company's policies and its managers' decisions.

■   If the forecasted percentage of sales for each item is the same as the percentage for the year preceding the forecast period, then each item will grow at the same rate as sales. This approach is called the *constant ratio method of forecasting*.

    □ Managers should strive to have improving, not constant ratios.

The percent of sales method involves projecting the asset requirements for the coming period, then projecting the liabilities and equity that will be generated under normal operations, and subtracting the projected liabilities and capital from the required assets to estimate the additional funds needed (AFN).

■   The first step is to forecast next year's income statement.

    □ A sales forecast is needed.

    □ The percent of sales method assumes initially that all costs except depreciation are a specified percentage of sales.

    □ Depreciation can be assumed to be a fixed percentage of net plant and equipment.

    □ The primary objective of this step is to determine how much income the company will earn and retain for reinvestment during the forecasted year.

        ● The addition to retained earnings in the first-pass forecasted income statement will turn out to be too high because it understates next year's actual interest and dividends.

■   The second step is to forecast next year's balance sheet.

    □ If sales are to increase, then assets will have to increase.

    □ Cash, accounts receivable, and inventory are assumed to increase proportionally with sales. They are expressed as a percentage of sales.

    □ In the long term, there is a relatively close relationship between sales and fixed assets for all companies. Therefore, as a first approximation, it is reasonable to assume that the long-term ratio of net plant and equipment to sales will be constant.

    □ Additional assets must be financed, so liabilities and equity must also increase.

        ● Some items on the liability side, such as accounts payable and accruals, can be expected to increase spontaneously with sales producing what are called *spontaneously generated funds*.

    □ Retained earnings will also increase, but not proportionately with sales. The new retained earnings will be determined from the projected income statement.

    □ Other financing accounts, such as notes payable, long-term debt, preferred stock, and common stock, are not directly related to sales. Changes in these accounts result from managerial financing decisions; they do not increase spontaneously as sales increase.

    □ The difference between projected total assets and projected liabilities and capital is the amount of *additional funds needed (AFN)*.

        ● AFN are funds that a firm must raise externally through some combination of debt, preferred stock, and common stock.

■ The third step is the decision on how to finance the additional funds required. The financial staff will base the financial mix on several factors, including the firm's target capital structure, the effect of short-term borrowing on its current ratio, conditions in the debt and equity markets, and restrictions imposed by existing debt agreements.

■ One complexity that arises in financial forecasting relates to *financing feedbacks*: The external funds raised to pay for new assets create additional expenses which must be reflected in the income statement, and that lowers the initially forecasted addition to retained earnings.

☐ Financing feedbacks are handled by forecasting the additional interest expense and dividends that result from external financings.

☐ In each iteration of the forecasted financial statements, the additional financing becomes smaller and smaller and eventually the AFN is essentially zero. Spreadsheet software can do this iteration process so fast that it appears to occur instantaneously.

■ Developing the forecasted financial statements is only the first part of a firm's total planning process.

☐ The projected statements must be analyzed to determine how much value the plan creates for shareholders, and whether they meet the firm's targets as set forth in the five-year financial plan.

☐ If the statements do not meet targets, then elements of the operating plan must be analyzed to see if changes should be made.

☐ The firm should estimate the expected value of its operations if it executes its preliminary operating plan.

● Management should compare the stock's current value to the value under the preliminary operating plan. The value of operations is the present value of expected free cash flows discounted at the weighted average cost of capital. The total value is the value of operations plus the value of any financial assets. Subtracting the value of preferred stock and debt results in the value of equity. Dividing by the number of shares gives the stock price.

● If the value under the plan is less than the stock's current value, changes need to be made.

■ Forecasting is an iterative process, both in the way the financial statements are generated and the way the financial plan is developed.

■ Managers use financial planning models for three important purposes.

☐ The models allow managers to measure the expected change in value, or stock price, based on different strategic and operating alternatives.

● This process often is called *value-based management*.

☐ The models help managers determine the amount of financing that will be required to support various operating plans.

☐ The models help identify appropriate targets for compensation plans.

Most firms' forecasts of capital requirements are made by constructing pro forma financial statements as described above. However, when the ratios are expected to remain constant, then a simple forecasting formula is sometimes used.

■ The formula is as follows:

$$\begin{matrix} \text{Additional} & & \text{Required} & & \text{Spontaneous} & & \text{Increase in} \\ \text{funds} & = & \text{increase} & - & \text{increase in} & - & \text{retained} \\ \text{needed} & & \text{in assets} & & \text{liabilities} & & \text{earnings} \end{matrix}$$

or

$$\text{AFN} = (A^*/S_0)\Delta S - (L^*/S_0)\Delta S - MS_1 (1 - d).$$

☐ A^*/S_0 = percentage of required assets to sales, which shows the required dollar increase in assets per \$1 increase in sales.

☐ L^*/S_0 = liabilities that increase spontaneously as a percentage of sales, or spontaneously generated financing per \$1 increase in sales.

☐ S_1 = total sales projected for next year (note that S_0 = last year's sales).

☐ ΔS = change in sales = $S_1 - S_0$.

☐ M = profit margin, or profit per \$1 of sales.

☐ d = the percentage of earnings paid out in common dividends (dividend payout ratio).

■ Inherent in the formula are the assumptions (1) that each asset item must increase in direct proportion to sales increases, (2) that accounts payable and accruals also grow at the same rate as sales, and (3) that the profit margin is constant.

☐ Obviously, these assumptions do not always hold, so the formula does not always produce reliable results.

☐ Therefore, the formula is used primarily to get a rough-and-ready forecast of financial requirements under "business as usual" conditions.

■ The faster a firm's growth rate in sales, the greater its need for additional financing.

☐ Higher growth rates require managers to plan very carefully to decide if the additional financing needed is actually available to the firm. Otherwise, they should reconsider the feasibility of the expansion plans.

☐ Dividend policy as reflected in the payout ratio also affects external capital requirements: the higher the payout ratio, the smaller the addition to retained earnings, and hence the greater the requirements for external capital. Dividend policy may be changed to satisfy internal financing requirements, but this may have a negative impact on stock price and may be met with resistance from investors.

☐ The amount of assets required per dollar of sales, $A*/S_0$, is often called the *capital intensity ratio*. This factor has a major effect on capital requirements. If the capital intensity ratio is low, then sales can grow rapidly without much outside capital. However, if a firm is capital intensive, even a small growth in output will require a great deal of new outside capital.

☐ Profit margin, M, also has an effect on capital requirements. The higher the profit margin, the lower the funds requirement, and the lower the profit margin, the higher the requirement. Thus, highly profitable firms can raise most of their capital internally.

The forecasting process is greatly complicated if the ratios of balance sheet items to sales are not constant at all levels of sales.

■ Where *economies of scale* occur in asset use, the ratio of that asset to sales will change over time as the size of the firm increases.

■ In many industries, technological considerations dictate that fixed assets be added in large, discrete units, often referred to as *lumpy assets*. This automatically creates excess capacity immediately after a plant expansion.

■ *Forecasting errors* can cause the actual asset/sales ratio for a given period to be quite different from the planned ratio. This situation can result in excess capacity.

If any of the above conditions apply (economies of scale, lumpy assets, or excess capacity), the $A*/S_0$ ratio will not be a constant, and the constant growth forecasting method should not be used. Rather, other techniques must be used to forecast asset levels to determine additional financing requirements. Two of these methods include simple linear regression and excess capacity adjustments.

■ If one assumes that the relationship between a certain type of asset and sales is linear, then one can use *simple linear regression* techniques to estimate the requirements for that type of asset for any given sales increase. An estimated regression equation is determined which provides an estimated relationship between a given asset account and sales.

■ If a firm's fixed assets are not operating at full capacity, then the calculation for the required level of fixed assets will need to be adjusted.

☐ *Full capacity sales* is defined as actual sales divided by the percentage of capacity at which the fixed assets were operated to achieve these sales:

$$\text{Full capacity sales } = \frac{\text{Actual sales}}{\begin{array}{c}\text{Percentage of capacity at which}\\\text{fixed assets were operated}\end{array}}.$$

☐ The *target fixed assets-to-sales ratio* is equal to actual fixed assets divided by full capacity sales:

$$\text{Target fixed assets-to-sales ratio} = \frac{\text{Actual fixed assets}}{\text{Full capacity sales}}.$$

☐ The *required level of fixed assets* is equal to the target fixed assets-to-sales ratio times projected sales:

$$\begin{array}{c}\text{Required level}\\\text{of fixed assets}\end{array} = \text{(Target fixed assets-to-sales ratio)(Projected sales)}.$$

☐ Theoretically, excess capacity could occur with other types of assets, but as a practical matter, excess capacity normally exists only with respect to fixed assets and inventories.

Although financial forecasting as described in this chapter can be done with a hand calculator, virtually all corporate forecasts are made using computerized forecasting models. Many models are based on spreadsheet programs, such as Lotus 1-2-3 and Microsoft Excel.

■ Spreadsheet models have two major advantages over pencil-and-paper calculations.
  ☐ It is much faster to construct a spreadsheet model than to make a "by hand" forecast if the forecast period extends beyond two or three years.
  ☐ A spreadsheet model can recompute the projected financial statements and ratios almost instantaneously when the input variables are changed, thus making it easy for managers to determine the effects of changes in variables such as sales.

SELF-TEST QUESTIONS

Definitional

1. If various asset categories increase, _____ and/or _____ must also increase.

2. Typically, certain liabilities will rise _____ with sales. These include accounts _____ and _____.

3. _____, _____ stock, _____ stock, and _____ earnings are examples of accounts that do not increase proportionately with higher levels of sales.

4. As the dividend _____ _____ is increased, the amount of earnings available to finance new assets is _____.

5. Retained earnings depend not only on next year's sales level and dividend payout ratio but also on the _____ _____.

6. The amount of assets that are tied directly to sales, A^*/S_0, is often called the _____ _____ _____.

7. A capital intensive industry will require large amounts of _____ capital to finance increased growth.

8. The _____ ____ _____ method involves projecting the asset requirements for the coming period, then projecting the liabilities and equity that will be generated under normal operations, and subtracting the projected liabilities and capital from the required assets to estimate the _____ _____ _____.

9. The assumption of constant percentage of sales ratios may not be accurate when assets must be added in discrete amounts, called _____ assets, or when _____ of scale are considered.

10. Two methods can be used to estimate external funding requirements: the _____ ____ _____ and the _____ methods.

11. One complexity that arises in financial forecasting relates to _____ _____, which are the effects on the income statement and balance sheet of actions taken to finance asset increases.

12. Forecasting is a(n) _____ process, both in the way financial statements are generated and the way the financial plan is developed.

13. The faster a firm's growth rate in sales, the _____ its need for additional financing.

14. If economies of scale, lumpy assets, or excess capacity exist, the capital intensity ratio will not be a constant, and the percent of sales method should not be used. Other techniques such as linear _____ and _____ _____ adjustments should be used.

15. _____ _____ _____ is defined as actual sales divided by the percentage of capacity at which fixed assets were operated to achieve those sales.

16. The _____ _____-to-_____ ratio is equal to actual fixed assets divided by full capacity sales.

17. The _____ level of _____ _____ is equal to the target fixed assets-to-sales ratio times projected sales.

18. _____ _____ _____ _____ are used for estimating future free cash flows, to plan for financing that will be required to execute operating plans, and to provide a basis for setting targets used in the firm's compensation plan.

19. A(n) _____ _____ is, in many ways, a condensed version of the firm's strategic plan.

20. Strategic plans usually begin with a statement of the overall _____ _____.

21. The _____ _____ set forth specific goals for management to attain.

22. The most commonly used technique for forecasting future balance sheets and income statements is the _____ ____ _____ method.

23. Companies often have what is called a(n) _____ _____ period, during which they can grow at rates higher than the long-term _____ growth rate.

24. Financial planning models allow managers to measure the expected change in value, or stock price, under different strategic and operating alternatives. This process is called _____-_____ _____.

Conceptual

25. An increase in a firm's inventory will call for additional financing unless the increase is offset by an equal or larger *decrease* in some other asset account.

   a. True   **b.** False

26. If the capital intensity ratio of a firm actually decreases as sales increase, use of the formula method will typically _overstate_ the amount of additional funds required, other things held constant.

   a. True   b. False

27. If the dividend payout ratio is 100 percent, all ratios are held constant, and the firm is operating at full capacity, then any increase in sales will require additional financing.

   a. True   b. False

28. One of the first steps in the percent of sales method of forecasting is to identify those asset and liability accounts that increase spontaneously with retained earnings.

   a. True   b. False

29. Which of the following would _reduce_ the additional funds required if all other things are held constant?

   a. An increase in the dividend payout ratio.
   b. A decrease in the profit margin.
   c. An increase in the capital intensity ratio.
   d. An increase in the expected sales growth rate.
   e. A decrease in the firm's tax rate.

30. Which of the following statements is most correct?

   a. Suppose economies of scale exist in a firm's use of assets. Under this condition, the firm should use the regression method of forecasting asset requirements rather than the percent of sales method.
   b. If a firm must acquire assets in lumpy units, it can avoid errors in forecasts of its need for funds by using the linear regression method of forecasting asset requirements because all the points will lie on the regression line.
   c. If economies of scale in the use of assets exist, then the AFN formula rather than the percent of sales method should be used to forecast additional funds requirements.
   d. Notes payable to banks are included in the AFN formula, along with a projection of retained earnings.
   e. One problem with the AFN formula is that it does not take account of the firm's dividend policy.

SELF-TEST PROBLEMS

1. United Products Inc. has the following balance sheet:

Current assets	$ 5,000	Accounts payable	$ 1,000
		Notes payable	1,000
Net fixed assets	5,000	Long-term debt	4,000
		Common equity	4,000
Total assets	$10,000	Total liabilities and equity	$10,000

Business has been slow; therefore, fixed assets are vastly underutilized. Management believes it can double sales next year with the introduction of a new product. No new fixed assets will be required, and management expects that there will be no earnings retained next year. What is next year's additional financing requirement?

a. $0 b. $4,000 c. $6,000 d. $13,000 e. $19,000

2. The 1998 balance sheet for American Pulp and Paper is shown below (in millions of dollars):

Cash	$ 3.0	Accounts payable	$ 2.0
Accounts receivable	3.0	Notes payable	1.5
Inventory	5.0		
Current assets	$11.0	Current liabilities	$ 3.5
Fixed assets	3.0	Long-term debt	3.0
		Common equity	7.5
Total assets	$14.0	Total liabilities and equity	$14.0

In 1998, sales were $60 million. In 1999, management believes that sales will increase by 20 percent to a total of $72 million. The profit margin is expected to be 5 percent, and the dividend payout ratio is targeted at 40 percent. No excess capacity exists. What is the additional financing requirement (in millions) for 1999 using the formula method?

a. $0.36 b. $0.24 c. $0 d. -$0.24 e. -$0.36

3. Refer to Self-Test Problem 2. How much can sales grow above the 1999 level of $60 million without requiring any additional funds?

a. 12.28% b. 14.63% c. 15.75% d. 17.65% e. 18.14%

4. Smith Machines Inc. has a net income this year of $500 on sales of $2,000 and is operating its fixed assets at full capacity. Management expects sales to increase by 25 percent next year and is forecasting a dividend payout ratio of 30 percent. The profit margin is not expected to change. If spontaneous liabilities are $500 this year and no excess funds are expected next year, what are Smith's total assets this year?

a. $1,000 **b.** $1,500 **c.** $2,250 **d.** $3,000 **e.** $3,500

(The following data apply to the next three Self-Test Problems.)

Crossley Products Company's 1998 financial statements are shown below:

Crossley Products Company
Balance Sheet as of December 31, 1998
(Thousands of Dollars)

Cash	$ 600	Accounts payable	$ 2,400
Receivables	3,600	Notes payable	1,157
Inventory	4,200	Accruals	840
Total current assets	$ 8,400	Total current liabilities	$ 4,397
		Mortgage bonds	1,667
		Common stock	667
Net fixed assets	7,200	Retained earnings	8,869
Total assets	$15,600	Total liabilities and equity	$15,600

Crossley Products Company
Income Statement for December 31, 1998
(Thousands of Dollars)

Sales	$12,000
Operating costs	10,261
EBIT	$ 1,739
Interest	339
Earnings before taxes	$ 1,400
Taxes (40%)	560
Net income	$ 840
Dividends (60%)	$ 504
Addition to retained earnings	$ 336

5. Assume that the company was operating at full capacity in 1998 with regard to all items except fixed assets; fixed assets in 1998 were utilized to only 75 percent of capacity. By what percentage could 1999 sales increase over 1998 sales without the need for an increase in fixed assets?

    a. 33%   **b.** 25%   **c.** 20%   **d.** 44%   **e.** 50%

6. Now suppose 1999 sales increase by 25 percent over 1998 sales. Assume that Crossley cannot sell any fixed assets. Use the percent of sales method to develop a pro forma balance sheet and income statement. Assume that any required financing is borrowed as notes payable, and ignore financing feedbacks. Use a pro forma income statement to determine the addition to retained earnings. How much additional external capital (in thousands) will be required?

    a. $825   **b.** $925   **c.** $750   **d.** $900   **e.** $850

7. Refer to Self-Test Problem 6. After the required financing is borrowed as notes payable, and ignoring any financing feedbacks, what is the firm's current and debt ratios?

    a. 1.73; 38.84%   **d.** 1.73; 43.64%
    b. 2.02; 38.84%   **e.** 2.02; 43.64%
    c. 1.73; 44.06%

(The following data apply to the next two Self-Test Problems.)

Taylor Technologies Inc.'s 1998 financial statements are shown below:

Taylor Technologies Inc.
Balance Sheet as of December 31, 1998

Cash	$ 90,000	Accounts payable	$ 180,000
Receivables	180,000	Notes payable	78,000
Inventory	360,000	Accruals	90,000
Total current assets	$ 630,000	Total current liabilities	$ 348,000
		Common stock	900,000
Net fixed assets	720,000	Retained earnings	102,000
Total assets	$1,350,000	Total liabilities and equity	$1,350,000

Taylor Technologies Inc.
Income Statement for December 31, 1998

Sales	$1,800,000
Operating costs	1,639,860
EBIT	$ 160,140
Interest	10,140
EBT	$ 150,000
Taxes (40%)	60,000
Net income	$ 90,000
Dividends (60%)	$ 54,000
Addition to retained earnings	$ 36,000

8. Suppose that in 1999, sales increase by 10 percent over 1998 sales. Construct the pro forma financial statements using the percent of sales method. Assume the firm operated at full capacity in 1998. How much additional capital will be required?

   a. $72,459 **b.** $70,211 **c.** $68,157 **d.** $66,445 **e.** $63,989

9. Refer to Self-Test Problem 8. Assume now that fixed assets are only being operated at 95 percent of capacity. Construct the proforma financial statements using the percent of sales method. How much additional capital will be required?

   a. $28,557 **b.** $32,400 **c.** $39,843 **d.** $45,400 **e.** $50,000

10. Your company's sales were $2,000 last year, and they are forecasted to rise by 50 percent during the coming year. Here is the latest balance sheet:

Cash	$ 100	Accounts payable	$ 200
Receivables	300	Notes payable	200
Inventory	800	Accruals	20
Total current assets	$ 1,200	Total current liabilities	$ 420
		Long-term debt	780
		Common stock	400
Net fixed Assets	800	Retained earnings	400
Total assets	$2,000	Total liabilities and equity	$2,000

Fixed assets were used to only 80 percent of capacity last year, and year-end inventory holdings were $100 greater than were needed to support the $2,000 of sales. The other current assets (cash and receivables) were at their proper levels. All assets would be a constant percentage of sales if excess capacity did not exist; that is, all assets would increase at the same rate as sales if no excess capacity existed. The company's profit margin will be 3 percent, and its payout ratio will be 80 percent. If all additional funds needed (AFN) are raised as notes payable and financing feedbacks are ignored, what will the current ratio be at the end of the coming year?

a. 2.47   b. 1.44   c. 1.21   d. 1.00   e. 1.63

11. The Bouchard Company's sales are forecasted to increase from $500 in 1998 to $1,000 in 1999. Here is the December 31, 1998, balance sheet:

Cash	$ 50	Accounts payable	$ 25
Receivables	100	Notes payable	75
Inventory	100	Accruals	25
Total current assets	$250	Total current liabilities	$125
		Long-term debt	200
		Common stock	50
Net fixed assets	250	Retained earnings	125
Total assets	$500	Total liabilities and equity	$500

Bouchard's fixed assets were used to only 50 percent of capacity during 1998, but its current assets were at their proper levels. All assets except fixed assets should be a constant percentage of sales, and fixed assets would also increase at the same rate if the current excess capacity did not exist. Bouchard's profit margin is forecasted to be 8 percent, and its payout ratio will be 40 percent. What is Bouchard's additional funds needed (AFN) for the coming year?

a. $102   b. $152   c. $197   d. $167   e. $183

ANSWERS TO SELF-TEST QUESTIONS

1. liabilities; equity
2. spontaneously; payable; accruals
3. Bonds; preferred; common; retained
4. payout ratio; decreased
5. profit margin
6. capital intensity ratio
7. external
8. percent of sales; additional funds needed
9. lumpy; economies
10. percent of sales; formula
11. financing feedbacks
12. iterative

13. greater
14. regression; excess capacity
15. Full capacity sales
16. fixed assets; sales
17. target; fixed assets
18. Pro forma financial statements
19. mission statement
20. corporate purpose
21. corporate objectives
22. percent of sales
23. competitive advantage; sustainable
24. value-based management

25. a. When an increase in one asset account is not offset by an equivalent decrease in another asset account, then financing is needed to reestablish equilibrium on the balance sheet. Note, though, that this additional financing may come from a spontaneous increase in accounts payable or from retained earnings.

26. a. A decreasing capital intensity ratio, A^*/S_0, means that fewer assets are required, proportionately, as sales increase. Thus, the external funding requirement is overstated. Always keep in mind that the formula method assumes that the asset/sales ratio is constant regardless of the level of sales.

27. a. With a 100 percent payout ratio, there will be no retained earnings. When operating at full capacity, *all* assets are spontaneous, but *all* liabilities cannot be spontaneous since a firm must have common equity. Thus, the growth in assets cannot be matched by a growth in spontaneous liabilities, so additional financing will be required in order to keep the financial ratios (the debt ratio in particular) constant.

28. b. The first step is to identify those accounts which increase spontaneously with sales.

29. e. Answers a through d would increase the additional funds required, but a decrease in the tax rate would raise the profit margin and thus increase the amount of available retained earnings.

30. a. Statement a is correct; economies of scale cause the ratios to change over time, which violates the assumption of the percent of sales method. Statement b is false; the points will not all lie on the regression line. Statement c is false; the AFN formula requires a constant percentage of sales over time. Statement d is false; the AFN formula includes only spontaneous liabilities, and notes payable do not spontaneously increase with sales. Statement e is false; the AFN formula includes the dividend payout, so dividend policy is included.

SOLUTIONS TO SELF-TEST PROBLEMS

1. b. Look at next year's balance sheet:

Current assets	$10,000	Accounts payable	$ 2,000
Net fixed assets	5,000	Notes payable	1,000
		Current liabilities	$ 3,000
		Long-Term debt	4,000
		Common equity	4,000
			$11,000
		AFN	4,000
Total assets	$15,000	Total liabilities and equity	$15,000

With no retained earnings next year, the common equity account remains at $4,000. Thus, the additional financing requirement is $15,000 − $11,000 = $4,000.

2. b. None of the items on the right side of the balance sheet rises spontaneously with sales except accounts payable. Therefore,

$$\text{AFN} = (A^*/S_0)(\Delta S) - (L^*/S_0)(\Delta S) - MS_1(1-d)$$
$$= (\$14/\$60)(\$12) - (\$2/\$60)(\$12) - (0.05)(\$72)(0.6)$$
$$= \$2.8 - \$0.4 - \$2.16 = \$0.24 \text{ million.}$$

The firm will need $240,000 in additional funds to support the increase in sales.

3.   d.   Note that g = Sales growth = $\Delta S/S_0$ and $S_1 = S_0(1 + g)$. Then,

$$
\begin{aligned}
AFN = \quad A^*g - L^*g - M[(S_0)(1 + g)](1 - d) \ &= 0 \\
\$14g - \$2g - 0.05[(\$60)(1 + g)](0.6) \ &= 0 \\
\$12g - [(\$3 + \$3g)(0.60)] \ &= 0 \\
\$12g - \$1.8 - \$1.8g \ &= 0 \\
\$10.20g \ &= \$1.80 \\
g \ &= 0.1765 = 17.65\%.
\end{aligned}
$$

4.   c.

$$
\begin{aligned}
0 &= (A^*/S_0)(\Delta S) - (L^*/S_0)(\Delta S) - MS_1(1 - d) \\
0 &= (A^*/\$2,000)(\$500) - (\$500/\$2,000)(\$500) - (\$500/\$2,000)(\$2,500)(1 - 0.3) \\
0 &= (\$500A^*/\$2,000) - \$125 - \$437.50 \\
0 &= (\$500A^*/\$2,000) - \$562.50 \\
\$562.50 &= 0.25A^* \\
A^* &= \$2,250.
\end{aligned}
$$

5.   a. $\dfrac{\text{Full capacity sales}}{} = \dfrac{\text{Actual sales}}{\text{\% of capacity at which FA were operated}} = \dfrac{\$12,000}{0.75} = \$16,000.$

$\dfrac{\text{Percent increase}}{} = \dfrac{\text{New sales} - \text{Old sales}}{\text{Old sales}} = \dfrac{\$16,000 - \$12,000}{\$12,000} = 0.33 = 33\%.$

Therefore, sales could expand by 33 percent before Crossley Products would need to add fixed assets.

6.   e.

Crossley Products Company
Pro Forma Income Statement
December 31, 1999
(Thousands of Dollars)

	1998	Forecast Basis[a]	1999 Forecast
Sales	$12,000	1.25	$15,000
Operating costs	10,261	0.8551	12,826
EBIT	$ 1,739		$ 2,174
Interest	339		339
EBT	$ 1,400		$ 1,835
Taxes (40%)	560		734
Net income	$ 840		$ 1,101
Dividends (60%)	$ 504		$ 661
Addition to RE	$ 336		$ 440

Crossley Products Company
Pro Forma Balance Sheet
December 31, 1999
(Thousands of Dollars)

	1998	Forecast Basis[a]	1999 Forecast	AFN	1999 After AFN
Cash	$ 600	0.05	$ 750		$ 750
Receivables	3,600	0.30	4,500		4,500
Inventory	4,200	0.35	5,250		5,250
Total current assets	$ 8,400		$10,500		$10,500
Net fixed assets	7,200		7,200[b]		7,200
Total assets	$15,600		$17,700		$17,700
Accts. payable	$ 2,400	0.20	$ 3,000		$ 3,000
Notes payable	1,157		1,157	+850	2,007
Accruals	840	0.07	1,050		1,050
Total current liab.	$ 4,397		$ 5,207		$ 6,057
Mortgage bonds	1,667		1,667		1,667
Common stock	667		667		667
Retained earnings	8,869	440[c]	9,309		9,309
Total liabilities and equity	$15,600		$16,850		$17,700
		AFN =	$ 850		

Notes:

[a]Sales are increased by 25%. Operating costs, all assets except fixed assets, accruals, and accounts payable are divided by 1998 sales to determine the appropriate ratios to apply to 1999 sales to calculate 1999 account balances.

[b]From Self-Test Problem 5 we know that sales can increase by 33 percent before additions to fixed assets are needed.

[c]See income statement.

7.   d.   Current ratio $= CA/CL$

$\qquad\qquad\quad= \$10,500/\$6,057$

$\qquad\qquad\quad= 1.73.$

$$\text{Debt/Asset ratio} = \frac{(\$6,057 + \$1,667)}{\$17,700}$$

$$= 43.64\%.$$

8.   c.   The projected balance sheet indicates that the AFN = $68,157.

Taylor Technologies Inc.
Pro Forma Income Statement
December 31, 1999

	1998	Forecast Basis[a]	1999 Forecast
Sales	$1,800,000	1.10	$1,980,000
Operating costs	1,639,860	0.9110	1,803,846
EBIT	$ 160,140		$ 176,154
Interest	10,140		10,140
EBT	$ 150,000		$ 166,014
Taxes (40%)	60,000		66,406
Net income	$ 90,000		$ 99,608
Dividends (60%)	$ 54,000		$ 59,765
Addition to RE	$ 36,000		$ 39,843

Taylor Technologies Inc.
Pro Forma Balance Sheet
December 31, 1999

	1998	Forecast Basis[a]	1999 Forecast
Cash	$ 90,000	0.05	$ 99,000
Receivables	180,000	0.10	198,000
Inventory	360,000	0.20	396,000
Total current assets	$ 630,000		$ 693,000
Net fixed assets	720,000	0.40	792,000
Total assets	$1,350,000		$1,485,000
Accts. payable	$ 180,000	0.10	$ 198,000
Notes payable	78,000		78,000
Accruals	90,000	0.05	99,000
Total current liabilities	$ 348,000		$ 375,000
Common stock	900,000		900,000
Ret. Earnings	102,000	39,843[b]	141,843
Total liabilities and equity	$1,350,000		$1,416,843
		AFN =	$ 68,157

Notes:

[a]Sales are increased by 10%. Operating costs, all assets, accruals, and accounts payable are divided by 1998 sales to determine the appropriate ratios to apply to 1999 sales to calculate 1999 account balances.

[b]See income statement.

9. a.

Taylor Technologies Inc.
Pro Forma Income Statement
December 31, 1999

	1998	Forecast Basis[a]	1999 Forecast
Sales	$1,800,000	1.10	$1,980,000
Operating costs	1,639,860	0.9110	1,803,846
EBIT	$ 160,140		$ 176,154
Interest	10,140		10,140
EBT	$ 150,000		$ 166,014
Taxes (40%)	60,000		66,406
Net income	$ 90,000		$ 99,608
Dividends (60%)	$ 54,000		$ 59,765
Addition to RE	$ 36,000		$ 39,843

Taylor Technologies Inc.
Pro Forma Balance Sheet
December 31, 1999

	1998	Forecast Basis[a]	1999 Forecast
Cash	$ 90,000	0.05	$ 99,000
Receivables	180,000	0.10	198,000
Inventory	360,000	0.20	396,000
Total current assets	$ 630,000		$ 693,000
Net fixed assets	720,000	32,400[b]	752,400
Total assets	$1,350,000		$1,445,400
Accts. payable	$ 180,000	0.10	$ 198,000
Notes payable	78,000		78,000
Accruals	90,000	0.05	99,000
Total current liabilities	$ 348,000		$ 375,000
Common stock	900,000		900,000
Ret. earnings	102,000	39,843[c]	141,843
Total liabilities and equity	$1,350,000		$1,416,843
		AFN =	$ 28,557

Notes:

[a]Sales are increased by 10%. Operating costs, all assets except fixed assets, accruals, and accounts payable are divided by 1998 sales to determine the appropriate ratios to apply to 1999 sales to calculate 1999 account balances.

$$^{b}\text{Full capacity sales} = \frac{\$1,800,000}{0.95} = \$1,894,737.$$

$$\text{Target fixed assets/ Sales ratio} = \frac{\$720,000}{\$1,894,737} = 38\%.$$

$$\text{Required level of fixed assets} = 0.38(\$1,980,000)$$

$$= \$752,400.$$

Necessary FA increase = $752,400 - $720,000 = $32,400.

[c]See income statement.

10. e.

	Current Year	Forecast Basis[a]	1st Pass	AFN	2nd Pass
Cash	$ 100	0.05	$ 150		$ 150
Receivables	300	0.15	450		450
Inventory	800	+250[b]	1,050		1,050
Total curr. assets	$1,200		$1,650		$1,650
Net fixed assets	800	+160[c]	960		960
Total assets	$2,000		$2,610		$2,610
Accts. Payable	$ 200	0.10	$ 300		$ 300
Notes payable	200		200	+482	682
Accruals	20	0.01	30		30
Total curr. liab.	$ 420		$ 530		$1,012
Long-term debt	780		780		780
Common stock	400		400		400
Ret. Earnings	400	+ 18[d]	418		418
Total liab./equity	$2,000		$2,128		$2,610

AFN = $ 482

Notes:

[a]Cash, receivables, accounts payable, and accruals are divided by current year's sales to determine the appropriate ratios to apply to next year's sales to calculate next year's account balances.

[b]Target inventory/assets = ($800 − $100)/$2,000 = 35%.
Target inventory level = 0.35($3,000) = $1,050.
Since we already have $800 of inventories, we need:
Additional inventories = $1,050 − $800 = $250.

[c]Capacity sales = Sales/Capacity factor = $2,000/0.8 = $2,500.
Target FA/S ratio = FA/Capacity sales = $800/$2,500 = 32%.
Required FA = (Target ratio)(Forecasted sales) = 0.32($3,000) = $960.
Since we already have $800 of fixed assets, we need:
Additional fixed assets = $960 − $800 = $160.

[d]Additions to RE = $M(S_1)(1 − \text{Payout ratio}) = 0.03($3,000)(0.2) = $18.$

The problem asks for the forecasted current ratio which is calculated as:
Forecasted current ratio = $1,650/$1,012 = 1.6304.

11.   b.

	1998	Forecast Basis[a]	1st Pass 1999
Cash	$ 50	0.10	$100
Receivables	100	0.20	200
Inventory	100	0.20	200
Total current assets	$250		$500
Net fixed assets	250	+0[b]	250
Total assets	$500		$750
Accounts payable	$ 25	0.05	$ 50
Notes payable	75		75
Accruals	25	0.05	50
Total current liabilities	$125		$175
Long-term debt	200		200
Common stock	50		50
Retained earnings	125	+48[c]	173
Total claims	$500		$598

AFN = $152

Notes:

[a]Cash, receivables, inventory, accounts payable, and accruals are divided by 1998 sales to determine the appropriate ratios to apply to 1999 sales to calculate 1999 account balances.

[b]Capacity sales = Actual sales/Capacity factor = $500/0.5 = $1,000.
  Target FA/S ratio = $250/$1,000 = 0.25.
  Target FA = 0.25($1,000) = $250 = Required fixed assets.
  Since Bouchard currently has $250 of FA, no new FA will be required.

[c]Addition to RE = $M(S_1)(1 - \text{Payout ratio}) = 0.08(\$1,000)(0.6) = \$48$.

OVERVIEW

One of the most perplexing issues facing financial managers is the relationship between capital structure, which is the mix of debt and equity financing, and stock prices. How does capital structure affect stock prices and the cost of capital? Should different industries, and different firms within industries, have different capital structures, and, if so, what factors lead to these differences? The next two chapters discuss both the theories that underlie capital structure decisions and more pragmatic approaches to the problem. Although the optimal capital structure decision is complex, and far from precise, an understanding of these chapters will help you deal with the issues involved.

OUTLINE

Two additional dimensions of risk are business risk and financial risk. Business and financial risk are examined within a stand-alone framework, which ignores the benefits of stockholder diversification.

- ■ *Business risk* is the riskiness of the firm's stock if it uses no debt.
  - ☐ This is the risk inherent in a firm's operations.

- ■ *Financial risk* is the additional risk placed on the common stockholders as a result of the firm's decision to use debt.

Business risk, in a stand-alone sense, is a function of the uncertainty inherent in projections of a firm's future return on invested capital (ROIC).

- ■ Return on invested capital (ROIC) is defined as follows:

$$\text{ROIC} = \frac{\text{NOPAT}}{\text{Capital}} = \frac{\text{Net income to common stockholders} + \text{After-tax interest payments}}{\text{Capital}}.$$

  - ☐ At zero debt ROIC = ROE.

■   The business risk of a *leverage-free firm* can be measured by the standard deviation of its ROE, σ_{ROE}.

■   Business risk varies not only from industry to industry but also among firms in a given industry. Further, business risk can change over time.

■   Business risk depends on a number of factors, the more important ones are listed below:
   ☐ Demand variability
   ☐ Sales price variability
   ☐ Input cost variability
   ☐ Ability to adjust output prices for changes in input costs
   ☐ Ability to develop new products in a timely, cost-effective manner
   ☐ Foreign risk exposure
   ☐ Extent to which costs are fixed: operating leverage

■   Each of these factors is determined partly by the firm's industry characteristics, but each of them is also controllable to some extent by management.
   ☐ Many firms also are using hedging techniques to reduce business risk.

■   *Operating leverage* is the degree to which a firm uses fixed cost inputs (as opposed to variable cost inputs) in its production processes.
   ☐ Firms that have a higher percentage of their total costs as fixed costs are said to have a high degree of operating leverage.
   ☐ Higher fixed costs are generally associated with more highly automated, capital intensive firms and industries.
   ☐ A high degree of operating leverage, other factors held constant, implies that a relatively small change in sales results in a large change in ROE.
   ☐ Other things held constant, the higher a firm's operating leverage, the higher its business risk (in a stand-alone sense).
   ☐ Production technology limits control over the amount of fixed costs and hence operating leverage. However, firms do have some control over the type of production processes they employ. Therefore, a firm's capital budgeting decisions can influence its operating leverage, hence its business risk.
   ☐ The breakeven quantity, Q_{BE}, is calculated as $Q_{BE} = F/(P - V)$.

Financial risk is the additional risk placed on the common stockholders as a result of the decision to finance with debt.

■   The use of debt concentrates the firm's business risk on its common stockholders.
   ☐ This concentration of business risk occurs because debtholders, who receive fixed interest payments, bear none of the business risk.

The use of financial leverage also increases the risk faced by the equity investors, and this higher risk will tend to offset the benefits of debt.

The greater the use of financial leverage, the more sensitive ROE is to changes in EBIT.

The use of debt increases a firm's expected ROE, provided the expected return on invested capital exceeds the after-tax interest rate.

The standard deviation of ROE if the firm uses zero financial leverage, $\sigma_{ROE(U)}$, is a measure of the firm's business risk, and σ_{ROE} at any debt level is a measure of the stand-alone risk borne by stockholders.

If the firm does not use any financial leverage, then $\sigma_{ROE} = \sigma_{ROE(U)}$.

If the firm does use debt, then $\sigma_{ROE} > \sigma_{ROE(U)}$, because business risk is being concentrated on stockholders.

$$\text{Financial risk} = \text{Stand-alone risk} - \text{Business risk} = \sigma_{ROE} - \sigma_{ROE(U)}.$$

Operating leverage and financial leverage normally work in the same way; both generally increase expected ROE, but they also increase the risk borne by stockholders.
- Operating leverage affects the firm's business risk, financial leverage affects the firm's financial risk, and both affect the firm's stand-alone risk.

Modern capital structure theory began in 1958, when Professors Franco Modigliani and Merton Miller (MM) published what has been called the most influential finance article ever written.

MM proved, but under a very restrictive set of assumptions, that a firm's value is unaffected by its capital structure. Thus, MM's results suggest that it does not matter how a firm finances its operations, because at least under their assumptions capital structure is irrelevant.

By indicating the conditions under which capital structure is irrelevant, MM provided us with some clues about what is required for capital structure to be relevant and hence to affect a firm's value. Consequently, MM's work was only the beginning of capital structure research, and subsequent research has focused on relaxing the MM assumptions to develop a more realistic theory of capital structure.

MM published a follow-up paper in which they relaxed the assumption that there are no corporate taxes. MM demonstrated that if all of their other assumptions hold, this differential treatment of the tax deductibility of interest versus the non-deductibility of dividend payments leads to a situation which calls for 100 percent debt financing.

■ Merton Miller then analyzed the effects of personal taxes. While an increase in the corporate tax rate makes debt look better to corporations because interest is tax deductible, an increase in the personal tax rate encourages additional equity financing because of the favorable capital gains tax treatment on stocks.

☐ It is difficult to say what the net effect of these two factors is. Most observers believe that interest deductibility has the stronger effect, hence that our tax system still favors the corporate use of debt.

■ Bankruptcy-related problems are most likely to arise when a firm has a lot of debt in its capital structure. Therefore, potential bankruptcy costs discourage firms from pushing their use of debt to excessive levels.

☐ Bankruptcy-related costs depend on three things: (1) the probability of bankruptcy, (2) the costs the firm will incur if financial distress arises, and (3) the adverse effects that the potential for bankruptcy has on current operations.

☐ Firms whose earnings are more volatile, all else equal, face a greater chance of bankruptcy and, therefore, should use less debt than more stable firms.

☐ Firms which would face high costs in the event of financial distress should rely less heavily on debt.

☐ A firm whose value primarily is due to growth opportunities and not to assets in place suffers from both a high cost of financial distress and from adverse effects on current operations.

■ The *trade-off theory of leverage* recognizes that firms trade off the *benefits* of debt financing (favorable corporate tax treatment) against higher interest rates and bankruptcy costs.

☐ Debt provides *tax shelter benefits* because interest is deductible.

☐ A disturbing empirical contradiction to capital structure theory is the fact that many large, successful firms use far less debt than the theory suggests. This point led to the development of the signaling theory.

■ *Signaling theory* recognizes the fact that investors and managers do *not* have the same information regarding a firm's prospects, as was assumed by the trade-off theory. This is called *asymmetric information*, and it has an important effect on the optimal capital structure.

☐ One would expect a firm with very favorable prospects to try to avoid selling stock and, rather, to raise any required new capital by other means, including using debt beyond the normal optimal capital structure.

- Firms with extremely good prospects prefer to finance with debt, whereas firms with poor prospects like to finance with stock.
  ☐ The announcement of a stock offering by a mature firm that has financing alternatives is taken as a signal that the firm's prospects as seen by its management are not bright.
  ☐ The implications of the signaling theory for capital structure decisions is that firms should, in normal times, maintain a *reserve borrowing capacity* which can be used in the event that some especially good investment opportunity comes along.
    - This means that firms should, in normal times, use less debt than is suggested by the tax benefit/bankruptcy cost trade-off model.

■ Agency conflicts are particularly likely when the firm's managers have too much cash at their disposal.
  ☐ Managers with constraints on free cash flow, such as commitments to make interest and principal payments, are less able to make wasteful expenditures. This is called *bonding* the free cash flow.

■ Firms can reduce, or bond, cash flow in a variety of ways:
  ☐ Funnel cash back to shareholders through higher dividends or stock repurchases.
  ☐ Shift the capital structure toward more debt in the hope that higher debt service requirements will force managers to become more disciplined. If debt is not serviced as required, the firm will be forced into bankruptcy.
    - *A leveraged buyout (LBO)* is one way to achieve this. An LBO bonds free cash flow by placing constraints on the cash flow.

■ Increasing debt to bond free cash flow has a downside: It increases the risk of bankruptcy, which can be costly.

■ In practice, capital structure decisions must be made by combining judgment and numerical analysis. An understanding of the theoretical issues can help you make better judgments on capital structure issues.

Capital structure theory suggests that each firm has an optimal capital structure, one that maximizes its value and minimizes its overall cost of capital. However, research on capital structure theory points out that there are many contradictory issues regarding capital structure decisions, and that theory cannot be used to specify a precisely optimal structure for a firm. However, one can get an idea of the capital structure range by quantitative analysis.

■ First, the costs of debt and equity are estimated for different debt levels, holding total assets constant.

■ As more debt is used, the estimated costs of debt and equity will rise, because the riskiness of these capital components is increasing.

■ The estimated component costs are then combined to find the weighted average cost of capital at each debt level.

■ The debt amount which produces the lowest overall weighted average cost of capital (WACC) is *optimal*, and this is the firm's *target capital structure*, because that capital structure which *minimizes* a firm's weighted average cost of capital also *maximizes* its stock price.

■ If one assumes that the firm's cash flows are perpetuities (a no-growth firm), the following equations can be used to determine a firm's total market value at different capital structures, and then to use this information to establish the firm's stock price as a function of its capital structure. This analysis focuses on the impact of leverage on a firm's total value and its stock price.

  □ Firm value: $V = D + S$.
  □ Equity value: $S = [(EBIT - k_dD)(1 - T)]/k_s$.
  □ Stock price: $P_0 = DPS/k_s = EPS/k_s$.
  □ Cost of capital: $WACC = (D/V)(k_d)(1 - T) + (S/V)(k_s)$.

■ EBIT is independent of financial leverage at "reasonable" debt levels, but at extreme degrees of leverage, EBIT is adversely affected.

■ Quite obviously, the situation in the real world is much more complex and less exact.

■ Although expected EPS is much higher if the firm uses financial leverage, the risk of low, or even negative, EPS is also higher if debt is used. Using leverage involves a risk/return tradeoff—higher leverage increases expected EPS, but it also increases the firm's risk. It is this increasing risk that causes k_s and k_d to increase at higher amounts of financial leverage.

■ Price per share and EPS will not both be maximized at the same debt level. Since management is primarily interested in *maximizing shareholder wealth*, the optimal capital structure should be based on value, or share price, and not on EPS.

■ Although conceptually simple, it is impossible to place much faith in these quantitative results, since (1) the values for k_d and k_s are very difficult to estimate; (2) the models are very sensitive to input estimates; (3) the quantitative analysis was restricted to the case of a no-growth firm; and (4) many firms are not publicly owned which causes still more difficulties.

Since one cannot determine a precise optimal capital structure, managers must apply judgment to their quantitative analyses. Several different factors should be taken into account in the judgmental analysis.

■   Managers often view financial distress with more concern than well-diversified investors because managers are typically not well diversified, and their careers, and thus the present value of their expected earnings, can be seriously affected by the onset of financial distress. Thus, it is not difficult to imagine that managers might be more "conservative" (*managerial conservatism*) in their use of leverage and might set a lower target capital structure than the one which maximizes stock price that the average stockholder would desire.

■   *Lenders' and rating agencies' attitudes* are frequently important determinants of financial structures.
   □   Lenders and rating agencies focus on *coverage ratios* to measure the risk of financial distress.
   □   Accordingly, considerable importance is placed on a firm's *times-interest-earned (TIE) ratio*:

$$\text{TIE} = \text{EBIT/Interest charges.}$$

   ●   The lower this ratio, the higher the probability that a firm will encounter financial distress.
   □   Another measure that is often used is the fixed charge coverage (FCC) ratio:

$$\text{FCC} = \frac{\text{EBIT} + \text{Lease payments}}{\underset{\text{charges}}{\text{Interest}} + \underset{\text{payments}}{\text{Lease}} + \dfrac{\text{Sinking fund payments}}{1 - T}}.$$

   ●   This ratio recognizes that there are fixed financial charges other than interest payments which could lead to financial distress.
   ●   *Sinking fund payments* are mandatory payments made to reduce debt. Note that this definition "grosses up" the sinking fund payments in recognition of the fact that these payments are made with after-tax dollars (net income). Interest and lease payments are fully deductible, hence they do not need to be grossed up.

■   Firms should maintain *reserve borrowing capacity* and *financing flexibility* to preserve their ability to issue debt on favorable terms. To maintain reserve borrowing capacity that permits new debt financings at favorable terms on short notice, firms generally use less debt under "normal" conditions, thus presenting a stronger financial picture than they would otherwise have. This is not suboptimal from a long-run standpoint.

■   The effect of debt on a management's *control position* may also influence the capital structure decision.

☐ If a firm's management just barely has majority control, but is not in a position to buy any more stock, debt may be the choice for new financing.

☐ A management group that is not concerned about voting control may decide to use equity rather than debt if the financial situation is so weak that the use of debt might subject the company to a serious risk of default.

☐ Control considerations do not necessarily suggest the use of debt or of equity, but the effects of financing decisions on control must certainly be taken into account.

■   The following additional considerations are relevant to the capital structure decision:

☐ *Business risk.* A firm that has relatively low business risk can take on more debt than can firms with high business risk.

☐ *Asset structure.* Firms whose assets are suitable as security for loans tend to use debt rather heavily.

☐ *Growth rate.* Firms with high growth rates need lots of capital. Since flotation costs are generally considerably lower for debt than for equity, rapidly growing firms tend to use somewhat more debt than slower-growth firms.

☐ *Profitability.* Firms that are highly profitable often have very low debt ratios. Although there is no theoretical justification, such firms simply do not need to sell much debt—they can do most of their financing through retained earnings.

☐ *Taxes.* The higher the firm's marginal tax rate, the greater the advantage of using debt.

☐ *Market conditions.* Conditions in the stock and bond markets undergo both long- and short-run changes that can affect a firm's optimal capital structure.

A pragmatic approach to setting the target capital structure requires judgmental assumptions, but it also requires managers to consider how alternative capital structures would affect future profitability, coverage, and external financing requirements under a variety of assumptions.

■   The starting point for the analysis is a forecasting model set up to test the effects of capital structure changes.

■   The financial manager begins by entering base year values plus data on expected unit sales growth rates, expected inflation rates, and other known or estimated operating input data.

■   Next, the debt/equity mix, the debt maturity structure, and the component costs of the capital must be entered. Note that the component costs must reflect the particular capital structure being analyzed—the higher the debt ratio, the higher the component costs.

■   The model then forecasts balance sheets and income statements, as well as ROE, EPS, DPS, WACC, and projected stock prices for a specified number of years.

■   The model is then used to analyze alternative scenarios. This analysis takes two forms: (1) changing the financing inputs to get an idea about how the financing mix affects the key outputs and (2) changing the operating inputs to see how economic conditions affect the key outputs under various financing strategies.

■   The model's outputs must be reviewed and analyzed, and a decision must be made as to the best capital structure. Particular attention should be paid to forecasted EPS, interest coverage, external funding requirements, and projected stock price.

■   It should be noted that while capital structure decisions do affect stock prices, those effects are generally small in comparison to the effects of operating decisions. Financial arrangements can facilitate or hamper operations, but the best of financial plans cannot overcome deficiencies in the operations area.

SELF-TEST QUESTIONS

Definitional

1.   High operating leverage implies that a relatively _____ change in sales will result in a large change in ROE.

2.   Business risk, in a stand-alone sense, is a function of the uncertainty inherent in projections of a firm's future _____ ____ _____ _____.

3.   One of the many factors that influence a firm's business risk is the extent to which costs are fixed, which is called _____ _____.

4.   Business risk represents the riskiness of the firm's operations if it uses no _____; financial risk represents the risk concentrated on the common stockholders as a result of using _____.

5.   Up to some point, expected EPS _____ as the debt/assets ratio increases.

6.   MM proved, but under a very restrictive set of assumptions, that a firm's value is unaffected by its _____ _____.

7.   Higher fixed costs are generally associated with more highly automated, _____ _____ firms and industries.

8.   MM demonstrated that if they relaxed the no tax assumption, and if all of their other assumptions held, the differential treatment of the tax deductibility of interest versus the non-deductibility of dividend payments leads to a situation which calls for 100 percent _____ financing.

9.   While an increase in the corporate tax rate makes _____ look better to corporations because _____ is tax deductible, an increase in the personal tax rate encourages additional _____ financing.

10.   _____ _____ discourage firms from pushing their use of debt to excessive levels.

11.   The _____-_____ theory of leverage recognizes the benefits of debt financing (favorable corporate tax treatment) versus higher interest rates and bankruptcy costs.

12.   _____ theory recognizes the fact that investors and managers do not have the same information regarding a firm's prospects.   This is called _____ _____, and it has an important effect on the optimal capital structure.

13.   The implications of the signaling theory for capital structure decisions is that firms should, in normal times, maintain _____ _____ _____ which can be used in the event that some especially good investment opportunity comes along.

14.   _____ _____ are particularly likely when the firm's managers have too much cash at their disposal.

15.   Firms whose assets are suitable as security for loans tend to use _____ rather heavily.

16.   The higher the firm's marginal tax rate, the _____ the advantage of using debt.

17.   While capital structure decisions do affect stock prices, those effects are generally small in comparison to the effects of _____ decisions.

18.   The same debt ratio that maximizes firm value also _____ the firm's cost of capital.

Conceptual

19. Firm A has higher business risk than Firm B. Firm A can offset this by increasing its operating leverage.

    a. True   **b.** False

20. Two firms, although operating in different industries, have the same expected ROE and the same standard deviation of expected ROE. Thus, in a stand-alone risk sense, the two firms must have the same financial risk.

    a. True   **b.** False

21. Assume a firm has zero debt. The use of some debt is bound to increase ROE.

    a. True   **b.** False

22. If a firm does use financial leverage, then $\sigma_{ROE} > \sigma_{ROE(U)}$, and the difference between the two is a measure of financial risk.

    a. True   **b.** False

23. Both price per share and EPS will be maximized at the same debt level; therefore, the optimal capital structure is determined at the debt level where both price and EPS are maximized.

    a. True   **b.** False

24. A decrease in the debt ratio will have _no_ effect on

    a. Financial risk.
    b. Stand-alone risk.
    c. Business risk.
    d. Market risk.
    e. Company-specific risk.

25. As a general rule, the capital structure that maximizes stock price also

 a. Maximizes the weighted average cost of capital.
 b. Maximizes EPS.
 c. Maximizes bankruptcy costs.
 d. Minimizes the weighted average cost of capital.
 e. Minimizes the required rate of return on equity.

26. Which of the following statements is most correct?

 a. If a firm is exposed to a high degree of business risk as a result of its high operating leverage, then it probably should offset this risk by using a larger-than-average amount of financial leverage. This follows because debt has a lower after-tax cost than equity.
 b. Financial risk can be reduced by replacing common equity with preferred stock.
 c. MM proved, under a very restrictive set of assumptions, that a firm's value is affected by its capital structure; therefore, it does matter how a firm finances its operations.
 d. The capital structure which minimizes the WACC also maximizes the firm's stock price and its total value, but generally not its expected EPS. One reason why debt is beneficial is that it shelters operating income from taxes, while a disadvantage of excessive debt has to do with costs associated with bankruptcy and financial distress generally.
 e. All of the statements above are false.

SELF-TEST PROBLEMS

1. The Fisher Company will produce 50,000 10-gallon aquariums next year. Variable costs will equal 40 percent of dollar sales, while fixed costs total $100,000. At what price must each aquarium be sold for the firm's EBIT to be $90,000?

 a. $5.00   b. $5.33   c. $5.50   d. $6.00   e. $6.33

2. The Diamond Company has identified two methods of producing playing cards. One method involves using a machine having a fixed cost of $20,000 and variable costs of $1.00 per deck. The other method would use a less expensive machine having a fixed cost of $5,000, but it would require variable costs of $2.00 per deck. If the selling price per deck will be the same under each method, at what level of output would the two methods produce the same net operating income (EBIT)?

 a. 5,000   b. 10,000   c. 15,000   d. 20,000   e. 25,000

3. Brown Products is a new firm just starting operations. The firm will produce backpacks which will sell for $22.00 each. Fixed costs are $500,000 per year, and variable costs are $2.00 per unit of production. The company expects to sell 50,000 backpacks per year, and its effective federal-plus-state tax rate is 40 percent. Brown needs $2 million to build facilities, obtain working capital, and start operations. If Brown borrows part of the money, the interest charges will depend on the amount borrowed as follows:

Amount Borrowed	Percentage of Debt in Capital Structure	Interest Rate on Total Amount Borrowed
$ 200,000	10%	9.00%
400,000	20	9.50
600,000	30	10.00
800,000	40	15.00
1,000,000	50	19.00
1,200,000	60	26.00

Assume that stock can be sold at a price of $20 per share on the initial offering, regardless of how much debt the company uses. Then after the company begins operating, its price will be determined as a multiple of its earnings per share. The multiple (or the P/E ratio) will depend upon the capital structure as follows:

Debt/Assets	P/E	Debt/Assets	P/E
0.0%	12.5×	40.0%	8.0×
10.0	12.0	50.0	6.0
20.0	11.5	60.0	5.0
30.0	10.0		

What is Brown's optimal capital structure, which maximizes stock price, as measured by the debt/assets ratio?

a. 10%   **b.** 20%   **c.** 30%   **d.** 40%   **e.** 50%

(The following data apply to the next six Self-Test Problems.)

United Producers (UP), an unleveraged firm, has a total market value of $10 million, consisting of 500,000 shares of common stock selling at $20 per share. Management is considering issuing $2 million of debt at a before-tax cost of 12 percent, and using the proceeds to repurchase stock at the new equilibrium market price. If the plan is carried out, the required rate of return on equity will increase by 2 percentage points to 16 percent. UP's marginal tax rate is 40 percent, and it pays out all earnings as dividends.

4. What are UP's earnings before interest and taxes (EBIT) in millions of dollars?

a. $1.4   **b.** $2.3   **c.** $3.0   **d.** $3.6   **e.** $4.2

5.	Regardless of your answer to Self-Test Problem 4, assume that UP's EBIT is $2,800,000. What is the value of the firm in millions of dollars if the restructuring occurs?

    a. $9.76   **b.** $10.00   **c.** $10.56   **d.** $11.00   **e.** $11.60

6.	Suppose a tax law change occurs which causes UP's marginal tax rate to decline to 30 percent. UP's EBIT remains at $2.8 million. Under these conditions, what is the value of the firm in millions of dollars at zero debt?

    a. $10   **b.** $11   **c.** $12   **d.** $13   **e.** $14

7.	Under the conditions of Self-Test Problem 6, what is the value of the firm in millions of dollars if restructuring occurs?

    a. $13.2   **b.** $14.0   **c.** $14.2   **d.** $14.6   **e.** $14.8

8.	Disregard the tax change in Self-Test Problem 6 and refer to the data in the original problem. Assume these data are correct, including an assumed EBIT of $2.8 million, except that use of financial leverage will increase the required rate of return on equity to only 15 percent, rather than 16 percent. What is the value of the firm in millions of dollars if the restructuring occurs?

    a. $9.4   **b.** $10.0   **c.** $12.2   **d.** $13.0   **e.** $13.1

9.	Under the conditions of Self-Test Problem 8, what will be the new number of shares outstanding if the restructuring occurs? (Hint: $P_1 = [V_1 - D_0]/n_0$.)

    a. 500,000   **b.** 478,642   **c.** 438,231   **d.** 418,301   **e.** 396,547

(The following data apply to the next four Self-Test Problems.)

Union Brick Inc. (UBI) has a total market value of $200 million, consisting of 2 million shares of common stock selling for $50 per share and $100 million of 10 percent perpetual bonds currently selling at par. UBI pays out all earnings as dividends, and its marginal tax rate is 40 percent. The firm's earnings before interest and taxes (EBIT) are $30 million. Management is considering increasing UBI's debt to $140 million. The additional funds will be used to repurchase stock at the new equilibrium price. At a debt level of $140 million UBI's cost of debt is estimated at 12 percent and its cost of equity is estimated to be 15 percent.

10. What is UBI's required rate of return on equity at its current debt level of $100 million?

    a. 11.0%   **b.** 12.0%   **c.** 13.0%   **d.** 14.0%   **e.** 15.0%

11. Assume that UBI will increase its outstanding debt by calling in the old debt and issuing new debt, resulting in a debt level of $140 million. What would be UBI's new firm value in millions of dollars?

    a. $52.8   **b.** $100.0   **c.** $140.0   **d.** $192.8   **e.** $200.0

12. Refer to Self-Test Problem 11. What would be UBI's new stock price? (Hint: $P_1 = [V_1 - D_0]/n_0$.)

    a. $40.00   **b.** $46.40   **c.** $50.00   **d.** $50.40   **e.** $52.60

13. Now assume that UBI will increase its outstanding debt by issuing $40 million of new debt—the debt outstanding will not be called. What would be UBI's new stock price? (Hint: $P_1 = [V_1 - D_0]/n_0$.)

    a. $40.00   **b.** $46.40   **c.** $50.00   **d.** $50.40   **e.** $52.60

(The following data apply to the next four Self-Test Problems.)

Tapley Dental Supplies Inc. is in a stable, no-growth situation. Its $1,000,000 of debt consists of perpetuities which have a 10 percent coupon and sell at par. Tapley's EBIT is $500,000; its cost of equity is 15 percent; it has 100,000 shares of common stock outstanding that sell for $16 per share; all earnings are paid out as dividends; and its federal-plus-state tax rate is 40 percent. Tapley could borrow an additional $500,000 at an interest rate of 13 percent without having to retire the original debt, and it would use the proceeds to repurchase stock at the new equilibrium price. The increased risk from the additional leverage will raise the cost of equity to 17 percent.

14. What is the firm's current value in millions of dollars at a debt level of $1 million?

    a. $1.6   **b.** $2.0   **c.** $2.6   **d.** $1.8   **e.** $2.3

15. What is the firm's new value in millions of dollars at a debt level of $1.5 million, assuming that the original debt is not retired?

    a. $2.25   **b.** $2.45   **c.** $2.68   **d.** $1.75   **e.** $1.18

16. If the recapitalization takes place, what is Tapley's new stock price? (Hint: $P_1 = [V_1 - D_0]/n_0$.)

   a. $16.50   b. $16.23   c. $17.10   d. $16.82   e. $17.45

17. After the recapitalization takes place, how many shares of common stock will remain?

   a. 70,273   b. 69,697   c. 70,760   d. 71,347   e. 69,193

ANSWERS TO SELF-TEST QUESTIONS

1. small
2. return on invested capital
3. operating leverage
4. debt (leverage); debt (leverage)
5. increases
6. capital structure
7. capital intensive
8. debt
9. debt; interest; equity

10. Bankruptcy costs
11. trade-off
12. Signaling; asymmetric information
13. reserve borrowing capacity
14. Agency conflicts
15. debt
16. greater
17. operating
18. minimizes

19. b. Increasing operating leverage will increase Firm A's business risk.

20. b. The two firms would have the same stand-alone risk. Each could have different combinations of business and financial risk.

21. b. Debt financing only increases ROE if the after-tax cost of debt is less than the return on invested capital.

22. a. This statement is correct.

23. b. Price per share and EPS will not both be maximized at the same debt level. The optimal capital structure occurs where price per share is maximized.

24. c. Business risk is solely dependent upon the basic riskiness of the assets, and not the financing mix.

25. d. The optimal capital structure balances risk and return to maximize the stock price. The structure that maximizes stock price also minimizes the firm's cost of capital.

26. d. Statement a is false; if a firm is exposed to a high degree of business risk this implies that it should offset this risk by using a lower amount of financial leverage. Statement b is false; preferred stock is a fixed-income security, and as such, would increase financial risk. Statement c is false; MM proved exactly the opposite. Under a very restrictive set of assumptions, MM proved a firm's value is not affected by its capital structure. Statement d is the correct choice.

SOLUTIONS TO SELF-TEST PROBLEMS

1. e. $\text{EBIT} = PQ - VQP - F$

$\$90,000 = P(50,000) - 0.4(50,000)P - \$100,000$

$30,000P = \$190,000$

$P = \$6.33.$

2. c. For the first method: $\text{EBIT} = PQ - \$1.00Q - \$20,000.$

For the second method: $\text{EBIT} = PQ - \$2.00Q - \$5,000.$

Now, equate the EBITs:

$PQ - \$1.00Q - \$20,000 = PQ - \$2.00Q - \$5,000$

$\$1.00Q = \$15,000$

$Q = 15,000.$

3.   b.   The first step is to calculate EBIT:

Sales in dollars [50,000($22)]	$1,100,000
Less: Fixed costs	500,000
Variable costs [50,000($2)]	100,000
EBIT	$ 500,000

The second step is to calculate the EPS at each debt/assets ratio using the formula:

$$EPS = \frac{(EBIT - I)(1 - T)}{Shares\ outstanding}.$$

Recognize (1) that I = Interest charges = (Dollars of debt)(Interest rate at each D/A ratio), and (2) that Shares outstanding = (Assets – Debt)/Initial price per share = ($2,000,000 – Debt)/$20.00.

D/A	EPS	D/A	EPS
0%	$3.00	40%	$3.80
10	3.21	50	3.72
20	3.47	60	2.82
30	3.77		

Finally, the third step is to calculate the stock price at each debt/assets ratio using the following formula: Price = (P/E)(EPS).

D/A	Price	D/A	Price
0%	$37.50	40%	$30.40
10	38.52	50	22.32
20	39.91	60	14.10
30	37.70		

Thus, a debt/assets ratio of 20 percent maximizes stock price. This is the optimal capital structure.

4. b. $V_0 = S_0 = 500,000(\$20) = \$10,000,000.$

$$S_0 = \frac{(EBIT - k_dD)(1-T)}{k_s}$$

$$S_0 = \frac{EBIT(1-T)}{k_s}.$$

$$\$10,000,000 = \frac{EBIT(0.6)}{0.14}$$
$$0.6(EBIT) = \$1,400,000$$
$$EBIT = \$2,333,333.$$

5. e. $S_1 = \frac{(EBIT - k_dD)(1-T)}{k_s}$

$$S_1 = \frac{[\$2,800,000 - 0.12(\$2,000,000)]0.6}{0.16} = \$9,600,000.$$

$V_1 = D_1 + S_1 = \$2,000,000 + \$9,600,000 = \$11,600,000.$

6. e. $S_0 = \frac{(EBIT - k_dD)(1-T)}{k_s}$

$$S_0 = \frac{(\$2,800,000 - \$0)(0.7)}{0.14} = \$14,000,000 = V_0.$$

Now, less money is paid in taxes, more remains for the shareholders, and the value of the firm is higher.

7. a. $S_1 = \frac{(EBIT - k_dD)(1-T)}{k_s}$

$$S_1 = \frac{[\$2,800,000 - 0.12(\$2,000,000)]0.7}{0.16} = \$11,200,000.$$

$V_1 = D_1 + S_1 = \$2,000,000 + \$11,200,000 = \$13,200,000.$

8.   c. $S_1 = \dfrac{(EBIT - k_d D)(1 - T)}{k_s}$

$S_1 = \dfrac{[\$2,800,000 - 0.12(\$2,000,000)]0.6}{0.15} = \$10,240,000.$

$V_1 = D_1 + S_1 = \$2,000,000 + \$10,240,000 = \$12,240,000.$

9.   d. First, find the equilibrium stock price:

$P_1 = \dfrac{V_1 - D_0}{n_0} = \dfrac{\$12,240,000 - \$0}{500,000} = \$24.48.$

Then, find the number of shares repurchased:

$\text{Shares repurchased} = \dfrac{\$2,000,000}{\$24.48} = 81,699.$

Finally, determine the shares remaining:

Shares remaining = 500,000 − 81,699 = 418,301.

10.   b. $k_s = \dfrac{(EBIT - k_d D)(1 - T)}{S} = \dfrac{[\$30 - 0.10(\$100)]0.6}{\$100} = 12.0\%.$

11.   d. $S_1 = \dfrac{(EBIT - k_d D)(1 - T)}{k_s} = \dfrac{[\$30 - 0.12(\$140)]0.6}{0.15} = \$52.8 \text{ million.}$

$V_1 = D_1 + S_1 = \$140 + \$52.8 = \$192.8 \text{ million.}$

12.   b. $P_1 = \dfrac{V_1 - D_0}{n_0} = \dfrac{\$192.8 - \$100}{2} = \$46.40.$

Note that stock price decreases with the increase in leverage. Thus, the change should not be made.

13.   d. $S_1 = \dfrac{\left(EBIT - k_d D - k_{d_1} D_1\right)(1 - T)}{k_s}$

$S_1 = \dfrac{[\$30 - 0.10(\$100) - 0.12(\$40)]0.6}{0.15} = \$60.8 \text{ million.}$

$V_1 = S_1 + D_0 + D_1.$

But the value of the old debt, D_0, decreases because its riskiness has increased:

$D_0 = \dfrac{0.1(\$100)}{0.12} = \$83.33 \text{ million.}$

Thus, $V_1 = \$60.8 + \$83.33 + \$40 = \$184.13$ million. Finally,

$P_1 = \dfrac{V_1 - D_0}{n_0} = \dfrac{\$184.13 - \$83.33}{2} = \$50.40.$

Note that the change should be made under these circumstances. Here some of the wealth of the old bondholders is being transferred to the shareholders.

14.   c. $S_0 = \dfrac{(EBIT - k_d D)(1 - T)}{k_s} = \dfrac{(\$500,000 - \$100,000)(0.6)}{0.15} = \$1.6 \text{ million.}$

$V_0 = S_0 + D_0 = \$1.6 \text{ million} + \$1.0 \text{ million} = \$2.6 \text{ million.}$

15.   b. $S_1 = \dfrac{\left(EBIT - k_d D - k_{d_1} D_1\right)(1 - T)}{k_s}$

$S_1 = \dfrac{[\$500,000 - \$100,000 - \$65,000](0.6)}{0.17} = \$1,182,353.$

$V_1 = S_1 + D_0 + D_1$

$D_0 = 0.1(\$1,000,000)/0.13 = \$769,231.$

$V_1 = \$1,182,353 + \$769,231 + \$500,000 = \$2,451,584.$

16.   d. $P_1 = (\$2,451,584 - \$769,231)/100,000 = \$16.82.$

17.   a.   Shares remaining $= 100,000 - \$500,000/\$16.82 = 70,273.$

OVERVIEW

Chapter 10 presented some basic material on capital structure, including a brief introduction to capital structure theory. Debt financing concentrates a firm's business risk on its stockholders, but debt also increases the expected return on equity. There is some optimal level of debt that maximizes a company's stock price, but it is next to impossible to identify that optimal capital structure. In this chapter, we go into more detail on capital structure theory. This will give you a deeper understanding of the benefits and costs associated with debt financing.

OUTLINE

Beginning in 1958, Modigliani and Miller (MM) addressed the capital structure issue in a rigorous, scientific fashion. The result is the well-known MM propositions. MM set off a chain of research that continues to this day.

- MM employed the concept of arbitrage to develop their theory.
  - ☐ Arbitrage occurs if two similar assets (leveraged and unleveraged stocks) sell at different prices. Arbitrageurs will buy the undervalued stock and simultaneously sell the overvalued stock, earning a profit in the process, and the process will continue until the prices of the two assets are equal.

- MM began with an initial set of assumptions including constant debt costs, zero brokerage costs, perpetual cash flows, and zero growth. Initially, they also assumed zero taxes. MM used an arbitrage proof to develop two propositions.
  - ☐ Proposition I:

$$V_L = V_U = EBIT/WACC = EBIT/k_{sU},$$

  where V_L = value of a leveraged firm, V_U = value of an unleveraged firm in the same risk class, and k_{sU} is the required rate of return for an unleveraged, or all-equity firm.

- Proposition I tells us that the value of a firm is established by capitalizing its expected net operating income (EBIT) at a constant rate (k_{sU}), which is based on the firm's risk class. Thus, Proposition I implies that the value of a firm is independent of its leverage.

- Proposition I also implies (1) that a firm's WACC is completely independent of its capital structure, and (2) that the WACC for a firm, regardless of the amount of debt it uses, is equal to the cost of equity it would have if it used no debt.

☐ Proposition II:

$$k_{sL} = k_{sU} + \text{Risk premium} = k_{sU} + (k_{sU} - k_d)(D/S).$$

- Here we see that the cost of equity to a leveraged firm, k_{sL}, is equal to the cost of equity to an unleveraged firm in the same risk class, k_{sU}, plus a risk premium whose size depends on both the differential between an unleveraged firm's costs of equity and debt and the amount of debt used.

- Proposition II states that as the firm's use of debt increases, its cost of equity also rises, and in a mathematically precise manner.

■ Taken together, the two MM propositions imply that the inclusion of more debt in the capital structure will not increase a firm's value, because the benefits of cheaper debt will be exactly offset by an increase in the riskiness, hence in the cost of its equity. Thus, MM argue that in a world without taxes, both the value of a firm and its WACC would be unaffected by its capital structure.

■ MM used an *arbitrage proof* to support their propositions. They showed that, under their assumptions, if two companies differed only (1) in the way they are financed and (2) in their total market values, then investors would sell shares of the higher-valued firm, buy those of the lower-valued firm, and continue this process until the companies had exactly the same market value.

☐ Each of MM's assumptions is necessary for the arbitrage proof to work.

☐ *Perfect arbitrage* occurs when you invest none of your own money, you have no risk, you have no future negative cash flows, but you end up with cash in your pocket.

MM reworked their theory in 1963 by adding corporate taxes. The result was two additional propositions. With corporate income taxes, they concluded that leverage will increase a firm's value. This occurs because interest on debt is a tax-deductible expense, hence more of a leveraged firm's operating income flows through to investors.

■ Proposition I:

$$V_L = V_U + TD = \text{EBIT}(1 - T)/k_{sU} + TD.$$

☐ The value of a leveraged firm is equal to the value of an unleveraged firm in the same risk class (V_U) plus the gain from leverage. The gain from leverage is the value of the tax savings, which equals the corporate tax rate (T) times the amount of debt (D) used.

☐ Note that for an unleveraged firm with perpetual cash flows, EBIT(1 – T) = Net income = Total dividends. Thus, the value of the unleveraged firm is equal to the perpetual dividend divided by k_{sU}.

☐ Also, note that the differential between V_U and V_L increases as the firm's use of debt increases, so a firm's value is maximized at virtually 100 percent debt financing.

■ Proposition II:

$$k_{sL} = k_{sU} + (k_{sU} - k_d)(1 - T)(D/S).$$

☐ The cost of equity to a leveraged firm is equal to (1) the cost of equity to an unleveraged firm in the same risk class plus (2) a risk premium whose size depends on the differential between the costs of equity and debt to an unleveraged firm, the amount of financial leverage used, and the corporate tax rate.

☐ Thus, when corporate taxes are introduced, the cost of equity rises less rapidly than it did in the absence of corporate taxes. Further, the cost of debt is reduced by the tax deductibility of interest payments. These two factors combine to produce the increase in firm value which is shown by Proposition I.

☐ MM's model with corporate taxes leads to the conclusion that firms should use almost 100 percent debt. Without taxes, both WACC and the firm's value (V) are constant. With corporate taxes, WACC declines and V rises as more and more debt is used, so the optimal capital structure, under MM with corporate taxes, is 100% debt.

In our discussion of business and financial risk, we focused on stand-alone risk. Now we shift our focus from a stand-alone risk perspective to a market risk perspective.

■ Robert Hamada, using the Capital Asset Pricing Model (CAPM) and the MM after-tax model, developed an expression for the cost of equity to a leveraged firm:

$$k_{sL} = \text{Risk-free rate} + \text{Business risk premium} + \text{Financial risk premium}$$
$$= k_{RF} + (k_M - k_{RF})b_U + (k_M - k_{RF})b_U(1 - T)(D/S).$$

☐ The Hamada equation partitions the required rate of return on a stock into three components:

• k_{RF}, the risk-free rate, which compensates shareholders for the time value of money.

• A premium for business risk as reflected by the term $(k_M - k_{RF})b_U$.

• A premium for financial risk as reflected by the term $(k_M - k_{RF})b_U(1 - T)(D/S)$.

■ Equating the SML equation with Hamada's equation for k_{sL}, we ultimately obtain:

$$b = b_U[1 + (1 - T)(D/S)].$$

   ☐ This equation analyzes the effect of financial leverage on beta.

■ Thus, under the MM and CAPM assumptions, the equity beta of any firm is equal to the equity beta the firm would have if it used zero debt, adjusted upward by a factor that depends on (1) the corporate tax rate and (2) the amount of financial leverage employed.

■ The stock's market risk, which is measured by b, depends on both the firm's business risk as measured by b_U and its financial risk as measured by $b - b_U = b_U(1 - T)(D/S)$.

■ The Hamada relationship can be used to help estimate a company's or a division's cost of equity by leveraging up or down the betas of comparable proxy firms to reflect the firm's or division's capital structure and tax rate.

   ☐ The result is an estimate of the firm's or division's equity beta, given (1) its business risk as measured by the equity betas of other firms in the same line of business and (2) its financial risk as measured by its own capital structure and tax rate.

In 1976, Miller presented a capital structure model which included not only corporate taxes, but personal taxes as well.

■ The *Miller Model* takes this form:

$$V_U = \frac{EBIT(1 - T_c)(1 - T_s)}{k_{sU}}, \text{ and } V_L = V_U + \left[1 - \frac{(1 - T_c)(1 - T_s)}{(1 - T_d)}\right]D.$$

   ☐ Here T_c is the corporate tax rate, T_s is the personal tax rate on stock income, and T_d is the personal tax rate on income from debt.
   ☐ The term in brackets, multiplied by D, is the gain from leverage. The bracketed term replaces the corporate tax rate, T, in the earlier MM model with corporate taxes, $V_L = V_U + TD$.
   ☐ If all taxes are ignored, then $T_c = T_s = T_d = 0$, and the model reduces to the original MM model without taxes.
   ☐ If we ignore personal taxes, then $T_s = T_d = 0$, and the model reduces to the MM model with corporate taxes.

■ The gain from leverage in the Miller model depends on the values of T_c, T_s, and T_d as well as the amount of debt financing.

   ☐ Because taxes on capital gains are both lower than on ordinary income and can be deferred, the effective tax rate on stock income is normally less than that on bond income.

☐ When $T_s < T_d$, the bracketed term is less than T_c, and the value of financial leverage is less than it would be in the absence of personal taxes.

Thus, Miller's model confirms the earlier MM conclusion that the use of corporate debt increases the value of a firm, but the advantage is clearly less than TD, and hence personal taxes reduce the benefits of corporate debt. Note, however, that the Miller model still prescribes close to 100 percent debt as the value-maximizing capital structure.

☐ In his paper, Miller argued that firms in the aggregate would issue a mix of debt and equity securities such that the before-tax yields on corporate securities and the personal tax rates of the investors who bought these securities would adjust until an equilibrium was reached. At equilibrium, the tax advantage of debt to the firm would be exactly offset by personal taxation, and capital structure would have no effect on a firm's value or its cost of capital.

While the conclusions of the two MM models and the Miller model follow logically from the initial assumptions, these theories lack support because (1) their assumptions do not reflect actual market conditions, and (2) more important, their prescriptions are not followed. Some of the main objections include the following:

Both MM and Miller assumed that personal and corporate leverage are perfect substitutes.

Homemade leverage puts stockholders in greater danger of bankruptcy than does corporate leverage.

Brokerage costs are assumed away, making the switch from leveraged to unleveraged costless.

MM initially assumed that corporations and investors can borrow at the risk-free rate.

Miller concluded that an equilibrium would be reached, but to reach equilibrium the tax benefit from corporate debt must be the same for all firms, and it must be constant for an individual firm regardless of the amount of leverage used.

MM and Miller assumed that there are no financial distress costs and they ignore agency costs.

MM and Miller assume that all market participants have identical information about firms' prospects.

A potential problem with the MM and Miller models is that they ignore financial distress and agency costs. Quite a few firms go bankrupt every year, and the costs of financial distress, as well as agency costs, can be significant.

■ Actual bankruptcy results in extraordinary costs such as forced sales of assets at below-market prices, deterioration of property, and court and administrative costs. The threat of financial distress also involves costs, since managers must spend more time on fending off bankruptcy than on making good operating decisions, as well as taking costly actions in attempts to ward off distress.

■ In general, the probability of *financial distress* increases as more debt is used. The greater the use of debt financing, and the larger the fixed interest charges, the greater the probability that a decline in earnings will lead to financial distress, and hence the higher the probability that costs associated with financial distress will be incurred.
  ☐ An increase in the probability of future financial distress lowers the current value of a firm and raises its cost of capital.
  ☐ The effects of financial distress are also felt by a firm's bondholders. Firms experiencing financial distress have a higher probability of defaulting on debt payments, so the higher the probability of financial distress, the higher the required return on debt.
  ☐ As a firm uses more and more debt, hence increasing the probability of distress, the value of k_d also increases.

■ *Agency costs* also tend to increase as more and more debt is used.
  ☐ Lost efficiency plus monitoring costs are agency costs that increase the cost of debt and thus reduces its advantage.

■ When these costs are considered, MM's Proposition I, with corporate taxes, becomes:

$$V_L = V_U + TD - \left(\begin{array}{c} \text{PV of expected} \\ \text{financial distress costs} \end{array} \right) - \left(\begin{array}{c} \text{PV of agency} \\ \text{costs} \end{array} \right).$$

■ This relationship is shown in Figure 1.

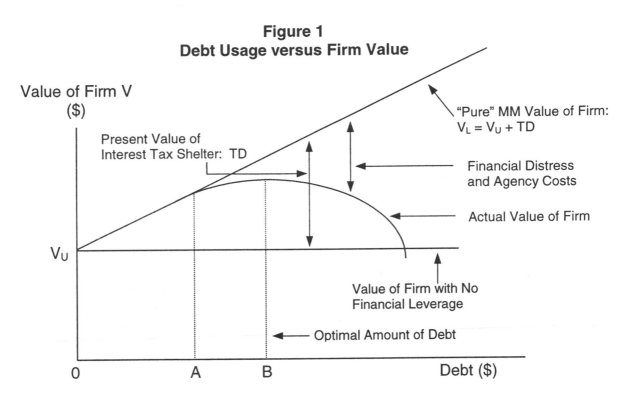

Figure 1
Debt Usage versus Firm Value

■ Here we see that the tax shelter effect dominates until debt reaches Point A. After Point A, the financial distress and agency costs begin to offset the tax advantages of debt financing. At Point B, the marginal tax benefits of debt are exactly offset by the marginal financial distress and agency costs, and beyond Point B, the disadvantages of using debt outweigh the benefits. However, the financial distress and agency costs cannot be estimated easily, and it is very difficult, if not impossible, to identify Point B in practice with any precision.

■ Note that financial distress and agency costs can also be added to the Miller model. When these are added, the relationship between value and debt is the same as when these costs are added to the MM with corporate taxes model. However, the "Pure" MM Value of Firm line would be less steep under Miller since the value of debt financing is reduced. Further, the Y intercept would be lowered because the addition of personal taxes reduces the value of the unleveraged firm.

Both the MM with corporate taxes and Miller models modified to include financial distress and agency costs are called trade-off models. That is, the optimal capital structure is found by balancing the tax shield benefits of leverage against the costs of leverage, and hence the costs and benefits are "traded off" against one another.

■ The trade-off models cannot be used to specify a firm's precise optimal capital structure, but they do enable us to make three statements about leverage:

- ☐ Firms with more business risk ought to use less debt than lower-risk firms, other things being equal, because the greater the business risk, the greater the probability of financial distress at any level of debt, hence the greater the expected costs of distress.
- ☐ Firms that have tangible, readily marketable assets can use more debt than firms whose value is derived primarily from intangible assets.
- ☐ Firms paying taxes at the highest rate gain the most benefit from debt financing and, hence, should carry more debt than firms with lower tax rates.

- ■ Although the trade-off models present a logical framework for thought, empirical support for the trade-off models is not strong, suggesting that factors that are not incorporated into the models are at work.

The signaling, or asymmetric information, theory of capital structure was developed by Professor Stewart Myers in an attempt to reconcile the MM/Miller theories with the pecking order method of financing observed by Professor Gordon Donaldson. By allowing that asymmetric (or different) information exists for different groups of market participants, certain actions may be implied for corporate financial policy.

- ■ Donaldson observed that there is a "pecking order" of financing, not a balanced approach as would result if the trade-off models accurately described real-world behavior.

- ■ The *signaling*, or *asymmetric information, theory* attempts to explain this "pecking order."
  - ☐ Information asymmetries often exist between managers and investors.
  - ☐ When asymmetric information exists, corporations should issue new shares only in the unlikely event that they have extraordinarily profitable investments that cannot be either postponed, signaled to investors, or financed by debt, or in situations where management thinks the shares are overvalued.
  - ☐ Investors recognize all this, so selling pressure drives down a company's share price when it announces plans to issue new shares.
  - ☐ The pecking order that Donaldson observed is rational when asymmetric information exists. It pays to retain a large fraction of earnings, and also to keep the equity ratio up and the debt ratio down, so as to maintain a "reserve borrowing capacity" which can be used to support the capital budget if and when an unusually large number of positive NPV projects come along, or if problems arise which require outside capital.

- ■ Signaling effects, and their impact on investor's perceptions, differ substantially across firms.
  - ☐ Industries which hold a significant amount of proprietary information, such as the drug or semiconductor industries, will have a higher degree of asymmetric information than the retailing or trucking industries.

□ Emerging firms with limited capital but good growth opportunities are recognized as having to use external financing, so the announcement of new stock offerings by a new company is not viewed with as much concern by investors as are offerings by mature firms with limited growth opportunities.

■ Although signaling affects all firms, its impact varies from firm to firm.

The great contribution of the trade-off models developed by MM, Miller, and their followers is that these models identified the specific benefits and costs of using debt. Prior to MM, no capital structure theory existed, so we had no systematic way of analyzing the effects of debt financing.

■ The trade-off view is summarized graphically in Figure 2.

Figure 2
Effects of Debt Financing

□ The left-hand graph shows the relationship between the debt ratio and capital costs. Both the cost of equity and cost of debt rise steadily with increasing leverage, but the rate of increase accelerates sharply at higher debt levels, reflecting agency costs and the increased probability of financial distress. The weighted average cost of capital first declines, then hits a minimum, and then begins to rise. Note, however, that the

WACC curve is shallow, indicating the debt ratio does not have a pronounced effect on WACC over a fairly wide range of values.

☐ The right-hand graph shows that firm value first rises with debt usage, hits a peak, and then falls. Again, the relationship is such that small deviations from the optimal debt ratio do not have a large impact on value.

☐ Note in the figure that the same debt ratio that minimizes the cost of capital also maximizes firm value. Thus, the optimal capital structure can be defined in terms of either cost minimization or value maximization because the same capital structure does both.

■ Little disagreement exists in either business or academic circles that the general situation described above is correct. However, details can only be discovered by empirical testing. Unfortunately, firms which differ only in capital structure do not exist, and future earnings are not known with any certainty. Thus, empirical tests have not produced conclusive results.

■ We believe that there is a net benefit to debt financing, at least out to some point, but we also believe that firms should maintain a borrowing reserve. Thus, firms use debt on the basis of their tax rates, asset structures, and inherent riskiness, but they also try to maintain the ability to issue new debt at favorable rates if it becomes necessary to raise external capital when chaotic market conditions exist.

Wide variations in the use of financial leverage occur both across industries and among the individual firms in each industry. In addition, capital structures also change over time.

Firms should focus on market value capital structures and base their cost of capital calculations on target market value weights. Because market values do change, it would be impossible to keep the actual capital structure on target at all times, but this fact in no way detracts from the validity of market value targets.

The Extensions to Chapter 11 provide the additional MM proofs for: (1) MM Proposition II without corporate taxes, (2) MM Proposition I with corporate taxes, and (3) MM Proposition II with corporate taxes.

SELF-TEST QUESTIONS

Definitional

1. The addition of financial distress and agency costs leads to a WACC curve which first _____, then reaches a _____, and then _____.

2.   The optimal capital structure is that structure at which the marginal _____ of leverage equal the marginal _____.

3.   The signaling, or asymmetric information, theory relaxes the MM models' assumption that _____ _____ exists.

4.   By allowing for asymmetric information, Donaldson's _____ _____ method of financing can be explained.

5.   Difficulties in estimating the relationship between _____ ratios and the costs of _____ and _____ have made some managers reluctant to rely heavily on quantitative analysis to set the target capital structure.

6.   Conservative financial managers may try to maintain a target capital structure that is _____ than optimal.

7.   External capital is particularly important to firms with high _____ _____.

8.   Owner/managers may prefer additional _____ as opposed to common stock in order to maintain _____ of the company.

9.   A firm's cost of capital should be based on _____ _____ _____ weights.

Conceptual

10.   While signaling, or asymmetric information, theory affects all firms, its impact varies from firm to firm.

       a. True   **b.** False

11.   As a general rule, the capital structure which *maximizes* stock price (firm value) also

       a. Maximizes earnings per share.
       b. Minimizes the probability of financial distress.
       c. Minimizes both the cost of equity and the cost of debt.
       d. Statements a, b, and c are true.
       e. Statements a, b, and c are false.

12. Firms should use *more* debt if

   a. They are in a lower tax bracket.
   b. They have stable expected returns on their assets (low business risk).
   c. They employ standardized, tangible assets.
   d. Answers b and c above are correct.
   e. Answers a, b, and c above are correct.

13. If information asymmetries exist, then management is motivated to issue new stock only if the stock is

   a. Overvalued.
   b. Undervalued.
   c. Fairly valued.

14. Which of the following statements is most correct?

   a. The "pure MM" theory of capital structure, when income taxes are considered, suggests that the value of a firm rises as it uses more and more debt and that this increase is due to tax savings. Thus, the optimal capital structure under MM theory calls for 100 percent debt.
   b. When the "pure MM" theory is modified to include bankruptcy costs, an optimal capital structure with some debt, but less than 100 percent debt, is found for the "typical" firm.
   c. Under the signaling, or asymmetric information, theory the issuance of new common stock by a mature company is taken by investors as bad news. As a result, new stock issues depress the stock price. This implies that firms should, under normal conditions, use less debt than they otherwise might so as to have a reserve borrowing capacity which would enable them to avoid issuing stock under most conditions.
   d. Statements a, b, and c are correct.
   e. Statements a, b, and c are incorrect.

SELF-TEST PROBLEMS

(The following data apply to the next two Self-Test Problems.)

A firm with no debt financing has a firm value of $20 million. It has a corporate marginal tax rate of 34 percent. The firm's investors are estimated to have marginal tax rates of 31 percent on interest income and a weighted average of 28 percent on stock income. The firm is planning to change its capital structure by issuing $10 million in debt, and repurchasing $10 million of common stock.

1. According to the Modigliani-Miller view with corporate taxes, what is the value in millions of dollars of the leveraged firm?

    a. $20.00   b. $22.44   c. $23.40   d. $26.40   e. $30.00

2. According to the Miller view with corporate and personal taxes, what is the gain from leverage in millions of dollars?

    a. $0.00   b. $3.11   c. $4.65   d. $6.48   e. $8.50

(The following data apply to the next three Self-Test Problems.)

The Ensyder Trading Company (ETC) is a zero growth firm with an EBIT of $250,000 and a corporate tax rate of 40 percent. ETC uses $1 million of debt financing, and the cost of equity to an unleveraged firm in the same risk class is 15 percent. The personal tax rates of ETC's investors are 30 percent on interest income and 20 percent (on average) on income from common stocks.

3. What is the value of ETC according to MM with corporate taxes?

    a. $1,000,000   b. $1,114,000   c. $1,314,000   d. $1,400,000   e. $2,000,000

4. What is ETC's value rounded to the nearest thousand according to Miller (including personal taxes)?

    a. $1,000,000   b. $1,114,000   c. $1,314,000   d. $1,600,000   e. $2,000,000

5. Suppose that the present value of financial distress costs is estimated to be $800,000, and that, at a debt level of $1 million, ETC has a 20 percent probability of going bankrupt. Further, assume that the present value of agency costs are $50,000 at a $1,000,000 debt level. What is the firm's value rounded to the nearest thousand if these costs are added to the Miller model?

    a. $904,000   b. $1,114,000   c. $1,314,000   d. $1,600,000   e. $2,000,000

(The following data apply to the next five Self-Test Problems.)

Unleveraged Corporation (Firm U) has a total market value of $500,000, a tax rate of 40 percent, and earnings before interest and taxes (EBIT) of $100,000. Leveraged Corporation (Firm L) is identical in all respects to Firm U, but Firm L has $200,000 market (and book) value of debt outstanding. Firm L pays total annual interest of $16,000 on this debt. Both firms satisfy the MM assumptions.

6.   What is the value of Firm L according to MM's Proposition I with corporate taxes?

   a. $500,000   **b.** $520,000   **c.** $540,000   **d.** $560,000   **e.** $580,000

7.   What is Firm U's cost of equity?

   a. 10.00%   **b.** 10.34%   **c.** 11.00%   **d.** 12.00%   **e.** 13.26%

8.   What is Firm L's cost of equity?

   a. 10.00%   **b.** 10.34%   **c.** 11.00%   **d.** 12.00%   **e.** 13.26%

9.   What is Firm L's weighted average cost of capital?

   a. 10.00%   **b.** 10.34%   **c.** 11.00%   **d.** 12.00%   **e.** 13.26%

10.   An alternative equation for a firm's cost of capital is

$$\text{WACC} = \frac{\text{EBIT}(1-T)}{V}.$$

   What is Firm L's weighted average cost of capital according to this formula?

   a. 10.00%   **b.** 10.34%   **c.** 11.00%   **d.** 12.00%   **e.** 13.26%

ANSWERS TO SELF-TEST QUESTIONS

1.   declines; minimum; rises
2.   benefits; costs
3.   perfect information
4.   pecking order
5.   debt; debt; equity

6.   less
7.   growth rates
8.   debt; control
9.   target market value

10.   a.   This statement is correct.

11.   e.   The capital structure which maximizes stock price also minimizes the firm's weighted average cost of capital. The probability of financial distress is minimized at zero debt. Also, note that neither the cost of debt nor the cost of equity is minimized at the optimal capital structure.

12. d. Firms gain the most benefits from using debt when they are in the highest tax bracket. Firms with highly variable expected returns and intangible, specialized assets should use lower levels of debt.

13. a. Management will want to issue new stock only if the excess value will benefit the existing stockholders and not be passed on to new investors.

14. d. Statements a, b, and c are all correct; therefore, statement d is the proper choice.

SOLUTIONS TO SELF-TEST PROBLEMS

1. c. $V_L = V_U + TD = \$20 + 0.34(\$10) = \$20 + \$3.4 = \$23.4$ million.

2. b. Gain from leverage $= \left[1 - \dfrac{(1 - T_c)(1 - T_s)}{(1 - T_d)}\right] D$

$= \left[1 - \dfrac{(1 - 0.34)(1 - 0.28)}{(1 - 0.31)}\right]\$10$

$= [1 - 0.689]\$10 = 0.311(\$10) = \$3.11$ million.

Note that the gain from leverage is reduced when personal taxes are added.

3. d. $V_L = V_U + TD = \dfrac{EBIT(1 - T)}{k_{sU}} + TD$

$= \dfrac{\$250,000(0.6)}{0.15} + 0.4(\$1,000,000)$

$= \$1,000,000 + \$400,000 = \$1,400,000.$

4. b. $V_L = V_U + \left[1 - \dfrac{(1 - T_c)(1 - T_s)}{(1 - T_d)}\right] D$

$= V_U + \left[1 - \dfrac{0.6(0.8)}{0.7}\right]\$1,000,000$

$= V_U + 0.3143(\$1,000,000) = V_U + \$314,286.$

Now, the addition of personal taxes also reduces the value of V_U:

$$V_U = \frac{EBIT(1 - T_c)(1 - T_s)}{k_{sU}} = \frac{\$250,000(0.6)(0.8)}{0.15} = \$800,000.$$

Thus, $V_L = \$800,000 + \$314,286 = \$1,114,286 \approx \$1,114,000.$

5. a. $V_L = V_{Miller} - PV$ (Financial distress costs) $- PV$ (Agency costs)
      $= \$1,114,286 - 0.2(\$800,000) - \$50,000 = \$904,286 \approx \$904,000.$

6. e. $V_L = V_U + TD = \$500,000 + 0.4(\$200,000) = \$500,000 + \$80,000 = \$580,000.$

7. d. $V_U = \dfrac{EBIT(1 - T)}{k_{sU}}$; $\$500,000 = \dfrac{\$100,000(0.6)}{k_{sU}}$; $k_{sU} = \dfrac{\$60,000}{\$500,000} = 12.0\%.$

8. e. First, note that Firm L's cost of debt is 8.0 percent:

    $k_d = \$16,000/\$200,000 = 8.0\%.$

    Next, note that $V_L = \$580,000$ and $D = \$200,000$. Thus, Firm L's equity value is $S = \$580,000 - \$200,000 = \$380,000$. Finally,

    $k_{sL} = k_{sU} + (k_{sU} - k_d)(1 - T)(D/S)$
    $\quad\quad = 12.0\% + (12.0\% - 8.0\%)(0.6)(\$200,000/\$380,000)$
    $\quad\quad = 12.0\% + 1.26\% = 13.26\%.$

9. b. $WACC = w_d k_d(1 - T) + w_{ce}k_s$
      $\quad\quad = (\$200,000/\$580,000)(8.00\%)(0.6) + (\$380,000/\$580,000)(13.26\%)$
      $\quad\quad = 10.34\%.$

10. b. $WACC = EBIT(1 - T)/V = \$100,000(0.6)/\$580,000 = 10.34\%.$

CHAPTER 12
DIVIDEND POLICY

OVERVIEW

Income earned by companies can be reinvested in operating assets, used to acquire securities, used to retire debt, or distributed to stockholders. If the decision is made to distribute income to stockholders, three key issues arise: (1) What percentage should be distributed? (2) Should the distribution be as cash dividends, or should the cash be passed on to shareholders by buying back some stock? (3) How stable should the distribution be; that is, should the funds paid out from year to year be stable and dependable, which stockholders would probably prefer, or be allowed to vary with the firm's cash flows and investment requirements, which would probably be better from the firm's standpoint? These three issues, as well as stock dividends and stock splits, are discussed in this chapter.

OUTLINE

Dividend policy involves the decision to pay out earnings versus retaining them for reinvestment in the firm. When deciding how much cash to distribute to stockholders, financial managers must keep in mind that the firm's objective is to maximize shareholder value.

- The *target payout ratio* is defined as the percentage of net income to be paid out as cash dividends, and it should be based in large part on investors' preferences for dividends versus capital gains.

- The constant growth stock valuation model, $P_0 = D_1/(k_s - g)$, shows that paying out more dividends will increase stock price. However, if D_1 is raised, then less money will be available for reinvestment, that will cause the expected growth rate to decline, and that would tend to lower the stock's price.

- Any change in payout policy will have two opposing effects. Therefore, the firm's *optimal dividend policy* must strike a balance between current dividends and future growth so as to maximize the stock price.

A number of theories have been proposed to explain how factors interact to determine a firm's optimal dividend policy. These theories include: (1) the dividend irrelevance theory, (2) the bird-in-the-hand theory, and (3) the tax preference theory.

■ Modigliani and Miller (MM), the principal proponents of the *dividend irrelevance theory*, argue that the value of the firm depends only on the income produced by its assets, not on how this income is split between dividends and retained earnings.

  ☐ MM prove their proposition, but only under a set of restrictive assumptions including the absence of taxes and brokerage costs.

  ☐ Obviously, taxes and brokerage costs do exist, so the MM conclusions on dividend irrelevance may not be valid under real-world conditions. The validity of a theory must be judged by empirical tests, not by the realism of its assumptions.

■ The principal conclusion of MM's dividend irrelevance theory is that dividend policy does not affect the required rate of return on equity, k_s. Relaxing this assumption provides the basis for the *bird-in-the-hand theory*.

  ☐ Myron Gordon and John Lintner argue that k_s decreases as the dividend payout is increased because investors are less certain of receiving the capital gains which are supposed to result from retaining earnings than they are of receiving dividend payments.

  ☐ MM call the Gordon-Lintner argument the *bird-in-the-hand fallacy* because Gordon and Lintner believe that investors view dividends in the hand as being less risky than capital gains in the bush. In MM's view, however, most investors plan to reinvest their dividends in the stock of the same or similar firms, and, in any event, the riskiness of the firm's cash flows to investors in the long run is determined by the riskiness of operating cash flows, not by dividend payout policy.

■ The *tax preference theory* states that investors may prefer to have companies retain most of their earnings because of various tax advantages. Investors then would be willing to pay more for low payout companies than for otherwise similar high payout companies.

  ☐ There are three tax-related reasons for thinking that investors might prefer a low dividend payout to a high payout.

    • Long-term capital gains are taxed at a maximum rate of 20 percent, whereas dividend income is taxed at effective rates which go up to 39.6 percent. Therefore, wealthy investors might prefer to have companies retain and plow earnings back into the business. Earnings growth would presumably lead to higher stock prices, and thus lower-taxed capital gains would be substituted for higher-taxed dividends.

    • Taxes are not paid on the gain until a stock is sold. Due to time value effects, a dollar of taxes paid in the future has a lower effective cost than a dollar paid today.

- If a stock is held by someone until he or she dies, no capital gains tax is due at all.

Empirical testing of the dividend theories has not produced definitive results regarding which theory is correct. Two reasons for this are: We cannot find a set of publicly owned firms that differ only in their dividend policies, nor can we obtain precise estimates of each sample firm's cost of equity.

- ■ No one can establish a clear relationship between dividend policy and the cost of equity.
  - ☐ Investors cannot be seen to uniformly prefer either higher or lower dividends.
  - ☐ However, *individual* investors do have strong preferences.

- ■ Both evidence and logic suggest that investors prefer firms which follow a *stable, predictable dividend policy* (regardless of the payout level).

There are two other issues which have a bearing on optimal dividend policy: (1) the information content, or signaling, hypothesis and (2) the clientele effect.

- ■ It has been observed that a dividend increase is often accompanied by an increase in the stock price, while a dividend cut generally leads to a stock price decline.
  - ☐ This might be interpreted by some to mean that investors prefer dividends over capital gains, thus supporting the Gordon-Lintner hypothesis.
  - ☐ However, MM argue that a higher-than-expected dividend increase is a signal to investors that the firm's management forecasts good future earnings. Conversely, a dividend reduction, or a smaller-than-expected increase, is a signal that management is forecasting poor earnings in the future. Thus, MM argued that investors' reactions to changes in dividend policy do not necessarily show that investors prefer dividends to retained earnings. Rather, they argue that price changes simply indicate that there is an important *information, or signaling, content* in dividend announcements.

- ■ MM also suggest that a *clientele effect* might exist.
  - ☐ Some stockholders (for example, retirees) prefer cash income; therefore, they would want the firm to pay out a high percentage of its earnings as dividends.
  - ☐ Other stockholders have no need for current investment income (for example, doctors in their peak earning years) and they would simply reinvest any dividends received, after first paying income taxes on the dividend income. Therefore, they would want the firm to retain most of its earnings.
  - ☐ Thus, a firm establishes a dividend policy and then attracts a specific clientele that is drawn to this dividend policy. Those who do not like the dividend policy can simply sell their shares to those that do.
  - ☐ To the extent that stockholders can switch firms, a firm can change from one dividend payout policy to another and then let stockholders who do not like the new policy sell

to other investors who do. However, frequent switching would be inefficient because of brokerage costs, the likelihood that stockholders who are selling will have to pay capital gains taxes, and a possible shortage of investors who like the firm's newly adopted dividend policy.
  □ MM and others have argued that one clientele is as good as another, so the existence of a clientele effect does not necessarily imply that one dividend policy is better than any other.

Dividend stability is important.

■ Profits and cash flows vary over time, as do investment opportunities. Taken alone, this suggests that corporations should vary their dividends over time, increasing them when cash flows are large and the need for funds is low and lowering them when cash is in short supply relative to investment opportunities.
  □ However, many stockholders rely on dividends to meet expenses, and they would be seriously inconvenienced if the dividend stream were unstable.
  □ Reducing dividends to make funds available for capital investment could send incorrect signals to investors who might then push down the stock price because they interpreted the dividend cut to mean that the company's future earnings prospects had been diminished.

■ Dividend stability has two components.
  □ How dependable is the growth rate?
  □ Can we count on at least receiving the current dividend in the future?

■ The most stable policy, from an investor's standpoint, is that of a firm whose dividend growth rate is predictable.
  □ Such a company's total return (dividend yield plus capital gains yield) would be relatively stable over the long run, and its stock would be a good hedge against inflation.

■ The second most stable policy is where stockholders can be reasonably sure that the current dividend will not be reduced—it may not grow at a steady rate, but management will probably be able to avoid cutting the dividend.

■ Investors prefer stocks that pay more predictable dividends to stocks which pay the same average amount of dividends but in a more erratic manner. Thus, the cost of equity will be minimized, and the stock price maximized, if a firm stabilizes its dividends as much as possible.

When deciding how much cash to distribute to stockholders, two points should be kept in mind: (1) The overriding objective is to maximize shareholder value, and (2) the firm's cash flows really belong to its shareholders, so management should refrain from retaining income unless it can be reinvested to produce returns higher than shareholders could themselves earn by investing the cash in investments of equal risk.

■ When establishing a dividend policy, one size does not fit all.

For a given firm, the optimal payout ratio is a function of four factors: (1) investors' preferences for dividends versus capital gains, (2) the firm's investment opportunities, (3) its target capital structure, and (4) the availability and cost of external capital.
☐ The last three elements are combined in the *residual dividend model*.

Residual dividend policy is based on the premise that investors prefer to have a firm retain and reinvest earnings rather than pay them out in dividends if the rate of return the firm can earn on reinvested earnings exceeds the rate of return investors can obtain for themselves on other investments of comparable risk. Further, it is less expensive for the firm to use retained earnings than it is to issue new common stock. A firm using the residual policy would follow these four steps:
☐ Determine the optimal capital budget.
☐ Determine the amount of equity needed to finance the optimal capital budget, given the firm's target capital structure.
☐ Use retained earnings to meet equity requirements to the extent possible.
☐ Pay dividends only if more earnings are available than are needed to support the optimal capital budget.

If a firm rigidly follows the residual dividend policy, then dividends paid in any given year can be expressed as follows:

Dividends = Net Income − [(Target Equity Ratio)(Total Capital Budget)].

Since investment opportunities and earnings will surely vary from year to year, strict adherence to the residual dividend policy would result in unstable dividends. Firms should use the residual policy to help set their *long-run target payout ratios*, but not as a guide to the payout in any one year.

■ Companies use the residual dividend model to help understand the determinants of an optimal dividend policy, but they typically use a computerized financial forecasting model when setting the target payout ratio.
☐ Most companies use the computer model to find a dividend pattern over the forecast period that will provide sufficient equity to support the capital budget without having

to sell new common stock or move the capital structure ratio outside the optimal range.

■ Some companies, especially those in cyclical industries, have difficulty maintaining in bad times a dividend that is really too low in good times. Such companies set a very low "regular" dividend and then supplement it with an "extra" dividend when times are good. This is called a *low-regular-dividend-plus-extras* policy.

■ Dividends clearly depend more on cash flows, which reflect the company's ability to pay dividends, than on current earnings, which are heavily influenced by accounting practices and which do not necessarily reflect the ability to pay dividends.

Firms usually pay dividends on a quarterly basis in accordance with the following payment procedures:

■ *Declaration date*. This is the day on which the board of directors declares the dividend. At this time they set the amount of the dividend to be paid, the holder-of-record date, and the payment date.

■ *Holder-of-record date*. This is the date the stock transfer books of the corporation are closed. Those shareholders who are listed on the company's books on this date are the holders of record and they receive the announced dividend.

■ *Ex-dividend date*. This date is four days prior to the holder-of-record date. Shares purchased after the ex-dividend date are not entitled to the dividend. This practice is a convention of the brokerage business which allows sufficient time for stock transfers to be made on the books of the corporation.

■ *Payment date*. This is the day when dividend checks are actually mailed to the holders of record.

Firms should try to establish a rational dividend policy and then stick with it. Dividend policy can be changed, but this can cause problems because such changes can inconvenience the firm's existing stockholders, send unintended signals, and convey the impression of dividend instability, all of which can have negative implications for stock prices. Still, economic circumstances do change, and occasionally such changes dictate that a firm should alter its dividend policy.

Many firms have instituted dividend reinvestment plans (DRIPs) whereby stockholders can automatically reinvest dividends received in the stock of the paying corporation. Income

taxes on the amount of the dividends must be paid even though stock rather than cash is received.

> There are two types of DRIPs.
> ☐ Plans which involve only "old stock" that is already outstanding.
> ☐ Plans which involve newly issued stock.

■ Stockholders choose between continuing to receive dividend checks or having the company use the dividends to buy more stock in the corporation.

> One interesting aspect of DRIPs is that they are forcing corporations to reexamine their basic dividend policies. A high participation rate in a DRIP suggests that stockholders might be better off if the firm simply reduced cash dividends, which would save stockholders some personal income taxes.

> Some companies have expanded their DRIPs by moving to *open enrollment*, whereby anyone can purchase the firm's stock directly and thus bypass brokers' commissions.

Regardless of the debate on the relevancy of dividend policy, it is possible to identify several factors that influence dividend policy. These factors are grouped into four broad categories.

> Constraints: (1) Bond indentures, (2) preferred stock restrictions, (3) impairment of capital rule, (4) availability of cash, and (5) penalty tax on improperly accumulated earnings.

> Investment opportunities: (1) Number of profitable investment opportunities and (2) possibility of accelerating or delaying projects.

> Alternative sources of capital: (1) Cost of selling new stock, (2) ability to substitute debt for equity, and (3) control.

> Effects of dividend policy on k_s: (1) Stockholders' desire for current versus future income, (2) perceived riskiness of dividends versus capital gains, (3) the tax advantage of capital gains over dividends, and (4) the information content of dividends (signaling).

Dividend policy decisions are exercises in informed judgment, not decisions that can be based on a precise mathematical model.

> Dividend policy is not an independent decision—the dividend decision is made jointly with capital structure and capital budgeting decisions. The underlying reason for this

joint decision process is asymmetric information, which influences managerial actions in two ways.

☐ In general, managers do not want to issue new common stock. Considering the total costs involved, including both issuance and asymmetric information costs, managers strongly prefer to use retained earnings as their primary source of new equity.

☐ Dividend changes provide signals about managers' beliefs as to their firms' future prospects. Thus, dividend reductions, or worse yet, omissions, generally have a significant negative effect on a firm's stock price. Consequently, managers try to set dollar dividends low enough so that there is only a remote chance that the dividend will have to be reduced in the future.

■ In setting dividend policy, managers should begin by considering the firm's future investment opportunities relative to its projected internal sources of funds.

■ The target long-term payout ratio should be designed to permit the firm to meet all of its equity capital requirements with retained earnings. Managers should use the residual dividend model to set dividends, but in a long-term framework.

■ The current dollar dividend should be set so that there is an extremely low probability that the dividend, once set, will ever have to be lowered or omitted.

■ In general, firms with superior investment opportunities should set lower payouts, hence retain more earnings, than firms with poor investment opportunities. The degree of uncertainty also influences the decision.

☐ If there is a great deal of uncertainty in the forecasts of free cash flows, then it is best to be conservative and to set a lower current dollar dividend.

☐ Firms with postponable investment opportunities can afford to set a higher dollar dividend, because, in times of stress, investments can be postponed for a year or two, thus increasing the cash available for dividends.

☐ Firms whose cost of capital is largely unaffected by changes in the debt ratio can also afford to set a higher payout ratio, because they can, in times of stress, more easily issue additional debt to maintain the capital budgeting program without having to cut dividends to issue stock.

■ Today's dividend decisions are constrained by policies that were set in the past, hence setting a policy for the next five years necessarily begins with a review of the current situation.

■ Because dividend policy still remains one of the most judgmental decisions that firms must make, it is always set by the board of directors. The financial staff analyzes the situation and makes a recommendation, but the board makes the final decision.

Stock dividends and stock splits are often used to lower a firm's stock price and, at the same time, to conserve its cash resources.

■ The effect of a *stock split* is an increase in the number of shares outstanding and a reduction in the par, or stated, value of the shares. For example, if a firm had 1,000 shares of stock outstanding with a par value of $100 per share, a 2-for-1 split would reduce the par value to $50 and increase the number of shares to 2,000.

☐ The total net worth of the firm remains unchanged.

☐ The stock split does not involve any cash payment, only additional certificates representing new shares.

☐ Stock splits often occur due to the widespread belief that there is an *optimal price range* for each stock.

☐ Stock splits are generally used after a sharp price run-up to produce a large price reduction.

■ A *stock dividend* requires an accounting entry transfer from retained earnings to common stock.

☐ Again, no cash is involved with this "dividend." Net worth remains unchanged, and the number of shares is increased.

☐ Stock dividends used on a regular annual basis will keep the stock price more or less constrained.

■ From a pure economic standpoint, stock dividends and splits are just additional pieces of paper. However, they provide management with a relatively low-cost way of signaling that the firm's prospects look good.

☐ All in all, it probably makes sense to employ stock dividends/splits when a firm's prospects are favorable especially if the price of its stock has gone beyond the normal trading range.

Stock repurchases are an alternative to dividends for transmitting cash to stockholders. They have become popular since they enhance shareholder value.

■ There are two principal types of repurchases: (1) Situations where the firm has cash available for distribution to its stockholders and it distributes this cash by repurchasing shares rather than by paying cash dividends, and (2) situations where the firm concludes that its capital structure is too heavily weighted with equity, and then it sells debt and uses the proceeds to buy back its stock.

■ Stock repurchased by the issuing firm is called *treasury stock*.

- ■ Advantages of repurchases include:
  - ☐ The repurchase is often motivated by management's belief that the firm's shares are undervalued.
  - ☐ The stockholder is given a choice of whether or not to sell his stock to the firm.
  - ☐ The repurchase can remove a large block of stock "overhanging" the market.
  - ☐ If an increase in cash flow is temporary, the cash can be distributed to stockholders as a repurchase rather than as a dividend that could not be maintained in the future.
  - ☐ The company has more flexibility in adjusting the total distribution than it would if the entire distribution were in the form of cash dividends, because repurchases can be varied from year to year without giving off adverse signals.
  - ☐ Repurchases can be used to produce large-scale changes in capital structures.
  - ☐ Companies that grant large numbers of options to employees can repurchase stock and then reissue those shares when options are exercised, thus avoiding the dilution that would occur if new shares were sold to cover exercised options.

- ■ Disadvantages of repurchases include:
  - ☐ Repurchases are not as dependable as cash dividends; therefore, the stock price may benefit more from cash dividends.
  - ☐ Selling stockholders may not be aware of all the implications of the repurchase; therefore, repurchases are usually announced in advance.
  - ☐ If a firm pays too high a price for the repurchased stock, it is to the disadvantage of the remaining stockholders.

- ■ Increases in the size and frequency of repurchases in recent years suggest that companies are doing more repurchases and paying out less cash as dividends.

SELF-TEST QUESTIONS

Definitional

1. MM argue that a firm's dividend policy has _____ _____ on a stock's price.

2. Gordon and Lintner hypothesize that investors value a dollar of _____ more highly than a dollar of expected _____ _____.

3. A company may be forced to increase its _____ ratio to avoid a tax on retained earnings deemed to be unnecessary for the conduct of the business.

4. Some stockholders prefer dividends to _____ _____ because of a need for current _____.

5.	If the _____ of a firm's stock increases with the announcement of an increase in dividends, it may be due to the _____ content in the dividend announcement rather than to a preference for dividends over capital gains.

6.	A firm with _____ earnings is most appropriate for using the policy of "extra" dividends.

7.	The stock transfer books of a corporation are closed on the _____-____-_____ date.

8.	The ____-_____ date occurs four days prior to the _____-____-_____ date and provides time for stock transfers to be recorded on the firm's books.

9.	Actual payment of a dividend is made on the _____ date as announced by the _____ ____ _____.

10.	Many firms have instituted _____ _____ plans whereby stockholders can use their dividends to purchase additional shares of the company's stock.

11.	A stock split involves a reduction in the _____ _____ of the common stock, but no accounting transfers are made between accounts.

12.	The assumption that some investors prefer a high dividend payout while others prefer a low payout is called the _____ effect.

13.	The residual dividend policy is based on the fact that new common stock is _____ _____ than retained earnings.

14.	Stock repurchased by the firm which issued it is called _____ _____.

15.	_____ _____ involves the decision to pay out earnings versus retaining them for reinvestment in the firm.

16.	The _____ _____ _____ is defined as the percentage of net income to be paid out as cash dividends, and should be based in large part on investors' preferences for dividends versus capital gains.

17.	The _____ _____ theory states that investors may prefer to have companies retain most of their earnings because of various tax advantages.

18.   Dividend _____ has two components: (1) How dependable is the growth rate and (2) can we count on at least receiving the current dividend in the future?

19.   The _____ _____ policy is based on the premise that investors prefer to have a firm retain and reinvest earnings rather than to pay them out in dividends, if the rate of return the firm can earn on reinvested earnings exceeds the rate of return investors can obtain for themselves on other investments of comparable risk.

20.   Some companies have expanded their DRIPs by moving to _____ _____ whereby anyone can purchase the firm's stock directly and bypass brokers' commissions.

21.   The dividend decision is made jointly with _____ _____ and _____ _____ decisions.

22.   _____ _____ are an alternative to dividends for transmitting cash to stockholders.

Conceptual

23.   An increase in cash dividends will always result in an increase in the price of the common stock because D_1 will increase in the stock valuation model.

    a. True   b. False

24.   A stock split will affect the amounts shown in which of the following balance sheet accounts?

    a. Common stock   d. Cash
    b. Pain-in capital   e. None of the above accounts.
    c. Retained earnings

25.   If investors prefer dividends to capital gains, then

    a. The required rate of return on equity, k_s, will not be affected by a change in dividend policy.
    b. The cost of capital will not be affected by a change in dividend policy.
    c. k_s will increase as the payout ratio is reduced.
    d. k_s will decrease as the retention rate increases.
    e. A policy conforming to the residual dividend model will maximize stock price.

26. Which of the following statements is most correct?

   a. Modigliani and Miller's theory of the effect of dividend policy on the value of a firm has been called the bird-in-the-hand theory, because MM argued that a dividend in the hand is less risky than a potential capital gain in the bush. After extensive empirical tests, this theory is now accepted by most financial experts.
   b. According to proponents of the dividend irrelevance theory, if a company's stock price rises after the firm announces a greater-than-expected dividend increase, the price increase occurs because of signaling effects, not because of investors' preferences for dividends over capital gains.
   c. Both statements a and b are correct.
   d. Both statements a and b are incorrect.

27. Which of the following statements is most correct?

   a. The residual dividend policy calls for the establishment of a fixed, stable dividend (or dividend growth rate) and then for the level of investment each year to be determined as a residual equal to net income minus the established dividends.
   b. According to the residual dividend policy, if a firm has a large number of profitable investment opportunities this will tend to produce a lower optimal dividend payout ratio.
   c. According to the text, a firm would probably maximize its stock price if it established a specific dividend payout ratio, say 40 percent, and then paid that percentage of earnings out each year because stockholders would then know exactly how much dividend income to count on when they planned their spending for the coming year.
   d. If you buy a stock after the ex-dividend date but before the dividend has been paid, then you, and not the seller, will receive the next dividend check the company sends out.
   e. Each of the above statements is incorrect.

28.   Which of the following statements is most correct?

   a. According to the asymmetric information, or signaling, theory of capital structure, the announcement of a new stock issue by a mature firm would generally lead to an *increase* in the price of the firm's stock.
   b. According to the asymmetric information, or signaling, theory of capital structure, the announcement of a new stock issue by a mature firm would generally lead to a *decrease* in the price of the firm's stock.
   c. If Firm A's managers believe in the asymmetric information theory, but Firm B's managers do not, then, other things held constant, Firm A would probably have the *higher* normal target debt ratio.
   d. There is no such thing as the asymmetric information theory of capital structure, at least according to the text.
   e. Both statements b and c are correct.

29.   Which of the following statements is most correct?

   a. According to the tax preference theory, investors prefer dividends and, as a result, the higher the payout ratio, the higher the value of the firm.
   b. According to the bird-in-the-hand theory, investors prefer cash to paper (stock), so if a company announces that it plans to repurchase some of its stock, this causes the price of the stock to increase.
   c. According to the dividend irrelevance theory developed by Modigliani and Miller, stock dividends (but not cash dividends) are irrelevant because they "merely divide the pie into thinner slices."
   d. According to the information content, or signaling, hypothesis, the fact that stock prices generally increase when an increase in the dividend is announced demonstrates that investors prefer higher to lower payout ratios.
   e. According to the text, the residual dividend policy is more appropriate for setting a company's long-run target payout ratio than for determining the payout ratio on a year-to-year basis.

30. Which of the following statements is most correct?

    a. Stock prices generally rise on the ex-dividend date, and that increase is especially great if the company increases the dividend.

    b. Dividend reinvestment plans are popular with investors because investors who do not need cash income can have their dividends reinvested in the company's stock and thereby avoid having to pay income taxes on the dividend income until they sell the stock.

    c. In the past, stock dividends and stock splits were frequently used by corporations which wanted to lower the prices of their stocks to an "optimal trading range." However, recent empirical studies have demonstrated that stock dividends and stock splits generally cause stock prices to decline, so companies today rarely split their stock or pay stock dividends.

    d. Statements a, b, and c are incorrect.

    e. Statements a, b, and c are correct.

SELF-TEST PROBLEMS

1. Express Industries' expected net income for next year is $1 million. The company's target and current capital structure is 40 percent debt and 60 percent common equity. The optimal capital budget for next year is $1.2 million. If Express uses the residual theory of dividends to determine next year's dividend payout, what is the expected payout ratio?

    a. 0%   **b.** 10%   **c.** 28%   **d.** 42%   **e.** 56%

2. Amalgamated Shippers has a current and target capital structure of 30 percent debt and 70 percent equity. This past year Amalgamated, which uses the residual dividend model, had a dividend payout ratio of 47.5 percent and net income of $800,000. What was Amalgamated's capital budget?

    a. $400,000   **b.** $500,000   **c.** $600,000   **d.** $700,000   **e.** $800,000

3. The Aikman Company's optimal capital structure calls for 40 percent debt and 60 percent common equity. The interest rate on its debt is a constant 12 percent; its cost of common stock is 18 percent; and its federal-plus-state tax rate is 40 percent. Aikman has the following investment opportunities:

    Project A: Cost = $5 million; IRR = 22%.
    Project B: Cost = $5 million; IRR = 14%.
    Project C: Cost = $5 million; IRR = 11%.

    Aikman expects to have net income of $7 million. If Aikman bases its dividends on the residual policy, what will its payout ratio be?

    a. 22.62%   **b.** 14.29%   **c.** 31.29%   **d.** 25.62%   **e.** 18.75%

4. Hiers Automotive Supply Inc.'s stock trades at $100 a share. The company is contemplating a 4-for-3 stock split. Assuming that the stock split will have no effect on the market value of its equity, what will be the company's stock price following the stock split?

    a. $50.00   **b.** $62.50   **c.** $70.00   **d.** $75.00   **e.** $80.00

5. Ridgdill Corporation has net income of $8,000,000 and it has 1,000,000 shares of common stock outstanding. The company's stock currently trades at $30 a share. Ridgdill is considering a plan where it will use available cash to repurchase 15 percent of its shares in the open market. The repurchase is expected to have no effect on either net income or the company's P/E ratio. What will be its stock price following the stock repurchase?

    a. $35.29   **b.** $32.00   **c.** $36.89   **d.** $35.15   **e.** $31.43

ANSWERS TO SELF-TEST QUESTIONS

1. no effect
2. dividends; capital gains
3. payout
4. capital gains; income
5. price (value); information
6. volatile (fluctuating)
7. holder-of-record
8. ex-dividend; holder-of-record
9. payment; board of directors
10. dividend reinvestment
11. par value
12. clientele
13. more costly
14. treasury stock
15. Dividend policy
16. target payout ratio

17.	tax preference	**20.**	open enrollment
18.	stability	**21.**	capital structure; capital budgeting
19.	residual dividend	**22.**	Stock repurchases

23.   b.   A dividend increase could be perceived by investors as signifying poor investment opportunities and hence lower growth in future earnings, thus reducing g in the DCF model. The net effect on stock price is uncertain.

24.   e.   A stock split will affect the par value and number of shares outstanding. However, no dollar values will be affected.

25.   c.   This is the Gordon-Lintner hypothesis. If investors view dividends as being less risky than potential capital gains, then the cost of equity is inversely related to the payout ratio.

26.   b.   Statement a is false; the proponents of this theory were Gordon and Lintner and empirical tests have not proven any of the dividend theories. Statement b is correct.

27.   b.   Statement a is false; the residual dividend policy calls for the determination of the optimal capital budget and then the dividend is established as a residual of net income minus the amount of retained earnings necessary for the capital budget. Statement b is correct. Statement c is false; a constant payout policy would lead to uncertainty of dividends due to fluctuating earnings. Statement d is false; if a stock is bought after the ex-dividend date the dividend remains with the seller of the stock.

28.   b.   The asymmetric information theory suggests that investors regard the announcement of a stock sale as bad news: If the firm had really good investment opportunities, it would use debt financing so that existing stockholders would get all the benefits from the good projects. Therefore, the announcement of a stock sale leads to a decline in the price of the firm's stock. In order to reduce the chances of having to issue stock, firms therefore set low target debt ratios, which give them "reserve borrowing capacity."

29.   e.   Statements a, b, c, and d are false, but statement e is true.

30.   d.   The statements are all false.

SOLUTIONS TO SELF-TEST PROBLEMS

1.   c.   The $1,200,000 capital budget will be financed using 40 percent debt and 60 percent equity. Therefore, the equity requirement will be 0.6($1,200,000) = $720,000. Since the expected net income is $1,000,000, $280,000 will be available to pay as dividends. Thus, the payout ratio is expected to be $280,000/$1,000,000 = 0.28 = 28%.

2.   c.   Of the $800,000 in net income, 0.475($800,000) = $380,000 was paid out as dividends. Thus, $420,000 was retained in the firm for investment. This is the equity portion of the total capital budget, or 70 percent of the total capital budget. Therefore, the total capital budget was $420,000/0.7 = $600,000.

3.   b.   WACC = 0.4(12%)(0.6) + 0.6(18%) = 13.68%.

       We see that the capital budget should be $10 million, since only Projects A and B have IRRs > WACC. We know that 60 percent of the $10 million should be equity. Therefore, the company should pay dividends of:

       Dividends = NI − Needed equity = $7,000,000 − $6,000,000 = $1,000,000.
       Payout ratio = $1,000,000/$7,000,000 = 0.1429 = 14.29%.

4.   d. $P_0 = \$100$; Split = 4 for 3; New $P_0 = ?$ $P_{0\,New} = \dfrac{\$100}{4/3} = \$75.00.$

5.   a.   NI = \$8,000,000; Shares = 1,000,000; P_0 = \$30; Repurchase = 15%; New P_0 = ?

Repurchase = 0.15 × 1,000,000 = 150,000 shares.

Repurchase amount = 150,000 × \$30.00 = \$4,500,000.

$$EPS_{Old} = \frac{NI}{Shares} = \frac{\$8,000,000}{1,000,000} = \$8.00.$$

$$P/E = \frac{\$30}{\$8} = 3.75\times.$$

$$EPS_{New} = \frac{\$8,000,000}{1,000,000 - 150,000} = \frac{\$8,000,000}{850,000} = \$9.41.$$

$Price_{New} = EPS_{New} \times P/E = \$9.41 \times 3.75 = \$35.29.$

CHAPTER 13
INVESTMENT BANKING AND FINANCIAL RESTRUCTURING

OVERVIEW

In this chapter topics related to long-term financing are discussed, including why firms sell equity to the public, how stocks and bonds are issued, the regulation of securities markets, and how bonds and preferred stocks are refunded.

OUTLINE

"Going public" means selling some of a company's stock to outside investors and then letting the stock trade in public markets.

■ *Going public* has the following advantages:
  □ By selling some of their stock in a public offering, the original owners are able to *diversify* their holdings, thereby reducing the riskiness of their personal portfolios.
  □ Public ownership *increases* the stock's *liquidity*.
  □ New corporate cash is more *easily raised* by a publicly owned company.
  □ Going public *establishes the firm's value* in the marketplace.

■ Going public has the following disadvantages:
  □ A publicly owned company must file quarterly and annual reports with various governmental agencies. These reports can be *costly*.
  □ Publicly owned firms must *disclose* operating and ownership data.
  □ The opportunities for owners/managers to engage in questionable, but legal, *self-dealings are reduced.*
  □ If a publicly held firm is very small, and if its shares will be *traded infrequently,* then its stock will not really be liquid, and the market price may be lower than the stocks' true value.
  □ Managers of publicly owned firms with *less than 50 percent* control must be concerned about tender offers and proxy fights. This sometimes leads to operating decisions that are not in the best long-run interests of the shareholders.

■   There are no hard-and-fast rules regarding if or when a company should go public. This is an individual decision that should be made on the basis of the company's and stockholders' own unique circumstances.

Stocks traded on organized exchanges are called listed stocks. While the decision to go public is significant, the decision to list is not a major event. In order to have a listed stock, a company must apply to an exchange, pay a relatively small fee, and meet the exchange's minimum requirements.

■   An exchange's minimum requirements relate to the following:
   ☐ Size of the company's net income. (Size qualifications increase as one moves from the regional exchanges to the AMEX and on to the NYSE.)
   ☐ Number of shares outstanding and in the hands of outsiders.
   ☐ Company must agree to disclose certain information to the exchange.

■   The company will have to file a few new reports with an exchange.

■   It will have to abide by the exchange's rules.

■   Firms benefit from listing their stock by *gaining liquidity, status,* and *free advertising* and *publicity.*
   ☐ By providing investors with these benefits, financial managers may be able to lower their firms' cost of equity and increase the value of their stock.
   ☐ However, due to improvements in telecommunications and computer technologies, the differences between the OTC market and the exchanges have become less distinct.

If stock is to be sold to raise new capital, the new shares may be sold in one of five ways:

■   If stockholders have a *preemptive right*, or if the firm chooses to do so, it can sell the additional stock to existing stockholders as a *rights offering*.
   ☐ The purpose of the preemptive right is twofold.
      • It protects the power of control of present stockholders.
      • It protects stockholders against dilutions of value.
   ☐ Each shareholder is issued an option to buy a certain number of new shares, and the terms of the option are listed on a certificate called a *stock purchase right*, or simply a *right*.
   ☐ If a stockholder does not wish to purchase any additional shares, then he or she can sell the rights to some other person who does want to buy the stock.
   ☐ Several issues confront the financial manager who is setting the terms of a rights offering:
      • How many rights will be required to purchase a share of the newly issued stock?

- • What is the value of each right?
- • What effect will the rights offering have on the price of the existing stock?
- • What will be the price of the stock if it is traded during the offering period? This depends on who will receive the rights, the old owners or the new.

☐ The company sets a "holder-of-record" date, then the stock goes *ex right* four trading days prior to the holder-of-record date.

☐ If the stock is sold prior to the ex-rights date, it is sold *rights on*; that is, the new owner will receive the rights.

☐ If the stock is sold on or after the ex-rights date, the old owner will receive them.

☐ While the stock is still selling rights on, the value at which the rights will sell when they are issued can be found by the following formula:

$$\frac{\text{Value of}}{\text{one right}} = \frac{\text{Market value of stock, rights on} - \text{Subscription price}}{\text{Number of rights required to purchase 1 share} + 1}.$$

$$R = \frac{M_o - S}{N + 1}.$$

☐ The value of a right on or after the ex-rights date can be found by the following formula:

$$\frac{\text{Value of}}{\text{one right}} = \frac{\text{Market value of stock, ex rights} - \text{Subscription price}}{\text{Number of rights required to purchase 1 share}}.$$

$$R = \frac{M_e - S}{N}.$$

☐ The price of the company's stock will be lower after a rights offering than prior to an offering.

- • Stockholders have not suffered a loss, however, because they receive the value of the rights.
- • The stock price decline is similar in nature to a stock split. The larger the underpricing in the rights offering, the greater the stock split effect, and the lower the final stock price.

■ If the preemptive right does not exist, the company can choose between a rights offering and a *public offering*.

■ In a *private placement*, securities are sold to one or a few investors, generally institutional investors. Private placements are most common with bonds, but they also occur with stocks.

☐ The primary advantages are lower flotation costs and greater speed, since the shares do not have to go through the SEC registration process.

☐ The most common type of private placement occurs when a company places securities directly with a financial institution.

☐ One type of private placement that is occurring with increasing frequency is where a large company makes an equity investment in a smaller supplier.

☐ The primary disadvantage of a private placement is that the securities generally do not go through the SEC registration process, so under SEC rules they cannot be sold except to another large, "sophisticated" purchaser in the event the original buyer wants to sell them.

■ Many companies have plans that allow employees to purchase stock on favorable terms.

☐ Under executive *stock option plans*, key managers are given options to purchase stock. If these managers perform well, the stock will go up, and the options will become valuable.

☐ There are also plans for lower-level employees in which they can allocate part of their salary to buy newly issued shares below market value.

☐ A third type of plan is an *Employee Stock Ownership Plan (ESOP),* in which the stock bought for the employees is purchased out of a share of the company's profits.

● ESOPs have the following advantages: (1) tax breaks, (2) anti-takeover defense, (3) pension cost control, and (4) productivity enhancement.

● Potential disadvantages are: (1) the balance of power is altered, (2) legal considerations regarding ESOP abuses, (3) retiree benefits becoming so dependent on the stock's price that retirees are vulnerable, and (4) private companies with ESOPs must repurchase stock at the current appraised value when employees quit or retire in a given year.

■ Although employee purchase plans are designed more to provide incentives to improve employee performance than to raise capital, these plans do produce a surprisingly large amount of new equity.

Common stock financing has advantages and disadvantages.

■ Financing with common stock has the following advantages to the corporation:

☐ Common stock *does not obligate* the firm to make *fixed payments* to investors.

☐ Common stock has *no maturity date.*

☐ Common stock *strengthens the position of creditors*. Its use improves access to debt markets and lowers the cost of debt.

☐ Common stock can often be *sold more easily* than debt.

● It typically carries a higher expected return than does preferred stock or debt.

● It provides investors with a better hedge against inflation than does preferred stock or bonds.

- Its returns are taxed as capital gains, and taxes can be deferred until the gains are realized.

■ Financing with common stock has the following disadvantages to the corporation:
  □ Issuing common stock *extends voting rights,* and thus *control*, to new stockholders.
  □ Common stock means that *more stockholders share in the firm's future profits* rather than a fixed payment as with creditors.
  □ The *costs of underwriting and distributing common stock* are higher than those for preferred stock or debt.
  □ The sale of new common stock may be perceived by investors as a *negative signal,* hence may cause the stock price to fall.

In a going private transaction, the entire equity of a publicly held firm is purchased by a small group of investors which usually includes the firm's current senior management.

■ When financing is arranged to purchase the publicly held stock, these deals are commonly known as *leveraged buyouts (LBOs)* or *leveraged managerial buyouts (MBOs).*

■ *Going private* simply rearranges the ownership structure.
  □ Going private can increase the value of the firm sufficiently to enrich both managers and public stockholders.
  □ The primary advantages to going private are:
    - Administrative cost savings.
    - Increased managerial incentives.
    - Increased managerial flexibility.
    - Increased shareholder participation.
    - Increased use of financial leverage, which reduces taxes.

In an equity carve-out (or partial public offering, or spin-out), a wholly-owned subsidiary becomes publicly owned but the parent retains full control of the subsidiary by retaining about 80 percent of the subsidiary's common stock.

■ The primary advantages to equity carve-outs are:
  □ Facilitate the evaluation of corporate growth opportunities on a line of business basis.
  □ Improve the ability of the parent's top management to offer incentives to a subsidiary's managers.
  □ Increase the effectiveness of capital allocation.
  □ Reduce the uncertainty faced by investors which can lower the cost of capital for the various units, and thus increase the aggregate value of the consolidated enterprise.

■ Equity carve-outs do have some associated costs:

☐ The underwriting commission involved in an equity carve-out is larger than for an equity offering by the parent. In addition, the potential for underpricing is great.

☐ Key managers of the subsidiary must spend a significant amount of time marketing the new stock.

☐ There are costs associated with the minority interest that is created in the carve-out.

☐ Additional costs including annual reports, SEC filings, and analyst presentations must now be borne by both the parent and subsidiary.

■ In essence, a carve-out is a form of corporate *securitization*, which is the issuance of public securities backed by assets that have been segregated from the remaining assets of the company.

☐ By creating such securities, and a liquid market for trading them, a corporation can potentially reduce investor risk and increase the value of the firm as a whole.

Most participants in the securities markets, including the organized exchanges, brokers, investment bankers, and dealers, are regulated by the federal government through the Securities and Exchange Commission (SEC) and, to a lesser extent, by state governments.

■ The SEC has jurisdiction over all *interstate public offerings* in amounts of $1.5 million or more.

■ New issues (stocks and bonds) must be registered with the SEC at least 20 days before they are publicly offered.

☐ The *registration statement* provides financial, legal, and technical information about the company to the SEC.

☐ A *prospectus* summarizes the registration statement information for investors.

☐ A preliminary, or "*red herring*," *prospectus* may be distributed to potential buyers during the 20-day waiting period, but no sales may be finalized during this time.

● It contains all the key information that will appear in the final prospectus except the price.

■ If the registration statement or prospectus contains *misrepresentations or omissions* of material facts, any purchaser who suffers a loss may sue for damages.

■ The SEC also regulates all national stock exchanges. Firms listed on these exchanges must file financial reports with both the SEC and the exchanges.

■ The SEC also monitors the stock transactions of corporate *insiders*.

■ The SEC has the power to prohibit *manipulation* by such devices as pools or wash sales.

The SEC has control over the *proxy statement* and the way the company uses it to solicit votes.

The Federal Reserve System controls credit used to buy securities through *margin requirements*.
   □ Margin requirements specify the maximum percentage of the purchase price someone can borrow.

States also have some control over the issuance of new securities within their boundaries.
   □ State laws relating to security sales are called *blue sky laws*, because they were put into effect to keep unscrupulous promoters from selling securities that offered the "blue sky" but which actually had little or no asset backing.

The securities industry itself realizes the importance of stable markets, sound brokerage firms, and the absence of stock manipulation. Therefore, the various exchanges work closely with the SEC to police transactions and to maintain the integrity and credibility of the system.
   □ The *National Association of Securities Dealers* (NASD) cooperates with the SEC to police trading in the OTC market.

In general, government regulation of securities trading, as well as industry self-regulation, is designed to ensure (1) that investors receive information that is as accurate as possible, (2) that no one artificially manipulates the market price of a given stock, and (3) that corporate insiders do not take advantage of their position to profit in their companies' stocks at the expense of other stockholders.

The financial manager must have a knowledge of the investment banking process, the process by which new securities are issued. The investment banking process takes place in two stages.

At *Stage I*, the firm itself makes some initial, preliminary decisions on its own.
   □ The *dollar amount* of new capital required is established.
   □ The *type of securities* to be offered is specified. Further, if common stock is to be issued, managers must decide whether a rights offering should be used.
   □ The basis on which to deal with the investment bankers, either by a *competitive bid* or a *negotiated deal,* is determined.
      • Except for the largest firms, offerings of stocks and bonds are generally on a negotiated basis.
   □ Finally, the *investment banking firm* must be *selected.*

The *Stage II* decisions are made jointly by the firm and its selected investment banker.
   □ First, the two parties will reevaluate the Stage I decisions.

☐ The firm and its investment banker must decide whether the banker will work on a "best efforts" basis or will "underwrite" the issue.

- On a *best efforts basis*, the banker does not guarantee that the securities will be sold or that the company will get the cash it needs, only that it will put forth its best efforts to sell the issue.

- On an *underwritten issue*, the company does get a guarantee. Essentially, the banker agrees to buy the entire issue and then resell the securities to its customers at a higher price. The banker bears significant risks in underwritten offerings.

☐ The investment banker's *compensation* must be *negotiated*, and other underwriting expenses must be estimated.

☐ The *offering price* must be set. The investment banker will have an easier job if the issue is priced relatively low; however, the issuer naturally wants as high a price as possible.

■ If *pressure* from the new shares and/or *negative signaling effects* drives down the stock's price, all shares outstanding, not just the new shares, are affected.

Once the company and its investment banker have decided how much money to raise, the type of securities to issue, and the basis for pricing the issue, they will prepare and file an SEC Registration statement and a prospectus.

■ Because they are exposed to large potential losses, investment bankers typically do not handle the purchase and distribution of issues single-handedly unless the issue is a very small one.

☐ If the sum of money involved is large, investment bankers form *underwriting syndicates* in an effort to minimize the risk each banker faces. The banking house which sets up the deal is called the *lead*, or *managing, underwriter*.

☐ In addition to the underwriting syndicate, on larger offerings still more investment bankers are included in a *selling group*, which handles the distribution of securities to individual investors.

- The underwriters act as wholesalers, while members of the selling group act as retailers.

■ A new selling procedure has recently emerged which does not require an underwriting syndicate. In this type of sale, called an *unsyndicated stock offering*, the managing underwriter, acting alone, sells the issue entirely to institutional investors.

■ Large well-known public companies which issue securities frequently may file a master registration statement with the SEC and then update it with a short-form statement just prior to each individual offering.

☐ This procedure is known as a *shelf registration* because, in effect, the company puts its new securities "on the shelf," and then sells them to investors when it feels the market is "right".

☐ Firms with less than $150 million in stock held by outside investors cannot use shelf registrations.

☐ Shelf registrations have two advantages over standard registrations: (1) lower flotation costs and (2) more control over the timing of the issue.

■ For new issues involving small companies, the investment banker will normally *maintain a market* in the shares after the public offering. This is done in order to provide liquidity for the shares and to maintain a good relationship with both the issuer and the investors who purchased the shares.

The last 15 years have witnessed many innovations in long-term debt financing. Three such innovations are zero coupon bonds, project financing, and securitization. Zero coupon bonds are the result of the extreme volatility in interest rates which has characterized the period. Project financing and securitization permit a firm to tie a debt issue to a specific asset.

■ *Zero coupon bonds*, pay no interest but are offered at a substantial discount below their par values and hence provide capital appreciation rather than interest income.

☐ A new form of zeros was created from U. S. Treasury bonds, *zero coupon U. S. Treasury Trust Certificates*. Coupons were clipped off and the "stripped" bond was sold as itself with the coupons used as collateral.

● In 1985 the Treasury Department began allowing investors to strip long-term U. S. Treasury bonds and directly register the newly created zero coupon bonds, called *STRIPs*, with the Treasury Department.

● Now virtually all U. S. Treasury zeros are held in the form of STRIPs.

☐ Zero coupon bonds are just one type of *original issue discount bond (OID)*. Any nonconvertible bond whose coupon rate is set below the going market rate at the time of its issue will sell at a discount, and it will be classified as an OID bond.

☐ Corporate and municipal zeros are generally callable at the option of the issuer after some stated call protection period.

● The call price is set at a premium over the accrued value at the time of the call.

● Stripped U. S. Treasury bonds are not callable. Thus, Treasury zeros are completely protected against reinvestment risk.

■ *Project financing* is another type of debt that has been used extensively in recent years.

☐ In project financing, the holders of the debt generally have claims only against the sponsor's equity in the project and the cash flows generated from the project, and not against the firm or firms that own the project (the sponsors).

☐ Project financings are generally characterized by large size and a high degree of complexity. However, since project financing is tied to a specific project, it can be tailored to meet the specific needs of both the creditors and the sponsors.

☐ Project financing offers several potential benefits over conventional debt financing.

- Project financing usually restricts the usage of the project's cash flows, which means that the lenders, rather than the managers, can decide whether to reinvest excess cash flows or to use them to reduce the loan balance by more than the minimum required.

- Conferring the above power on lenders reduces their risks.

☐ Project financings also have advantages for borrowers.

- Because risks to the lenders are reduced, the interest rate built into a project financing deal may be relatively low.

- Project financings insulate the firm's other assets from risks associated with the project being financed.

☐ Project financings increase the number and type of investment opportunities, hence they make capital markets "more complete."

☐ Project financings reduce the costs to investors of obtaining information and monitoring the borrower's operations.

☐ Project financings also permit firms whose earnings are below the minimum requirements specified in their existing bond indentures to obtain additional debt financing.

☐ Project financings increase the ability of a firm to maintain confidentiality.

☐ Project financings can improve incentives for key managers by enabling them to take direct ownership stakes in the operations under their control.

■ As the term is generally used, a *security* refers to a publicly traded financial instrument, as opposed to a privately placed instrument. Thus, securities tend to have high liquidity. In recent years, procedures have been developed to securitize various types of debt instruments, thus *increasing their liquidity*, *lowering the cost of capital to borrowers*, and generally *increasing the efficiency of the financial markets*.

☐ Securitization has occurred in two ways.

- Some debt instruments that were formerly rarely traded are now being actively traded. Examples are commercial paper and junk bonds.

- In *asset securitization*, or the creation of *asset-backed securities*, individual assets are pledged as collateral, but then typically combined into pools to reduce risk. The oldest type of asset securitization is the mortgage-backed security, but today, such things as accounts receivable and automobile loans are also used as collateral.

☐ The process of securitization has, in general, *lowered costs* and *increased the availability of funds* to borrowers, *decreased risks* to lenders, and *created new investment opportunities* for many investors.

Long-term debt financing has several advantages and disadvantages to the issuer.

■ The major advantages are as follows:
  ☐ The cost of debt is independent of earnings, so debtholders do not participate if profits soar.
  ☐ The effective risk-adjusted cost of debt is lower than that of common stock when the deductibility of interest payments is considered.
  ☐ The corporate owners do not share their control with debtholders.

■ The primary disadvantages are as follows:
  ☐ Since debt service is a fixed charge, a decline in operating income may result in insufficient cash flow to meet debt service requirements. This can lead to bankruptcy.
  ☐ Financial leverage increases the firm's riskiness, hence raises its cost of both debt and equity.
  ☐ Debt normally has a fixed maturity date, and hence the firm must repay the principal at some future date.
  ☐ Long-term debt indenture agreements are much more stringent than those in a short-term credit agreement.
  ☐ Widely accepted lending standards dictate the maximum amount of debt that is considered "reasonable," and the cost of debt beyond this limit becomes prohibitive.

Many factors influence a firm's long-term financing decisions. Their relative importance varies among firms at any point in time and also for any given firm over time, but all should be considered when a firm raises capital.

■ One of the most important factors in any financing decision is the relationship between the firm's actual capital structure and its *target capital structure.*
  ☐ Over the long haul, firms try to maintain their target structures.
  ☐ However, from year to year, firms may stray from the target to minimize flotation costs, to take advantage of market conditions, or because of their own internal situation.
    • Small fluctuations about the optimal capital structure have little effect on the WACC, investors recognize that this procedure is prudent, and the firm saves substantial amounts of flotation costs by financing in this manner.

■ Firms also must consider the *maturity of the assets being financed.*
  ☐ If a firm uses 30-year bonds to finance 10-year assets, the bond payments would continue long after the assets were retired.
  ☐ If a firm uses 10-year bonds to finance 30-year assets, it would have to "roll over" the debt after 10 years.
  ☐ Each of the above strategies involves significant risks. In general, the best all-around financing strategy is to match debt maturities with asset maturities.

- Firms generally do place great emphasis on maturity matching, and this factor often dominates the debt portion of the financing decision.

■ *Current interest rate levels and forecasts of future interest rates* also play an important role in the financing decision.
  - ☐ If current rates are high, and are expected to drop, it might be wise to use short-term financing until rates drop, and then lock in the lower rates with long-term financing.
  - ☐ Conversely, if current rates are low and expected to rise, use long-term financing now to lock in the rates.
  - ☐ However, interest rates are difficult, if not impossible, to forecast. Thus, pursuing one of the above strategies could prove to be disastrous if the forecasts were wrong.
  - ☐ Financial managers ought to arrange their capital structures in such a manner that they can ride out almost any economic storm, and this generally calls for (1) using some "reasonable" mix of debt and equity and (2) using debt with maturities which more or less match the maturities of the assets being financed.

■ The *firm's current condition and earnings outlook* also have an effect on the choice of securities.
  - ☐ A firm may delay debt financing which would trigger a review by the rating agencies.
  - ☐ Debt issued when in a poor financial condition would probably cost more and have more severe restrictive covenants.

■ The amount of financing required and the availability of assets that could be pledged as collateral also impact the financing decision.

Corporations that issue callable debt or preferred stock during high interest rate periods often replace the issue with a lower cost issue when interest rates drop. This operation is called refunding.

■ Refunding decisions involve two separate questions: (1) Is it profitable to call an outstanding issue in the current period and replace it with a new issue; and (2) even if refunding is currently profitable, would the value of the firm be increased even more if the refunding were postponed to a later date?

■ The decision to refund a security is analyzed in much the same way as a capital budgeting expenditure.
  - ☐ The costs of refunding (the investment outlays) are (1) the call premium paid for the privilege of calling the old issue, (2) the tax savings from writing off the unexpensed flotation costs on the old issue, and (3) the net interest that must be paid while both issues are outstanding.

☐ The annual cash flows, in a capital budgeting sense, are the interest payments that are saved each year plus the net tax savings which the firm receives for amortizing the flotation expenses.

■ The *net present value method* is used to analyze the advantages of refunding.
   ☐ The future cash flows are discounted back to the present, and then this discounted value is compared with the cash outlays associated with the refunding.
   ☐ The firm should refund the bond only if the present value of the savings exceed the cost—that is, if the NPV of the refunding operation is positive.

■ In the discounting process, the *after-tax cost of the new debt* should be used as the discount rate.
   ☐ The reasons for this are (1) there is relatively little risk to the savings—cash flows in a refunding are known with relative certainty and (2) the cash outlay required to refund the old issue is generally obtained by increasing the amount of the new issue.

■ If the refunding operation is advantageous to the firm, it must be disadvantageous to bondholders.
   ☐ This points out the danger of the call provision to bondholders, and it also explains why bonds without a call provision command higher prices than callable bonds.

■ The mechanics of calculating the NPV of a refunding are simple, but the decision on when to refund is not a simple one at all, because it requires a forecast of future interest rates. Thus, refunding now versus waiting for a possibly more favorable future refunding is a judgmental decision.

■ Financial managers making bond refunding decisions can now use the values of derivative securities to estimate the value of the bond issue's *embedded call option.*
   ☐ If the call option is worth *more* than the NPV of refunding today, the issue should not be immediately refunded.
   ☐ The issuer should either delay the refunding to take advantage of the information obtained from the derivative market or actually create a derivative transaction to lock in the value of the call option.

SELF-TEST QUESTIONS

Definitional

1. _____ _____ refers to the sale of shares of a closely held business to the general public.

2. Going public establishes the firm's _____ in the marketplace.

3. Securities traded on an organized exchange are known as _____ securities.

4. Before an interstate issue of stock amounting to $1.5 million or more can be sold to the public, it must be _____ with and approved by the _____.

5. In a(n) _____ _____ securities are sold to one or a few investors, generally institutional investors. The primary advantages are lower flotation costs and greater speed, since shares do not have to go through the SEC registration process.

6. Setting the _____ price for a stock issue may present a conflict of interest between the issuer and the _____ _____.

7. In order to spread the risk of underwriting a sizable common stock issue, investment bankers will form a(n) _____ _____.

8. In a(n) _____ _____ _____ plan stock is bought for the employees out of a share of the company's profits.

9. In a(n) _____ _____ _____ the managing underwriter, acting alone, sells the issue entirely to institutional investors, thus bypassing both retail stockbrokers and individual investors.

10. On a(n) _____ _____ _____, the investment banker does not guarantee that the securities will be sold or that the company will get the cash it needs; while on a(n) _____ issue the company does get a guarantee.

11. _____ _____ _____ are offered at a substantial discount below their par values and pay no interest.

12. The oldest type of asset securitization is the _____-_____ _____.

13. Over the long run, a firm should finance in accordance with its _____ _____ _____.

14. The least risky financing strategy is to match the debt _____ with the _____ maturity.

15. It is very _____, if not _____, to forecast interest rates.

16. In _____ _____, the holders of the debt generally have claims only against the sponsor's equity in the project and the cash flows generated from the project, and not against the firm or firms that own the project.

17. If stockholders have a(n) _____ _____, it sells additional stock to existing stockholders as a rights offering.

18 If a stock is sold prior to the ex rights date, it is sold _____ ____; that is, the new owner will receive the rights.

19. The price of the company's stock will be _____ after a rights offering than prior to an offering.

20. In a(n) _____ _____ transaction, the entire equity of a publicly held firm is purchased by a small group of investors which usually includes the firm's current senior management.

21. In a(n) _____ _____ - _____, a wholly-owned subsidiary becomes publicly owned but the parent retains full control of the subsidiary by retaining about 80 percent of the subsidiary's common stock.

22. In essence, a carve-out is a form of corporate _____, which is the issuance of public securities backed by assets that have been segregated from the remaining assets of the company.

23. A(n) _____ refers to a publicly traded financial instrument, as opposed to a privately placed instrument.

24. Corporations that issue callable debt or preferred stock during high interest rate periods often replace the issue with a lower cost issue when interest rates drop; this operation is called _____.

25. A(n) _____ _____ _____ contains all the key information that will appear in the final prospectus except the price.

Conceptual

26. A firm may go public, yet the firm itself may not receive any additional funds in the process.

    a. True   b. False

27. Flotation costs are generally higher for bond issues than for stock issues.

    a. True   **b.** False

28. When new shares are being sold, if it appears that the investment bankers will be unable to sell the entire issue at the initial offering price, the only way the entire issue can be sold is to lower the price.

    a. True   **b.** False

29. Which of the following statements is most correct?

    a. Stocks traded on organized exchanges are called listed stocks. Both the decision to go public and to list are major events for the firm.

    b. Whenever a publicly-owned firm decides to issue new common stock, it must register the stock with the SEC, and prospective stockholders must be given a copy of the prospectus. The SEC must approve the prospectus, and one key aspect of this approval is that the SEC must agree that the price at which the shares are to be offered is fair to investors.

    c. Once a company "goes public," it must file periodic statements with the SEC. These periodic statements are called prospectuses, or, sometimes, "red herring" prospectuses.

    d. One important recent innovation is "shelf registration," whereby large companies can register securities in advance, in effect putting them "on the shelf" of an investment banking house, which can then sell them at any time, in whole or in part, when the market is receptive to the securities. Theoretically, either stock or bonds could be sold through shelf registrations, but, because of the preemptive right, as a practical matter, only bonds are involved.

    e. All of the above statements are false.

30. Which of the following statements is most correct?

   a. Large companies such as IBM and Exxon are exempt from SEC listing requirements, but small companies (assets below $10 million) are not. Hence, small companies have listed stock, while large companies have unlisted stock.

   b. If a company's stock is publicly owned, and if its price has been established in the market and is quoted in a source such as *The Wall Street Journal*, then the price of any new issue of stock will be based on the current market price. However, if the stock is not traded, and if the company is going public for the first time, then the Securities and Exchange Commission (SEC) must approve the price at which the stock is to be offered to the public.

   c. In the United States, most new stock issues are sold through the investment banking departments of large commercial banks, such as Barnett Bank or Citibank.

   d. The SEC must normally approve the prospectuses relating to new stock offerings by companies whose securities are listed on the New York Stock Exchange before the new stock can be sold to the public.

   e. Statements b and d are both correct.

31. Which of the following statements is most correct?

   a. A disadvantage to the issuer of long-term debt financing is that the cost of debt is fixed, so debtholders do not participate if profits soar.

   b. If current interest rates are high, and are expected to drop, it might be wise to use long-term financing until rates drop, and then lock in the lower rates with short-term financing.

   c. The primary advantage of zero coupon bonds to investors, especially to wealthy individual investors, is that the investor gets his or her returns in the form of capital gains rather than interest income. Since capital gains (1) are taxed at relatively low rates and (2) are deferred until the bond matures or is sold, zero coupon corporate bonds have a significant advantage over regular coupon bonds.

   d. The bond refunding decision is analyzed like a capital budgeting decision. The investment cost consists of the call premium plus the flotation cost on the new issue, and the cash flow benefits consist of the interest saved each year as a result of substituting low rate debt for high rate debt. Rational companies constantly monitor the situation, and they call callable bonds immediately if the NPV on the refunding decision is positive.

   e. The above statements are false.

SELF-TEST PROBLEMS

1. J.C. Nickel is planning a zero coupon bond issue. The bond has a par value of $1,000, matures in 10 years, and will be sold at an 80 percent discount, or for $200. The firm's marginal tax rate is 40 percent. What is the annual after-tax cost of debt to Nickel on this issue? (Hint: You will need to use a financial calculator.)

    a. 10.48%   **b.** 10.00%   **c.** 11.62%   **d.** 14.79%   **e.** 17.46%

2. Assume that the City of Miami sold an issue of $1,000 maturity value, tax exempt (muni), zero coupon bonds 10 years ago. The bonds had a 30-year maturity when they were issued, and the interest rate built into the issue was a nominal 12 percent, but with semiannual compounding. The bonds are now callable at a premium of 12 percent over the accrued value. What effective annual rate of return would an investor who bought the bonds when they were issued and who still owns them earn if they are called today? (Hint: You will need to use a financial calculator.)

    a. 13.33%   **b.** 12.00%   **c.** 12.37%   **d.** 11.76%   **e.** 13.64%

3. The City of Tampa issued $1,000,000 of 12 percent coupon, 25-year, semiannual payment, tax-exempt muni bonds 10 years ago. The bonds had 10 years of call protection, but now Tampa can call the bonds if it chooses to do so. The call premium would be 11 percent of the face amount. New 15-year, 10 percent, semiannual payment bonds can be sold at par, but flotation costs on this issue would be 3 percent, or $30,000. What is the net present value of the refunding?

    a. $13,011   **b.** $12,262   **c.** $15,121   **d.** $13,725   **e.** $14,545

4. Assume that the Tennessee Valley Power Authority (which is exempt from income taxes) issued $100,000 of 30-year maturity, 10 percent coupon, semiannual payment, tax-exempt bonds on January 1, 1989. The bonds were callable after 10 years, or after January 1, 1999, at a price that is 10 percent above the bonds' par value. On January 1, 1999, the Power Authority learns that it can issue $100,000 of new 20-year, semiannual payment, 8 percent coupon bonds at par. Costs associated with selling the new issue will amount to $2,000. What is the NPV of the refunding decision?

    a. -$7,485.46   **b.** $9,285.48   **c.** -$4,334.60   **d.** $7,792.77   **e.** $6,982.74

5. Assume that the City of Pensacola has $10 million of 12 percent, 20-year, $1,000 par value, semiannual payment bonds outstanding that can be called at a price of $1,100 per bond. New 20-year, 10 percent, semiannual payment bonds can be sold at a flotation cost of $600,000, or 6 percent. What is the NPV of the refunding operation?

    a. $115,909   **b.** $120,606   **c.** $125,505   **d.** $130,707   **e.** $135,808

ANSWERS TO SELF-TEST QUESTIONS

1.	Going public	**14.**	maturity; asset
2.	value	**15.**	difficult; impossible
3.	listed	**16.**	project financings
4.	registered; SEC	**17.**	preemptive right
5.	private placement	**18.**	rights on
6.	offering; investment banker	**19.**	lower
7.	underwriting syndicate	**20.**	going private
8.	employee stock ownership	**21.**	equity carve-out
9.	unsyndicated stock offering	**22.**	securitization
10.	best efforts basis; underwritten	**23.**	security
11.	Zero coupon bonds	**24.**	refunding
12.	mortgage-backed security	**25.**	red herring prospectus
13.	target capital structure		

26.   a. An example is that of the Ford Foundation selling stock to the general public. Also, a firm may go public if its managers sell off a portion of their stock holdings. Then, the funds obtained go to the managers rather than the firm.

27.   b. The investment banker normally must expend greater effort in selling stocks, thus must charge a higher fee. Also, a new common stock issue may lower stock price because of negative signaling effects and/or supply/demand price pressure.

28.   b. The investment bankers may be able to increase the demand for the stock by promoting the issue. If not, then a price reduction may be required.

29.   e. Statement a is false; while the decision to go public is a major event, the decision to list is not. Statement b is false; the SEC is responsible for making sure the information in the registration and prospectus is adequate; however, it does not determine the fairness of the offering price. Statement c is false; prospectuses accompany any sales solicitations. Statement d is false; shelf registrations are also applicable to common stock. Thus, statement e is the correct choice.

30. d. All companies are subject to the SEC's listing requirements, which makes statement a false. The SEC does not have to approve offering prices for initial public offerings. Therefore, statement b is false. Finally, statement c is false because commercial banks are barred from participating in investment bank activities at the present time.

31. e. Statement a is false; this is an advantage to the issuer. Statement b is false; the firm should use short-term financing until interest rates drop and then lock in the lower rates with long-term financing. Statement c is false; investors must impute interest income in each year on zero coupon bonds even though the interest is not received until maturity. The advantage to investors is that there is no reinvestment rate risk with zeros. Statement d is false; companies do not necessarily call callable bonds immediately if the NPV on the refunding decision is positive because if interest rates decrease further it may be beneficial to wait awhile. Therefore, the correct choice is statement e.

SOLUTIONS TO SELF-TEST PROBLEMS

1. a. Maturity = N = 10; Issue price = PV = 200; PMT = 0; Maturity value = FV = 1000; Corporate tax rate = 40%.

Enter into a financial calculator: N = 10, PV = -200, PMT = 0, and FV = 1000, and then solve for $k_d = I = 17.46\%$. However, this is a before-tax cost of debt. $k_d (1 - T)$ $= 17.46\%(1 - 0.4) = 10.48\%$.

Alternatively, set the analysis up on a time line:

	0	1	2	3	4	5	6	7	8	9	10 Years
Year-end accrued value[1]	200.00	234.92	275.94	324.12	380.71	447.18	525.25	616.96	724.69	851.22	1,000.00
Interest deduction[2]		34.92	41.02	48.18	56.59	66.47	78.07	91.71	107.73	126.53	148.78
Tax savings (40%)[3]		13.97	16.41	19.27	22.64	26.59	31.23	36.68	43.09	50.61	59.51
Cash flow[4]	200.00	13.97	16.41	19.27	22.64	26.59	31.23	36.68	43.09	50.61	-940.49

After-tax cost of debt: 10.48%.

Notes:
[1]Year-end accrued value = Issue price $\times (1 + k_d)^n$.
[2]Interest in Year n = Accrued value$_n$ – Accrued value$_{n-1}$.
[3]Tax savings = (Interest deduction)(T).
[4]Cash flow in Year 10 = Tax savings – Maturity value.

2.   e.

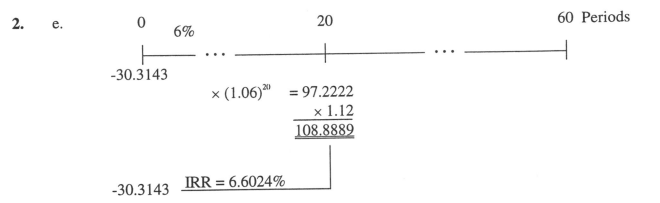

Periodic rate = 6.6024%.

$EAR = (1.066024)^2 - 1 = 0.1364 = 13.64\%.$

The solution to this problem requires three steps:

1. Solve for the PV of the original issue. Using a financial calculator, enter N = 60, I = 6, PMT = 0, and FV = 1000, and then solve for PV = $30.3143.

2. Determine the accrued value at the end of 20 periods, and multiply by the call premium.

$$\$30.3143 \times (1.06)^{20} \times 1.12 = \$108.8889.$$

3. Solve for the EAR to an investor if the bonds are called today. Using a financial calculator, enter N = 20, PV = -30.3143, PMT = 0, and FV = 108.8889, and then solve for $k_d/2 = I = 6.6024\%$.

$$EAR = (1.066024)^2 - 1 = 0.1364 = 13.64\%.$$

3.   d.   Interest on old bond per 6 months: $120,000/2 = $ 60,000
       Interest on new bond per 6 months: $100,000/2 =   50,000
       Savings per six months $ 10,000

       Cost: Call premium = 11% = $110,000
                     Flotation cost = 3% =   30,000
                     Total investment outlay $140,000

$k_d/2 = 10\%/2 = 5\%$ per 6 months.

$$NPV = \sum_{t=1}^{30} \frac{\$10,000}{(1.05)^t} - \$140,000 = \$153,725 - \$140,000 = \$13,725.$$

Alternatively, input the cash flows into the cash flow register, enter I = 5, and then solve for NPV = $13,725.

4.   d.   Cost of refunding = Call premium + Flotation cost
                      = 0.10($100,000) + $2,000 = $12,000.

Savings each 6 months = Interest on old bonds – Interest on new bonds
                           = 0.05($100,000) – 0.04($100,000)
                           = $5,000 – $4,000 = $1,000.

$k_d/2 = 8.0\%/2 = 4.0\%$ = Discount rate for NPV.

$$NPV = \sum_{t=1}^{40} \frac{\$1,000}{(1.04)^t} - \$12,000 = \$19,792.77 - \$12,000 = \$7,792.77.$$

5.   a.   Cost of refunding = Call premium + Flotation cost

$$= (\$1,100 - \$1,000)10,000 + \$600,000 = \$1,600,000.$$

Savings each 6 months = Interest on old bonds – Interest on new bonds

$$= 0.06(\$1,000)(10,000) - 0.05(\$1,000)(10,000)$$

$$= \$100,000.$$

Using a time line, the cash flows are shown below:

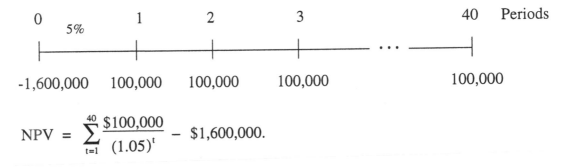

$$NPV = \sum_{t=1}^{40} \frac{\$100,000}{(1.05)^t} - \$1,600,000.$$

Using a financial calculator, input the cash flows into the cash flow register, enter I = 5, and then solve for NPV = \$115,908.64, or approximately \$115,909.

OVERVIEW

Firms generally own fixed assets and report them on their balance sheets, but it is the use of assets that is important, not their ownership per se. One way to obtain the use of facilities and equipment is to buy them, but an alternative is to lease them. Prior to the 1950s, leasing was generally associated with real estate—land and buildings. Today, however, it is possible to lease virtually any kind of fixed asset, and currently over 30 percent of all new capital equipment is financed through lease arrangements.

OUTLINE

There are two parties to every lease agreement, and there are several different types of leases.

■ The *lessor* is the owner of the leased property. The lessor receives the tax benefit of ownership through depreciation tax savings.

■ The *lessee* buys the right to use the property in exchange for one or more *lease*, or *rental*, *payments* to the lessor.

■ Leasing takes several different forms, the four most important include:
  □ *Operating leases.* These leases are sometimes called *services leases* and generally provide for both financing and maintenance.
  ● Operating leases require the lessor to maintain and service the leased equipment, and the cost of the maintenance is built into the lease payments.
  ● Operating leases are not fully amortized. In other words, the rental payments required under the lease contract are not sufficient for the lessor to recover the full cost of the asset.
  ● The lease contract is written for a period considerably less than the expected economic life of the asset, and the lessor expects to recover all costs either by

subsequent renewal payments, by re-leasing the asset to other lessees, or by selling the asset.

- Operating leases often contain a *cancellation clause* to protect the lessee against obsolescence or a change in the lessee's business.

☐ *Financial, or capital, leases.* These leases are fully amortized; they do not provide for maintenance; and they are not cancellable.

- Equipment is purchased by the lessor from the manufacturer or distributor, and the lessee simultaneously executes an agreement to lease the equipment.

- The terms of the lease generally call for full amortization of the lessor's investment, plus a rate of return on the unamortized balance which is close to the percentage rate the lessee would have paid on a secured loan.

- The lessee generally pays the property taxes and insurance on the leased property. Since the lessor receives a return after, or net of, these payments, this type of lease is often called a "net, net" lease.

☐ *Sale and leaseback arrangements.* In this type of lease, a firm owning an asset sells the property to another firm and simultaneously leases it back for a stated period under specific terms.

- The sale and leaseback is an alternative to a mortgage.

- The seller immediately receives the purchase price, but retains the use of the property in exchange for rental payments.

- The lease payments are sufficient to return the purchase price to the lessor plus provide a specified return on the investment.

- A sale and leaseback may be thought of as a special type of financial lease.

☐ *Combination leases.* This type of lease combines features of both operating and financial leases.

Lease payments are deductible expenses for income tax purposes, provided the IRS agrees that the contract is a genuine lease and not an installment loan called a lease.

■   A lease that complies with all IRS requirements is called a *guideline,* or *tax-oriented, lease*, and the tax benefits of ownership (depreciation and any investment tax credits) belong to the lessor. The main provisions of the tax guidelines are as follows:

☐ The lease term (including any extensions or renewals at a fixed rental rate) must not exceed 80 percent of the estimated useful life of the equipment at the commencement of the lease transaction.

☐ The equipment's estimated residual value (in constant dollars without adjustment for inflation) at the expiration of the lease must equal at least 20 percent of its value at the start of the lease.

□ Neither the lessee nor any related party can have the right to purchase the property at a predetermined fixed price at the lease's inception. However, the lessee can be given an option to buy the asset at its fair market value.

□ Neither the lessee nor any related party can pay or guarantee payment of any part of the price of the leased equipment.

□ The leased equipment must not be "limited use" property, defined as equipment that can only be used by the lessee or a related party at the end of the lease.

■ If just any type of contract could be called a lease and given tax treatment as a lease, then the timing of the tax shelters could be speeded up as compared with ownership depreciation tax shelters. This speedup would benefit companies, but it would be costly to the government.

■ A lease that does not meet the tax guidelines is called a *non-tax-oriented lease*.

□ For this type of lease, the lessee is (1) the effective owner of the leased property, (2) can depreciate it for tax purposes, and (3) can deduct only the interest portion of each lease payment.

Lease financing is financially comparable to debt financing because both subject the firm to a contractual series of payments, and failure to make these payments could lead to bankruptcy.

■ Leasing is sometimes referred to as *off balance sheet financing* because, under certain conditions, neither the leased assets nor the lease liabilities appear directly on the firm's balance sheet.

■ A firm with extensive lease arrangements not appearing directly on the firm's balance sheet would have both its assets and its liabilities understated in comparison with a firm which borrowed to purchase the assets, and hence, the firm that leases would show a lower debt ratio. Note, however, that these lease obligations must be disclosed in the notes to the financial statements.

■ FASB Statement 13 requires firms to *capitalize* certain financial (or capital) leases, and thus to restate their balance sheets to report the leased asset as a fixed asset and the present value of the future lease payments as a liability, if certain conditions exist.

□ The logic behind FASB Statement 13 is as follows. If a firm signs a financial lease, its obligation to make lease payments is just as binding as if it had signed a loan agreement—the failure to make lease payments can bankrupt a firm just as fast as the failure to make principal and interest payments on a loan.

□ For all intents and purposes, a financial lease is identical to a loan.

□ If a firm signs a financial lease agreement, this has the effect of raising its true debt ratio, and thus its true capital structure is changed.

- A lease is capitalized if one or more of the following conditions exist:
  - ☐ Ownership of the property is effectively transferred from the lessor to the lessee.
  - ☐ The lessee can purchase the property at less than its true market value when the lease expires.
  - ☐ The lease runs for a period equal to or greater than 75 percent of the asset's life.
  - ☐ The present value of the lease payments is equal to or greater than 90 percent of the initial value of the asset.

- Leases are regarded as debt for capital structure purposes, and they have the same effects as debt on k_d and k_s.
  - ☐ Therefore, leasing is not likely to permit a firm to use more financial leverage than could be obtained with conventional debt.

- The lease decision is a *financing decision,* and not a capital budgeting decision. Thus, lease analysis is not generally conducted unless the decision has already been made to acquire the asset.

Leases must be evaluated by both the lessee and the lessor. For the lessee, the analysis focuses on whether leasing the asset is less costly than buying the asset, and the lessor must decide whether the lease payments provide a satisfactory return on the invested funds.

- Whether or not to acquire the asset is *not* part of the typical lease analysis. In a lease analysis, we are concerned simply with whether to obtain the use of the asset by lease or by purchase.

- The leasing analysis should compare the cost of leasing with the cost of debt financing regardless of how the asset purchase is actually financed.
  - ☐ The asset may be purchased with available cash if not leased, but since leasing is a substitute for debt financing, and has the same capital structure effect, the appropriate comparison would still be with debt financing.

- In an NPV-type analysis, the lessee estimates the cost of leasing and the cost of owning, assuming that the asset is financed solely with debt. If the cost of leasing is less than the cost of owning, the asset should be leased.
  - ☐ All cash flows must reflect tax effects.
  - ☐ Since leasing is a substitute for debt financing, and since lease cash flows have approximately the same risk as debt cash flows, the *appropriate discount rate is the after-tax cost of debt.*
  - ☐ In a lease analysis, the PV cost of owning less the PV cost of leasing is called the *net advantage to leasing (NAL).*
  - ☐ The financing method that produces the smaller present value of costs is the one that should be selected.

- ☐ This analysis focuses on the dollar cost of leasing versus borrowing and buying, which is analogous to the NPV method used in capital budgeting.

- ▬ A second method that lessees can use to evaluate leases focuses on the percentage cost of leasing and is analogous to the IRR method used in capital budgeting. The *percentage cost analysis* is discussed in the Extensions to this chapter.

The lessor views the lease transaction as an investment, and hence, the lessor's analysis focuses on the return on the lease transaction.

- ■ Any potential lessor needs to know the rate of return on the capital invested in the lease, and this information is also useful to the prospective lessee: Lease terms on large leases are generally negotiated, so the lessee should know what return the lessor is earning.

- ■ The lessor's analysis involves:
  - ☐ Determining the net cash outlay, which is usually the invoice price of the leased equipment less any lease payments made in advance.
  - ☐ Determining the periodic cash inflows, which consist of the lease payments minus both income taxes and any maintenance expense the lessor must bear.
  - ☐ Estimating the after-tax residual value of the property when the lease expires.
  - ☐ Determining whether the rate of return on the lease exceeds the lessor's opportunity cost of capital or, equivalently, whether the NPV of the lease exceeds zero.

- ■ The lessor compares the return on the lease with the return available on alternative investments of similar risk. If the return expected on the lease is greater than that available on alternatives of similar risk, the lease should be written.

- ■ The analysis is similar to that of the lessee, in that the cash flows are laid out on a time line.
  - ☐ All tax effects must be considered.
  - ☐ If the lessor's NPV is positive, then the lease should be written.
  - ☐ The lessor's IRR can also be examined, and if it is greater than the after-tax return on comparable investments, the lease transaction should be completed.

In large leases the parties generally sit down and work out an agreement on the size of the lease payments, with these payments being set so as to provide the lessor with some specific required rate of return.

- ■ In situations where the lease terms are not negotiated, the lessor must still go through the same type of analysis, setting terms which provide a target rate of return, and then offering these terms to the potential lessee on a take-it-or-leave-it basis.

■ Leasing is not always a zero sum game, but if the inputs to the lessee and the lessor are identical, then a positive NAL to the lessee implies an equal but negative NPV to the lessor.

■ However, conditions are often such that leasing can provide net benefits to both parties.
  □ This situation arises because of differentials, generally in taxes, in estimated residual values, or in the ability to bear the residual value risk.

■ The lessor can, under certain conditions, increase the return on the lease by borrowing some of the funds used to purchase the leased asset. Such a lease is called a *leveraged lease*.
  □ Whether or not a lease is leveraged has no effect on the lessee's analysis, but it can have a significant effect on the cash flows to the lessor, hence on the lessor's expected return.
  □ Leveraged leases are discussed in the Extensions to this chapter.

Other issues often arise in leasing decisions.

■ The value of the asset at lease termination is called its *residual value*.
  □ Superficially, it might first appear that assets with large residual values would most likely be owned since the owner gets the residual value.
  □ However, competition among leasing companies and other financing sources forces lease contracts to fully recognize expected residual values. Thus, large residual value assets are not necessarily more suitable for buying than for leasing.

■ It is sometimes argued that firms which lease a significant portion of their assets can get more favorable debt terms than firms which do not.
  □ This premise rests upon the assumption that credit analysts do not recognize the full impact of leasing on a firm's financial strength.
  □ However, this contention is of *questionable validity* for firms with audited financial statements.
  □ Leasing can be a way to circumvent existing loan covenants. If restrictive covenants prohibit a firm from issuing more debt but fail to restrict lease payments, then the firm could effectively increase its leverage by leasing additional assets.
  □ Firms in very poor financial condition and facing possible bankruptcy may be able to obtain lease financing at a lower cost than comparable debt financing.
    • Lessors often have a more favorable position than lenders should the lessee actually go bankrupt.
    • Lessors that specialize in certain types of equipment may be in a better position to dispose of repossessed equipment than banks or other lenders.

■ The lease-versus-purchase analysis discussed here is just as applicable for real estate as for equipment—conceptually, there is no difference.

■ Lease analysis, like capital budgeting, is particularly well suited for spreadsheets.

■ The ability to structure leases that are advantageous to both lessor and lessee depends in large part on tax laws. The four major factors that influence leasing are (1) investment tax credits, (2) depreciation rules, (3) tax rates, and (4) alternative minimum taxes.

☐ The *investment tax credit (ITC)* is a direct reduction of taxes that occurs when a firm purchases new capital equipment. Current tax laws do not allow an ITC, but they once did, and it is possible they will do so again in the future.

☐ Owners recover their investments in capital assets through *depreciation*, which is tax deductible. Recent tax laws have tended to slow depreciation write-offs, thus reducing the value of ownership.

☐ The value of depreciation depends on the firm's *tax rate*, because the depreciation tax savings equals the amount of depreciation multiplied by the tax rate. Higher tax rates mean greater ownership tax savings, and hence more incentive for tax-driven leases.

☐ The *alternative minimum tax (AMT)* also impacts leasing activity.

● Previously, some corporations were able to pay little or no taxes by using accelerated depreciation for tax purposes, and yet report high earnings to stockholders by using straight line depreciation. The AMT now requires companies to pay a minimum tax equal to approximately 20 percent of their reported earnings.

● A company can reduce its reported income, and hence its AMT liability, by using short-term, fully amortized leases on long-term assets—such leases need not meet the requirements for ordinary tax deductibility.

In addition to tax motivations, there are many other reasons why firms might lease assets rather than purchase them.

■ Many assets are leased, particularly through operating leases, because it is less risky for the firm to lease the asset than to commit to ownership.

☐ Leasing provides *operating flexibility*.

☐ Assets that face rapid and uncertain *technological obsolescence* are often leased. Lessees benefit because they are more easily able to acquire the most advanced equipment. Although the risk of obsolescence is passed to the lessor, lessors may be better able to bear this risk because of (1) diversification across a wide variety of assets and (2) being better able to assess residual values and market the used assets.

☐ If the life of the project is in doubt, then it may be better to lease the asset, since it might be easier to dispose of the asset in the event of *premature termination* of the project.

■ The leasing industry recently introduced a type of lease that even transfers some of a project's operating risk from the lessee to the lessor, and also motivates the lessor to maintain the leased equipment in good working order.

  ☐ In the health care industry, such leases are called *per-procedure leases*.

  ☐ Instead of making a fixed rental payment, the lessee pays a fee each time the leased equipment is used. By using a per-procedure lease, the company is converting a fixed cost for the equipment into a variable cost, hence reducing the machine's operating leverage and breakeven point.

■ Some companies also find leasing attractive because the lessor is able to provide servicing on favorable terms.

■ A sound lease decision must begin with a quantitative analysis, and then qualitative factors can be considered before making the final lease-or-buy decision.

The Extensions to Chapter 14 discuss percentage cost analysis, the feedback effect of leasing on capital budgeting, and leveraged lease analysis.

■ The lease-versus-purchase decision can also be analyzed using the *percentage cost analysis*.

  ☐ The after-tax cost rate implied in the lease contract is determined.

  ☐ The asset should be leased if the after-tax cost rate of the lease is less than the after-tax cost of debt.

■ If the cost of leasing is less than the cost of debt, the overall cost of capital for an asset with lease financing would be less than that for a nonleased asset of similar risk. Thus, assets that were marginally unacceptable could have a positive NPV if lower cost lease financing were available.

  ☐ There are two possible polar positions, depending on the firm's opportunity to substitute lease financing for regular debt financing:

    ● The debt component of all projects can be financed by leasing on similar terms. In this case, the firm should never borrow—all "debt" financing should come from leasing, and all projects should be evaluated at a WACC based on the debt cost implied in the lease contracts.

    ● The project under consideration is unique—it is the only one for which favorable lease terms are available. If the project's cost does not exceed the company's incremental debt capacity, the project's NPV for capital budgeting purposes should be determined as:

$$\begin{array}{c} \text{Adjusted} \\ \text{NPV} \end{array} = \begin{array}{c} \text{NPV based on} \\ \text{``regular'' WACC} \end{array} + \begin{array}{c} \text{Project's} \\ \text{NAL} \end{array}.$$

■ When the lessor borrows to purchase the leased property, the lease is called a *leveraged lease*.

☐ Whether or not a lease is leveraged is unimportant from the lessee's standpoint.

☐ Typically, leveraged leases provide the lessor with higher expected rates of return (IRRs) and higher NPVs per dollar of invested capital than unleveraged leases. However, the riskiness to the lessor is increased by the leveraging.

SELF-TEST QUESTIONS

Definitional

1. Conceptually, leasing is similar to _____, and it provides the same type of financial _____.

2. Under a(n) _____ _____ _____ arrangement, the seller receives the purchase price of the asset but retains the _____ of the property.

3. _____ leases include both financing and maintenance arrangements.

4. A(n) _____, or _____, lease is similar to a sale and leaseback arrangement, but generally apply to the purchase of _____ equipment directly from the manufacturer.

5. The IRS would disallow a "lease" which pays for the asset in a relatively _____ period, and then permits the lessee to retain the asset for a(n) _____ payment.

6. If the IRS allows the lease, then the _____ _____ is fully deductible.

7. FASB Statement 13 requires that firms _____ certain financial leases, and hence restate their _____ _____.

8. Capitalizing a lease requires that the asset be listed under _____ _____, and that the _____ _____ of the future lease payments be shown as a(n) _____.

9. The value of an asset at the end of the lease term is referred to as its _____ _____.

10. _____ among leasing companies will tend to force leasing rates down to the point where _____ values are fully recognized in the lease rates.

11. Since some leases do not appear on the _____ _____, a firm may be able to use more _____ than if it did not lease.

12. The leasing decision is a(n) _____ decision rather than a(n) _____ _____ decision.

13. _____ _____ are often an important motive behind financial leases.

14. The _____ _____ _____ is designed to ensure that corporations reporting high earnings will pay some taxes.

15. _____ leases contain features of both operating and financial leases.

16. A lease that complies with all the IRS requirements for a genuine lease is called a(n) _____, or _____-_____, lease.

17. Since leasing is a substitute for debt financing, and since lease cash flows have approximately the same risk as debt cash flows, the appropriate discount rate is the _____-_____ _____ ____ _____.

18. When the lessor borrows to purchase the leased property, the lease is called a(n) _____ lease.

19. Assets that face rapid and uncertain _____ _____ are often leased.

Conceptual

20. Capital leases typically include both financing and maintenance arrangements.

   a. True   **b.** False

21. Leveraged leases typically provide the lessor with higher NPVs per dollar of investment than do unleveraged leases.

   a. True   **b.** False

22. When one is evaluating a lease proposal, cash flows should be discounted at a relatively high rate because lease flows are fairly certain.

   a. True   **b.** False

23. Generally, operating leases are fully amortized, and the lease is written for the expected life of the asset.

    a. True   b. False

24. A firm which uses extensive lease financing may have a substantially lower reported debt ratio than a firm which borrows to finance its assets.

    a. True   b. False

25. Firms may or may not capitalize a financial lease.

    a. True   b. False

26. The more stringent alternative minimum tax (AMT) has generated new leasing business.

    a. True   b. False

27. Which of the following statements is most correct?

    a. Some years ago leasing was called "off balance sheet financing" because the leased asset and the corresponding lease obligation did not appear directly on the balance sheet. Today, though, that situation has changed materially because all leases must be capitalized and reported on the balance sheet, along with the value of the leased asset.
    b. In a lease-versus-purchase analysis, cash flows should generally be discounted at the weighted average cost of capital (WACC).
    c. Lease payments are deductible expenses for income tax purposes, provided the IRS agrees that the contract is a genuine lease and not an installment loan called a lease.
    d. Each of the above statements is true.
    e. Each of the above statements is false.

SELF-TEST PROBLEMS

(The following data apply to the next four Self-Test Problems.)

Treadmill Trucking Company is negotiating a lease for five new tractor/trailer rigs with Leasing International. Treadmill has received its best offer from Betterbilt Trucks for a total price of $1 million. The terms of the lease offered by International Leasing call for a payment of $205,000 at the beginning of each year of the 5-year lease. As an alternative to leasing, the firm can borrow from a large insurance company and buy the trucks. The $1 million would be borrowed on a simple interest term loan at a 10 percent interest rate for 5 years. The trucks fall into the MACRS 5-year class and have an expected residual value of $100,000. Maintenance costs would be included in the lease. If the trucks are owned, a maintenance contract would be purchased at the beginning of each year for $10,000 per year. Treadmill plans to buy a new fleet of trucks at the end of the fifth year. Leasing International has a 40 percent federal-plus-state marginal tax rate, while Treadmill Trucking has a total tax rate of 20 percent.

1.   What is Treadmill's present value of the cost of owning?

   a. $802,468   b. $805,265   c. $807,189   d. $817,197   e. $829,668

2.   What is Treadmill's present value of the cost of leasing?

   a. $702,468   b. $705,265   c. $707,189   d. $729,668   e. $735,419

3.   Treadmill should lease the trucks.

   a. True   b. False

4.   Assume that the lessor's alternative to leasing is to invest in a 5-year certificate of deposit which pays 9 percent before taxes. The lessor should

   a. Write the lease; it has an IRR of 3 percent.
   b. Not write the lease; it has an IRR of 3 percent.
   c. Write the lease; its NPV is $78,625.
   d. Not write the lease; its NPV is -$78,625.
   e. Be indifferent between the lease and the alternative investment.

(The following data apply to the next four Self-Test Problems.)

Walton Publishing Company (WPC) is evaluating a potential lease agreement on a printing press that costs $250,000 and falls into the MACRS 3-year class. The firm can borrow at an 8 percent rate on a 4-year amortized loan, if WPC decided to borrow and buy rather than lease. The press has a 4-year economic life, and its estimated residual value is $25,000 at the end of Year 4. If WPC buys the press, it would purchase a maintenance contract which costs $5,000 per year, payable at the beginning of each year. The lease terms, which include maintenance, call for a $71,000 lease payment at the beginning of each year. WPC's tax rate is 40 percent. (Hint: Use a financial calculator.)

5. Should the firm lease or buy?

    a. Lease; it costs $842 less than buying.
    b. Lease; it costs $1,576 less than buying.
    c. Buy; it costs $1,576 less than leasing.
    d. Buy; it costs $842 less than leasing.
    e. Neither lease nor buy; the truck's NPV is negative.

6. Assume that the lessor is in the 40 percent tax bracket. Further, the lessor's investment alternatives of similar risk yield 8 percent before taxes. Should the lessor write the lease?

    a. Yes, its NPV is $1,577.
    b. No, its NPV is -$1,577.
    c. Yes, its NPV is $842.
    d. No, its NPV is -$842.
    e. The lessor is indifferent.

7. At what lease payment would the lessee be indifferent between owning and leasing?

    a. $42,178   **b.** $68,348   **c.** $69,572   **d.** $70,898   **e.** $70,296

Chapter 14 Extensions

14E-1. Assume that the lessor's NPV on the lease investment is $1,600. Further, assume that the lessor could obtain financing on 80 percent of his cost of $250,000. If the lessor leverages, assume his NPV on the lease investment would drop to $800. Should the lessor leverage the lease?

    a. Yes   **b.** No

ANSWERS TO SELF-TEST QUESTIONS

1.	borrowing; leverage	**9.**	residual value
2.	sale and leaseback; use	**10.**	Competition; residual
3.	Operating	**11.**	balance sheet; leverage (debt)
4.	financial; capital; new	**12.**	financing; capital budgeting
5.	short; small (nominal)	**13.**	Tax considerations
6.	lease payment	**14.**	alternative minimum tax
7.	capitalize; balance sheets	**15.**	Combination
8.	fixed assets; present value; liability	**16.**	guideline; tax-oriented

17. after-tax cost of debt   **19.** technological obsolescence

18. leveraged

20. b. Operating leases include both financing and maintenance arrangements, while financial, or capital, leases typically do not provide maintenance services. However, many leases written today are combination leases, which combine some of the features of both operating and financial leases.

21. a. However, this only holds true if the cost of leveraging is less than the return on the lease. Further, note that leveraging increases the lessor's risk.

22. b. The cash flows are fairly certain, so they should be discounted at a relatively low rate, generally, the after-tax cost of debt.

23. b. Operating leases are not fully amortized. The lessor expects to recover all costs either in subsequent leases or through the sale of the used equipment at its residual value.

24. a. But analysts would recognize that leases are as risky as debt financing, and thus include the impact of lease financing on the firm's debt costs and capital structure.

25. b. FASB #13 spells out in detail the conditions under which leases must be capitalized.

26. a. Firms have been seeking ways to lower their AMT liability. Leasing for short periods and hence making high lease payments will reduce the company's reported earnings and meet this need.

27. c. Statement a is false; only certain leases that meet the FASB #13 criteria for capitalization have to be reported on the balance sheet. Statement b is false; the discount rate in a borrow-versus-lease decision is the after-tax cost of debt because the cash flows are fairly certain. Statement c is correct; lease payments are tax deductible under the circumstances stated.

SOLUTIONS TO SELF-TEST PROBLEMS

1. d. Place the cash flows associated with ownership on a time line:

	0 8%	1	2	3	4	5 Years
AT loan payments		-80,000	-80,000	-80,000	-80,000	-1,080,000
Dep. tax savings[a]		40,000	64,000	38,000	24,000	22,000
Maintenance (AT)[b]	-8,000	-8,000	-8,000	-8,000	-8,000	
Residual value (AT)[c]						92,000
	-8,000	-48,000	-24,000	-50,000	-64,000	-966,000

PV cost of owning at the firm's 8 percent after-tax cost of debt is $817,197.

Notes:
[a]Depreciation schedule:

Year	Factor	Depreciation Expense	Tax Savings
1	0.20	$ 200,000	$ 40,000
2	0.32	320,000	64,000
3	0.19	190,000	38,000
4	0.12	120,000	24,000
5	0.11	110,000	22,000
6	0.06	60,000	12,000
		$1,000,000	$200,000

[b]After-tax maintenance cash flow = $10,000(1 – T) = $8,000.
[c]Net residual value = $100,000 – ($100,000 – $60,000)(T) = $92,000.

2. c. Place the cash flows associated with leasing on a time line:

	0 8%	1	2	3	4	5 Years
Lease payments (AT)[a]		-164,000	-164,000	-164,000	-164,000	-164,000

PV cost of leasing at the firm's 8 percent after-tax cost of debt is $707,189.

Notes:
[a]$205,000(1 – T) = $164,000.

3. a. The Net Advantage to Leasing (NAL) is $817,197 – $707,189 = $110,008, and hence the trucks should be leased.

4. d. Place the lessor's cash flows on a time line:

	0 5.4%	1	2	3	4	5 Years
Outlay[a]	-1,000,000					
Dep. tax savings[b]		80,000	128,000	76,000	48,000	44,000
Lease pymt (AT)[c]	123,000	123,000	123,000	123,000	123,000	
Residual value (AT)[d]						84,000
Maintenance (AT)[e]	-6,000	-6,000	-6,000	-6,000	-6,000	
	-883,000	197,000	245,000	193,000	165,000	128,000

The lessor's NPV of the lease investment is the PV of the net cash flows when discounted at the after-tax opportunity cost of capital or $9\%(1 - T) = 9\%(0.6) = 5.4\%$. NPV = -$78,625.

Notes:

[a]Cost of purchasing the trucks.

[b]This is each year's depreciation expense times the lessor's tax rate of 40 percent.

[c]After-tax lease payment = $205,000(1 - 0.40) = $123,000.

[d]After-tax residual value = $100,000 - ($100,000 - $60,000)(T) = $84,000.

[e]After-tax maintenance payment = $10,000(1 - T).

5. c. Cost of owning: Net investment = $250,000.

	0 4.8%	1	2	3	4 Years
Loan Payments[a]		-75,480.20	-75,480.20	-75,480.20	-75,480.20
Interest tax savings[b]		8,000.00	6,224.63	4,307.24	2,236.45
Maintenance (AT)[c]	-3,000	-3,000.00	-3,000.00	-3,000.00	
Dep. tax savings[d]		33,000.00	45,000.00	15,000.00	7,000.00
Residual value (AT)[e]					15,000.00
	-3,000	-37,480.20	-27,255.57	-59,172.96	-51,243.75

PV cost of owning at 4.8% = $157,470.

Notes:

[a]Loan amortization schedule:

Year	Beg. Bal.	PMT	Int.	Prin. Repymt.	End. Bal.
1	$250,000.00	$ 75,480.20	$20,000.00	$ 55,480.20	$194,519.80
2	194,519.80	75,480.20	15,561.58	59,918.62	134,601.18
3	134,601.18	75,480.20	10,768.09	64,712.11	69,889.07
4	69,889.07	75,480.20	5,591.13	69,889.07	0.00
		$301,920.80	$51,920.80	$250,000.00	

[b]Interest tax savings = Interest$(1 - T)$.
[c]After-tax maintenance cash outflow = $5,000$(1 - T)$ = $3,000.
[d]Depreciation schedule:

Year	Factor	Depreciation Expense	Tax Savings
1	0.33	$ 82,500	$ 33,000
2	0.45	112,500	45,000
3	0.15	37,500	15,000
4	0.07	17,500	7,000
	1.00	$250,000	$100,000

[e]Residual value (AT) = $25,000$(1 - T)$ = $15,000.

Cost of leasing:

	0 4.8%	1	2	3	4 Years
Lease payments (AT)[a]	-42,600	-42,600	-42,600	-42,600	

PV cost of leasing at 4.8% = $159,046.

Notes:
[a]$71,000$(1 - T)$ = $42,600.

Thus, owning is $157,470 − $159,046 = $1,576 less costly than leasing, so the firm should purchase the printing press.

6.   a.   Lessor's analysis:

	0 4.8%	1	2	3	4 Years
Net cost	-250,000				
Maintenance	-3,000	-3,000	-3,000	-3,000	
Dep. tax savings		33,000	45,000	15,000	7,000
Net residual value					15,000
Lease payment	42,600	42,600	42,600	42,600	
	-210,400	72,600	84,600	54,600	22,000

The lessor's NPV at 4.8 percent = $1,577.

7.   e.   The lessee would be indifferent if the cost of leasing were equal to $157,470, the PV of owning. Thus,

$$157{,}470 = \text{PMT}(\text{PVIFA}_{4.8\%,4})(1.048)$$
$$\text{PMT} = \$42{,}177.74.$$

Note that this payment is after taxes, so it must be "grossed up" to calculate the lease payment before taxes. Lease payment (BT) = $42,177.74/0.6 = $70,296.23, or approximately $70,296.

Chapter 14 Extensions

14E-1. a.   If the lessor can finance 80 percent of his cost, the lease would only require an investment of 0.2($250,000) = $50,000. Thus, the lessor could write 5 leases for the same $250,000 original investment, and his total NPV would be 5($800) = $4,000, which is significantly higher than the assumed $1,600 NPV available on the $250,000 unleveraged lease.

CHAPTER 15
HYBRID FINANCING

OVERVIEW

In earlier chapters, we examined common stock, various types of long-term debt, and leasing. In this chapter, we examine three other sources of long-term capital: preferred stock, which is a hybrid security that represents a cross between debt and common equity; warrants, which are derivative securities; and convertibles, which are hybrids between debt (or preferred stock) and warrants.

OUTLINE

Preferred stock is a hybrid—it is similar to bonds in some respects and to common stock in others.

■ Accountants classify preferred stock as equity, and hence show it on the balance sheet as an equity account.

■ However, from a finance perspective preferred stock lies somewhere between debt and common equity—it imposes a fixed charge and thus increases the firm's financial leverage, yet omitting the preferred dividend does not force a company into bankruptcy.

■ Some of the basic features of preferred stock are listed below.
  □ The dividend is either stated as a percentage of par, as so many dollars per share, or both ways. If the preferred dividend is not earned, the company does not have to pay it.
  □ Most preferred issues are *cumulative*, meaning that the cumulative total of all unpaid preferred dividends must be paid before dividends can be paid on the common stock.
  □ Unpaid dividends are called *arrearages*. Dividends in arrears do not earn interest; they only grow from additional nonpayments of the preferred dividend.
  □ Preferred stock normally has no voting rights. However, most preferred issues stipulate that the preferred stockholders can elect a minority of the directors if the preferred dividend is passed (omitted).

- Passing the dividend makes it difficult to raise capital by selling bonds, and virtually impossible to sell more preferred or common stock.

■ Preferred stock is less risky than bonds from the viewpoint of the issuing corporation.

■ For investors preferred stock is riskier than bonds for the following reasons:
  ☐ Preferred stockholders' claims are subordinated to those of bondholders in the event of liquidation.
  ☐ Bondholders are more likely to continue receiving income during hard times than are preferred stockholders.

■ Investors require a higher after-tax rate of return on a given firm's preferred stock than on its bonds.

■ Since 70 percent of preferred dividends is exempt from corporate taxes, preferred stock is attractive to corporate investors.

■ About half of all preferred stock issued in recent years has been convertible into common stock.

■ Some preferred stocks are similar to perpetual bonds in that they have no maturity date, but most new issues now have specified maturities.
  ☐ Many preferred issues are callable by the issuing corporation, which can also limit the life of the preferred.

■ Nonconvertible preferred stock is virtually all owned by corporations, which can take advantage of the 70 percent dividend exclusion to obtain a higher after-tax yield on preferred stock than on bonds.
  ☐ Individuals should not own preferred stocks (except convertible preferreds). They can get higher yields on safer bonds.
  ☐ As a result of this ownership pattern, the volume of preferred stock financing is geared to the supply of money in the hands of corporate investors.

■ For issuers, preferred stock has a tax disadvantage relative to debt—interest expense is deductible, but preferred dividends are not.

■ Preferred stock has the following advantages from the issuer's standpoint:
  ☐ The obligation to pay preferred dividends is not contractual; passing a preferred dividend cannot force a firm into bankruptcy.
  ☐ The firm avoids the dilution of common equity that occurs when common stock is sold.

☐ Since preferred stock sometimes has no maturity, and since preferred sinking fund payments, if present, are typically spread over a long period, preferred issues reduce the cash flow drain from repayment of principal that occurs with debt issues.

■ Preferred also has the following disadvantages from the issuer's standpoint:
☐ Since preferred dividends are not tax deductible, preferred stock usually has a higher after-tax cost than debt financing. However, the tax advantage of preferred stocks to corporate purchasers lowers their pre-tax cost and thus their effective cost.
☐ Preferred dividends are considered to be a fixed cost. Therefore, their use, like that of debt, increases financial risk and thus the cost of common equity.

A warrant is a certificate issued by a company which gives the holder the right to buy a stated number of shares of the company's stock at a specified price for some specified length of time.

■ Generally, warrants are distributed with debt as an incentive for investors to buy long-term debt with a lower coupon rate than would otherwise be required.
☐ Warrants are long-term *call options* that have value because holders can buy the firm's common stock at the exercise price regardless of how high the market price climbs.
☐ The option offsets the low interest rate on the bonds and makes the package of low-yield bonds plus warrants attractive to investors.

■ The key issue in setting the terms of a bond-with-warrants is valuing the warrants.
☐ The straight-debt value can be estimated quite accurately.
☐ The Black-Scholes Model cannot be used to value a warrant. Instead, more sophisticated and accurate models are used.
☐ Price paid for bond-with-warrants = Straight-debt value of bond + Value of warrants.
  • There is a major difference between call options and warrants. When call options are exercised, the stock provided to the optionholder comes from the secondary market, but when warrants are exercised, the stock provided to the warrantholders are newly issued shares.
  • The exercise of warrants dilutes the value of the original equity, which could cause the value of the original warrant to differ from the value of a similar call option.

■ Warrants generally are used by small, rapidly growing firms as "sweeteners" when they sell debt or preferred stock. However, after AT&T became the first large and financially strong corporation to use warrants, their use by such firms became commonplace.

■   A bond-with-warrants has some characteristics of debt and some characteristics of equity. It is a *hybrid security* that provides the financial manager with an opportunity to expand the firm's mix of securities and thus to appeal to a broader group of investors.

■   Most warrants are *detachable* and can be traded separately from the bond or preferred stock with which they were issued.
      □   Even after the warrants have been exercised, the bond remains outstanding.

■   Warrants generate additional equity capital when they are exercised.
      □   The *exercise price* on warrants is generally set 20 to 30 percent above the market price of the stock on the date the bond is issued.

■   There are three conditions which encourage holders to exercise their warrants:
      □   If the market price is above the exercise price, and the warrants are about to expire, holders will exercise their options and purchase stock.
      □   Since warrants pay no dividends, holders will be inclined to exercise them and obtain common stock as the common dividend is increased.
      □   A *stepped-up exercise price* will also induce holders to exercise their warrants.

■   Warrants generally bring in funds only if funds are needed. Warrants generally produce needed funds as the company grows and as the stock price increases over the exercise price.

■   The component cost of an issue with warrants can be estimated by placing the expected cash flows associated with the issue on a time line and then calculating the IRR of the stream.
      □   The expected rate of return to investors is the before-tax cost to the company.
      □   The return on the bond-with-warrants is higher than the return on straight debt. This reflects that it is riskier because some of the return is expected to come in the form of stock price appreciation.

■   Although the interest rate on the bond will be less than the rate on a similar straight-debt issue, the total cost rate of the issue, including the opportunity cost of the warrants, will usually be somewhere between the firm's costs of straight debt and equity because the riskiness of a bond-with-warrants falls between that of debt and equity.

Convertible securities are bonds or preferred stocks which, under specified terms and conditions, can be exchanged for common stock at the option of the holder.

■   Conversion of a bond or preferred stock, unlike the exercise of a warrant, does not provide capital: debt (or preferred stock) is simply replaced on the balance sheet by common stock. However, conversion does lower the debt ratio improving the firm's financial strength and making it easier to raise additional capital.

The *conversion ratio (CR)* specifies the number of common shares that will be received for each bond or share of preferred stock that is converted.

The *conversion price,* P_c, is the effective price paid for the common stock when conversion occurs. For example, if a bond is issued at its par value of $1,000 and can be converted into 40 shares of common stock, the conversion price would be

$$P_c = \$1,000/CR = \$1,000/40 = \$25 \text{ per share.}$$

The conversion price of a bond is typically set at about 20 to 30 percent above the prevailing market price of the common stock at the time the convertible issue is sold. Thus, if the common stock is selling for $20.83 at the time the convertible is issued, the conversion price might be set at 1.2($20.83) = $25. This would produce a conversion ratio of CR = 40:

$$CR = \$1,000/P_c = \$1,000/\$25 = 40.$$

☐ A standard feature of almost all convertibles is the clause protecting the convertible against dilution from stock splits, stock dividends, and the sale of common stock at prices below the conversion price.

The actual market price of a convertible bond can never fall below the higher of its straight-debt value or its conversion value. The higher of those two values is called the *floor price*.

The bond's market value will typically exceed its floor value.
☐ It will exceed the straight-bond value because the option to convert is worth something.
☐ The convertible's price will also exceed its conversion value because holding the convertible is equivalent to holding a call option, and, prior to expiration, the option's true value is higher than its expiration (or conversion) value.

Like a bond-with-warrants, the expected cost rate on convertible debt can be estimated by placing the issue's expected cash flows on a time line. Also, like debt-with-warrants, the costs should lie between the issuing firm's cost of straight debt and its cost of common stock, because, from the investors' viewpoint, a convertible is riskier than straight debt but less risky than common stock.

Convertible issues have two important advantages from the issuer's standpoint:

- ☐ By giving investors an opportunity to realize capital gains, a firm can sell debt with a lower interest rate or preferred stock with a lower dividend yield.
  - ☐ Convertibles provide a way of selling common stock in the future at prices higher than those currently prevailing.

- From the standpoint of the issuer, convertibles have three important disadvantages:
  - ☐ If the stock price does not increase, investors will not convert and the company will be stuck with debt (or preferred) rather than equity in its capital structure.
  - ☐ Convertibles typically have a low coupon interest rate, and the advantage of this low-cost debt will be lost when conversion occurs.
  - ☐ If the firm's stock price rises sharply, it would have been better off if the company had used straight debt in spite of its higher cost and then sold the common shares at the higher price and refunded the debt.

- Typically, convertibles contain a call provision that enables the issuing firm to force holders to convert.

- When convertible debt is issued, actions to increase the company's riskiness may increase the convertible debt's value as well as the common stock's value. Thus, some of the gains to shareholders from taking on high-risk projects may be transferred to convertible bondholders. This reduction in benefits to shareholders decreases the incentive for managers to substitute assets, and hence lowers agency costs. This same general logic applies to convertible preferred and warrants.

Convertible debt can be thought of as straight debt with nondetachable warrants. Thus, it might appear that debt-with-warrants and convertible debt are more or less interchangeable. However, a closer examination reveals differences.

- The exercise of warrants brings in new equity capital, while the conversion of convertibles results only in an accounting transfer.

- A second difference involves flexibility. Most convertible issues contain a call provision that allows the issuer either to refund the debt or to force conversion, depending on the relationship between the conversion value and call price. However, most warrants are not callable, so firms generally must wait until maturity for the warrants to generate new equity capital.

- Generally, maturities also differ between warrants and convertibles. Warrants typically have much shorter maturities than convertibles, and warrants typically expire before their accompanying debt matures.

■   Warrants usually provide for fewer future common shares than do convertibles because with convertibles all of the debt is converted to common whereas debt remains outstanding when warrants are exercised.

■   In general, firms that issue debt-with-warrants are smaller and riskier than those that issue convertibles.

■   Bonds with warrants typically require issuance costs that are about 1.2 percentage points more than the flotation costs for convertibles.

The Extensions to Chapter 15 discuss adjustable rate and market auction preferred stocks, reporting earnings when warrants or convertibles are outstanding, calling convertible issues, and some innovative new hybrids.

■   Two important innovations in preferred stock financing have occurred in recent years.
　　□ *Adjustable rate preferred stocks (ARPs)* tie their dividends to the rate on Treasury securities instead of paying fixed dividends.
　　□ *Money market,* or *market auction, preferred stocks* are, from the investor's point of view, a low risk, largely tax-exempt, 7-week maturity security which can be sold between auction dates at close to par value.

■   Firms with warrants or convertible securities outstanding must reflect these securities when they report earnings per share to stockholders. A firm could report earnings per share in one of three ways:
　　□ *Basic EPS,* where earnings available to common stockholders are divided by the average number of shares actually outstanding during the period.
　　□ *Primary EPS,* where earnings available are divided by the average number of shares that would be outstanding if those warrants and convertibles "likely to be converted in the near future" had actually been exercised or converted.
　　□ *Diluted EPS,* which is similar to primary EPS except that *all* warrants and convertibles are assumed to be exercised or converted, regardless of the likelihood of exercise or conversion.
　　□ Under SEC rules, firms are required to report both basic and diluted EPS.

■   Most convertible issues have provisions that allow the issuer to call the issue prior to maturity.
　　□ If a convertible is called when its conversion value is less than the stock price, convertible holders will elect to receive the call price. In this situation, the firm will have to pay out cash to redeem the issue, and no new equity will appear on the balance sheet.
　　□ If the call is made when the conversion value exceeds the stock price, convertible holders will convert their bonds. In this case, the firm will not need to use cash to

retire the convertibles, and a balance sheet transfer will be made from debt or preferred to common equity.

- When a convertible is converted into common stock, the difference between the convertible's conversion price and the stock's current market price constitutes a wealth transfer from current stockholders to convertible holders.
- Theory dictates that the optimal call policy is to call the convertible issue as soon as the issue's conversion value reaches the call price.

■ Investment bankers have devised some new preferred stock hybrids having significant appeal to both issuers and investors.

☐ New hybrids offer yields higher than those set on the firm's debt securities and also offer longer maturities.

☐ Changes in the economic environment, coupled with increased volatility in interest and exchange rates, have fueled the surge.

SELF-TEST QUESTIONS

Definitional

1. Preferred stock has characteristics similar to both _____ and _____ _____.

2. The _____ _____ feature means that preferred stockholders must receive all dividends in arrears before common dividends may be paid.

3. Warrants and convertibles may make a company's securities more attractive to a broader range of _____ and hence lower its _____ ____ _____.

4. A(n) _____ is a long-term call option to buy a stated number of shares of _____ _____ at a specified _____.

5. Warrants are often attached to a(n) _____ issue in order to induce investors to purchase the issue at a relatively low _____ rate.

6. The _____ price of a warrant is generally set at about ____ to ____ percent above the stock's market price.

7. When they are exercised, warrants add additional _____ _____ to a firm's capital structure.

8. Warrants will certainly be exercised if the stock's market price is above the _____ price and the warrant is about to _____.

9. Holders of warrants will have an extra incentive to convert to _____ _____ as the company increases the _____ on its common shares.

10. Almost all warrants are _____ and can be traded separately from the debt or preferred stock with which they were issued.

11. Convertible bonds or preferred stocks may be exchanged for _____ _____ at the option of the holder.

12. The _____ _____ specifies the number of shares of common stock that will be received for each bond that is converted.

13. The _____ _____ is the effective price paid for one share of common stock upon conversion.

14. When a convertible bond is issued, the conversion price is determined by dividing the _____ _____ of the bond by the number of shares received on conversion.

15. Selling a convertible issue may have the effect of selling _____ _____ at a price higher than the market price prevailing at the time the convertible is issued.

16. If a firm's stock price does increase, the company can force _____ of convertible bonds by including a(n) _____ _____ in the bond indenture.

17. It may be unwise for a firm to sell a convertible issue if it anticipates that its _____ _____ will increase rapidly in the near future.

18. In reporting its earnings, a firm with warrants and convertible securities must report both _____ EPS and _____ EPS.

19. The higher of a convertible bond's straight-debt value or its conversion value is called the _____ _____.

20. _____ _____ _____ _____ tie their dividends to the rate on Treasury securities instead of paying fixed dividends.

Conceptual

21. Preferred stock is generally viewed as equity by bondholders and as debt by common stockholders.

    a. True   **b.** False

22. The coupon interest rate on convertible bonds is generally set higher than the rate on similar nonconvertible issues.

    a. True   **b.** False

23. Primary EPS shows what EPS would have been if all warrant and convertibles had been converted prior to the reporting date.

    a. True   **b.** False

24. Investors are willing to accept lower interest (or dividend) yields on convertible securities in the hopes of later realizing capital gains.

    a. True   **b.** False

25. The conversion of a convertible bond replaces debt with common equity on a firm's balance sheet, but it does not bring in any additional capital.

    a. True   **b.** False

26. The market price of a warrant may be substantially above its expiration value.

    a. True   **b.** False

27. The advantage to the corporation of using preferred stock financing is:

    a. Preferred dividends are tax deductible.
    b. Preferred stockholders bear no risk of ownership.
    c. The returns on preferred stock are always higher than on bonds.
    d. The firm can retain control and limit the profit sharing of new investors.
    e. Preferred stockholders always have voting rights.

SELF-TEST PROBLEMS

1. The Clayton Corporation has warrants outstanding that permit the holder to purchase one share of common stock per warrant at $30. What is the expiration value of Clayton's warrants if the common stock is currently selling at $20 per share?

   a. -$20   **b.** -$10   **c.** $5   **d.** $10   **e.** $20

2. Refer to Self-Test Problem 1. Calculate the expiration value if the common stock is now selling at $40 per share.

   a. -$20   **b.** -$10   **c.** $0   **d.** $10   **e.** $20

3. White Corporation has just sold a bond issue with 10 warrants attached to each bond. The bonds have a 20-year maturity, an annual coupon rate of 12 percent, and they sold at the $1,000 initial offering price. The current yield to maturity on bonds of equal risk, but without warrants, is 15 percent. What is the value of each warrant?

   a. $22.56   **b.** $21.20   **c.** $20.21   **d.** $19.24   **e.** $18.78

(The following data apply to the next four Self-Test Problems.)

Central Food Brokers is considering issuing a 20-year convertible bond that will be priced at its par value of $1,000 per bond. The bonds have a 12 percent annual coupon interest rate, and each bond could be converted into 40 shares of common stock. The stock currently sells at $20 per share, has an expected annual dividend of $3.00, and is growing at a constant 5 percent per year. The bonds are callable after 10 years at a price of $1,050, with the price declining by $5 per year thereafter. If, after 10 years, the conversion value exceeds the call price by at least 20 percent, management will call the bonds.

4. What is the conversion price?

   a. $20   **b.** $25   **c.** $33   **d.** $40   **e.** $50

5. If the yield to maturity on similar nonconvertible bonds is 16 percent, what is the straight-debt value?

   a. $1,000.00   **b.** $907.83   **c.** $812.22   **d.** $762.85   **e.** $692.37

6. What is the conversion value in Year 10?

    a. $800.73   **b.** $1,000.50   **c.** $1,148.01   **d.** $1,222.18   **e.** $1,303.12

7. If an investor expects the bond issue to be called in Year 10, and he plans on converting it at that time, what is the investor's expected rate of return upon conversion?

    a. 12.0%   **b.** 12.2%   **c.** 13.6%   **d.** 14.4%   **e.** 15.3%

ANSWERS TO SELF-TEST QUESTIONS

1.	bonds (debt); common stock (equity)	**11.**	common stock
2.	cumulative dividends	**12.**	conversion ratio
3.	investors; cost of capital	**13.**	conversion price
4.	warrant; common stock; price	**14.**	par value
5.	debt; interest	**15.**	common stock
6.	exercise (strike); 20; 30	**16.**	conversion; call provision
7.	common equity	**17.**	stock price
8.	exercise (strike); expire	**18.**	basic; diluted
9.	common stock; dividend	**19.**	floor price
10.	detachable	**20.**	Adjustable rate preferred stock

21.   a. Preferred stock is treated as debt by common stockholders since preferred dividends must be paid before common dividends. Bondholders have a priority claim on cash flows over preferred stockholders and also priority in the event of liquidation and therefore view preferred stock as equity.

22.   b. The coupon interest rate is lower because investors expect some capital gains return upon conversion. Note, however, that the overall required rate of return is higher for the convertible issue.

23.   b. Primary EPS includes only those shares from warrants and convertibles likely to be converted in the near future. Diluted EPS includes all shares.

24.   a. However, the investor is including the expected capital gain as part of his required return, so the total required return on convertibles is higher than on a straight security with similar other features.

25.   a. The bond is turned in to the company and replaced with common stock. No cash is exchanged.

26. a. A warrant is a call option, and hence its value depends not only on its expiration value, but also on its time to maturity, the price volatility of the underlying stock, and the risk-free rate.

27. d. By setting a fixed dividend, management can limit the degree of profit sharing by preferred stockholders and also retain control since preferred stockholders normally do not have voting rights.

SOLUTIONS TO SELF-TEST PROBLEMS

1. b. Expiration value = Market price − Exercise price. When $P_0 = \$20$, the Expiration value = $\$20 − \$30 = -\$10$.

2. d. When $P_0 = \$40$, the Expiration value = $\$40 − \$30 = \$10$.

3. e. First, find the straight-debt value:

$$V = INT(PVIFA_{k,n}) + M(PVIF_{k,n}) = \$120(PVIFA_{15\%,20}) + \$1,000(PVIF_{15\%,20})$$
$$= \$812.22.$$

Thus the value of the attached warrants is $\$1,000 − \$812.22 = \$187.78$. Since each bond has 10 warrants, each warrant must have a value of $\$18.78$.

4. b. P_c = Par value/Shares received = $\$1,000/40 = \$25.00$.

5. d. $V = INT(PVIFA_{k,n}) + M(PVIF_{k,n})$
$$= \$120(PVIFA_{16\%,20}) + \$1,000(PVIF_{16\%,20}) = \$762.85.$$

6. e. $C_t = P_tCR$; $C_{10} = P_{10}CR = \$20(1.05)^{10}(40) = \$1,303.12$.

7.   c.   This is solved by finding the value of k_c in the equation:

$$\text{Price paid} = \text{INT}\left(\text{PVIF}_{k_c,n}\right) + \text{Expected conversion value}\left(\text{PVIF}_{k_c,n}\right)$$

$$\$1,000 = \$120\left(\text{PVIF}_{k_c,10}\right) + \$1,303.12\left(\text{PVIF}_{k_c,10}\right)$$

$$k_c = 13.6\%.$$

CHAPTER 16
CURRENT ASSET MANAGEMENT

OVERVIEW

About 60 percent of a typical financial manager's time is devoted to working capital management, and many students' first jobs will involve working capital. This is particularly true in smaller businesses, where most new jobs in the U. S. are being created. Therefore, working capital is an essential topic.

Working capital policy involves two basic questions: (1) What is the appropriate amount of current assets for the firm to carry, both in total and for each specific account, and (2) how should current assets be financed? This chapter addresses the first question, while the next chapter addresses the second question.

OUTLINE

It is useful to begin by reviewing some basic definitions and concepts.

■   *Working capital*, sometimes called *gross working capital*, simply refers to current assets used in operations.

■   *Net working capital* is defined as current assets minus current liabilities.

■   *Net operating working capital (NOWC)* is defined as non-interest bearing current assets minus non-interest charging current liabilities. Generally, NOWC is equal to cash, accounts receivable, and inventories less accounts payable and accruals.

■   The *current ratio*, which is calculated as current assets divided by current liabilities, is intended to measure liquidity.

■   The *quick ratio*, which also attempts to measure liquidity, is calculated as current assets less inventories, divided by current liabilities. The quick ratio is an "acid test" of a company's ability to meet its current obligations.

■ The best and most comprehensive picture of a firm's liquidity position is obtained by examining its *cash budget*. The cash budget forecasts a firm's cash inflows and outflows, and thus focuses on what really counts, the firm's ability to generate sufficient cash inflows to meet its required cash outflows.

■ *Working capital policy* refers to the firm's policies regarding target levels for each category of current assets and how current assets will be financed.

■ *Working capital management* involves both setting working capital policy and carrying out that policy in day-to-day operations.

A firm's current asset levels rise and fall with business cycles and seasonal trends. At the peak of such cycles, businesses carry their maximum amounts of current assets.

■ There are three alternative policies regarding the total amount of current assets carried. Each policy differs with regard to the amount of current assets carried to support any given level of sales, hence in the turnover of those assets.

   ☐ A *relaxed current asset investment policy* is one where relatively large amounts of cash, marketable securities, and inventories are carried, and where sales are stimulated by the use of a credit policy that provides liberal financing to customers and a corresponding high level of receivables.

   ☐ A *restricted current asset investment policy* is one where holdings of cash, securities, inventories, and receivables are minimized. Current assets are turned over more frequently, so each dollar of current assets is forced to "work harder."

   ☐ A *moderate current asset investment policy* is between the two extremes.

   ☐ Generally, the decision on the current assets level involves a risk/return tradeoff. The relaxed policy minimizes risk, but it also has the lowest expected return. On the other hand, the restricted policy offers the highest expected return coupled with the highest risk. The moderate policy falls in between the two extremes in terms of expected risk and return.

   ☐ Changing technology can lead to dramatic changes in the optimal current asset investment policy.

■ Working capital consists of four main components: cash, marketable securities, inventory, and accounts receivable.

■ For each type of asset, firms face a fundamental tradeoff: current assets are necessary to conduct business, and the greater the holdings of current assets, the smaller the danger of running out, hence the lower the firm's operating risk. However, holding working capital is costly. So, there is pressure to hold the amount of working capital to the minimum consistent with running the business without interruption.

Firms typically follow a cycle where they purchase inventory, sell goods on credit, and then collect accounts receivable. This cycle is referred to as the cash conversion cycle, and it is discussed in Chapter 18.

Sound working capital policy is designed to minimize the time between cash expenditures on materials and the collection of cash on sales.

In today's world of intense global competition, working capital management is receiving increasing attention from managers striving for peak efficiency. In fact, the goal of many leading companies today is zero working capital.

Proponents of *zero working capital* claim that a movement toward this goal not only generates cash but also speeds up production and helps businesses make more timely deliveries and operate more efficiently.

The concept has its own definition of working capital: Inventories + Receivables – Payables.
- The rationale here is (1) inventories and receivables are the keys to making sales, but (2) inventories can be financed by suppliers through accounts payable.

Reducing working capital and thus increasing turnover has two major financial benefits.
- Every dollar freed up by reducing inventories or receivables, or by increasing payables, results in a one-time contribution to cash flow.
- A movement toward zero working capital permanently raises a company's earnings.

The most important factor in moving toward zero working capital is increased speed. The best companies are able to start production after an order is received yet still meet customer delivery requirements. This system is known as *demand flow,* or *demand-based management*, and it builds on the just-in-time method of inventory control.
- Demand flow management is broader than just-in-time because it requires that all elements of a production system operate quickly and efficiently.

A focus on minimizing receivables and inventories while maximizing payables will help a firm lower its investment in working capital and achieve financial and production economies.

Cash is a nonearning asset. Excessive cash balances reduce the rate of return on equity and hence the value of a firm's stock. Thus, the goal of the cash manager is to minimize the amount of cash the firm must hold for use in conducting its normal business activities, yet at the same time, to have sufficient cash (1) to take trade discounts, (2) to maintain its credit rating, and (3) to meet unexpected cash needs.

■ Firms hold cash for two primary reasons:

☐ *Transactions balances* are held to provide the cash needed to conduct normal business operations.

☐ *Compensating balances* are often required by banks for providing loans and services.

■ Two secondary reasons are also cited:

☐ *Precautionary balances* are held in reserve for random, unforeseen fluctuations in cash inflows and outflows.

☐ *Speculative balances* are held to enable the firm to take advantage of bargain purchases that might arise.

■ Firms do not segregate funds for each of these motives, because the same money often serves more than one purpose, but firms do consider all four factors in setting their overall cash positions.

■ An ample cash balance should be maintained to take advantage of *trade discounts* and favorable business opportunities, to help the firm maintain its credit rating, and to meet emergency needs.

A cash budget projects cash inflows and outflows over some specified period of time.

■ The basis for a cash budget is the sales forecast, the level of fixed assets and inventory that will be required to meet the forecasted sales level, and the times when payment must be made.

■ Cash budgets can be created for any time interval, but firms typically use a daily cash budget forecasted over the next month, plus less detailed monthly cash budgets for the coming year.

☐ The monthly cash budgets are used for planning purposes, and the daily or weekly budgets for actual cash control.

■ A typical cash budget consists of three sections.

☐ The *collections and purchases worksheet* summarizes the firm's cash collections from sales and cash purchases for materials.

☐ The *cash gain or loss section* lays out the cash inflows and outflows, and the "bottom line" of this section is the net cash gain or loss.

☐ The *loan requirement or cash surplus section* summarizes the firm's cumulative need for loans and cumulative surplus cash.

If the firm's cash inflows and outflows are not uniform over the budget interval, say monthly, the cash budget could seriously understate the firm's peak financing requirements.

The cash budget can be used to help set the firm's *target cash balance*, the desired cash balance that a firm plans to maintain in order to conduct business. This is accomplished by incorporating uncertainty into the budget, and then setting a target balance which provides a cushion against adverse conditions.

Note that the cash budget focuses on the physical movement of cash, and hence depreciation cash flow does not appear directly in the budget. It does, however, affect the amount of taxes shown.

Since the cash budget represents a forecast, all the values in the table are *expected* values.

Spreadsheet programs such as *Lotus 1-2-3* and *Microsoft Excel*, are particularly well suited for preparing and analyzing the cash budget.

■ The target cash balance probably will be adjusted over time, rising and falling with seasonal patterns and with long-term changes in the scale of the firm's operations.

Cash management has changed significantly over the last two decades as a result of an upward trend in interest rates and technological developments.

From the early 1970s to the mid-1980s, there was an upward trend in interest rates that increased the opportunity cost of holding cash. This encouraged financial managers to search for more efficient ways of managing cash.

Technological developments, particularly computerized electronic funds transfer mechanisms, changed the way cash is managed.

Effective cash management encompasses proper management of cash inflows and outflows, which entails (1) improving forecasts of cash flows, (2) synchronizing cash inflows and outflows, (3) using float, (4) accelerating collections, (5) getting available funds to where they are needed, and (6) controlling disbursements.

Synchronizing cash inflows and outflows provides cash when it is needed and thus enables firms to reduce cash balances, decrease bank loans, lower interest expense, and boost profits.

■   *Check clearing* is the process of converting a check that has been written and mailed into cash in the payee's account.

■   *Float* is defined as the difference between the balance shown in a firm's (or individual's) checkbook and the balance on the bank's records. A firm's *net float* is a function of its ability to speed up collections on checks received (*collections float*) and to slow down collections on checks written (*disbursement float*).
      ☐ Delays that cause float arise because it takes time for checks (1) to travel through the mail (mail float), (2) to be processed by the receiving firm (processing float), and (3) to clear through the banking system (clearing, or availability, float).

Several techniques are now used to speed collections and to get funds where they are needed. Included are lockbox plans established close to customers and requiring large customers to pay by wire or automatic debit.

■   A *lockbox plan* is a procedure which speeds up collections and reduces float through the use of post office boxes in payers' local areas.
      ☐ Customers mail checks to a post office box in a specified city. A local bank then collects the checks, deposits them, starts the clearing process, and notifies the selling firm that payment has been received.
      ☐ Processing time is further reduced because it takes less time for banks to collect local checks.

■   Firms are increasingly demanding payments of larger bills by wire, or even by automatic electronic debits, whereby funds are automatically deducted from one account and added to another.

Marketable securities typically provide much lower yields than a firm's operating assets, yet they are often held in sizable amounts.

■   In many cases companies hold marketable securities for the same reasons they hold cash.

■   While these securities are not as liquid as cash, in most cases they can be converted to cash on very short notice.

■   Marketable securities provide at least a modest return, while cash yields nothing.

■   William Baumol first recognized that the tradeoff between cash and marketable securities is similar to the one firms face when setting the optimal inventory level.
      ☐ He applied the EOQ inventory model to determine the optimal level of cash balances.

☐ He suggested that cash holdings should be higher if costs are high and the time to liquidate marketable securities is long, but that those holdings should be lower if interest rates are low.

Inventories, which may be classified as supplies, raw materials, work-in-process, and finished goods, are an essential part of virtually all business operations.

■ Inventory levels depend heavily upon sales. Since inventory is acquired before sales can take place, an accurate sales forecast is critical to effective inventory management.

■ Errors in the establishment of inventory levels quickly lead either to lost sales or to excessive carrying costs.

■ Proper inventory management requires close coordination among the sales, purchasing, production, and finance departments. The sales/marketing department is generally the first to spot changes in demand. These changes must be worked into the company's purchasing and manufacturing schedules, and the financial manager must arrange any financing needed to support the inventory buildup. Lack of coordination among departments, poor sales forecasts, or both, can lead to disaster.

The twin goals of inventory management are (1) to ensure that the inventories needed to sustain operations are available, but (2) to hold the costs of ordering and carrying inventories to the lowest possible level.

■ Inventory costs are divided into three categories: carrying costs, ordering and receiving costs, and the costs that are incurred if the firm runs short of inventory.
  ☐ *Carrying costs* generally rise in direct proportion to the average amount of inventory held. Carrying costs associated with inventory include cost of the capital tied up, storage and handling costs, insurance, property taxes, and depreciation and obsolescence.
  ☐ *Ordering costs*, which are considered to be fixed costs, decline as average inventory increase, that is, as the number of orders decrease. Ordering costs include the costs of placing and receiving orders.
  ☐ The *costs of running short* include loss of sales, loss of customer goodwill, and disruption of production schedules.

Inventory management requires the establishment of an inventory control system. These systems vary from the extremely simple to the very complex, depending on the size of the firm and the nature of its inventory.

■ One simple control procedure is the *red-line method*. A red line is drawn inside the bin where the inventory is stocked. When the red line shows, an order is placed.

■ The *two-bin method* has inventory items stocked in two bins. When the working bin is empty, an order is placed and inventory is drawn from the second bin.

■ Large companies employ much more sophisticated *computerized inventory control systems*. The computer starts with an inventory count in memory. As withdrawals are made, they are recorded by the computer, and the inventory balance is revised. Orders are automatically placed once the reorder point is reached.

  □ A good inventory control system is dynamic, not static.

■ The *just-in-time (JIT) system* coordinates a manufacturer's production with suppliers' so that raw materials arrive from suppliers just as they are needed in the production process. It also requires that component parts be perfect; therefore, JIT inventory management has been developed in conjunction with total quality management (TQM).

■ Another important development related to inventory is *out-sourcing*, which is the practice of purchasing components rather than making them in-house. Out-sourcing is often combined with just-in-time systems to reduce inventory levels.

■ A final point relating to inventory levels is the *relationship between production scheduling and inventory levels*. Inventory policy must be coordinated with the firm's manufacturing and procurement policies, because the ultimate goal is to *minimize total production and distribution costs*, and inventory costs are just one part of total costs.

Carrying receivables has both direct and indirect costs, but it also has an important benefit—granting credit will increase sales.

■ *Accounts receivable* are created when a firm sells goods or performs services on credit rather than on a cash basis. When cash is received, accounts receivable are reduced by the same amount.

■ The total amount of accounts receivable outstanding is determined by (1) the volume of credit sales and (2) the average length of time between sales and collections.

■ The investment in receivables, like any asset, must be financed in some manner, but the entire amount of receivables does not have to be financed because the profit portion does not represent a cash outflow.

Receivables must be actively managed to ensure that the firm's receivables policy is effective. There are two commonly used methods to monitor a firm's receivables.

■ The *days sales outstanding (DSO)*, also sometimes called the average collection period (ACP), measures the average length of time it takes a firm's customers to pay off their credit purchases.
   □ The DSO is calculated by dividing the receivables balance by average daily credit sales.
   □ The DSO can be compared with the industry average and the firm's own credit terms to get an indication of how well customers are adhering to the terms prescribed and how customers' payments, on average, compare with the industry average.

■ An *aging schedule* breaks down a firm's receivables by the ages of the accounts, and it points out the percentage of receivables due that are attributable to late paying customers.

■ Management should constantly monitor both the DSO and the aging schedule to detect trends, to see how the firm's collection experience compares with its credit terms, and to see how effectively the credit department is operating in comparison with other firms in the industry.

■ Both the DSO and aging schedule can be distorted if sales are seasonal or if a firm is growing rapidly. A deterioration in either the DSO or the aging schedule should be taken as a signal to investigate further, but not necessarily as a sign that the firm's credit policy has weakened.

The success or failure of a business depends primarily on the demand for its products. The major controllable determinants of demand are sales prices, product quality, advertising, and the firm's credit policy. The credit policy consists of (1) the credit period, (2) credit standards, (3) collection policy, and (4) discounts.

■ The *credit period* is the length of time for which credit is granted. Increasing the credit period often stimulates sales, but there is a cost involved in carrying the increased receivables.
   □ A firm's regular *credit terms* include the credit period and discount.

■ *Credit standards* refer to the financial strength and creditworthiness a customer must exhibit in order to qualify for credit.
   □ Setting credit standards requires a measurement of *credit quality*, which is defined in terms of the probability of a customer's default.

□ Credit evaluation is a well-established practice, and a good credit manager can make reasonably accurate judgments of the probability of default by different classes of customers.

□ Computerized information systems can assist in making better credit decisions, but in the final analysis, most credit decisions are really exercises in informed judgment.

■ *Collection policy* refers to the procedures the firm follows to collect past-due accounts. The collection process can be expensive in terms of both out-of-pocket expenditures and lost goodwill, but at least some firmness is needed to prevent an undue lengthening of the collection period and to minimize outright losses. A balance must be struck between the costs and benefits of different collection policies.

■ The last variable in the credit policy decision is the firm's *cash discount policy*. Cash discounts attract customers and encourage early payment but reduce the dollar amount received on each discount sale.

□ Offering discounts should cause a reduction in the days sales outstanding, because some existing customers will pay more promptly in order to get the discount.

□ If sales are seasonal, a firm may use *seasonal dating* on discounts. Seasonal dating is the offering of terms to induce customers to buy early by not requiring payment until the purchaser's selling season, regardless of when the goods are shipped.

■ Other conditions may also influence a firm's overall credit policy.

□ It is sometimes possible to sell on credit and assess a carrying charge on the receivables that are outstanding, making credit sales more profitable than cash sales.

□ It is illegal for a firm to charge prices or to set credit terms that discriminate between customers unless these differential prices are cost-justified.

• The same holds true for credit—it is illegal to offer more favorable credit terms to one customer or class of customers than to another, unless the differences are cost justified.

SELF-TEST QUESTIONS

Definitional

1. Current assets used in operations are also referred to as _____ _____.

2. _____ working capital is defined as _____ assets minus current _____.

3. The goal of the cash manager is to _____ the amount of _____ the firm must hold for use in conducting its normal business activities.

4. Precautionary balances are maintained in order to allow for random, unforeseen fluctuations in cash _____ and _____.

5. _____ balances are maintained to pay banks for services they perform.

6. Efficient cash management is often concerned with speeding up the _____ of checks received and slowing down the _____ of checks issued.

7. One method for speeding the collection process (through the use of post office boxes in payers' local areas) is the use of a(n) _____ system.

8. The difference between a firm's balance on its own books and its balance as carried on the bank's books is known as _____.

9. Inventory is usually classified as _____, _____ _____, _____-____-_____, and _____ _____.

10. The twin goals of inventory management are to provide the inventory needed for operations at the _____ _____.

11. Storage costs, obsolescence, and other costs that _____ with larger inventory are known as _____ costs.

12. Ordering and receiving costs are _____ related to average inventory size.

13. Inventory control systems that require suppliers to deliver items as they are needed are called _____-____-_____ systems.

14. _____ _____ are created when goods are sold or services are performed on credit.

15. A firm's outstanding accounts receivable will be determined by the _____ of credit sales and the length of time between _____ and _____.

16. Sales volume and the collection period will be affected by a firm's _____ _____.

17. Extremely strict credit standards will result in lost _____.

18. Credit terms generally specify the _____ for which credit is granted and any _____ _____ that is offered for early payment.

19.   The optimal credit terms involve a tradeoff between increased _____ and the cost of carrying additional _____ _____.

20.   _____ policy refers to the manner in which a firm tries to obtain payment from past-due accounts.

21.   Two popular methods for monitoring receivables are _____ _____ and the _____ _____ _____.

22.   Credit sales may be especially profitable if a(n) _____ charge is assessed on accounts receivable.

23.   The best and most comprehensive picture of a firm's liquidity position is obtained by examining its _____ _____, which forecasts a firm's cash inflows and outflows.

24.   _____ _____ _____ refers to the firm's policies regarding target levels for each category of current assets and how current assets will be financed.

25.   A(n) _____ current asset investment policy is one where relatively large amounts of cash, marketable securities, and inventories are carried, and where sales are stimulated by the use of a credit policy that provides liberal financing to customers and a corresponding high level of receivables.

26.   A(n) _____ current asset investment policy is one where holdings of cash, securities, inventories, and receivables are minimized.

27.   Firms hold cash for two primary reasons: _____ and _____ balances.

28.   _____ _____ _____ defines working capital as inventories plus receivables less payables.

29.   _____ _____ management is a system where firms are able to start production after an order is received, yet still meet customer delivery requirements, and it builds on the just-in-time method of inventory control.

30.   A typical cash budget consists of three sections: the _____ and _____ worksheet, the cash _____ or _____ section, and the cash surplus or loan requirement section.

31.   The _____ cash balance is the desired cash balance that a firm plans to maintain in order to conduct business.

32.   _____ _____ typically provide much lower yields than a firm's operating assets, yet they are often held in sizable amounts and are held for the same reasons firms hold cash.

33.   _____-_____ is the practice of purchasing components rather than making them in-house.

34.   _____ _____ is defined in terms of the probability of a customer's default.

Conceptual

35.   A firm changes its credit policy from 2/10, net 30, to 3/10, net 30. The change is to meet competition, so no increase in sales is expected. The firm's average investment in accounts receivable will probably increase as a result of the change.

       a. True   **b.** False

36.   An aging schedule is constructed by a firm to keep track of when its accounts payable are due.

       a. True   **b.** False

37.   If a credit policy change increases the firm's accounts receivable, the entire increase must be financed by some source of funds.

       a. True   **b.** False

38.   Which of the following actions would *not* be consistent with good cash management?

       a. Increasing the synchronization of cash flows.
       b. Using lockboxes in funds collection.
       c. Maintaining an average cash balance equal to that required as a compensating balance or that which minimizes total cost.
       d. Minimizing the use of float.
       e. None of the above; all are consistent with good cash management.

39. The costs of a stock-out do *not* include

    a. Disruption of production schedules.
    b. Loss of customer goodwill.
    c. Depreciation and obsolescence.
    d. Loss of sales.
    e. Answers c and d above.

40. The goal of credit policy is to

    a. Minimize bad debt losses.
    b. Minimize DSO.
    c. Maximize sales.
    d. Minimize collection expenses.
    e. Extend credit to the point where marginal profits equal marginal costs.

SELF-TEST PROBLEMS

1. The Mill Company has a daily average collection of checks of $250,000. It takes the company 4 days to convert the checks to cash. Assume a lockbox system could be employed which would reduce the cash conversion period to 3 days. The lockbox system would have a net cost of $25,000 per year, but any additional funds made available could be invested to net 8 percent per year. Should Mill adopt the lockbox system?

    a. Yes; the system would free $250,000 in funds.
    b. Yes; the benefits of the lockbox system exceed the costs.
    c. No; the benefit is only $10,000.
    d. No; the firm would lose $5,000 per year if the system were used.
    e. The benefits and costs are equal; hence the firm is indifferent toward the system.

(The following data apply to the next three Self-Test Problems.)

Simmons Brick Company sells on terms of 3/10, net 30. Gross sales for the year are $1,200,000 and the collections department estimates that 30 percent of the customers pay on the tenth day and take discounts; 40 percent pay on the thirtieth day; and the remaining 30 percent pay, on average, 40 days after the purchase. Assume 360 days per year.

2. What is the days sales outstanding?

    a. 10 days   **b.** 13 days   **c.** 20 days   **d.** 27 days   **e.** 40 days

3. What is the current receivables balance?

    a. $60,000   **b.** $70,000   **c.** $75,000   **d.** $80,000   **e.** $90,000

4. What would be the new receivables balance if Simmons toughened up on its collection policy, with the result that all nondiscount customers paid on the thirtieth day?

    a. $60,000   **b.** $70,000   **c.** $75,000   **d.** $80,000   **e.** $90,000

5. Haberdash Inc. last year reported sales of $12 million and an inventory turnover ratio of 3. The company is now adopting a just-in-time inventory system. If the new system is able to reduce the firm's inventory level and increase the firm's inventory turnover ratio to 7.5, while maintaining the same level of sales, how much cash will be freed up?

    a. $2,400,000   **b.** $1,600,000   **c.** $4,000,000   **d.** $3,000,000   **e.** $5,250,000

ANSWERS TO SELF-TEST QUESTIONS

1. working capital
2. Net; current; liabilities
3. minimize; cash
4. inflows; outflows
5. Compensating
6. collection; payment
7. lockbox
8. float
9. supplies; raw materials; work-in-process; finished goods
10. lowest cost
11. increase; carrying
12. inversely
13. just-in-time
14. Accounts receivable
15. volume; sales; collections
16. credit policy
17. sales

18. period; cash discount
19. sales; accounts receivable
20. Collection
21. aging schedules; days sales outstanding
22. carrying
23. cash budget
24. Working capital policy
25. relaxed
26. restricted
27. transactions; compensating
28. Zero working capital
29. Demand flow (based)
30. collections; purchases; gain; loss
31. target
32. Marketable securities
33. Out-sourcing
34. Credit quality

35. b. No new customers are being generated. The current customers pay either on Day 10 or Day 30. The increase in trade discount will induce some customers who are now paying on Day 30 to pay on Day 10. Thus, the days sales outstanding is shortened which, in turn, will cause a decline in accounts receivable.

36. b. The aging schedule breaks down accounts receivable according to how long they have been outstanding.

37. b. Receivables are based on sales price which presumably includes some profit. Only the actual cash outlays associated with receivables must be financed. The remainder, or profit, appears on the balance sheet as an increase in retained earnings.

38. d. Management should try to maximize float.

39. c. Depreciation and obsolescence are inventory carrying costs.

40. e. The goal of credit policy is to maximize overall profits. This is achieved when the marginal profits equal the marginal costs.

SOLUTIONS TO SELF-TEST PROBLEMS

1. d. Currently, Mill has 4($250,000) = $1,000,000 in unavailable collections. If lockboxes were used, this could be reduced to $750,000. Thus, $250,000 would be available to invest at 8 percent, resulting in an annual return of 0.08($250,000) = $20,000. If the system costs $25,000, Mill would lose $5,000 per year by adopting the system.

2. d. 0.3(10 days) + 0.4(30 days) + 0.3(40 days) = 27 days.

3. e. Receivables = (DSO)(Sales/360) = 27($1,200,000/360) = $90,000.

4. d. New days sales outstanding = 0.3(10) + 0.7(30) = 24 days.
Sales per day = $1,200,000/360 = $3,333.33.
Receivables = $3,333.33(24 days) = $80,000.00.

Thus, the average receivables would drop from $90,000 to $80,000. Furthermore, sales may decline as a result of the tighter credit and reduce receivables even more.

Also, some additional customers may now take discounts, which would further reduce receivables.

5.   a.   Inventory turnover ratio$_{Old}$ = Sales/Inventory

$$3 = \$12{,}000{,}000/I$$
$$3I = \$12{,}000{,}000$$
$$I = \$4{,}000{,}000.$$

Inventory turnover ratio$_{New}$ = Sales/Inventory

$$7.5 = \$12{,}000{,}000/I$$
$$I = \$12{,}000{,}000/7.5$$
$$I = \$1{,}600{,}000.$$

Cash freed up = $\$4{,}000{,}000 - \$1{,}600{,}000 = \$2{,}400{,}000.$

OVERVIEW

In the last chapter, we discussed the first step in working capital management—determining the optimal level for each type of current asset. Now we turn to the second step—financing current assets. This chapter first explains alternative current asset financing policies and the advantages and disadvantages of short-term financing. Then the nature of accruals and trade credit and their respective costs are covered. Finally, the cost of bank loans, how to choose a bank, the use of commercial paper, and the use of security in short-term financing are considered.

OUTLINE

A firm's current asset levels and financing requirements rise and fall with business cycles and seasonal trends. At the peak of such cycles, businesses carry their maximum amounts of current assets. Similar fluctuations in financing needs can occur over these cycles, typically, financing needs contract during recessions and they expand during booms.

■ Current assets rarely drop to zero, and this fact has led to the development of the idea of *permanent current assets*. These are the current assets on hand at the low point of the cycle.

■ Seasonal current assets are defined as *temporary current assets*.

■ The manner in which the permanent and temporary current assets are financed is called the firm's *current asset financing policy*.
  □ The *maturity matching, or "self-liquidating," approach* matches asset and liability maturities. Defined as a moderate current asset financing policy, this would use permanent financing for permanent assets (permanent current assets and fixed assets), and use short-term financing to cover seasonal and/or cyclical temporary assets (fluctuating current assets).

□ The *aggressive approach* is used by a firm which finances all of its fixed assets with long-term capital but part of its permanent current assets with short-term, nonspontaneous credit.

□ A *conservative approach* would be to use permanent capital to meet some of the cyclical demand, and then hold the temporary surpluses as marketable securities at the trough of the cycle (storing liquidity). Here, the amount of permanent financing exceeds permanent assets.

■ The aggressive policy calls for the greatest use of short-term debt, while the conservative policy calls for the least.

Although short-term credit is generally riskier than long-term credit, using short-term funds does have some significant advantages. The pros and cons of short-term financing are discussed below.

■ A short-term loan can be obtained much faster than long-term credit.

■ Short-term debt is more flexible since it may be repaid if the firm's financing requirements decline. Long-term debt can be retired, but this will probably involve a prepayment penalty. In addition, flotation costs are higher for long-term debt than for short-term credit and long-term loan agreements always contain provisions that constrain the firm's future actions.

■ Short-term interest rates are normally lower than long-term rates. Therefore, financing with short-term credit usually results in lower interest costs.

■ Short-term debt is generally more risky than long-term debt for two reasons.
□ Short-term interest rates fluctuate widely while long-term rates tend to be more stable and predictable, and hence the interest rate on short-term debt could increase dramatically over a short period.
□ Short-term debt comes due every few months. If a firm does not have the cash to repay debt when it comes due, and if it cannot refinance the loan, it may be forced into bankruptcy.

Different types of short-term funds have different characteristics. One source of short-term funds is accrued wages and taxes, which increase and decrease spontaneously as a firm's operations expand and contract.

■ This type of debt is "free" in the sense that no explicit interest is paid on funds raised through accruals.

■ However, a firm cannot ordinarily control its accruals.
   ☐ The timing of wage payments is set by economic forces and industry custom, while tax payment dates are established by law.

Accounts payable, or trade credit, is the largest single category of short-term debt. Trade credit is a "spontaneous" source of funds because it arises from ordinary business transactions. Most firms make purchases on credit, recording the debt as an account payable.

■ An increase in sales will be accompanied by an increase in inventory purchases, which will automatically generate additional financing.

■ The cost of trade credit is made up of discounts lost by not paying invoices within the discount period.
   ☐ For example, if credit terms are 2/10, net 30, the cost of 20 additional days' credit is 2 percent of the dollar value of the purchases made.
   ☐ The following equation may be used to calculate the nominal percentage cost, on an annual basis, of not taking discounts:

$$\begin{array}{c} \text{Nominal annual} \\ \text{cost} \end{array} = \frac{\text{Discount \%}}{100 - \text{Discount \%}} \times \frac{360}{\begin{array}{c}\text{Days credit is}\\\text{outstanding}\end{array} - \begin{array}{c}\text{Discount}\\\text{period}\end{array}}.$$

   ☐ For example, the nominal cost of not taking the discount when the credit terms are 2/10, net 30, is

$$\begin{array}{c}\text{Nominal}\\\text{annual}\\\text{cost}\end{array} = \frac{2}{98} \times \frac{360}{30-10} = 0.0204(18) = 0.367 = 36.7\%.$$

   ☐ In effective annual interest terms, the rate is even higher. Note that the first term on the right-hand side of the nominal cost equation is the periodic cost, and the second term is the number of periods per year. Thus, the effective annual rate is:

$$(1.0204)^{18} - 1.0 = 1.439 - 1.0 = 43.9\%.$$

■ Trade credit can be divided into two components: *Free trade credit* is that credit received during the discount period. *Costly trade credit* is obtained by foregoing discounts. This costly component should be used only when it is less expensive than funds obtained from other sources.
   ☐ Firms should always use the free component, but they should use the costly component only after analyzing the cost of this capital to make sure that it is less than the cost of funds which could be obtained from other sources.

☐ Competitive conditions may permit firms to do better than the stated credit terms by taking discounts beyond the discount period or by simply paying late. Such practices, called *stretching accounts payable*, reduce the cost of trade credit, but they also result in poor relationships with suppliers.

Bank loans appear on a firm's balance sheet as notes payable and are second in importance to trade credit as a source of short-term financing. Bank loans are not generated spontaneously but must be negotiated and renewed on a regular basis.

■ About two-thirds of all bank loans mature in a year or less, although banks do make longer-term loans.

■ When a firm obtains a bank loan, the agreement is executed by signing a *promissory note*. The following key elements are contained in most promissory notes: the amount borrowed, the interest rate, the maturity date, the repayment schedule, any collateral offered as security, any loan guarantees, and other terms and conditions to which the bank and the borrower have agreed.

■ Banks normally require regular borrowers to maintain *compensating balances* equal to 10 to 20 percent of the face amount of the loan. Such required balances increase the effective interest rate on the loan.

■ A *line of credit* is an informal agreement between a bank and a borrower indicating the maximum credit the bank will extend to the borrower.
   ☐ Many lines of credit have a "clean-up" clause requiring the borrower to have a zero balance on the loan for some period during the year.
   ☐ The clean-up clause prevents the line of credit from becoming a permanent source of financing.

■ A *revolving credit agreement* is a formal line of credit often used by large firms. Normally, the borrower will pay the bank a commitment fee to compensate the bank for guaranteeing that the funds will be available. This fee is paid in addition to the regular interest charge on funds actually borrowed.
   ☐ Note that a revolving credit agreement is very similar to an informal line of credit, but with an important difference: The bank has a *legal obligation* to honor a revolving credit agreement, and for this it receives a commitment fee. Neither the legal obligation nor the fee exists under the informal line of credit.

The interest cost of loans will vary for different types of borrowers at any given point in time and for all borrowers over time. Bank rates charged will vary depending on economic

conditions, the risk of the borrower, and the size of the loan. Interest charges on bank loans can be calculated in one of several ways listed below.

■ *Regular, or simple, interest.* The nominal interest rate is divided by the number of days in the year to get the interest rate per day. This rate is then multiplied by the actual number of days during the specific payment period, and then this result is multiplied by the amount of the loan.

$$\text{Interest rate per day} = \frac{\text{Nominal rate}}{\text{Days in year}}.$$

Interest charge for period = (Days in period)(Rate per day)(Amount of loan).

☐ The effective interest rate on a loan depends on how frequently interest must be paid—the more frequently, the higher the effective rate. The best procedure to use is to lay out all the cash flows on a time line and solve for the interest rate.

■ *Discount interest.* Under this method, the bank deducts interest in advance. The effective annual rate of interest on a discount loan is always higher than the rate on an otherwise similar simple interest loan.
☐ To find the effective interest rate on a discount loan, lay out all the cash flows on a time line (remembering to subtract out the interest paid in advance) and solve for the interest rate.
☐ The firm actually receives less than the face amount of the loan.

Funds received = Face amount of loan (1.0 – Nominal interest rate).

☐ The face amount of the loan can be calculated as follows:

$$\text{Face amount of loan} = \frac{\text{Funds received}}{1.0 - \text{Nominal rate (decimal)}}.$$

☐ Shortening the period of a discount loan lowers the effective rate of interest.
☐ If the bank requires a compensating balance, and if the amount of the required balance exceeds the amount the firm would normally hold on deposit, then the excess must be deducted at t = 0 and then added back when the loan matures.

■ *Installment loans: add-on interest.* Interest charges are calculated and then added on to the amount received to determine the loan's face value, which is paid off in equal installments. The borrower has use of the full amount of the funds received only until the first installment is paid.
☐ To determine the effective rate of an add-on loan, lay out all the cash flows on a time line and solve for the interest rate.

☐ The payments are calculated as the amount to be repaid, which consists of principal plus the total interest divided by 12.

☐ *Annual percentage rate (APR)* is a rate reported by banks and other lenders on loans when the effective rate exceeds the nominal rate of interest.

APR = (Periods per year)(Rate per period).

Choosing a bank involves an analysis of the following variables:

■ *Willingness to assume risks.* Some banks are quite conservative, while others are more willing to make risky loans.

■ *Advice and counsel.* A bank's ability to provide counsel is particularly important to firms in their early and formative years.

■ *Loyalty to customers.* This variable deals with a bank's willingness to support customers during difficult economic times.

■ *Specialization.* A bank may specialize in making loans to a particular type of business. Firms should seek out a bank which is familiar with their particular type of business.

■ *Maximum loan size.* This is an important consideration for large companies when establishing a borrowing relationship because most banks cannot lend to a single customer more than 15 percent of the bank's capital accounts (capital stock plus retained earnings).

■ *Merchant banking.* Originally the term applied to banks which not only loaned depositors' money but also provided its customers with equity capital and financial advice. In recent years, commercial banks have been attempting to get back into merchant banking, in part because their foreign competitors offer such services, and U. S. banks compete with foreign banks for multinational corporations' business.

☐ Currently, the larger banks, often though subsidiaries, are being permitted to get back into merchant banking, at least to a limited extent.

■ *Other services.* The availability of services such as providing cash management services, assisting with electronic funds transfers, and helping firms obtain foreign exchange should also be taken into account when selecting a bank.

Commercial paper, another source of short-term credit, is an unsecured promissory note. It is generally sold to other business firms, to insurance companies, to banks, and to money market mutual funds. Only large, financially strong firms are able to tap the commercial paper market.

■   Maturities of commercial paper range from a few days to nine months, with an average of about five months.

    ☐   Interest rates on prime commercial paper generally range from 1 1/2 to 3 percentage points below the stated prime rate, and about 1/8 to 1/2 of a percentage point above the T-bill rate. However, rates fluctuate daily with supply and demand conditions in the marketplace.

    ☐   A disadvantage of the commercial paper market vis-a-vis bank loans is that the impersonal nature of the market makes it difficult for firms to use commercial paper at times when they are in temporary financial distress.

For a strong firm, borrowing on an unsecured basis is generally cheaper and simpler than on a secured loan basis because of the administrative costs associated with the use of security. However, lenders will refuse credit without some form of collateral if a borrower's credit standing is questionable.

The Extensions to Chapter 17 discuss procedures for using accounts receivable and inventory as security for short-term loans. Accounts receivable financing involves either the pledging of receivables or the selling of receivables (factoring). Credit can also be secured by business inventory. Blanket liens, trust receipts, and warehouse receipts are methods for using inventory as security.

■   The *pledging of accounts receivable,* or putting accounts receivable up as security for a loan, is characterized by the fact that the lender not only has a claim against the receivables but also has *recourse* to the borrower: If the person or firm that bought the goods does not pay, the selling firm must take the loss.

■   *Factoring,* or selling accounts receivable, involves the purchase of accounts receivable by the lender, generally without recourse to the borrower, which means that if the purchaser of the goods does not pay for them, the lender rather than the seller of the goods takes the loss.

■   The *inventory blanket lien* gives the lending institution a lien against all the borrower's inventories. However, the borrower is free to sell inventories, and thus the value of the collateral can be reduced below the level that existed when the loan was granted.

■   The *trust receipt* is an instrument acknowledging that the goods are held in trust for the lender. Under this method, the borrowing firm, as a condition for receiving funds from the lender, signs and delivers a trust receipt for the goods.

■ *Warehouse receipt financing* uses inventory as a security and requires public notification, physical control of the inventory, and supervision by a custodian of the field warehousing concern.

SELF-TEST QUESTIONS

Definitional

1. In the maturity matching approach to working capital financing, permanent assets should be financed with _____ capital, while _____ assets should be financed with short-term credit.

2. Some firms use short-term financing to finance permanent assets. This approach maximizes _____ _____, but also has the _____ _____.

3. Short-term borrowing provides more _____ for firms that are uncertain about their future borrowing needs.

4. Short-term borrowing will be less expensive than borrowing long-term if the yield curve is _____ sloping.

5. Short-term interest rates fluctuate _____ than long-term rates.

6. _____ wages and taxes are a common source of short-term credit. However, most firms have little control over the _____ of these accounts.

7. Accounts payable, or _____ _____, is the largest single source of short-term credit for most businesses.

8. Trade credit is a(n) _____ source of funds in the sense that it automatically increases when sales increase.

9. Trade credit can be divided into two components: _____ trade credit and _____ trade credit.

10. Free trade credit is that credit received during the _____ period.

11. _____ trade credit should only be used when the cost of the trade credit is less than the cost of _____ sources.

12.	The instrument signed when bank credit is obtained is called a(n) _____ _____.

13.	Many banks require borrowers to keep _____ _____ on deposit with the bank equal to 10 or 20 percent of the loan's face amount.

14.	Maturities on commercial paper generally range from _____ to _____ months, with interest rates set about 1 1/2 to 3 percentage points _____ the _____ rate.

15.	A(n) _____ loan is one where collateral such as _____ or _____ have been pledged in support of the loan.

16.	A(n) _____ _____ _____ is an informal agreement between a bank and a borrower as to the maximum loan that will be permitted.

17.	The fee paid to a bank to secure a revolving credit agreement is known as a(n) _____ fee.

18.	If interest charges are deducted in advance, this is known as _____ interest, and the effective rate is higher than the _____ interest rate.

19.	With a(n) _____ loan, interest charges are calculated and then added on to the amount received to determine the loan's face value, and then it is paid off in equal amounts per period.

20.	Commercial paper can only be issued by _____, _____ _____ firms.

21.	_____ current assets are those current assets on hand at the low point of a business cycle.

22.	Seasonal current assets are defined as _____ current assets.

23.	Competitive conditions may permit firms to do better than the stated credit terms by taking discounts beyond the discount period or by simply paying late; such practices are called _____ _____ _____.

24.	A(n) _____ _____ _____ is a formal line of credit often used by large firms.

25.	_____ the period of a discount loan lowers the effective rate of interest.

26.   _____ _____ _____ is reported by banks and other lenders on loans when the effective rate exceeds the nominal rate of interest, and its is calculated as the number of periods per year times the rate per period.

27.   The _____ of accounts receivable is characterized by the fact that the lender not only has a claim against receivables but also has recourse to the borrower.

28.   _____, or selling accounts receivable, involves the purchase of accounts receivable by the lender, generally without recourse to the borrower.

29.   The _____ _____ is an instrument acknowledging that the goods are held in trust for the lender.

30.   _____ _____ financing uses inventory as a security and requires public notification.

Conceptual

31.   The matching of asset and liability maturities is considered desirable because this strategy minimizes interest rate risk.

    a. True   **b.** False

32.   Accruals are "free" in the sense that no interest must be paid on these funds.

    a. True   **b.** False

33.   The effect of compensating balances is to decrease the effective interest rate of a loan.

    a. True   **b.** False

34.   Which of the following statements concerning commercial paper is most correct?

    a. Commercial paper is secured debt of large, financially strong firms.
    b. Commercial paper is sold primarily to individual investors.
    c. Maturities of commercial paper generally exceed nine months.
    d. Commercial paper interest rates are typically 1 1/2 to 3 percentage points above the stated prime rate.
    e. None of the above statements is correct.

35. Which of the following statements is most correct?

    a. If you had just been hired as Working Capital Manager for a firm with but one stockholder, and that stockholder told you that she had all the money she could possibly use, hence that her primary operating goal was to avoid even the remotest possibility of bankruptcy, then you should set the firm's working capital financing policy on the basis of the "Maturity Matching, or Self-Liquidating, Approach."

    b. Due to the existence of positive maturity risk premiums, at most times short-term debt carries lower interest rates than long-term debt. Therefore, if a company finances primarily with short-term as opposed to long-term debt, its expected TIE ratio, hence its overall riskiness, will be lower than if it finances with long-term debt. Therefore, the more conservative the firm, the greater its reliance on short-term debt.

    c. If a firm buys on terms of 2/10, net 30, and pays on the 30th day, then its accounts payable may be thought of as consisting of some "free" and some "costly" trade credit. Since the percentage cost of the costly trade credit is lowered if the payment period is reduced, the firm should try to pay earlier than on Day 30, say on Day 25.

    d. Suppose a firm buys on terms of 2/10, net 30, but it normally pays on Day 60. Disregarding any "image" effects, it should, if it can borrow from the bank at an effective rate of 14 percent, take out a bank loan and start taking discounts.

    e. Each of the above statements is false.

SELF-TEST PROBLEMS

(The following data apply to the next three Self-Test Problems.)

A firm buys on terms of 2/10, net 30, but generally does not pay until 40 days after the invoice date. Its purchases total $1,080,000 per year.

1. How much "non-free" trade credit does the firm use on average each year?

    a. $120,000   **b.** $90,000   **c.** $60,000   **d.** $30,000   **e.** $20,000

2. What is the nominal cost of the "non-free" trade credit?

    a. 16.2%   **b.** 19.4%   **c.** 21.9%   **d.** 24.5%   **e.** 27.4%

3. What is the effective cost rate of the costly credit?

    a. 16.2%   **b.** 19.4%   **c.** 21.9%   **d.** 24.5%   **e.** 27.4%

4.   Lawton Pipelines Inc. has developed plans for a new pump that will allow more economical operation of the company's oil pipelines. Management estimates that $2,400,000 will be required to put this new pump into operation. Funds can be obtained from a bank at 10 percent discount interest, or the company can finance the expansion by delaying payment to its suppliers. Presently, Lawton purchases under terms of 2/10, net 40, but management believes payment could be delayed 30 additional days without penalty; that is, payment could be made in 70 days. Which means of financing should Lawton use? (Use the nominal cost of trade credit.)

   a. Trade credit, since the cost is about 12.24 percent.
   b. Trade credit, since the cost is about 3.13 percentage points less than the bank loan.
   c. Bank loan, since the cost is about 1.13 percentage points less than trade credit.
   d. Bank loan, since the cost is about 3.13 percentage points less than trade credit.
   e. The firm could use either since the costs are the same.

(The following data apply to the next four Self-Test Problems.)

You plan to borrow $10,000 from your bank, which offers to lend you the money at a 10 percent nominal, or stated, rate on a 1-year loan.

5.   What is the effective interest rate if the loan is a discount loan?

   a. 11.1%   **b.** 13.3%   **c.** 15.0%   **d.** 17.5%   **e.** 20.0%

6.   What is the effective interest rate if the loan is an add-on interest loan with 12 monthly payments?

   a. 11.5%   **b.** 13.3%   **c.** 15.0%   **d.** 17.5%   **e.** 19.5%

7.   What is the effective interest rate if the loan is a discount loan with a 15 percent compensating balance?

   a. 11.1%   **b.** 13.3%   **c.** 15.0%   **d.** 17.5%   **e.** 20.0%

8.   Under the terms of the previous problem, how much would you have to borrow to have the use of $10,000?

   a. $10,000   **b.** $11,111   **c.** $12,000   **d.** $13,333   **e.** $15,000

9. Gibbs Corporation needs to raise $1,000,000 for one year to supply working capital to a new store. Gibbs buys from its suppliers on terms of 4/10, net 90, and it currently pays on the 10th day and takes discounts, but it could forego discounts, pay on the 90th day, and get the needed $1,000,000 in the form of costly trade credit. Alternatively, Gibbs could borrow from its bank on a 15 percent discount interest rate basis. What is the effective annual cost rate of the lower cost source?

    a. 20.17%   **b.** 18.75%   **c.** 17.65%   **d.** 18.25%   **e.** 19.50%

Chapter 17 Extensions

(The following data apply to the next two Self-Test Problems.)

Douglas Industries needs an additional $500,000, which it plans to obtain through a factoring arrangement. The factor would purchase Douglas's accounts receivable and advance the invoice amount, minus a 4 percent commission, on the invoices purchased each month. Douglas sells on terms of net 30 days. In addition, the factor charges a 14 percent annual interest rate on the total invoice amount, to be deducted in advance.

17E-1. What amount of accounts receivable must be factored to net $500,000?

    a. $527,241   **b.** $515,464   **c.** $530,441   **d.** $525,367   **e.** $518,989

17E-2. If Douglas can reduce credit expenses by $10,000 per month and avoid bad debt losses of 3.5 percent on the factored amount, what is the total annual dollar cost of the savings that results from the use of the factoring arrangement?

    a. $12,353   **b.** $11,076   **c.** $14,544   **d.** $13,767   **e.** $11,841

ANSWERS TO SELF-TEST QUESTIONS

1.	permanent (long-term); temporary	**9.**	free; costly
2.	expected return; greatest risk	**10.**	discount
3.	flexibility	**11.**	Costly; alternative
4.	upward	**12.**	promissory note
5.	more	**13.**	compensating balances
6.	Accrued; size (amount)	**14.**	one; nine; below; prime
7.	trade credit	**15.**	secured; receivables; inventory
8.	spontaneous	**16.**	line of credit

17.	commitment	24.	revolving credit agreement
18.	discount; simple (or nominal or stated)	25.	Shortening
		26.	Annual percentage rate
19.	installment	27.	pledging
20.	large; financially strong	28.	Factoring
21.	Permanent	29.	trust receipt
22.	temporary	30.	Warehouse receipt
23.	stretching accounts payable		

31. b. The matching of maturities minimizes default risk, or the risk that the firm will be unable to pay off its maturing obligations, and reinvestment rate risk, or the risk that the firm will have to roll over the debt at a higher rate.

32. a. Neither workers nor the IRS require interest payments on wages and taxes that are not paid as soon as they are earned.

33. b. Compensating balances increase the effective rate because the firm is required to maintain excess non-interest-bearing balances.

34. e. Commercial paper is the unsecured debt of strong firms. It generally has a maturity from one to nine months and is sold primarily to other corporations and financial institutions. Rates on commercial paper are typically below the prime rate.

35. d. Statement a is false; the conservative approach would be the safest current asset financing policy. Statement b is false; short-term debt fluctuates more than long-term debt, thus, the greater the firm's reliance on short-term debt, the riskier the firm. Statement c is false; it makes no difference in the cost if the firm pays on Day 25 versus Day 30 in this instance. Statement d is true; if the firm can "stretch" its payables the nominal cost is 14.69% (the effective cost is 15.66%). Thus, the firm should obtain the 14% bank loan to take discounts as this is the lowest cost to the firm.

SOLUTIONS TO SELF-TEST PROBLEMS

1. b. $1,080,000/360 = $3,000 in purchases per day. Typically, there will be $3,000(40) = $120,000 of accounts payable on the books at any given time. Of this, $3,000(10) = $30,000 is "free" credit, while $3,000(30) = $90,000 is "non-free" credit.

2.   d.   Nominal cost $= \dfrac{\text{Discount \%}}{100 - \text{Discount \%}} \times \dfrac{360}{\substack{\text{Days credit is} \\ \text{outstanding}} - \substack{\text{Discount} \\ \text{period}}}$

$$= \frac{2}{100-2} \times \frac{360}{40-10} = \frac{2}{98} \times \frac{360}{30} = 24.5\%.$$

3.   e.   The periodic rate is 2/98 = 2.04%, and there are 360/30 = 12 periods per year. Thus, the effective annual rate is 27.4 percent:

$$\left(1 + \frac{k_{Nom}}{m}\right)^{12} - 1.0 = (1.0204)^{12} - 1.0$$
$$= 1.2742 - 1.0 = 0.2742 = 27.4\%.$$

4.   c.   Face amount $= \dfrac{\$2,400,000}{1 - 0.10}$
$$= \$2,666,667.$$

Interest to be deducted in advance $= 0.10 \times \$2,666,667 = \$266,667.$

Using a financial calculator, enter N = 1, PV = 2400000, PMT = 0, and FV = -2666667; and then solve for I to get the effective cost of the loan, 11.11%.

Credit terms are 2/10, net 40, but delaying payments 30 additional days is the equivalent of 2/10, net 70. Assuming no penalty, the nominal cost is as follows:

$$\text{Nominal cost} = \frac{\text{Discount \%}}{100 - \text{Discount \%}} \times \frac{360}{\substack{\text{Days credit is} \\ \text{outstanding}} - \substack{\text{Discount} \\ \text{period}}}$$

$$= \frac{2}{100-2} \times \frac{360}{70-10} = \frac{2}{98} \times \frac{360}{60} = 0.0204(6) = 12.24\%.$$

Therefore, the loan cost is 1.13 percentage points less than trade credit.

5.   a.   Face amount $= \dfrac{\$10,000}{1-0.10}$

                    $= \$11,111.$

Interest to be deducted in advance $= 0.1 \times \$11,111 = \$1,111.$

$$
\begin{array}{l}
11,111 \\
\underline{-\ 1,111} \\
\underline{10,000}
\end{array}
$$

Using a financial calculator, enter N = 1, PV = 10000, PMT = 0, and FV = -11111; and then solve for I to get the effective cost of the loan, 11.11%.

6.   e.   The amount to be repaid is $10,000 plus $1,000 of interest, or $11,000. The monthly payment is $11,000/12 = $916.67.

The time line for the loan is:

With a financial calculator, enter N = 12, PV = 10000, PMT = -916.67, FV = 0, and solve for I = 1.49767%. However, this is a monthly rate. The effective rate is found as $(1 + 0.0149767)^{12} - 1 = 19.529\% \approx 19.5\%.$

7. **b.** Face amount of loan $= \dfrac{\$10,000}{1-0.10-0.15}$

$= \$13,333.$

Interest to be deducted in advance $= 0.1 \times \$13,333 = \$1,333.$
Compensating balance $= 0.15 \times \$13,333 = \$2,000.$

```
   0   I = ?                                 1  Year
   ├────────────────────────────────────────┤
 13,333                                   -13,333
 -  1,333                                 +  2,000
 -  2,000                                 -11,333
  10,000
```

Using a financial calculator, enter N = 1, PV = 10000, PMT = 0, and FV = -11333; and then solve for I to get the effective cost of the loan, 13.3%.

8. **d.** $\dfrac{\$10,000}{1-0.15-0.10} = \$13,333.$

0.15($13,333) = $2,000 is required for the compensating balance, and 0.10($13,333) = $1,333 is required for the immediate interest payment.

9.   c.   Accounts payable:
Nominal cost = (4/96)(360/80) = 0.04167(4.5) = 18.75%.
EAR cost = $(1.04167)^{4.5} - 1.0 = 20.17\%$.

Cost of notes payable:

Face amount of loan $= \dfrac{\$1,000,000}{1-0.15}$
$= \$1,176,471.$

Interest to be deducted in advance = $0.15 \times \$1,176,471 = \$176,471.$

0   I = ?   1 Year

1,176,471   -1,176,471
- 176,471
1,000,000

Using a financial calculator, enter N = 1, PV = 1000000, PMT = 0, and FV = -1176471; and then solve for I to get the effective cost of the loan, 17.65%.

Chapter 17 Extensions

17E-1. a. $\dfrac{\text{Accounts receivable}}{\text{needed to factor}} = \dfrac{\$500,000}{1-\left(\dfrac{0.14}{12}+0.04\right)} = \$527,241.$

17E-2. c.   Monthly costs:
Commission = $527,241(0.04) = $21,090
Interest = $527,241(0.14/12)   =   6,151
                                                           $27,241

Monthly savings:
Credit expense $10,000
Bad debt losses = $527,241(0.035) =   18,453
                                                          $28,453

The factoring arrangement will result in a savings of $28,453 - $27,241 = $1,212 per month, or $1,212(12) = $14,544 per year.

CHAPTER 18
OTHER TOPICS IN WORKING CAPITAL MANAGEMENT

OVERVIEW

In Chapters 16 and 17, the basic elements of current asset management and short-term financing were presented. Now, in Chapter 18, we present a more in-depth treatment of several working capital topics, including (1) the cash conversion cycle, (2) the target cash balance, (3) accounting for inventory, (4) the EOQ model, and (5) monitoring the receivables position.

OUTLINE

The concept of working capital management originated with the old Yankee peddler, who would borrow to buy inventory, sell the inventory to pay off the bank loan, and then repeat the cycle. That general concept has been applied to more complex businesses, and the cash flow cycle concept is used for analyzing the effectiveness of a firm's working capital management.

- The *cash conversion cycle* model analyzes the length of time between when the company makes payments and when it receives cash. The following terms are used in the model.
  - ☐ The *inventory conversion period* is the average length of time required to convert materials into finished goods and then to sell those goods. It is calculated as Inventory/Sales per day.
  - ☐ The *receivables collection period*, also called the *days sales outstanding (DSO)*, is the average length of time required to convert receivables into cash, that is, to collect cash following a sale. It is calculated as Receivables/(Sales/360).
  - ☐ The *payables deferral period* is the average length of time between the purchase of materials and labor and the payment of cash for them. It is calculated as Payables/Credit purchases per day.

- The cash conversion cycle nets out the inventory conversion period, the receivables collection period, and the payables deferral period.

☐ It equals the length of time between the firm's actual cash expenditures for productive resources and its own cash receipts from the sale of products—the average length of time a dollar is tied up in current assets.

☐ The longer the cash conversion cycle, the larger the amount of capital tied up in working capital, hence the higher the firm's capital costs.

☐ Cash conversion cycle = Inventory conversion period + Receivables collection period – Payables deferral period.

☐ The cash conversion cycle can be shortened if the firm can reduce the inventory conversion period by processing and selling goods more quickly, if it can reduce the receivables collection period by speeding up collections, or if it can lengthen the payables deferral period by slowing down its own payments. To the extent that these actions can be taken without increasing costs or depressing sales, they should be carried out.

One of the key elements in a firm's cash budget is the target cash balance. The target cash balance is normally set as the larger of the firm's transactions balances plus precautionary balances or its required compensating balances. The Baumol model applies inventory methodology (EOQ model) to cash balances.

■ The optimal cash holdings to be transferred from marketable securities or to be borrowed, C*, can be found by the equation:

$$C^* = \sqrt{\frac{2(F)(T)}{k}}.$$

Here, F = fixed costs of borrowing or of converting marketable securities into cash, T = total amount of net new cash needed for transactions during the entire period, usually a year, and k = the opportunity cost of holding cash, set equal to either the rate of return foregone on marketable securities or the cost of borrowing to hold cash.

■ Assuming no precautionary balances, the optimal average cash balance is C*/2.

■ The optimal cash balance increases less than proportionately with increases in the amount of cash needed for transactions. This suggests that there are economies of scale in holding cash balances, and this, in turn, gives larger firms an edge over smaller ones.

■ The *Baumol model* is simplistic in many respects, but it can provide a useful starting point for establishing a target cash balance.

☐ It assumes relatively stable, predictable cash inflows and outflows, and it does not take into account seasonal or cyclical trends.

■ Although the Baumol model and other theoretical models provide insights into the optimal cash balance, they are generally not practical for actual use. Rather, firms generally set their target cash balances as some "safety stock" of cash that holds the risk of running out of money to some acceptably low level. One commonly used procedure is *Monte Carlo simulation.*

When finished goods are sold, the firm must assign a cost of goods sold. Four methods can be used to value the cost of goods sold, and hence to value remaining inventory.

■ Under *specific identification,* a unique cost is attached to each item in inventory.
  ☐ This method is used only when the items are high cost and move relatively slowly.

■ In the *first-in, first-out (FIFO)* method, the units sold during a given period are assumed to be the first units that were placed in inventory. As a result, the cost of goods sold is based on the cost of the older inventory items, and the remaining inventory consists of the newer goods.
  ☐ When costs are increasing, FIFO gives the lowest cost of goods sold and thus the highest net income. FIFO also shows the highest inventory value, so it produces the strongest apparent liquidity position as measured by net working capital or the current ratio.

■ The *last-in, first-out (LIFO)* method is the opposite of FIFO. The cost of goods sold is based on the last units placed in inventory, while the remaining inventory consists of the first goods placed in inventory.
  ☐ When costs are increasing, LIFO produces the highest cost of goods sold, the lowest reported profits, and the weakest apparent liquidity position.
  ☐ When taxes are considered, LIFO provides the greatest tax deductibility, and thus it results in the lowest tax burden.

■ The *weighted average* method involves the computation of the weighted average unit cost of goods available for sale from inventory, and this average cost is then applied to the goods sold to determine the cost of goods sold.
  ☐ This method results in a cost of goods sold and an ending inventory that falls somewhere between the FIFO and LIFO methods.

Inventories are obviously necessary; however, a firm's profitability will suffer if it has too much or too little inventory. As a starting point in the process, it is useful for managers to consider the insights provided by the economic ordering quantity (EOQ) model.

■ *Carrying costs* generally rise in direct proportion to the average amount of inventory held.

- □ Carrying costs include the following: Cost of the capital tied up in inventories, storage costs, insurance costs, property taxes, and depreciation and obsolescence.
- □ If TCC = total carrying cost, C = annual carrying cost as a percentage of inventory value, P = purchase price per unit of inventory, and A = average number of units held in inventory, then

$$TCC = (C)(P)(A).$$

- ■ *Ordering costs*, which are considered to be fixed costs, decline as average inventories increase, that is, as the number of orders decrease.
  - □ Ordering costs include the costs of placing and receiving orders.
  - □ If TOC = total ordering cost, F = fixed costs associated with placing and receiving an order, and N = the number of orders placed per year, then

$$TOC = (F)(N).$$

- ■ The costs of running short of inventory, or *stock-out costs*, may well be the most important element of inventory costs. These costs will be added later, when safety stocks are discussed.

- ■ *Total inventory costs, TIC*, equal the sum of total carrying costs and total ordering costs:

$$TIC = TCC + TOC = (C)(P)(A) + (F)(N).$$

- □ Now recognize that if Q units are ordered each time an order is placed, and assuming that inventories are used evenly over the year and inventory levels are run down to zero immediately prior to receipt of the next order, then the average inventory level is one-half the number ordered:

$$A = Q/2.$$

- □ Further, if Q units are ordered each time, and S units are required over the year, then

$$N = S/Q.$$

- □ Using these relationships for A and N, the total inventory cost equation can be rewritten as

$$TIC = (C)(P)\left(\frac{Q}{2}\right) + (F)\left(\frac{S}{Q}\right).$$

- ■ The *EOQ model,* which is derived by minimizing total inventory costs, is

$$EOQ = \sqrt{\frac{2(F)(S)}{(C)(P)}},$$

where:
- □ EOQ is the optimal quantity to be ordered each time an order is placed.
- □ F = fixed costs of placing and receiving an order.
- □ S = annual sales in units.
- □ C = carrying cost expressed as a percentage of inventory value.
- □ P = purchase price the firm must pay per unit of inventory.

■ The assumptions of the model are as follows:
- □ Sales can be forecasted perfectly.
- □ Sales are evenly distributed over time.
- □ Orders are received when expected.

■ With instantaneous order delivery, the order point is zero. However, if the instantaneous order delivery assumption is dropped, the order point is found as follows:
- □ Find the daily rate of usage.
- □ The lead time is the number of days required to place an order and receive delivery.
- □ Order point equals daily usage times lead time.

■ Demand, rate of usage, and order lead time cannot always be known with certainty. Therefore, firms add a *safety stock* to their inventories to avoid running out of inventory and suffering stock-out costs.
- □ At the optimal level of safety stock, the probable cost of running out of inventory is just offset by the cost of carrying the additional inventory.
- □ The optimal safety stock *increases* with the uncertainty of demand forecasts, with the costs (in terms of lost sales and lost goodwill) that result from inventory shortages, and with the probability that delays will occur in receiving shipments.
- □ The optimal safety stock *decreases* as the cost of carrying this additional inventory increases.
- □ The costs of a stock-out include customer ill will, production delays, and lost sales.
- □ The probability of a stock-out is influenced by fluctuations in usage rate and delivery time.
- □ Inclusion of a safety stock does not affect the EOQ.
  - The average inventory with the safety stock is

$$A = (EOQ/2) + \text{Safety stock.}$$

  - The order point is increased by the amount of the safety stock.
  - Total inventory costs are increased by the carrying cost of the safety stock.

■ Suppliers often offer discounts for ordering large quantities; such discounts are called *quantity discounts*. To evaluate taking or not taking a quantity discount, the savings of the quantity discount is compared against the increased costs of ordering (and holding) a nonoptimal amount.

■ Moderate inflation—3% per year—can largely be ignored for purposes of inventory management, but higher inflation rates must be explicitly considered.
  □ If the inflation rate in the types of goods the firm stocks tends to be relatively constant, it can be dealt with quite easily—simply deduct the expected annual rate of inflation from the carrying cost percentage, C, and use this modified version of the EOQ model to establish the ordering quantity.
  □ On balance, there is no evidence that inflation either raises or lowers the optimal inventories of firms in the aggregate. Inflation should still be explicitly considered, however, for it will raise the individual firm's optimal holdings if the inflation rate for its own inventories is above average.

■ For most firms, it is unrealistic to assume that demand for an inventory item is uniform throughout the year. Thus, the EOQ model cannot be used on an annual basis, but it can be used on a seasonal basis, with inventories either run down or built up during the transition between seasons.

■ Small deviations from the EOQ quantity do not appreciably affect total inventory costs, and, consequently, the optimal ordering quantity should be viewed more as a range than as a single value.

The days sales outstanding and aging schedules are useful receivables monitoring methods, especially for monitoring an individual customer's account, but neither method is totally suitable for monitoring the aggregate payment performance of all of a firm's credit customers, especially for a firm that experiences fluctuating credit sales.

■ The primary point in analyzing the aggregate accounts receivable situation is to see if customers, on average, are paying more slowly.
  □ The DSO and aging schedules are useful in monitoring credit operations, but both are affected by increases and decreases in a firm's sales level.

■ Changes in sales levels, including normal seasonal or cyclical changes, can change a firm's DSO and aging schedule even though its customers' payment behavior has not changed at all. For this reason, the *payments pattern approach* has been developed to measure any changes that might be occurring in customers' payment behavior.
  □ The payments pattern approach permits us to remove the effects of seasonal and/or cyclical sales variation and to construct a more accurate measure of customers' payments patterns.

■ Another basic tool used to monitor receivables is the *uncollected balances schedule*. At the end of each quarter, the dollar amount of receivables remaining from each of the three month's sales is divided by the month's sales to obtain three receivables-to-sales ratios. The sum of the receivables-to-sales ratio, the total uncollected balances percentage, is obtained and if it has increased it will alert the firm's managers that customers are paying more slowly.

  □ The uncollected balances schedule permits a firm to monitor its receivables better, and it can also be used to forecast future receivables balances.

Changes in credit policy must be analyzed. For example, easing the credit policy normally stimulates sales. As sales rise, costs also rise (1) to produce the extra required goods, (2) to carry the additional receivables outstanding, and (3) because bad debt expenses may rise.

■ The question to answer when considering a credit policy change, therefore, is whether sales revenues will rise more than costs.

■ One way to answer this question is to compare projected income statements and, hence, focus on the *incremental changes* in expected sales revenues and costs that would result from a proposed change in the credit policy.

  □ In this analysis, determine the firm's *cost of carrying receivables* before and after the change in credit policy.

  □ The cost of carrying receivables is the product of the days sales outstanding, sales per day, the variable cost ratio, and the cost of funds.

$$\text{Cost of carrying receivables} = \text{DSO} \times \frac{\text{Sales}}{\text{per day}} \times \frac{\text{Variable}}{\text{cost ratio}} \times \frac{\text{Cost of}}{\text{funds}} \ .$$

  □ Only *variable costs* are considered because only this portion needs to be financed; the remainder is profit.

  □ The change in the level of *bad debt losses* and the dollar value of the *discounts* taken must also be determined.

  □ If expected sales revenues less expected expenses are greater after the proposed change in credit policy than before, the change in credit policy should be undertaken, unless the riskiness of the change is disproportionate to the benefits.

■ The second approach to analyzing changes in credit policy, *the incremental analysis approach*, uses a set of algebraic equations which focus directly on the incremental changes.

  □ The following equations are used:

Sales increase: $\Delta I = [(\text{DSO}_N - \text{DSO}_0)(S_0/360)] + V[(\text{DSO}_N)(S_N - S_0)/360]$.

Sales decrease: $\Delta I = [(\text{DSO}_N - \text{DSO}_0)(S_N/360)] + V[(\text{DSO}_0)(S_N - S_0)/360]$.

$$\Delta P = (S_N - S_0)(1 - V) - k(\Delta I) - (B_N S_N - B_0 S_0) - (D_N S_N P_N - D_0 S_0 P_0).$$

☐ The symbols used, as well as the application of these equations, are discussed fully in the text.

■ There is quite a bit of uncertainty in credit policy change analysis because the variables are very difficult to estimate. Further, the end result depends on the reactions of competitors. Thus, the final decision is based on the quantitative analysis plus a great deal of informed judgment.

SELF-TEST QUESTIONS

Definitional

1. The _____ _____ applies inventory methodology (the EOQ model) to cash balances.

2. The _____ _____ period is the average length of time required to convert materials into finished goods and then to sell those goods.

3. The _____ _____ period is the average length of time required to convert the firm's receivables into cash, that is, to collect cash following a sale.

4. The _____ _____ period is the average length of time between the purchase of materials and labor and the cash payment for them.

5. The _____ _____ _____ is the average length of time a dollar is tied up in current assets.

6. The optimal cash balance increases _____ than proportionately with increases in the amount of cash needed for transactions. This suggests that there are _____ ____ _____ in holding cash balances, and this, in turn, gives _____ firms an edge over _____ firms.

7. Besides using the Baumol model to give insights into the optimal cash balance, a commonly used method for setting the target cash balance is _____ _____ simulation.

8. Under _____ _____, a unique cost is attached to each item in inventory.

9. In the _____-____, _____-_____ method, the units sold during a given period are assumed to be the first units that were placed in inventory.

10. _____ costs generally rise in direct proportion to the average amount of inventory held.

11. _____ costs, which are considered to be fixed costs, decline as average inventories increase.

12. Besides the payments pattern approach, another basic tool used to monitor receivables is the _____ _____ _____. With this method, at the end of each quarter, the dollar amount of receivables remaining from each of the three month's sales is divided by the month's sales to obtain receivables-to-sales ratios.

13. _____ the credit policy normally stimulates sales.

14. If expected sales revenues less expected expenses are _____ after the proposed change in credit policy than before, the change in credit policy should be undertaken.

15. The _____ _____ approach removes the effects of seasonal and/or cyclical sales variations and measures any changes that might be occurring in customers' payment behavior.

16. The _____ _____ quantity minimizes the total costs of ordering and holding inventories.

17. When the level of inventories reaches the _____ _____, the EOQ amount should be ordered.

18. _____ _____ must be maintained in order to allow for shipping delays and uncertainty in the rate of _____.

19. Running out of an item of inventory is called a(n) _____-_____.

20. The optimal ordering quantity should be thought of more as a(n) _____ than as a point value.

Conceptual

21. The economic ordering quantity is the order quantity that provides the minimum total cost; that is, both the ordering and carrying cost components are minimized.

    a. True   **b.** False

22. To evaluate taking or not taking a quantity discount, the savings of the quantity discount should be compared against the increased costs of ordering and holding a non optimal amount.

    a. True   **b.** False

23. There is evidence to suggest that inflation lowers the optimal inventories of firms in the aggregate.

    a. True   **b.** False

24. The addition of a safety stock to the EOQ model

    a. Increases the EOQ proportionately.
    b. Raises the order point.
    c. Lowers the order point.
    d. Does not change the total inventory costs.
    e. Results in greater variability in the time required to receive deliveries.

SELF-TEST PROBLEMS

1. The Ryder Company has been practicing cash management for some time by using the Baumol model to determine cash balances. Recently, when the interest rate on marketable securities was 10 percent, the model called for an average cash balance of $1,000. A rapid increase in interest rates has driven this rate up to 15 percent. The firm incurs a cost of $20 per transaction. Ryder does not carry any precautionary balances. What is the appropriate average cash balance now?

    a. $596.97   **b.** $604.73   **c.** $816.50   **d.** $1,632.99   **e.** $1,333.33

(The following data apply to the next three Self-Test Problems.)

Stanton Industries projects that cash outlays of $1.5 million will occur uniformly throughout the year. Stanton plans to meet its cash requirements by periodically selling marketable securities from its portfolio. The firm's marketable securities are invested to earn 9 percent, and the cost per transaction of converting securities to cash is $18.

2. Using the Baumol model, what is the optimal transaction size for transfers from marketable securities to cash?

   a. $24,495   **b.** $33,271   **c.** $20,876   **d.** $23,154   **e.** $27,989

3. What will be Stanton's average cash balance?

   a. $13,994.50   **b.** $16,635.50   **c.** $11,577.00   **d.** $10,438.00   **e.** $12,247.50

4. How many transfers per year will be required?

   a. 45.08   **b.** 61.24   **c.** 53.59   **d.** 71.85   **e.** 64.78

(The following data apply to the next three Self-Test Problems.)

Furston Inc., a retail firm, currently has sales of $1 million. Its credit period and days sales outstanding are both 30 days, and 1 percent of its sales end up as bad debts. Furston's credit manager estimates that, if the firm extends its credit period to 45 days so that its days sales outstanding increases to 45 days, sales will increase by $100,000, but its bad debt losses on the incremental sales would be 3 percent. Variable costs are 40 percent, and the cost of carrying receivables, k, is 15 percent. Assume a tax rate of 40 percent and 360 days per year. (Hint: Use the first approach given in the *Study Guide* for analyzing changes in credit policy.)

5. What would be the *incremental* investment required to finance the increase in receivables if the change were made?

   a. $3,250   **b.** $41,667   **c.** $21,667   **d.** $50,000   **e.** $56,667

6. What would be the *incremental* cost of carrying receivables?

   a. $5,000   **b.** $3,250   **c.** $8,250   **d.** $10,000   **e.** $0

7. What would be the *incremental* change in net income?

   a. $32,250   **b.** $26,875   **c.** $20,000   **d.** $10,550   **e.** $15,875

(The following data apply to the next two Self-Test Problems.)

Hodes Furniture currently has annual sales of $2,000,000. Its days sales outstanding is 40 days, and bad debts are 5 percent of sales. The credit and collection manager is considering instituting a stricter collection policy, whereby bad debts would be reduced to 2 percent of total sales, and the days sales outstanding would fall to 30 days. However, sales would also fall by an estimated $250,000 annually. Variable costs are 60 percent of sales and the cost of carrying receivables is 12 percent. Assume a tax rate of 40 percent and 360 days per year. (Hint: Use the first approach given in the *Study Guide* for analyzing changes in credit policy.)

8. What would be the *incremental* investment required to finance the increase in receivables if the change were made?

    a. -$16,667   **b.** -$27,167   **c.** -$48,611   **d.** -$45,833   **e.** -$72,431

9. What would be the *incremental* change in net income?

    a. -$16,667   **b.** -$17,700   **c.** -$20,250   **d.** -$25,750   **e.** -$15,000

(The following data apply to the next four Self-Test Problems.)

The South Florida Lawn Supply Company is reviewing its inventory policy regarding lawn seed. The following relationships and conditions exist:

(1) Orders must be placed in multiples of 100 bags.
(2) Requirements for the year are 16,200 bags.
(3) The purchase price per bag is $5.00.
(4) The carrying cost is 20 percent of inventory value.
(5) The fixed costs per order are $25.
(6) The desired safety stock is 300 units; this amount is on hand initially.
(7) Five days are required for delivery.
(8) Assume 360 days per year.

10. What is the economic ordering quantity?

    a. 600 bags   **b.** 700 bags   **c.** 800 bags   **d.** 900 bags   **e.** 1,000 bags

11. How many orders should South Florida Lawn Supply place each year?

    a. 22   **b.** 20   **c.** 18   **d.** 16   **e.** 14

12. What is the order point?

    a. 750 bags   **b.** 525 bags   **c.** 345 bags   **d.** 300 bags   **e.** 225 bags

13. What is the average inventory level?

    a. 750 bags   **b.** 525 bags   **c.** 345 bags   **d.** 300 bags   **e.** 225 bags

(The following data apply to the next six Self-Test Problems.)

The Magnuson Company is trying to determine its optimal inventory policy. The following relationships and conditions exist for the firm:

(1) Annual sales are 120,000 units.
(2) The purchase price per unit is $500.
(3) The carrying cost is 20 percent of inventory value.
(4) The fixed costs per order are $600.
(5) The optimal safety stock is 500 units, which are already on hand.
(6) Assume 360 days per year.

14. What is the economic ordering quantity?

    a. 600 units   **b.** 800 units   **c.** 1,000 units   **d.** 1,200 units   **e.** 1,400 units

15. What is the maximum inventory the company will hold?

    a. 1,300 units   **b.** 1,400 units   **c.** 1,500 units   **d.** 1,600 units   **e.** 1,700 units

16. What is the average inventory the company will hold?

    a. 600 units   **b.** 850 units   **c.** 1,100 units   **d.** 1,200 units   **e.** 1,700 units

17. How often will the company order?

    a. Every 2.0 days   **d.** Every 2 weeks
    b. Every 3.60 days   **e.** Continually
    c. Every 5.25 days

18. What are the firm's annual total inventory costs disregarding the safety stock?

    a. $50,000   **b.** $120,000   **c.** $150,000   **d.** $170,000   **e.** $200,000

19. What are the annual total inventory costs including the safety stock?

    a. $50,000   **b.** $120,000   **c.** $150,000   **d.** $170,000   **e.** $200,000

20. The Hamilton Company has a variable operating cost ratio of 60 percent, its cost of capital is 12 percent, and current sales are $20,000. All of its sales are on credit, and it currently sells on terms of net 30. Its accounts receivable balance is $3,000. Hamilton is considering a new credit policy with terms of net 45. Under the new policy, sales will increase to $24,000, and accounts receivable will rise to $5,000. If Hamilton changes its credit policy to net 45, by how much will its cost of carrying receivables increase? Assume a 360-day year. (Hint: Use the first approach given in the *Study Guide* for analyzing changes in credit policy.)

    a. $144   **b.** $127   **c.** $118   **d.** $135   **e.** $168

21. Your company sells on terms of net 40, sales (all on credit) are $500 per year, and accounts receivable average $50. You are considering a new credit policy, with terms of net 20, under which you expect sales of $475 and an average receivables balance of $25. Your variable cost ratio is 80 percent, and your cost of capital is 10 percent. Use 360 days per year, assume that fixed costs are the same under each credit policy, and assume all dollars are in millions. By how much would your *pre-tax profits* (in millions) change if the new credit policy is employed? (Hint: Use the first approach given in the *Study Guide* for analyzing changes in credit policy.)

    a. $1.00   **b.** -$2.00   **c.** -$1.00   **d.** $3.00   **e.** -$3.00

ANSWERS TO SELF-TEST QUESTIONS

1.	Baumol model	11.	Ordering
2.	inventory conversion	12.	uncollected balances schedule
3.	receivables collection	13.	Easing
4.	payables deferral	14.	greater
5.	cash conversion cycle	15.	payments pattern
6.	less; economies of scale; larger; smaller	16.	economic ordering
		17.	order point
7.	Monte Carlo	18.	Safety stocks; usage
8.	specific identification	19.	stock-out
9.	first-in first-out	20.	range
10.	Carrying		

21. b. The total cost, or sum of ordering and carrying costs, is minimized, but neither of the component costs is minimized. For example, to minimize carrying costs, no inventory would be kept on hand at all.

22. a. This is a correct statement.

23. b. On balance, there is no evidence that inflation either raises or lowers the optimal inventories of firms in the aggregate. Inflation should still be explicitly considered, however, for it will raise the individual firm's optimal holdings if the inflation rate for its own inventories is above average.

24. b. The addition of a safety stock increases the order point by the amount of the safety stock.

SOLUTIONS TO SELF-TEST PROBLEMS

1. c. The model is

$$C^* = \sqrt{\frac{2(F)(T)}{k}}.$$

Initially, the average cash balance, $C^*/2$, is $1,000, thus $C^* = $2,000$. Therefore,

$$\$2,000 = \sqrt{\frac{2(\$20)(T)}{0.10}}$$

$$\$4,000,000 = \frac{2(\$20)(T)}{0.10}$$

$$\$4,000,000 = \$400\,T$$

$$\$10,000 = T.$$

Therefore, the new average cash balance is

$$C^* = \sqrt{\frac{2(\$20)(\$10,000)}{0.15}}$$

$$C^* = \$1,632.99$$

$$C^*/2 = \$816.50.$$

2. a. $C^* = \sqrt{\dfrac{2(F)(T)}{k}}$ = Optimal transaction size.

F = $18; T = $1,500,000; k = 9%.

$C^* = \sqrt{\dfrac{2(\$18)(\$1,500,000)}{0.09}} = \$24,494.90 \approx \$24,495.$

3. e. Average cash balance = $24,495/2 = $12,247.50.

4. b. Transfers per year = $1,500,000/$24,495 = 61.24.

5. c. The incremental receivable investment is calculated as follows:

Old credit policy: $\text{DSO} \times \dfrac{\text{Sales}}{\text{per day}} \times \dfrac{\text{Variable}}{\text{cost ratio}}$

$(30)\left(\dfrac{\$1,000,000}{360}\right)(0.4) = \$33,333.$

New credit policy: $\text{DSO} \times \dfrac{\text{Sales}}{\text{per day}} \times \dfrac{\text{Variable}}{\text{cost ratio}}$

$(45)\left(\dfrac{\$1,100,000}{360}\right)(0.4) = \$55,000.$

The incremental investment in receivables is $55,000 – $33,333 = $21,667.

6. b. The incremental cost of carrying receivables would be calculated as follows:

Old credit policy: $\text{DSO} \times \dfrac{\text{Sales}}{\text{per day}} \times \dfrac{\text{Variable}}{\text{cost ratio}} \times \dfrac{\text{Cost of}}{\text{funds}}$.

$(30)\left(\dfrac{\$1,000,000}{360}\right)(0.4)(0.15) = \$5,000.$

or $\$33,333(0.15) = \$5,000.$

New credit policy:

$$(45)\left(\frac{\$1,100,000}{360}\right)(0.4)(0.15) = \$8,250.$$

or $\qquad \$55,000(0.15) = \$8,250.$

Thus, the incremental cost is $8,250 - $5,000 = $3,250.

7. a.

	Income Statement under Current Policy	Effect of Change	Income Statement under New Policy
Gross sales	$1,000,000	$ 100,000	$1,100,000
Less discounts	0	0	0
Net sales	$1,000,000	$ 100,000	$1,100,000
Production costs	400,000	40,000	440,000
Profit before credit costs and taxes	$ 600,000	$ 60,000	$ 660,000
Credit related costs:			
Cost of carrying receivables	5,000	3,250	8,250
Collection expenses			
Bad debt losses	10,000	3,000	13,000
Profit before taxes	$ 585,000	$ 53,750	$ 638,750
Taxes (40%)	234,000	21,500	255,500
Net income	$ 351,000	$ 32,250	$ 383,250

8. d. The incremental change in receivable investment would be calculated as follows:

$$\text{Old credit policy} : \text{DSO} \times \frac{\text{Sales}}{\text{per day}} \times \frac{\text{Variable}}{\text{cost ratio}}$$

$$(40)\left(\frac{\$2,000,000}{360}\right)(0.6) = \$133,333.$$

$$\text{New credit policy} : \text{DSO} \times \frac{\text{Sales}}{\text{per day}} \times \frac{\text{Variable}}{\text{cost ratio}}$$

$$(30)\left(\frac{\$1,750,000}{360}\right)(0.6) = \$87,500.$$

The incremental change in receivables is $87,500 - $133,333 = -$45,833.

9. b.

	Income Statement under Current Policy	Effect of Change	Income Statement under New Policy
Sales	$2,000,000	($250,000)	$1,750,000
Less discounts	0	0	0
Net sales	$2,000,000	($250,000)	$1,750,000
Production costs	1,200,000	(150,000)	1,050,000
Profit before credit costs and taxes	$ 800,000	($100,000)	$ 700,000
Credit related costs:			
Cost of carrying receivables	16,000	(5,500)	10,500
Collection expenses			
Bad debt losses	100,000	(65,000)	35,000
Profit before taxes	$ 684,000	($ 29,500)	$ 654,500
Taxes (40%)	273,600	(11,800)	261,800
Net income	$ 410,400	($ 17,700)	$ 392,700

10. d. $$EOQ = \sqrt{\frac{2(F)(S)}{(C)(P)}} = \sqrt{\frac{2(\$25)(16,200)}{0.20(\$5)}} = \sqrt{\frac{\$810,000}{\$1.00}} = 900 \text{ bags}.$$

11. c. $$\frac{16,200 \text{ bags per year}}{900 \text{ bags per order}} = 18 \text{ orders per year}.$$

12. b. Daily rate of use = 16,200/360 = 45 bags.

Order point = 300 + 5(45) = 525 bags.

Thus, South Florida Lawn Supply Company will have 1,200 bags on hand immediately after a shipment is received, will use 45 bags per day, will reorder when the stock is down to 525 bags (which is 5 days' requirement, plus the safety stock), and will be down to 300 bags just before a shipment arrives.

13. a. Average inventory level = EOQ/2 + Safety stock = 900/2 + 300 = 750 bags.

Note that the inventory fluctuates between 1,200 and 300 bags.

14. d. $EOQ = \sqrt{\dfrac{2(F)(S)}{(C)(P)}} = \sqrt{\dfrac{2(\$600)(120,000)}{0.20(\$500)}} = \sqrt{\dfrac{\$144,000,000}{\$100}} = 1,200 \text{ units}.$

15. e. Maximum inventory = EOQ + Safety stock = 1,200 + 500 = 1,700 units.

16. c. Average inventory = EOQ/2 + Safety stock = 600 + 500 = 1,100 units.

17. b. $\dfrac{120,000 \text{ units per year}}{1,200 \text{ units per order}} = 100 \text{ orders per year}.$

$\dfrac{360 \text{ days per year}}{100 \text{ orders per year}} = 3.60 \text{ days}.$

The firm must place one order every 3.60 days.

18. b. $TIC = (C)(P)(Q/2) + \dfrac{(F)(S)}{Q}$

$= 0.2(\$500)(1,200/2) + \dfrac{\$600(120,000)}{1,200}$

$= \$60,000 + \$60,000 = \$120,000.$

Note that total carrying costs equal total ordering costs at the EOQ.

19. d. Now, the average inventory is EOQ/2 + Safety stock = 1,100 units rather than EOQ/2 = 600 units.

$TIC = 0.2(\$500)(1,100) + \dfrac{\$600(120,000)}{1,200} = \$110,000 + \$60,000 = \$170,000.$

Another way of looking at this is:
TIC = Cost of working inventory + Cost of safety stock
$= \$120,000 + 500(\$500)(0.2) = \$120,000 + \$50,000 = \$170,000.$

20.   a.   Cost of carrying accounts receivable at present:

DSO = Receivables/(Sales/360) = \$3,000/(\$20,000/360) = 54 days.

$$\begin{matrix} \text{Cost of carrying receivables} \\ \text{under current policy} \end{matrix} = \text{DSO(Sales/360)(V)(k)}$$

$$= 54(\$55.556)(0.6)(0.12) = \$216.$$

Cost of carrying accounts receivable if credit policy is changed:

DSO = \$5,000/(\$24,000/360) = \$5,000/\$66.667 = 75 days.

Credit cost of new policy = 75(\$66.667)(0.6)(0.12) = \$360.

Change in cost of carrying accounts receivable = \$360 – \$216 = \$144.

21.   e.   Cost of carrying accounts receivable (in millions) at present:

DSO = Receivables/(Sales/360) = \$50/(\$500/360) = \$50/\$1.389 = 36 days.

$$\begin{matrix} \text{Credit cost (in millions)} \\ \text{at present} \end{matrix} = \text{DSO(Sales/360)(V)(k)} = 36(\$1.389)(0.8)(0.1) = \$4.00.$$

Cost of carrying receivables (in millions) if credit policy is changed:

DSO = \$25/(\$475/360) = \$25/\$1.319 = 18.95 days.

Credit cost (in millions) of new policy = 18.95(\$1.319)(0.8)(0.1) = \$2.00.

Change in cost of carrying accounts receivable = \$2.00 – \$4.00 = -\$2.00.

Here are the partial income statements (in millions):

	Current Policy	Change	New Policy
Sales	\$500	(\$25)	\$475
Variable costs (80%)	400	(20)	380
Fixed costs	NA	NA	NA
Pretax profit before credit costs	\$100	(\$ 5)	\$ 95
Credit costs	4	(2)	2
Pretax profit after credit costs	\$ 96	(\$ 3)	\$ 93

Change (in millions) in pre-tax profits: -\$3.00.

CHAPTER 19
DERIVATIVES AND RISK MANAGEMENT

OVERVIEW

Risk management can mean many things, but in business it involves identifying events that could have adverse financial consequences and then taking actions to prevent and/or minimize the damage caused by these events. Years ago, corporate risk managers dealt primarily with insurance—they made sure the firm was adequately insured against fire, theft, and other casualties and that it had adequate liability coverage. More recently, however, the scope of risk management has been broadened to include such things as controlling the costs of key inputs or protecting against changes in interest rates or exchange rates. In addition, risk managers try to insure that actions designed to hedge against risks are not actually increasing risks.

Since perhaps the most important aspect of risk management involves derivative securities, we begin the chapter with a discussion of derivatives. Derivatives are securities whose values are determined, in whole or in part, by the market price (or interest rate) of some other asset. Derivatives include options, whose values depend on the price of some underlying asset; interest rate and exchange rate futures and swaps, whose values depend on interest rate and exchange rate levels; and commodity futures, whose values depend on commodity prices.

OUTLINE

Investors dislike risk. Most investors hold well-diversified portfolios, so at least in theory the only "relevant risk" is systematic risk.

■ You might expect a corporate executive to say that beta is the type of risk they were concerned about. However, the executive would probably define risk as: "The possibility that our future earnings and free cash flows will be significantly lower than we expect."

■ The long-run value of a stock depends on the present value of its expected future free cash flows, discounted at the weighted average cost of capital (WACC).
   □ WACC will change only if a particular action causes a change in the cost of debt or equity, or the target capital structure.

■ If investors use *"homemade" hedging*, then the stock of a company that hedges its own operations should be the same as it would be if the company did not hedge its operations.

■ A 1995 survey reported that 59 percent of firms with market values greater than $250 million engage in *risk management*, and that percentage is surely much higher today. Although there is no proof that risk management adds value, there are several good reasons for companies to manage risk.

  ☐ *Debt capacity.* Risk management can reduce the volatility of cash flows, and this decreases the probability of bankruptcy.

  ☐ *Maintaining the optimal capital budget over time.* Smoothing out the cash flows can alleviate the problem of not meeting capital needs in the most efficient manner.

  ☐ *Financial distress.* Risk management can reduce the likelihood of low cash flows, hence of financial distress.

  ☐ *Comparative advantages in hedging.* Firms generally have lower transactions cost due to a larger volume of hedging activities. Also, managers know more about the firm's risk exposure than outside investors, hence managers can create more effective hedges. Effective risk management requires specialized skills and knowledge that firms are more likely to have.

  ☐ *Borrowing costs.* Firms can sometimes reduce input costs, especially the interest rate on debt, through the use of derivative instruments called "swaps". Any such reduction adds value to the firm.

  ☐ *Tax effects.* Companies with volatile earnings pay more taxes than more stable companies due to the treatment of tax credits and the rules governing corporate loss carry-forwards and carry-backs.

  ☐ *Compensation systems.* Many compensation systems establish "floors" and "ceilings" on bonuses or else reward managers for meeting targets. So, even if hedging does not add much value for stockholders, it may still be beneficial to managers.

Derivatives are securities whose values are determined by the market price of some other asset. Derivatives include options, whose values depend on the price of some underlying asset; interest rate and exchange rate futures and swaps, whose values depend on interest rate and exchange rate levels; and commodity futures, whose values depend on commodity prices.

■ *Hedging* with futures lowered aggregate risk in the economy.

  ☐ The earliest futures dealings were between two parties who arranged transactions between themselves. Soon, though, middlemen came into the picture, and trading in futures was established.

  ☐ The Chicago Board of Trade was an early market place for this dealing, and *futures dealers* helped make a market in futures contracts. This improved the efficiency and lowered the cost of hedging operations.

☐ *Speculators* then entered the scene. Speculators add capital and players to the derivatives market, and this tends to stabilize the market. Risk to the speculators themselves is high, but their bearing that risk makes the derivatives markets more stable for the hedgers.

■ *Natural hedges* are situations where aggregate risk can be reduced by derivatives transactions between two parties (called *counterparties*). These exist for many commodities, for foreign currencies, for interest rates on securities with different maturities, and even for common stocks where portfolio managers want to "hedge their bets."

☐ Hedging can also be done in situations where no natural hedge exists. Here one party wants to reduce some type of risk, and another party agrees to sell a contract which protects the first party from a specific event or situation.

☐ With nonsymmetric hedges, risks are generally transferred rather than eliminated.

■ The derivatives markets have grown more rapidly than any other major market in recent years for a number of reasons.

☐ Analytical techniques have been developed to help establish "fair" prices, and having a better basis for pricing hedges makes the counterparties more comfortable with deals.

☐ Computers and electronic communications make it much easier for counterparties to deal with one another.

☐ Globalization has greatly increased the importance of currency markets and the need for reducing the exchange rate risks brought on by global trade.

■ Derivatives do have a potential downside. These instruments are highly leveraged, so small miscalculations can lead to huge losses. Also, they are complicated, hence not very well understood by most people. This makes mistakes more likely than with less complex instruments and, importantly, it makes it harder for a firm's top management to understand and exercise proper control over derivatives transactions.

An option is a contract which gives its holder the right to buy (or sell) an asset at some predetermined price within a specified period of time. Financial managers should understand option theory both for risk management and also because such an understanding will help them structure warrant and convertible financings.

■ The *strike*, or *exercise*, *price* is the price that must be paid for a share of common stock when an option is exercised.

■ A *call option* gives you the right to purchase a stock at a specified price within some future period.

■ The seller of an option is called the *option writer*.

■ An investor who "writes" call options against stock held in his or her portfolio is said to be selling *covered options*. Options sold without the stock to back them up are called *naked options*.

■ When the exercise price exceeds the current stock price, a call option is said to be *out-of-the-money*. When the exercise price is below the current price of the stock, a call option is *in-the-money*.

■ An option which gives you the right to sell a stock at a specified price within some future period is called a *put option*.

■ In addition to options on individual stocks, options are also available on several stock indexes. Index options permit one to hedge (or bet) on a rise or fall in the general market as well as on individual stocks.

■ Options can be used to create *hedges* which protect the value of an individual stock or portfolio.

■ Conventional options are generally written for 6 months or less, but a new type of option called a *Long-Term Equity Anticipation Security* (LEAPS) has been trading in recent years.
   □ Like conventional options, LEAPS are listed on exchanges and are tied both to individual stocks and to stock indexes.
   □ LEAPS are long-term options having maturities of up to 2 1/2 years.

■ Corporations on whose stocks options are written have nothing to do with the option market. Corporations do not raise money in the option market, nor do they have any direct transactions in it.

■ There are at least three factors which affect a call option's value.
   □ For a given strike price, the higher the stock's market price in relation to the strike price, the higher will be the call option price.
   □ For a given stock price, the higher the strike price, the lower the call option price.
   □ The longer the option period, the higher will be the option price. This occurs because the longer the time before expiration, the greater the chance that the stock price will climb substantially above the exercise price.

■ A call option's *exercise value* is equal to the current stock price less the strike price.

☐ The calculated exercise value of a call option could be negative, but realistically the minimum "true" value of an option is zero, because no one would exercise an out-of-the-money option.

☐ The actual market price of the option lies above the exercise value at each price of the common stock, although the premium declines as the price of the stock increases.

- Options enable individuals to gain a high degree of personal leverage when buying securities.

- The leverage effect and loss protection feature of options decline at high stock prices. This helps explain why the premium diminishes as the price of the common stock rises.

■ In addition to the stock price and the exercise price, the price of an option depends on three other factors: (1) the option's term to maturity, (2) the variability of the stock price, and (3) the risk-free rate.

☐ The longer a call option has to run, the greater its value and the larger its premium.

☐ An option on an extremely volatile stock is worth more than one on a very stable stock. If the stock price rarely moves, then there is only a small chance of a large gain. Stock underlying the call option provides no dividends or other distributions during the life of the option.

☐ The value of the option is the present value of an expected future payoff. The higher the discount rate used to find the PV, the lower the value of the call option.

The Black-Scholes Model is a widely used but complex option pricing model. Some basic principles that will help you to understand the model are listed below.

■ All option pricing models are based on the concept of a *riskless hedge*.

☐ An investor buys a stock and simultaneously sells a call option on that stock. If the stock's price goes up, the investor will earn a profit, but the holder of the option will exercise it, and that will cost the investor money. If the stock goes down, the investor will lose on his or her investment in the stock, but gain from the option (which will expire worthless if the stock price declines.)

☐ It is possible to set things up such that the investor will end up with a riskless position—regardless of what the stock does, the value of the investor's portfolio will remain constant.

☐ A riskless investment must, in equilibrium, yield the riskless rate. If it offered a higher rate of return, arbitrageurs would buy it and in the process push the rate of return down, and vice versa, if it offered less than the riskless rate.

■ Given the price of the stock, its potential volatility, the option's exercise price, the life of the option, and the risk-free rate, there is but one price for the option if it is to meet the equilibrium condition, namely, that a portfolio which consists of the stock and the call option will earn the riskless rate.

The Black-Scholes Option Pricing Model (OPM) is widely used by option traders to estimate the value of a call option. The derivation of the Black-Scholes model rests on the concept of a riskless hedge.

■   The assumptions made in the OPM are:
  □ The stock underlying the call option provides no dividends or other distributions during the life of the option.
  □ There are no transaction costs for buying or selling either the stock or the option.
  □ The short-term, risk-free interest rate is known and is constant during the life of the option.
  □ Any purchaser of a security may borrow any fraction of the purchase price at the short-term, risk-free interest rate.
  □ Short selling is permitted, and the short seller will receive immediately the full cash proceeds of today's price for a security sold short.
  □ The call option can be exercised only on its expiration date.
  □ Trading in all securities takes place continuously, and the stock price moves randomly.

■   The Black-Scholes model consists of the following three equations:

$$V = P[N(d_1)] - X e^{-k_{RF}t} [N(d_2)].$$

$$d_1 = \frac{\ln(P/X) + [k_{RF} + (\sigma^2/2)]t}{\sigma\sqrt{t}}.$$

$$d_2 = d_1 - \sigma\sqrt{t}.$$

  □ V = current value of the call option.
  □ P = current price of the underlying stock.
  □ $N(d_i)$ = probability that a deviation less than d_i will occur in a standard normal distribution. Thus, $N(d_1)$ and $N(d_2)$ represent areas under a standard normal distribution function.
  □ X = exercise, or strike, price of the option.
  □ $e \approx 2.7183$.
  □ k_{RF} = risk-free interest rate.
  □ t = time until the option expires (the option period).
  □ $\ln(P/X)$ = natural logarithm of P/X.
  □ σ^2 = variance of the rate of return on the stock.

Put and call options represent an important class of derivative securities, but there are other types of derivatives, including forward contracts, futures, swaps, structured notes, inverse floaters, and a host of other "exotic" contracts.

- ■ *Forward contracts* are agreements where one party agrees to buy a commodity at a specific price on a specific future date and the other party agrees to make the sale.
  - ☐ Goods are actually delivered under forward contracts.

- ■ A *futures contract* is similar to a forward contract, but with three key differences.
  - ☐ Futures contracts are "marked to market" on a daily basis, meaning that gains and losses are noted and money must be put up to cover losses. This greatly reduces the risk of default that exists with forward contracts.
  - ☐ With futures, physical delivery of the underlying asset is virtually never taken—the two parties simply settle up with cash for the difference between the contracted price and the actual price on the expiration date.
  - ☐ Futures contacts are generally standardized instruments that are traded on exchanges, whereas forward contracts are generally tailor-made, are negotiated between two parties, and are not traded after they have been signed.

- ■ In a *swap* two parties agree to swap something, generally obligations to make specified payment streams. Most swaps today involve either interest payments or currencies.
  - ☐ Originally, swaps were arranged between companies by money center banks, which would match up counterparties. Such matching still occurs, but today most swaps are between companies and banks, with the banks then taking steps to ensure that their own risks are hedged.

- ■ A *structured note* generally means a debt obligation which is derived from some other debt obligation.
  - ☐ Zeros formed by stripping T-bonds were one of the first types of structured notes.
  - ☐ Another important type of structured note is backed by the interest and principal payments on mortgages, *collateralized mortgage obligations*.
  - ☐ A variety of structured notes can be created, ranging from notes whose cash flows can be predicted with virtual certainty to other notes whose payment streams are highly uncertain.
  - ☐ Investment bankers can create notes called IOs, for Interest Only, which provide cash flows from the interest component of the mortgage amortization payments, and POs, for Principal Only, which are paid from the principal repayment stream.
  - ☐ Structured notes permit a partitioning of risks to give investors what they want.

- ■ A *floating rate note* has an interest rate that rises and falls with some interest rate index. With an *inverse floater*, the rate paid on the note moves counter to market rates.

☐ Thus, if interest rates in the economy rose, the interest rate paid on an inverse floater would fall, lowering its cash interest payments.

☐ At the same time, the discount rate used to value the inverse floater's cash flows would rise along with other rates.

☐ The combined effect of lower cash flows and a higher discount rate would lead to a very large decline in the value of the inverse floater. Thus, inverse floaters are exceptionally vulnerable to increases in interest rates.

Risk can be classified in many ways and different classifications are commonly used in different industries.

■ Here's one list that provides an idea of the wide variety of risks to which a firm can be exposed: pure risks, speculative risks, demand risks, input risks, financial risks, property risks, personnel risks, environmental risks, liability risks, and insurable risks.

Firms often use the following three-step approach to risk management: (1) identify the risks faced by the firm, (2) measure the potential impact of the risks identified, and (3) decide how each relevant risk should be handled.

■ There are several techniques to help minimize risk exposure:

☐ *Transfer the risk to an insurance company.* Often, it is advantageous to insure against, and hence transfer, a risk. However, insurability does not necessarily mean that a risk should be covered by insurance. Thus, it might be better for the company to *self-insure*, which means bearing the risk directly rather than paying to have another party bear the risk.

☐ *Transfer the function that produces the risk to a third party.* In some situations, risks can be reduced most easily by passing them on to some other company that is not an insurance company.

☐ *Purchase derivative contracts to reduce risk.* Firms use derivatives to hedge risk.

☐ *Reduce the probability of occurrence of an adverse event.* The expected loss arising from any risk is a function of both the probability of occurrence and the dollar loss if the adverse event occurs. In some instances, it is possible to take action to reduce the probability that an adverse event will occur.

☐ *Reduce the magnitude of the loss associated with an adverse event.*

☐ *Totally avoid the activity that gives rise to the risk.*

■ Risk management decisions, like all corporate decisions, should be based on a cost/benefit analysis for each feasible alternative. The same financial management techniques applied to other corporate decisions can also be applied to risk management decisions.

Firms are subject to numerous risks related to interest rate, stock price, and exchange rate fluctuations in the financial markets. For an investor, one of the most obvious ways to reduce financial risks is to hold a broadly diversified portfolio of stocks and debt securities. However, derivatives can also be used to reduce the risks associated with financial and commodity markets.

■　　One of the most useful tools for reducing both *security and commodity price exposure* is to *hedge* in the futures markets.

    ☐　Futures contracts are divided into two classes, *commodity futures* and *financial futures*.

       ●　Commodity futures are contracts that are used to hedge against price changes for input materials.

       ●　Financial futures are contracts that are used to hedge against fluctuating interest rates, stock prices, and exchange rates.

    ☐　When futures contracts are purchased, the purchaser does not have to put up the full amount of the purchase price; rather, the purchaser is required to post an initial *margin*. However, investors are required to maintain a certain value in the margin account, called a *maintenance margin*.

    ☐　The value of the contract is checked at the end of every working day, and margin account adjustments are made at that time. This is called "marking to market."

    ☐　An *option* is similar to a futures contract, but it merely gives someone the right to buy (call) or sell (put) an asset, but the holder of the option does not have to complete the transaction. A futures agreement, on the other hand, is a definite agreement on the part of one party to buy something on a specific date and a specific price, and the other party agrees to sell on the same terms.

■　　Firms are exposed to losses due to changes in security prices when securities are held in investment portfolios, and they are also exposed during times when securities are being issued. In addition, firms are exposed to risk when floating rate debt is used to finance an investment that produces a fixed income stream. These types of risk can be reduced by using *derivatives*. *Futures and swaps* are two types of derivatives used to manage security price exposure.

    ☐　*Futures markets* are used for both speculation and hedging: *Speculation* involves betting on future price movements; *hedging* is done by a firm or individual to protect against a price change that would otherwise negatively affect profits.

       ●　There are two basic types of hedges: (1) *long hedges*, in which futures contracts are *bought* in anticipation of (or to guard against) price increases, and (2) *short hedges*, where a firm or individual *sells* futures contracts to guard against price declines.

       ●　A *perfect hedge* occurs when the gain or loss on the hedged transaction exactly offsets the loss or gain on the unhedged position.

- The futures and options markets permit flexibility in the timing of financial transactions, because the firm can be protected, at least partially, against changes that occur between the time a decision is reached and the time when the transaction will be completed.

    □ A *swap* is another method for reducing financial risks. It is an exchange of cash payment obligations, in which each party to the swap prefers the payment type or pattern of the other party.

    □ Standardized contracts have been developed for the most common types of swaps, and this has had two effects:

    - Standardized contracts lower the time and effort involved in arranging swaps, and thus lower transactions costs.

    - The development of standardized contracts has led to a secondary market for swaps, which has increased the liquidity and efficiency of the swaps market.

■ Although the corporate use of derivatives to hedge risk is a relatively new phenomenon, it has caught on like wild fire. In fact, more than 90 percent of large U. S. companies use derivatives on a regular basis.

    □ There is, however, a downside to derivatives. Hedging is invariably cited by authorities as a "good" use of derivatives, whereas speculating with derivatives is often cited as a "bad" use.

    □ Hedging allows managers to concentrate on running their core business without having to worry about interest rate, currency, and commodity price variability. However, if derivatives are improperly constructed or used for speculative purposes, they have the potential to create very large losses in very short periods.

■ CFOs, CEOs, and board members should be reasonably knowledgeable about the derivatives their firms use, should establish policies regarding when they can and cannot be used, and should establish audit procedures to ensure that the policies are actually carried out. Moreover, a firm's derivatives position should be reported to stockholders.

The Extensions to Chapter 19 describe ways in which companies can use insurance to manage certain types of risks, such as property and liability loss exposure. In addition, some types of interest rate risk can be managed through the use of immunization.

■ The first step in a corporate insurance program is to identify all potential losses. The second step is to assess their likelihoods of occurrence and loss potentials.

■ *Loss frequency* (probability) and *loss severity* (dollar value of each loss) are used to measure a firm's degree of exposure to identified risks.

    □ Two measures of loss severity are (1) the *maximum loss approach*, and (2) the *average loss approach*.

■ Property losses are an important part of corporate risk management.
- ☐ Property is divided into two classes: (1) real property and (2) personal property.
- ☐ Property losses are classified as either direct or indirect.
- ☐ The perils associated with property losses are (1) physical perils, (2) social perils, and (3) economic perils.

■ Companies risk liability losses thorough five categories of exposure: (1) bailee exposure, (2) ownership exposure, (3) business operation exposure, (4) employee action exposure, and (5) professional exposure.

■ Bond portfolios can be *immunized* against interest rate and reinvestment rate risk.
- ☐ *Duration* is the key to immunization.

SELF-TEST QUESTIONS

Definitional

1. _____ _____ generally involves the management of unpredictable events that have adverse financial consequences for the firm.

2. There are six reasons risk management might increase the value of a firm. Risk management allows corporations (1) to increase their _____ ____ _____, (2) to maintain their capital budget over time, (3) to avoid costs associated with _____ _____, (4) to utilize their comparative advantages in hedging relative to the hedging ability of individual investors, (5) to reduce both the risks and costs of borrowing by using _____, and (6) to reduce the higher _____ that result from fluctuating earnings.

3. Firms often use a three-step approach to risk management: (1) _____ the risks faced by the firm, (2) _____ the potential impact of the risks identified, and (3) decide how each relevant risk should be handled.

4. If an investment is riskless, it must, in equilibrium yield the _____ _____.

5. To _____-_____ means bearing the risk directly rather than paying to have another party bear the risk.

6. Risk management decisions, like all corporate decisions, should be based on a(n) _____/_____ analysis for each feasible alternative.

7. All option pricing models are based on the concept of a _____ _____.

8. When the exercise price exceeds the current stock price a call option is said to be _____-_____-_____-_____; however, when the exercise price is less than the current price of the underlying stock, a call option is _____-_____-_____.

9. In addition to the stock price and the exercise price, the price of an option depends on three other factors: (1) the option's _____ ____ _____, (2) the _____ of the stock price, and (3) the risk-free rate.

10. The _____-_____ _____ _____ _____ is widely used by option traders to estimate the value of a call option.

11. _____ are generally standardized instruments that are traded on exchanges and that are "marked to market" daily, but where physical delivery of the underlying asset is virtually never taken.

12. Futures markets are used for both hedging and speculation: _____ involves betting on future price movements, while _____ is done by a firm or individual to protect against price changes that could otherwise negatively affect profits.

13. _____ are securities whose values are determined by the market price (or interest rate) of some other asset.

14. A(n) _____ is an exchange of cash payment obligations, in which each party to the transaction prefers the payment type or pattern of the other party.

15. A(n) _____ _____ often means a debt obligation which is derived from some other debt obligation, for example, collateralized mortgage obligations.

16. The two parties involved in derivatives transactions are called _____.

17. _____ _____ are situations where aggregate risk can be reduced by derivatives transactions between two parties.

18. A(n) _____ is a contract which gives its holder the right to buy (or sell) an asset at some predetermined price within a specified period of time.

19. The _____, or _____, price is the price that must be paid for a share of common stock when an option price is exercised.

20. The seller of an option is called the option _____.

21. An investor who writes call options against stock held in his or her portfolio is said to be selling _____ options.

22. Options sold without the stock to back them up are called _____ options.

23. An option which gives you the right to sell a stock at a specified price within some future period is called a(n) _____ option.

24. Conventional options are generally written for 6 months or less, but a new type of option called a(n) _____-_____ _____ _____ Security has a maturity of up to 2½ years.

25. A call option's _____ _____ is equal to the current price less the strike price.

26. _____ _____ are agreements where one party agrees to buy a commodity at a specific price on a specific future date and the other party agrees to make the sale.

27. A floating rate note has an interest rate that rises and falls with some interest rate index. With a(n) _____ _____, the rate paid on the note moves counter to market rates.

28. _____ futures are contracts that are used to hedge against price changes for input materials.

29. _____ futures are contracts that are used to hedge against fluctuating interest rates, stock prices, and exchange rates.

30. There are two basic types of hedges: (1) _____ hedges, in which futures contracts are bought in anticipation of (or to guard against) price increases, and (2) _____ hedges, where a firm or individual sells futures contracts to guard against price declines.

Conceptual

31. The two basic types of hedges involving the futures market are long hedges and short hedges, where the words "long" and "short" refer to the maturity of the hedging instrument. For example, a long hedge might use stocks, while a short hedge might use 3-month T-bills.

    a. True   b. False

32. Speculators add capital and players to the derivatives market; thus, this tends to make the market unstable.

    a. True   **b.** False

33. A perfect hedge occurs when the gain or loss on the hedge transaction exactly offsets the loss or gain on the unhedged position.

    a. True   **b.** False

34. A swap is a method for reducing financial risk. Which of the following statements about swaps, if any, is _incorrect_?

    a. A swap involves the exchange of cash payment obligations.
    b. The earliest swaps were currency swaps, in which companies traded debt denominated in different currencies, say dollars and pounds.
    c. Swaps are generally arranged by a financial intermediary, who may or may not take the position of one of the counterparties.
    d. A problem with swaps is the lack of standardized contracts, which limits the development of a secondary market.
    e. None of the statements are incorrect; all of the above statements are correct.

35. Which of the following statements regarding futures and forward contracts is most correct?

    a. Futures contracts are similar to forward contracts except for the length of time the contract is outstanding.
    b. Forward contracts are "marked to market" on a daily basis, while futures contracts are not "marked to market."
    c. With forward contracts, physical delivery of the underlying asset is virtually never taken.
    d. Forward contracts are generally standardized instruments that are traded on exchanges, whereas futures contracts are generally tailor-made, are negotiated between two parties, and are not traded after they have been signed.
    e. All of the above statements are incorrect.

36. Which of the following statements is most correct?

    a. Recently, the scope of risk management has been broadened to include things like controlling the costs of key inputs or protecting against changes in interest rates on exchange rates.

    b. Hedging with futures raises the aggregate risk in the economy.

    c. Corporations on whose stocks options are written have nothing to do with the option market.

    d. The actual market price of an option lies below the exercise value at each price of the common stock, although the premium rises as the stock price increases.

    e. Statements a and c are correct.

SELF-TEST PROBLEMS

1. A call option on the stock of Heuser Enterprises has a market price of $15. The stock sells for $38 a share, and the option has an exercise price of $30 a share. What is the exercise value of the call option?

    a. $5.00   **b.** $6.25   **c.** $7.00   **d.** $7.50   **e.** $8.00

2. Refer to Self-Test Problem 1. What is the premium on the option?

    a. $5.00   **b.** $6.25   **c.** $7.00   **d.** $7.50   **e.** $8.00

3. Assume you have been given the following information on Detweiler Industries:

Current stock price = $27.50   Option's exercise price = $27.50
Time to maturity of option = 3 months   Risk-free rate = 8%
Variance of stock price = 0.14 $d_1 = 0.20045$
$d_2 = 0.01336$ $N(d_1) = 0.57942$
$N(d_2) = 0.50533$

Using the Black-Scholes Option Pricing Model, what would be the option's value?

    a. $2.00   **b.** $2.31   **c.** $2.73   **d.** $3.18   **e.** $3.75

4. What is the implied interest rate on a Treasury bond ($100,000) futures contract that settled at 101-2?

    a. 7.89%   **b.** 7.55%   **c.** 8.25%   **d.** 8.05%   **e.** 7.73%

5. Refer to Self-Test Problem 4. If the interest rate was 8.50 percent, what would be the contract's new value?

    a. $101,062.50   **b.** $100,235.33   **c.** $97,875.42   **d.** $95,230.68   **e.** $99.189.44

ANSWERS TO SELF-TEST QUESTIONS

1. Risk management
2. use of debt; financial distress; swaps, taxes
3. identify; measure
4. riskless rate
5. self-insure
6. cost/benefit
7. riskless hedge
8. out-of-the-money; in-the-money
9. term to maturity; variability
10. Black-Scholes Option Pricing Model
11. Futures
12. speculation; hedging
13. Derivatives
14. swap
15. structured note
16. counterparties
17. Natural hedges
18. option
19. strike; exercise
20. writer
21. covered
22. naked
23. put
24. Long-Term Equity Anticipation
25. exercise value
26. Forward contracts
27. inverse floater
28. Commodity
29. Financial
30. long; short

31. b. Long hedges are futures contracts bought to guard against price increases, while short hedges are futures contracts sold to guard against price declines.

32. b. These very things tend to stabilize the market.

33. a. This statement is correct.

34. d. This is not a problem with swaps.

35. e. Futures contracts are similar to forward contracts except for three key differences. (1) Futures contracts are "marked to market." (2) With futures contracts, physical delivery of the underlying asset is virtually never taken. (3) Futures contracts are standardized instruments that are traded on the exchange.

36. e. Statement b is false because hedging lowers the aggregate risk in the economy. Statement d is false because an option's market value lies above its exercise value at each price of the common stock, although the premium declines as the stock price increases. Since statement a and c are correct, the proper choice is statement e.

SOLUTIONS TO SELF-TEST PROBLEMS

1. e. Exercise value $=$ Current stock price $-$ Strike price
$\qquad\qquad\qquad\quad = \$38 - \$30$
$\qquad\qquad\qquad\quad = \$8.$

2. c. Premium $=$ Option's market price $-$ Exercise value
$\qquad\qquad\qquad = \$15 - \$8$
$\qquad\qquad\qquad = \$7.$

3. b. $V = P[N(d_1)] - Xe^{-k_{RF}t}[N(d_2)]$
$\qquad = \$27.50(0.57942) - \$27.50e^{-0.02}[0.50533]$
$\qquad = \$15.93 - \$13.62$
$\qquad = \$2.31.$

4. a. Futures contract settled at 101 2/32% of $100,000 contract value, so PV = 1.010625 × $1,000 = 1,010.625 × 100 bonds = $101,062.50. Using a financial calculator, we can solve for k_d as follows:

N = 40; PV = -1010.625; PMT = 40; FV = 1000; solve for I = k_d = 3.9467% × 2 = 7.8935% ≈ 7.89%.

5. d. If the interest rate was 8.50%, then we would solve for PV as follows:

N = 40; I = 8.50/2 = 4.25; PMT = 40; FV = 1000; solve for PV = $952.3068 × 100 = $95,230.68.

OVERVIEW

The financial manager of a failing firm must know how to ward off his or her firm's total collapse and thereby reduce its losses. The ability to hang on during rough times often means the difference between the firm's forced liquidation versus its rehabilitation and eventual success. At the same time, an understanding of business failures and bankruptcies, their causes, and their possible remedies is also critical to the managers of healthy firms, because they must know the best way to handle things when their customers or suppliers face the threat of bankruptcy.

OUTLINE

A number of factors combine to cause business failures. Case studies show that financial difficulties are usually the result of a series of errors, misjudgments, and interrelated weaknesses that can be attributed directly or indirectly to management. Signs of potential financial distress are generally evident in a ratio analysis long before the firm actually fails. Researchers use ratio analysis to predict the probability that a given firm will go bankrupt.

■ Although bankruptcies are more common among smaller firms, it is clear that large firms are not immune. It is interesting to note that whereas the failure rate per 10,000 businesses fluctuates with the state of the economy, the average liability per failure has tended to increase over time. This is due primarily to inflation, but it also reflects the fact that some very large firms have failed in recent years.

■ Government and industry seek to avoid failure among larger firms. In the case of banks, the main reason is to prevent an erosion of confidence and a consequent run on the banks. The fact that bankruptcy is a very expensive process gives private industry strong incentives to avoid outright bankruptcy.

Financial distress begins when a firm is unable to meet scheduled payments or when cash flow projections indicate that it will soon be unable to do so.

■ Several questions arise as to how a firm should proceed:
- ☐ Is the situation a temporary cash flow problem or a permanent problem?
- ☐ If temporary, can an agreement with creditors be worked out? If permanent, who should bear the losses, and who should get whatever value remains?
- ☐ Is the company "worth more dead than alive"?
- ☐ Should the firm file for bankruptcy or use informal procedures?
- ☐ Who should control the firm while it is being liquidated or rehabilitated?

Because of costs associated with formal bankruptcy, including the disruptions that occur when a firm's customers, suppliers, and employees learn that it has filed under the Bankruptcy Act, it is desirable to reorganize (or liquidate) a firm outside formal bankruptcy through use of informal settlement procedures.

■ *Informal reorganization* can be used in the case of an economically sound company in temporary distress. Voluntary plans, commonly called *workouts,* usually require some type of *restructuring* of the firm's debt, because current cash flows are insufficient to service the existing debt.
- ☐ A debt restructuring begins with a meeting between the failing firm's managers and creditors. An *adjustment bureau* run by the local creditor managers' association often arranges the meeting. A great deal of negotiation is involved to reach a final debt restructuring agreement.
  - Management draws up a list of creditors with the amounts of debt owed.
  - The company develops information showing the value of the firm under different scenarios.
  - The information is then shared with the firm's bankers and other creditors. This information, when presented in a credible manner, will often convince creditors that they would be better off accepting something less than the full amount of their claims rather than holding out for the full face amount.
- ☐ Creditors often prefer an *extension* because it promises eventual payment in full. In an extension, creditors postpone the dates of required interest or principal payments, or both.
- ☐ In a *composition*, creditors voluntarily reduce their fixed claims on the debtor by accepting a lower principal amount, by reducing the interest rate on the debt, by taking equity for debt, or by some combination of these changes.
- ☐ Such voluntary settlements are not only informal and simple, but also relatively inexpensive because legal and administrative expenses are held to a minimum. Creditors generally recover more money, and sooner, than if the firm were to file for bankruptcy.
- ☐ The biggest problem with informal reorganizations is getting all the parties to agree to the voluntary plan. This problem is called the *holdout problem.*

■ *Informal liquidation* is the result of determining that a firm is more valuable dead than alive. *Assignment* is an informal procedure for liquidating a firm, and it usually yields creditors a larger amount than they would receive in a formal bankruptcy liquidation. In an assignment, the title to the debtor's assets is transferred to a third party, known as an *assignee* or *trustee*. The assignee is instructed to liquidate the assets through a private sale or public auction and then to distribute the proceeds among the creditors on a pro rata basis. Assignments are feasible only if the firm is small and its affairs are not too complex.

☐ Assignment does not automatically discharge the debtor's obligations, nor does it protect the creditors against fraud.

☐ Assignment has some advantages over liquidation in federal bankruptcy courts in terms of time, legal formality, and expense.

A firm is officially bankrupt when it files for bankruptcy with a federal court. Formal bankruptcy proceedings are designed to protect both the firm and its creditors. Chapter 11 of the 1978 Bankruptcy Reform Act deals with business reorganization.

■ If the problem is temporary insolvency, then the firm may use bankruptcy proceedings to gain time to solve its cash flow problems without asset seizure by its creditors.

■ If the firm is truly bankrupt in the sense that liabilities exceed assets, the creditors can use bankruptcy procedures to stop the firm's managers from continuing to operate, lose more money, and thus deplete assets which should go to creditors.

■ Bankruptcy law is flexible in that it provides scope for negotiations between a company, its creditors, and its stockholders.

☐ A bankruptcy petition may be either *voluntary* or involuntary; that is, it may be filed either by the firm's management or by its creditors.

Two problems often arise to stymie informal reorganizations and thus force debtors into formal Chapter 11 bankruptcy.

■ The *common pool problem* is that, in the absence of protection under the Bankruptcy Act, individual creditors have an incentive to foreclose on the firm even though it is worth more collectively as an ongoing concern. A solution to the common pool problem is the Chapter 11 *automatic stay provision*, which is forced on all creditors in a bankruptcy and limits the ability of creditors to foreclose to collect their individual claims.

■ *Fraudulent conveyance* statutes, which are part of debtor-creditor law, protect creditors from unjustified transfers of property by a firm in financial distress.

■ The *holdout problem* can also make it difficult to reorganize a firm's debts. If all creditors agreed to a reorganization plan, it would benefit the creditors and the firm simultaneously. However, there is an advantage for a creditor to "hold out" since his or her claim would be higher than that of those who would agree to a lower settlement. Thus, it is likely that none of the creditors would accept the offer. Because of this problem, it is easier for a firm with few creditors to informally reorganize than it is for a firm with many creditors.

☐ The holdout problem is mitigated in bankruptcy proceedings by the bankruptcy court's ability to lump creditors into classes.

In bankruptcy, it is much easier to gain acceptance of a reorganization plan, because the bankruptcy court will lump the creditors into classes.

Each class is considered to have accepted a reorganization plan if two-thirds of the amount of debt and one-half the number of claimants vote for the plan, and it is deemed "fair and equitable" to dissenting parties.

A *cramdown* is a procedure in which the court mandates a reorganization plan in spite of dissent.

Filing for bankruptcy under Chapter 11 has several other features which help the bankrupt firm.

Interest and principal payments may be delayed without penalty until a reorganization plan is approved.

The firm is permitted to issue *debtor in possession (DIP) financing* which enhances the ability of the firm to borrow funds for short-term liquidity purposes, because such loans are, under the law, senior to all previous unsecured debt.

The debtor firm's managers are given the exclusive right for 120 days after filing to submit a reorganization plan, plus another 60 days to obtain agreement on the plan from the parties affected.

Under the early bankruptcy laws, most formal reorganization plans were guided by the *absolute priority doctrine*. This doctrine holds that creditors should be compensated for their claims in a rigid hierarchical order, and that senior claims must be paid in full before junior claims can receive even a dime.

An alternative position, the *relative priority doctrine*, holds that more flexibility should be allowed in a reorganization, and that balanced consideration should be given to all claimants. Current law represents a movement away from absolute priority and toward relative priority.

The primary role of the bankruptcy court in a reorganization is to determine the fairness and the feasibility of proposed plans of reorganization.

The *fairness* doctrine states that claims must be recognized in the order of their legal and contractual priority.

Feasibility means that there is a reasonable chance that the reorganized company will be viable.
□ The primary test of feasibility in a reorganization is whether the fixed charges after reorganization will be adequately covered by earnings.

Recently a new type of reorganization called *prepackaged bankruptcy* combines the advantages of both the informal workout and formal Chapter 11 reorganization.
□ Here the debtor firm gets all, or most of, the creditors to agree to the reorganization plan prior to filing for bankruptcy. Then, a reorganization plan is filed along with the bankruptcy petition. If enough creditors have signed on before the filing, a cramdown can be used to bring reluctant creditors along.
□ The three primary advantages of a prepackaged bankruptcy are (1) reduction of the holdout problem, (2) preserving creditors' claims, and (3) taxes.

If a company is "too far gone" to be reorganized, then it must be liquidated.

Liquidation should occur when the business is worth more dead than alive, or when the possibility of restoring it to financial health is remote and the creditors are exposed to a high risk of greater loss if operations are continued.

Chapter 7 of the Federal Bankruptcy Reform Act addresses three important problems during a *liquidation in bankruptcy:*
□ It provides safeguards against fraud by the debtor.
□ It provides for an equitable distribution of the debtor's assets among the creditors.
□ It allows insolvent debtors to discharge all their obligations and thus be able to start new businesses unhampered by the burden of prior debt.

Formal liquidation is time consuming and costly, and it extinguishes the business.

The distribution of assets in a liquidation under Chapter 7 is governed by the following priority of claims: (1) Past due property taxes, (2) secured creditors, (3) trustee's costs, (4) expenses incurred after an involuntary case has begun but before a trustee is appointed, (5) wages due workers if earned within 3 months prior to filing the bankruptcy petition, (6) claims for unpaid contributions to employee pension plans, (7) unsecured claims for customer deposits, (8) taxes due, (9) unfunded pension plan liabilities, (10) general (unsecured) creditors, (11) preferred stockholders, and (12) common stockholders.

Normally, bankruptcy proceedings originate after a company cannot meet its current obligations. However, bankruptcy law also permits a company to file for bankruptcy if its financial forecasts indicate that a continuation of current conditions would lead to insolvency.

■　　Bankruptcy law has also been used to hasten settlements in major product liability suits.

Many critics today claim that current bankruptcy laws are not doing what they were intended to do.

■　　Before 1978, most bankruptcies ended quickly in liquidation. Then Congress rewrote the laws, giving companies more opportunity to stay alive, believing that this was best for managers, employees, creditors, and stockholders.

■　　Critics believe that bankruptcy is good business for consultants, lawyers, and investment bankers, who reap hefty fees during bankruptcy proceedings, and for managers, who continue to collect their salaries and bonuses as long as the business is kept alive.

■　　Bankruptcy cases can drag on in court for many years, depleting assets that could be sold to pay off creditors and shareholders. In effect, critics say, maintaining companies on life support does not serve the interests of the parties that bankruptcy laws were meant to protect.

■　　Other critics think the entire bankruptcy system of judicial protection and supervision needs to be scrapped. Some have proposed a kind of auction procedure, where shareholders and creditors would have the opportunity to gain control of a bankrupt company by raising the cash needed to pay the bills.

The Extensions to Chapter 20 discuss recent business failures and how Multiple Discriminant Analysis can be used to predict bankruptcy.

■　　*Multiple Discriminant Analysis (MDA)* is a statistical tool which can predict the possibility of bankruptcy, thus allowing firms to take steps to avoid bankruptcy or at least reduce its impact. MDA uses a set of economic variables, such as the current ratio and debt ratio, to establish the possibility of failure.

■   In a classic paper, Edward Altman applied MDA to a sample of corporations, and he developed the following discriminant function:

$$Z = 0.012X_1 + 0.014X_2 + 0.033X_3 + 0.006X_4 + 0.999X_5.$$

☐   Here, X_1 = net working capital divided by total assets; X_2 = retained earnings divided by total assets; X_3 = EBIT divided by total assets; X_4 = market value of common and preferred stock divided by book value of debt; and X_5 = sales divided by total assets.

☐   Altman's *zone of ignorance* was from $Z = 1.81$ to $Z = 2.99$; and the higher the Z score, the lower the probability of bankruptcy.

SELF-TEST QUESTIONS

Definitional

1.   _____ _____ can be used in the case of an economically sound company in temporary distress. Voluntary plans, called _____, usually require some type of restructuring of the firm's debt.

2.   Creditors often prefer a(n) _____ because it promises eventual payment in full.

3.   In a(n) _____, creditors agree to reduce their fixed claims on the debtor.

4.   _____ is an informal procedure for liquidating a firm, and it usually yields creditors a larger amount than they would receive in a formal bankruptcy liquidation.

5.   Two problems often arise to stymie informal reorganizations and thus force debtors into formal Chapter 11 bankruptcy: the _____ _____ _____ and the _____ _____.

6.   A(n) _____ is a procedure in which the court mandates a reorganization plan in spite of dissent.

7.   _____-____-_____ financing enhances the ability of the firm to borrow funds for short-term liquidity purposes, because such loans are, under law, senior to all other unsecured debt.

8.   The _____ doctrine states that claims must be recognized in the order of their legal and contractual priority, while the primary test of _____ in a reorganization is whether the fixed charges after reorganization will be adequately covered by earnings.

9. _____ _____ _____ is a statistical tool which can predict the possibility of bankruptcy, thus allowing firms to take steps to avoid bankruptcy or at least reduce its impact.

Conceptual

10. Financial distress begins when a firm is unable to meet scheduled payments to creditors, not when the firm's cash flow projections indicate that it will soon be unable to do so.

    a. True   **b.** False

11. Bankruptcies are more common among larger firms than smaller firms.

    a. True   **b.** False

12. Informal reorganization can be used in the case of an economically sound company in temporary distress. One type of voluntary plan is called a workout.

    a. True   **b.** False

13. Which of the following statements is most correct?

    a. In an extension, creditors voluntarily reduce their fixed claims on the debtor by accepting a lower principal amount, by reducing the interest rate on the debt, by taking equity for debt, or by some combination of these changes.
    b. Technical insolvency occurs when a firm's book value of total liabilities exceeds the true market value of its assets.
    c. Although many people use the term bankruptcy to refer to any firm that has "failed," a firm is not legally bankrupt unless it has filed for bankruptcy under federal law.
    d. Both statements a and c are true.
    e. All of the statements are false.

14. Which of the following statements is most correct?

    a. The automatic stay provision provided for in Chapter 11 is only granted to certain debtors in bankruptcy. It limits the ability of creditors to foreclose unilaterally on the debtor to collect their individual claims and, as a result, it provides a solution to the holdout problem.

    b. Fraudulent conveyance statutes, which are a part of debtor-creditor law, protect creditors from unjustified transfers of property by a firm in financial distress.

    c. In a cramdown, creditors postpone the dates of required interest or principal payments, or both.

    d. The common pool problem occurs because individual creditors have an incentive to foreclose on the firm even though the firm is worth more collectively as an ongoing concern.

    e. Both statements b and d are true.

15. Which of the following statements is most correct?

    a. Chapter 11 of the Federal Bankruptcy Reform Act addresses liquidation, while Chapter 7 deals with business reorganization.

    b. Preferred stockholders have priority over general, or unsecured, creditors in the distribution of claims in a liquidation.

    c. In Multiple Discriminant Analysis the higher the Z-score, the higher the probability of bankruptcy.

    d. Multiple Discriminant Analysis is a statistical tool which can predict the possibility of bankruptcy, thus allowing firms to take steps to avoid bankruptcy or at least reduce its impact.

    e. All of the above statements are true.

SELF-TEST PROBLEMS

1. The Stanton Marble Company has the following balance sheet:

Current assets	$15,120	Accounts payable	$ 3,240
		Notes payable (to bank)	1,620
		Accrued taxes	540
		Accrued wages	540
		Total current liabilities	$ 5,940
Net fixed assets	8,100	First mortgage bonds	2,700
		Second mortgage bonds	2,700
		Total mortgage bonds	$ 5,400
		Subordinated debentures	3,240
		Total long-term debt	$ 8,640
		Preferred stock	1,080
		Common stock	7,560
Total assets	$23,220	Total liabilities and equity	$23,220

The debentures are subordinated only to the notes payable. Suppose Stanton Marble goes bankrupt and is liquidated with $5,400 being received from the sale of the fixed assets, which were pledged as security for the first and second mortgage bonds, and $8,640 received from the sale of current assets. The trustee's costs total $1,440. How much will the holders of subordinated debentures receive?

a. $2,052   **b.** $2,448   **c.** $3,240   **d.** $2,709   **e.** $3,056

(The following data apply to the next three Self-Test Problems.)

The Lockwood Corporation's balance sheet and income statement are as follows (in millions of dollars). Lockwood and its creditors have agreed upon a voluntary reorganization plan. In this plan, each share of the $6 preferred will be exchanged for one share of $2.40 preferred with a par value of $37.50 plus one 8 percent subordinated income debenture with a par value of $75. The $10.50 preferred issue will be retired with cash.

Balance Sheet:

Current assets	$336	Current liabilities	$ 84
Net fixed assets	306	Advance payments	156
Goodwill	30	Reserves	12
		$6 preferred stock, $112.50 par value (2,400,000 shares)	270
		$10.50 preferred stock, no par, callable at $150 (120,000 shares)	18
		Common stock, $1.50 par value (12,000,000 shares)	18
		Retained earnings	114
Total assets	$672	Total claims	$672

Income Statement:

Net sales	$1,080.0
Operating expense	1,032.0
Net operating income	$ 48.0
Other income	6.0
EBT	$ 54.0
Taxes (50%)	27.0
Net income	$ 27.0
Dividends on $6 preferred	14.4
Dividends on $10.50 preferred	1.3
Income available to common stockholders	$ 11.3

2. What is the value (in millions of dollars) of total assets on the balance sheet?

   a. $680 **b.** $620 **c.** $636 **d.** $654 **e.** $645

3. What is the value (in millions of dollars) of the new preferred stock?

   a. $105 **b.** $90 **c.** $110 **d.** $80 **e.** $95

4. What is the net income available to common stockholders (in millions of dollars) after the proposed recapitalization takes place?

   a. $17 **b.** $11 **c.** $14 **d.** $13 **e.** $16

(The following data apply to the next six Self-Test Problems.)

At the time it defaulted on its interest payments and filed for bankruptcy, the Southeastern Manufacturing Company (SMC) had the following balance sheet (in thousands of dollars). The court, after trying unsuccessfully to reorganize the firm, decided that the only recourse was liquidation under Chapter 7. Sale of the fixed assets, which were pledged as collateral to the mortgage bondholders, brought in $1,600,000, while the current assets were sold for another $800,000. Thus, the total proceeds from the liquidation sale were $2,400,000. Trustee's costs amounted to $200,000; no single worker was due more than $2,000 in wages; and there were no unfunded pension plan liabilities.

Current assets	$1,600	Accounts payable	$ 200
		Accrued taxes	160
		Accrued wages	120
		Notes payable	720
		Total current liabilities	$1,200
Net fixed assets	2,400	First mortgage bonds[a]	1,200
		Second mortgage bonds[a]	800
		Debentures	800
		Subordinated debentures[b]	400
		Common stock	200
		Retained earnings	(600)
Total assets	$4,000	Total claims	$4,000

Notes:

[a]All fixed assets are pledged as collateral to the mortgage bonds.
[b]Subordinated to notes payable.

5. How much of the proceeds (in thousands of dollars) from the sale of assets remain to be distributed to general creditors after distribution to priority claimants?

   a. $432   b. $500   c. $375   d. $300   e. $320

6. How much of the proceeds (in thousands of dollars) do the second mortgage holders receive after distribution to general creditors and subordination adjustments are made?

   a. $400   b. $451   c. $51   d. $375   e. $500

7. How much of the proceeds (in thousands of dollars) do the holders of the subordinated debentures receive after distribution to general creditors and subordination adjustments are made?

   a. $51   **b.** $102   **c.** $142   **d.** $0   **e.** $25

8. How much of the proceeds (in thousands of dollars) from the liquidation do the common stockholders receive?

   a. $0   **b.** $51   **c.** $25   **d.** $102   **e.** $142

9. SMC's EBIT was $320,000 based on sales of $4,800,000, and its common stock market value was $800,000. What Z-score is obtained when using Altman's multiple discriminant function, $Z = 0.012X_1 + 0.014X_2 + 0.033X_3 + 0.006X_4 + 0.999X_5$.

   a. 1.22   **b.** 1.72   **c.** 1.48   **d.** 1.33   **e.** 1.66

10. Assume that you used Altman's multiple discriminant function in Self-Test Problem 9 and calculated a Z-score of 1.48. What does this score mean?

    a. The Z-score falls in the zone of ignorance, which means that we are uncertain about how the firm should be classified.
    b. Because the Z-score falls below 1.81, there is a likelihood that the firm will not go bankrupt: the lower the Z-score, the lower the probability of bankruptcy.
    c. Because the Z-score falls below 1.81, there is a likelihood that the firm will go bankrupt: the higher the Z-score, the lower the probability of bankruptcy.
    d. All the statements are false.

ANSWERS TO SELF-TEST QUESTIONS

1. Informal reorganization; workouts
2. extension
3. composition
4. Assignment
5. common pool problem; holdout problem

6. cramdown
7. Debtor-in-possession
8. fairness; feasibility
9. Multiple Discriminant Analysis (MDA)

10. b. Financial distress also begins when the firm's cash flow projections indicate that it will soon be unable to meet scheduled payments to creditors.

11. b. Just the reverse is true; however, large firms are not immune to bankruptcy.

12. a. This statement is correct.

13. c. Statement a is false; it describes a composition, not an extension. Statement b is false; a firm is considered technically insolvent if it cannot meet its current obligations as they fall due. Statement c is true. Thus, statements d and e are both incorrect.

14. e. Statement a is false; automatic stay is granted to all debtors in bankruptcy and it is a solution for the common pool problem. Statement b is true. Statement c describes an extension, not a cramdown. Statement d is true; thus, statement e is correct.

15. d. Statement a is false; the chapters have been reversed. Statement b is false; general, or unsecured, creditors have priority over preferred stockholders in the distribution of claims. Statement c is false; the higher the Z score, the lower the probability of bankruptcy. Statement d is true. Thus, statement e is false.

SOLUTIONS TO SELF-TEST PROBLEMS

1. a.

Claimant	Claim Amount (1)	Priority Distribution and General Creditor (2)	Subordinate Adjustment (3)	Percent of Claim (4)
Accounts payable	$ 3,240	$ 2,448	$ 2,448	75.56%
Notes payable	1,620	1,224	1,620	100.00
Accrued taxes	540	540	540	100.00
Accrued wages	540	540	540	100.00
1st mortgage bonds	2,700	2,700	2,700	100.00
2nd mortgage bonds	2,700	2,700	2,700	100.00
Subord. debentures	3,240	2,448	2,052	63.33
Preferred stock	1,080	0	0	0.00
Common stock	7,560	0	0	0.00
Trustee	1,440	1,440	1,440	100.00
Total	$ 24,660	$ 14,040	$ 14,040	56.93%

Explanation of the columns:
(1) Values are taken from the balance sheet.
(2) Since the firm's total debt obligations (including trustee costs) equals $16,020 and only $14,040 is received from the sale of assets, the preferred and common stockholders are wiped out. These stockholders receive nothing.

The $5,400 from the sale of fixed assets is immediately allocated to the mortgage bonds. The holders of the first mortgage bonds are paid off first, so they receive $2,700. The remaining $2,700 from the sale of fixed assets is allocated to the second mortgage bonds, so these bondholders are also paid off.

By law, trustee expenses have first claim on the remaining available funds, wages have second priority, and taxes have third priority. Thus, these claims are paid in full.

We now have $6,120 remaining and claims of $8,100, so the general creditors will receive 75.56 cents on the dollar:

$$\frac{\text{Funds available}}{\text{Unsatisfied debt}} = \frac{\$14,040 - \$5,400 - \$1,080 - \$1,440}{\$3,240 + \$1,620 + \$3,240} = 0.7556.$$

General creditors are now initially allocated 75.56 percent of their original claims.

(3) This column reflects a transfer of funds from the subordinated debentures to the notes payable to the bank. Since subordinated debentures are subordinate to bank debt, notes payable to the bank must be paid in full before the debentures receive anything. The notes are paid in full by transferring the difference between their book value and initial allocation ($1,620 − $1,224 = $396) from subordinated debentures to notes payable. This reduces the allocation to subordinated debentures and increases the allocation to notes payable by $396.

(4) Column 3 ÷ Column 1.

2. d. The pro forma balance sheet follows (in millions of dollars):

Current assets[a]	$318	Current liabilities	$ 84
Net fixed assets	306	Advance payments	156
Goodwill	30	Reserves	12
		Subordinated debentures[b]	180
		$2.40 preferred stock, $37.50 par value (2,400,000 shares)[c]	90
		Common stock, $1.50 par value (12,000,000 shares)	18
		Retained earnings	114
Total assets	$654	Total claims	$654

Notes:

[a]$336 million - $18 million = $318 million. $18 million used to retire the $10.50 preferred stock.

[b]2,400,000 shares × $75 par value = $180 million.

[c]2,400,000 shares × $37.50 par value = $90 million.

3.   b.   See the balance sheet shown in response to Self-Test Problem 2.

4.   c.   The pro forma income statement (in millions of dollars) follows:

Net sales	$1,080.0
Operating expense	1,032.0
Net operating income	$ 48.0
Other income	6.0
EBIT	$ 54.0
Interest expense[a]	14.4
EBT	$ 39.6
Taxes (50%)	19.8
Net income	$ 19.8
Dividends on $2.40 preferred[b]	5.8
Income available to common stockholders	$ 14.0

Notes:

[a]0.08($180 million par value) = $14.4 million.
[b]$2.40(2,400,000 shares) = $5.76 million ≈ $5.8 million.

5. e. Distribution to priority claimants (in thousands of dollars):

Proceeds from the sale of assets	$2,400
Less:	
1. First mortgage (paid from sale of fixed assets)	1,200
2. Second mortgage (paid from sale of fixed assets)	400
3. Fees and expenses of bankruptcy	200
4. Wages due to workers	120
5. Taxes due	160
Funds available for distribution to general creditors	$ 320

Distribution to general creditors (in thousands of dollars):

General Creditor Claims	Amount of Claim	Pro Rata Distribution[a]	Distrib.After Subord.Adj.[b]	% of Orig. Claim Received
Unsat. 2nd mortgage	$ 400	$ 51	$ 51	56.4%[c]
Accounts payable	200	25	25	12.5
Notes payable	720	91	142	19.7
Debentures	800	102	102	12.8
Subord. debentures	400	51	0	0.0
Total	$2,520	$320	$320	

Notes:

[a]Pro rata distribution: $320/$2,520 = 0.127 = 12.7%.

[b]Subordinated debentures are subordinated to notes payable. The unsatisfied portion of notes payable is greater than the subordinated debenture distribution, so subordinated debentures receive $0.

[c]Includes $400 from sale of fixed assets received in priority distribution.

6. b. See the distribution worksheet shown in response to Self-Test Problem 5.

7. d. See the distribution worksheet shown in response to Self-Test Problem 5.

8. a. Because the amount of funds available for distribution to general creditors is $320,000 and the total claims of these general creditors is $2,520,000, the common stockholders will receive nothing.

9.   c.   First, compute the five variables required in the Altman model (in thousands of dollars):

X_1 = Net working capital/Total assets = ($1,600 − $1,200)/$4,000 = 0.10 = 10%.
X_2 = Retained earnings/Total assets = -$600/$4,000 = -0.15 = -15%.
X_3 = EBIT/Total assets = $320/$4,000 = 0.08 = 8%.
X_4 = Mkt. value of common and pref. stk./Book value of debt
       = $800/$4,400 = 0.18 = 18%.
X_5 = Sales/Total assets = $4,800/$4,000 = 1.20.

Next, determine the Z-score:
Z = 0.012(10) + 0.014(-15) + 0.033(8) + 0.006(18) + 0.999(1.2) = 1.48.

10.   c.   Finally, compare the Z-score of 1.48 with Altman's standard:

Bankrupt	Zone of Ignorance	Nonbankrupt
1.81		2.99

A Z-score of 1.48 indicates a likelihood of bankruptcy—the higher the Z-score, the lower the probability of bankruptcy.

OVERVIEW

Most corporate growth occurs by internal expansion, which takes place when a firm's existing divisions grow through normal capital budgeting activities. However, the most dramatic examples of growth, and often the largest increases in firms' stock prices, result from mergers.

Leveraged buyouts, or LBOs, occur when a firm's stock is acquired by a small group of investors rather than by another operating company. Since LBOs are similar to mergers in many respects, they are also covered here. Conditions change over time, causing firms to sell off, or divest, major divisions to other firms that can better utilize the divested assets. Divestitures are also discussed in the chapter. Finally, we discuss the holding company form of organization, wherein one corporation owns the stock of one or more other companies.

OUTLINE

The primary motives behind corporate mergers are listed below.

■ The primary motivation for most mergers is *synergy*, to increase the value of the combined enterprise.

  □ If Companies A and B merge to form Company C, and if C's value exceeds that of A and B taken separately, then synergy is said to exist.

  □ Synergism can arise from four sources:

   • Operating economies

   • Financial economies

   • Differential management efficiency

   • Increased market power

  □ Operating and financial economies, as well as increases in managerial efficiency, are socially desirable. However, mergers that reduce competition are socially undesirable and illegal.

■   *Tax considerations* have stimulated a number of mergers.

     ☐   A highly profitable firm might merge with a firm that has accumulated tax losses so as to put these losses to immediate use.

     ☐   A firm with excess cash and a shortage of internal investment opportunities might seek a merger rather than pay the cash out as dividends, which would result in the shareholders paying immediate taxes on the distribution.

■   Occasionally, a firm will merge with another because it thinks it has found a "bargain," that is, *assets can be purchased below their replacement cost.*

     ☐   However, if the capital markets are efficient, stock prices represent the fair market value of the underlying assets.

     ☐   The fact that a firm's market value is far below its replacement or book value does not, in itself, make the firm an attractive acquisition candidate.

■   *Diversification* is often cited by managers as a reason for mergers.

     ☐   Diversification may bring some real benefits to the firm, especially by reducing the variability of the firm's earnings, which benefits the firm's managers, creditors, and other stakeholders.

     ☐   However, by simply holding portfolios of stocks, stockholders can generally diversify more easily and efficiently than can firms.

■   Financial economists like to think that business decisions are based only on economic considerations, especially maximization of firms' values. However, some business decisions are based more on managers' personal motivations than on economic analyses.

     ☐   Some mergers occur because managers want to increase the size of their firms, and hence gain more power, prestige, and monetary compensation.

     ☐   Other mergers occur because managers want to keep their jobs, so they merge with other firms to make the firm less attractive to hostile suitors. This type of merger is called a *defensive merger.*

■   Firms are generally valued in the markets as ongoing firms. However, some firms are worth more if they are broken up and then sold off separately. Thus, some acquisitions are motivated by the fact that a firm's *breakup value* is greater than its current market value.

Economists classify mergers into four types.

■   A *horizontal merger* occurs when one firm combines with another in the same line of business.

■   A *vertical merger* exists when firms combine in a producer-supplier relationship.

■ A *congeneric merger* occurs when the merging companies are somewhat related, but not to the extent required for a horizontal or a vertical merger.

■ A *conglomerate merger* occurs when completely unrelated enterprises combine.

Five major "merger waves" have occurred in the United States. The high level of merger activity that is still going on has been sparked by several factors.

■ Five major "merger waves" have occurred in the U. S.
  □ In the late 1800s consolidations occurred in the oil, steel, tobacco, and other basic industries.
  □ In the 1920s the stock market boom helped financial promoters consolidate firms in a number of industries, including utilities, communications, and autos.
  □ In the 1960s conglomerate mergers were the rage.
  □ In the 1980s LBO firms and others began using junk bonds to finance all manner of acquisitions.
  □ Currently, strategic alliances are being designed to enable firms to compete better in the global economy.

■ In general, the mergers in the 1990s have been significantly different from those of the 1980s.
  □ Most 1980s mergers were financial transactions in which buyers sought companies that were selling at less than their true values as a result of incompetent or sluggish management.
  □ In the 1990s most of the mergers have been strategic in nature. Companies are merging to gain economies of scale or scope and thus be better able to compete in the world economy.
  □ Other differences between mergers in the 1980s and the 1990s are the way they were financed and how the target firms' stockholders were compensated.
  □ In the 1990s there has been an increase in cross-border mergers. Many of these mergers have been motivated by large shifts in the value of the world's leading currencies.

In most mergers, one company, the target company, is acquired by another, the acquiring company.

■ In a *friendly merger*, the management of the target company approves the merger and recommends it to their stockholders.
  □ Under these circumstances a suitable price is determined, and the acquiring company will simply buy the target company's shares through a friendly *tender offer*.

☐ Payment will be made either in cash, in the stock or debt of the acquiring firm, or some mix of cash and securities.

■ A *hostile merger* is one in which the target firm's management resists the takeover. The target firm's management either believes the price offered is too low, or it may simply want to remain independent.

☐ Under these circumstances, the acquiring company may make a hostile tender offer for the target company's shares. This is a direct appeal to the target firm's stockholders asking them to exchange their shares for cash, bonds, or stock in the acquiring firm.

☐ The number of hostile tender offers has increased greatly during the past several years.

● An all-cash offer that is high enough will generally overcome any resistance by the target firm's management.

● Strategic buyers often begin the hostile bidding process with a "preemptive" or "blowout" bid.

● If a hostile bid is eventually accepted by the target's board, the deal ends up as "friendly."

Mergers are regulated by both the state and federal governments.

■ Because of the unfair situation that existed due to corporate raiders' well-planned raids, Congress passed the Williams Act in 1968. This law had two main objectives.

☐ To regulate the way acquiring firms can structure takeover offers.

☐ To force acquiring firms to disclose more information about their offers.

● Basically, Congress wanted to put target managements in a better position to defend against hostile offers.

■ Federal laws place four restrictions on acquiring firms.

☐ Acquirers must disclose their current holdings and future intentions within 10 days of amassing at least 5 percent of a company's stock.

☐ Acquirers must disclose the source of the funds to be used in the acquisition.

☐ Target shareholders must be given at least 20 days to tender their shares.

☐ If the tender price is increased during the 20-day open period, all shareholders who tendered prior to the new offer must receive the higher price.

● These restrictions were intended to reduce the acquiring firm's ability to surprise management and to stampede target shareholders into accepting an inadequate offer.

■ Many states now have merger laws which restrict the actions that can be taken by raiders.

□ One such law restricts the ability of a raider to vote the shares they have acquired; that is, the merger must be approved by disinterested shareholders.

□ Other state laws limit the use of *golden parachutes,* onerous debt-financing plans, and some types of *poison pills* to protect target stockholders from their own managers.

While merger analysis may appear simple, there are a number of complex issues involved.

■ The acquiring firm must perform a capital budgeting-type analysis. If it appears that the target firm can be purchased for less than its intrinsic value, then the offer should be made.

■ The target firm's shareholders must believe that a "fair" price is being offered. Otherwise, they will not tender their shares.

■ Several methodologies are used to value firms. Two commonly-used methods are the *discounted cash flow analysis* and the *market multiple method.* Regardless of the valuation methodology, two factors must be recognized.

□ Any changes in operations occurring as a result of the proposed merger that will impact the value of the business must be considered in the analysis.

□ The goal of merger valuation is to value the target firm's equity, because a firm is acquired from its owners, not from its creditors.

● Although the phrase "valuing the firm" is used, the focus is on the value of the equity rather than on total value.

■ The *discounted cash flow approach* to valuing a business involves the application of capital budgeting procedures to an entire firm rather than to a single project.

□ To apply this method, two key items are needed: (1) pro forma statements that forecast the incremental free cash flows expected to result from the merger, and (2) a discount rate, or cost of capital, to apply to these projected cash flows.

□ In a pure *financial merger*, in which no synergies are expected, the incremental postmerger cash flows are simply the expected cash flows of the target firm.

□ In an *operating merger*, in which the two firms' operations are to be integrated, forecasting future cash flows is more difficult.

■ Merger cash flows, unlike capital budgeting cash flows *must include* interest expense in the cash flow forecast.

□ The target firm usually has embedded debt that will be assumed by the acquiring company.

□ The acquisition is often financed partially by debt.

- ☐ If the subsidiary is to grow in the future, new debt will have to be issued over time to support its expansion. Thus, the easiest way to properly account for the complexities of merger debt is for it to be explicitly included in the cash flow analysis.

- ■ With debt costs included in the cash flow analysis, the resulting net cash flows accrue solely to the equity holders of the acquiring firm; thus, we are using the *equity residual method.*
  - ☐ This is in contrast to the corporate value model where the free cash flows, which belong to all investors not just shareholders, are discounted at the WACC.
  - ☐ Both methods lead to the same estimate of equity value.

- ■ The *appropriate discount rate is a cost of equity* rather than an overall cost of capital. The cost of equity used must reflect the underlying riskiness of the target company's assets and the riskiness of the financing mix used for the acquisition.

- ■ A risk analysis could be performed on the cash flows.
  - ☐ Sensitivity analysis, scenario analysis, and/or Monte Carlo simulation could be used to get a feel for the risks involved with the acquisition.

- ■ *Due diligence* is the careful investigation of the books and assets, and it is an essential part of any merger analysis.

- ■ The Security Market Line can then be used to determine the target firm's postmerger cost of equity.

- ■ The present value of the incremental merger cash flows is the maximum price that the acquiring firm should pay for the target company.
  - ☐ In a merger analysis, the value of the target consists of the target's premerger value plus any value created by operating or financial synergies.

- ■ Another method of valuing a target company is *market multiple analysis*, which applies a market-determined multiple to some measure of earnings such as net income or earnings per share. The basic premise is that the value of any business depends on the earnings that the business produces.
  - ☐ Note that measures other than net income can be used in the market multiple approach. Another commonly used measure is *earnings before interest, taxes, depreciation, and amortization (EBITDA).*

- ■ The terms of a merger include three important elements:
  - ☐ *The price to be paid* determines whether the shareholders of the acquiring company or the shareholders of the target company reap the greater benefits from the merger.

- If there were no synergistic benefits, the maximum bid would be equal to the current value of the target company. The greater the synergistic gains, the greater the gap between the target's current price and the maximum the acquiring company could pay.

- The greater the synergistic gains, the more likely a merger is to be consummated.

- The issue of how to divide the synergistic benefits is critically important in any merger analysis.

- Where in the range the actual price will be set depends on the negotiating skills of the two management teams and on the bargaining positions of the two parties as determined by fundamental economic conditions.

- The acquiring firm keeps its maximum bid secret, and it plans its bidding strategy carefully and consistently with the situation.

☐ *Postmerger control of the firm* is of great interest to managers due to their concern for their jobs.

☐ *The structure of the offer* is how to pay for the merger—in cash, in securities of the acquiring firm, or some combination of the two.

Once the value of the target is estimated, the acquiring firm must decide on the structure of the takeover bid.

■ The structure of the bid is extremely important since it affects:
   ☐ The capital structure of the postmerger firm.
   ☐ The tax treatment of both the acquiring firm and the target firm's stockholders.
   ☐ The ability of the target firm's stockholders to benefit from future merger-related gains.
   ☐ The types of federal and state regulations to which the acquiring firm will be subjected.

■ Target shareholders do not have to pay taxes on their takeover proceeds if their shares are paid for by stock in the acquiring firm (at least 50 percent of the payment must be in stock). If the offer is predominantly cash or debt securities, taxes will have to be paid.

■ If the acquiring firm writes up the target company's assets for tax purposes, then the target company must pay capital gains taxes in the year the merger occurs. However, it can then depreciate the assets from their new, higher value.

■ Securities laws also have an effect on the construction of the offer.
   ☐ Whenever a corporation bids for control of another firm through the exchange of equity or debt, the entire process must take place under the scrutiny of the SEC.

Mergers are handled in either of two basic ways: (1) as a pooling of interests or (2) as a purchase. The method used can have a significant effect on postmerger reported profits, and this, in turn, can influence the desirability of the merger.

■ In theory, a *pooling of interests* is a merger among equals, hence the consolidated balance sheet is simply the sum of the two merging company's balance sheets.

■ Under the *purchase* method, one firm is assumed to have bought another in much the same way a firm would buy any capital asset, paying for it with cash, debt, or stock of the acquiring company.

  □ If the price paid is exactly equal to the acquired firm's *net asset value*, which is defined as its total assets minus its liabilities, then the consolidated balance sheet will be identical to that under pooling.

  □ If the price paid exceeds the net asset value, then asset values will be increased to reflect the price actually paid, whereas if the price paid is less than the net asset value, then assets must be written down when preparing the consolidated balance sheet.

■ Significant differences can also arise in reported profits under the two accounting methods.

  □ If asset values are increased, this must be reflected in a higher depreciation charge and also in a higher cost of goods sold if inventories are written up.

  □ Also, *goodwill* represents the excess paid for a firm over its adjusted net asset value. Goodwill is written off, or amortized, over a period corresponding to not more than 40 years.

    • The write-off of goodwill is also reflected in earnings per share. The greater the amount of goodwill, the larger is the write-off and the more significant is the dilution in reported earnings per share.

■ Several conditions must be met to use the pooling method, the most important of which is that the acquisition must be paid for with common stock of the acquiring firm.

  □ Nevertheless, about 90 percent of all recent acquisitions over $100 million have used pooling, which does not lower the combined firm's reported earnings.

In many situations it is hard to identify an acquirer and a target firm. Thus, the merger appears to be a true "merger of equals." There are several steps to go through in this type of analysis.

■ Develop pro forma financial statements for the consolidated corporation.

  □ The key set of figures is the projected consolidated free cash flows available to stockholders.

Estimate the new company's cost of equity, and use that rate to discount the equity flows of the consolidated company.
- ☐ This is the value of the equity of the consolidated company.

Decide how to allocate the new company's stock between the two sets of old stockholders.
- ☐ A key issue is how to divide the synergistic-induced value between the two sets of stockholders.
  - ● One basis for the allocation is the relative pre-announcement values of the two companies.
- ☐ Control of the consolidated company is also a key issue.

Investment bankers play an important role in merger activities.

The major investment banking firms have merger and acquisition (M&A) departments which help to match merger partners.

These same investment bankers can also help a firm fend off an unwanted suitor.
- ☐ Sometimes a *white knight* will be lined up to acquire a firm that is trying to avoid being taken over by an unfriendly suitor.
- ☐ In other situations, a *white squire* may be sought to buy shares in the target firm, hold them, and then vote in favor of current management.
- ☐ Investment bankers can also recommend *poison pills*, which are actions that effectively destroy the value of the firm in the event of a merger, and hence drive off unwanted suitors.

Investment bankers are often used to help establish the offering price. Generally, both the acquiring and target firms will use investment bankers to help establish a price and also to participate in the negotiations.

To be successful in the mergers and acquisitions business, an investment banker must be able to offer a financing package to clients, whether they are acquirers who need capital to take over companies or target companies trying to finance stock repurchase plans or other defenses against takeovers.

Investment banking firms also engage in *risk arbitrage*, which means speculating in the stocks of companies that are likely takeover targets.

Recent merger activity has raised two questions: (1) Do corporate acquisitions really create value, and, (2) if so, how is this value shared between the parties?

■   Researchers attempt to answer questions such as this by examining the relative stock price performance of merging firms around the merger announcement date.

■   On average, the stock prices of target companies have increased by 20-30 percent upon the merger announcement.

■   However, the stock prices of acquiring firms, on average, remain constant.

■   Thus, the evidence strongly indicates that acquisitions do create value, but that shareholders of target firms reap virtually all of the benefits.

Mergers are one way for two companies to completely join assets and management, but many firms are striking cooperative deals which fall short of merging. Such cooperative amalgamations are called corporate, or strategic, alliances, and they occur in many forms.

■   *Joint ventures* are an important type of alliance.
   □ Parts of companies are joined to achieve specific, limited objectives.
   □ Joint ventures are controlled by a combined management team formed by the parent companies.
   □ Joint ventures are operated independently from the parent companies.

In a leveraged buyout (LBO), a small group of investors, usually including current management, acquires a firm in a transaction financed largely by debt.

■   The debt is serviced with funds generated by the acquired company's operations and, often, by the sale of some of its assets.
   □ In other instances, the LBO firm plans to sell off divisions to other firms that can gain synergies.
   □ The heavy debt burden forces management to operate very efficiently.

■   Usually, after several years of being privately held, the firm has been streamlined and made more efficient. Then, the owners recover their equity investment by going public again.

Although corporations do more buying than selling of productive assets, selling, or divestiture, does take place.

■   There are four types of *divestitures*:
   □ A division may be *sold to another firm*. This is the most common form of divestiture.
   □ In a *spin-off*, a division may be set up as a corporation, with the parent firm's stockholders then being given stock in the new corporation on a pro rata basis.

- ☐ In a *carve-out*, a minority interest in a corporate subsidiary is sold to new share-holders, so the parent gains new equity financing yet retains control.
- ☐ In a *liquidation*, the assets of a division are sold off piecemeal, rather than as a single entity.

■ There are a variety of reasons cited for divestitures:
- ☐ It appears that, on occasion, investors do not properly value some assets when they are part of a large conglomerate. Thus, divestiture can occur to enhance firm value.
- ☐ Often, firms will need to raise large amounts of cash to finance expansion in their core business, or to reduce an onerous debt burden, and divestitures can raise the needed cash.
- ☐ Sometimes, assets are just no longer profitable and must be liquidated.
- ☐ Firms that are struggling against bankruptcy often have to divest profitable divisions just to stay alive.
- ☐ The government sometimes mandates divestiture on antitrust grounds.

A holding company is a firm that holds large blocks of stock in other companies and exercises control over those firms. The holding company is often called the parent company and the controlled companies are known as subsidiaries or operating companies. Holding companies may be used to obtain some of the same benefits that could be achieved through mergers and acquisitions. However, the holding company device has some unique disadvantages as well as unique advantages.

■ Advantages of holding companies include the following:
- ☐ *Control with fractional ownership.* Effective control of a company may be achieved with far less than 50 percent ownership of the common stock.
- ☐ *Isolation of risks.* Claims on one unit of the holding company may not be liabilities to the other units. Each element of the holding company organization is a separate legal entity.

■ Disadvantages of holding companies include the following:
- ☐ *Partial multiple taxation.* Consolidated tax returns may be filed only if the holding company owns 80 percent or more of the voting stock of the subsidiary. Otherwise, intercorporate dividends will be taxed. Note, though, that firms that own over 20 percent but less than 80 percent of another corporation can deduct 80 percent of the dividends received from taxable income, while firms that own less than 20 percent may deduct only 70 percent of the dividends received.
- ☐ *Ease of enforced dissolution.* It is much easier for the Justice Department to require disposal of a stock position than to demand the separation of an integrated business operation.

■   The holding company device can be used to control large amounts of assets with a relatively small equity investment.   The substantial leverage involved in such an operation may result in high returns, but it also involves a high degree of risk.

SELF-TEST QUESTIONS

Definitional

1.   If the value of two firms, in combination, is greater than the sum of their separate values, then _____ is said to exist.

2.   Synergistic effects may result from either _____ economies or _____ economies.

3.   The Justice Department may be concerned about the _____ implications of a proposed merger.

4.   A(n) _____ merger takes place when two firms in the same line of business combine, while the combination of a steel company with a coal company would be an example of a(n) _____ merger.

5.   The merger of two completely unrelated enterprises is referred to as a(n) _____ merger.

6.   A firm which seeks to take over another company is commonly called the _____ company, while the firm it seeks to acquire is referred to as the _____ company.

7.   A merger may be described as "friendly" or "hostile," depending upon the attitude of the _____ of the target company.

8.   A(n) _____ _____ is a request by the acquiring company to the target company's _____ to submit their shares in exchange for a specified price or specified number of shares of stock.

9.   A(n) _____ merger combines the business activity of the two firms with the expectation of _____ benefits.

10.   _____ mergers do not combine the business operations of two firms, and no operating economies are expected.

11. Merger analysis is very similar to _____ _____ analysis.

12. In valuing the target firm, the analysis focuses on the cash flows that accrue to the stockholders of the _____ firm.

13. A(n) _____ _____ occurs when two firms combine parts of their companies to accomplish specific, limited objectives.

14. A pro rata distribution of stock in a new firm which was formerly a subsidiary is called a(n) _____.

15. Unless a holding company owns at least _____ percent of the shares of a subsidiary company, it may be subject to multiple _____ on a portion of any intercorporate _____.

16. A(n) _____ merger is a merger that occurs to make the firm less attractive to hostile suitors.

17. A(n) _____ merger occurs when the merging companies are somewhat related, but not to the extent required for a horizontal or vertical merger.

18. A(n) _____ merger is one in which the target firm's management resists the takeover.

19. Two commonly-used methods to value firms are _____ _____ _____ and _____ _____ analyses.

20. Merger cash flows, unlike capital budgeting cash flows, must include _____ expenses.

21. A(n) _____ _____ is sometimes lined up to acquire a firm that is trying to avoid being taken over by an unfriendly suitor.

22. A(n) _____ _____ may be sought to buy enough of the target firm's shares to block a merger.

23. _____ _____ are actions that effectively destroy the value of the firm in the event of a merger, and hence drive off unwanted suitors.

24. Investment banking firms engage in _____ _____, which means speculating in the stock of companies that are likely takeover targets.

25. In a(n) _____ _____ a small group of investors, usually including top management, acquires a firm in a transaction financed largely by debt.

26. _____ occurs when the assets of a division are sold off piecemeal, rather than as an operating entity.

27. Mergers are handled in either of two basic ways: (1) as a(n) _____ ____ _____ or as a(n) _____.

28. _____ represents the excess paid for a firm over its adjusted net asset value.

29. In a(n) _____-_____, a minority interest in a corporate subsidiary is sold to new shareholders, so the parent gains new equity financing yet retains control.

30. The most common form of _____ is where a division is sold to another firm.

Conceptual

31. In a financial merger, the expected postmerger cash flows are generally the sum of the cash flows of the separate companies.

    a. True   b. False

32. Interest expense must be explicitly included in the incremental cash flow analysis for a merger.

    a. True   b. False

33. The holding company device can be used to take advantage of the principle of financial leverage. Thus, the holding company can control a great deal of assets with a limited amount of top-tier equity.

    a. True   b. False

SELF-TEST PROBLEMS

(The following data apply to the next four Self-Test Problems.)

TransCorp, a large conglomerate, is evaluating the possible acquisition of the Chip Company, a transistor manufacturer. TransCorp's analyst projects the following postmerger incremental cash flows (in millions of dollars):

	1999	2000	2001	2002
Net sales	$200	$230	$250	$270
Cost of goods sold	130	140	145	150
Selling/admin. expense	20	25	30	32
EBIT	$ 50	$ 65	$ 75	$ 88
Interest	10	12	13	14
EBT	$ 40	$ 53	$ 62	$ 74
Taxes (40%)	16	21	25	30
Net income	$ 24	$ 32	$ 37	$ 44
Retained earnings	12	13	14	15
Cash available to stockholders	$ 12	$ 19	$ 23	$ 29
Terminal value				400
Net CF	$ 12	$ 19	$ 23	$429

The acquisition, if made, would occur on January 4, 1999. All cash flows above are assumed to occur at the end of the year. Chip currently has a market value capital structure of 10 percent debt, but TransCorp would increase the debt to 50 percent if the acquisition were made. Chip, if independent, pays taxes at 30 percent, but its income would be taxed at 40 percent if consolidated. Chip's current market-determined beta is 1.80. Its estimated postmerger beta is 2.67.

The cash flows above include the additional interest payments due to increased leverage and asset expansion, and the full taxes paid by TransCorp on the Chip income stream. Depreciation-generated funds would be used to replace worn-out equipment, so they would not be available to TransCorp's shareholders. Retained earnings would be used, in addition to new debt, to finance required asset expansion. Thus, the net cash flows are the flows that would accrue to TransCorp's stockholders. The risk-free rate is 10 percent and the market risk premium is 5 percent.

1. What is the appropriate discount rate for valuing the acquisition?

    a. 10.00%   **b.** 15.00%   **c.** 19.00%   **d.** 21.75%   **e.** 23.35%

2. What is the value (in millions of dollars) of the Chip Company to TransCorp?

    a. $197.73   **b.** $206.42   **c.** $219.78   **d.** $322.85   **e.** $429.00

3. Chip has 5 million shares outstanding. Chip's current market price is $32.50. What is the maximum price per share that TransCorp should offer?

    a. $32.50   **b.** $37.50   **c.** $41.37   **d.** $43.96   **e.** $46.93

4. TransCorp should offer Chip's stockholders $32.625 per share.

    a. True   **b.** False

ANSWERS TO SELF-TEST QUESTIONS

1.	synergy	**16.**	defensive
2.	operating; financial	**17.**	congeneric
3.	antitrust	**18.**	hostile
4.	horizontal; vertical	**19.**	discounted cash flow; market multiple
5.	conglomerate	**20.**	interest
6.	acquiring; target	**21.**	white knight
7.	management	**22.**	white squire
8.	tender offer; stockholders	**23.**	Poison pills
9.	operating; synergistic	**24.**	risk arbitrage
10.	Financial	**25.**	leveraged buyout
11.	capital budgeting	**26.**	Liquidation
12.	acquiring	**27.**	pooling of interests; purchase
13.	joint venture	**28.**	Goodwill
14.	spinoff	**29.**	carve-out
15.	80; taxation; dividends	**30.**	divestiture

31. a. In a financial merger, no synergistic effects are anticipated.

32. a. The target firm generally has embedded debt that is being assumed by the acquiring firm. Since these costs are not marginal, they must be specifically included in the analysis.

33. a. This statement is true, but the leveraging which occurs in a holding company organization significantly increases the riskiness of the firm.

SOLUTIONS TO SELF-TEST PROBLEMS

1. e. $k_s = 10\% + (5\%)2.67 = 23.35\%$.

2. c. $V = \dfrac{\$12\,\text{million}}{(1.2335)^1} + \dfrac{\$19\,\text{million}}{(1.2335)^2} + \dfrac{\$23\,\text{million}}{(1.2335)^3} + \dfrac{\$429\,\text{million}}{(1.2335)^4}$

    $= \$219.78\,\text{million}$.

3. d. \$219.78 million/5 million = \$43.96.

4. b. It does not make sense to offer Chip's shareholders just a little above the current market price. Not enough shares would be tendered to gain control, the expenses would be for naught, and other firms could be induced to make competing bids.

OVERVIEW

As the world economy becomes more integrated, the role of multinational firms is increasing. Managers of multinational companies must deal with a wide range of issues that are not present when a company operates in a single country. Although the same basic principles of financial management apply to multinational corporations as well as to domestic ones, financial managers of multinational firms face a much more complex task. The primary problem, from a financial standpoint, is the fact that the cash flows must cross national boundaries.

These flows may be constrained in various ways, and, equally important, their values in dollars may rise or fall depending on exchange rate fluctuations. This means that the multinational financial manager must be constantly aware of the many complex interactions among national economies and their effects on international operations. In this chapter, the key differences between multinational and domestic corporations are highlighted, and the impact these differences have on the financial management of multinational businesses is discussed.

OUTLINE

A multinational, or global, corporation is the term used to describe a firm that operates in an integrated fashion in a number of countries. The growth of multinationals has greatly increased the degree of worldwide economic and political interdependence.

- Companies, both U. S. and foreign, go "global" for six primary reasons:
  - □ *To broaden their markets.* After a company has saturated its home market, growth opportunities are often better in foreign markets.
  - □ *To seek raw materials.* Many of the present multinational firms began their international operations because raw materials were located abroad.
  - □ *To seek new technology.* Because no single nation holds a commanding advantage in all technologies, companies are scouring the globe for leading scientific and design ideas.

☐ *To seek production efficiency.* Still other firms have moved their manufacturing facilities overseas to take advantage of cheaper production costs in low-cost countries.

☐ *To avoid political and regulatory hurdles.* Firms can avoid political and regulatory hurdles by moving production to other countries.

☐ *To diversify.* Finally, firms go international so that they can diversify, and consequently, cushion the impact of adverse economic trends in any single country.

■ Over the past 10 to 15 years, there has been an increasing amount of investment in the United States by foreign corporations, and in foreign nations by U. S. corporations. These developments suggest an increasing degree of mutual influence and interdependence among business enterprises and nations, to which the United States is not immune.

In theory, financial concepts and procedures are valid for both domestic and multinational operations. However, there are six major factors which distinguish financial management in firms operating entirely within a single country from firms that operate globally.

■ *Different currency denominations.* Cash flows will be denominated in different currencies, making exchange rate analysis necessary for all types of financial decisions.

■ *Economic and legal ramifications.* Economic and legal differences among countries can cause significant problems when the corporation tries to coordinate and control worldwide operations of its subsidiaries.

■ *Language differences.* The ability to communicate is critical in all business transactions. U. S. citizens are often at a disadvantage because we are generally fluent only in English.

■ *Cultural differences.* Values and the role of business in society reflect the cultural differences that may vary dramatically from one country to the next.

■ *Role of governments.* Financial models based on the traditional assumption of a competitive marketplace must often be modified to include political (governmental) and other noneconomic facets of the decision.

■ *Political risk.* This is seldom negotiable and may be as extreme as *expropriation.* Political risk must be explicitly addressed in financial analysis and it varies from country to country.

An exchange rate specifies the number of units of a given currency that can be purchased with one unit of another currency.

■ An *exchange rate* listed as the number of U. S. dollars required to purchase one unit of foreign currency is called a *direct quotation*. An exchange rate listed as the number of units of foreign currency that can be purchased for one U. S. dollar is called an *indirect quotation*. Normal practice in the U. S. is to use indirect quotations for all currencies other than British pounds, for which direct quotations are given.

■ Converting from one foreign currency to another foreign currency may require the use of *cross rates*. For example, if the direct quotation between pounds and dollars is $1.7875 and the indirect quotation between francs and dollars is FF5.6344, the cross rate between pounds and francs can be calculated as follows:

$$\text{Cross rate} = \frac{\text{Dollars}}{\text{Pound}} \times \frac{\text{Francs}}{\text{Dollar}} = \frac{\text{Francs}}{\text{Pound}}$$
$$= 1.7875 \text{ dollars per pound} \times 5.6344 \text{ francs per dollar}$$
$$= 10.0715 \text{ francs per pound}.$$

■ The tie-in with the dollar ensures that all currencies are related to one another in a consistent manner. If this consistency did not exist, currency traders could profit by buying undervalued and selling overvalued currencies. This process, known as *arbitrage*, works to bring about an equilibrium.
   ☐ Currency traders are constantly operating in the market. The traders' existence enables the rest of us to assume that currency markets are in equilibrium and that, at any point in time, cross rates are all internally consistent.
   ☐ If the Europeans' plans remain on track, currency conversions within Europe will soon be unnecessary, for one European currency, the *Euro*, will replace francs, marks, and so forth.

The International Monetary Fund (IMF) was the center of a fixed exchange rate system that operated for 25 years after World War II.

■ Under this system, the U. S. dollar, which was linked to gold by a fixed price of $35 per ounce, was the base currency, and the relative values of all other currencies to the dollar were controlled within narrow limits, but then adjusted periodically.
   ☐ Currency fluctuations depend on supply and demand and capital movements. However, these fluctuations were kept within limits by the actions of the various central banks, which bought or sold currency to maintain specific prices.
   ☐ If a country *devalued* its currency, then fewer units of another currency would be required to buy one unit of the devalued currency. Its "price" would be reduced, making the country's goods cheaper and thus stimulating exports and discouraging imports. A country could devalue its currency only with the approval of the IMF.

■ In 1971, the *fixed exchange rate system* was replaced by a system under which the U. S. dollar was permitted to "float."

□ A *floating exchange rate system* is one under which currency prices are allowed to seek their own levels without much governmental intervention.

□ The present managed floating system permits currency rates to move without any specific limits, but central banks do buy and sell currencies to smooth out exchange rate fluctuations.

■ The inherent volatility of exchange rates under a floating system increases the uncertainty of the cash flows for a multinational corporation. This uncertainty is known as *exchange rate risk*, and it is a major factor differentiating a global corporation from a purely domestic one.

■ Concerns about exchange rate risk have led to attempts to stabilize currency movements. In 1979, the European Monetary System (EMS) was formed.

□ Participants agreed to limit fluctuations in their exchange rates so that rates stayed within a prespecified range.

□ It was felt that this arrangement would prevent the frequent disruptions to international trade and economic health that were caused by the vagaries of a floating foreign exchange market.

■ European nations are now moving toward an alternative to the EMS. Under the Treaty of Maastricht, participants in the European Monetary Union (EMU) agreed to move to a common currency, the Euro, that will replace the currencies of the member countries.

□ It is hoped that this arrangement will be more successful than past arrangements in terms of creating a stable international economic environment.

■ In today's floating exchange rate environment, many countries have chosen to peg their currencies to one or more major currencies.

□ Countries with *pegged exchange rates* establish a fixed exchange rate with some major currency, and then the values of the pegged currencies move together over time.

■ Not all currencies are *convertible*. A currency is convertible when the nation which issued it allows it to be traded in the currency markets and is willing to redeem it at market rates.

□ This means that, except for limited central bank influence, the issuing government loses control over the value of its currency.

□ A lack of convertibility creates major problems for international trade.

Importers, exporters, tourists, and governments buy and sell currencies in the foreign exchange market. The foreign exchange market consists of a network of brokers and banks based in New York, London, Tokyo, and other financial centers.

■ The rate paid for delivery of currency no more than two days after the day of trade is called the *spot rate*.

■ When currency is bought or sold and is to be delivered at some agreed-upon future date, usually 30, 90, or 180 days into the future, a *forward exchange rate* is used.

  □ If one can obtain *more* of the foreign currency for a dollar in the forward market than in the spot market, then the forward currency is *less valuable* than the spot currency, and the forward currency is said to be selling at a *discount*.

  □ If a dollar will buy *fewer* units of a currency in the forward market than in the spot market, then the forward currency is worth *more* dollars than the spot currency, and the forward currency is said to be selling at a *premium*.

Market forces determine whether a currency sells at a forward premium or discount, and the general relationship between spot and forward exchange rates is specified by a concept called interest rate parity.

■ *Interest rate parity* holds that investors should earn the same return on security investments in all countries after adjusting for risk.

  □ It recognizes that when you invest in a country other than your home country, you are affected by two forces—returns on the investment itself and changes in the exchange rate.

  □ Your overall return will be *higher* than the investment's stated return if the currency your investment is denominated in *appreciates* relative to your home currency.

■ Interest rate parity is expressed as follows:

$$\frac{\text{Forward exchange rate}}{\text{Spot exchange rate}} = \frac{1 + k_h}{1 + k_f}.$$

  □ Both the forward and spot rates are expressed in terms of the amount of home currency received per unit of foreign currency.

  □ k_h and k_f are the periodic interest rates in the home country and foreign country.

■ Interest rate parity shows why a particular currency might be at a forward premium or discount.

  □ A currency is at a forward premium whenever domestic interest rates are higher than foreign interest rates.

  □ Discounts prevail if domestic interest rates are lower than foreign interest rates.

  □ If these conditions do not hold, arbitrage forces interest rates back to parity.

Over the long run, market forces work to ensure that similar goods sell for similar prices in different countries after taking exchange rates into account. This relationship is known as purchasing power parity.

■ *Purchasing power parity (PPP)*, sometimes referred to as the *law of one price*, implies that the level of exchange rates adjusts so that identical goods cost the same amount in different countries.

■ The equation for purchasing power parity is

$$P_h = (P_f)(\text{Spot rate}) \text{ or Spot rate} = \frac{P_h}{P_f}.$$

  □ P_h is the price of the good in the home country.
  □ P_f is the price of the good in the foreign country.
  □ The spot market exchange rate is expressed as the number of units of home currency that can be exchanged for one unit of foreign currency.

■ PPP assumes that there are no transportation or transaction costs, or import restrictions, all of which limit the ability to ship goods between countries. In many cases, these assumptions are incorrect, which explains why PPP is often violated.
  □ Products in different countries are rarely identical. Frequently, there are real or perceived differences in quality, which can lead to price differences in different countries.

■ Companies and investors must anticipate changes in interest rates, inflation, and exchange rates, and they often try to *hedge* the risks of adverse movements in these factors. Parity relationships are extremely useful when anticipating future conditions.

Relative inflation rates, or the rates of inflation in foreign countries compared with that in the home country, have many implications for multinational financial decisions. Relative inflation rates will greatly influence future production costs at home and abroad. Equally important, inflation has a dominant influence on relative interest rates and exchange rates.

■ A foreign currency will, on average, *depreciate* at a percentage rate approximately equal to the amount by which its inflation rate *exceeds* the U. S. inflation rate. Conversely, foreign currencies in countries with *less* inflation than the U. S. will, on average, *appreciate* relative to the U. S. dollar.

■ Countries experiencing higher rates of inflation than the United States tend to have higher interest rates. The reverse is true for countries with lower inflation rates.

■ Gains from borrowing in countries with low interest rates can be offset by losses from currency appreciation in those countries.

There exists a well developed system of international capital markets.

■ Americans can invest in world markets by investing in the stock of U. S. multinational corporations or by buying the bonds and stocks of large corporations (or governments) headquartered outside the United States.
  □ Investment by U. S. firms in physical assets is called *direct investment.*
  □ Investment in foreign security investments is called *portfolio investment.*

■ The *Eurodollar market* is essentially a short-term market for handling dollar-denominated loans and deposits made outside the United States.
  □ A *Eurodollar* is a U. S. dollar deposited in a bank outside the United States.
  □ The major difference between Eurodollar deposits and regular U. S. time deposits is their geographic locations. The two types of deposits do not involve different currencies, so exchange rate considerations do not apply. However, Eurodollars are outside the direct control of the U. S. monetary authorities, so U. S. banking regulations, including reserve requirements and FDIC insurance premiums, do not apply.
  □ If interest rates in the United States are above Eurodollar rates, these funds will be sent back and invested in the United States, while if Eurodollar deposit rates are significantly above U. S. interest rates, more dollars will be sent out of the United States.
  □ Interest rates on Eurodollar deposits (and loans) are tied to a standard rate known as the *London Interbank Offer Rate (LIBOR)*, the rate of interest offered by the largest and strongest London banks on dollar deposits of significant size.

■ Two international bond markets have developed which trade in long-term funds. Any bond sold outside the country of the borrower is called an *international bond.*
  □ *Foreign bonds* are bonds sold by a foreign borrower but denominated in the currency of the country in which the issue is sold.
  □ *Eurobonds* are bonds issued in one country but denominated in the currency of some other country.
  □ Eurobonds appeal to investors for several reasons.
    ● Generally, they are issued in bearer form rather than as registered bonds, so the names and nationalities of investors are not recorded.
    ● Most governments do not withhold taxes on interest payments associated with Eurobonds.

■ New issues of stock are sold in international markets for a variety of reasons.
  ☐ Firms are able to tap a much larger source of capital than their home countries.
  ☐ Firms want to create an equity market presence to accompany operations in foreign countries.
  ☐ Large multinational companies also occasionally issue new stock simultaneously in multiple countries.

■ In addition to new issues, outstanding stocks of large multinational companies are increasingly being listed on multiple international exchanges.

■ In addition to direct listing, U. S. investors can invest in foreign companies through *American Depository Receipts (ADRs)*, which are certificates representing ownership of foreign stock held in trust.

There are several important differences in the capital budgeting analysis of foreign versus domestic operations.

■ Cash flow estimation is more complex for overseas investments.
  ☐ Firms set up separate subsidiaries in each foreign country in which they operate, and the relevant cash flows for the parent company are the dividends and royalties paid by the subsidiaries to the parent.
  ☐ Any dividends or royalties repatriated by the subsidiary must be converted into the parent company's currency, hence they are subject to exchange rate risk.
  ☐ Dividends and royalties are normally taxed by both foreign and home-country governments.
  ☐ A foreign government may place restrictions, or exchange controls, on the amount of cash that may be repatriated to the parent company. Such restrictions are normally intended to force multinational firms to reinvest earnings in the foreign country, although restrictions are sometimes imposed to prevent large currency outflows, which might disrupt the exchange rate.
  ☐ The cash flows relevant for foreign investment analysis are the cash flows that the subsidiary actually expects to send back to the parent.

■ The cost of capital may be different for a foreign project than for an equivalent domestic project, because foreign projects may be more or less risky.
  ☐ *Exchange rate risk* refers to the fact that exchange rates may fluctuate, increasing the uncertainty about cash flows to the parent company.
  ☐ *Political risk* refers to the possibility of *expropriation*, but it also includes less drastic actions that reduce the value of the parent firm's investment in the foreign subsidiary, including higher taxes, tighter repatriation or currency controls, and restrictions on prices charged.

■ Companies can take steps to reduce the potential loss from expropriation in three major ways.
  ☐ Finance the subsidiary with local capital.
  ☐ Structure operations so that the subsidiary has value only as a part of the integrated corporate system.
  ☐ Obtain insurance against economic losses from expropriation from a source such as the Overseas Private Investment Corporation (OPIC).

Companies' capital structures vary among countries. Evidence suggests that companies in Germany and the United Kingdom tend to have less leverage, whereas firms in Canada appear to have more leverage, relative to firms in the United States, France, Italy, and Japan.

The objectives of working capital management in the multinational corporation are similar to those in the domestic firm but the task is more complex.

■ The objectives of cash management in the multinational corporation are: (1) to speed up collections, slow down disbursements, and thus maximize net float; (2) to shift cash as rapidly as possible from those parts of the business where it is not needed to those parts where it is needed; and (3) to maximize the risk-adjusted, after-tax rate of return on temporary cash balances. Multinational companies use the same general procedures for achieving these goals as domestic firms, but because of longer distances and more serious mail delays, lockbox systems and electronic funds transfers are especially important.

■ Granting credit is more risky in an international context because, in addition to the normal risks of default, the multinational corporation must also worry about exchange rate changes between the time a sale is made and the time a receivable is collected. Credit policy is generally more important for a multinational firm than for a domestic firm. Much of the U. S.'s trade is with poorer, less-developed countries; thus, granting credit is generally a necessary condition for doing business.
  ☐ Nations whose economic health depends upon exports often help their manufacturing firms compete internationally by granting credit to foreign countries.

■ The physical location of inventories is a complex consideration for the multinational firm. The multinational firm must weigh a strategy of keeping inventory concentrated in a few areas from which they can be shipped, and thus minimize the total amount of inventory needed to operate the global business, with the possibility of delays in getting goods from central locations to user locations around the world. Exchange rates, import/export quotas or tariffs, the threat of expropriation, and taxes all influence inventory policy.

SELF-TEST QUESTIONS

Definitional

1. The _____ _____ determines the number of units of one currency that can be exchanged for another.

2. International financial transactions were carried out under a(n) _____ _____ _____ system from the end of World War II until 1971.

3. The organization that controlled the fixed exchange rate system was the _____ _____ _____, which served as a world central bank.

4. Under the fixed rate system, the relative values of various currencies were based on the ____ ____ _____, and were controlled within narrow limits, but then adjusted periodically.

5. Countries with export surpluses and a strong currency might have to _____ their currencies upward.

6. In 1971, the _____ rate system was replaced by one that permitted the U. S. dollar to _____ against other currencies.

7. Evaluation of foreign investments involves the analysis of dividend and royalty cash flows that are _____ to the parent company.

8. Some foreign governments restrict, or block, the amount of income that can be repatriated to encourage _____ in the foreign country.

9. _____ risk refers to the possibility of restrictions on cash flows or the outright _____ of property by a foreign government.

10. A dollar deposited in a non-U. S. bank is often called a(n) _____.

11. Investment by U. S. firms in foreign physical assets is called _____ investment, while the purchase of foreign security investments by U. S. citizens or firms is called _____ investment.

12. _____ bonds are bonds sold by a foreign borrower but denominated in the currency of the country in which the issue is sold.

13. A(n) _____ corporation is a firm that operates in an integrated fashion in a number of countries.

14. An exchange rate listed as the number of U. S. dollars required to purchase one unit of foreign currency is called a(n) _____ quotation. An exchange rate listed as the number of units of foreign currency that can be purchased for one U. S. dollar is called a(n) _____ quotation.

15. _____ is the process that works to bring about an equilibrium among exchange rates.

16. A currency is _____ when the nation which issued it allows it to be traded in the currency markets and is willing to redeem it at market rates.

17. Countries with _____ exchange rates establish a fixed exchange rate with some major currency, and then the values of these currencies move together over time.

18. The rate paid for delivery of currency no more than two days after the day of trade is called the _____ rate.

19. When currency is bought or sold and is to be delivered at some agreed-upon future date a(n) _____ exchange rate is used.

20. _____ _____ parity holds that investors should earn the same return on security investments in all countries after adjusting for risk.

21. _____ _____ parity, sometimes referred to as the law of one price, implies that the level of exchange rates adjusts so that identical goods cost the same amount in different countries.

22. The _____ _____ _____ rate is the interest rate offered by the largest and strongest London banks on dollar deposits of significant size.

23. _____ are bonds issued in one country but denominated in the currency of some other country.

24. _____ _____ _____ are certificates representing ownership of foreign stock held in trust.

25. A currency is at a(n) _____ premium whenever domestic interest rates are higher than foreign interest rates.

Conceptual

26. Financial analysis is not able to take into account political risk.

  a. True   **b.** False

27. When a central bank of a country buys and sells its currency to smooth out fluctuations in the exchange rate, the system is referred to as a managed floating system.

  a. True   **b.** False

28. A foreign currency will, on average, appreciate at a percentage rate approximately equal to the amount by which its inflation rate exceeds the inflation rate in the United States.

  a. True   **b.** False

29. The cost of capital is generally lower for a foreign project than for an equivalent domestic project since the possibility of exchange gains exists.

  a. True   **b.** False

30. Which of the following statements concerning multinational cash flow analysis is _not_ correct?

  a. The relevant cash flows are the dividends and royalties repatriated to the parent company.
  b. The cash flows must be converted to the currency of the parent company and, thus, are subject to future exchange rate changes.
  c. Dividends and royalties are normally taxed only by the government of the country in which the subsidiary is located.
  d. Foreign governments may restrict the amount of the cash flows that may be repatriated.

SELF-TEST PROBLEMS

1. The "spot rate" for Greek drachmas is 0.0313 U. S. dollars per drachma. What would the exchange rate be expressed in drachmas per dollar?

    a. 0.0313 drachmas per dollar   d. 319.4890 drachmas per dollar
    b. 3.1300 drachmas per dollar   e. 400.0000 drachmas per dollar
    c. 31.9489 drachmas per dollar

2. The U. S. dollar can be exchanged for 942.1432 Italian lire today. The Italian currency is expected to appreciate by 10 percent tomorrow. What is the expected exchange rate tomorrow expressed in lire per dollar?

    a. 836.1935 lire per dollar   d. 958.2334 lire per dollar
    b. 841.3167 lire per dollar   e. 965.9813 lire per dollar
    c. 856.4938 lire per dollar

3. You are considering the purchase of a block of stock in Galic Steel, a French steel producer. Galic just paid a dividend of 10 francs per share; that is, $D_0 = 10$ francs. You expect the dividend to grow indefinitely at a rate of 15 percent per year, but because of a higher expected rate of inflation in France than in the United States, you expect the franc to depreciate against the dollar at a rate of 5 percent per year. The exchange rate is currently 5 francs per U. S. dollar, but this ratio will change as the franc depreciates. For a stock with this degree of risk, including exchange rate risk, you feel that a 20 percent rate of return is required. What is the most, in dollars, that you should pay for the stock?

    a. $20.90   b. $31.70   c. $46.00   d. $53.60   e. $60.34

4. Refer to Self-Test Problem 3. Now assume that the franc is expected to appreciate against the dollar at the rate of 1 percent per year. All other facts are unchanged. Under these conditions, what should you be willing to pay for the stock?

    a. $20.90   b. $31.70   c. $46.00   d. $53.60   e. $60.34

5. A currency trader observes that in the spot exchange market, one U. S. dollar can be exchanged for 130.99 Spanish pesetas or for 1.3395 Swiss francs. How many Swiss francs would you receive for every peseta exchanged?

    a. 0.005699   b. 0.010226   c. 63.468975   d. 97.790220   e. 175.461105

6. A deluxe refrigerator costs $1,300 in the United States. The same refrigerator costs 2,250 Dutch guilders. If purchasing power parity holds, what is the spot exchange rate between guilders and the dollar? In other words, according to the spot rate calculated, how many guilders would you receive for every dollar exchanged?

    a. 0.5778   **b.** 0.6375   **c.** 1.2349   **d.** 1.7308   **e.** 2.0345

7. Six-month U. S. T-bills have a nominal rate of 8 percent, while default-free German bonds that mature in 6 months have a nominal rate of 6 percent. In the spot exchange market, one German mark equals $0.70. If interest rate parity holds, what is the 6-month forward exchange rate? In other words, how many U. S. dollars would you receive for every German mark exchanged in 6 months?

    a. $0.7068   **b.** $0.7280   **c.** $0.7498   **d.** $0.6933   **e.** $0.6875

ANSWERS TO SELF-TEST QUESTIONS

1.	exchange rate	**14.**	direct; indirect
2.	fixed exchange rate	**15.**	Arbitrage
3.	International Monetary Fund (IMF)	**16.**	convertible
4.	U. S. dollar	**17.**	pegged
5.	revalue	**18.**	spot
6.	fixed; "float"	**19.**	forward
7.	repatriated	**20.**	Interest rate
8.	reinvestment	**21.**	Purchasing power
9.	Political; expropriation	**22.**	London Interbank Offer
10.	Eurodollar	**23.**	Eurobonds
11.	direct; portfolio	**24.**	American Depository Receipts
12.	Foreign		(ADRs)
13.	multinational	**25.**	forward

26. b. Political risk must be explicitly addressed by international financial managers.

27. a. This statement is correct.

28. b. The foreign currency will depreciate if its inflation rate is higher than that of the United States.

29. b. The cost of capital is generally higher because of exchange rate risk and political risk.

30. c. Dividends and royalties will generally also be taxed by the U. S. government, but the total taxes paid to both governments will not exceed that which would be paid had the earnings occurred in the United States.

SOLUTIONS TO SELF-TEST PROBLEMS

1. c. The exchange rate for drachmas per dollar would be the reciprocal of the exchange rate of dollars per drachma: 1/(0.0313 dollars per drachma) = 31.9489 drachmas per dollar.

2. c. 942.1432(1.10)/$1.00 = 856.4938 lire per dollar.

3. a. First, the valuation equation must be modified to convert the expected dividend stream to dollars:

$$D_t = D_0(1 + g)(ER),$$

where ER = exchange ratio. ER = 1/5 today, but if francs depreciate at a rate of 5 percent, it will take more francs to buy a dollar in the future. The value of ER at some future time (t) will be

$$ER_t = \frac{Dollars}{Francs} = \frac{1}{5(1.05)^t}.$$

Therefore, D_t in dollars may be calculated as follows:

$$
\begin{aligned}
D_t \text{ (in dollars)} &= (10 \text{ francs})(1 + g)^t (ER_t) \\
&= \frac{\$10(1.15)^t}{5(1.05)^t} \\
&= \frac{\$2(1.15)^t}{(1.05)^t} \\
&= \$2\left(\frac{1.15}{1.05}\right)^t \\
&= \$2(1.0952)^t.
\end{aligned}
$$

Thus, if the dividend in francs is expected to grow at a rate of 15 percent per year, but the franc is expected to depreciate at a rate of 5 percent per year against the dollar, then the growth rate, in dollars, of dividends received will be 9.52 percent. We can now calculate the value of the stock in dollars:

$$\hat{P}_0 = \frac{D_1}{k_s - g} = \frac{\$2(1.0952)}{0.20 - 0.0952} = \frac{\$2.1904}{0.1048} = \$20.90.$$

4.   e.   Solve the problem as above: $ER_t = 1(1.01)^t/5$.

$$D_t \text{ (in dollars)} = (10 \text{ francs})(1 + g)^t \left(\frac{(1.01)^t}{5} \right)$$
$$= (\$10/5)(1.15)^t (1.01)^t$$
$$= \$2(1.1615)^t.$$

Thus, the franc dividend is expected to increase at a rate of 15 percent per year, and the value of these francs is expected to rise at the rate of 1 percent per year, so the expected annual growth rate of the dollar dividend is 16.15 percent. We can now calculate the stock price:

$$\hat{P}_0 = \frac{D_1}{k_s - g} = \frac{\$2(1.1615)}{0.20 - 0.1615} = \frac{\$2.3230}{0.0385} = \$60.34.$$

5.   b. $1 = 130.99 Spanish pesetas; $1 = 1.3395 Swiss Francs; Swiss francs/peseta = ?

$$\text{Cross rate:} \quad \frac{\text{Dollar}}{\text{Peseta}} \times \frac{\text{Swiss Franc}}{\text{Dollar}} = \frac{\text{Swiss Franc}}{\text{Peseta}}.$$

Note that an indirect quotation is given for the Spanish peseta; however, the cross rate formula requires a direct quotation. The indirect quotation is the reciprocal of the direct quotation. Since $1 = 130.99 Spanish pesetas, then 1 peseta = $0.007634.

$$\frac{\text{Swiss Franc}}{\text{Peseta}} = 0.007634 \times 1.3395 = 0.010226 \text{ Swiss francs per peseta.}$$

6.   d. $P_h = P_f \text{ (Spot rate)}$
$$1,300 = 2,250 \text{(Spot rate)}$$
$$\frac{1,300}{2,250} = \text{Spot rate}$$
$$\text{Spot rate} = \$0.5778.$$

1 guilder = $0.5778. This is a direct quotation. However, the problem asks for how many guilders would you receive for every dollar exchanged, an indirect quote. To obtain the answer, take the reciprocal of 0.5778 = 1/0.5778 = 1.7308 guilders per 1 U. S. dollar.

7. a. $$\frac{\text{Forward exchange rate}}{\text{Spot exchange rate}} = \frac{1 + k_h}{1 + k_f}$$

$$k_h = \frac{8\%}{2} = 4\%.$$

$$k_f = \frac{6\%}{2} = 3\%.$$

Spot exchange rate = $0.70.

$$\frac{\text{Forward exchange rate}}{\$0.70} = \frac{1.04}{1.03}$$

1.03(Forward exchange rate) = $0.7280

Forward exchange rate = $0.7068.

OVERVIEW

Pension plans are an important component of the U. S. financial system for five reasons: (1) Pension funds, which have an aggregate market value of more than $6 trillion, are important participants in the financial markets. (2) Pension plans provide employees with the majority of their retirement income. (3) Contributions to pension plans are an important component of most compensation plans, and they affect labor productivity, morale, and economic stability. (4) The rate of return on pension plan assets can have a major effect on corporate earnings, employees' retirement incomes, or both. (5) Because pension plans are large owners of corporate stocks, their managers play an important role in the direction and control of corporate policy. In this chapter different types of pension plans, their management and regulation, and their effects on both individuals and firms are discussed.

OUTLINE

Most companies, and practically all government units, have some type of employee pension plan.

■ The *chief financial officer (CFO)* typically administers the plan.
  ☐ He or she has three specific responsibilities: (1) deciding on the general nature of the plan, (2) determining the required annual payments into the plan, and (3) managing the plan's assets.

■ The company does not have total control over these decisions. Employees, often through their unions, have a major say about the plan's structure, and the federal government imposes strict rules on certain aspects of all plans.

■ Under a typical pension plan, the company (or governmental unit) agrees to provide retirement payments to employees. These promised payments constitute a liability, and the employer is required to establish, under the pension plan, a *pension fund* and place money in it each year, in order to have sufficient assets to meet the pension payments as they come due.

■ Pension plan assets represent a very large fraction of total assets for many firms.

■ Because pension fund administration requires so much specialized technical knowledge, companies typically hire specialized consulting firms to help design, modify, and administer their plans.

    ☐ Because the plans are under the general supervision of the financial staff, and because they have such significant implications for the firm as a whole, it is important that financial managers understand the basics of pension plan management.

There are four principal types of pension plans: (1) defined contribution plans, (2) defined benefit plans, (3) profit sharing plans, and (4) cash balance plans.

■ A *defined contribution plan* is one in which a company agrees to make specific payments into a retirement fund and then retirees receive benefits from the plan that depend on the plan's investment success.

    ☐ A defined contribution plan is, in effect, a savings plan that is funded by employers, although many plans also permit additional contributions by employees.

    ☐ The firm is obligated, in bad times as well as in good, to make the specified contributions on behalf of participating employees.

    ☐ Such plans are *portable* in that the assets belong to the employee and can be carried forward whenever he or she changes jobs.

    ☐ Because the sponsoring firm does not guarantee any specific dollar payments to participants upon retirement, participants in a defined contribution plan bear all of the investment risk associated with poor portfolio performance. However, participants can often choose among several investment alternatives, so each individual can accommodate his or her own risk preference.

    ☐ No taxes are paid on income contributed to the plan at the time of contribution, nor when any income or capital gains are generated by the retirement account. However, income taxes must be paid when retirees receive retirement benefits.

    ☐ Funds cannot be left in a retirement account indefinitely. IRS regulations require that withdrawals begin when the retiree is 70 1/2.

■ Under a *defined benefit plan,* the employer agrees to give retirees a specifically defined benefit, such as $500 per month, 50 percent of his or her last salary, or 2.5 percent of his or her highest annual salary for each year of employment.

    ☐ The sponsoring firm, not the participants, bears the risk of poor portfolio performance. Thus, the company has a firm obligation to its retirees that must be met regardless of how well or poorly the pension plan investments perform.

☐ Defined benefit participants generally bear purchasing-power risk, the risk that inflation will eat away at the purchasing power of a fixed pension payment.

- Sometimes payments are indexed to rise with inflation.

■ A *profit sharing plan* calls for the employer to make payments into the retirement fund, but with the payments varying with the level of corporate profits.

☐ These plans are operated like defined contribution plans in the sense that each employee's funds are maintained in a separate account, and benefits depend on the plan's performance.

☐ Payments to the plan rise or fall depending on the level of the firm's profits.

☐ These plans can be operated separately or in conjunction with defined benefit or defined contribution plans.

■ A *cash balance plan* is like a defined benefit plan in some respects and like a defined contribution plan in others.

☐ An account is created for each employee.

☐ The company promises to put a specified percentage of the employee's monthly salary into the plan, and to pay a specified return on the plan's assets, often the T-bill rate.

☐ Employers like the plans because their payment obligations are fixed and known.

The following terms and concepts are used frequently in discussions of pension plans.

■ If employees have a right to receive pension benefits even if they leave the company prior to retirement, then their pension rights are said to be *vested*. If the employee loses his or her pension rights by leaving the company prior to retirement, the rights are said to be *nonvested*.

☐ Defined contribution and profit sharing plans generally provide immediate vesting.

☐ Most defined benefit plans have *deferred vesting,* which means that pension rights are nonvested for the first few years, but become fully vested if the employee remains with the company for a prescribed period.

- The costs to the company are clearly lower for plans with deferred vesting.

- Deferred vesting tends to reduce turnover, which, in turn, lowers training costs.

- It is much easier to recruit employees if the plan offers early vesting.

☐ Companies with defined benefit plans are required to vest participants at least as fast as either the five-year rule (*cliff vesting*) or the 3-to-7-year rule (partial vesting).

■ A *portable* pension plan is one that an employee can carry from one firm to another. It is extremely important in occupations such as construction, where workers move from one employer to another fairly frequently.

☐ Defined contribution plans are always portable, because the plan's assets are held in the employees' names.

- [ ] For a defined benefit plan to be portable, both the old employer and the new employer must be part of the same plan.
- [ ] Cash balance plans are completely portable.

- A plan is said to be *fully funded* if the present value of expected retirement benefits is equal to assets on hand. If assets exceed the present value of benefits, the plan is *overfunded*. Conversely, if the present value of benefits exceeds assets, the plan is *underfunded*, and an *unfunded pension liability* exists.

- The discount rate used to determine the present value of future benefits under a defined benefit plan is called the *actuarial rate of return*.
  - [ ] Higher actuarial rate assumptions lead to lower current contribution requirements for two reasons: (1) the present value of benefits will be lower, and (2) the plan's assets will be assumed to earn more, hence to grow at a faster rate. Thus, the actuarial rate of return has a significant impact on the plan's annual contributions.

- The *Employee Retirement Income Security Act of 1974 (ERISA)* is the basic federal law governing the structure and administration of corporate pension plans. ERISA requires that companies fully fund their defined benefit pension plans, although it gives them up to 30 years to correct for underfunding of past service benefits.
  - [ ] ERISA mandates that pension funds be managed according to the "prudent man" rule, which focuses on diversification as the cornerstone of portfolio management.
  - [ ] ERISA sets the mandatory vesting requirements to prevent situations whereby long-term employees are fired or laid off just before their benefits are vested.

- The *Pension Benefit Guarantee Corporation (PBGC)* was established by ERISA to insure corporate defined benefit pension funds. The PBGC steps in and takes over payments to retirees of bankrupt companies with underfunded pension plans. However, a number of restrictions apply:
  - [ ] PBGC does not cover company-promised health insurance for retirees.
  - [ ] PBGC payments are capped at about $33,000 (in 1997 dollars) per year per plan, which for some highly paid workers, is considerably less than their plan originally promised.
  - [ ] PBGC does not guarantee pensions that are paid by annuities purchased by plans from insurance companies.

- Actuaries calculate annually how much a company must pay into its defined benefit fund in order to keep it fully funded.
  - [ ] These contributions are a tax-deductible expense.
  - [ ] Payments depend on the investment performance of the pension fund.

- If a fund's managers do a good job of investing its assets, then required annual contributions will be reduced, and vice versa if the fund's investment performance is poor.
- ☐ During the 1990s, as a result of the greatest bull market in history, many corporations' pension plans are overfunded to such an extent that they do not have to make any annual contributions.

■ Both the Financial Accounting Standards Board (FASB) and the SEC have established rules that require firms operating pension plans to report specific information in its annual report. While the reporting of defined contribution plans is relatively straightforward, the reporting of defined benefit plans is much more complex.

The calculation of the present value of expected future benefits is of primary importance for defined benefit pension plans. This calculation determines both the required contribution to the fund for the year and the reported unfunded liability or surplus.

■ The rate of return assumed makes a substantial difference in the annual contribution. Assumptions about how long the worker will live, years before retirement, and, if the payment is based on salary, annual raises will have similarly large effects on the required annual contribution.

Different types of plans differ with regard to the certainty of cash contributions, investment earnings, and promised benefits at retirement.

■ In a *defined contribution or cash balance plan,* the corporation, or *plan sponsor,* contributes a guaranteed amount which will be invested for eventual retirement payments to the beneficiaries. No guarantee is made about either the rate of return earned on the funds contributed or the final payments. Thus, the beneficiaries assume the risk of fluctuations in the rate of return on the invested money, so they must bear a risk regarding the level of their retirement incomes.

■ A *profit sharing plan* is similar, except that the sponsor's cash contributions are also uncertain. This increases the risk to the beneficiaries. Retirees' incomes could be quite large or quite small, depending on (1) how profitable the corporation is and (2) how well the plan's assets are managed.

■ In a *defined benefit plan,* the corporate sponsor bears all risks of unexpected variations in rates of return on investment. The resulting annual contributions could vary if the defined benefits are based on some average of the final years' salaries. Further, these contributions cannot be reduced if the corporation's profits fall, as they could be with a profit sharing plan.

■ A defined benefit plan is by far the riskiest from the standpoint of the sponsoring corporation, but the least risky from the standpoint of the employees.

■ Risks to a corporation under a defined benefit plan can be divided into (1) uncertainty about the annual cash contribution and (2) uncertainty about the firm's obligations in the event it goes bankrupt.

☐ The *minimum annual cash contribution* is the sum of (1) the amount needed to fund projected future benefit payments that were accrued during the current period, (2) the amount that must be contributed to make up for not having funded all benefits for service that occurred prior to the current period, and (3) an additional amount required to offset unexpected deviations from the plan's actuarial assumptions, especially deviations in the earned rate of return and in employee turnover and wage rates.

☐ There are three key types of actuarial assumptions which reflect real-world risks:

● *personnel assumptions,* which allow the actuary to adjust annually for the probability that any employee will leave the company;

● *future salary assumptions,* which take into account expected future average wage increases, which will affect the final salary and hence defined benefit payments based on the final salary; and

● *discount rate assumptions,* which explicitly forecast the portfolio's expected future rate of return, which is used both to compound the fund's growth from investment and to discount and thus find the present value of future benefits.

☐ At the end of each year, the assumptions are examined and modified if necessary, and actuaries determine the present value of expected future benefits.

☐ Prior to the passage of ERISA, employees had no claim against a corporation's assets in the event of bankruptcy. By passing ERISA, Congress elevated the priority of unfunded vested pension liabilities in the event of bankruptcy. In the event of a pension plan termination due to bankruptcy, unfunded vested pension liabilities have a lien with the same priority as federal taxes on up to 30 percent of the stockholders' equity.

☐ The value of a firm's stock is affected by its pension plan.

● Researchers have examined the relationship between corporations' market values and their pension fund liabilities. They concluded that investors recognize the existence of unfunded pension liabilities and lower firms' values accordingly.

■ Not all risks associated with defined benefit pension plans are borne by the PBGC or corporate sponsor; its participants can also face uncertainties. For example, bankruptcy of a firm still imposes hardships on workers; it has been a major factor in unions' acceptance of reduced wages and benefits in situations where corporate bankruptcy with corresponding layoffs would otherwise have occurred.

As an employee, choosing between either a defined benefit or a defined contribution plan is not an easy decision to make. It depends on both the specifics of the plans being offered and the unique situation of the individual making the decision.

- A young employee who has a high probability of moving would be better off under a defined contribution plan.

- A cash balance plan would also be better for a potentially mobile employee.

- The economic consequences of changing jobs are much worse under the defined benefit plan because benefits are frozen rather than increased with inflation.

- It is much more costly to a firm to hire older workers if it operates under a defined benefit plan than if it operates under a defined contribution plan.
  - ☐ Defined benefit plans carry with them an economic incentive to discriminate against older workers in hiring, while defined contribution plans are neutral in this regard.

- Employees are generally exposed to more risks under a defined contribution plan, while employers face more risks under a defined benefit plan.
  - ☐ The pension benefits under the defined contribution plan are highly sensitive to changes in the rate of return earned on the pension fund's investments.

- Other factors held constant, there is an economic incentive for employers to discriminate against women in their hiring practices if they use defined benefit plans. Defined contribution plans are again neutral in this regard.

The actual choice of a plan type is often dictated by competitive conditions in the labor market.

- Unions generally seek defined benefit plans to cushion beneficiaries from investment risks inherent in defined contribution and profit sharing plans.

- A defined benefit plan provides tax-planning flexibility because firms can vary the fund contribution from year to year. Thus, in highly profitable years, firms can make large contributions, which decrease taxable income, hence taxes.
  - ☐ Defined contribution plans do not afford such flexibility, because the specified contributions must be made each year regardless of the firm's profitability. However, defined contribution plans do not require firms to increase contributions if the fund's investment performance is poor.

■ In recent years, new firms have tended to adopt defined contribution or profit sharing plans. The regulatory burden of ERISA has driven many older firms to replace defined benefit with defined contribution plans.

■ Assuming a firm has decided on a defined benefit plan, proper strategic planning requires integrating the plan's funding and investment policies into the company's general corporate operations.

   □ The *funding strategy* involves deciding how fast should any unfunded liability be reduced, and what rate of return should be assumed in the actuarial calculations.

   □ The *investment strategy* must determine how a portfolio that minimizes the risk of not achieving an assumed actuarial rate of return should be structured.

   □ Pension fund managers use *asset allocation models* when making funding and investment strategies. Several conclusions emerge from such model runs.

      ● The safety of principal is a paramount consideration, so pension fund managers ought not to "reach" for the highest possible returns.

      ● For a given level of return, the inclusion of more types of assets generally reduces the portfolio's risk, because asset types are not perfectly correlated.

      ● Choices among the possible portfolios are limited by the introduction of managerial constraints.

Three factors have a major influence on pension funds' investments: (1) the dollar amount of assets, (2) the mix of a fund's liabilities between those attributable to active workers and those attributable to retired beneficiaries, and (3) the tax situation facing the corporate sponsor.

■ A common investment tactic involves segregating pension fund assets into two parts: a "retiree portfolio" that provides income to current retirees and a "worker portfolio" that builds value for current workers. Then, as current workers retire, the assets of the fund are shifted from the worker portfolio to the retiree portfolio.

   □ The *retiree portfolio* is usually invested in fixed-income securities that are chosen to produce a cash stream that matches the required retiree pension payments.

      ● In managing the retiree portfolio, fund managers often use *immunization techniques* such as *duration* to eliminate, or at least significantly reduce, the risk associated with changing interest rates.

      ● Matching the duration of the portfolio to the duration of the required payments ensures that any loss of market value due to rising interest rates is offset by additional interest income, and vice versa.

   □ The *worker portfolio* usually includes some relatively risky assets such as stocks and real estate, along with some lower-risk assets such as bonds. To reduce the risk inherent in such a portfolio, pension fund managers often use a hedging technique called *portfolio insurance*, which does not appreciably affect upside potential but limits the downside risk.

- Portfolio insurance involves buying or selling options or futures contracts that would gain about the same amount of value that the portfolio loses if the market takes a sudden fall.

- Pension fund sponsors generally evaluate the performance of portfolio managers on a regular basis and then use this information when allocating the fund's assets among portfolio managers.
  - *Alpha analysis* adds substantially to a pension manager's knowledge about his or her equity portfolio's results.
    - Alpha measures the vertical distance of a portfolio's return above or below the Security Market Line.
    - Alpha is the portfolio's extra return (positive or negative) after adjusting for the portfolio's market risk.
  - Several shortcomings of alpha analysis must be recognized.
    - Alpha is based on the CAPM which in theory requires all risky assets be included in the market portfolio. Market proxies result in some degree of measurement error.
    - The statistical significance of alpha is often too low to make strong statements about the portfolio's relative performance.
    - All of the measurements are based on ex post results which contain both expected returns and unanticipated returns caused by random economic events. Thus, a large positive alpha may indicate good luck rather than good management.
  - Another way to measure portfolio performance is *peer comparison*. At the end of each year, managers with similar investment objectives can be ranked on the basis of total realized return.

There is an ongoing debate about whether excess assets in a defined benefit plan belong to the sponsoring company or to the employees. Legally, they belong to the company, but a number of union leaders have argued that they ought to belong to the workers.

With the population aging and health care costs soaring, at many companies the liability of estimated future costs represents 20 to 40 percent of the firm's net worth.

- Corporate planners and consultants say that changes to retiree health care benefits are likely to become more prevalent and more profound.
  - Possibilities range from cutting back benefits for retirees, forcing them into managed care plans, or even eliminating retiree health care altogether.

■ The most important factor forcing companies to consider health care benefits is the FASB rule, FASB Statement 106, that requires companies to set up a reserve for future medical benefits of retirees.

■ The rationale behind FASB Statement 106 is clear: Retiree health care costs should be reported just like pension costs—at the time the benefits are earned by workers.

SELF-TEST QUESTIONS

Definitional

1. The _____ _____ _____ typically administers the pension plan.

2. A(n) _____ _____ plan is one in which a company agrees to make specific payments into a retirement fund and then retirees receive benefits from the plan that depend on the plan's investment success.

3. Under a(n) _____ _____ plan the employer agrees to give retirees a specific amount, such as $500 per month or 50 percent of his or her last salary.

4. A(n) _____ _____ plan calls for the employer to make payments into the retirement fund, but with the payments varying with the level of corporate profits.

5. Under a(n) _____ _____ plan the company promises to put a specified percentage of the employee's monthly salary into the plan, and to pay a specified return on the plan's assets.

6. If employees have a right to receive pension benefits even if they leave the company prior to retirement, then their pension rights are said to be _____; if the employee loses pension rights if he or she leaves the company prior to retirement, the rights are said to be _____.

7. Most defined benefit plans today have _____ _____, where pension rights are nonvested for the first few years, but become fully vested if the employee remains with the company for a prescribed period.

8. A(n) _____ pension plan is one that an employee can carry from one firm to another.

9. A plan is said to be _____ _____ if the present value of expected retirement benefits is equal to assets on hand.

10. If assets exceed the present value of benefits, the plan is _____.

11. If the present value of benefits exceeds assets, the plan is _____, and a(n) _____ _____ _____ exists.

12. The _____ _____ _____ _____ _____ of 1974 is the basic federal law governing the structure and administration of corporate pension plans.

13. The _____ _____ _____ _____ was established to insure corporate defined benefit pension funds.

14. In a defined benefit plan, the _____ _____ assumes all risks of unexpected variations in rates of return on investments.

15. The _____ _____ _____ _____ is the sum of the amount needed to fund projected future benefit payments that were accrued during the current period, the amount that must be contributed to make up for not having funded all benefits for service that occurred prior to the current period, and an additional amount required to offset unexpected deviations from the plan's actuarial assumptions.

16. There are three key types of actuarial assumptions which reflect real-world risks— _____ assumptions, which allow the actuary to adjust annually for the probability that any employee will leave the company, _____ _____ assumptions, and _____ _____ assumptions.

17. Three factors have a major influence on pension funds' investments: (1) the _____ _____ of assets, (2) the _____ of a fund's liabilities between those attributable to active workers and those attributable to retired beneficiaries, and (3) the _____ situation facing the corporate sponsor.

Conceptual

18. Under a defined benefit plan, employees agree to contribute some percentage of their salaries, up to 20 percent, to the firm's pension fund.

    a. True   b. False

19. If employees have a right to receive pension benefits even if they leave the company prior to retirement, their pension rights are said to be deferred.

   a. True   **b.** False

20. From a pure cost standpoint, a firm with a defined benefit plan would be more likely to hire older workers than a firm with a defined contribution plan.

   a. True   **b.** False

21. The performance measurement of stock portfolio managers must recognize the risk inherent in the investment portfolio. One way to incorporate risk into performance measurement is to examine the portfolio's z-score, which measures the vertical distance of the portfolio's return above or below the Security Market Line.

   a. True   **b.** False

22. Which of the following statements about pension plans is most correct?

   a. A defined contribution plan is, in effect, a savings plan that is funded by employers, although many plans also permit additional contributions by employees.
   b. Under a defined benefit plan, the employer agrees to give retirees a specifically defined benefit, such as $500 per month or 50 percent of his or her last salary.
   c. A portable pension plan is one that an employee can carry from one employer to another.
   d. An employer's obligation is satisfied under a defined benefit plan when it makes the required contributions to the plan. The risk of inadequate investment returns is borne by the employee.
   e. Statements a, b, and c are all correct.

23.   Which of the following statements about defined contribution plans is *incorrect*?

    a. A defined contribution plan places the risk of poor pension portfolio performance on the employee.

    b. In general, employees can choose the investment vehicle under a defined contribution plan. Thus, highly risk-averse employees can choose low-risk investments, while more risk-tolerant employees can choose high-risk investments.

    c. In a defined contribution plan, the employer must make larger-than-average contributions to the pension plan when investment returns have been below expectations.

    d. Large corporations tend to use defined benefit plans, while small corporations tend to use defined contribution plans.

24.   Which of the following statements about pension plan portfolio performance is *incorrect*?

    a. Pension fund sponsors must evaluate the performance of their portfolio managers periodically as a basis for future asset allocations.

    b. Alpha analysis, which relies on the Capital Asset Pricing Model, considers the risk of the portfolio when measuring performance.

    c. Peer comparison examines the relative performance of portfolio managers with different investment objectives.

    d. A portfolio annual return of 12 percent from one investment advisor is not necessarily better than a return of 10 percent from another advisor.

    e. Index fund managers are evaluated against the index whose returns they attempt to match.

SELF-TEST PROBLEMS

1.   The Apex Company has just hired Mr. Smith, who is age 25 and is expected to retire at age 60. Mr. Smith's current salary is $30,000 per year, but his wages are expected to increase by 5 percent annually over the next 35 years. Apex has a defined benefit pension plan in which workers receive 1.5 percent of their final year's wages for each year of employment. Assume a world of certainty. Further, assume that all payments occur at year-end. What is Mr. Smith's approximate expected annual retirement benefit rounded to the nearest thousand?

    a. $35,000   **b.** $57,000   **c.** $87,000   **d.** $116,000   **e.** $132,000

2.   Midwest Investment Consultants (MIC) operates several stock investment portfolios that
      are used by firms for investment of pension plan assets. Last year, one portfolio had a
      realized return of 12.6 percent and a beta coefficient of 1.25. The average T-bond rate
      was 7 percent and the realized rate of return on the S&P 500 was 12 percent. What was
      the portfolio's alpha?

      a. -0.65%   **b.** -0.25%   **c.** 0%   **d.** +0.25%   **e.** +0.65%

3.   The Ritz Company has a 40-year old employee that will retire at age 60 and live to age
      75. The firm has promised a retirement income of $20,000 at the end of each year
      following retirement until death. The firm's pension fund is expected to earn 7 percent
      annually on its assets. What is Ritz's annual pension contribution for this employee?
      (Assume certainty and end-of-year cash flows.)

      a. $2,756   **b.** $3,642   **c.** $4,443   **d.** $4,967   **e.** $5,491

ANSWERS TO SELF-TEST QUESTIONS

1. chief financial officer
2. defined contribution
3. defined benefit
4. profit sharing
5. cash balance
6. vested; nonvested
7. deferred vesting
8. portable
9. fully funded
10. overfunded
11. underfunded; unfunded
      pension liability

12. Employee Retirement Income
      Security Act
13. Pension Benefit Guarantee
      Corporation
14. corporate sponsor
15. minimum annual cash
      contribution
16. personnel; future salary;
      discount rate
17. dollar amount; mix; tax

18. b. Under a defined benefit plan, the employer agrees to give retirees a specifically
      defined benefit.

19. b. The employee's pension rights are vested.

20. b. It is much more costly to a company to hire older workers if it operates under a
      defined benefit plan than if it operates under a defined contribution plan.

21. b. Alpha analysis adds substantially to a pension manager's knowledge about his or her equity portfolio's results. Alpha measures the vertical distance of a portfolio's return above or below the Security Market Line.

22. e. The risk of inadequate investment returns in a defined benefit plan are borne by the corporate sponsor.

23. c. In a defined contribution plan, the corporate sponsor agrees to make *specific* payments.

24. c. Peer comparison examines the relative performance of portfolio managers with similar investment objectives.

SOLUTIONS TO SELF-TEST PROBLEMS

1. c. Final year's salary = $30,000(1.05)^{35}$ = \$165,480.46.
   Salary multiplier = 35(1.5%) = 52.5%.
   Pension benefit = 0.525($165,480.46) = $86,877.24 \approx $87,000.

2. a. Portfolio's required rate of return $= k_{RF} + (k_M - k_{RF})b$
   $$= 7\% + (12\% - 7\%)1.25$$
   $$= 7\% + (5\%)1.25 = 13.25\%.$$

   Alpha = 12.6% - 13.25% = -0.65%.

3. c. Find the PV (at retirement) of the 15-year pension payment:
   $20,000(PVIFA_{7\%,\ 15\ years})$ = \$182,158.28.

   Alternatively, using a financial calculator input the following: N = 15, I = 7, PMT = 20000, FV = 0, and then solve for PV = \$182,158.28.

   Find the annual payment needed to accumulate the above amount over 20 years:
   Annual payment = $182,158.28(FVIFA_{7\%,\ 20\ years})$ = \$4,443.37.

   Alternatively, using a financial calculator input the following: N = 20, I = 7, PV = 0, FV = 182158.28, and then solve for PMT = \$4,443.37.

OVERVIEW

Financial management is also important in not-for-profit businesses, defined as corporations which charge a fee for their services and are expected to generate enough revenues to cover costs, but which have neither outstanding stock nor stockholders. Indeed, the healthcare industry, which is one of the fastest growing sectors of the economy, includes thousands of not-for-profit businesses. Such firms require the same financial management skills as do investor-owned firms, but they do not have stockholders, and their goal is not shareholder wealth maximization. This difference in goals between profit and not-for-profit businesses leads to some interesting contrasts in the financial management of the two types of organizations.

OUTLINE

Not-for-profit businesses differ considerably from for-profit, or investor-owned, firms.

- ■ *Investor-owned firms* have three key characteristics.
  - □ The owners (stockholders) are well defined, and they exercise control by voting for the firm's board of directors.
  - □ The firm's residual earnings belong to its stockholders, so management is responsible to the stockholders for the firm's profitability.
  - □ The firm is subject to taxation at the federal, state, and local levels.

- ■ Unlike an investor-owned firm, a *not-for-profit firm* can qualify as a *tax-exempt* corporation if it fits the definition of a charitable organization and hence qualifies as a *501(c)(3) corporation.*
  - □ In addition to being organized for a charitable purpose, a not-for-profit corporation must be administered so that (1) it operates exclusively for the public, (2) none of the profits is used for private inurement, (3) no political activity is conducted, and (4) if liquidation occurs, the assets will continue to be used for a charitable purpose.

☐ Since not-for-profit businesses have no shareholders, no group of individuals has ownership rights to the firm's residual earnings. No outside group exercises control of the firm; rather, control is exercised by a *board of trustees* which is not constrained by outside oversight.

☐ Individual contributions to 501(c)(3) corporations can be deducted from taxable income by the donor, so not-for-profit businesses have access to tax-advantaged contribution capital.

■ There are almost an unlimited number of ways of organizing within the corporate structure.

☐ At the most basic level, a not-for-profit business can be a single entity with one operating unit. All financial management decisions are performed by a single set of managers who must raise the needed capital and decide how to allocate it within the organization.

☐ Alternatively, corporations can be set up with separate operating divisions or as holding companies, with wholly owned or partially owned subsidiaries.

● Holding companies are especially useful when a corporation is engaged in both for-profit and not-for-profit activities.

■ The inherent differences between investor-owned and not-for-profit organizations have profound implications for many elements of financial management, including defining the goals of the firm and making financing and capital budgeting decisions.

Since not-for-profit businesses do not have stockholders, shareholder wealth maximization cannot be the goal of such organizations. Rather, not-for-profit businesses serve and are served by a number of stakeholders, which include all parties that have an interest (financial or otherwise) in the organization.

■ Managers of not-for-profit businesses must try to please all the *stakeholders* because there is no single, well-defined group which exercises control.

■ Typically, the goal of a not-for-profit business is stated in terms of some *mission*.

☐ Typically, the mission statement provides managers and employees with a framework for developing specific goals and objectives.

☐ Financially weak organizations cannot continue to accomplish their stated missions over the long run.

Cost of capital estimation for not-for-profit businesses parallels that for investor-owned businesses, but there are two major differences: (1) Since not-for-profit businesses pay no taxes, there are no tax effects associated with debt financing. (2) Not-for-profit businesses raise the equivalent of equity capital, called fund capital.

■ *Fund capital* is raised in three ways: (1) by earning profits, which by law must be retained within the business, (2) by receiving grants from governmental entities, and (3) by receiving contributions from individuals and companies.

■ Fund capital is fundamentally different from equity capital.

■ Determining the *opportunity cost of fund capital* has been controversial. Historically, at least four positions have been taken with regard to the cost of fund capital:

☐ Fund capital has zero cost, since contributors do not expect a monetary return on their contributions, and the firm's other stakeholders do not require an explicit return on the capital retained by the firm.

☐ In addition to a zero cost, it has been recognized that, when inflation exists, fund capital must earn a return sufficient to enable the organization to replace existing assets as they wear out.

☐ Fund capital has some cost but it is not very high, probably roughly equal to the return available on a portfolio of short-term, low-risk securities such as T-bills.

☐ Fund capital to not-for-profit businesses has about the same cost as the cost of retained earnings to similar investor-owned firms. This "opportunity cost" can be defined as the return available from investing the fund capital in alternative investments of similar risk.

■ In general, the *opportunity cost principle* applies to all fund capital—this capital has a cost which is equal to the cost of retained earnings to similar investor-owned firms.

☐ However, contributions that are designated for a specific purpose may indeed have a zero cost. Since the funds are *restricted* to a particular project, the firm does not have the opportunity to invest them in other alternatives.

When making capital structure decisions within not-for-profit businesses, managers must decide to what extent capital structure theory applies to their own not-for-profit businesses.

■ Although not-for-profit businesses do not pay taxes, many of these businesses have access to the tax-exempt debt market. As a result, not-for-profit businesses have about the same effective cost of debt as do investor-owned firms.

■ Not-for-profit businesses are subject to the same types of financial distress and agency costs that are borne by investor-owned firms. Therefore, we would expect the *trade-off theory* to be applicable to not-for-profit businesses.

☐ Such businesses should have *optimal capital structures* which are defined as a trade-off between the costs and benefits of debt financing.

☐ Problems can arise, however in practice: Not-for-profit firms do not have access to the equity markets—their sole source of "equity" capital is through government grants, private contributions, and profits.

■ Managers of not-for-profit businesses do not have the same degree of flexibility in either capital investment or capital structure decisions as do their counterparts in for-profit firms.
   ☐ For this reason, it is often necessary for not-for-profit businesses to delay new projects because of funding insufficiencies, and to use more than the theoretically optimal amount of debt.

The primary goal of a not-for-profit business is to provide some service to society, not to maximize shareholder wealth. Thus, capital budgeting decisions must consider many factors besides the project's profitability. Noneconomic factors such as the community's well-being must also be taken into account, and these factors may outweigh financial considerations.

■ Nevertheless, good decision making, designed to ensure the future viability of the organization, requires that the financial impact of each capital investment be fully recognized.

In general, the same project analysis techniques that are applicable to investor-owned firms are also applicable to not-for-profit businesses. However, project analysis should consider social value along with financial, or cash flow, value.

■ When *social value* is considered, the total net present value (TNPV) can be expressed as

$$TNPV = NPV + NPSV,$$

where NPV is the standard net present value of the project's cash flow stream, and NPSV is the net present social value of the project.

■ A project is deemed to be acceptable if its TNPV is greater than or equal to zero.

■ To ensure the financial viability of the firm, the sum of the NPVs of all projects initiated in a planning period, plus the value of the unrestricted contributions received, must equal or exceed zero.
   ☐ If this restriction were not imposed, social value could displace financial value over time. This would not be a sustainable situation because a firm cannot continue to provide social value unless its financial integrity is maintained.

■   In estimating a project's NPSV, it is necessary (1) to quantify the social value of the services provided by the project in each year, and (2) to determine the discount rate that is to be applied to those services.

■   Not-for-profit businesses are often subject to *capital rationing*.

Risk analysis of not-for-profit firms differs in many ways from that of investor-owned firms.

■   For not-for-profit businesses, stand-alone risk would be relevant if a firm had only one project. However, most not-for-profit businesses offer a myriad of different products or services; thus, they can be thought of as having a large number of individual projects. Thus, the *relevant risk* of a new project is its *corporate risk*, which is the contribution of the project to the firm's overall risk as measured by the impact of the project on the variability of the firm's overall profitability.

■   As with investor-owned firms, in most situations it is very difficult to develop accurate quantitative assessments of projects' corporate risk. Therefore, managers are often left with only an assessment of a project's stand-alone risk plus a subjective notion about how it fits into the firm's other operations.

■   Capital budgeting decisions in not-for-profit organizations require the blending of objective and subjective factors to reach a conclusion about a project's risk, social value, effects on debt capacity, profitability, and overall acceptability.

While not-for-profit businesses have access to many of the same types of capital as do investor-owned firms, there are two major differences: (1) not-for-profit firms can issue tax-exempt debt, but (2) they cannot issue equity, although they can solicit tax-exempt contributions, and their earnings are not taxable and must be retained.

■   Not-for-profit businesses can issue *tax-exempt*, or *municipal*, *bonds*, generally called "munis."
  □ There are several types of munis:
      ● *General obligation bonds* are secured by the full faith and credit of a government unit, whereas *special tax bonds* are secured by a specific tax.
      ● *Revenue bonds* are those bonds where the revenues derived from such projects as roads, bridges, airports, water and sewage systems, and not-for-profit healthcare facilities are pledged as security for the bonds.
  □ Most municipal bonds are sold in *serial* form, which means that a portion of the issue comes due periodically, generally every six months or every year, over the life of the issue.

☐ In contrast to regular corporate bonds, municipal issues are not required to be registered with the SEC.

☐ About half of all munis outstanding are held by individual investors, in large part because of the munis' exemption from federal and state (in the state of issue) taxes.

☐ Unique to municipal bonds, *credit enhancement,* or *bond insurance,* is used for upgrading an issue's rating to AAA.

- A bond insurance company guarantees that bondholders will receive the promised interest and principal payments, regardless of the inherent credit rating of the issuer. Thus, bond insurance protects investors against default by the issuer.

- The bond carries the credit rating of the insurance company, not the issuer.

- There is a premium charged for this insurance.

■ While not-for-profit businesses can retain earnings, they cannot sell stock to raise equity capital. They can, however, raise equity capital through *charitable contributions.*

☐ Charitable contributions are often *restricted,* which means that they can be used only for a designated purpose.

SELF-TEST QUESTIONS

Definitional

1. Unlike an investor-owned firm, a _____-_____-_____ firm can qualify as a _____-_____ corporation if it fits the definition of a charitable organization and hence qualifies as a 501(c)(3) corporation.

2. In addition to being organized for a _____ _____, a not-for-profit corporation must be administered so that it operates exclusively for the _____, none of the profits are used for _____ _____, no political activity is conducted, and, if liquidation occurs, the assets will continue to be used for a _____ _____.

3. No outside group exercises control of the not-for-profit business; rather, control is exercised by a _____ ____ _____, which is not constrained by outside oversight.

4. Since not-for-profit businesses do not have stockholders, _____ _____ _____ cannot be the goal of such organizations. Rather, not-for-profit businesses serve and are served by a number of _____, which include all parties that have an interest in the organization.

5. Typically, the goal of a not-for-profit business is stated in terms of some _____.

6. Cost of capital estimation for not-for-profit businesses is similar to investor-owned businesses, but there are two major differences: (1) Since not-for-profit businesses pay no taxes, there are no tax effects associated with _____ _____. (2) Not-for-profit businesses raise the equivalent of equity capital, called _____ _____.

7. Fund capital is raised in three ways: (1) by _____ _____, which by law must be retained within the business; (2) by _____ _____ from governmental entities; and (3) by _____ _____ from individuals and companies.

8. In general, the opportunity cost principle applies to all fund capital—this capital has a cost which is equal to the cost of _____ _____ to similar _____- _____ _____.

9. Although not-for-profit businesses do not pay taxes, many of these businesses have access to the _____-_____ _____ market. Thus, not-for-profit businesses have about the same effective cost of debt as do _____-_____ _____.

10. Capital budgeting decisions in the not-for-profit firm must consider many factors besides the project's profitability. _____ factors such as the community's well-being must also be taken into account, and these factors may outweigh _____ considerations.

11. Project analysis within the not-for-profit firm should consider _____ _____ along with _____, or cash flow, value.

12. To ensure the financial viability of the firm, the sum of the _____ of all projects initiated in a planning period, plus the value of the _____ _____ received, must equal or exceed zero.

13. _____ _____ bonds are secured by the full faith and credit of a government unit, whereas _____ _____ bonds are secured by a specified tax.

14. Unique to municipal bonds, _____ _____, or _____ _____, is used for upgrading an issue's rating to AAA.

15. In contrast to regular corporate bonds, _____ _____ are not required to be registered with the SEC.

Conceptual

16. The primary goal of investor-owned firms is shareholder wealth maximization, while the primary goal of not-for-profit firms is to maximize managers' utility.

    a. True   **b.** False

17. Not-for-profit firms have fund capital in place of equity capital. Since fund capital does not have to provide a return to stockholders, its appropriate cost is the return available on short-term Treasury securities.

    a. True   **b.** False

18. Not-for-profit firms do not pay taxes, but they still receive tax benefits from debt financing because they can issue municipal (tax-exempt) debt.

    a. True   **b.** False

19. The net present social value model formally recognizes that not-for-profit firms must consider the social value along with the financial value of proposed new projects, but it does not recognize the time value of social value.

    a. True   **b.** False

20. Which of the following statements about project risk analysis in not-for-profit firms is *false*?

    a. The market risk of a project is not relevant to not-for-profit firms.
    b. A project's corporate beta measures the contribution of the project to the overall corporate risk of the firm.
    c. A project's corporate beta is found (at least conceptually) by regressing returns on the project against returns on the firm.
    d. A project's corporate beta is defined as $(\sigma_P/\sigma_F)r_{PF}$, where σ_P is the standard deviation of the project's returns, σ_F is the standard deviation of the firm's returns, and r_{PF} is the correlation among the two sets of returns.
    e. In practice, it is usually easy to directly measure a project's corporate risk, so stand-alone risk plays no role in project risk analysis.

21. Which of the following statements about municipal bond financing is most correct?

    a. In contrast to corporate bonds, municipal bond issues are not required to be registered with the Securities and Exchange Commission.

    b. Whereas the vast majority of Treasury and corporate bonds are held by institutions, about half of all municipal bonds are held by individual investors.

    c. The primary attraction of municipal bonds to individual investors is their high before-tax yields.

    d. Municipal bonds issued in one state are free from state taxes in all states.

    e. Statements a and b are correct.

22. Which of the following statements about a not-for-profit firm's ownership is most correct?

    a. Not-for-profit firms are governed by a board of trustees whose members are elected by the community at large.

    b. The residual earnings (profits) of not-for-profit firms can be distributed to the firm's top managers.

    c. Not-for-profit firms are exempt from federal, state, and local taxes, including property taxes.

    d. Upon liquidation of a not-for-profit firm, the proceeds from the sale of its assets are distributed, on a pro rata basis, to the firm's employees.

    e. Not-for-profit firms issue municipal debt directly to investors.

23. Which of the following statements about a not-for-profit firm's cost of capital estimate is most correct?

    a. Since a not-for-profit firm has no shareholders, its WACC estimate does not include a cost of equity (fund capital) estimate.

    b. The capital structure weights for a not-for-profit firm are set at 50/50, because such firms can raise $1 of debt financing for each dollar of retained earnings.

    c. The cost of tax-exempt debt issued by not-for-profit firms is increased ("grossed up") by 1 - T in the WACC estimate to reflect the fact that such firms do not pay taxes.

    d. Equity (fund) capital has a cost that is roughly equivalent to the cost of retained earnings to similar investor-owned companies.

    e. None of the statements above are correct.

24.   Which of the following statements about a not-for-profit firm's fund capital is most correct?

    a. Fund capital is equivalent to equity capital in investor-owned firms.
    b. The sources of fund capital include the excess of revenues over expenses, contributions, and government grants.
    c. Fund capital, like equity capital, has an opportunity cost associated with it.
    d. Only statements a and c are correct.
    e. Statements a, b, and c are correct.

25.   Which of the following statements about a not-for-profit firm's sources of capital is most correct?

    a. Since not-for-profit firms are tax exempt, there is no tax advantage to debt capital.
    b. Fund capital is obtained by retaining earnings—if all earnings are paid out as dividends, no fund capital is created.
    c. Preferred stock is never used by not-for-profit firms.
    d. Statements a and b are correct.
    e. Statements a, b, and c are correct.

ANSWERS TO SELF-TEST QUESTIONS

1.   not-for-profit; tax-exempt
2.   charitable purpose; public; private inurement; charitable purpose
3.   board of trustees
4.   shareholder wealth maximization; stakeholders
5.   mission
6.   debt financing; fund capital
7.   earning profits; receiving grants; receiving contributions
8.   retained earnings; investor-owned firms
9.   tax-exempt debt; investor-owned firms
10.   Noneconomic; financial
11.   social value; financial
12.   NPVs; unrestricted contributions
13.   General obligation; special tax
14.   credit enhancement; bond insurance
15.   municipal issues

16.   b.   Typically, the goal of a not-for-profit business is stated in terms of some mission.

17.   b.   In general, the opportunity cost principle applies to all fund capital—this capital has a cost which is equal to the cost of retained earnings to similar investor-owned firms.

18.   a.   This statement is correct.

19. b. The total net present value of a project can be expressed as the net present value of the project's cash flow stream and the net present social value of the project.

20. e. In most situations, it is very difficult, if not impossible, to develop accurate quantitative assessments of projects' corporate risk.

21. e. The primary attraction of most municipal bonds is their exemption from federal and state (in the state of issue) taxes.

22. c. Not-for-profit firms are controlled by a board of trustees but not elected by the community; residual earnings must be retained within the firm; and if the firm is liquidated, the assets must continue to be used for a charitable purpose.

23. d. In general, the opportunity cost principle applies to all fund capital.

24. e. Statements a, b, and c are correct.

25. c. Since individuals cannot benefit from not-for-profit corporations' profits, such organizations cannot pay dividends; therefore, no common or preferred stock is sold.

CHAPTER 25
RISK AND RETURN I

OVERVIEW

Risk is an important concept in financial analysis, especially in terms of how it affects security prices and rates of return. Investment risk is associated with the probability of low or negative future returns.

The riskiness of an asset can be considered in two ways: (1) on a stand-alone basis, where the asset's cash flows are analyzed all by themselves, or (2) in a portfolio context, where the cash flows from a number of assets are combined and then the consolidated cash flows are analyzed.

In a portfolio context, an asset's risk can be divided into two components: (1) a diversifiable risk component, which can be diversified away and hence is of little concern to diversified investors, and (2) a market risk component, which reflects the risk of a general stock market decline and which cannot be eliminated by diversification, hence does concern investors. Only market risk is relevant; diversifiable risk is irrelevant to most investors because it can be eliminated.

An attempt has been made to quantify market risk with a measure called beta. Beta is a measurement of how a particular firm's stock returns move relative to overall movements of stock market returns. The Capital Asset Pricing Model (CAPM), using the concept of beta and investors' aversion to risk, specifies the relationship between market risk and the required rate of return. This relationship can be visualized graphically with the Security Market Line (SML). The slope of the SML can change, or the line can shift upward or downward, in response to changes in risk or required rates of return.

In this chapter, we define precisely what the term risk means as it relates to investments, examine procedures managers use to measure risk, and discuss the relationship between risk and return.

OUTLINE

With most investments, an individual or business spends money today with the expectation of earning even more money in the future. The concept of return provides investors with a convenient way of expressing the financial performance of an investment.

■   One way of expressing an investment return is in *dollar terms*.

Dollar return = Amount received − Amount invested.

- ☐ Expressing returns in dollars is easy, but two problems arise.
- ☐ To make a meaningful judgment about the adequacy of the return, you need to know the scale (size) of the investment.
- ☐ You also need to know the timing of the return.

■ The solution to the scale and timing problems of dollar returns is to express investment results as *rates of return*, or *percentage returns*.

$$\text{Rate of return} = \frac{\text{Amount received} - \text{Amount invested}}{\text{Amount invested}}.$$

- ☐ The rate of return calculation "standardizes" the return by considering the return per unit of investment.
- ☐ Expressing rates of return on an annual basis solves the timing problem.
- ☐ Rate of return is the most common measure of investment performance.

Risk refers to the chance that some unfavorable event will occur. Investment risk is related to the probability of actually earning less than the expected return; thus, the greater the chance of low or negative returns, the riskier the investment.

■ An asset's risk can be analyzed in two ways: (1) on a *stand-alone basis,* where the asset is considered in isolation, and (2) on a *portfolio basis,* where the asset is held as one of a number of assets in a portfolio.
- ☐ An asset's *stand-alone risk* is the risk an investor would face if he or she held only this one asset.

■ No investment will be undertaken unless the expected rate of return is high enough to compensate the investor for the perceived risk of the investment.

■ The *probability distribution* for an event is the listing of all the possible outcomes for the event, with mathematical probabilities assigned to each.
- ☐ An event's *probability* is defined as the chance that the event will occur.
- ☐ The sum of the probabilities for a particular event must equal 1.0, or 100 percent.

■ The *expected rate of return* ($\hat{k}$) is the sum of the products of each possible outcome times its associated probability—it is a weighted average of the various possible outcomes, with the weights being their probabilities of occurrence:

$$\text{Expected rate of return} = \hat{k} = \sum_{i=1}^{n} P_i\, k_i .$$

☐ Where the number of possible outcomes is virtually unlimited, *continuous probability distributions* are used in determining the expected rate of return of the event.

☐ The tighter, or more peaked, the probability distribution, the more likely it is that the actual outcome will be close to the expected value, and, consequently, the less likely it is that the actual return will end up far below the expected return. Thus, the tighter the probability distribution, the lower the risk assigned to a stock.

■ One measure for determining the tightness of a distribution is the *standard deviation, σ.*

$$\text{Standard deviation} = \sigma = \sqrt{\sum_{i=1}^{n} (k_i - \hat{k})^2 P_i}.$$

☐ The standard deviation is a probability-weighted average deviation from the expected value, and it gives you an idea of how far above or below the expected value the actual value is likely to be.

■ Another useful measure of risk is the *coefficient of variation (CV)*, which is the standard deviation divided by the expected return. It shows the risk per unit of return, and it provides a more meaningful basis for comparison when the expected returns on two alternatives are not the same:

$$\text{Coefficient of variation (CV)} = \frac{\sigma}{\hat{k}}.$$

☐ Because the coefficient of variation captures the effects of both risk and return, it is a better measure for evaluating risk in situations where investments have substantially different expected returns.

■ Most investors are *risk averse.* This means that for two alternatives with the same expected rate of return, investors will choose the one with the lower risk.

■ In a market dominated by risk-averse investors, riskier securities must have higher expected returns, as estimated by the marginal investor, than less risky securities. If this situation does not hold, buying and selling in the market will force it to occur.

An asset held as part of a portfolio is less risky than the same asset held in isolation. This is important, because most financial assets are not held in isolation; rather, they are held as parts of portfolios. From the investor's standpoint, what is important is the return on his or her portfolio, and the portfolio's risk—not the fact that a particular stock goes up or down. Thus, the risk and return of an individual security should be analyzed in terms of how it affects the risk and return of the portfolio in which it is held.

■ The expected return on a portfolio, $\hat{k}_p$, is the weighted average of the expected returns on the individual assets in the portfolio, with the weights being the fraction of the total portfolio invested in each asset:

$$\hat{k}_p = \sum_{i=1}^{n} w_i \hat{k}_i.$$

■ The riskiness of a portfolio, σ_p, is generally *not* a weighted average of the standard deviations of the individual assets in the portfolio; the portfolio's standard deviation will be smaller than the weighted average of the assets' σs. The riskiness of a portfolio depends not only on the standard deviations of the individual stocks, but also on the *correlation between the stocks.*

☐ The tendency of two variables to move together is called *correlation.*

☐ The *correlation coefficient, r,* measures the tendency of two variables to move together. With stocks, these variables are the individual stock returns.

☐ Diversification does nothing to reduce risk if the portfolio consists of *perfectly positively correlated* stocks.

☐ As a rule, the riskiness of a portfolio will decline as the number of stocks in the portfolio increases.

☐ In the real world, where the correlations among the individual stocks are generally positive but less than +1.0, some, but not all, risk can be eliminated.

☐ In the real world, it is impossible to form completely riskless stock portfolios. *Diversification* can reduce risk, but cannot eliminate it.

■ While very large portfolios end up with a substantial amount of risk, it is not as much risk as if all the money were invested in only one stock. Almost half of the riskiness inherent in an average individual stock can be eliminated if the stock is held in a reasonably well-diversified portfolio, which is one containing 40 or more stocks.

☐ *Diversifiable risk* is that part of the risk of a stock which can be eliminated. It is caused by events that are unique to a particular firm.

☐ *Market risk* is that part of the risk which cannot be eliminated, and it stems from factors which systematically affect most firms, such as war, inflation, recessions, and high interest rates.

• It can be measured by the degree to which a given stock tends to move up or down with the market.

• Market risk is the *relevant* risk, which reflects a security's contribution to the portfolio's risk.

☐ The *Capital Asset Pricing Model* is an important tool for analyzing the relationship between risk and rates of return.

- The model is based on the proposition that any stock's required rate of return is equal to the risk-free rate of return plus a risk premium, which reflects only the risk remaining after diversification.
- Its primary conclusion is: The relevant riskiness of an individual stock is its contribution to the riskiness of a well-diversified portfolio.

The risk that remains after diversifying is market risk, or the risk that is inherent in the market, and it can be measured by the degree to which a given stock tends to move up or down with the market. The tendency of a stock to move with the market is reflected in its beta coefficient, b, which is a measure of the stock's volatility relative to that of an average stock.

■ An *average-risk stock* is defined as one that tends to move up and down in step with the general market. By definition it has a beta of 1.0.

■ A stock that is twice as volatile as the market will have a beta of 2.0, while a stock that is half as volatile as the market will have a beta coefficient of 0.5.

■ Since a stock's beta measures its contribution to the riskiness of a portfolio, beta is the theoretically correct measure of the stock's riskiness.

■ The beta coefficient of a portfolio of securities is the weighted average of the individual securities' betas:

$$b_p = \sum_{i=1}^{n} w_i b_i.$$

The Capital Asset Pricing Model (CAPM) employs the concept of beta, which measures risk as the relationship between a particular stock's movements and the movements of the overall stock market. The CAPM uses a stock's beta, in conjunction with the average investor's degree of risk aversion, to calculate the return that investors require, k_s, on that particular stock.

■ The *Security Market Line (SML)* shows the relationship between risk as measured by beta and the required rate of return for individual securities. The SML equation can be used to find the required rate of return on Stock i:

$$\text{SML: } k_i = k_{RF} + (k_M - k_{RF})b_i.$$

■ Here k_{RF} is the rate of interest on risk-free securities, b_i is the *i*th stock's beta, and k_M is the return on the market or, alternatively, on an average stock.

□ The term $k_M - k_{RF}$ is the *market risk premium, RP_M*. This is a measure of the additional return over the risk-free rate needed to compensate investors for assuming an average amount of risk.

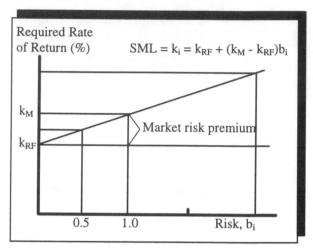

□ In the CAPM, the market risk premium, $k_M - k_{RF}$, is multiplied by the stock's beta coefficient to determine the additional premium over the risk-free rate that is required to compensate investors for the risk inherent in a particular stock.

□ This premium may be larger or smaller than the premium required on an average stock, depending on the riskiness of that stock in relation to the overall market as measured by the stock's beta.

□ The risk premium calculated by $(k_M - k_{RF})b_i$ is added to the risk-free rate, k_{RF} (the rate on Treasury securities), to determine the total rate of return required by investors on a particular stock, k_s.

□ The slope of the SML, $(k_M - k_{RF})$, shows the increase in the required rate of return for a one unit increase in risk. It reflects the degree of risk aversion in the economy.

■ Both the Security Market Line and a company's position on it change over time due to changes in interest rates, investor's aversion to risk, and individual companies' betas.

■ The risk-free (also known as the nominal, or quoted) rate of interest consists of two elements: (1) a real inflation-free rate of return, k^*, and (2) an inflation premium, IP, equal to the anticipated rate of inflation.

□ The real rate on long-term Treasury bonds has historically ranged from 2 to 4 percent, with a mean of about 3 percent.

□ As the expected rate of inflation increases, a higher premium must be added to the real risk-free rate to compensate for the loss of purchasing power that results from inflation.

□ The same inflation premium is built into the required rate of return of both riskless and risky assets.

■ As risk aversion increases, so do the risk premium and, thus, the slope of the SML. The greater the average investor's aversion to risk, then (1) the steeper the slope of the SML, (2) the greater the risk premium for all stocks, and (3) the higher the required rate of return on all stocks.

■ Many factors can affect a company's beta. When such changes occur, the required rate of return also changes.
  □ A firm can influence its market risk, hence its beta, through changes in the composition of its assets and also through its use of debt.
  □ A company's beta can also change as a result of external factors such as increased competition in its industry, the expiration of basic patents, and the like.

For a management whose primary goal is stock price maximization, the overriding consideration is the riskiness of the firm's stock, and the relevant risk of any physical asset must be measured in terms of its effect on the stock's risk as seen by investors.

A number of recent studies have raised concerns about the validity of the CAPM.

■ A recent study by Fama and French found no relationship between stocks' historical returns and their market betas.
  □ They found two variables that are consistently related to stock returns: (1) a firm's size and (2) its market/book ratio.
  □ After adjusting for other factors, they found that smaller firms have provided relatively high returns, and that returns are higher on stocks with low market/book ratios.
  □ However, they found no relationship between a stock's beta and its return.

■ As an alternative to the traditional CAPM, researchers and practitioners have begun to look to more general multi-beta models that extend the CAPM and address its shortcomings.
  □ In the multi-beta model, risk is measured relative to a set of factors that determine the behavior of asset returns, whereas the CAPM gauges risk only relative to the market return.
  □ The risk factors in multi-beta models are all nondiversifiable sources of risk.
  □ Practitioners and academicians have long recognized the limitations of the CAPM, and they are constantly looking for ways to improve it. The multi-beta model is a potential step in that direction.

Earnings volatility does not necessarily imply risk. You have to think about the causes of the volatility before reaching any conclusions as to whether earnings volatility indicates investment risk. However, stock price volatility does signify risk (except for stocks that are negatively correlated with the market, which are few and far between, if they exist at all).

SELF-TEST QUESTIONS

Definitional

1. Investment risk is associated with the _____ of low or negative returns; the greater the chance of loss, the riskier the investment.

2. A listing of all possible _____, with a probability assigned to each, is known as a probability _____.

3. Weighting each possible outcome of a distribution by its _____ of occurrence and summing the results give the expected _____ of the distribution.

4. One measure of the tightness of a probability distribution is the _____ _____, a probability-weighted average deviation from the expected value.

5. Investors who prefer outcomes with a high degree of certainty to those that are less certain are described as being _____ _____.

6. Owning a portfolio of securities enables investors to benefit from _____.

7. Diversification of a portfolio can result in lower _____ for the same level of return.

8. Diversification of a portfolio is achieved by selecting securities that are not perfectly _____ correlated with each other.

9. That part of a stock's risk that can be eliminated is known as _____ risk, while the portion that cannot be eliminated is called _____ risk.

10. The _____ coefficient measures a stock's relative volatility as compared with that of an average stock.

11. A stock that is twice as volatile as the market would have a beta coefficient of _____, while a stock with a beta of 0.5 would be only _____ as volatile as the market.

12. The beta coefficient of a portfolio is the _____ _____ of the betas of the individual stocks in that portfolio.

13. The minimum expected return that will induce investors to buy a particular security is the _____ rate of return.

14. The security used to measure the _____-_____ rate is the return available on U. S. Treasury securities.

15. The risk premium for a particular stock may be calculated by multiplying the market risk premium times the stock's _____ _____.

16. A stock's required rate of return is equal to the _____-_____ rate plus the stock's _____ _____.

17. The risk-free rate on a short-term Treasury security is made up of two parts: the _____ _____-_____ rate plus a(n) _____ premium.

18. Changes in investors' risk aversion alter the _____ of the Security Market Line.

19. The concept of _____ provides investors with a convenient way of expressing the financial performance of an investment.

20. An event's _____ is defined as the chance that the event will occur.

21. Investment returns can be expressed in _____ terms or as _____ ____ _____, or percentage returns.

22. The _____ ____ _____ shows the risk per unit of return, and it provides a more meaningful basis for comparison when the expected returns on two alternatives are not the same.

Conceptual

23. The Y-axis intercept of the Security Market Line (SML) indicates the required rate of return on an individual stock with a beta of 1.0.

    a. True   b. False

24. If a stock has a beta of zero, it will be riskless when held in isolation.

    a. True   b. False

25. A group of 200 stocks each has a beta of 1.0. We can be certain that each of the stocks was positively correlated with the market.

    a. True   b. False

26. Refer to Self-Test Question 25. If we combined these same 200 stocks into a portfolio, market risk would be reduced below the average market risk of the stocks in the portfolio.

    a. True   **b.** False

27. Refer to Self-Test Question 26. The standard deviation of the portfolio of these 200 stocks would be lower than the standard deviations of the individual stocks.

    a. True   **b.** False

28. Suppose $k_{RF} = 7\%$ and $k_M = 12\%$. If investors became more risk averse, k_M would be likely to decrease.

    a. True   **b.** False

29. Refer to Self-Test Question 28. The required rate of return for a stock with $b = 0.5$ would increase more than for a stock with $b = 2.0$.

    a. True   **b.** False

30. Refer to Self-Test Questions 28 and 29. If the expected rate of inflation increased, the required rate of return on a $b = 2.0$ stock would rise by more than that of a $b = 0.5$ stock.

    a. True   **b.** False

31. Which is the best measure of risk for an asset held in a well-diversified portfolio?

    a. Variance   **d.** Semi-variance
    b. Standard deviation   **e.** Expected value
    c. Beta

32. In a portfolio of three different stocks, which of the following could _not_ be true?

    a. The riskiness of the portfolio is less than the riskiness of each stock held in isolation.
    b. The riskiness of the portfolio is greater than the riskiness of one or two of the stocks.
    c. The beta of the portfolio is less than the beta of each of the individual stocks.
    d. The beta of the portfolio is greater than the beta of one or two of the individual stocks.
    e. The beta of the portfolio is equal to the beta of one of the individual stocks.

33. If investors expected inflation to increase in the future, and they also became more risk averse, what could be said about the change in the Security Market Line (SML)?

   a. The SML would shift up and the slope would increase.
   b. The SML would shift up and the slope would decrease.
   c. The SML would shift down and the slope would increase.
   d. The SML would shift down and the slope would decrease.
   e. The SML would remain unchanged.

34. Which of the following statements is most correct?

   a. The SML relates required returns to firms' market risk. The slope and intercept of this line _cannot_ be controlled by the financial manager.
   b. The slope of the SML is determined by the value of beta.
   c. If you plotted the returns of a given stock against those of the market, and if you found that the slope of the regression line was negative, then the CAPM would indicate that the required rate of return on the stock should be less than the risk-free rate for a well-diversified investor, assuming that the observed relationship is expected to continue on into the future.
   d. If investors become less risk averse, the slope of the Security Market Line will increase.
   e. Statements a and c are both correct.

35. Which of the following statements is most correct?

   a. Normally, the Security Market Line has an upward slope. However, at one of those unusual times when the yield curve on bonds is downward sloping, the SML will also have a downward slope.
   b. The market risk premium, as it is used in the CAPM theory, is equal to the required rate of return on an average stock minus the required rate of return on an average company's bonds.
   c. If the marginal investor's aversion to risk decreases, then the slope of the yield curve would, other things held constant, tend to increase. If expectations for inflation also increased at the same time risk aversion was decreasing—say the expected inflation rate rose from 5 percent to 8 percent—the net effect could possibly result in a parallel upward shift in the SML.
   d. According to the text, it is theoretically possible to combine two stocks, each of which would be quite risky if held as your only asset, and to form a 2-stock portfolio that is riskless. However, the stocks would have to have a correlation coefficient of expected future returns of -1.0, and it is hard to find such stocks in the real world.
   e. Each of the above statements is false.

36. Which of the following statements is most correct?

    a. The expected future rate of return, $\hat{k}$, is always *above* the past realized rate of return, $\overline{k}$, except for highly risk-averse investors.

    b. The expected future rate of return, $\hat{k}$, is always *below* the past realized rate of return, $\overline{k}$, except for highly risk-averse investors.

    c. The expected future rate of return, $\hat{k}$, is always *below* the required rate of return, k, except for highly risk-averse investors.

    d. There is no logical reason to think that any relationship exists between the expected future rate of return, $\hat{k}$, on a security and the security's required rate of return, k.

    e. Each of the above statements is false.

37. Which of the following statements is most correct?

    a. Someone who is highly averse to risk should invest in stocks with high betas (above +1.0), other things held constant.

    b. The returns on a stock might be highly uncertain in the sense that they could actually turn out to be much higher or much lower than the expected rate of return (that is, the stock has a high standard deviation of returns), yet the stock might still be regarded by most investors as being less risky than some other stock whose returns are less variable.

    c. The standard deviation is a better measure of risk when comparing securities than the coefficient of variation. This is true because the standard deviation "standardizes" risk by dividing each security's variance by its expected rate of return.

    d. Market risk can be reduced by holding a large portfolio of stocks, and if a portfolio consists of all traded stocks, market risk will be completely eliminated.

    e. The market risk in a portfolio declines as more stocks are added to the portfolio, and the risk decline is linear, that is, each additional stock reduces the portfolio's risk by the same amount.

SELF-TEST PROBLEMS

1. Stock A has the following probability distribution of expected returns:

Probability	Rate of Return
0.1	-15%
0.2	0
0.4	5
0.2	10
0.1	25

What is Stock A's expected rate of return and standard deviation?

a. 8.0%; 9.5%   d. 5.0%; 6.5%
b. 8.0%; 6.5%   e. 5.0%; 9.5%
c. 5.0%; 3.5%

2. If $k_{RF} = 5\%$, $k_M = 11\%$, and $b = 1.3$ for Stock X, what is k_X, the required rate of return for Stock X?

a. 18.7%   b. 16.7%   c. 14.8%   d. 12.8%   e. 11.9%

3. Refer to Self-Test Problem 2. What would k_X be if investors expected the inflation rate to increase by 2 percentage points?

a. 18.7%   b. 16.7%   c. 14.8%   d. 12.8%   e. 11.9%

4. Refer to Self-Test Problem 2. What would k_X be if an increase in investors' risk aversion caused the market risk premium to increase by 3 percentage points? k_{RF} remains at 5 percent.

a. 18.7%   b. 16.7%   c. 14.8%   d. 12.8%   e. 11.9%

5. Refer to Self-Test Problem 2. What would k_X be if investors expected the inflation rate to increase by 2 percentage points _and_ their risk aversion increased by 3 percentage points?

a. 18.7%   b. 16.7%   c. 14.8%   d. 12.8%   e. 11.9%

6. Jan Middleton owns a 3-stock portfolio with a total investment value equal to $300,000.

Stock	Investment	Beta
A	$100,000	0.5
B	100,000	1.0
C	100,000	1.5
Total	$300,000	

What is the weighted average beta of Jan's 3-stock portfolio?

a. 0.9   b. 1.3   c. 1.0   d. 0.4   e. 1.2

7. The Apple Investment Fund has a total investment of $450 million in five stocks.

Stock	Investment (Millions)	Beta
1	$130	0.4
2	110	1.5
3	70	3.0
4	90	2.0
5	50	1.0
Total	$450	

What is the fund's overall, or weighted average, beta?

a. 1.14   b. 1.22   c. 1.35   d. 1.46   e. 1.53

8. Refer to Self-Test Problem 7. If the risk-free rate is 12 percent and the market risk premium is 6 percent, what is the required rate of return on the Apple Fund?

a. 20.76%   b. 19.92%   c. 18.81%   d. 17.62%   e. 15.77%

9. Stock A has a beta of 1.2, Stock B has a beta of 0.6, the expected rate of return on an average stock is 12 percent, and the risk-free rate of return is 7 percent. By how much does the required return on the riskier stock exceed the required return on the less risky stock?

a. 4.00%   b. 3.25%   c. 3.00%   d. 2.50%   e. 3.75%

10. You are managing a portfolio of 10 stocks which are held in equal dollar amounts. The current beta of the portfolio is 1.8, and the beta of Stock A is 2.0. If Stock A is sold and the proceeds are used to purchase a replacement stock, what does the beta of the replacement stock have to be to lower the portfolio beta to 1.7?

a. 1.4   b. 1.3   c. 1.2   d. 1.1   e. 1.0

11. Consider the following information for the Alachua Retirement Fund, with a total investment of $4 million.

Stock	Investment	Beta
A	$ 400,000	1.2
B	600,000	-0.4
C	1,000,000	1.5
D	2,000,000	0.8
Total	$4,000,000	

The market required rate of return is 12 percent, and the risk-free rate is 6 percent. What is its required rate of return?

a. 9.98%   **b.** 10.45%   **c.** 11.01%   **d.** 11.50%   **e.** 12.56%

12. You are given the following distribution of returns:

Probability	Return
0.4	$30
0.5	25
0.1	-20

What is the coefficient of variation of the expected dollar returns?

a. 206.2500   **b.** 0.6383   **c.** 14.3614   **d.** 0.7500   **e.** 1.2500

13. If the risk-free rate is 8 percent, the expected return on the market is 13 percent, and the expected return on Security J is 15 percent, then what is the beta of Security J?

a. 1.40   **b.** 0.90   **c.** 1.20   **d.** 1.50   **e.** 0.75

ANSWERS TO SELF-TEST QUESTIONS

1. probability
2. outcomes; distribution
3. probability; return
4. standard deviation
5. risk averse
6. diversification
7. risk
8. positively
9. diversifiable; market
10. beta
11. 2.0; half
12. weighted average
13. required
14. risk-free
15. beta coefficient
16. risk-free; risk premium
17. real risk-free; inflation
18. slope

19. return

20. probability

21. dollar; rates of return

22. coefficient of variation

23. b. The Y-axis intercept of the SML is k_{RF}, which is the required rate of return on a security with a beta of zero.

24. b. A zero beta stock could be made riskless if it were combined with enough other zero beta stocks, but it would still have company-specific risk and be risky when held in isolation.

25. a. By definition, if a stock has a beta of 1.0 it moves exactly with the market. In other words, if the market moves up by 7 percent, the stock will also move up by 7 percent, while if the market falls by 7 percent, the stock will fall by 7 percent.

26. b. Market risk is measured by the beta coefficient. The beta for the portfolio would be a weighted average of the betas of the stocks, so b_p would also be 1.0. Thus, the market risk for the portfolio would be the same as the market risk of the stocks in the portfolio.

27. a. Note that with a 200-stock portfolio, the actual returns would all be on or close to the regression line. However, when the portfolio (and the market) returns are quite high, some individual stocks would have higher returns than the portfolio, and some would have much lower returns. Thus, the range of returns, and the standard deviation, would be higher for the individual stocks.

28. b. RP_M, which is equal to $k_M - k_{RF}$, would rise, leading to an increase in k_M.

29. b. The required rate of return for a stock with b = 0.5 would increase less than the return on a stock with b = 2.0.

30. b. If the expected rate of inflation increased, the SML would shift parallel due to an increase in k_{RF}. Thus, the effect on the required rates of return for both the b = 0.5 and b = 2.0 stocks would be the same.

31. c. The best measure of risk is the beta coefficient, which is a measure of the extent to which the returns on a given stock move with the stock market.

32. c. The beta of the portfolio is a weighted average of the individual securities' betas, so it could not be less than the betas of all of the stocks. (See Self-Test Problem 6.)

33. a. The increase in inflation would cause the SML to shift up, and investors becoming more risk averse would cause the slope to increase. (This can be demonstrated by graphing the SML lines on the same graph in Self-Test Problems 2 through 5.)

34. e. Statement b is false because the slope of the SML is $k_M - k_{RF}$. Statement d is false because as investors become less risk averse the slope of the SML decreases. Statement a is correct because the financial manager has no control over k_M or k_{RF}. ($k_M - k_{RF}$ = slope and k_{RF} = intercept of the SML.) Statement c is correct because the slope of the regression line is beta and beta would be negative; thus, the required return would be less than the risk-free rate.

35. d. Statement a is false. The yield curve determines the value of k_{RF}; however, SML = $k_{RF} + (k_M - k_{RF})b$. The average return on the market will always be greater than the risk-free rate; thus, the SML will always be upward sloping. Statement b is false because RP_M is equal to $k_M - k_{RF}$. k_{RF} is equal to the risk-free rate, not the rate on an average company's bonds. Statement c is false. A decrease in an investor's aversion to risk would indicate a downward sloping yield curve. A decrease in risk aversion and an increase in inflation would cause the SML slope to decrease and to shift upward simultaneously.

36. e. All the statements are false. For equilibrium to exist, the expected return must equal the required return.

37. b. Statement b is correct because the stock with the higher standard deviation might not be highly correlated with most other stocks, hence have a relatively low beta, and thus not be very risky if held in a well-diversified portfolio. The other statements are simply false.

SOLUTIONS TO SELF-TEST PROBLEMS

1. e. $\hat{k}_A = 0.1(-15\%) + 0.2(0\%) + 0.4(5\%) + 0.2(10\%) + 0.1(25\%) = 5.0\%$.

$$\begin{aligned} \text{Variance} &= 0.1(-0.15 - 0.05)^2 + 0.2(0.0 - 0.05)^2 + 0.4(0.05 - 0.05)^2 \\ &\quad + 0.2(0.10 - 0.05)^2 + 0.1(0.25 - 0.05)^2 \\ &= 0.009. \end{aligned}$$

Standard deviation = $\sqrt{0.009} = 0.0949 = 9.5\%$.

2.   d. $k_X = k_{RF} + (k_M - k_{RF})b_X = 5\% + (11\% - 5\%)1.3 = 12.8\%$.

3.   c. $k_X = k_{RF} + (k_M - k_{RF})b_X = 7\% + (13\% - 7\%)1.3 = 14.8\%$.

        A change in the inflation premium does _not_ change the market risk premium ($k_M - k_{RF}$) since both k_M and k_{RF} are affected.

4.   b. $k_X = k_{RF} + (k_M - k_{RF})b_X = 5\% + (14\% - 5\%)1.3 = 16.7\%$.

5.   a. $k_X = k_{RF} + (k_M - k_{RF})b_X = 7\% + (16\% - 7\%)1.3 = 18.7\%$.

6.   c. The calculation of the portfolio's beta is as follows:

$$b_p = (1/3)(0.5) + (1/3)(1.0) + (1/3)(1.5) = 1.0.$$

7.   d. $b_p = \sum_{i=1}^{5} w_i\, b_i$

$$= \frac{\$130}{\$450}(0.4) + \frac{\$110}{\$450}(1.5) + \frac{\$70}{\$450}(3.0) + \frac{\$90}{\$450}(2.0) + \frac{\$50}{\$450}(1.0) = 1.46.$$

8.   a. $k_p = k_{RF} + (k_M - k_{RF})b_p = 12\% + (6\%)1.46 = 20.76\%$.

9.   c. We know $b_A = 1.20$, $b_B = 0.60$; $k_M = 12\%$, and $k_{RF} = 7\%$.

        $k_i = k_{RF} + (k_M - k_{RF})b_i = 7\% + (12\% - 7\%)b_i$.

        $k_A = 7\% + 5\%(1.20) = 13.0\%$.

        $k_B = 7\% + 5\%(0.60) = 10.0\%$.

        $k_A - k_B = 13\% - 10\% = 3\%$.

10. e. First find the beta of the remaining 9 stocks:

$1.8 = 0.9(b_R) + 0.1(b_A)$
$1.8 = 0.9(b_R) + 0.1(2.0)$
$1.8 = 0.9(b_R) + 0.2$
$1.6 = 0.9(b_R)$
$b_R = 1.78$.

Now find the beta of the new stock that produces $b_p = 1.7$.

$1.7 = 0.9(1.78) + 0.1(b_N)$
$1.7 = 1.6 + 0.1(b_N)$
$0.1 = 0.1(b_N)$
$b_N = 1.0$.

11. c. Determine the weight each stock represents in the portfolio:

Stock	Investment	w_i	Beta	$w_i \times$ Beta
A	400,000	0.10	1.2	0.1200
B	600,000	0.15	-0.4	-0.0600
C	1,000,000	0.25	1.5	0.3750
D	2,000,000	0.50	0.8	0.4000

$b_p = \underline{0.8350}$ = Portfolio beta

Write out the SML equation, and substitute known values including the portfolio beta. Solve for the required portfolio return.

$k_p = k_{RF} + (k_M - k_{RF})b_p = 6\% + (12\% - 6\%)0.8350$
$ = 6\% + 5.01\% = 11.01\%$.

12. b. Use the given probability distribution of returns to calculate the expected value, variance, standard deviation, and coefficient of variation.

P_i	k_i	$P_i k_i$	k_i	$\hat{k}$		$(k_i - \hat{k})$	$(k_i - \hat{k})^2$	$P(k_i - \hat{k})^2$
0.4	× $30	= $12.0	$30 - $22.5	=		$ 7.5	$ 56.25	$ 22.500
0.5	× 25	= 12.5	25 - 22.5	=		2.5	6.25	3.125
0.1	× -20	= -2.0	-20 - 22.5	=		-42.5	1,806.25	180.625

$\hat{k} = \underline{\$22.5}$

σ^2 = Variance = $\underline{\$206.250}$

The standard deviation (σ) of $\hat{k}$ is $\sqrt{\$206.25} = \$14.3614$.

Use the standard deviation and the expected return to calculate the coefficient of variation: $\$14.3614/\$22.5 = 0.6383$.

13.   a.   Use the SML equation, substitute in the known values, and solve for beta. k_{RF} =   8%; k_M = 13%; k_J = 15%.

$$k_J = k_{RF} + (k_M - k_{RF})b_J$$
$$15\% = 8\% + (13\% - 8\%)b_J$$
$$7\% = (5\%)b_J$$
$$b_J = 1.4.$$

OVERVIEW

In Chapter 25 we presented the key elements of risk and return analysis. There we saw that much of the risk inherent in a stock can be eliminated by diversification, so rational investors should hold portfolios of stocks rather than just one stock. We also introduced the Capital Asset Pricing Model (CAPM), which links risk and required rates of return, using a stock's beta coefficient as the relevant measure of risk.

In this chapter, we extend the Chapter 25 material by presenting an in-depth treatment of portfolio concepts and the CAPM. We continue the discussion of risk and return by adding a risk-free asset to the set of investment opportunities. This leads all investors to hold the same well-diversified portfolio of risky assets, and then to account for differing degrees of risk aversion by combining the risky portfolio in different proportions with the risk-free asset. Additionally, we show how betas are actually calculated, and we discuss an alternative view of the risk/return relationship, the Arbitrage Pricing Theory (APT).

OUTLINE

The riskiness of a portfolio, which may itself be considered as a single asset held in isolation, is measured by the standard deviation of its return distribution. This equation is exactly the same as the one for the standard deviation of a single asset, except that here the asset is a portfolio of assets (for example, a mutual fund).

$$\text{Portfolio standard deviation} = \sigma_p = \sqrt{\sum_{i=1}^{n} \left(k_{pi} - \hat{k}_p\right)^2 P_i}.$$

Two key concepts in portfolio analysis are covariance and the correlation coefficient.

■ *Covariance* is a measure of the general movement relationship between two variables. It combines the variance (or volatility) of a stock's returns with the tendency of those returns to move up or down at the same time other stocks move up or down. The following equation defines the covariance (Cov) between Stocks A and B:

$$\text{Covariance} = \text{Cov (AB)} = \sum_{i=1}^{n} (k_{Ai} - \hat{k}_A)(k_{Bi} - \hat{k}_B)P_i.$$

☐ If the returns move together, the terms in parentheses will both be positive or both be negative, hence the product of the two terms will be positive, while if the returns move counter to one another, the products will tend to be negative.

☐ If either stock has a zero standard deviation, hence is riskless, then all of its deviations will be zero, and Cov(AB) also will be zero.

☐ Cov(AB) will be large and positive if two assets have large standard deviations and tend to move together; it will be large and negative for two high σ assets which move counter to one another; and it will be small if the two assets' returns move randomly, rather than up or down with one another, or if either of the assets has a small standard deviation.

■ It is difficult to interpret the magnitude of the covariance term, so a related statistic, the *correlation coefficient*, is generally used to measure the degree of comovement between two variables. The relationship between covariance and the correlation coefficient can be expressed as

$$\text{Correlation coefficient(AB)} = r_{AB} = \frac{\text{Cov(AB)}}{\sigma_A \sigma_B}.$$

☐ The correlation coefficient standardizes the covariance.

☐ The sign of the correlation coefficient is the same as the sign of the covariance, so a positive sign means that the variables move together, a negative sign indicates that they move in opposite directions, and if r is close to zero, they move independently of one another.

☐ Its values are limited to the range from -1.0 (perfect negative correlation) to +1.0 (perfect positive correlation).

■ Under the assumption that the distributions of returns on the individual securities are normal, the following equation can be used to determine the riskiness of a two-asset portfolio:

$$\text{Portfolio SD} = \sigma_p = \sqrt{x^2 \sigma_A^2 + (1-x)^2 \sigma_B^2 + 2x(1-x)r_{AB}\sigma_A\sigma_B}.$$

☐ Here x is the fraction of the portfolio invested in Security A, so $(1 - x)$ is the fraction invested in Security B.

One important use of portfolio risk concepts is to select efficient portfolios. An efficient portfolio provides the highest expected return for any degree of risk, or the lowest degree of risk for any expected return.

> While the riskiness of a multi-asset portfolio usually decreases as the number of stocks increase, the portfolio's risk depends on the degree of correlation among the stocks.

> In general, the average correlation between two stocks is +0.5 to +0.7, and hence holding stocks in portfolios will reduce, but not eliminate, risk.

> The *attainable*, or *feasible, set of portfolios* represents all portfolios that can be constructed from a given set of stocks.

The optimal portfolio is found by determining the efficient set of portfolios and then choosing from the efficient set the single portfolio that is best for the individual investor.

> The efficient set of portfolios is also called the *efficient frontier*.
>> ☐ Portfolios to the left of the efficient set are not possible because they lie outside the attainable set.
>> ☐ Portfolios to the right of the boundary line (interior portfolios) are inefficient because some other portfolio would provide either a higher return with the same degree of risk or lower risk for the same rate of return.

> An *indifference curve* (or risk/return trade-off function) reflects an individual investor's attitude towards risk.
>> ☐ The steeper the slope of an investor's indifference curve, the more risk averse the investor.

> The optimal portfolio for each investor is found at the *tangency point* between the efficient set of portfolios and one of the investor's indifference curves.
>> ☐ This tangency point marks the highest level of satisfaction the investor can attain.

The Capital Asset Pricing Model (CAPM) specifies the relationship between risk and required rates of return on assets when they are held in well-diversified portfolios.

> As in all financial theories, a number of assumptions were made in the development of the CAPM. These assumptions are:
>> ☐ All investors focus on a single holding period, and they seek to maximize the expected utility of their terminal wealth.
>> ☐ All investors can borrow or lend an unlimited amount at a given risk-free rate of interest, k_{RF}.

□ Investors have homogeneous expectations.
□ All assets are perfectly divisible and perfectly liquid.
□ There are no transactions costs.
□ There are no taxes.
□ All investors are price takers.
□ The quantities of all assets are given and fixed.

■ Theoretical extensions in finance literature have relaxed some of the assumptions, and in general these extensions have led to conclusions that are reasonably consistent with the basic theory. However, even the extensions contain assumptions which are both strong and unrealistic, so the validity of the model can only be established through empirical tests.

The Capital Market Line (CML) specifies a linear relationship between expected return and risk for efficient portfolios.

■ The equation of the CML may be expressed as follows:

$$\hat{k}_p = k_{RF} + \left(\frac{\hat{k}_M - k_{RF}}{\sigma_M} \right) \sigma_p.$$

Here $\hat{k}_p$ is the expected (and in equilibrium, required) rate of return on an efficient portfolio, k_{RF} is the rate of interest on risk-free securities, $\hat{k}_M$ is the return on the market portfolio, σ_M is the standard deviation of the market portfolio, and σ_p is the standard deviation of the efficient portfolio in question.

■ In words, the expected rate of return on an efficient portfolio (that is, a portfolio on the CML) is equal to the riskless rate plus a risk premium, and the risk premium is equal to $(\hat{k}_M - k_{RF}) / \sigma_M$ multiplied by the portfolio's standard deviation, σ_p.

■ The slope of the CML reflects the aggregate attitude of investors toward risk.

■ An *efficient portfolio* is one that is well diversified, hence all of its unsystematic risk has been eliminated and its only remaining risk is market risk.
□ Unlike individual stocks, the riskiness of an efficient portfolio is measured by its standard deviation, σ_p.

The relevant measure of risk for use in the Security Market Line (SML) equation is the stock's beta coefficient, which measures the volatility of a stock relative to that of a portfolio containing all stocks.

■   *Beta* is estimated by plotting historical returns on a particular stock versus returns on a market index. The slope of the regression line, or *characteristic line*, is the stock's beta coefficient. The statistical equation for beta is:

$$b_j = \frac{Cov(\overline{k}_j, \overline{k}_M)}{\sigma_M^2} = \frac{r_{jM}\sigma_j\sigma_M}{\sigma_M^2} = r_{jM}\left(\frac{\sigma_j}{\sigma_M}\right),$$

where,

b_j = the slope, or beta coefficient, for Stock j.

$\overline{k}_j$ = the historical (realized) rate of return on Stock j.

$\overline{k}_M$ = the historical (realizcd) rate of return on the market.

r_{jM} = the correlation between Stock j and the market.

σ_j = the standard deviation of Stock j.

σ_M = the standard deviation of the market.

☐ A stock's beta, hence its market risk, depends on its correlation with the stock market as a whole, r_{jM}, and its own variability, σ_j, relative to the variability of the market, σ_M.

☐ We assume that the historical relationship between Stock j and the market as a whole, as given by its characteristic line, will continue into the future.

☐ Besides general market movements, each firm also faces events that are unique to it and independent of the general economic climate. This component of total risk is the stock's *diversifiable*, or *company-specific, risk*, and rational investors will eliminate its effects by holding diversified portfolios of stocks.

☐ An individual stock tends to move with the market as economic conditions change. This component of total risk is the stock's *market*, or *non-diversifiable, risk*. Even well-diversified portfolios contain some market risk.

☐ Total risk (variance) equals market risk plus diversifiable risk.

$$\frac{\text{Total}}{\text{risk}} = \frac{\text{Market}}{\text{risk}} + \frac{\text{Diversifiable}}{\text{risk}}$$

$$\sigma_j^2 = b_j^2\sigma_M^2 + \sigma_{e_j}^2.$$

☐ If all the points plotted on the characteristic line, then all of the stock's total risk would be market risk. On the other hand, if the points are widely scattered about the regression line, much of the stock's total risk would be diversifiable.

☐ If the stock market never fluctuated, then stocks would have no market risk.

☐ Beta is the measure of relative market risk, but the stock's actual risk depends on both its beta (market risk), and on the volatility of the market.

☐ The diversifiable risk can and should be eliminated by diversification, so the *relevant risk* is market risk, not total risk.

☐   A stock's risk premium, $(k_M - k_{RF}) b_j$, depends only on its market risk, not its total risk.

Since the CAPM depends on some unrealistic assumptions, it must be tested empirically to determine if it gives accurate estimates of k_i.

■   Betas are generally calculated for some past period, and the assumption is made that the relative volatility of a stock will remain constant in the future. However, conditions may change and alter a stock's future volatility, which is the item of real concern to investors.

☐   Betas of individual stocks are unstable, hence past betas for individual securities are not good estimators of their future risk, but the betas of portfolios of ten or more randomly selected stocks are reasonably stable, hence that past portfolio betas are good estimators of future portfolio volatility.

☐   The CAPM should use expected (future) data, yet only historical data are generally available.

☐   Studies indicate that the CAPM is a better concept for structuring investment portfolios than it is for purposes of estimating the cost of capital for individual securities.

☐   Studies of the CAPM based on the slope of the SML have generally showed a significant positive relationship between realized returns and systematic risk and that the relationship between risk and return appears to be linear. The slope of the relationship is usually less than that predicted by the CAPM.

☐   According to the CAPM, high-beta stocks should provide higher returns than low-beta stocks. However, the Fama-French study revealed no relationship between historical betas and historical returns—low-beta stocks provided about the same returns as high-beta stocks.

The CAPM is extremely appealing at an intellectual level.

☐   The CAPM framework is clearly a useful way to think about the riskiness of assets. Thus, as a conceptual model, the CAPM is of truly fundamental importance.

☐   Estimates of k_i found through the use of the CAPM are subject to potentially large errors, because we do not know precisely how to measure any of the inputs required to implement the CAPM.

■ Because the CAPM is logical in the sense that it represents the way risk-averse people ought to behave, the model is a useful conceptual tool.

■ It is appropriate to think about many financial problems in a CAPM framework. However, it is equally important to recognize the limitations of the CAPM when using it in practice.

The CAPM assumes that required rates of return depend on only one risk factor, the stock's beta coefficient, but required returns may be a function of several risk factors. An approach called the Arbitrage Pricing Theory (APT) can include any number of risk factors.

$$\overline{k}_i = \hat{k}_i + \left(\overline{F}_1 - \hat{F}_1\right)b_{i1} + \cdots + \left(\overline{F}_j - \hat{F}_j\right)b_{ij} + e_i,$$

where,

> $\overline{k}_i$ = the realized rate of return on Stock i.
>
> $\hat{k}_i$ = the expected rate of return on Stock i.
>
> $\overline{F}_j$ = the realized value of economic Factor j.
>
> $\hat{F}_j$ = the expected value of Factor j.
>
> b_{ij} = the sensitivity of Stock i to economic Factor j.
>
> e_i = the effect of unique events on the realized return of Stock i.

■ This equation shows that the realized return on any stock is equal to the stock's expected return, increases or decreases which depend on unexpected changes in fundamental economic factors times the sensitivity of the stock to these changes, and a random term which reflects changes unique to the firm or industry.

■ Theoretically, one could construct a portfolio such that (1) the portfolio was riskless and (2) the net investment in it was zero. Such a zero investment portfolio must have a zero expected return, or else arbitrage operations would occur that would cause the prices of the underlying assets to change until the portfolio's expected return was zero.

■ The end result is APT:

$$k_i = k_{RF} + \left(k_1 - k_{RF}\right)b_{i1} + \cdots + \left(k_j - k_{RF}\right)b_{ij},$$

where k_j is the required rate of return on a portfolio that is sensitive only to the jth economic factor ($b_j = 1.0$) and has zero sensitivity to all other factors.

■ The primary theoretical advantage of the APT is that it permits several economic factors to influence individual stock returns, whereas the CAPM assumes that the impact of all factors, except those unique to the firm, can be captured in a single measure, the volatility of the stock with respect to the market portfolio.

   ☐ The APT requires fewer assumptions than the CAPM and hence is a more general theory.

   ☐ The APT does not assume that all investors hold the market portfolio, a CAPM requirement that clearly is not met in practice.

■ However, the APT does not identify the relevant factors, nor does it even tell us how many factors should appear in the model.

   ☐ The APT's proponents argue that it is not actually necessary to identify the relevant factors.

      ● Researchers use a complex statistical procedure called *factor analysis* to develop the APT parameters.

■ The APT is in an early stage of development, and there are still many unanswered questions.

The Extensions to Chapter 26 illustrate risk/return concepts for continuous probability distributions.

■ A *uniform distribution* is a continuous distribution in which each possible outcome has the same probability of occurrence as any other outcome.

■ A *triangular distribution* is a continuous distribution that has a clustering of values around the most likely outcome, and the probability of occurrence declines in each direction from the most likely outcome.

■ The most commonly used continuous distribution is the *normal distribution*, which is symmetric about the expected value and its tails extend out to plus and minus infinity.

SELF-TEST QUESTIONS

Definitional

1. _____ is a measure of the general movement relationship between two variables, while the _____ _____ also measures the degree of comovement between two stocks but its values are limited from -1.0 to +1.0.

2. A(n) _____ _____ is that portfolio which provides the highest expected return for any given degree of risk, or the lowest degree of risk for any expected return.

3. The _____, or _____, set of portfolios represents all portfolios that can be constructed from a given set of stocks.

4. The _____ _____ is found by determining the efficient set of portfolios and then choosing from the efficient set the single portfolio that is best for the individual investor.

5. The efficient set of portfolios is also called the _____ _____.

6. A(n) _____ _____ (or risk/return trade-off function) reflects an individual investor's attitude towards risk.

7. The _____ _____ _____ _____ specifies the relationship between risk and required rates of return on assets when they are held in well-diversified portfolios.

8. The _____ _____ _____ specifies a linear relationship between expected return and risk for efficient portfolios.

9. The relevant measure of risk for use in the Security Market Line (SML) equation is the stock's _____ _____, which measures the volatility of a stock relative to that of a portfolio containing all stocks.

10. Beta is estimated by plotting historical returns on a particular stock versus returns on a market index. The slope of the regression line, or _____ _____, is the stock's beta coefficient.

11. Besides general market movements, each firm also faces events that are unique to it and independent of the general economic climate. This component of total risk is the stock's _____, or _____-_____, risk, and rational investors will eliminate its effects by holding diversified portfolios of stocks.

12. The relevant risk is _____ risk, not total risk.

13. Studies indicate that the CAPM is a better concept for structuring _____ _____ than it is for purposes of estimating the cost of capital for individual securities.

14. The _____ _____ _____ uses several risk factors for determining the required return on a stock.

15. The most commonly used continuous distribution is the _____ _____, which is symmetric about the expected value and its tails extend out to plus and minus infinity.

16. The _____ _____ standardizes the covariance.

17. The sign of the correlation coefficient is the _____ as the sign of the covariance. A(n) _____ sign means that the variables move together, a(n) _____ sign indicates that they move in opposite directions, and if r is close to zero, they move _____ of one another.

18. Portfolios to the _____ of the efficient set are not possible because they lie outside the attainable set, while portfolios to the _____ of the boundary line are inefficient because some other portfolio would provide either a higher return with the same degree of risk or lower risk for the same rate of return.

19. The _____ of the CML reflects the aggregate attitude of investors toward risk.

20. An individual stock tends to move with the market as economic conditions change. This component of total risk is the stock's _____, or _____-_____ risk.

21. _____ risk equals market risk plus diversifiable risk.

22. A stock's risk premium depends only on its _____ risk, not its total risk.

Conceptual

23. The standard deviation of a portfolio is not the weighted average of the standard deviations of the individual stocks in the portfolio.

    a. True   **b.** False

24. If the correlation coefficient between two stocks is +1.0, risk can be completely diversified away.

    a. True   **b.** False

25. Total risk is relevant only for assets held in isolation.

    a. True   **b.** False

26. The Arbitrage Pricing Theory identifies the relevant factors for determining the required return beforehand.

    a. True   **b.** False

27. Which of the following statements is most correct?

    a. It is difficult to interpret the magnitude of the correlation coefficient, so a related statistic, the covariance, is often used to measure the degree of comovement between two variables.

    b. The sign of the correlation coefficient is the same as the sign of the covariance, so a positive sign means that the variables move together, a negative sign indicates that they move in opposite directions, and if the correlation coefficient is close to zero, they move independently of one another.

    c. Attainable portfolios are defined as those portfolios which provide the highest expected return for any degree of risk, or the lowest degree of risk for any expected return.

    d. The efficient set of portfolios is also called the efficient frontier.

    e. Statements b and d are both correct.

28. Which of the following statements is most correct?

    a. The Capital Market Line (CML) specifies a curvilinear relationship between expected return and risk, whereas the Security Market Line (SML) specifies a linear relationship between expected return and risk.

    b. An efficient portfolio is one that is well diversified, so like individual stocks, all the riskiness of an efficient portfolio is measured by its standard deviation, σ_p.

    c. A stock's beta coefficient is the y-intercept of its characteristic line.

    d. Empirical tests of the stability of beta coefficients have indicated that the betas of individual stocks are stable, hence that past betas for individual securities are good estimators of their future risk, while betas of portfolios of ten or more randomly selected stocks are not stable, hence that past portfolio betas are not good estimators of future portfolio volatility.

    e. All of the above statements are false.

SELF-TEST PROBLEMS

1. You are evaluating two potential investment opportunities: Stocks A and B. The expected rate of return on Stock A is 15.8% and its standard deviation is 2.8%. Stock B's expected rate of return is 20.5% with a standard deviation of 3.5%. What is the coefficient of variation (CV) for Stocks A and B, respectively?

   a. 0.12; 0.12   **b.** 0.18; 0.12   **c.** 0.18; 0.17   **d.** 0.25; 0.17   **e.** 0.25; 0.25

2. Refer to Self-Test Problem 1. Assume that Stocks A and B have a correlation coefficient of 0.65. What is the covariance between Stocks A and B?

   a. 3.89   **b.** 4.35   **c.** 5.12   **d.** 6.37   **e.** 7.19

3. Refer to Self-Test Problem 1. Assume that Stocks A and B have a covariance of -5.4. What is the correlation coefficient between Stocks A and B?

   a. -0.55   **b.** -0.70   **c.** -0.85   **d.** -0.92   **e.** -1.00

4. Given the information below, calculate the betas for Stocks A and B.

Year	Stock A	Stock B	Market
1	-5%	10%	-10%
2	10	20	10
3	25	30	30

   (Hint: Think rise over run.)

   a. 1.0; 0.5   **b.** 0.75; 0.5   **c.** 0.75; 1.0   **d.** 0.5; 0.5   **e.** 0.75; 0.25

   (The following data apply to the next two Self-Test Problems.)

   You are given the following information:

Year	Stock N	Market
1	-5%	10%
2	-8	15
3	7	-10

   The risk-free rate is equal to 7 percent, and the market required return is equal to 10 percent.

5. What is Stock N's beta coefficient?

    a. 1.00   **b.** -0.50   **c.** 0.60   **d.** -0.75   **e.** -0.60

6. What is Stock N's required rate of return?

    a. 6.40%   **b.** 5.20%   **c.** 8.80%   **d.** 5.90%   **e.** 7.00%

7. Stock Y and the Market had the following rates of return during the last 4 years. What is Stock Y's beta? (Hint: You will need a financial calculator to calculate the beta coefficient.)

Year	Y	Market
1995	10.0%	10.0%
1996	16.0	13.5
1997	-7.5	-4.0
1998	0.0	5.5

    a. 1.25   **b.** 0.75   **c.** 1.00   **d.** 1.34   **e.** 1.57

8. Stock Y, Stock Z, and the Market had the following rates of return during the last 4 years:

Year	Y	Z	Market
1995	10.0%	10.0%	10.0%
1996	16.0	11.5	13.5
1997	-7.5	1.0	-4.0
1998	0.0	6.0	5.5

The expected future return on the market is 15 percent, the real risk-free rate is 3.75 percent, and the expected inflation rate is a constant 5 percent. If the market risk premium rises by 3 percentage points, what will be the change in the required rate of return of the riskier stock?

    a. 4.01%   **b.** 3.67%   **c.** 4.88%   **d.** 3.23%   **e.** 4.66%

ANSWERS TO SELF-TEST QUESTIONS

1.	Covariance; correlation coefficient	5.	efficient frontier
2.	efficient portfolio	6.	indifference curve
3.	attainable; feasible	7.	Capital Asset Pricing Model
4.	optimal portfolio	8.	Capital Market Line

9. beta coefficient
10. characteristic line
11. diversifiable; company-specific
12. market
13. investment portfolios
14. Arbitrage Pricing Theory
15. normal distribution
16. correlation coefficient

17. same; positive; negative; independently
18. left; right
19. slope
20. market; non-diversifiable
21. Total
22. market

23. a. The standard deviation of a portfolio depends on the correlations among the stocks as well as their individual standard deviations. The calculation for the portfolio standard deviation is:

$$\sigma_p = \sqrt{\sum_{i=1}^{n} \left(k_{pi} - \hat{k}_p\right)^2 P_i}.$$

24. b. A correlation coefficient of -1.0 is required to combine two stocks into a riskless portfolio.

25. a. When assets are combined into portfolios, then the relevant risk is an asset's market risk, which is the contribution of the asset to the riskiness of the portfolio.

26. b. The APT does not identify the relevant factors beforehand, nor does it even tell how many factors should appear in the model.

27. e. Statement a is false. It is difficult to interpret the magnitude of the covariance, so the correlation coefficient is used to measure comovement between two variables. Statement c is false; this statement is true only for efficient portfolios. Both statements b and d are true, so statement e is the correct choice.

28. e. Statement a is false. The CML specifies the relationship between risk and return for efficient portfolios, while the SML specifies the relationship between risk and return for individual securities. Statement b is false. The standard deviation of an individual stock should not be used to measure the stock's riskiness because some of its risk as reflected in the standard deviation can be eliminated by diversification. Statement c is false; beta is the slope of the characteristic line. Statement d is false; just the reverse is true. Betas of portfolios of 10 or more randomly selected stocks have been shown to be stable, while the betas of individual securities have been shown to be unstable. Consequently, statement e is the correct choice.

SOLUTIONS TO SELF-TEST PROBLEMS

1. c. Stock A: CV = 2.8%/15.8% = 0.18. Stock B: CV = 3.5%/20.5% = 0.17. Since the CV for Project A is higher, it has more risk per unit of expected return.

2. d. Cov(AB) = 0.65 (2.8) (3.5) = 6.37.

3. a. r_{AB} = -5.4/[(2.8)(3.5)] = -0.55.

4. b. Stock A: b_A = Rise/Run = [10 – (-5)]/[10 – (-10)] = 15/20 = 0.75.
        Stock B: b_B = Rise/Run = [20 – 10]/[10 – (-10)] = 10/20 = 0.50.

    This problem can also be worked using most financial calculators having statistical functions.

5. e. b_N = Rise/Run = [-8) – (-5)]/(15 – 10) = -3/5 = -0.60.

    Again, this problem can also be worked using most financial calculators having statistical functions.

6. b. k_N = 7% + (10% – 7%)(-0.60) = 7% + (-1.80%) = 5.20%.

7. d. Use the regression feature of the calculator. Enter data for the market and Stock Y, and then find $Beta_Y$ = 1.3374 rounded to 1.34.

8.   a.   We know $k_M = 15\%$; $k^* = 3.75\%$; $IP = 5\%$.

Original $RP_M = k_M - k_{RF} = 15\% - (3.75\% + 5\%) = 6.25\%$.

RP_M increases by 3% to 9.25%.

Find the change in $k = \Delta k$ for the riskier stock.

First, find the betas for the two stocks. Enter data in the regression register, then find $b_Y = 1.3374$ and $b_Z = 0.6161$.

Y is the riskier stock. Originally, its required return was $k_Y = 8.75\% + 6.25\%(1.3374) = 17.11\%$. When RP_M increases by 3 percent, $k_Y = 8.75\% + (6.25\% + 3\%)(1.3374) = 21.12\%$. Difference $= 21.12\% - 17.11\% = 4.01\%$.

CHAPTER 27
BOND VALUATION

OVERVIEW

This chapter presents a discussion of the key characteristics of bonds, and then uses time value of money concepts to determine bond values. Bonds are one of the most important types of securities to investors, a major source of financing for corporations and governments.

The value of any financial asset is the present value of the cash flows expected from that asset. Therefore, once the cash flows have been estimated, and a discount rate determined, the value of the financial asset can be calculated.

A bond is valued as the present value of the stream of interest payments (an annuity) plus the present value of the par value which is received by thc investor on the bond's maturity date. Depending on the relationship between the current interest rate and the bond's coupon rate, a bond can sell at its par value, at a discount, or at a premium. The total rate of return on a bond is comprised of two components: interest yield and capital gains yield.

The bond valuation concepts developed earlier in the chapter are used to illustrate interest rate and reinvestment rate risk. In addition, default risk, various types of corporate bonds, bond ratings, and bond markets are discussed.

OUTLINE

A bond is a long-term contract under which a borrower agrees to make payments of interest and principal, on specific dates, to the holders of the bond. Bonds are classified into four main types: Treasury, corporate, municipal, and foreign. Each type differs with respect to expected return and degree of risk.

- *Treasury bonds*, sometimes referred to as government bonds, are issued by the Federal government and are not exposed to default risk.
    - However, Treasury bond prices decline when interest rates rise, so they are not free of all risk.

- *Corporate bonds* are issued by corporations and are exposed to default risk.

☐ Different corporate bonds have different levels of default risk, depending on the issuing company's characteristics and on the terms of the specific bond.

☐ Default risk often is referred to as "credit risk," and the larger the default or credit risk, the higher the interest rate the issuer must pay.

■ *Municipal bonds, or "munis,"* are issued by state and local governments.

☐ The interest earned on most municipal bonds is exempt from federal taxes, and also from state taxes if the holder is a resident of the issuing state.

☐ Municipal bonds carry interest rates that are considerably lower than those on corporate bonds with the same default risk.

■ *Foreign bonds* are issued by foreign governments or foreign corporations.

☐ These bonds are not only exposed to default risk, but are also exposed to an additional risk if the bonds are denominated in a currency other than that of the investor's home currency.

Differences in contractual provisions, and in the underlying strength of the companies backing the bonds, lead to major differences in bonds' risks, prices, and expected returns. It is important to understand both the key characteristics, which are common to all bonds, and how differences in these characteristics affect the values and risks of individual bonds.

■ The *par value* is the stated face value of a bond, usually $1,000. This represents the amount of money the firm borrows and promises to repay on the maturity date.

■ The *coupon interest payment* is the dollar amount that is paid annually to a bondholder by the issuer for use of the $1,000 loan. This payment is a fixed amount, established at the time the bond is issued.

☐ The *coupon interest rate* is obtained by dividing the coupon payment by the par value of the bond.

☐ In some cases, a bond's coupon payment may vary over time. These bonds are called *floating rate,* or *indexed, bonds.* Floating rate debt is popular with investors because the market value of the debt is stabilized. It is advantageous to corporations because firms can issue long-term debt without committing themselves to paying a historically high interest rate for the entire life of the loan.

☐ *Zero coupon bonds* pay no coupons at all, but are offered at a substantial discount below their par values, and hence, provide capital appreciation rather than interest income.

☐ In general, any bond originally offered at a price significantly below its par value is called an *original issue discount bond (OID).*

■ The *maturity date* is the date on which the par value must be repaid. Most bonds have *original maturities*, the maturity at the time the bond is issued, of from 10 to 40 years, but any maturity is legally permissible.

■ Most bonds contain a *call provision*, which gives the issuing corporation the right to call the bonds for redemption. The call provision generally states that if the bonds are called, the company must pay the bondholders an amount greater than the par value, which is termed a *call premium*.

☐ Bonds are often not callable until several years after they are issued. This is known as a *deferred call*, and the bonds are said to have *call protection*.

☐ A call provision is valuable to the firm but potentially detrimental to investors. Investors lose when interest rates go up, but don't reap the gains when rates fall. To induce an investor to take this type of risk a new issue of callable bonds must provide a higher interest rate than an otherwise similar issue of noncallable bonds.

☐ The process of using the proceeds of a new low-rate bond issue to retire a high-rate issue and reduce the firm's interest expense is called a *refunding operation*.

■ Bonds that are *redeemable at par* at the holder's option protect the holder against a rise in interest rates.

☐ *Event risk* is the risk that some sudden action, such as an LBO, will occur and increase the credit risk of the company, hence lower the firm's bond rating and the value of its outstanding bonds.

☐ In an attempt to control debt costs, a new type of protective covenant was devised to minimize event risk. This covenant, called a *super poison put*, enables a bondholder to turn in, or "put" a bond back to the issuer at par in the event of a takeover, merger, or major recapitalization.

■ A *sinking fund provision* facilitates the orderly retirement of a bond issue.

☐ A sinking fund call typically requires no call premium, but only a small percentage of the issue is normally callable in any one year.

☐ A sinking fund call can be achieved in one of two ways, and the firm will choose the least-cost method.

● The company can call in for redemption (at par value) a certain percentage of bonds each year.

● The company may buy the required amount of bonds on the open market.

☐ Bonds that have a sinking fund are regarded as being safer than those without such a provision, so at the time they are issued sinking fund bonds have lower coupon rates than otherwise similar bonds without sinking funds.

■ *Convertible bonds* are securities that are convertible into shares of common stock, at a fixed price, at the option of the bondholder.

☐ Convertibles have a lower coupon rate than nonconvertible debt, but they offer investors a chance for capital gains in exchange for the lower coupon rate.

■ Bonds issued with *warrants* are similar to convertibles. Warrants are options which permit the holder to buy stock for a stated price, thereby providing a capital gain if the stock price rises.
   ☐ Like convertibles, they carry lower coupon rates than straight bonds.

■ *Income bonds* pay interest only if the interest is earned.
   ☐ These securities cannot bankrupt a company, but from an investor's standpoint they are riskier than "regular" bonds.

■ The interest rate of an *indexed, or purchasing power, bond* is based on an inflation index such as the consumer price index (CPI), so the interest paid rises automatically when the inflation rate rises, thus protecting the bondholders against inflation.

The value of any financial asset is simply the present value of the cash flows the asset is expected to produce. The cash flows from a specific bond depend on its contractual features.

■ A "regular" bond represents an annuity plus a lump sum, and its value is found as the present value of this payment stream:

$$\text{Bond value} = \sum_{t=1}^{N} \frac{\text{INT}}{\left(1+k_d\right)^t} + \frac{M}{\left(1+k_d\right)^N}$$
$$= \text{INT}\left(\text{PVIFA}_{k_d,N}\right) + M\left(\text{PVIF}_{k_d,N}\right).$$

Here INT = dollars of interest paid each year, M = par, or maturity, value, which is typically $1,000, k_d = interest rate on the bond, and N = number of years until the bond matures.

■ For example, consider a 15-year, $1,000 bond paying $150 annually, when the appropriate interest rate, k_d, is 15 percent. Utilizing the PVIFA and PVIF tables in the text, we find:

$$V_B = \$150(5.8474) + \$1,000(0.1229)$$
$$= \$877.11 + \$122.90$$
$$= \$1,000.01 \approx \$1,000.$$

☐ Using a financial calculator, enter N = 15, k_d = I = 15, PMT = 150, and FV = 1000, and then press the PV key for an answer of -$1,000.

☐ Excel and other spreadsheet software packages provide specialized functions for bond prices.

■ At the time a coupon bond is issued, the coupon is generally set at a level that will cause the market price of the bond to equal its par value.

■ A *new issue* is the term applied to a bond that has just been issued.

☐ Once the bond has been on the market for a while, it is classified as an outstanding bond, or a *seasoned issue*.

■ Bond prices and interest rates are *inversely* related; that is, they tend to move in the opposite direction from one another.

☐ A fixed-rate bond will sell at par when its coupon interest rate is equal to the going rate of interest, k_d.

☐ When the going rate of interest is above the coupon rate, a fixed-rate bond will sell at a *discount* below its par value.

☐ If current interest rates are below the coupon rate, a fixed-rate bond will sell at a *premium* above its par value.

☐ Your percentage rate of return on a bond consists of an *interest yield*, or *current yield*, plus a *capital gains yield*.

☐ The market value of a bond will always approach its par value as its maturity date approaches, provided the firm doesn't go bankrupt.

The expected interest rate on a bond is also called its "yield." Unlike the coupon interest rate, which is fixed, the bond's yield varies from day to day depending on current market conditions. Moreover, it can be calculated in three different ways.

■ The rate of return earned on a bond if it is held until maturity is known as the *yield to maturity (YTM)*.

☐ The YTM for a bond that sells at par consists entirely of an interest yield, but if the bond sells at a price other than its par value, the YTM consists of the interest yield plus a positive or negative capital gains yield.

☐ The yield to maturity can also be viewed as the bond's *promised rate of return*, which is the return that investors will receive if all the promised payments are made.

☐ The yield to maturity equals the expected rate of return only if (1) the probability of default is zero and (2) the bond cannot be called.

- If current interest rates are well below an outstanding bond's coupon rate, then a *callable bond* is likely to be called, and investors should estimate the most likely rate of return on the bond as the *yield to call (YTC)* rather than as the yield to maturity.
  - ☐ To calculate the YTC, solve this equation for k_d:

$$\text{Price of bond} = \sum_{t=1}^{N} \frac{\text{INT}}{(1 + k_d)^t} + \frac{\text{Call price}}{(1 + k_d)^N}.$$

- The *current yield* is the annual interest payment divided by the bond's current price.
  - ☐ The current yield provides information about the cash income a bond will generate in a given year, but since it does not take account of capital gains or losses that will be realized if the bond is held until maturity (or call), it does not provide an accurate measure of the total expected return.

The bond valuation model must be adjusted when interest is paid semiannually:

$$V_B = \sum_{t=1}^{2N} \frac{\text{INT}/2}{(1 + k_d/2)^t} + \frac{M}{(1 + k_d/2)^{2N}}$$

$$= (\text{INT}/2)(\text{PVIFA}_{k_d/2,2N}) + M(\text{PVIF}_{k_d/2,2N}).$$

Interest rates fluctuate over time, and an increase in interest rates leads to a decline in the value of an outstanding bond.

- People or firms who invest in bonds are exposed to risk from changing interest rates, or *interest rate risk*. The longer the maturity of the bond, the greater the exposure to interest rate risk.
  - ☐ To induce an investor to take this extra risk, long-term bonds must have a higher expected rate of return than short-term bonds. This additional return is the *maturity risk premium*.
  - ☐ An upward sloping yield curve is consistent with the idea that longer maturity bonds must have a higher expected rate of return to compensate for their higher risk.

- The shorter the maturity of the bond, the greater the risk of a decrease in interest rates. The risk of a decline in income due to a drop in interest rates is called *reinvestment rate risk*.

- Interest rate risk relates to the *value* of the bonds in a portfolio, while reinvestment rate risk relates to the *income* the portfolio produces.
  - ☐ No fixed-rate bond can be considered totally riskless. Bond portfolio managers try to balance these two risks, but some risk always exists in any bond.

Another important risk associated with bonds is default risk. If the issuer defaults, investors receive less than the promised return on the bond. Default risk is affected by both the financial strength of the issuer and the terms of the bond contract, especially whether collateral has been pledged to secure the bond.

■ The greater the default risk, the higher the bond's yield to maturity.

■ A corporation can affect default risk by the terms of the bond contract.
   □ An *indenture* is a legal document that spells out the rights of both bondholders and the issuing corporation.
   □ A *trustee* is an official who represents the bondholders and makes sure the terms of the indenture are carried out.
   □ *Restrictive covenants* are typically included in the indenture and cover such points as the conditions under which the issuer can pay off the bonds prior to maturity, the level at which the issuer's TIE ratio must be maintained if the company is to issue additional debt, and restrictions against the payment of dividends unless earnings meet certain specifications.

■ Corporations can affect the default risk of their bonds by changing the type of bonds they issue.
   □ Under a *mortgage bond*, the corporation pledges certain assets as security for the bond.
   □ A *debenture* is an unsecured bond, and as such, it provides no lien against specific property as security for the obligation. Debenture holders are, therefore, general creditors whose claims are protected by property not otherwise pledged.
   □ *Subordinated debentures* have claims on assets, in the event of bankruptcy, only after senior debt as named in the subordinated debt's indenture has been paid off. Subordinated debentures may be subordinated to designated notes payable or to all other debt.
   □ Some companies may be in a position to benefit from the sale of either *development bonds* or *pollution control bonds*.
      ● State and local governments may set up both industrial development agencies and pollution control agencies.
      ● The agencies are allowed, under certain circumstances, to sell *tax-exempt bonds*, then to make the proceeds available to corporations for specific uses deemed by Congress to be in the public interest.

■ Municipalities can have their bonds insured. An insurance company guarantees to pay the coupon and principal payments should the issuer default.
   □ This reduces risk to investors, who will thus accept a lower coupon rate for an insured bond vis-a-vis an uninsured one.

■ Bond issues are normally assigned quality ratings by major rating agencies, such as Moody's Investors Service and Standard & Poor's Corporation. These ratings reflect the probability that a bond will go into default. Aaa (Moody's) and AAA (S&P) are the highest ratings.

☐ Rating assignments are based on qualitative and quantitative factors including the firm's debt/assets ratio, current ratio, and coverage ratios.

☐ Bond ratings are important both to firms and to investors.

☐ Because a bond's rating is an indicator of its default risk, the rating has a direct, measurable influence on the bond's interest rate and the firm's cost of debt capital.

☐ Most bonds are purchased by institutional investors rather than individuals, and many institutions are restricted to *investment-grade* securities, securities with ratings of Baa/BBB or above.

☐ Changes in a firm's bond rating affect both its ability to borrow long-term capital and the cost of that capital. Rating agencies review outstanding bonds on a periodic basis, occasionally *upgrading* or *downgrading* a bond as the issuer's circumstances change. Also, if a company issues more bonds, this will trigger a review by the rating agencies.

■ *Junk bonds* are high-risk, high-yield bonds issued to finance leveraged buyouts, mergers, or troubled companies.

☐ The emergence of junk bonds as an important type of debt is another example of how the investment banking industry adjusts to and facilitates new developments in capital markets.

☐ The development of junk bond financing has done much to reshape the U. S. financial scene. The existence of these securities has led directly to the loss of independence of some companies, and has led to major shake-ups in other companies.

Corporate bonds are traded primarily in the over-the-counter market. Most bonds are owned by and traded among the large financial institutions, and it is relatively easy for the over-the-counter bond dealers to arrange the transfer of large blocks of bonds among the relatively few holders of the bonds.

■ Information on bond trades in the over-the-counter market is not published, but a representative group of bonds is listed and traded on the bond division of the NYSE.

SELF-TEST QUESTIONS

Definitional

1. A(n) _____ is a long-term contract under which a borrower agrees to make payments of interest and principal on specific dates.

2. _____ bonds are issued by state and local governments, and the _____ earned on these bonds is exempt from federal taxes.

3. The stated face value of a bond is referred to as its _____ value and is usually set at $_____.

4. The "coupon interest rate" on a bond is determined by dividing the _____ _____ by the _____ _____ of the bond.

5. The date at which the par value of a bond is repaid to each bondholder is known as the _____ _____.

6. A(n) _____ _____, or _____, bond is one whose interest rate fluctuates with shifts in the general level of interest rates.

7. A(n) _____ _____ bond is one that pays no annual interest but is sold at a discount below par, thus providing compensation to investors in the form of capital appreciation.

8. The legal document setting forth the terms and conditions of a bond issue is known as the _____.

9. In meeting its sinking fund requirements, a firm may _____ the bonds or purchase them on the _____ _____.

10. Except when the call is for sinking fund purposes, when a bond issue is called, the firm must pay a(n) _____ _____, which is an amount in excess of the _____ value of the bond.

11. A bond with annual coupon payments represents an annuity of INT dollars per year for N years, plus a lump sum of M dollars at the end of N years, and its value, V_B, is the _____ _____ of this payment stream.

12.   At the time a bond is issued, the coupon interest rate is generally set at a level that will cause the _____ _____ and the _____ _____ of the bond to be approximately equal.

13.   Market interest rates and bond prices move in _____ directions from one another.

14.   The rate of return earned by purchasing a bond and holding it until maturity is known as the bond's _____ _____ _____.

15.   To adjust the bond valuation formula for semiannual coupon payments, the _____ _____ and _____ _____ must be divided by 2, and the number of _____ must be multiplied by 2.

16.   A bond secured by real estate is known as a(n) _____ bond.

17.   _____ bonds are issued by the Federal government and are not exposed to default risk.

18.   _____ bonds pay interest only if the interest is earned.

19.   The interest rate of a(n) _____, or _____ _____, bond is based on an inflation index, so the interest paid rises automatically when the inflation rate rises, thus protecting the bondholders against inflation.

20.   Any bond originally offered at a price significantly below its par value is called a(n) _____ _____ _____ bond.

21.   Once a bond has been on the market for a while, it is classified as an outstanding bond, or a(n) _____ _____.

22.   The _____ _____ is the annual interest payment divided by the bond's current price.

23.   Bonds are often not callable until several years after they are issued. This is known as a(n) _____ _____, and the bonds are said to have _____ _____.

24.   To induce investors to take on the risk of a callable bond, a new issue of callable bonds must provide a(n) _____ interest rate than an otherwise similar issue of noncallable bonds.

25.   _____ are options sold with bonds which permit the holder to buy stock for a stated price, thereby providing a capital gain if the stock price rises.

26.   _____ risk is the risk that some sudden action, such as an LBO, will occur and increase the credit risk of the company, hence lower the firm's bond rating and the value of its outstanding bonds.

27.   To induce an investor to take on the extra risk of investing in long-term bonds, they must have a higher expected rate of return than short-term bonds. The additional return is the _____ _____ _____.

28.   A(n) _____ is an official who represents the bondholders and makes sure the terms of the indenture are carried out.

29.   _____ bonds are high-risk, high-yield bonds issued to finance leveraged buyouts, mergers, or troubled companies.

Conceptual

30.   Changes in economic conditions cause interest rates and bond prices to vary over time.

   a. True   b. False

31.   If the appropriate rate of interest on a bond is greater than its coupon rate, the market value of that bond will be above par value.

   a. True   b. False

32.   A 20-year, annual coupon bond with one year left to maturity has the same interest rate risk as a 10-year, annual coupon bond with one year left to maturity. Both bonds are of equal risk, have the same coupon rate, and the prices of the two bonds are equal.

   a. True   b. False

33.   There is a direct relationship between bond ratings and the required rate of return on bonds; that is, the higher the rating, the higher is the required rate of return.

   a. True   b. False

34. The "penalty" for having a low bond rating is less severe when the Security Market Line is relatively steep than when it is not so steep.

    a. True   **b.** False

35. Which of the following statements is _false_? In all of the statements, assume that "other things are held constant."

    a. Price sensitivity—that is, the change in price due to a given change in the required rate of return—increases as a bond's maturity increases.

    b. For a given bond of any maturity, a given percentage point increase in the going interest rate (k_d) causes a _larger_ dollar capital loss than the capital gain stemming from an identical decrease in the interest rate.

    c. For any given maturity, a given percentage point increase in the interest rate causes a _smaller_ dollar capital loss than the capital gain stemming from an identical decrease in the interest rate.

    d. From a borrower's point of view, interest paid on bonds is tax deductible.

    e. A 20-year zero-coupon bond has less reinvestment rate risk than a 20-year coupon bond.

36. Which of the following statements is most correct?

    a. Ignoring interest accrued between payment dates, if the required rate of return on a bond is less than its coupon interest rate, and k_d remains below the coupon rate until maturity, then the market value of that bond will be below its par value until the bond matures, at which time its market value will equal its par value.

    b. Assuming equal coupon rates, a 20-year original maturity bond with one year left to maturity has more interest rate risk than a 10-year original maturity bond with one year left to maturity.

    c. Regardless of the size of the coupon payment, the price of a bond moves in the same direction as interest rates; for example, if interest rates rise, bond prices also rise.

    d. For bonds, price sensitivity to a given change in interest rates generally increases as years remaining to maturity increases.

    e. Because short-term interest rates are much more volatile than long-term rates, you would, in the real world, be subject to more interest rate risk if you purchased a 30-_day_ bond than if you bought a 30-_year_ bond.

37. Which of the following statements is most correct?

   a. Bonds C and Z both have a $1,000 par value and 10 years to maturity. They have the same default risk, and they both have an effective annual rate (EAR) = 8%. If Bond C has a 15 percent annual coupon and Bond Z a zero coupon (paying just $1,000 at maturity), then Bond Z will be exposed to more *interest rate risk*, which is defined as the *percentage* loss of value in response to a given increase in the going interest rate.

   b. If the words "interest rate risk" were replaced by the words "reinvestment rate risk" in Statement a, then the statement would be true.

   c. The interest rate paid by the state of Florida on its debt would be lower, other things held constant, if interest on the debt were not exempt from federal income taxes.

   d. Given the conditions in Statement a, we can be sure that Bond Z would have the higher price.

   e. Statements a, b, c, and d are false.

38. If a company's bonds are selling at a *discount*, then:

   a. The YTM is the return investors probably expect to earn.

   b. The YTC is probably the expected return.

   c. Either a or b could be correct, depending on the yield curve.

   d. The current yield will exceed the expected rate of return.

   e. The after-tax cost of debt to the company will have to be less than the coupon rate on the bonds.

SELF-TEST PROBLEMS

1. Delta Corporation has a bond issue outstanding with an annual coupon rate of 7 percent and 4 years remaining until maturity. The par value of the bond is $1,000. Determine the current value of the bond if present market conditions justify a 14 percent required rate of return. The bond pays interest annually.

   a. $1,126.42   **b.** $1,000.00   **c.** $796.06   **d.** $791.00   **e.** $536.42

2. Refer to Self-Test Problem 1. Suppose the bond had a semiannual coupon. Now what would be its current value?

   a. $1,126.42   **b.** $1,000.00   **c.** $796.06   **d.** $791.00   **e.** $536.42

3. Refer to Self-Test Problem 1. Assume an annual coupon but 20 years remaining to maturity. What is the current value under these conditions?

    a. $1,126.42   **b.** $1,000.00   **c.** $796.06   **d.** $791.00   **e.** $536.42

4. Refer to Self-Test Problem 3. What is the bond's current yield?

    a. 12.20%   **b.** 13.05%   **c.** 13.75%   **d.** 14.00%   **e.** 14.50%

5. Acme Products has a bond issue outstanding with 8 years remaining to maturity, a coupon rate of 10 percent with interest paid annually, and a par value of $1,000. If the current market price of the bond issue is $814.45, what is the yield to maturity, k_d?

    a. 12%   **b.** 13%   **c.** 14%   **d.** 15%   **e.** 16%

6. You have just been offered a bond for $863.73. The coupon rate is 8 percent, payable annually, and interest rates on new issues with the same degree of risk are 10 percent. You want to know how many more interest payments you will receive, but the party selling the bond cannot remember. If the par value is $1,000, how many interest payments remain?

    a. 10   **b.** 11   **c.** 12   **d.** 13   **e.** 14

7. Bird Corporation's 12 percent coupon rate, semiannual payment, $1,000 par value bonds which mature in 20 years are callable at a price of $1,100 five years from now. The bonds sell at a price of $1,300, and the yield curve is flat. Assuming that interest rates in the economy are expected to remain at their current level, what is the best estimate of Bird's *nominal interest rate* on the new bonds? (Hint: You will need a financial calculator to work this problem.)

    a. 8.46%   **b.** 6.16%   **c.** 9.28%   **d.** 6.58%   **e.** 8.76%

8. The Graf Company needs to finance some new R&D programs, so it will sell new bonds for this purpose. Graf's currently outstanding bonds have a $1,000 par value, a 10 percent coupon rate, and pay interest semiannually. The outstanding bonds have 25 years remaining to maturity, are callable after 5 years at a price of $1,090, and currently sell at a price of $700. The yield curve is expected to remain flat. On the basis of these data, what is the best estimate of Graf's *nominal interest rate* on the new bonds it plans to sell? (Hint: You will need a financial calculator to work this problem.)

    a. 21.10%   **b.** 14.48%   **c.** 15.67%   **d.** 16.25%   **e.** 18.29%

9. Suppose Hadden Inc. is negotiating with an insurance company to sell a bond issue. Each bond has a par value of $1,000, it would pay 10 percent per year in quarterly payments of $25 per quarter for 10 years, and then it would pay 12 percent per year ($30 per quarter) for the next 10 years (Years 11-20). The $1,000 principal would be returned at the end of 20 years. The insurance company's alternative investment is in a 20-year mortgage which has a nominal rate of 14 percent and which provides monthly payments. If the mortgage and the bond issue are equally risky, how much should the insurance company be willing to pay Hadden for each bond? (Hint: You will need a financial calculator to work this problem.)

    a. $750.78   **b.** $781.50   **c.** $804.65   **d.** $710.49   **e.** $840.97

ANSWERS TO SELF-TEST QUESTIONS

1.	bond	16.	mortgage
2.	Municipal; interest	17.	Treasury
3.	par; 1,000	18.	Income
4.	coupon payment; par value	19.	indexed; purchasing power
5.	maturity date	20.	original issue discount
6.	floating rate; indexed	21.	seasoned issue
7.	zero coupon	22.	current yield
8.	indenture	23.	deferred call; call protection
9.	call; open market	24.	higher
10.	call premium; par	25.	Warrants
11.	present value	26.	Event
12.	market price; par value	27.	maturity risk premium
13.	opposite	28.	trustee
14.	yield to maturity	29.	Junk
15.	coupon payment; interest rate; years		

30. a. For example, if inflation increases, the interest rate (or required return) will increase, resulting in a decline in bond price.

31. b. It will sell at a discount.

32. a. Both bonds are valued as 1-year bonds regardless of their original issue dates, and since they are of equal risk and have the same coupon rate, their prices must be equal.

33. b. The relationship is inverse. The higher the rating, the lower is the default risk and hence the lower is the required rate of return. Aaa/AAA is the highest rating, and as we go down the alphabet, the ratings are lower.

34. b. A steeper SML implies a higher risk premium on risky securities and thus a greater "penalty" on lower-rated bonds.

35. b. Statements a, d, and e are true. To determine which of the remaining statements is false, it is best to use an example. Assume you have a 10-year, 10 percent annual coupon bond which sold at par. If interest rates increase to 13 percent, the value of the bond decreases to $837.21, while if interest rates decrease to 7 percent, the value of the bond increases to $1,210.71. Thus, the capital gain is greater than the capital loss and statement b is false.

36. d. Statement a is false because the bond would have a premium and thus sell above par value. Statement b is false because both bonds would have the same interest rate risk because they both have one year left to maturity. Statement c is false because the price of a bond moves in the opposite direction as interest rates. Statement e is false because the 30-year bond would have more interest rate risk than the 30-day bond. Statement d is correct. As years to maturity increase for a bond, the number of discount periods used in finding the current bond value also increases. Therefore, bonds with longer maturities will have more price sensitivity to a given change in interest rates.

37. a. Statement a is correct. Bond C has a high coupon (hence its name), so bondholders get cash flows right away. Bond Z has a zero coupon, so its holders will get no cash flows until the bond matures. Since all of the cash flows on Z come at the end, a given increase in the interest rate will cause this bond's value to fall sharply relative to the decline in value of the coupon bond.

You could also use the data in the problem to find the value of the two bonds at two different interest rates, and then calculate the percentage change. For example, at k_d = 15%, V_C = $1,000 and V_Z = $247.18. At k_d = 20%, V_C = $790.38 and V_z = $161.51. Therefore, Bond Z declines in value by 34.66 percent, while Bond C declines by only 20.96 percent. Note that Bond Z is exposed to *less* reinvestment rate risk than Bond C.

38. a. When bonds sell at a discount, the going interest rate (k_d) is above the coupon rate. If a company called the old discount bonds and replaced them with new bonds, the new coupon would be above the old coupon. This would increase a firm's interest cost; hence, the company would not call the discount bonds. Therefore, the YTM would be the expected rate of return. The shape of the yield curve would have no effect on the situation described in this question, but if the bonds had been selling at a premium, making the YTC the relevant yield, then the yield curve in a sense would have an effect. The YTC would be below the cost if the company were to sell new long-term bonds, if the yield curve were steeply upward sloping. Statement d is false because the expected rate of return would include a current yield component and a capital gains component (because the bond's price will rise from its current discounted price to par as maturity approaches). Therefore, the current yield will _not_ exceed the expected rate of return. The after-tax cost of debt is the expected rate adjusted for taxes, $k_d(1 - T)$. Because the bonds are selling at a discount, the coupon rate could be quite low, even zero, so we know that statement e is false. Therefore, statement a is correct.

SOLUTIONS TO SELF-TEST PROBLEMS

1. c. $V_B = INT(PVIFA_{k_d,N}) + M(PVIF_{k_d,N})$
$$= \$70(PVIFA_{14\%,4}) + \$1,000(PVIF_{14\%,4})$$
$$= \$70(2.9137) + \$1,000(0.5921) = \$796.06.$$

Calculator solution: Input N = 4, I = 14, PMT = 70, FV = 1000, and solve for PV = -$796.04.

2. d. $V_B = (INT/2)(PVIFA_{k_d/2,2N}) + M(PVIF_{k_d/2,2N})$
$$= \$35(PVIFA_{7\%,8}) + \$1,000(PVIF_{7\%,8})$$
$$= \$35(5.9713) + \$1,000(0.5820) = \$791.00.$$

Calculator solution: Input N = 8, I = 7, PMT = 35, FV = 1000, and solve for PV = -$791.00.

3. e. $V_B = INT(PVIFA_{k_d,N}) + M(PVIF_{k_d,N})$
$$= \$70(PVIFA_{14\%,20}) + \$1,000(PVIF_{14\%,20})$$
$$= \$70(6.6231) + \$1,000(0.0728) = \$536.42.$$

Calculator solution: Input N = 20, I = 14, PMT = 70, FV = 1000, and solve for PV = -$536.38.

4.   b.   From Self-Test Problem 3 we know that the current price of the bond is $536.38.

$$\text{Therefore, the current yield} = \frac{\text{Annual Interest}}{\text{Current Price}}$$

$$= \frac{\$70}{\$536.38}$$

$$= 13.05\%.$$

5.   c. $V_B = INT(PVIFA_{k_d,N}) + M(PVIF_{k_d,N})$

$814.45 = \$100(PVIFA_{k_d,8}) + \$1,000(PVIF_{k_d,8})$.

Now use trial and error techniques. Try $I = k_d = 12\%$:
$814.45 = \$100(4.9676) + \$1,000(0.4039) = \$900.66$.

Since $814.45 \neq \$900.66$, the yield to maturity is not 12 percent. The calculated value is too large. Therefore, increase the value of I to 14 percent to lower the calculated value: $814.45 = \$100(4.6389) + \$1,000(0.3506) = \$814.49$. This is close enough to conclude that k_d = yield to maturity = 14%.

Calculator solution: Input N = 8, PV = -814.45, PMT = 100, FV = 1000, and solve for $I = k_d = 14.00\%$.

6.   c. $V_B = INT(PVIFA_{k_d,N}) + M(PVIF_{k_d,N})$

$863.73 = \$80(PVIFA_{10\%,N}) + \$1,000(PVIF_{10\%,N})$

Now use trial and error to find the value of N for which the equality holds. For N = 12, $80(6.8137) + \$1,000(0.3186) = \$863.70$. Or using a financial calculator, input I = 10, PV = -863.73, PMT = 80, FV = 1000, and solve for N = 12.

7.   d.   The bond is selling at a large premium, which means that its coupon rate is much higher than the going rate of interest. Therefore, the bond is likely to be called—it is more likely to be called than to remain outstanding until it matures. Thus, it will probably provide a return equal to the YTC rather than the YTM. So, there is no point in calculating the YTM; just calculate the YTC. Enter these values: N = 10, PV = -1300, PMT = 60, and FV = 1100. The periodic rate is 3.29 percent, so the nominal YTC is 2(3.29%) = 6.58%. This would be close to the going rate, and it is about what Bird would have to pay on new bonds.

8.   b.   Investors would expect to earn either the YTM or the YTC, and the expected return on the old bonds is the cost Graf would have to pay in order to sell new bonds.

YTM: Enter N = 2(25) = 50; PV = -700; PMT = 100/2 = 50; and FV = 1000. Press I to get I = $k_d/2$ = 7.24%. Multiply 7.24%(2) = 14.48% to get the YTM.

YTC: Enter N = 2(5) = 10, PV = -700, PMT = 50, FV = 1090, and then press I to get I=10.55%. Multiply by 2 to get YTC = 21.10%.

Would investors expect the company to call the bonds? Graf currently pays 10 percent on its debt (the coupon rate). New debt would cost at least 14.48 percent. Because k_d >10% coupon rate, it would be stupid for the company to call, so investors would not expect a call. Therefore, they would expect to earn 14.48 percent on the bonds. This is k_d, so 14.48 percent is the rate Graf would probably have to pay on new bonds.

9.   a.   Time line:

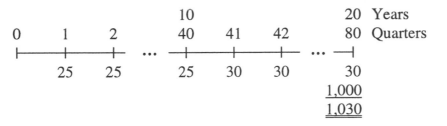

1. You could enter the time line values into the cash flow register, but one element is missing: the interest rate. Once we have the interest rate, we could press the NPV key to get the value of the bond.

2. We need a *periodic* interest rate, and it needs to be a quarterly rate, found as the annual nominal rate divided by 4: $k_{Per} = k_{Nom}/4$. So, we need to find k_{Nom} so that we can find k_{Per}.

3. The insurance company will insist on earning at least the same effective annual rate on the bond issue as it can earn on the mortgage. The mortgage pays 14 percent monthly, which is equivalent to an EAR = 14.93%. Using a financial calculator, enter NOM% = 14, P/YR = 12, and press EFF% to obtain 14.93%. So, the bond issue will have to have a k_{Nom}, with quarterly payments, which translates into an EAR of 14.93 percent.

4. EAR = 14.93% is equivalent to a quarterly nominal rate of 14.16 percent; that is, a nominal rate of 14.16 percent with quarterly compounding has an EAR of 14.93 percent. You can find this by entering EFF% = 14.93, P/YR = 4, and pressing the NOM% key to get NOM% = 14.16%. If this nominal rate is set on the bond issue, the insurance company will earn the same effective rate as it can get on the mortgage. (Don't forget to set your calculator back to P/YR = 1.)

5. The periodic rate for a 14.16 percent nominal rate, with quarterly compounding, is 14.16%/4 = 3.54%. This 3.54% is the rate to use in the time line calculations.

With an HP-10B calculator, enter the following data:
$CF_0 = 0$, $CF_j = 25$; $N_j = 40$; $CF_j = 30$; $N_j = 39$; $CF_j = 1030$; $I = 3.54$.
Solve for NPV = $750.78 = Value of each bond.

With an HP-17B calculator, enter the following data:
Flow(0) = 0 Input; Flow(1) = 25 Input; # Times = 40 Input; Flow(2) = 30 Input; # Times = 39 Input; Flow(3) = 1030 Input; # Times = 1 Input; Exit; Calc; $I = 3.54$.
Solve for NPV = $750.78 = Value of each bond.

If each bond is priced at $750.78, the insurance company will earn the same effective rate of return on the bond issue as on the mortgage.

CHAPTER 28
STOCK VALUATION

OVERVIEW

Common stock constitutes the ownership position in a firm. As owners, common stockholders have certain rights and privileges, including the right to control the firm through election of directors and the right to the firm's residual earnings.

Firms generally begin corporate life as closely held companies, with all the common stock held by the founding managers. Then, as the company grows, it is often necessary to sell stock to the general public (that is, to go public) to raise more funds. Eventually, the firm may choose to list its stock on one of the organized exchanges.

A common stock is valued as the present value of its expected future dividend stream. The total rate of return on a stock is comprised of a dividend yield plus a capital gains yield. If a stock is in equilibrium, its total expected return must equal the average investor's required rate of return.

Preferred stock is a hybrid—it is similar to bonds in some respects and to common stock in others. The value of a share of preferred stock which is expected to pay a constant dividend forever is found as the dividend divided by the required rate of return.

OUTLINE

The corporation's common stockholders are the owners of the corporation, and as such, they have certain rights and privileges.

■ Common stockholders have control of the firm through their election of the firm's directors, who in turn elect the officers who manage the business.
   □ In a large, publicly owned firm, the managers typically have some stock, but their personal holdings are generally insufficient to give them voting control.
   □ Thus, stockholders must vote for directors, and the voting process is regulated by both state and federal laws.
   □ Stockholders who are unable to attend annual meetings may still vote by means of a *proxy*. Proxies can be solicited by any party seeking to control the firm.

☐ If earnings are poor and stockholders are dissatisfied, an outside group may solicit the proxies in an effort to overthrow management and take control of the business. This is known as a *proxy fight*.

☐ A *takeover* is an action whereby a person or group succeeds in ousting a firm's management and taking control of the company by purchasing a majority of the outstanding stock.

☐ A *poison pill* makes a possible acquisition unattractive and wards off hostile takeover attempts.

■ The *preemptive right* gives the current shareholders the right to purchase any new shares issued in proportion to their current holdings.

☐ The preemptive right may or may not be required by state law.

☐ When granted, the preemptive right enables current owners to maintain their proportionate share of ownership and control of the business.

☐ It also prevents the sale of shares at low prices to new stockholders, which would dilute the value of the previously issued shares.

Special classes of common stock are sometimes created by a firm to meet special needs and circumstances. If two classes of stock were desired, one would normally be called "Class A" and the other "Class B."

■ Class A might be entitled to receive dividends before dividends can be paid on Class B stock.

■ Class B might have the exclusive right to vote.

☐ Note that Class A and Class B have no standard meanings.

■ *Founders' shares* are stock owned by the firm's founders that have sole voting rights but restricted dividends for a specified number of years.

■ The right to vote is often a distinguishing characteristic between different classes of stock. As you would expect, the stock with voting rights would be more valuable.

Some companies are so small that their common stocks are not actively traded; they are owned by only a few people, usually the companies' managers. Such firms are said to be privately owned, or closely held, corporations, and their stock is called closely held stock. In contrast, the stocks of most larger companies are owned by a large number of investors, most of whom are not active in management. Such companies are called publicly owned corporations, and their stock is called publicly held stock.

■ Larger, publicly owned companies generally apply for listing on an *organized security exchange*, and they and their stocks are said to be *listed*.

■ Stock market transactions may be separated into three distinct categories.
  □ The *secondary market* deals with trading in previously issued, or outstanding, shares of established, publicly owned companies. The company receives no new money when sales are made in this market.
  □ The *primary market* handles additional shares sold by established, publicly owned companies. Companies can raise additional capital by selling in this market.
  □ The primary market also handles new public offerings of shares in firms that were formerly closely held. Capital for the firm can be raised by *going public*, and this market is often termed the *initial public offering (IPO) market*.

■ Initial offerings are generally *oversubscribed*, which means that the demand for shares at the offering price exceeds the number of shares issued. Investors can buy the stock in the after-market, but evidence suggests that if you do not get in on the ground floor, the average IPO underperforms the overall market over the longer run.

Common stocks are valued by finding the present value of the expected future cash flow stream.

■ People typically buy common stock expecting to earn *dividends* plus a *capital gain* when they sell their shares at the end of some holding period. The capital gain may or may not be realized, but most people expect a gain or else they would not buy stocks.
  □ The expected dividend yield on a stock during the coming year is equal to the expected dividend, D_1, divided by the current stock price, P_0.
  □ $\left(\hat{P}_1 - P_0\right)/P_0$ is the expected capital gains yield.
  □ The expected dividend yield plus the expected capital gains yield equals the expected total return.

■ The value of the stock today is calculated as the present value of an infinite stream of dividends. For any investor, cash flows consist of dividends plus the expected future sales price of the stock. This sales price, however, depends on dividends expected by future investors:

$$\text{Value of stock} = \hat{P}_0 = \text{PV of expected future dividends}$$

$$= \frac{D_1}{(1+k_s)^1} + \frac{D_2}{(1+k_s)^2} + \cdots + \frac{D_\infty}{(1+k_s)^\infty}$$

$$= \sum_{t=1}^{\infty} \frac{D_t}{(1+k_s)^t}.$$

Here k_s is the discount rate used to find the present value of the dividends.

■   If expected dividend growth is zero ($g = 0$), the value of the stock is found as follows:

$$\hat{P}_0 = D/k_s.$$

☐ Since a zero growth stock is expected to pay a constant dividend, it can be thought of as a *perpetuity*.

☐ The expected rate of return is simply the dividend yield: $\hat{k}_s = D / P_0$.

■   For many companies, earnings and dividends are expected to grow at some normal, or constant, rate. Dividends in any future Year t may be forecasted as $D_t = D_0(1 + g)^t$, where D_0 is the last dividend paid and g is the expected growth rate.

☐ For a company which last paid a $2.00 dividend and which has an expected 6 percent constant growth rate, the estimated dividend one year from now would be $D_1 = $2.00(1.06) = 2.12; D_2 would be $$2.00(1.06)^2 = 2.25, and the estimated dividend 4 years hence would be $D_t = D_0(1 + g)^t = $2.00(1.06)^4 = 2.525.

☐ Using this method of estimating future dividends, the current price, P_0, is determined as follows:

$$\hat{P}_0 = D_0 \sum_{t=1}^{\infty} \frac{(1+g)^t}{(1+k_s)^t} = \frac{D_0(1+g)}{k_s - g} = \frac{D_1}{k_s - g}.$$

This equation for valuing a constant growth stock, the *constant growth model*, is often called the *Gordon Model*, after Myron J. Gordon, who developed it.

☐ If growth is zero, this is simply a special case of constant growth.

☐ A necessary condition is that k_s must be greater than g.

☐ Growth in dividends occurs primarily as a result of growth in earnings per share.

  ● Earnings growth results from a number of factors including (1) inflation, (2) the amount of earnings the company retains and reinvests, and (3) the rate of return the company earns on its equity (ROE).

■   For all stocks, the total expected return is composed of an expected dividend yield plus an expected capital gains yield. For a constant growth stock, the formula for the total expected return can be written as:

$$\hat{k}_s = \frac{D_1}{P_0} + g.$$

☐ For a *constant growth stock*, the following conditions must hold:

  ● The dividend is expected to grow forever at a constant rate, g.

  ● The stock price is expected to grow at that same rate.

  ● The expected dividend yield is a constant.

- The expected capital gains yield is also a constant, and it is equal to g.
- The expected total return, $\hat{k}_s$, is equal to the expected dividend yield plus the expected growth rate.

Firms typically go through periods of nonconstant growth, after which time their growth rate settles to a rate close to that of the economy as a whole. These firms are called *supernormal,* or *nonconstant, growth* firms. The value of such a firm is equal to the present value of its expected future dividends. To find the value of such a stock, we proceed in three steps:
- ☐ Find the present value of the dividends during the period of nonconstant growth.
- ☐ Find the price of the stock at the end of the nonconstant growth period, at which point it has become a constant growth stock, and discount this price back to the present.
- ☐ Add these two components to find the stock's present value.

The relationship between a stock's required and expected rates of return determines the equilibrium price level where buying and selling pressures will just offset each other.

If the expected rate of return is less than the required rate, investors will desire to sell the stock; there will also be a tendency for the price to decline.

When the expected rate of return is greater than the required rate, investors will try to purchase shares of the stock; this will drive the price upward.

Only at the *equilibrium price*, where the expected and required rates are equal, will the stock be stable.

It is the marginal investor who establishes the actual market price.

Equilibrium will generally exist for a given stock because security prices, especially those of large companies, adjust rapidly to new information.

Changes in the equilibrium price can be brought about by (1) a change in risk aversion, (2) a change in the risk-free rate, (3) a change in the stock's beta coefficient, or (4) a change in the stock's expected growth rate.

The *Efficient Markets Hypothesis (EMH)* holds that stocks are always in equilibrium and that it is impossible for an investor to consistently "beat the market." If markets are efficient, stock prices will rapidly reflect all available information.
- ☐ The *weak-form* of the EMH states that all information contained in past price movements is fully reflected in current market prices.

□ The *semistrong-form* of the EMH states that current market prices reflect all *publicly available* information. If this is true, no abnormal returns can be gained by analyzing stocks.

• Another implication of semistrong-form efficiency is that whenever information is released to the public, stock prices will respond only if the information is different from what had been expected.

□ The *strong-form* of the EMH states that current market prices reflect all pertinent information, whether publicly available or privately held (inside information).

• If this form holds, even insiders would find it impossible to earn abnormal returns in the stock market.

■ In general, stocks are neither overvalued nor undervalued—they are fairly priced and in equilibrium.

■ Empirical tests have shown that EMH is, in its weak and semistrong forms, valid.

Anyone who has ever invested in the stock market knows that there can be, and generally are, large differences between expected and realized prices and returns.

■ Investors always expect positive returns from stock investments or else they would not buy them. However, in some years negative returns are actually earned.

■ Even in bad years, some individual stocks do well, and the "name of the game" in security analysis is to pick the winners. Financial managers are trying to take those actions that will help put their companies in the winners' column, but they don't always succeed.

■ When investing overseas, you are making two bets: (1) that foreign stocks will increase in their local markets and (2) that the currencies in which you will be paid will rise relative to the dollar.
□ Foreign investments improve diversification.

Preferred stock is a hybrid—it is similar to bonds in some respects and to common stock in other respects.

■ Preferred dividends are similar to interest payments on bonds in that they are fixed in amount and generally must be paid before common stock dividends can be paid.

■ If the preferred dividend is not earned, the directors can omit (or "pass") it without throwing the company into bankruptcy. So, although preferred stock has a fixed payment like bonds, a failure to make this payment will not lead to bankruptcy.

■ Most preferred stocks entitle their owners to regular fixed dividend payments. If the payments last forever, the issue is a *perpetuity* whose value, V_{ps}, is found as follows:

$$V_{ps} = \frac{D_{ps}}{k_{ps}}.$$

☐ Here D_{ps} is the dividend to be received in each year and k_{ps} is the required rate of return on the preferred stock.

The Extensions to Chapter 28 provide the derivations of the valuation equations presented in this chapter.

SELF-TEST QUESTIONS

Definitional

1. One of the fundamental rights of common stockholders is to elect a firm's _____, who in turn elect the firm's operating management.

2. If a stockholder cannot vote in person, participation in the annual meeting is still possible through a(n) _____.

3. The preemptive right protects stockholders against loss of _____ of the corporation as well as _____ of market value from the sale of new shares below market value.

4. Firms may find it desirable to separate the common stock into different _____. Generally, this classification is designed to differentiate stock in terms of the right to receive _____ and the right to _____.

5. A(n) _____ _____ corporation is one whose stock is held by a small group, normally its management.

6. The trading of previously issued shares of a corporation takes place in the _____ market, while new issues are offered in the _____ market.

7. _____ _____ refers to the sale of shares of a closely held business to the general public.

8. Securities traded on the organized exchanges are known as _____ securities.

9. Like other financial assets, the value of common stock is the _____ value of a future stream of income.

10. The income stream expected from a common stock consists of a(n) _____ yield and a(n) _____ _____ yield.

11. If the future growth rate of dividends is expected to be _____, the rate of return is simply the _____ yield.

12. Investors always expect a(n) _____ return on stock investments, but in some years _____ returns may actually be earned.

13. Preferred stock is referred to as a hybrid because it is similar to _____ in some respects and to _____ _____ in others.

14. If earnings are poor and stockholders are dissatisfied, an outside group may solicit the votes of stockholders unable to attend the annual meeting in an effort to overthrow management and take control of the business. This is known as a(n) _____ _____.

15. A(n) _____ is an action whereby a person or group succeeds in ousting a firm's management and taking control of the company.

16. A(n) _____ _____ makes a possible acquisition unattractive and wards off hostile takeover attempts.

17. The market where capital is raised for firms that were formerly closely held companies is often termed the _____ _____ _____ market.

18. _____ is the term used when the demand for shares at the offering price exceeds the number of shares issued.

19. A zero growth stock can be thought of as a(n) _____.

20. If the expected rate of return on a stock is less than its required rate of return, investors will desire to _____ the stock; there will also be a tendency for the stock's price to _____.

21. Only at the _____ price, where the expected and required rates of return are equal, will the stock's price be stable.

22. The _____ _____ _____ holds that stocks are always in equilibrium and that it is impossible for an investor to consistently "beat the market."

23. The _____-form of the EMH states that all information contained in past price movements is fully reflected in current market prices.

24. When investing overseas, you are making two bets: (1) that foreign stock prices will _____ in their local markets and (2) that the currencies in which you will be paid will _____ relative to the dollar.

25. Growth in dividends occurs primarily as a result of growth in _____ _____ _____.

26. Although preferred stock has a fixed payment like bonds, a failure to make this payment will not lead to _____.

Conceptual

27. According to the valuation model developed in this chapter, the value that an investor assigns to a share of stock is independent of the length of time the investor plans to hold the stock.

    a. True   b. False

28. Which of the following assumptions would cause the constant growth stock valuation model to be invalid? The constant growth model is given below:

$$\hat{P}_0 = \frac{D_0(1+g)}{k_s - g}.$$

    a. The growth rate is negative.
    b. The growth rate is zero.
    c. The growth rate is less than the required rate of return.
    d. The required rate of return is above 30 percent.
    e. None of the above assumptions would invalidate the model.

29. Assume that a company's dividends are expected to grow at a rate of 25 percent per year for 5 years and then to slow down and to grow at a constant rate of 5 percent thereafter. The required (and expected) total return, k_s, is expected to remain constant at 12 percent. Which of the following statements is most correct?

    a. The dividend yield will be higher in the early years and then will decline as the annual capital gains yield gets larger and larger, other things held constant.
    b. Right now, it would be easier (require fewer calculations) to find the dividend yield expected in Year 7 than the dividend yield expected in Year 3.
    c. The stock price will grow each year at the same rate as the dividends.
    d. The stock price will grow at a different rate each year during the first 5 years, but its average growth rate over this period will be the same as the average growth rate in dividends; that is, the average stock price growth rate will be $(25 + 5)/2$.
    e. Statements a, b, c, and d are false.

30. Which of the following statements is most correct?

    a. According to the text, the constant growth model is especially useful in situations where g is greater than 15 percent and k_s is 10 percent or less.
    b. According to the text, the constant growth model can be used as one part of the process of finding the value of a stock which is expected to experience a very rapid rate of growth for a few years and then to grow at a constant ("normal") rate.
    c. According to the text, the constant growth model cannot be used unless g is greater than zero.
    d. According to the text, the constant growth model cannot be used unless the constant g is greater than k.
    e. Statements a, b, c, and d are correct.

31. When stockholders assign their right to vote to another party, this is called

    a. A privilege.
    b. A preemptive right.
    c. An ex right.
    d. A proxy.
    e. A takeover.

SELF-TEST PROBLEMS

1. Stability Inc. has maintained a dividend rate of $4 per share for many years. The same rate is expected to be paid in future years. If investors require a 12 percent rate of return on similar investments, determine the present value of the company's stock.

    a. $15.00   **b.** $30.00   **c.** $33.33   **d.** $35.00   **e.** $40.00

2. Your sister-in-law, a stockbroker at Invest Inc., is trying to sell you a stock with a current market price of $25. The stock's last dividend (D_0) was $2.00, and earnings and dividends are expected to increase at a constant growth rate of 10 percent. Your required return on this stock is 20 percent. From a strict valuation standpoint, you should:

    a. Buy the stock; it is fairly valued.
    b. Buy the stock; it is undervalued by $3.00.
    c. Buy the stock; it is undervalued by $2.00.
    d. Not buy the stock; it is overvalued by $2.00.
    e. Not buy the stock; it is overvalued by $3.00.

3. Lucas Laboratories' last dividend was $1.50. Its current equilibrium stock price is $15.75, and its expected growth rate is a constant 5 percent. If the stockholders' required rate of return is 15 percent, what is the expected dividend yield and expected capital gains yield for the coming year?

    a. 0%; 15%   **b.** 5%; 10%   **c.** 10%; 5%   **d.** 15%; 0%   **e.** 15%; 15%

4. The Canning Company has been hard hit by increased competition. Analysts predict that earnings (and dividends) will decline at a rate of 5 percent annually into the foreseeable future. If Canning's last dividend (D_0) was $2.00, and investors' required rate of return is 15 percent, what will be Canning's stock price *in 3 years*?

    a. $8.15   **b.** $9.50   **c.** $10.00   **d.** $10.42   **e.** $10.96

(The following data apply to the next three Self-Test Problems.)

The Club Auto Parts Company has just recently been organized. It is expected to experience no growth for the next 2 years as it identifies its market and acquires its inventory. However, Club will grow at an annual rate of 5 percent in the third year and, beginning with the fourth year, should attain a 10 percent growth rate which it will sustain thereafter. The first dividend (D_1) to be paid at the end of the first year is expected to be $0.50 per share. Investors require a 15 percent rate of return on Club's stock.

5. What is the current equilibrium stock price?

    a. $5.00   **b.** $8.75   **c.** $9.56   **d.** $12.43   **e.** $15.00

6. What will Club's stock price be at the end of the first year $\left(\hat{P}_1\right)$?

    a. $5.00   **b.** $8.75   **c.** $9.56   **d.** $12.43   **e.** $15.00

7. What dividend yield and capital gains yield should an investor in Club expect for the first year?

    a. 7.5%; 7.5%   **b.** 4.7%; 10.3%   **c.** 5.7%; 9.3%   **d.** 10.5%; 4.5%   **e.** 11.5%; 3.5%

8. Johnson Corporation's stock is currently selling at $45.83 per share. The last dividend paid (D_0) was $2.50. Johnson is a constant growth firm. If investors require a return of 16 percent on Johnson's stock, what do they think Johnson's growth rate will be?

    a. 6%   **b.** 7%   **c.** 8%   **d.** 9%   **e.** 10%

9. Assume that the average firm in your company's industry is expected to grow at a constant rate of 7 percent and its dividend yield is 8 percent. Your company is about as risky as the average firm in the industry, but it has just successfully completed some R&D work which leads you to expect that its earnings and dividends will grow at a rate of 40 percent [$D_1 = D_0(1 + g) = D_0(1.40)$] this year and 20 percent the following year, after which growth should match the 7 percent industry average rate. The last dividend paid (D_0) was $1. What is the current value per share of your firm's stock?

    a. $22.47   **b.** $24.15   **c.** $21.00   **d.** $19.48   **e.** $22.00

10. Assume that as investment manager of Maine Electric Company's pension plan (which is exempt from income taxes), you must choose between Exxon bonds and GM preferred stock. The bonds have a $1,000 par value; they mature in 20 years; they pay $35 each 6 months; they are callable at Exxon's option at a price of $1,150 after 5 years (ten 6-month periods); and they sell at a price of $815.98 per bond. The preferred stock is a perpetuity; it pays a dividend of $1.50 each quarter, and it sells for $75 per share. Assume interest rates do not change. What is the most likely *effective annual rate of return (EAR)* on the *higher* yielding security? (Hint: You will need a financial calculator to work this problem.)

    a. 9.20%   **b.** 8.24%   **c.** 9.00%   **d.** 8.00%   **e.** 8.50%

11. Chadmark Corporation is expanding rapidly, and it currently needs to retain all of its earnings, hence it does not pay any dividends. However, investors expect Chadmark to begin paying dividends, with the first dividend of $0.75 coming 2 years from today. The dividend should grow rapidly, at a rate of 40 percent per year, during Years 3 and 4. After Year 4, the company should grow at a constant rate of 10 percent per year. If the required return on the stock is 16 percent, what is the value of the stock today?

    a. $16.93   **b.** $17.54   **c.** $15.78   **d.** $18.87   **e.** $16.05

12. Some investors expect Endicott Industries to have an irregular dividend pattern for several years, and then to grow at a constant rate. Suppose Endicott has $D_0 = \$2.00$; no growth is expected for 2 years ($g_1 = 0$); then the expected growth rate is 8 percent for 2 years; and finally the growth rate is expected to be constant at 15 percent thereafter. If the required return is 20 percent, what will be the value of the stock?

    a. $28.53   **b.** $25.14   **c.** $31.31   **d.** $21.24   **e.** $23.84

ANSWERS TO SELF-TEST QUESTIONS

1.	directors		14.	proxy fight
2.	proxy		15.	takeover
3.	control; dilution		16.	poison pill
4.	classes; dividends; vote		17.	initial public offering
5.	closely held (privately-owned)		18.	Oversubscribed
6.	secondary; primary		19.	perpetuity
7.	Going public		20.	sell; decline
8.	listed		21.	equilibrium
9.	present		22.	Efficient Markets Hypothesis
10.	dividend; capital gains		23.	weak
11.	zero; dividend		24.	increase; increase
12.	positive; negative		25.	earnings per share
13.	debt; common stock		26.	bankruptcy

27.   a. The model considers all future dividends. This produces a current value which is appropriate for all investors independent of their expected holding period.

28.   e. The model would be invalid, however, if the growth rate *exceeded* the required rate of return.

29. b. Statement b is correct. We know that after Year 5, the stock will have a constant growth rate, and the capital gains yield will be equal to that growth rate. We also know that the total return is expected to be constant. Therefore, we could find the expected dividend yield in Year 7 simply by subtracting the growth rate from the total return: Dividend yield = 12% – 5% = 7% in Year 7.

The other statements are all false. This could be confirmed by thinking about how the dividend growth rate starts high, ends up at the constant growth rate, and must lie between these two rates and be declining between Years 1 and 5. The average growth rate in dividends during Years 1 through 5 will be (25 + 5)/2 = 15%, which is above k_s = 12%, so statements c and d must be false.

30. b. Statement b is correct. In the case of a nonconstant growth stock which is expected to grow at a constant rate after Year N, we would find the value of D_{N+1} and use it in the constant growth model to find P_N. The other statements are all false. Note that the constant growth model can be used for g = 0, g < 0, and g < k.

31. d. Recently, there has been a spate of proxy fights, whereby a dissident group of stockholders solicits proxies in competition with the firm's management. If the dissident group gets a majority of the proxies, then it can gain control of the board of directors and oust existing management.

SOLUTIONS TO SELF-TEST PROBLEMS

1. c. This is a zero-growth stock, or perpetuity: $\hat{P}_0 = D/k_s = \$4.00/0.12 = \$33.33$.

2. e. $\hat{P}_0 = \dfrac{D_0(1+g)}{k_s - g} = \dfrac{\$2.00(1.10)}{0.20 - 0.10} = \$22.00$.

Since the stock is currently selling for $25.00, the stock is not in equilibrium and is overvalued by $3.00.

3. c. $\dfrac{\text{Dividend}}{\text{yield}} = \dfrac{D_1}{P_0} = \dfrac{D_0(1 + g)}{P_0} = \dfrac{\$1.50(1.05)}{\$15.75} = 0.10 = 10\%$.

$\dfrac{\text{Capital}}{\text{gains yield}} = \dfrac{\hat{P}_1 - P_0}{P_0} = \dfrac{P_0(1+g) - P_0}{P_0} = \dfrac{\$16.54 - \$15.75}{\$15.75} = g = 5\%$.

4.   a. $\hat{P}_0 = \dfrac{D_0(1+g)}{k_s - g} = \dfrac{\$2.00(0.95)}{0.15 - (-0.05)} = \dfrac{\$1.90}{0.20} = \$9.50.$

$\hat{P}_3 = \hat{P}_0(1+g)^3 = \$9.50(0.95)^3 = \$9.50(0.8574) = \$8.15.$

The Gordon model can also be used:

$\hat{P}_3 = \dfrac{D_4}{k_s - g} = \dfrac{D_0(1+g)^4}{0.15 - (-0.05)} = \dfrac{\$2.00(0.95)^4}{0.20} = \dfrac{\$2.00(0.8145)}{0.20} = \$8.15.$

5.   b.   To calculate the current value of a nonconstant growth stock, follow these steps:

1. Determine the expected stream of dividends during the nonconstant growth period. Also, calculate the expected dividend at the end of the first year of constant growth that will be used later to calculate stock price.

$$D_1 = \$0.50.$$
$$D_2 = D_1(1+g) = \$0.50(1 + 0.0) = \$0.50.$$
$$D_3 = D_2(1+g) = \$0.50(1.05) \quad = \$0.525.$$
$$D_4 = D_3(1+g) = \$0.525(1.10) \quad = \$0.5775.$$

2. Discount the expected dividends during the nonconstant growth period at the investor's required rate of return to find their present value.

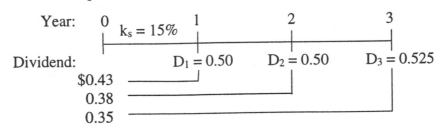

3. Calculate the expected stock price at the end of the final year of nonconstant growth. This occurs at the end of Year 3. Use the Gordon model for this calculation.

$$\hat{P}_3 = \dfrac{D_4}{k_s - g} = \dfrac{\$0.5775}{0.15 - 0.10} = \$11.55.$$

Then discount this stock price back 3 periods at the investor's required rate of return to find its present value.

$$PV = \$11.55(PVIF_{15\%,3}) = \$11.55(0.6575) = \$7.59.$$

4. Add the present value of the stock price expected at the end of Year 3 plus the dividends expected in Years 1, 2, and 3 to find the present value of the stock, P_0.

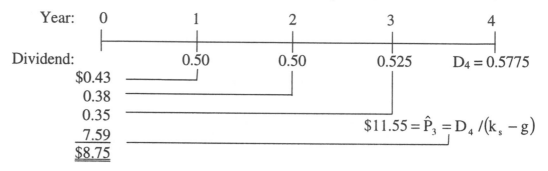

Alternatively, input 0, 0.5, 0.5, 12.075(0.525 + 11.55) into the cash flow register, input I = 15, and then solve for NPV = $8.75.

6.   c.   To calculate the expected stock price at the end of Year 1, $\hat{P}_1$, follow the same procedure you did to find the value of the nonconstant growth stock in Self-Test Problem 5. However, discount values to Year 1 instead of Year 0. Also, remember that the dividend in Year 1, D_1, is not included in the valuation because it has already been paid and therefore adds nothing to the wealth of the investor buying the stock at the end of Year 1.

Alternatively, input 0, 0.5, 12.075 (0.525 + 11.55) into the cash flow register, input I = 15, and then solve for NPV = $9.57.

7.   c. $\dfrac{\text{Dividend}}{\text{yield}} = \dfrac{D_1}{P_0} = \dfrac{\$0.50}{\$8.75} = 5.7\%.$

$\dfrac{\text{Capital}}{\text{gains yield}} = \dfrac{\hat{P}_1 - P_0}{P_0} = \dfrac{\$9.56 - \$8.75}{\$8.75} = 9.3\%.$

The Total yield = Dividend yield + Capital gains yield = 5.7% + 9.3% = 15%. The total yield must equal the required rate of return. Also, the capital gains yield is not equal to the growth rate during the nonconstant growth phase of a nonconstant growth stock. Finally, the dividend and capital gains yields are not constant until the constant growth state is reached.

8.   e.

$$P_0 = \frac{D_0(1+g)}{k_s - g}$$

$$\$45.83 = \frac{\$2.50(1+g)}{0.16 - g}$$

$\$7.33 - \$45.83g = \$2.50 + \$2.50g$

$\$48.33g = \$4.83$

$g = 0.0999 \approx 10\%.$

9.   d. $D_0 = \$1.00$; $k_s = 8\% + 7\% = 15\%$; $g_1 = 40\%$; $g_2 = 20\%$; $g_n = 7\%$.

$$*\hat{P}_2 = \frac{\$1.7976}{0.15 - 0.07} = \$22.47.$$

10.   a.   Exxon bonds: Price = $815.98, Maturity = 20 years, PMT = $35 per 6 months, and they are callable at $1,150 after 10 periods (5 years).

Will the bond's YTM or YTC be applicable? The bond is selling at a discount, so $k_d >$ Coupon interest rate. Therefore, the bond is not likely to be called, so calculate the YTM.

Input N = 40, PV = -815.98, PMT = 35, FV = 1000, and solve for I = $k_d/2$ = 4.5%. EAR = $(1.045)^2 - 1 = 9.2\%$.

Preferred: $D = \$1.50$ per quarter and $P_0 = \$75$.

$k_{ps} = \$1.50/\$75 = 2\% =$ periodic rate. $EAR = (1.02)^4 - 1 = 8.24\%$.

Thus, the Exxon bonds provide the higher effective annual rate of return.

11.   a.   To calculate Chadmark's current stock price, follow the following steps: (1) Determine the expected stream of dividends during the nonconstant growth period. You will need to calculate the expected dividend at the end of Year 5, which is the first year of constant growth. This dividend will be used in the next step to calculate the stock price. (2) Calculate the expected stock price at the end of the final year of nonconstant growth. This occurs at the end of Year 4. Use the Gordon model for this calculation. (3) Add the value obtained in Step 2 to the dividend expected in Year 4. (4) Put the values obtained in the prior steps on a time line and discount them at the required rate of return to find the present value of Chadmark's stock. These steps are shown below.

$D_0 = \$0$; $D_1 = \$0$; $D_2 = \$0.75$; $D_3 = \$0.75(1.4) = \$1.05$; $D_4 = \$0.75(1.4)^2 = \$1.47$; $D_5 = \$0.75(1.4)^2(1.10) = \$1.617$.

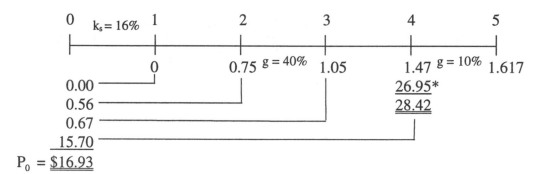

$* \hat{P}_4 = \$1.617/(0.16 - 0.10) = \$26.95$.

$CF_0 = 0$; $CF_1 = 0$; $CF_2 = 0.75$; $CF_3 = 1.05$; $CF_4 = 28.42$.

Alternatively, using a financial calculator you could input the cash flows as shown above into the cash flow register, input $I = 16$, and press NPV to obtain the stock's value today of $16.93.

12.   c.   First, set up the time line as follows. Note that D_5 is used to find $\hat{P}_4$, which is treated as part of the cash flow at t = 4:

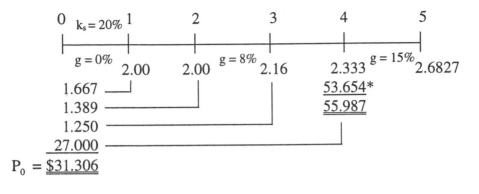

$*\hat{P}_4 = \$2.6827/(0.20 - 0.15) = \$53.654.$

Enter the time line values into the cash flow register, with I = 20, to find NPV = $31.31. Be sure to enter $CF_0 = 0$. Note that $\hat{P}_4$ is the PV, at t = 4, of dividends from t = 5 to infinity; that is, the PV of the dividends after the stock is expected to become a constant growth stock.